Frontier Faith

The Story of the Pioneer Congregations of

Fort Wayne, Indiana, 1820 - 1860

Joseph Pierre de Bonnecamps, S. J. — the first recorded clergyman to traverse the Miami-Wabash portage — visited Fort Miami in 1749.
[Original Illustration by Kenneth B. Dutton]

Frontier Faith

The Story of the

Pioneer Congregations of

Fort Wayne, Indiana

1820 - 1860

By George Ross Mather

With illustrations by Kenneth B. Dutton

The Allen County-Fort Wayne Historical Society
Fort Wayne, Indiana

FRONTIER FAITH
The Story of the Pioneer Congregations of Fort Wayne, Indiana, 1820-1860

Printed in the United States of America by
Fairway Press, 628 South Main Street, Lima, Ohio 45804.

Library Of Congress Catalogue Card Number: 92-35676

Suggested Cataloging Data

Mather, George Ross, 1930-
   Frontier Faith: the story of the pioneer congregations of Fort Wayne, Indiana, 1820-1860. — Fort Wayne, Indiana: Allen County-Fort Wayne Historical Society, 1992.
   x., 342 p.: ill.; 28 cm.
   Includes bibliographical references and index.

   1. Fort Wayne (Ind.) — History. 2. Fort Wayne (Ind.) — Church history. 3. Church and social problems — Indiana — Fort Wayne. 4. Missions — Indiana — Fort Wayne — History. 5. Miami Indians — Indiana — Fort Wayne — Missions. 6. Women and religion — Indiana — Fort Wayne. 7. Afro-Americans — Indiana — Fort Wayne — History. I. Title.

ISBN 1-55673-526-X   977.274

Dedicated to present-day religious pioneers
who venture to carry their faith to the
challenges of new frontiers.

Contents

Preface

The parameters of any historical work are essentially defined by the interests of the author and the nature of the sources. This author's research has focused primarily on the establishment of the two missions to the Native Americans and the fourteen congregations of the early settlers in Fort Wayne, Indiana, between 1800 and 1860. The several years of research and writing have been sustained by a fascination with the manner in which the first Catholic, Protestant, and Jewish settlers faced the moral, as well as the physical challenges of the western frontier—challenges not unlike those faced by their descendents nearly two centuries later. Removed from the relative homogeneity of their New England or European villages, most of the new arrivals were instantly confronted with the need to relate positively to a polyglot community of Native Americans, old French Americans, Anglo-Saxon-Celtic Americans, African-Americans, and European immigrants—and, for many, a bewildering variety of religious persuasions. The author's purpose has been to go beyond a narration of congregational organization and development, and to examine the spiritual dynamics and religious convictions of these faith communities, especially their response to the emerging causes for moral reform, such as abolition, temperance, and woman's rights. As a result, the narrative closely follows the activities of the local religious leaders, especially those clergy who volunteered to serve in Fort Wayne. It has been the intent of the author to allow their voices to speak again to a community which is preparing to celebrate its two hundredth anniversary.

The documentary sources are surprisingly rich and varied: each of the first missionaries to the Miami Indians kept detailed diaries; a majority of the congregations have preserved some of their original parish records; many of the reports from the first clergy to visit the area were saved, either by the mission societies or published in the denominational journals; and a surprising number of relevant personal letters and diaries have survived. In addition, most of the newspapers published in Fort Wayne in the 1840s and 1850s

are available, and many of the early denominational journals and records are now in archival collections. Three of the local parishes published histories at their fiftieth anniversaries: two of these are in German and, like all of the handwritten records of the German-speaking congregations, had never been translated. Most of the letters of the Catholic priests and sisters were written in French.

Except for the section on the Women's Societies, the chapters are arranged chronologically according to the year in which each denomination commenced its activity in the area. Readers seeking information about a particular denomination should consult the index for additional material in other chapters.

This research project would not have been possible without the generous assistance of the librarians and archivists at Allen County-Fort Wayne Historical Society, Fort Wayne, Indiana; Allen County Public Library, Fort Wayne, Indiana; American Baptist Historical Society, Rochester, New York; American Jewish Archives, Cincinnati, Ohio; Andover-Harvard Theological Library, Cambridge, Massachusetts; Archives of the Episcopal Church, Austin, Texas; Archives of the Evangelical Lutheran Church in America, Chicago, Illinois; Archives of Indiana United Methodism, DePauw University, Greencastle, Indiana; Clements Library, Ann Arbor, Michigan; Concordia Historical Institute, St. Louis, Missouri; Concordia Theological Seminary, Fort Wayne, Indiana; Congregation of Holy Cross, Indiana Province Archives, Notre Dame, Indiana; Disciples of Christ Historical Society, Nashville, Tennessee; Earlham College Library, Richmond, Indiana; Franklin College Library, Franklin, Indiana; Hanover College Library, Hanover, Indiana; Indiana Historical Society, Indianapolis, Indiana; Indiana Jewish Historical Society, Fort Wayne, Indiana; Indiana State Library, Indianapolis, Indiana; Lancaster Central Archives and Library, Lancaster, Pennsylvania; Lilly Library, Bloomington, Indiana; Miami University Library, Oxford, Ohio; Ohio Synod Archives,

Wittenberg University Library, Springfield, Ohio; Presbyterian Historical Society, Philadelphia, Pennsylvania; Princeton Theological Seminary Library, Princeton, New Jersey; St. Mary-of-the-Woods Archives, Terre Haute, Indiana; State Historical Society of Wisconsin, Madison, Wisconsin; Swedenborg Library, Academy of the New Church, Bryn Athyn, Pennsylvania; United Library of Garrett-Evangelical and Seabury-Western Theological Seminaries, Chicago, Illinois; University of Notre Dame Archives, Notre Dame, Indiana.

Several friends transcribed and translated the German documents: Carl H. Amelung, Frances Lowens, Antonius Holtmann, Herbert A. Just, and Annelie Moxter-Collie. Of invaluable assistance in the search for primary sources were Charles H. Banet, John D. Beatty, Virgil V. Bjork, Herbert G. Bredemeier, Dennis C. Dickerson, Walter Font, Richard G. Frazier, Richard L. Hamm, Thomas D. Hamm, Robert H. Klopfenstein, Ethel Johnson, Richard Langhinrichs, Joseph Levine, William O. Harris, Robert E. Mason, Sarah McNair-Vosmeier, Charlene Pettit, Melvin R. Phillips, C. Corydon Randall, Clifford H. Richards, Coy D. Robbins, Peggy B. Seigel, Aurele J. Violette, and Matthew N. Vosmeier. Most of these scholars and friends also read individual chapters and made helpful suggestions, as did Carl L. Bradley, James J. Divita, Richard B. Dutton, Steven C. Fortriede, William J. Lester, Rudolph F. Rehmer, Richard B. Safran, Hermine J. van Nuis, and D. Newell Williams. I am especially grateful to those historians who read the entire manuscript: Michael C. Hawfield, J. Randolph Kirby, Mark E. Neely, Jr., L. C. Rudolph, and Clifford H. Scott.

Kenneth B. Dutton spent many hours in research and consultation for his excellent illustrations. Catherine A. Mather and Becki S. Tapp were most conscientious in preparing the typescript. My labors were sustained by my supportive children, Catherine and Geoffrey; and, last but first, by my wife, Doris, — an alert researcher, a gentle critic, and a careful editor — whose enthusiasm for this project contributed significantly to its fruition.

Introduction

What forces transformed Fort Wayne from a rough military post and center of Indian trade in the early 1800s into a community which, in 1852, described itself as a "City of Churches?"[1] Most histories of northern Indiana focus primarily on the military, political, and economic forces that shaped the new settlements, and generally ignore the role of the religious congregations in creating a moral tone and social climate that attracted a new class of stable settlers. Michael C. Hawfield, a Fort Wayne historian, has said, "The establishment of the early religious congregations in places like Fort Wayne was the single most important force in the shaping of the communities of the frontier."[2]

The first voluntary organizations to be established on any scale in Fort Wayne were religious—and all of those early churches and synagogues are flourishing today. The first public buildings of any consequence to be erected in the town were churches, some of which occasionally served the community as a school house, lecture hall, or court room. The churches and synagogues organized most of the schools, founded the town's first institutions of higher learning, and established all of the orphanages and hospitals. Most of the movements for social reform were nurtured in these early congregations, and the zeal of individual members advanced the antislavery, temperance, and woman's rights causes. The only agencies to send teachers to the Native Americans of the region were the religious denominations.

Religious faith was in ferment during the first half of the nineteenth century. A Protestant evangelical revival, emphasizing personal religious experience, gained strength on the western frontier. Just as the political situation in America between 1830 and the Civil War became increasingly sectional, the religious scene became more sectarian: denominational loyalty was emphasized and divisions became common.

At the same time, great waves of immigrants from Europe (especially Germany, France, and Ireland) were arriving to challenge the Anglo-Protestant hegemony. The new settlers, whether from the eastern states or western Europe, usually found in one of the local congregations a caring and supportive fellowship. Their admission to membership depended solely on their sharing of a common faith. For newly arrived German Jews, the synagogue quickly became the center of their social as well as spiritual life, and the members became the immigrants' adopted family. German Lutherans, Reformed, and Catholics—who may have had only a nominal relationship with their state-sponsored village church in Europe—now found that any of the four German parishes in Fort Wayne would not only minister to their spiritual life, but also preserve their ethnic identity, provide education for their children, and help them to adapt to the American environment.

African-Americans especially found in their local congregation a source of comfort in the midst of a segregated society. With the support of their denomination, they gained the courage to protest oppressive measures and to assist their brothers and sisters in distress.

The congregations that were founded in Fort Wayne between 1820 and 1860 reflected the heterogeneity of the settlers and the variety of their religious persuasions. Undergirding this diversity of religious expression, however, was a unity of purpose: all congregations held a common core of spiritual values which respected faith in God and held a high standard of personal morality. All believed that improved private morals would enhance public morality; some lobbied their state legislators for such measures as prohibition and public education—and even succeeded in electing a local clergyman to Congress.

The story of the pioneer congregations of Fort Wayne is first of all a story of individual people: dedicated lay members who strove to create a viable fellowship of believers, and pioneer pastors, most of whom came from the eastern states or Europe to serve as missionaries on the western frontier. It is also the story of a pioneer community that wished to be known as "A City of Churches."

Philip Dennis, a Quaker argicultural missionary, prepares the land for plowing.
[Original illustration by Kenneth B. Dutton]

1
Missions to the Miamis

"Brothers, it is our wish that the Great Spirit will enable you to render to your Red Brethren that service which you appear to be so desirous of doing them, and which their women and children are so much in need of."

Chief Little Turtle, 1803

During the early 1800s, two missions, Quaker and Baptist, were established for the Miami tribe (Miamiaki) in northeastern Indiana at the confluence of the St. Mary's, St. Joseph, and Maumee rivers. Both were inaugurated, not by any plan of the denominations, but in response to the urgent requests of the tribal leaders: Chief Little Turtle (Meshekenaque) in 1802 and Chief Richardville (Pishewa) in 1819. These chiefs—who had seen their people defeated by the American army's weapons, degraded by the local traders' whiskey, and threatened by the settlers' wagons—hoped that the American farmer's knowledge of agriculture and the Christian missionary's concern for education and temperance would strengthen their tribe. Many groups in nineteenth-century America could have assisted these Native Americans; only the churches would.

The Early Jesuit Missionaries

Much of what is known about the Miamis is found in the letters and records of the first French missionaries who were active in northern Indiana during the seventeenth century—those intrepid Jesuit fathers who followed a vision to make of the native North American people "a great Christian nation which would purify the world."[1] The Reverend Jacques Marquette, in the 1670s, praised the character of the Miamis, and René Robert Cavelier, Sieur de LaSalle, judged

them as "the most civilized of all nations of Indians —neat of dress, splendid in bearing, haughty of manner, holding all other tribes as inferiors."[2] The Reverend Claude Jean Allouez referred to them as "gentle, affable and sedate, with a language in harmony with their dignity."[3] Despite their outstanding success with the Canada and Maine Indians, as well as with the Illinois tribes and the Potawatomis, the seventeenth-century Jesuits largely failed in their efforts to Christianize the Miamis. As a result, after the time of Allouez (who died in 1689 when the Miamis were still in western Indiana) the Jesuit records have little to say of the tribe because so few had become Christians.[4]

None of the early missionaries left any comprehensive description of traditional Miami religion. Recent scholarship suggests that the supreme power for the Miamis was the sun, while the Great Spirit, or Manito, was the power for good and evil residing in both the animate and inanimate. Upon death, the human soul was released from the body to inhabit both this world, as an observer and occasional participant in the affairs of mortals, and the spirit world. The tribe's chief religious leader, called a Meda, practiced the art of healing and prophecy by releasing the spirit of Manito in charms and fetishes, either to banish evil spirits or reveal portents of the future. Miami religious beliefs controlled all areas of tribal life from birth to death and agriculture to warfare.[5] Every significant communal activity was accompanied with propitiatory rituals; Miami scholar Bert Anson notes: "Raids were preceded by elaborate ritualistic preparation. After each raid, appropriate ceremonies—mourning, torturing, and burning of captives, adoption or enslavement of accepted prisoners—were properly observed . . . and cannibalism was practiced on some occasions."[6] Artist George Winter, who visited Indiana in the 1830s, observed that the Potawatomis "cultivated a more religious sentiment [than the Miamis], hence the missionary work was marked by greater success. . . . I never succeeded very well in making many sketches among the Miami people. They were so superstitious that I was an object of terror among them. . . . In physical characteristics the Miamis were superior to the Potawatomis. But the latter had claims in moral qualities over the former."[7]

During the seventeenth century, the Miamis had been forced out of their village called Kiskaton (or Kekionga) by the Iroquois nation who were resisting French settlement in the area. By 1701, however, the French had concluded a

"A Miami Indian," by George Winter, ca. 1838

temporary peace with the Iroquois and proceeded to re-establish their Miami allies in their former lands in the Wabash and Maumee valleys. Little persuasion was needed for the tribe to return to their old lands with its abundance of fur, especially beaver. The French governor—confronted by unfriendly tribes to the north and English efforts to gain a foothold in the Wabash and Maumee valleys—soon determined to establish a strong post at the confluence of the St. Mary's and St. Joseph rivers. Completed in May of 1722, the new fort was seen by Governor de Vaudreuil to be a potential center of Christian missionary activity; in October, he

reported to Quebec: "The log Fort Miami. . . is the finest in the upper county. . . . The post, which is of considerable worth, ought to have a missionary. One could be sent here in 1724 if next year the Council will send the four Jesuits I ask."[8] There is, however, no record of a priest ever being stationed at Fort Miami or of any Catholic chapel or school being established for the native people of the region. In practice, the only Catholic missionaries to the Miamis during the French occupation were those traders who settled in the area and married native women—and thereby brought the Catholic faith, along with the French language and culture, to the native society.[9]

Fort Miami never attracted any other type of entrepreneur than the trader. When the British took control of the outpost in 1760, there were no white farmers or craftsmen, much less persons of education or refinement. After 1763, when the British were driven out by Chief Pontiac's Miami allies, no permanent military garrison was stationed there—and no British (or American) missionary attempted to enter the region. Charles Poinsatte, a Fort Wayne historian, noted: "Over this period of thirty-one years . . . the region . . . gradually became the rendezvous of a defiant mixture of Indian warriors, lawless renegades. . . English and French traders and their families, French 'engages', and Miami, Delaware, and Shawnee tribes. . . . In the heart of Indian country, Miamitown [as it was now called] was also the principal point from which the Indian raiding parties harassed the frontier. Twenty-six war parties left Miamitown in a period of six months during 1786."[10] In retaliation, a determined American Army, in 1790, burned Miamitown to the ground. The Indians retreated under scorched earth tactics, but raids on American settlements continued. Finally, in 1794, at Fallen Timbers near Toledo, General Anthony Wayne defeated the Indian confederacy, and then proceeded up the Maumee to defend the Northwest Territory by building an American stronghold to be named Fort Wayne.

Little Turtle Seeks Assistance

The defeat of the Indians by the weapons of war was soon followed by a more insidious attack on them by the wiles and whiskey of the traders. The Miami chief, Little Turtle, spoke of this new danger during his visit to the East in 1801-1802. Riding horseback to Washington with William Wells[11] as interpreter, he appealed personally to President Jefferson to halt the traffic of liquor with his people. The president in turn asked the Ohio and Kentucky legislatures to enact and enforce such laws as Little Turtle requested. Upon his return, the Miami chief visited both of those territorial legislatures and renewed his appeal to suppress the sale of whiskey and promote agriculture: "We had better be at war with the white people. This liquor that they introduce into our country, is more to be feared than the tomahawk. There are more of us dead since the treaty of Greenville than we lost in the wars before, and it is owing to the introduction of this liquor among us."[12]

While passing through Baltimore in December 1801, Little Turtle was invited to address the Indian Affairs Committee of the Baltimore Society of Friends, in whom he expressed a rare trust: "Almost every white man that comes

Chief Little Turtle (Meshekenaque)
[Drawing by B. F. Griswold, 1917]

among us endeavors to cheat us. . . . But your talks, brothers, are different, and we believe you." When the Quakers asked how they might help their "red brothers," Little Turtle asked them to use their influence to embargo the shipment of liquor into Indian Territory. The Baltimore Society initiated a variety of petitions, but the whiskey trade in the three rivers region continued to flourish. John Johnston, the local Indian factor (whose wife was a Quaker), reported to the Baltimore Friends in 1808 that there was no enforcement of the regulations forbidding the sale of liquor: "[Whiskey] is sometimes sold to the Indians at this Post yet no notice has been taken of it. The white people treat this Law with great contempt, many alleging that the sooner the Indians are destroyed the better, and scarcely care by what means this is affected."[13]

Little Turtle had also asked the Baltimore Friends to help his people modernize their farming methods. In response,

the Society's Indian Affairs Committee sent agricultural implements to Fort Wayne in 1803—including plows, harness, axes, and hoes.[14] The Miamis were, in fact, quite skilled in agriculture. General Anthony Wayne had been impressed with their well-developed plantings and wrote:

John Johnston
[Drawing by B. F. Griswold, 1917]

"The very extensive and highly-cultivated fields and gardens show the work of many hands. The margins of those beautiful rivers, the Miamis of the Lake [Maumee] and Auglaize appear like one continued village for a number of miles both above and below this place; nor have I ever before beheld such immense fields of corn in any part of America, from Canada to Florida."[15] Miami agriculture was primarily managed by the women of the tribe using hand tools of traditional design, and the crops were generally limited to corn, beans, squash, and melons. Little Turtle, on his trips to the East, had observed the white settlers using steel implements with animal power on farms that were flourishing with a wide variety of produce.

When the Quaker gifts of plows and harness arrived in Fort Wayne, the chief perceived that they would lie idle without instruction and motivation, and so, in September 1803, he joined with Chief Five Medals of the Potawatomis in a written appeal to the Baltimore Friends:

Brothers and Friends of our hearts: We have received your speech from the hand of our friend,

5

William Wells, with the implements of husbandry, that you were so kind to send to his care,— all in good order.

Brothers, it is our wish that the Great Spirit will enable you to render to your Red Brethren that service which you appear to be so desirous of doing them, and which their women and children are so much in need of . . . .

Brothers, we are sorry to say that the minds of our people are not so much inclined towards the cultivation of the earth as we could wish them.

Brothers, our Father, the President of the United States, has prevented our traders from selling liquor to our people, which is the best thing he could do for his Red Children.

Brothers, our people appear dissatisfied because our traders do not, as usual, bring them liquor, and, we believe, will request our Father to let the traders bring the liquor; and if he does, your Red Brethren are all lost forever.

Brothers, you will see, from what we have said, that our prospects are bad at present, though we hope the Great Spirit will change the minds of our people, and tell them it will be better for them to cultivate the earth than to drink whiskey.

Brothers, we hope the Great Spirit will permit some of you to come and see us,—when you will be able to know whether you can do anything for us or not.

Brothers, we delivered you the sentiments of our hearts, when we spoke to you at Baltimore, and shall say nothing more to you at present. We now take you by the hand, and thank you for the articles you were so kind to send us.[16]

The Baltimore Friends immediately made plans to send an agriculturalist, Philip Dennis, in time for spring planting, accompanied by two members of the Indian Committee, Gerald T. Hopkins and George Ellicott. Before their departure, Secretary of War Henry Dearborn came from Washington to give the delegation letters of introduction to "the commanding officer at Fort Wayne, Mr. John Johnson, Indian Factor, and Mr. William Wells, Indian Agent." Dearborn wrote that the Quakers would be "visiting the Indians in the western country for the laudable purpose of affording them assistance in the introduction of the arts of civilization. . . and are entitled to all the civilities in your power to bestow."[17]

The Quaker Agricultural Mission

The Quaker deputation arrived at the headwaters of the Maumee on March 30, 1804, and was greeted by the commanding officer and lodged in the "house of a Canadian trader." After a meeting with Johnson and Wells, a message was sent to the chiefs, suggesting they confer as soon as possible. As the following day was Sunday, the Quakers attempted to find someone in the fort or village with whom they might join for worship; Hopkins wrote in his journal: "This is the first day of the week, and the inhabitants of Fort Wayne appear to pay no respect to it. The soldiers are on duty, and the Canadians who are settled here are busied with their several occupations."[18] On the next day, Little Turtle arrived to join Five Medals in a meeting with the Friends. Hopkins told the chiefs: "We have not come merely to talk, but we hope we have come prepared to do a little for the welfare of our red brethren." Five Medals responded: "Brothers, your brethren the Indians do business not as the white people do. We convene our chiefs, and things of importance are considered by them. . . . Our young men are out hunting, and our women and children are now at work at their sugar camps. The time is not far off when they will all return to our town, when it is usual to meet together. We hope, brothers, that you will not be in a hurry." The Quakers knew that, to make their agricultural school and demonstration farm a success, the corn had to be planted before June. Chief Five Medals then remarked that "they could easily convene a considerable number of their indolent people, who were too lazy to hunt or make sugar . . . but their industrious young men and women were too far from home to be convened in so short a time."[19]

A week later, Little Turtle sent word to the Quakers that he and Ossomit, a brother of Five Medals, would assemble on the morrow with some of their people to learn more of the plans. At the meeting Hopkins strove to inspire the tribal leaders to endorse a conscientious effort to till the land:

> Brothers and Friends: We are not ashamed to acknowledge that the time was when our forefathers rejoiced at finding a wild plum tree, or at killing a little game, and that they wandered up and down, living on the uncertain supplies of fishing and hunting. But, brothers, for your encouragement, we now mention that, by turning their attention to the cultivation of the earth . . . they soon had orchards of many kinds of good fruits—instead of wild game, they soon had large numbers of cattle, horses, sheep, hogs, and other valuable animals, and in many places, instead of their forests, they had large fields of corn and other grain . . . .

> Brothers . . . we will now tell you that we have not come merely to talk to you. We have come prepared to render you a little assistance. Our beloved brother, Philip Dennis, who is now present, has come along with us. His desire is to cultivate for you a field of corn; also, to show you how to raise some of the other production of the

6

earth . . . . Brothers, he has left a farm; he has left a wife and five small children, who are very dear to him; he has come from a sincere desire to be useful to our red brothers. His motives are pure; he will ask no reward from you for his services; his greatest reward will be in the satisfaction he will feel in finding you inclined to take hold of the same tools which he takes hold of, to receive from him instruction in the cultivation of your land . . . . All the corn, and other productions of the earth, which Philip Dennis may raise, we wish our red brethren to accept as a token of our friendship.

Hopkins knew that unless the young men of the tribe endorsed farming as an appropriate activity for men, their effort would be in vain: "Brothers, there is one thing more which we wish to add. The white people, in order to get their land cultivated, find it necessary that their young men should be employed in it, and not their women. Women . . . are not as strong as men. They are not as able to endure fatigue as men. It is the business of our women to be employed in our houses."[20]

Little Turtle's reply, taken down in shorthand by Hopkins, was cautiously optimistic: "I, as well as some others of my brother chiefs have been endeavoring to turn the minds of our people towards the cultivation of the earth, but I am afraid that we have not yet been able to effect anything . . . . We hope we shall finally be able to convince our young men that this is the plan we ought to adopt to get our living. . . . Brothers, tell your old chiefs . . . that this is a work which cannot be done *immediately*—that we are *that way disposed,* and we hope it will take place gradually." Little Turtle then announced that he and Five Medals had already decided that Dennis "should be at neither of our villages, lest our younger brothers be jealous. We have determined to place him on the Wabash, where some of our families will follow him— where our young men I hope will flock to him, and where he will be able to instruct them as he wishes. This is all I have to say."[21]

Little Turtle then bade the Quakers farewell. On the following day, guided by William Wells and Massanonga— who said he would be the first to take hold of the plow—the three men journeyed to the assigned site, thirty-two miles southwest of Fort Wayne; Hopkins wrote: "We are pleased to find . . . about twenty-five acres of land clear. . . . About half a mile below, a handsome creek falls into the river . . . it affords a good mill seat . . . . Bearing no name, we called it Dennis' Creek in honor of Philip Dennis . . . . At 9 o'clock we wrapped ourselves in our blankets and laid down to sleep before the fire . . . . In the night the otters were very noisy along the river; the deer also approached our fire and made a whistling noise; the wolves howled and, at the dawn of day, turkeys gobbled in all directions."[22] The next day Hopkins

and Ellicott "bade both a joyful and sorrowful farewell to Philip Dennis . . . [and] embarked for Detroit" in a pirogue manned by two soldiers of the fort.[23]

From an agricultural standpoint, the farm was a great success: the land was fertile and produced a large crop of corn and other products. As a school of agriculture, however, the enterprise was a failure. The Quakers later wrote: "After [Dennis] had, with some assistance from the Indians, enclosed his plantation with a rude fence, only one, or at the most two, of the red men evinced any disposition to labor. They would take a seat either on the fence, or in the trees, near the premises, and watch him with apparent interest in his daily engagement of ploughing and hoeing, but without offering to lend a helping hand." In the autumn, Dennis put his harvested crops in the storehouse he had built and informed the nearby village chiefs that these were given "as a winter supply for the necessitous members of the tribes."[24] He then returned to his home in Maryland.[25]

Several factors contributed to the lack of Indian participation. The location, although ideal for farming, was isolated: few Miamis lived between Fort Wayne and the demonstration farm, and the closest villages were Little Turtle's town, eighteen miles to the north, and Mississinawa, thirty miles to the south. Also, the chiefs had done little to prepare their young men for the arrival of the Quaker farmer, and did nothing to support his efforts by their presence or example. Perhaps, if the farm had been attached to a village whose chief was enthusiastic, enough of the people would have come to appreciate its value, and taken over the work the following year.

The most negative factor, however—over which neither the chiefs nor the Quakers had any control—was Miami culture, which did not respect farming as a noble activity, worthy of a hunter or a warrior. The stand of Little Turtle for peace, temperance, and agriculture won for him the admiration of many whites, but brought him only scorn from many of his tribe. General William H. Harrison, writing in 1814, two years after the chief's death, observed that his loss of standing with the tribes was due to his attempts to lead his braves to lay aside the scalping knife and take up the plow: "It [the rejection of white culture] was the rock upon which the popularity of Tecumseh was founded and that upon which the influence of Little Turtle was wrecked."[26] Tecumseh spoke against the treaties, the peace chiefs, and any other change in the traditional way of life. His brother, the Prophet (Tenskwatawa), temporarily assumed leadership in 1805 and asserted that he had received a revelation from the "Master of Life" declaring that the Indians could recover their lands and integrity by abstaining from alcohol and other perversions of white civilization, and by uniting against the white invader. His dream died in 1811 at the Battle of Tippecanoe and, discredited as a prophet, he fled to British Canada.

Most land-hungry Easterners preferred Tecumseh's image of the hunter-warrior to Little Turtle's image of the peaceful farmer, as it reinforced their contention that northern Indiana—which until 1818 was considered Indian territory—should no longer remain the exclusive hunting and gathering preserve for a few thousand Indians. Jesse L. Williams, an early Fort Wayne settler and church elder, summed up the local view of the American destiny ethic when he wrote in 1860: "The earth is for cultivation, not permanently for the chase. For great and beneficent providential ends—the greatest good to the greatest number—civilization and religion were to be introduced and the Redman has passed away."[27]

Isaac McCoy
[Courtesy of Allen County-Fort Wayne Historical Society]

The Baptist Mission School

If the Indians were not eager to adopt the ways of white "civilization and religion" it may have been in reaction to the character of many of the Americans with whom they came in contact. As federal treaty monies began to flow into the region, scores of unscrupulous traders rushed in to get every dollar, and their entrepreneurial activities sometimes created the atmosphere of a mythic orgy. James Riley, a surveyor working in the area in the fall of 1820, reported to the Surveyor General on the behavior of the traders at the annual distribution of the annuity to the Indians gathered at Fort Wayne:

There are now assembled, as I should judge, at least one thousand persons from Ohio, Michigan,

Christiana Polk McCoy (Mrs. Isaac)
[Courtesy of Allen County-Fort Wayne Historical Society]

Indiana, and New York whose object is stated to be that of trade with the Indians, in order to carry off some of their specie, paid them by the Government. They have brought whiskey in abundance, which they pretend to deposit with the agent, until he shall have finished his business with the Indians, but yet contrive to deal out large quantities from their deposits in the woods, so that the savages are kept continually drunk, and unfit for any business. Horse racing, drinking, gambling, and every kind of debauchery, extravagance and waste, are the order of the day, and night too; and in my opinion, the savages themselves are the most christianized, the least savage, of the two classes now congregated here. Here the whites set example to the Indians too indelicate to mention, and that cannot fail to produce in their minds disgust for the American character.[28]

It was to change this scene and improve the lot of the Indian that the Reverend Isaac McCoy had come to Fort Wayne in the spring. The young Baptist clergyman had previously been a daily witness to the degradation and sufferings of the Indians encamped about the post in Vincennes. The effect was profound, and the result was a life-long dedication: "My wife and I consecrated our lives and labor to the improvement of the condition of the Indians."[29]

McCoy was born in western Pennsylvania in 1784 and moved with his family to Kentucky when he was five years of age. At seventeen he joined the Baptist Church and began to preach; two years later he married Christiana Polk—whose mother and sisters had once been captured by Indians—and moved into southwestern Indiana. By trade he was a wheelwright and wagon maker; initially he supported his family by making spinning wheels and serving as keeper of the Vincennes jail. He had received little formal schooling and was not considered a powerful preacher; he was, however, judged to be a person of high character, and, in 1809, was ordained as the first pastor of the newly organized Maria Creek Church. Among the Articles of Faith adopted by this congregation was one of the first public statements enunciated in the Indiana Territory against slavery: "We believe that African Slavery as it exists in some parts of the United States is unjust in its origin and oppressive in its consequences, and is inconsistent with the spirit of the Gospel."[31]

McCoy's deep concern for persons of color led him to organize a society for domestic missions. Then, in 1817, he offered his services to the Baptist Triennial Convention (which had taken over the work of his mission society) and was given a one-year appointment to work with the Indians. Not every Indiana Baptist encouraged his calling: those of predestinarian persuasion considered missions to be contrary to God's eternal decrees, believing that only the elect would be saved; a more insidious opposition, however, came from the white traders near his Raccoon Creek mission at Montezuma, who immediately saw the missionary to be a threat to their activities. McCoy wrote: "The influence of certain individuals whose interest it is to keep them [the Indians] in ignorance, is so great that I sometimes tremble for the cause . . . . There are serious difficulties . . . the capricious disposition of the Indians, and the interest of the traders."[31] After two years of discouraging labor, McCoy became convinced that his mission could succeed only if it were sufficiently removed from the degrading influence of whites, and hoped that he might be appointed superintendent of one of the mills which the government proposed to erect within the Miami reserve in north-central Indiana.

In Fort Wayne, those associated with the Department of Indian Affairs perceived the benefit of an Indian School, and the Indian agent, William Turner,[32] urged the McCoys to settle there. McCoy wrote that he would rather have settled "at the Miami villages on the Massassinawa. But the agent, the principal Miami chief [Richardville], and many others, were united in endeavoring to bring us to Fort Wayne, and I was under the necessity of consenting."[33] In the spring of 1820, his family of eight, along with six Indian foster children, trekked north, driving fifteen head of cattle and forty-three swine. At one point, when he was scouting ahead, McCoy was attacked by a party of drink-crazed Indians; Louis Godfroy, a Miami, saved his life, and the next day Chief Jean Baptiste de Richardville met the party and conducted them safely to Fort Wayne.

The McCoys were well received by the people of the village and quarters were arranged in the fort, which had

Chief Jean Baptiste de Richardville
[Courtesy of Allen County-Fort Wayne Historical Society]

been decommissioned in 1819. He later recalled: "I preached to them in my own house on every Sabbath. On the twenty-ninth of May [1820] our school was opened; I was teacher myself. We commenced with ten English scholars, six French, eight Indians, and one Negro; the latter, we hoped, would one day find his way to Liberia,[34] in Africa . . . . Besides the care of the eight Indian children, and six of our own, the whole charge of the family, consisting of about twenty persons, devolved on Mrs. McCoy; she also endeavored to instruct neighboring Indian females in the art of knitting, and other domestic labors."[35]

In addition to the traditional classroom subjects, the students were instructed in "mechanical trades and agricul-

Isaac McCoy opened his school — the first established in the area — in the decommissioned fort.
[Original illustration by Kenneth B. Dutton]

ture"— and to appreciate the value of manual labor:

> As a matter of economy . . . we cultivated about thirty acres of corn, and mowed hay on the prairies. In attending to this . . . we sometimes employed the boys of our school. When they worked, I had to work with them, not only for the purpose of teaching them and of preventing idleness, but also to satisfy both them and their parents that we did not esteem labour disgraceful. . . . We have found his [the Indian's] mistaken sense of honor, esteeming it degrading to labour, a formidable obstacle to his improvement . . . . The Indians, discovering that the employees [of traders] were treated as menials, naturally drew the conclusion that manual labor was generally esteemed to be degrading among the whites. We found it necessary, therefore, to correct this impression by our own example.[36]

A schoolteacher was soon hired and enrollment in the school steadily increased to about fifty "scholars." Over the two years of its existence, five teachers arrived and soon departed; most found frontier life less romantic, and teaching Indian children more difficult, than they had imagined. Most of the students, however, including a grandson of Chief Richardville, wanted to learn; Thomas Scattergood Teas, who traveled through Fort Wayne in 1821, was impressed with the school and wrote:

> There is a school for the Indian children in the Fort, under the auspices of the Baptist Society. It is conducted on the Lancasterian System;[37] the teacher's name is Montgomery. On my arrival, as the school was the principal object of curiosity, I waited on the missionary whose name is McKoy(sic), and requested him to accompany me to it, which he did; and during my stay in Fort Wayne, treated me with an attention as unexpected as it was gratifying. There are about forty scholars. It is pleasing to see the order in which the school is kept, and the delight that the scholars seem to take in their studies. There are two boys of the Potawatomi tribe, who had been only two weeks at school, who were spelling words of four letters. As soon as they begin to learn their letters, they are furnished with a slate and form letters on it in imitation of printed type. Their improvement is such as to remove all doubts as to their capacity.[38]

McCoy Pleads for Teachers and Funds

It was this belief in the "capacity" of Indian children to learn the American "Rs" that sustained an optimism that the Native American could eventually be brought into nineteenth century "civilized society." McCoy, however, was one lone candle in northeastern Indiana. His teaching assistants lacked his commitment, and financial support for his mission was thin and sporadic. In November, he and his wife lay ill: "We were in much affliction; our circumstances had become such that we could not afford a comfortable meal for a sick person. Mrs. McCoy and myself needed little else, for the restoration of our health, than suitable food and a little *rest*. But our great distress was, lest for want of missionary and pecuniary aid, the children of our charge, and everything else, would exhibit such a ragged and ordinary appearance that the institution would become contemptible in the eyes of the Indians."[39]

McCoy now realized that he had to raise the funds for the mission himself, and made horseback trips to Dayton and Detroit to beg and borrow money. Gradually, as word of his pioneer mission became known in wider church circles, a few gifts of money and clothing trickled in; the first was from "a worthy Presbyterian brother, a Mr. Hudson, an entire stranger," in Detroit. These contributions, however, were soon spent, and so, in February 1821, McCoy rode to Detroit to plead for assistance from the Governor of the Michigan Territory, Lewis Cass. On the way, he wrote in his journal: "My mind is oppressed with anxiety. We are deeply in debt. Our wants have long since, and often, been made known to the [mission] board, but no relief has arrived . . . . Old debts are becoming due . . . and, should we not obtain relief soon, our mission must be broken up." McCoy was persuasive, and the governor furnished four hundred and fifty dollars' worth of clothing and food for the "Indian scholars." This contribution saved the day, but not the year; McCoy still lacked any dependable income with which he could plan ahead, and lamented: "We often had to create a debt with one person to procure the means of paying the other."[40]

McCoy also requested Governor Cass to send a teacher of agriculture to the village of White Raccoon (located fifteen miles to the west of Fort Wayne), explaining that they had "manifested a laudable disposition to improve their circumstances . . . [and] wished to procure a suitable white man to aid them." The governor assented, but none was ever sent. Another Indian leader who pleaded for McCoy's assistance was Menominee, who had led his village to abstain from alcoholic beverages, and wanted the missionary to settle among them to reinforce their resolve. McCoy, however, whose mission was seventy miles from the village, was unable to help or even offer the hope that someone else would come. He felt overwhelmed with his responsibilities, and discouraged that "among three or four hundred thousand of our denomination in the United States, none manifested a willingness to make his home in the desert, and teach these poor anxious inquirers the path to heaven."[41]

In Fort Wayne, progress on the "path to heaven" was

11

noticeable. McCoy's first Indian convert was Ann Turner (Ahpezahquah), the wife of the Indian agent. She was the daughter of William Wells and Sweet Breeze (Manwangopath), and a granddaughter of Little Turtle.[42] With her sister, Rebecca Hackley (Pemesahquah), she had been educated at a Catholic school in Kentucky. McCoy respected them:

> Their relations among the Miamis were influential, for the improvement of the condition of whom, and for the welfare of all the Indians, these women manifested a commendable solicitude . . . . Previous to our going to Fort Wayne, [Mrs. Turner's] mind had become much exercised upon the subject of religion . . . . In reading those passages in the Bible which spoke of God's displeasure with the heathen she supposed that, as she was an Indian, they applied to her, and therefore she had no hope for mercy. [Now] upon the subject of baptism her mind was clear,[43] but, on account of the scruples of her husband, her baptism was deferred for several months, and until he consented.

> About this time her sister, Mrs. Hackley, also gave satisfactory evidence of conversion to the faith of the Lord Jesus. Her baptism took place on the 18th of June [1821]. The scene was novel to all, both white and red, and on that account excited the more interest. At ten o'clock I preached on the subject of baptism. We then assembled at the fort gate, about sixty yards from the brink of the river Maumee. As the procession moved to the water, we sung "Thee, Great Jehovah, we adore, Who came the lost to seek and save."[44]

A hymn was composed for the occasion, which connected the baptism with the site of the bloody defeat of General Harmar's army at the river some thirty years before:

> This very stream was lately stained
> With blood from strangling soldier drained;
> Now, strange to tell, the Prince of Peace
> In it displays his sovereign grace.

> Ye oaks, which shook while cannons roar'd,
> Now bow your heads and praise the Lord;
> Tell the wild man beneath your shade
> Why Christ in Jordan's stream was laid.

> Those warlike towers on yonder wall,
> Like those of Jericho, must fall,
> While deathful weapons dormant lie—

> Shout, saints, the Ark is passing by.[45]

Fort Wayne had never before witnessed a river baptism. McCoy wrote: "The mixed assembly, consisting of whites and Indians, behaved well; many appeared serious, and some shed tears. As the candidate came out of the water, an elderly white woman, who in earlier life had been prisoner many years with the Indians, took her by the hand and said, 'I wish it was my case.' The afternoon's service was better attended than usual. This was a good day to a couple of poor missionaries."[46]

In conducting worship, McCoy had modified his preaching style to the custom of the Indians, who disdained shouting and gesticulating. He observed that, on a trip to Dayton, Ohio, a student who accompanied him looked in on a preaching service and was amazed "that the people hallooed, and jumped, and fell down, and were in confusion, 'like a company fighting.' At one time we were a while in the company of a preacher . . . whose gesticulations were more violent and less natural than those of an Indian. As soon as he had left, the lad asked me if that man was not intoxicated."[47]

Not long after news of the founding of a Baptist Mission at Fort Wayne had spread abroad, three priests, who were traveling through the area, paused on their journey to minister to the Catholic residents. McCoy wrote:

> Some of the few white people about Fort Wayne were French Catholics. These were visited by three priests, who came to administer the sacrament, &c. On Sunday, the 21st of April [1821], after worship at our house, I took our family, including our Indian pupils, to their meeting, and heard one of them preach. His subject was Baptism, and his discourse was directed against Baptist sentiments . . . . It happened that our white neighbors about Fort Wayne were exceedingly affectionate and friendly towards us; and in the attentions bestowed on the priests, the few days that they remained at our place, we were frequently invited to participate. This afforded them an opportunity of discovering that I would not be otherwise than friendly, and if my conjecture respecting their design was correct, it was entirely frustrated. At our request, they visited our school and drank tea with us.[48]

A Congregation Is Organized and Moves North

After a year in Fort Wayne, McCoy was still convinced that his mission should be located closer to the Indians and farther from the whites. Then, in 1821, when the government signed the Treaty of Chicago with the Miami, Potawatomi, and Ottowa tribes—agreeing to provide mills, schools, and other benefits to the Indians—McCoy made a four-week trip on horseback to Philadelphia to discuss with his mission board the new opportunities this treaty afforded. The Potawatomis had already requested McCoy to be their teacher, and asked that a mission, as well as a mill, be established at their reserve on the St. Joseph River (near the present site of Niles, Michigan). The board received McCoy's plan with enthusiasm and gave him the authority to select missionaries, hire assistants, and employ agents—and voted five hundred dollars for the erection of a mission house at the site. They also directed him to leave Fort Wayne whenever he should deem it expedient. McCoy immediately rode to Washington, accompanied by three of the board, and laid their proposal before the Secretary of War, John C. Calhoun. The Secretary declared his willingness to grant their requests when the treaty was ratified.[49]

Near the end of his return journey to Fort Wayne—by horseback in the dead of winter—McCoy became "so unwell as to be scarcely able to travel." Then, upon his approach to the village, he learned that, two days before, a Potawatomi Indian had almost murdered his nine-year-old daughter. He wrote in his journal: "This circumstance puts our missionary zeal to the test. O, how hard it is to regard a people affectionately, who, while we are toiling and suffering solely for their benefit and not our own, thus cruelly requite us . . . . But, alas! this abuse of my dear little daughter, who could not provoke insult. . . has taught me a lesson of human frailty . . . . We concluded to leave vengeance to Him to whom alone it belongs, and reflected that we should not regard *even life itself,* should we be called to sacrifice it in the work upon which we have entered."[50]

At this time McCoy had become increasingly concerned about the negative influence of the illegal liquor traffic with the Indians around Fort Wayne, and attempted to organize the local citizenry to combat this "most formidable obstacle to Indian reform":

> On the 12th of June [1822] we had a general meeting of the white inhabitants of the neighborhood, and formed a society. . . [which] resolved to solicit co-operation of all traders in the Indian country . . . . The individual who refused . . . was soon after detected in selling liquor to the Indians, with proof positive, which made him liable to fines for three offences . . . . The cases were. . . to be decided by the court in the village of Winchester, about eighty miles from Fort Wayne. The matter was, by the society, placed in the hands of the proper civil officers, and there it ended. Finding it impracticable to induce the execution of laws forbidding the sale of ardent spirits to the Indians, the society was not a little discouraged.[51]

If McCoy was displeased with the lack of cooperation by local authorities, he was encouraged by the speed with which the Secretary of War prepared his commission as "superintendent of the establishment" for the Potawatomis. In July, Governor Cass detailed his responsibilities:

> As teacher, you will give such instruction to the Indians, old and young, as you may deem best suited to their capacity, habits and condition. What portion of these instructions shall be moral and religious, must be referred to your own discretion . . . . It will be a paramount duty to inculcate proper sentiments towards the Government and citizens of the United States . . . .

> All attempts to meliorate the condition of the Indians must prove abortive so long as ardent spirits are freely introduced into the country. Their continued intoxication is the bane of all our efforts . . . . At the treaty concluded September last, at Chicago, Topenebe, principal chief of the Potawatomis, a man nearly eighty years of age, irritated at the continual refusal, on the part of the commissioners, to gratify his importunities for whiskey, exclaimed in the presence of his tribe, "We care not for the land, the money, or the goods; it is the whiskey we want—give us the whiskey." Under such circumstances, your efforts must be unceasingly directed to prevent the introduction of ardent spirits into Indian country . . . . It will be necessary for you to observe the conduct of the traders, and report any infractions of the laws . . . .

> It is impossible for the different tribes to support themselves by the product of the chase, and it is highly important that their attention should be directed to agriculture . . . . Without this radical change in their habits and views, their declension must be rapid, and their final extinction near and certain . . . . Endeavor, therefore, by precept and example, to reclaim them from the life of the hunter.[52]

By mid-summer, a minister, two schoolteachers, and a blacksmith had arrived in Fort Wayne with their families to join McCoy in the new mission enterprise. As a first step, the missionary families, under McCoy's leadership, organized themselves as a church. Baptist tradition was carefully observed. McCoy had invited several clergy in Ohio to assist, and one responded, the Reverend Corbly Martin (whom McCoy had baptized when he served as teacher at the Raccoon Creek Mission); Martin preached the constituting sermon on the text: "The wilderness and the solitary place shall be glad for them." Joining with the missionaries in signing the statement of faith were three local residents: "Wiskehelaehqua, a Delaware woman; Ann Turner, a Miami woman; Jesse Cox, a black man."[53] No local white settlers were invited to unite with the congregation, because McCoy knew that their presence would intimidate the Indians from participating fully—a sentiment vocalized by Wiskehelaehqua, who lived forty miles from Fort Wayne in Ohio, and said she "preferred joining the church at Fort Wayne, because that was intended for the Indians."[54]

The little congregation continued to meet regularly until preparations for the move were completed. Then, in late 1822, they scattered. Both the recently arrived clergyman and blacksmith, after a few months at the Fort Wayne mission, decided that they had misjudged their calling as missionaries and returned east, and one of the teachers died of typhus. McCoy, however, with his wife and children, carried the church charter with them to their new station and made it the nucleus of their new Carey Mission.[55] Then, in 1838, they saw the congregation move again when the Potawatomis were forced to trek to the West. The next year McCoy reported from Indian Territory: "The Potawatomi Baptist Mission Church, constituted at Fort Wayne, in the state of Indiana, August 3rd, 1822, which afterwards met at Carey, in Michigan Territory... now meets here."[56]

McCoy's work in Fort Wayne was as fruitful as any missionary in Indiana. He gained the confidence of the Indians and learned several of their languages; he won the respect of the settlers and equally important, he earned the confidence of federal officials and established a viable church-state partnership for the spiritual and material betterment of the Native American. In spite of enormous obstacles, McCoy never lost hope in the cause and never ceased working for its fulfillment.[57]

Chief Richardville's Judgment

One unhappy consequence for any future Protestant mission in the area devolved from a misconception of McCoy's work. Chief Richardville's grandson, who had attended the mission school, later became an alcoholic. Richardville projected blame for the young man's demise on the school, and then declared that none of his tribe would be allowed to attend any school except one taught by a Catholic.[58] As a result, the opportunity of any other Indian school being established in Fort Wayne was closed for the next decade, because no Catholic priest resided in the area until 1836,[59] and no Catholic school was established until 1844. In addition, Bishop Benedict Joseph Flaget—whose diocese of Bardstown, Kentucky, included Indiana (until 1835)— did not consider Indian missions to be a priority or even a possibility. In a letter to the Society of Paris-Lyon in 1828, he expressed the stereotype of the native peoples that was held by most whites of the region:

It is untrue to say that I have no Indians in my diocese; many nations of these poor barbarians live in Indiana and Illinois, two states that come under my jurisdiction. But I have such a scarcity of priests for the Catholics near me that it is impossible to occupy that mission which is so totally different from that which I conduct. The repugnance so unconquerable that the savages have for civilization, their intellectual faculties degraded and stupefied, their hate and vengeance implacable, their drunkenness so constant and disgusting, their laziness insurmountable, their wandering and vagabonded life more necessary today because the presence of the white man drives away the game . . . make the work of the missionary less fruitful.[60]

As a result of the bishop's attitude, the only opportunity for a Miami youth to receive a Catholic education was to study out of the state. At the urging of a Catholic priest, Richardville sent two other sons to Catholic schools, one in Louisville and the other in Montreal. A local resident reported: "When they returned to their home near Fort Wayne, they were as bright and interesting young fellows as could be found anywhere. Such they did not long continue. They had lost their taste for Indian life, and they had no disposition to engage in the pursuits of white men. They soon passed from listlessness to dissipation, and became the most degraded of the young men of the tribe. 'Education,' said their disappointed father, 'very good for white boys; bad, very bad, for Indians.' "[61]

Richardville had been raised in the Catholic faith by his parents, Joseph Drouet de Richardville, a French-Canadian trader from Vincennes, and Taucumwah (baptized Maria Louise), who was half-French and was called a "Chieftess." The Reverend Julien Benoit of St. Augustine's Church in Fort Wayne, however, noted with some disappointment that, when he celebrated mass in the Richardvilles' home, all the family received the sacrament except the old chief.[62] Hugh McCulloch remembered him as "a man of great natural shrewdness and sagacity, of whom no one got the better in a trade . . . . He was watchful of the interests of his own people, but by no means unmindful of his own. In all treaties, large reservations of the choicest land were secured to him, and not a few boxes of silver were set aside for his special use."[63] When Richardville died in 1841 at the age of eighty-one, he was the richest Indian in America and the wealthiest man in Fort Wayne. He was buried near the wall of St. Augustine's Church.[64]

Richardville had once said he trusted no one but Allen Hamilton and Julien Benoit. This priest, whom Richardville appointed to settle his estate, had a reputation of acting as friend and advocate of the Indians, especially during the distribution of their government annuities. On one occasion, Benoit is said to have compelled a Fort Wayne trader to refund seventy-five thousand dollars which had been fraudulently taken from the Miamis.[65] On the other hand, Allen Hamilton, who in 1841 became the government subagent for the Miami tribe, proceeded to tarnish his own reputation by dealing with some of Richardville's estate in a manner that enriched his own. A double standard of business ethics had long prevailed in frontier trading towns: merchants often dealt unscrupulously with the Indians, while treating their white customers with the expected standards of fairness and honesty. Hugh McCulloch, who once worked as a cashier in Allen Hamilton's bank, wrote: "There has been a good deal of Indian trade outside of the agencies in which the Indians have been cheated. Nothing surprised me more, as I became acquainted with the manner in which this was carried on, than the fact that men who had the reputation of dealing fairly with white men did not hesitate to practice the most shameful impositions in their dealing with Indians. I have known many men who were engaged in the Indian trade, but I cannot remember more than two or three who dealt with them with perfect fairness."[66]

The Removal of the Miamis

A formal agreement between the Miami Indians and the federal government was signed in 1840, in which Richardville and other chiefs of the Miami tribe agreed to cede their last reserve, located southwest of Fort Wayne along the Wabash River. For this concession the Miamis were granted $550,000, with the understanding that, in five years, they would relocate to the lands assigned to them near the Kansas-Missouri border. Richardville seems to have acceded to the inevitable: the Delawares had already been moved west in 1820 and the Potawatomis in 1838; only the Miamis were left. The Miami leader, however, had nothing to lose and much to gain by signing the treaty: not only would he and his family be exempted from the removal, but, as the civil chief, he would personally receive a substantial monetary reward from the government for inducing his people to assent.

The local white population was somewhat divided on the issue of Indian removal. The remaining Indian lands were coveted by a variety of Anglo-Americans, from rich speculators to poor squatters. Many Fort Wayne merchants, however, who had built their businesses on the flow of cash from the regular distribution of annuities to the Indians, were loath to see their golden goose deported. William G. Ewing, long active in the Indian trade, expressed the sentiments of most of the local businessmen when he wrote: "Would it not be well to suffer them [the Miamis] to occupy back and unimportant situations for a while, as their increased annuity will be of material benefit in the first settling of our country—and there is yet room for all."[67]

A fear of Indians still existed in the minds of some residents, and there were enough incidents of scattered violence by drunken Indians to reinforce these people's anxieties. Some remembered when refugees fled through town in the wake of the Black Hawk War in the spring of 1832. The Reverend Stephen Badin, a Catholic missionary to the Potawatomis near the Michigan border, was in Fort Wayne at the time and expressed the anxieties of most white settlers when he wrote:

> We have found ourselves unsettled on account of
> . . . the Indian War . . . . The alarm excited by
> Indian hostilities, promoted my friends to make
> me delay the prosecution of my journey to St.
> Joseph, as several families had passed through
> the town [Fort Wayne], flying from St. Joseph.
> But I set out on the 29th [of May], and we arrived
> safe at Bertrand's . . . . As I approached the place,
> I sang French cantiques, well known to the family
> with a view of not surprising them. But the means
> taken to prevent alarm caused a contrary effect, in
> the women at least, whose minds had been much
> agitated on that day by the assemblage at Niles,
> and the departure of 200 Militia for Chicago, near
> which some hostilities and murders by the Indi-
> ans had taken place.[68]

Although Black Hawk's warriors never threatened northeast Indiana, the sight of pioneer families fleeing to Ohio, and the report that the citizens of nearby LaPorte were building defensive blockhouses,[69] was unsettling. The bloody war in Illinois convinced most local residents that Indian removal was best, a sentiment later kept alive by newspaper accounts of Indian and settler confrontations in the newly opened lands to the west. As a result, no white voices were raised in defense of Indian rights east of the Mississippi. The general policy of the Federal Government, beginning with the presidency of Thomas Jefferson, was based on the conviction that the red and white races could not live together in harmony, and that an Indian reservation system, established west of the Mississippi River, was the only permanent solution to the Indian "problem."[70]

No responsible religious leaders had advocated the forcible deportation of the native Americans from their eastern treaty lands. Many, however, saw the Indians' relocation to be the lesser of two evils, because most of the tribes were not thriving in close proximity to the ever encroaching white settlements. In 1840, Isaac McCoy commented on the decline of the Miami since his departure from Fort Wayne eighteen years before:

> Most of the tribe continue on the same ground to
> this present time, in wretched condition and con-
> stantly diminishing in number. It is now too late
> to help them in that place, where they are closely
> hemmed in on every side by the white population,
> and are subject to the wasting influence of the
> causes which have injured all tribes surrounded

by white people. Their recovery can only be hoped for by their removal, and by vigorous humane efforts for their relief.

The tribe was once powerful, but it is now feeble; a few are located in the Indian territory west of the Mississippi; possibly this western settlement may prove to be a germ from which the tribe may again thrive, and outlive its present wretchedness.[71]

Generally, the American churches reluctantly agreed that relocation was the only solution to an intractable situation and, in the same breath, dedicated themselves to establish mission schools and churches on each new reservation. The Protestants planned their new Indian missions cooperatively, so that each denomination would have specific tribal reservations as a unique responsibility with no overlapping competition.

The Miamis naturally feared the federal government's plan for their removal to Kansas and tried legal means to prevent or postpone their deportation. As a result, the August 1844 deadline for their withdrawal had to be extended to May 1845; even then, the Indians refused to assemble for their transportation while their new chief, Francis LaFontaine, was pleading their cause in Washington, D. C. In addition, the Miamis' natural resistance to removal was secretly encouraged by the avarice of the local traders, whose future fortunes depended on the Indians receiving their annuity payments in Indiana where their trading licences were legal.

When all hope was extinguished, the Indians declared that they would not leave unless their priest, Julien Benoit, accompanied them. The request was not without precedent. The Miamis knew that, in 1838, the Reverend Benjamin Petit had accompanied the Potawatomi tribe on their infamous "Trail of Death" when they were forced to march from the St. Joseph River near South Bend to the Osage River in the West.[72] In addition to the heartfelt pleas of the Miamis, Benoit also was subjected to pressure from the commander of the Federal troops who had been sent to effect the deportation. The officer told Benoit: "Unless you go with them, they will not go and I will be obliged to hunt them down like wild beasts and kill them."[73]

In September 1846, a detachment of Federal troops came through Fort Wayne to remove the last of the Miami Indians from their historic homeland. Just three months before, two quickly formed companies of United States Army recruits had left Fort Wayne to fight in the Mexican War. In both actions, American soldiers were deployed to acquire more land for those westward-driving white settlers whose two-tiered morality had excluded Native Americans from national constitutional guarantees of liberty and justice for all.

Finally, in October 1846 at Peru, the move began in a

scene of high emotion and extraordinary confusion as Miami families assembled and exempted relatives[74] came to say farewell. The *Fort Wayne Sentinel* reported: "A detachment of U. S. soldiers, under the command of Capt. Jouett arrived here on Wednesday last and proceeded to Peru. Capt. Jouett is said to be a thoroughgoing, prompt, energetic old soldier, who will carry out his instructions to the letter, without fear or favor—just the kind of man to make short work of a job of this kind. He has had some experience in this business,

Chief Francis LaFontaine
[Courtesy of Allen County-Fort Wayne Historical Society]

having been engaged in the removal of the Cherokees and some other tribes."[75] A local resident later remembered: "Many of the Indians had to be brought forcibly to the place of rendezvous previous to taking their departure. Many had to be hunted down like wild animals; some were actually found in the tops of trees, others secreted themselves in swamps, and many fled from the locality, coming back only after the emigration had taken place, only to be forwarded as prisoners to their new home in the eastern part of Kansas."[76] There was a similar scene at the St. Mary's and Eel rivers as families packed to join the large contingent at Fort Wayne.

Many of the local populace, relatives, friends, and sensation seekers, gathered along the canal to watch the last of the Indians leave by canal boat for the West. A Fort Wayne citizen later wrote: "Well I remember the sober, saddened faces, the profusion of tears, as I saw them hug to their bosoms a little handful of earth which they had gathered from the graves of their dead kindred . . . and, as the canal boat that bore them to the Ohio River loosed her moorings, many a bystander was moved to tears at the evidences of grief he saw before him."[77] A twentieth-century historian of the Miamis said of the process of removal: "At least it was a ceremonial exodus—more humane, more worthy of both the federal government and the Indians than the herded caravans of the 1830s."[78]

The morally sensitive people of Fort Wayne were divided in their judgments of this forced exodus to the promised land in the West. Some saw, or wanted to see, the relocation as a benefit to the Indians by resettling them closer to a natural environment and farther from the vices of white culture. One local citizen rationalized: "No doubt these people would be more prosperous and happy west of the Missouri, among their old friends the Shawnees, Delawares, Potawatomis, and other emigrated tribes, than among the whites, and under laws they do not understand."[79]

Some Protestant Christians in Fort Wayne, however, saw the Indian removal as an indictment of their local congregations' failure to have reached out to their Miami neighbors with sincere invitations to worship together in love and friendship, on the excuse that all of the Indians were Catholic. One such distressed Protestant, six months before the deportation, was so moved by the impending exile to write "An Appeal for the Miamis":

> Why should every Christian's gold
>   Across the ocean flow?
> While souls at home each sin do hold,
>   Unask'd "why do ye so?"
>   Dark Nature's child,
>   In wigwam wild,
>   Can often hear
>   Our church-bells near,
> But never hears a Savior's love
> That brought him down from realms above,
>   To save poor sinners lost.
>
> What would be thought of parent proud,
>   Who gave his thousands out,
> When Fame would sound the deed aloud,
>   And hand his name about?—
>   Yet ne'er supplied
>   His wretched bride,
>   And helpless brood,
>   With clothes and food!
> None needs to know. I ask again,

> Will not some view with hearts of pain,
>   Our own soil's children here?
>
> Bleeds, bleeds my soul, to see them there,
>   In villages and glens,
> The young, the old, the brave, the fair,
>   Friends, victims, for all Sins.
>   With minds untrained,
>   Passions unchained,
>   With liquor swill'd,
>   (By hell distill'd)
> By white men — hold! to God, belongs
> The arm of vengeance for their wrongs,
>   I dare, but will not speak.
>
> Some may assert: "They're Papists, all,
>   And therefore out of reach,"
> But find me ten that you would call
>   Aught versed in what they teach!
>   Great kings of old,
>   Were very bold
>   To hold vast lands
>   At their commands
> By right of mere discovery!
> That's near the way that Popery
>   Doth hold these Savages.
>
> O Savior! Thou, who hast the hearts
>   Of all men in thine hands,
> Incline some, now, to act right parts,
>   In well directed plans:
>   To teach the youth
>   In Learning's truth,
>   To give to all,
>   Salvation's call;
> And thus obey thy last behest,
> And make themselves and others blest,
>   Now and forever more.[80]

For others in Fort Wayne the removal of the Indians was an event to be ignored; one local newspaper, the *Times and People's Press,* chose to disregard the deportation by printing a scant two-sentence announcement. The *Sentinel* said more, reflecting the irritation of many people who felt that the Indians had delayed too long in fulfilling their treaty obligations: "It is no doubt a great hardship to these poor Indians—the last remnant of a once mighty tribe—to have to leave the homes of their fathers, and give up possession of the rich and beautiful country they have so long owned; but these lands were years ago sold to the Government of the United States for an ample consideration, part of which has been received by the Indians; the time they were to be allowed to remain has been extended; every indulgence had been shown to them, and it is but justice they should now comply with their treaty stipulations."[81] A week later this editor gleefully reported: "Their lands—the finest portion of this State . . . are now open for settlement . . . . In the meantime, settlers are flocking in from all quarters to secure pre-emption rights and but a few years will lapse before the 'Miami Reserve' will be one of the richest and best parts of the state."[82] In an adjacent column it was reported that Federal troops had just captured Santa Fe with the declaration "New Mexico is ours." Ironically, the retreating army of four thousand Mexicans was mostly Indians, and the remaining New Mexican tribes, like their Miami cousins, would soon learn what little of their historic lands they would be allowed to keep.

Three hundred and twenty-four Miamis left Fort Wayne on canal boats and followed the Wabash and Erie waterway to its junction with the Miami and Erie Canal in Ohio; they then went south through Dayton to Cincinnati where the entire party was transferred to a steamboat to travel down the Ohio River. At St. Louis they changed vessels and steamed up the Missouri River, disembarking at Kansas Landing (now Kansas City) on November 1. Then, traveling overland they reached the Osage subagent eight days later, where they were met by Joseph Comparet of Fort Wayne who had successfully transported ninety of their horses from Indiana to Kansas.

Chief LaFontaine immediately called a council, apologized to the Indian agent for their fractiousness at Peru, and said they were pleased with their new home. The council then declared that education was of first importance and, in their new home, they wanted a school operated by the Catholic Church.[83] The chiefs had previously resolved in council "not to allow any whites to settle among them, or on their lands, except the missionaries and teachers."[84] The continued care and concern of both Protestant and Catholic missionaries was so valued by the tribe that, by 1848, most of the Miamis had moved a few miles from their original location on Sugar Creek over to the east bank of the Marais de Cynes River in order to be nearer to their new Baptist and Catholic missions,[85] as well as farther from the Missouri border where grog shops abounded with that old nemesis of the Miamis.

Julien Benoit stayed with the tribe in Kansas for two weeks and then returned to Fort Wayne in a non-stop nine-day trip by stage coach. His pastoral concern for the Indians was now directed toward those exempt Miamis of mixed blood, whose status in Indiana was yet to be fixed. In 1831, the Indiana General Assembly had proposed a constitutional amendment that would have given citizenship to all Indians in the state. It was defeated; hence any person who was only "one-eighth" Indian was legally denied the right to buy land, vote, or hold public office. In 1846, the newest emigrants from Europe could easily buy the expropriated lands of the Miamis, but these Native Americans had no equal right to control any land transactions for themselves. Finally, on December 5, 1848, the Indiana General Assembly granted the right of land conveyance to Indians upon a petition through the county probate court. All sales, however, were to be made through a bonded agent. In Allen County, Benoit was appointed to that position because of the great trust the Indians put in him. As a successful entrepreneur in real estate, as well as the executor of the estates of Chief Richardville and Chief LaFontaine (who had died the year before), Benoit was well equipped to assist the Indians in their land transactions.[86]

Epilogue

The final chapter of the Indians at Fort Wayne was recorded by the Sisters of Providence who taught the young girls of the local Miami families who had been exempted from the deportation. All of the daughters of James Godfroy, who later became chief, were educated at St. Augustine's Academy for Girls, as were Mary Richardville and Esther LaFontaine, who went on to study at the order's school at St. Mary-of-the-Woods. None were full-blooded Miamis and several had the blue eyes and fair complexion of Richardville. Benoit noticed that they were often ill and once told the sisters at the school: "You would not have so much sickness were it not for these wild birds of the forest."[87] Their health continued to be fragile and most of the Richardville and LaFontaine children were short lived; only Archange LaFontaine (Engleman) lived to an old age.

Thus closed the Indiana chapter of the Miamis who had once dominated the three rivers area. A Fort Wayne leader later said: "There is cause for national humiliation in the fact that their disappearance has been hastened by the vices, the cupidity, the injustice, the inhumanity of people claiming to be Christians."[88]

2

Early Presbyterians

1822 - 1843

"I am . . . convinced none would be so useful as a minister from the Presbyterian Church—in as much as they are generally better educated."

Allen Hamilton, 1828

The Presbyterian Church, in 1822, was the first Protestant denomination to send a clergyman to the residents of the newly platted town of Fort Wayne. Although a Baptist minister had established a short-lived mission church for the Indians, it was the Presbyterians who founded the town's first Sunday School, organized the first continuing congregation, erected the first church building, and opened the first church-related school. Its pastors founded the community's first total temperance, tract, and Bible societies, and were the first to advocate the abolition of slavery; its members were leaders in the new causes of moral reform, and were the only local congregation to grant full voting privileges to women.

John Ross Preaches at the Fort

In the final weeks of 1822, the residents of Fort Wayne witnessed the departure of the area's last missionary to the Native Americans and the arrival of the first Protestant pastor to the Anglo-Americans. The Reverend John Ross, affectionately titled "Father" Ross in his later years,[1] arrived in Fort Wayne on a bitter cold night in December. Ross was a forty-year-old native of Dublin, Ireland, who, at the age of nineteen, had been seized by a press-gang in Liverpool and put on board a British man-of-war. In Barbados he escaped a third impressment, stowed away on an American vessel, and landed in New London, Connecticut—"hatless, shoeless, and penniless." A nominal Roman Catholic, Ross soon became active in the religious life of the community, experienced a profound conversion, and declared his desire to enter the Protestant ministry. His sincerity and potential were recognized and, with the aid of a women's society, he pursued theological studies at Middlebury College and Princeton Seminary. After serving congregations in Pennsylvania, Ross came to Ohio, and in 1822 was ministering at the New Jersey settlement in Butler County, Ohio. His visit to Fort Wayne was by appointment of the Presbyterian General Assembly to labor for three months "as missionary among the destitutions of this [St. Mary's River valley] frontier region."[2] Ross depended entirely upon the churches in the East to support his missionary labors, and "often said that, during these years he was missionating thro' the West, the money he received for preaching would not have clothed one of his children."[3]

In later years, Ross described in detail his first trip to Fort Wayne. He had arranged to travel with Matthew Griggs, a Presbyterian merchant from Lebanon, Ohio, who was transporting a cargo of hats and dried fruit in his light, two-horse wagon. Their first night's sleep in the woods north of Dayton was made fitful by the "howling of wolves on every side"; the next day a snow storm broke upon them "with intense cold," freezing the wheels of the wagon fast in the mud. Unable "to strike a fire from the flint," they left the wagon under guard of Grigg's dog and, leading the horses—"the cold being too severe to ride"—they walked the rest of the way, arriving late on a Saturday night at the home of Samuel

John Ross, caught in a snowstorm, helps Matthew Griggs unhitch the horses to walk to Fort Wayne.
[Original Illustration by Kenneth B. Dutton]

Hanna. Ross recollected: "The next day being the Sabbath, I preached in the Fort morning and afternoon, because there was no other convenient place to preach in . . . . I visited the place five times from 1822 to 1826. I was once sent out to Fort Wayne by the Synod of Ohio. In all my visitations I preached in St. Mary's, Shane's Prairie, and Willshire, and scattered religious tracts and Bibles. There was no place that appeared to me so unpromising as Fort Wayne."[4]

John Ross was not the first Presbyterian minister to conduct services within the palisades of Fort Wayne. During the War of 1812, the Reverend Matthew Wallace, a Presbyterian pastor from Ohio, served as chaplain to the army under General William Henry Harrison and accompanied the troops in their march to the relief of the Fort Wayne garrison.[5] The visit of a chaplain, so common in today's military, seems to have been totally absent in the life of the fort at that time. John Johnston, who served as the first Indian factor at Fort Wayne from 1802 to 1811, said, "There was not a Protestant clergyman of any denomination that performed divine service at the post . . . . The only officer of the army, within my knowledge, who publicly professed Christianity, was Col. Vose, who commanded at Fort Wayne about the year 1816 or 17. This noble Christian soldier was in the constant practice of assembling his men on the Sabbath day to read the scriptures and converse with them relative to their duties and the salvation of their souls—a rare instance of Christian fidelity and the power of divine grace. I never knew to what denomination he belonged. The conduct of such a man and under such circumstances, can only be appreciated by persons familiar with the allurements and temptations of military life."[6]

James Hanna Starts a Sunday School

The spiritual seeds sown by John Ross between 1822 and 1826 were nurtured by another Irish Presbyterian, James Hanna, who founded the first Sunday school in Fort Wayne. Born in 1753 in Ballyboy, Ireland, Hanna immigrated to America at the age of ten when his parents joined with their entire Presbyterian congregation to sail to America and settle in Pennsylvania.[7] Both his parents had died by the time he was thirteen; he was then bound out to a neighboring Presbyterian family in Bucks County where he learned the weaving trade. Hanna married, moved to Kentucky and then to Ohio, where he established a thriving weaving business in Dayton. On the day the Dayton Presbyterian Church was organized, Hanna was elected an elder; he took an equally active part in founding the local Moral Society, the first schools, and the Bible Society. Thus, when James Hanna, at the age of seventy-two, journeyed to Fort Wayne in 1825 to visit his son Samuel and daughter Nancy Barnett (and possibly son Hugh), he was well equipped to organize the settlement's first Sunday school.[8]

The Sunday school movement had been born in England in the eighteenth century and had begun to flourish in most American Protestant churches in the early nineteenth century. Study materials for Sunday school scholars were provided by several interdenominational organizations, especially the American Bible Society (founded in 1821) and the American Tract Society (begun in 1825); during the next thirty-five years these agencies published more than two

James Hanna
[Courtesy of Allen County-Fort Wayne Historical Society]

hundred million books and tracts. The American Sunday School Union (founded in 1824) awakened the eastern churches to the spiritual needs of the western settlements and, at its annual assembly in 1839, resolved to "establish within two years a Sunday school in every destitute place where it is practical throughout the Valley of the Mississippi."[9] The Reverend Isaac Reed—another product of Middlebury College, who labored forty years in Indiana and founded more churches there than any other eastern missionary—said that the Sunday school of sixty members he organized in New Albany in 1818 in the "miserable log school house [was] the first ever formed in Indiana."[10] The Sunday school founded by James Hanna in 1825, which met in the storeroom of Samuel Hanna's store, was probably the first to be formed in the new lands of northern Indiana—one in which "for some years all Protestant denominations united."[11]

Josiah H. Vose, commandment of Fort Wayne from 1817 to 1819, converses with his men after Sunday worship.

[Original Illustration by Kenneth B. Dutton]

Allen Hamilton Petitions for a Minister

The interchurch agency which had the greatest potential to aid the "destitution" at Fort Wayne was the American Home Missionary Society. Founded in 1826, this new organization was a merger of several voluntary groups who were dedicated to provide pastors for the new settlements of the American West. Well financed by eastern Congrega-

Allen Hamilton
[Courtesy of Allen County Public Library]

tionalists and Presbyterians, it became an enthusiastic patron of domestic missionaries, especially in Ohio, Indiana, Illinois, Iowa, Michigan, and Wisconsin. Between 1829 and 1850, funds from the Home Missionary Society partially supported the first four Presbyterian ministers, as well as three of the first German speaking pastors in Fort Wayne. The Society's aim was to place full-time working ministers in the frontier towns as quickly as possible. Their preachers were not to ride circuits in general, but develop specific congregations with local support. These organized churches would then apply to the Home Missionary Society for aid, with the understanding that its assistance would diminish as local support increased.

In 1828, Allen Hamilton, a red-haired Irish-born settler, was selected to write to the headquarters of the American Home Missionary Society in New York City for their assistance in providing a minister for Fort Wayne.[12] Hamilton

had come to Fort Wayne in 1823 to become Deputy Registrar of Land Titles. The following year, the Governor appointed him sheriff of Allen County, a position from which he resigned two years later, perhaps to devote more time to his new commercial partnership with Samuel Hanna and James Barnett. All three were Scotch-Irish and Presbyterians. In October 1828, Hamilton had married Emerine Jane Holman of Aurora; three weeks later he wrote the first of many letters that would be sent by Fort Wayne church people to the headquarters of the American Home Missionary Society in New York City:

> The remoteness of this situation deprives us the benefit of hearing the word of God preached by a regular minister of the gospel . . . . There has been no resident minister since the time the town was laid out — the Revd. Isaac McCoy, a Baptist missionary with the Indians leaving here at that time . . . . I cannot say I have any prepossessions in favor of the tenets of any denomination. I am, however, convinced none would be so useful as a minister from the Presbyterian Church—in as much as they are generally better educated, and others here having predilections in favor of that order— their connections being members of that church in other parts.[13]

The spiritual benefit accruing from the presence of a minister and a church at Fort Wayne was not the only motive in the minds of the merchants and landowners in Fort Wayne; all knew that significant material benefits would be reaped from an influx of new settlers, and that the establishment of a church was essential in making their "remote settlement" appear appropriately civilized: "The unwillingness of farmers who are regular members of the church to move here and be deprived of regular worship . . . with other inducements yet stronger, gives me a great solicitude to have a regular minister amongst us." Hamilton also understood the economics of church development, and concluded his letter with assurances that the community would support a minister: "I doubt not a sum could be raised in part to aid in his support. I would cheerfully add my might and pledge my best exertions in promoting the same—we cannot however expect to be able to meet the necessary sum without aid from the board for one or two years, after which time I doubt not a church can be formed which will be enabled to support themselves without any other aid."[14]

Charles Furman Arrives

The Home Missionary Society considered Fort Wayne's spiritual needs to be worthy of its support, and on November 13, 1829, Charles Edwin Furman arrived from Ohio where

**Matthew Wallace, chaplain to the army under William Henry Harrison, greet soldiers
of the Fort Wayne garrison during the War of 1812.**
[Original Illustration by Kenneth B. Dutton]

he had been serving as an agent for the American Tract Society since his graduation from Auburn Theological Seminary the year before. As a seminary graduate without a formal pastoral charge, he was termed a licentiate, awaiting a congregation's call in order to be ordained. He came, therefore, with full ecclesiastical authority to preach, teach, and officiate at weddings and funerals; he could not, however, organize a church, as he was not allowed to administer the sacraments or moderate a church session.[15]

Most of the Society's missionaries, such as Furman, were educated in the colleges and seminaries of the East, until such western schools as Hanover, Wabash, and Lane became effective. All, with a few exceptions, were Presbyterians and Congregationalists who approved of the "Plan of Union of 1801" between the two denominations, a scheme which had been designed to eliminate competition and foster cooperation on the frontier. Theoretically, Presbyterian churches could call Congregational ministers and Congregational churches could call Presbyterian ministers; in Fort Wayne, although half of the first Presbyterian ministers had been raised in Congregational churches, all became Presbyterians.[16]

The Missionary Society had well defined expectations of its clergy on the frontier. Ministers were to hold meetings in whatever places were convenient to the scattered population, which, in the greater Fort Wayne area, meant establishing as many as eight preaching points around the county. In addition, they were to promote education in both the Sabbath schools and community schools, form praying societies and missionary associations, promote the temperance movement, distribute Bibles, religious books, and tracts, convert unbelievers, build up churches, and generally improve the moral quality of the community.

Finding a suitable place for worship in Fort Wayne was always a challenge: Ross and McCoy preached at the fort; private homes usually accommodated visiting Catholic priests; the back room of Hanna's store sheltered the Sunday school; but, when news of the impending arrival of a resident minister spread through the area, the people set themselves to refurbish the town's schoolhouse. In February 1830, Furman was able to report:

> We have a schoolhouse which will hold 250 if they are well stood.[17] Immediately after I came, the people prepared the house for worship by plastering it and seating it. I preached two or three times and expected that I should, like my predecessors, be neglected. But from the first two weeks the house had been full and sometimes crowded; last Sabbath the house was as full as it would hold; many on the outside and many returned home, the ground being very wet. I never knew for the same number of inhabitants, in any place, so many attendants upon preaching

of the Gospel . . . . There is a Masonic Hall which will be fitted up early in the summer designed for public worship which will hold more by a third than our present house. And the people already say that, with two or three years at most, they must have a house built exclusively for the worship of God and must support their minister themselves.

Samuel Hanna
[Courtesy of Allen County Public Library]

Furman, who had been accompanied by James Hanna on his journey to Fort Wayne, was awed by the isolation of the settlement: "From this place one hundred miles in every direction it is almost a perfect wilderness. There is no Presby. Church or minister nearer than Piqua, Indianapolis, Logansport or Monroe near Detroit. The county only contains seven or eight hundred inhabitants, between three and four hundred of whom live in town." He also concluded that the wilderness had not shielded the inhabitants from "dissipation." "This has been a place of Indian trade and formerly a garrison of soldiers was stationed here. The people who came here were enterprising and have done well in business, whiskey having been a principal article of traffic. Many have fallen and are still falling prey to dissipation. Indians knowing no Sabbath, the dealers . . . would even choose to trade upon the Sabbath . . . [which] was much the most noisy day of the seven . . . . When I came here almost all the stores were kept open constantly, but . . . now there is a great difference and . . . a reformation in the external conduct of men is rapidly working. The people were formerly under no religious restraint and had run wild as the foxes."

Furman then reported on his labors in preaching and teaching, visiting and organizing: "Without a library, excepting a very small selection of tracts, I have a small, though interesting, Sabbath school. I have attached to the school a young men's Bible class, and also a female B[ible] C[lass] which I attend every Thursday afternoon. I preach regularly upon the Sabbath at 11 A.M., at candle lighting and generally Wednesday evening. I visit very much and am familiar with almost all in town. There are about 7 or 8 who have been professors of religion . . . and I think now a church might be formed of at least a dozen members."

Furman knew that the success of his missionary enterprise depended on the receptiveness of the people, which, in part, was conditioned by their religious persuasions. "I do not know of any Deists in the place. There are as many as three or four who say they have thought that the doctrine of universalism might be true . . . . There are no newlights or Unitarians . . . a few Baptists, all of whom are very friendly to me and constantly attend my preaching. There are a few Methodists tho' no church of any kind exists here, and I think that I may safely say that the might of influence is on the side of the Presbyterians. The people are hospitable and have more intelligence and liberality of feeling than any similar town I have found in the Western country. . . . I had forgotten to say that there is a small population of Catholicks here, some of which attend punctually my preaching."[18]

The Temperance Society

In addition to encouraging Fort Wayne citizens to observe the more sedate traditions of Protestant Sabbath observance, Furman took up the equally controversial cause of temperance. In May 1830, he was able to report that, in spite of some opposition, he had organized a temperance society with "more than forty members with the prospect of a number more, and there is at least one half diminution in the amount of ardent spirits consumed by the white population."[19]

Sabbath observance was a religious practice endorsed by the first Puritans, but abstinence from alcoholic beverages was a new issue for the churches; the Biblical commandments, which were unequivocal on keeping the Sabbath holy, were silent on drinking. Scotch whisky had been regularly served at meetings of the Philadelphia Presbytery throughout the eighteenth century and, until the year 1800, most of the ordinations and installations of Protestant pastors were accompanied by liberal libations of beverage alcohol. Silas C. Jones, son of the Reverend Daniel Jones who preached in the Presbyterian Church in 1836, noted the clergy's sharp change of attitude by 1825: "When father

started to prepare for the ministry, a bottle of gin was a part of his outfit, but when temperance societies first started in this country, father was the first man in the town where he lived to sign the temperance pledge, and was ever after a warm friend to the cause."[20]

It was physicians, however, not clergy, who launched the temperance movement. In 1788, Dr. Benjamin Rush, the first Surgeon General, published a striking paper which discouraged the consumption of distilled spirits and suggested the alternative use of beer and wine. He further prescribed a mixture of the opiate laudanum with wine for those who found the change from ardent spirits too painful. In 1826, the American Society for the Promotion of Temperance was founded and, by 1833, it counted six thousand local societies with one million members who had signed its pledge. The temperance movement quickly became a moral tidal wave which rolled across the Appalachians and broke with force on the village of Fort Wayne in 1830, and continued to roil until the passage of the Prohibition Amendment ninety years later.

Initially, the aim of the temperance movement focused on responsible moderation, but when the social problems of alcohol abuse seemed untouched by this philosophy, the movement's leaders increasingly advocated total abstinence. At first, individuals who joined a local society registered their total abstinence position by writing a "T" after their name, to be ever after termed "T-totalers." Members of Presbyterian, Baptist, Methodist, and Congregational churches could expect their pastors to be teetotalers, as well as their elders and deacons. Indiana church historian L. C. Rudolph noted: "Churches . . . came to make total abstinence a condition of church membership. Most of the new churches formed by American Home Missionaries were formed on this basis."[21] The result of this hardening of the categories was to create a body of regular church attenders who declined to join its membership in order to avoid any censure from the pastor or church officers. A second consequence was the splintering of the temperance movement in Fort Wayne into two societies, the teetotalers and the moderationists, who occasionally expended as much energy fighting each other as they did "demon rum."

Charles Furman was committed to temperance, but he was not committed to Fort Wayne. He had told the Home Missionary Society in his first report that he wanted to be ordained in his native state, and at the end of May he departed for the East. By the end of the summer he had been ordained by the Presbytery of Skaneateles, New York, installed as pastor of the Presbyterian Church in Clarkson, New York, and married. Furman had followed his own advice; in his final report to the Mission Society he had counseled: "Tell your missionaries to get married—I certainly believe it best. I am told that many [in Fort Wayne] object to support [me] because, say they, 'We do not know that he will stay with us.'"[22]

Furman was the first clergyman since Isaac McCoy to remain in Fort Wayne for as long as six months. As a result, many residents became accustomed to regular Sunday worship, and saw the spiritual and moral climate of the town elevated by the presence of a minister. They now wanted more of the same, and immediately petitioned the Home Missionary Society for another pastor equally eager and conscientious, but one already settled in marriage and comfortable with frontier life.

James Chute: Fort Wayne's First "Settled" Pastor

There was no waiting list of Presbyterian clergy eager to assume a vacant pastorate on the western frontier, and the embryonic congregation remained without spiritual leadership during the remainder of 1830. Then, in early 1831, the need for a missionary in Fort Wayne came to the attention of the Reverend James Chute, who was at the time serving as chaplain to the State Prison at Columbus under appointment by the Synod of Ohio. Chute was forty-two years of age and married with four children. A native of Rowley, Massachusetts, he attended the Drummer Academy and was graduated from Dartmouth College, New Hampshire, in 1813; soon afterwards, he migrated to Cincinnati, Ohio, where he first began a business and later established a school. In 1821, he was ordained a ruling elder in the First Presbyterian Church of Cincinnati and grew in the conviction that he should enter the ministry. His pastor, the Reverend Joshua L. Wilson, encouraged this inclination by directing his private studies in theology. After he was licensed to preach, Chute supplied vacant churches in the Cincinnati area until 1828, when he was called to the prison chaplaincy and subsequently ordained.[23]

At the invitation of the Presbyterians at Fort Wayne, Chute made a three-week visit to the community, arriving during the last week of June 1831. He was well received and a dozen of the residents immediately announced their desire to be organized into a congregation. On Saturday, July 1, the pastor met at the Masonic Hall with seven of the group—five women and two men—who presented certificates of membership from their churches in the East. After hymns, scripture, and prayer, these members then elected the two men as ruling elders. On the following day, during Sunday worship, the elders were ordained; then, after services, the pastor and elders constituted themselves as the church session, electing Chute as moderator and Smalwood Noel as clerk. The officers were then able to examine and receive into the day-old congregation four additional members who had no active church membership—as well as one other by letter of transfer.[24]

The little congregation—the first organized in Fort Wayne for the settlers—represented a variety of backgrounds. Smalwood Noel, the Justice of the Peace, and his wife Nancy were natives of Virginia. Nancy Barnett was the daughter of James Hanna; her husband, James, had first visited the fort as a boy in 1797, later as a soldier in 1812, and settled there in 1818—and was now in a business partnership with his brother-in-law, Samuel Hanna. Elder John McIntosh had settled as a farmer in Adams Township in 1823. Ann Turner and Rebecca Hackley, granddaughters of Chief Little Turtle, had joined Isaac McCoy's Baptist Indian mission congregation nine years before.[25] Hugh McCulloch especially admired Mrs. Hackley as "very interesting and intelligent . . . . I hardly know of the lady who appears more mild, amiable, polite, and sensible than she."[26]

Smalwood Noel
[Drawing by B. F. Griswold, 1917]

Although formal membership in the church was Presbyterian, financial support for the minister was interdenominational. Knowing well that their little band could not support a settled pastor and his family, the congregation circulated a subscription among all interested citizens in the village. Except for the visits of a Methodist circuit rider, there was no other clergyman, Protestant or Catholic, within fifty miles of Fort Wayne, and the prospect of a minister moving to the community was appealing to many residents. In a few days, more than forty-four citizens pledged a total of $258 "in aid of the support of Rev. James Chute for one year at this place." James Barnett—who seems to have organized the appeal—pledged twenty dollars; Henry Rudisill—who would later seek assistance from the Presbyterians in support of a Lutheran pastor—promised five dollars; and John Dubois of the French Catholic community subscribed the same amount.[27]

Chute was encouraged not only by the broad community support represented in the subscriptions, but also by the special spirit of his newborn congregation. He wrote: "On the first Sabbath in July...I administered the sacrament here for the first time it ever was administered in this place. The congregation was respectable and very solemn. The season [of communion] was one of great interest. I spent three

James Barnett
[Drawing by B. F. Griswold, 1917]

Sabbaths among this people, preached nine or ten times, organized a church, ordained two elders, held a number of prayer meetings, and addressed the Sabbath School a number of times. The people were anxious I should return and settle among them."[28]

At the end of July, Chute returned to Columbus and began preparations to move his family to Fort Wayne on September 1. The American Home Missionary Society agent in Cincinnati had previously assured Chute that it would provide a two-hundred-dollar annual stipend if he accepted the position. The elders at Fort Wayne, however, believed that $250 would be needed; Smalwood Noel explained: "$5.00 will give a family no better support in this place than $3.00 in many parts of Ohio."[29] Chute later commented on frontier inflation: "I find every article of living extremely high and difficult to obtain, but the people very friendly and willing to afford me all the aid in their power."[30] The Chutes made the trip from Columbus to Fort

Wayne, "a tedious journey of twelve days," in a large Pennsylvania covered wagon drawn by four horses. By conviction they did not travel on the Sabbath, but rested that day in Troy, Ohio. On the evening of September 12, they arrived in Fort Wayne and were entertained in the home of Samuel and Eliza Hanna.[31]

From the church's beginning, Samuel Hanna was totally devoted to the success of the congregation and, in October 1831, he visited the headquarters of the Home Missionary Society in New York City to plead the cause of the new church. Neither the Hannas nor the Hamiltons, however, had yet formally joined the church. Eliza Hanna affiliated in 1832, and Emerine Hamilton, whose father was president the Indiana Baptist General Association, joined in 1837. Allen Hamilton put off his formal affiliation until 1840[32] and Samuel Hanna finally united with the congregation in 1843. Most likely, Chute's strong advocacy of temperance caused the men to shy away from formal affiliation—a step which would make them liable to the censure of the session and suspension from the church when they joined in the traditional political toasting. After the election of 1836, a young member of the congregation noted: "Judge Hanna and his oldest son were both carried home drunk with champagne. Mr. Hamilton and most of the [bank] directors are very much mortified and wish it to be kept still, for they are members of the temperance society, but not of the total abstinence... Mrs. Hanna has been weeping almost constantly since election and, as Judge Hanna repents of his conduct, I think he will not give her occasion again."[33] Hanna soon became an ardent advocate of total abstinence and served for many years as president of the Allen County Temperance Society.

During the fall of 1832, the Chutes remained in temporary housing; then, in the spring, the new pastor signaled his determination to stay in the area by purchasing twenty-eight acres of land adjoining the town—and with his own hands built a double log house.[34] In Columbus, Chute had supplemented his salary by teaching a few classes of Latin and higher mathematics; in Fort Wayne, with the price of food so high, he determined to protect his marginal income by farming his land. Staples, such as flour, were not always available on the frontier; Chute once wrote: "For more than two weeks my family lived without bread of any description and most of the people in this place were in similar circumstances."[35]

Solving his own housing problem was easier than finding a home for the new congregation. "There being no meeting house, the Presbyterians and Methodists have but one place of worship which is the Free Mason Hall, which was built with a view of making it a place of worship. The Methodists claim it one-half time, and consequently we cannot worship in it but once on the Sabbath.... I have therefore appointed preaching once on the Sabbath, at three different places in the country." With the encouragement of the Home Missionary Society, Chute maintained as many as seven preaching points in the surrounding countryside. These rural meetings were usually held in the homes of the settlers who had begun to arrive soon after the land was opened for sale in 1823; Chute found these gatherings to be especially

The Hanna Family, by Horace Rockwell, ca. 1843. The painting depicts Samuel and Eliza Taylor Hanna with their children (clockwise from lower left): William W., James B., Samuel T., (standing) Amos T., Henry C., Hugh T., Eliza Taylor Hanna (Mrs. Samuel), Samuel Hanna, Charles, and Horace H.
[Courtesy of the Fort Wayne Museum of Art]

challenging: "A few weeks ago I preached in a part of the country where perhaps a sermon never before was preached, and where the neighborhood is notoriously intemperate. I carried out some tracts, adapted to their situation, and one of my elders, who was with me, remarked that I had probably offended most all the people present; but, to my surprise, one week had not elapsed before a special message was sent to me, requesting I should make another appointment, and that a room should always be provided for my accommodation." Chute also noted that attendance, in both town and country, diminished in the winter months, "owing to the inclemency of the weather and the want of shoes, which are high and difficult to obtain in this place."[36]

Except for the Sunday school, which Chute found to be "nearly extinct," every other aspect of congregational life had to be started from scratch: "I have found a great deficiency in this place in sacred music and have thought it a duty to spend one night in the week in its cultivation. I gave a general invitation for all to attend, and am happy to say that many have readily embraced the opportunity, and the prospect is that we shall soon have a respectable choir of singers." Besides rehearsing the choir each Friday evening, he lectured at the prayer meeting each Wednesday evening, taught a weekly Bible class, organized a tract society for a monthly distribution of religious literature, and established a "reading room for the diffusions of knowledge on religion, temperance, and morality."[37]

In his home visitations, Chute found many residents wary of reflecting on their own faith: "Considerable time has been spent in visiting from house to house. In these labors, we learn much of mankind and the natural disposition of the heart. If the great and all important subject of salvation be urged, very likely it will be parried off by some curious and frivolous question, as 'What was Paul's thorn in the flesh?' or 'Who was Melchizedek?' or 'How were the weeds wrapped about Jonah in the whale?' Almost anything suits the carnal heart better than the question, 'What must I do to be saved?'"[38]

The Canal Brings New Challenges

Chute judged the mood of the community to be politely spiritual on the surface, but aggressively materialistic underneath: "This place seems destined by nature to be a place of considerable importance, but most of those who have come here, have come from worldly considerations and appear very careless about the 'one thing needful.' Many are anxious for the commencement of the contemplated canal, but few for the salvation of their souls." The proposed canal was seen by most to be a harbinger of prosperity; Chute sensed their anxious hopes: "The general inquiry is, 'how shall I make my future?' Some are for taking contracts, some for speculating in land, and others for establishing groceries and selling whiskey." The sale of whiskey, legally or illegally, had always been a profitable business in Fort Wayne since the early days of the Indian trade; now, with canal workers moving closer to Fort Wayne, a new threat to the cause of temperance was perceived on the eastern horizon. During February and March 1832, both local temperance societies—whose membership had doubled since Chute's arrival[39]—were meeting weekly in emergency sessions to formulate plans. Chute reported that among nineteen new members who had signed the pledge were "some of the most influential men in the place . . . . They are determined . . . to persuade, if possible, every contractor on the canal not to give whiskey to any of their hands. One contract has already been made and the contractor, tho' not a member of the temperance society and the owner of a distillery, has promised not to allow his men whiskey, and is seriously contemplating giving up his distillery."[40]

Alcohol consumption had risen steadily during the early nineteenth century and, by 1830, the annual per capita consumption in the United States exceeded five gallons —

nearly triple the rate in the twentieth century.[41] A local resident reported that Fort Wayne in 1833 had "about a dozen dry goods stores and as many groceries, alias dram shops."[42] Joining in the work to advance the cause of temperance was the local Methodist circuit rider, the Reverend Richard S. Robinson; Chute wrote: "We have endeavored to belabor together, and not put down what the other builds up." The two ministers coordinated their efforts with other temperance groups across the state, and their growing influence was soon felt at the spring session of the Indiana legislature—which passed a law "prohibiting any person from giving or selling whiskey to the Indians under heavy penalty." The new settlers of the 1830s were not as tolerant of the abuses of the whiskey trade with the Indians as had been the older residents a decade before; in 1831, Chute had written: "There is great room for reformation .... Some will sell it to the Indians who resort here to trade .... Last week one Indian was stabbed by another in a drunken frolic, and still the whiskey was dealt out to them by the pail full."[43]

After winning a legislative victory to halt the flow of liquor to the Indians, Chute then directed the energies of his temperance forces to persuade the canal commission to forbid all contractors from distributing whiskey under penalty of forfeiting their contract: "This is a measure I urged upon the commissioners with all my feeble powers, and thanks to the Disposer of all things, it has been thus far accomplished." In Fort Wayne, the influence of the pastors and the temperance societies had changed many people's drinking patterns: in 1833, a physician told Chute that, among the local residents, "two years ago a gallon of whiskey was drunk to one pint now," and that "some in this place who were most notorious [in selling whiskey to the Indians] have given up the practice."[44] Hugh McCulloch marked the beginning of the town's improvement with the arrival of a resident minister and the establishment of a church; he told his fiancée in 1833: "The town was settled at an early day by Indian traders but it never began decidedly to improve till about 2 years ago, since which time it has rapidly advanced .... The morals of the place have ... been low, but they are rapidly changing for the better. There are many fine families here and there is no lack for [prayer] meetings. Mr. Chute, the Presbyterian minister, I think you will like. He is a well educated and rather liberal man and ... a Yankee."[45]

By 1833, Chute had organized a Bible Society and, with thirty dollars collected, reported that "the town has been fully supplied with Bibles." The congregation's membership had now doubled, mostly by persons connected with the development of the canal. The pastor noted, however, that only a few of the new arrivals were interested in church: "Within a year our population has considerably increased, but they add very little toward the support of the gospel. Speculators and those who regard the things of the world ... compose the great mass of emigrants to this country.

... There are, however, a few exceptions."[46] Among these was Jesse L. Williams, the canal's chief engineer. Raised in a Quaker family in North Carolina, Williams soon joined the church and, at the age of twenty-six, was elected to the eldership at the next congregational meeting.[47] Hugh McCulloch admired Williams: "His labors as chief engineer of the Wabash and Erie Canal, and other public works in Indiana, were prodigious, but he never failed to be equal to them. Week after week and month after month, every day

Jesse L. Williams
[Courtesy of Allen County-Fort Wayne Historical Society]

except Sunday, on which he always rested, he could be found upon the line of the public works, usually in the saddle, and in the evening, and until midnight, at this desk."[48] Williams strongly supported the prohibition of whiskey along the canal line: "Mr. J. L. Williams, the engineer, who is a pious and worthy man, has informed me that the rule has been strictly attended to. No instance to his knowledge has occurred in which ardent spirits have been given to the workmen. I am confident the contractors have no desire to be released from their obligations; if no higher motive, self interest would prompt them to adhere to the rule." The rule, however, was hard to enforce, and not all contractors were vigilant; in early 1834 Chute sadly reported: "The influx of strangers into this part of our county to labor in our canal has been very unfavorable to the cause of virtue and temperance. A large portion of these emigrants are Irish and Scotch Catholics, ignorant, superstitious, and vicious. The contractors upon the canal obligated themselves not to give ardent spirits, but in some instances they have broken over, being too much influenced by the character of their workmen."[49]

One of the contractors who supported the temperance rule along the canal line was Marshall W. Wines. A native of New York he arrived in Fort Wayne in 1832 and, like Williams, immediately united with the Presbyterian church and was elected an elder. McCulloch described Wines as "a man of extraordinary enterprise and force."[50] His wife, Elizabeth, was remembered for her tireless ministrations to

Elizabeth Wines (Mrs. Marshall)
[Courtesy of First Presbyterian Church of Fort Wayne]

the many sick workers along the canal line: "When a malignant fever broke out among a large number of emigrants, some of whom were in his employ, she devoted herself for weeks to the care of the sick."[51]

Illness Along the Canal

One who succumbed to this fever during the summer of 1833 was the pastor's wife, Martha. In his grief, Chute wrote to the secretary of the Missionary Society: "Yes, my dear brother, she who was the participator in my joys and sorrows . . . took her flight to the world of spirits, and we have reason to hope to a world where sin and sorrow never enter, and where all tears shall be wiped from every eye. Pray, my brother, that this afflictive providence may be sanctified to my spiritual good, that I might be quickened in duty, feel more deeply impressed with the shortness and uncertainty of life, and the necessity of a continual preparation for death."[52]

In spite of personal loss and prevalent sickness, Chute continued to preach occasionally along the canal line where "nearly one thousand" were now employed—ministering especially to those Protestants from northern Ireland. The canal seemed to attract sickness; one resident recollected: "In the fall of 1838 we remember to have taken a trip on horseback following down the Maumee river . . . . The sick and paleface Irish laborers and settlers then seen, seemed enough to appall the stoutest heart. Fever and ague prevailed, and much interrupted the public work. To say the Maumee was not a sickly valley, is to be ignorant of the truth."[53]

Sickness also stalled the effort to build a worship facility. When the Freemasons, in 1833, disbanded their lodge in the wake of a national scandal[54] and sold their hall to a printer, the Presbyterians moved out to uncertain accommodations. At first the congregation crowded "in the back room of Judge Hanna's store"; soon they moved to Hanna and Edsell's carpenter shop, with the work bench for a pulpit; later they rented a room in a tavern. Jesse Williams recollected some Sunday morning ramblings: "On . . . more than one occasion, the congregation were compelled, after the services had commenced, to go forth from one of their humble sanctuaries, and were seen following their pastor, with Bible and hymnbook in hand, in search of a place of less discomfort—having been sorely persecuted, not by Pope or King, but by the . . . chimney builder."[55] In the summer of 1833, and in 1835 and early 1836, the congregation occupied the courthouse, sometimes sharing it with the Methodists on alternate Sundays. The courthouse was a sorry structure and other facilities were small; in early 1835, Chute lamented: "Our congregations of late have been unusually large. At our last meeting in town, a considerable number went away, because there was no room for them in our house of worship. We need a meeting house very much. Last year a subscription of about twelve hundred dollars was raised and the timber got out and brought on the ground, but owing to the unusual sickness, all further operations were suspended. We are now making another effort."[56]

Chute's faith in the subscription process may have been weakened when, after laboring for over six months in Fort Wayne, not one of the forty-four subscribers to his salary had yet remitted a dollar for his subsistence. Smalwood Noel, in an appeal to the Missionary Society, had confessed that "our subscription has been rather nominal than real, and . . . his salary has been somewhat deficient."[57]

In addition to the prevalence of sickness and an absence of salary, most ministers on the frontier experienced professional isolation. Chute had only two visits from fellow clergymen during his tenure in Fort Wayne: a pastor traveling though on his way north and the Indiana agent of the Home Missionary Society.[58] It was only by attending the distant meetings of his presbytery and synod that Chute stayed in touch with his denomination and clergy colleagues.

He travelled 120 miles to his first presbytery meeting in Dayton, Ohio, when his newly organized congregation was formally received by the Miami Presbytery on October 14, 1831. Travel to and from these meetings took three weeks and Chute honored the custom of preaching along the route in such "destitute" settlements as St. Mary's, Ohio. On one such trip to Dayton in October 1834, he married Mrs. Mary H. Crane, the widow of the Reverend Samuel Crane, who had been a missionary to the Tuscarora Indians near Niagara Falls. The new Mrs. Chute brought into her husband's home three children to add to the four Chute offspring.[59]

The fever which had struck down Martha Chute worsened the following summer; Chute wrote: "Though we have been exempt from the cholera, yet other diseases have been very prevalent and swept many of our citizens into the world of the spirits, some of whom were active members of our church . . . . My time has been almost entirely occupied in preaching and visiting from house to house, conversing and praying with the sick . . . . Probably about 80 souls during the last quarter have gone to their accounts . . . . This amount of sickness is not usual in this country. Heretofore it has been very healthy; but, in the early part of summer, floods of rain fell and excessively wet weather immediately succeeded and continued . . . doubtless the instrumental cause of this heavy calamity."[60] In August, Chute reported that he and his wife were "taken down with the bilious fever. Three times her life was despaired of. Once I have been brought to the borders of grace."[61] While convalescing from this illness, Chute caught a severe cold which caused a relapse; he died December 28, 1835, and was buried on his homestead by the side of his first wife.[62]

James Chute was one of those rare Easterners who became totally dedicated to the western missionary enterprise. More than a few young clergyman, such as Charles Furman, took a quick turn around the West and then returned to the East, but not Chute. In one of his last letters—written to a nephew, a theological student at Andover, Massachusetts—he expressed his devotion to the cause: "The call for ministers in the West is loud and pressing. Men who can endure hardness as good soldiers of Christ are much wanted. There are many destitute churches in the West, and many more ought to be formed. The country is settling with great rapidity. Great exertions are required that the moral improvement should keep pace with the material. Men are wanted who can adapt themselves to the circumstances of the people; who can preach in a barn, log cabin, school house, or grove, as well as a church, either with or without notes."[63] Unconsciously, Chute had delineated his own character. Never a spellbinding evangelist, he was a sound preacher who built people patiently and solidly into a strong community of faith; he was remembered as an excellent teacher, an effective organizer, and a caring pastor. Years later, Jesse Williams wrote: "The labors of James Chute were continued in humble, self-denying, faithfulness . . . . His memory is

blessed."[64]

The Interim Preachers: Daniel Jones and Jesse Hoover

During the first six months of 1836, the vacant pulpit was supplied by the Reverend Daniel Jones, a Presbyterian minister at Leasburg who was supported by the Home

Daniel Jones
[Courtesy of First Presbyterian Church of Fort Wayne]

Missionary Society. Jones was a thirty-five-year-old native of London, England, who had learned to read and write in a Baptist Sabbath school. At the age of seventeen he came to New York with his parents, and soon began studies for the ministry. His son remembered Jones as "anti-slavery in his sentiments. He never voted for a President who was elected until he voted for Abraham Lincoln . . . . When he came to the West in 1835, he came up the Maumee River in a pirogue (or log dugout) from Toledo, Ohio to Fort Wayne, Ind., and from Fort Wayne to Leasburg (about fifty miles). He had his family and goods taken in a wagon drawn by a yoke of cattle and a span of horses. It took him about seven days to go from Fort Wayne to Leasburg . . . . Father has lived on potatoes without salt for three weeks together. He has also traveled thirty miles in a day in attending a funeral when the mercury was fourteen degrees below zero." [65]

Jones enjoyed his relation with people in Fort Wayne, and appears to have aspired to the pastorate. The church officers handled the situation diplomatically; Jones wrote:

"The elders . . . at Fort Wayne informed me in the spring that the people had expressed a wish that I might be called to settle among them, and that the only reason why they had not done it was because they questioned the propriety of remov-

Alexander McJunkin
[Courtesy of First Presbyterian Church of Fort Wayne]

ing me from my present field and doubted whether I should be at liberty to abandon it."[66]

In the summer of 1836, the Reverend Jesse Hoover, a Pennsylvania-born Lutheran pastor, arrived in town and was quickly pressed into service by the Presbyterians, both as principal of their school and preacher in their pulpit. The arrangement was reluctantly accepted by the local German Lutherans: their own denomination had declined to offer them any financial support and, as a result, they were unable to provide their pastor with anything close to a minimum salary. During Hoover's interim preaching at the Presbyterian Church, Jones returned occasionally to administer the sacraments and moderate the session meetings; for over twelve months, however, the Lutheran pastor preached on most Sundays, first in English, and then in German.[67]

In the summer of 1837, Hoover declined to continue teaching at the Presbyterian academy; the trustees then named as principal William W. Steevens, formerly an English clergyman of no recorded denomination, and Alexander McJunkin as teacher. McJunkin was a defrocked Presbyterian minister who had recently come to Fort Wayne from Detroit. At the time, the Presbyterians were unaware that, in

July, he had been excommunicated for "grossly scandalous conduct: secretly engaging himself to be married to three single persons at the same time, and while he was himself a married man."[68] In late September, when the Detroit newspapers arrived in Fort Wayne with details of McJunkin's ecclesiastical trial, the townspeople buzzed, wondering what action the school trustees would take. Hugh McCulloch told Susan Man, who had formerly taught in the school, that McJunkin "denies the engagement. He states that his wife left him of her own accord and that he knows not what has become of her and that he expects soon to be regularly divorced from her. Mrs. Hoover states that he has engaged himself to Miss Waugh (the impudent puppy!). This, however, is known to but few and is now to be kept 'sub umbra.' . . . I do not know what course the Trustees and Church will take."[69] McJunkin, however, was too good a schoolmaster to be summarily dismissed; the academy was filled to capacity and he was well liked. One student later wrote: "Mr. McJunkin was capable of teaching any branch of a college curriculum. A noble man, respected and held in fond remembrance by the many who went out from his school fitted to engage in any profession or business."[70] John S. Irwin, who later became a public school trustee, remembered him as a "fine scholar, a strong judicious instructor, and a stern, rigidly strict disciplinarian; he most forcibly impressed his ideas and teachings on the minds of his scholars, and not infrequently with equal force on their bodies."[71]

Alexander T. Rankin: Abolitionist

After twenty months without a regular minister, the Presbyterian congregation called to the pastorate, the Reverend Alexander Taylor Rankin. In September 1837, the young clergyman arrived in Fort Wayne with his family and "was undoubtedly the most controversial and controversy-provoking Protestant minister of the period."[72] As pastor of the First Presbyterian Church, he led the congregation in significant growth, not only in numbers, but also in spiritual commitment and ethical awareness; as a prophetic voice in the community, Rankin was a fearless advocate of the temperance cause and became the first leader in Fort Wayne to publicly advance the antislavery movement.

Chute had been loved for his faithful service and Hoover was admired as a popular preacher, but Rankin evoked both awe and enthusiasm. Hugh McCulloch wrote to his fiancée: "Mr. Rankin, our Presbyterian minister, has at length arrived. He preached last Sunday and I was delighted with him. He is not a very well educated man, but I think him very interesting. He has a fine voice, is sufficiently animated and, if I mistake not, possesses an original, clear, and discriminating mind."[73] McCulloch's enthusiasm did not diminish; a few weeks later, he wrote:

Mr. Rankin . . . is a great favorite of mine. He is decidedly the best preacher I have heard in the West. Concise and forcible in argument, clear and correct in language, animated and eloquent, I listen to him with a delight which I have not experienced under the preaching of any other

Alexander T. Rankin
[Courtesy of First Presbyterian Church of Fort Wayne]

man since I left New England. His personal appearance is very fine and his manner of speaking is particularly bold and impulsive.

His brother John Rankin is a very distinguished abolitionist and I am disposed to think that, on the subject of slavery, they sympathize with each other, both in feeling and sentiment. He (our preacher) is composed of the right kind of material for an abolitionist. Uncommonly fearless in expressing his sentiments, with a mind deeply imbued with the great principles of natural equality and civil liberty, he will be, I think at all times, the prompt, decided and fearless champion of the oppressed, and the advocate of the slaves. At the same time, his clearness of understanding and soundness of judgement will preserve him from

the impudent trash measures which have so deeply excited the community against Garrison and his following.[74]

McCulloch was a debater by instinct and welcomed an opportunity to draw Rankin into discussion, especially on the subject of slavery on which he had previously commented in his Fourth of July address at the Canal Inauguration ceremonies in 1835. In Rankin, he found a formidable advocate: "This is our Thanksgiving Day, the first that has ever been appointed in Indiana. Mr. Rankin gave us a most excellent discourse upon the occasion. He took for his subject that part of the Declaration of Independence which speaks of the natural equality of men, and from it he took occasion to speak freely of the liberty of free discussions, and the efforts that have been made of late to suppress it throughout our country. His theory was that of the abolitionists, and yet there was not one word to which a reasonable slaveholder could object. We took tea together at Col. Wines. There was some little sharpshooting between us—nothing serious, however."[75] Hugh McCulloch's "sharpshooting" was not at the principles, but at the practicalities of an antislavery position, a concept with which he struggled up to the moment he joined President Lincoln's cabinet. His Presbyterian fiancée wrote, "I should like to hear one of Mr. Rankin's abolition sermons . . . . I hope Mr. Rankin will make an antislavery man of you."[76]

Rankin's abolitionism was a deeply held religious conviction nurtured by his Pennsylvania-born Scotch-Irish parents, who had settled near Mount Horeb in Jefferson (now Washington) County, Tennessee. His older brother, John Rankin, had moved to Ohio immediately upon the completion of his theological studies because he would not live in a slave state. In Ripley, Ohio, John established a flourishing congregation, an underground railway to aid runaway slaves, an antislavery tract and book society, and a theological school for clergy. To this school came Alexander and another brother; both, in turn, married sisters of John's wife.[77] Of Alexander, the teacher-brother wrote: "He studied under me both science and theology. He possessed superior talents and is a popular preacher . . . [and] ever maintained a high rank among public speakers. In the church at Felicity he was very successful as a minister." Alexander was equally active in the antislavery cause; when the Cincinnati Presbytery was scheduled to meet in his church in Felicity, Ohio, he invited his brother John to give a public lecture on slavery. His elders, however, refused to allow the church to be used for that purpose; John Rankin later commented: "This measure of the session was very unpopular, for I had founded that church. The Methodists gave their church and it was crowded with hearers, and the members of the Presbytery attended. At the close of the lecture sixty names were given to form an Antislavery Society and that village was a stronghold of Abolitionism to the end of the

War."[78]

Six months before his arrival in Fort Wayne, Rankin was physically attacked by an anti-abolitionist mob in Dayton, Ohio. His account of the incident was printed in more than one antislavery newspaper:

Hugh McCulloch
[Matthew Brady Photograph]

Messr. Editors,— I have commenced my labors [lecturing] again. The injury received in the mob scrape, on the 13th, kept me pretty closely confined until the 21st; but the effects are now nearly removed.

The opposers of abolitionism are supremely deluded in their measures to arrest the progress of anti-slavery principles. One would think that the blindness of fanaticism itself would be more judicious in the selection of means. Never was more strikingly verified the old maxim, "whom God intends to destroy, he first makes mad," than in the late disgraceful riot in Dayton. The influence of that affair, unquestionably, has made more abolitionists in that place than I could have done in a dozen lectures. How true it is that God sometimes makes even the wrath of man to further his inscrutable purposes . . . .

Everything has been done to prejudice the community against me and the cause of human liberty, but the spirit of inquiry cannot be intimidated— the people will think and determine for themselves. If the father of lies had been there, himself in person, his fruitful genius could not have exceeded the invention of his dutiful subjects in fabricating and retailing slander. As a specimen of the false statements, take the following. One man is said to be willing to swear that I said publicly, "that I was not only in favor of amalgamation, but intended to marry a black wife"— the most unlikely thing in the world for a man to say who has a wife and children at home. But, whether the opposers throw eggs, beat me, lie, or be still, inquiry goes on; our cause advances.

The result reminds me of a remark once made by an opponent. He said abolition was the most singular thing he had known. For, whether the lecturers were opposed by arguments, or their meetings broken up by mobs, or were attended in peace, the cause advanced.[79]

When the congregation of First Presbyterian Church elected the thirty-three-year-old Rankin as their pastor, they were fully aware of his wide reputation as a fearless advocate of abolition, and understood that they would be welcoming to their pulpit one of the West's most prophetic voices for the "cause of human liberty." Soon after Rankin arrived in Fort Wayne—accompanied by his wife Mary and their two young sons—he perceived the need for a broad based abolition organization, and, in 1838, became one of the founding directors of the Indiana Anti-Slavery Society. Rankin and his abolitionist colleagues also confronted discrimination in the North, and resolved "to remove the prejudice that has kept free men of color from a participation in the rights and privileges of citizens . . . . Prejudice against any portion of the human family on account of their condition, or the color of their skins, is rebellion against God, who has created, in his likeness, all the tribes of men."[80]

Rankin's antislavery stance in Fort Wayne worried the local Lutheran pastor, Jesse Hoover, who described the Presbyterian minister as "a warm abolitionist . . . . I fear this will injure him some day."[81] Lutheran ministers tended to be much more cautious on controversial social issues than their Methodist, Presbyterian, Quaker, or Baptist colleagues. Just as some of the Pennsylvania-German Lutherans had found it difficult to embrace the patriot cause during the American Revolution—against what they believed to be a divinely established government—so they now found it difficult to criticize established authority, and saw the Presbyterians again preaching in a manner that might lead to another rebellion.

Other Fort Wayne residents saw Rankin to be stepping over the line separating the preacher's pulpit from the politician's stump. The anti-abolitionist *Marion* (Indiana) *Herald Democrat* advertised in the equally conservative Democratic *Fort Wayne Sentinel* for a copy of the sermon "this clerical politician secretly circulated among the abolitionists." The editor then threatened: "If the letter purports to contain the matter we are advised it does, his clerical robes shall not screen him from the lash."[82]

Rankin's abolitionist sermon may have been carried to Marion by some of the people of the rural areas he regularly visited. At the end of his first year in Fort Wayne, he reported: "I have visited different neighborhoods in other counties frequently on weekdays to preach. There are many points in every part of the land where there are few Christians."[83] His missionary spirit was broadly ecumenical and he worked hard to secure adequate funding from the Home Missionary Society for the community's first Lutheran pastors, Jesse Hoover and Friedrich Wyneken.[84]

Apparently, Rankin's activism for these causes did him no harm in his congregation. His attention to pastoral duties was conscientious, attendance at Sunday worship doubled during his first year, and new members were added to the fellowship. Rankin set high standards and, in 1840, became discouraged at his people's seeming indifference to spiritual matters: "We have to lament a general state of coldness in the church. There is a regular attendance on the means of grace, but very little interest manifested. No church needs a revival of religion more than this one."[85] Then something happened and, a month later, Rankin wrote: "This . . . is the most interesting[86] time this church has ever witnessed. God has answered our prayer and poured out his Spirit upon the church and congregation. Though we cannot say we enjoy a revival, yet the members are more alive to the importance of laboring for the conversion of sinners than I ever have seen them; and there are more persons in the congregation inquiring than I ever have known at one time."[87]

The Church Is Finished

By the fall of 1837, the finishing touches on the interior of Fort Wayne's first church building were finally completed.[88] The new Presbyterian house of worship, on the south side of East Berry Street, east of Lafayette Street, was a white wooden structure forty feet square, surmounted by a large belfry and a small spire. Its church bell was the first to summon worshippers in Fort Wayne since French boys rang cow bells through the village streets fifty years before. The final installation of the interior furnishings was not without incident. The Female Sewing Society had raised funds "for the benefit of the unfinished church";[89] their president, however, refused to pay the bill for one item which failed to meet the women's expectations. Jesse Hoover reported:

"The pulpit was put in the house last week. Miss [Sally C.] Vance is boss. She has the money of the Sewing Society and refuses to give it up because they won't make the pulpit circular! She is an odd genius. She says she is president of the society and she takes 'responsibility' upon herself."[90]

First Presbyterian Church (first building), erected on the southside of Berry Street east of Lafayette Street, was Fort Wayne's first house of worship. In this building a school was established in 1836, Baptists organized in 1837, Episcopalians worshipped in 1839, the county court held sessions in 1842, St. John's German Reformed Church worshipped during 1843, and the Methodist North Indiana Conference was organized in 1844. Trinity English Lutheran Church purchased the facility in 1846, and has installed its original bell in successive steeples.

[Courtesy of First Presbyterian Church of Fort Wayne]

When the shaky courthouse was deemed unsafe, the new church building was engaged by the courts on weekdays.[91] The populace seemed to carry their fear of a building collapse into the new facility, for an eye witness reported: "One day, when court was in session and a large crowd present, a rumor gained currency that the steeple of the church was not securely supported and would come crashing down to the destruction of all below . . . . When the room was crowded, there came a crash and roar, and the people rushed to the doors and windows to escape the ruins. One man clasped the Bible under his arms and crawled under the bench. Discovering the steeple was still in place, the crowd came back to find the long stove pipe, which stretched from the front to back, had fallen—only that and nothing more."[92]

The Panic of 1837

The new church was not paid for and the congregation had difficulty paying their new pastor regularly. The Panic of 1837 had created an economic depression which continued to worsen; during the next two years, work on the canal eventually came to a halt when the state could not pay the contractors who, in turn, could not pay their laborers or suppliers. Rankin wrote in early 1840: "There is great pressure here in money matters, greater than ever has been known since the settlement of this place. It appears as if there was no money in the country. Not one in ten of the people is able to meet his engagements." He then told of the people's frustration with their politicians: "All eyes were turned to the legislature for some relief; but they have spent the winter in wrangling about party politics and have adjourned without doing anything that will be effectual. It seems as if our leading men, in state affairs, are more interested in president-making than in the prosperity of their constituents. No better times are to be expected until after the fall elections, if then. All the energies of state are embarked in electioneering. The demon of politics is sweeping over the land like the plague. From present appearance, the contest is to be hotter and more pernicious than anything of the kind that has been seen in this country."[93]

The offering plates of most congregations reflected the hard times, and Rankin feared for the future: "Unless the Lord have mercy on his church in the West . . . her suffering must be great, and her prospect will be blighted. . . . The sufferings of ministers, and especially of missionaries, this season . . . probably will surpass anything they may have experienced heretofore. It is impossible for the people to pay their subscriptions." Six months later, Rankin judged that conditions had worsened: "The general distress in money matters here is unparalleled in the history of the country. There is an entire prostration of business of all kinds. It has been impossible to collect my salary for the last year. . . . It does seem as if ministers in new settlements like this will have to resort to secular business to obtain a support."[94] To add to Rankin's hardship, the American Home Missionary Society, in the fall of 1840, cut off its aid to his salary. Possibly the Society felt that, after ten years of subsidy, it was time for the congregation to assume full responsibility for its pastor. On the darker side, the Society may have discontinued its aid because Rankin and the church session had chosen the Old School side of the denomination's break with the New School group. In a long and tangled conflict, the Presbyterian Church had divided in 1837, and one of the sharpest disputes was over support for the denomination's own Board of Missions over against the independent, pow-erful American Home Missionary Society. In 1837, the Presbyterian General Assembly voted "that the organization and operations of the so-called American Home Missionary Society. . . are exceedingly injurious to the peace and purity of the Presbyterian Churches. We recommend accordingly, that they should cease to operate within any of our churches."[95] The Old School and New School controversy was now alive in Indiana and would appear in Fort Wayne in 1844, in a dramatic confrontation initiated by Henry Ward Beecher.[96]

Elders Stand Trial

While this denominational schism stayed at a safe distance during Rankin's Fort Wayne pastorate, he had no trouble finding other issues to address, from dancing to secret societies. Like the Catholic priest, Stephen Badin, and the Lutheran pastor, Jesse Hoover, before him, Rankin disapproved of dancing,[97] and his public remarks on this subject provoked one indignant citizen to declare: "If this gentleman would let both fiddling and dancing alone and mind his own business, he would not only advance his temporal interests in the community. . . he would be much the gainer in a spiritual point of view."[98] Another resident observed that Rankin, "if not exactly an anti-mason, looks upon this venerable association . . . with a suspicious eye."[99]

Temperance, however, was the preeminent social issue to which most evangelical Protestant churches directed their moral energies. Soon after Rankin arrived, he was distressed to discover that there were "two temperance societies in the village: one of them on the total abstinence principle, the other on the old pledge."[100] To Rankin, the moderationist position of the "old pledge" was anathema; immediately he threw the weight of his office and oratory into the cause of total abstinence: "The advocates of temperate drinking have marshalled their strength. They now dispute every inch of ground."[101] These temperance debates were advertised in the local newspapers and were well attended. One editor complained: "The Rev. Mr. Rankin spoke at great length . . . occupying much more time than all others . . . . We think it no person should speak to exceed half an hour."[102]

The subject of temperance also took a good deal of the church session's time and energies. New members were required to take a pledge of total abstinence, and the elders were expected to discipline those who violated the pledge. In 1834, Elder John McIntosh was one of a committee of elders appointed to counsel with Elder James Barnett about his alleged intemperance; then, four years later, John McIntosh was cited by his fellow elders for his intemperance. Their concern was more pastoral than punitive, and therefore resolved and read from the pulpit "that, in consequence of his confession of his sin and purpose of new obedience. . . he is continued [in the communion of the church] and recommended to the fellowship and sympathy of the brethren."[103]

Elder McIntosh's drinking problem, however, surfaced the following year, and again he was cited; but, as no witness appeared, the matter was dropped. Then, in 1841, McIntosh was again charged by "common fame with unchristian conduct: first, with visiting tippling houses, and second, with being drunk on the last Saturday evening of the Allen County Circuit Court."[104] The accused and the witnesses were cited and, after some delays, the case was set for trial.

John McIntosh
[Courtesy of Allen County-Fort Wayne Historical Society]

Rankin, as moderator of the session, presided. The witnesses were elder Marshall S. Wines, the canal contractor; elder Nathan Farrand,[105] who had served a term on Fort Wayne's Board of Trustees; and James H. Jacoby, a local merchant in partnership with Farrand. The presenting issue for the elders was not that one of their members occasionally imbibed, but that, as a ruling elder of the church, McIntosh had scandalized the church for his frequent drinking at local "tippling houses" or "groceries."

At the conclusion of the trial, the clerk of session, Smalwood Noel,[106] read aloud his verbatim notes, which were approved by the witnesses. Then, "Mr. McIntosh withdrew from the session in a very abrupt and contemptuous manner, stating that he would make no defense—that he must go and look after his boy whom he had left at a grocery and go home—that, if it was an offence to go to a grocery, they would have another charge against him as he was going directly to one—that they might just do with his case as they pleased." The session then "unanimously resolved that the charges as specified against Mr. McIntosh are sustained by the testimony. . . [and] that John McIntosh be and is hereby suspended from communion with the church until he repent.

The moderator is directed to publish this decision from the pulpit."[107] John McIntosh never returned to the church.

Such trials took much of the session's time and placed severe strains on the bonds of congregational fellowship. Presbyterian ministers and elders, in their ordination vows, promised "to be zealous and faithful in maintaining the . . . purity and peace of the church";[108] in seeking to purify the congregation, however, they often disturbed its peace. In 1843, James H. Jacoby was accused by Matthew Griggs of "unchristian conduct: overcharging goods and keeping false books." The session would not sustain those specific charges, but did rule that the offending merchant had dealt with his fellow member "in direct violation of the gospel of Christ, which enjoins honesty in all our dealings . . . an offense so unjustifiable as to require the severity of censure . . . . Therefore, resolved, that James H. Jacoby be excluded from the communion of the Church . . . until he give satisfactory evidence of repentance."[109]

Six weeks later Jacoby requested a meeting with the same triumvirate, and asked what was required to be restored to the full fellowship of the church. The pastor, with elders Jesse L. Williams and Smalwood Noel, informed Jacoby "that it would be necessary for him to give satisfactory evidence of sincere and ingenuous repentance; that this evidence must be such as will satisfy the church, against which he had sinned; and that he could only be accepted and pardoned by God, in the exercise of Godly sorrow." Jacoby then replied "at considerable length as to his feelings; . . . that he had been brought to see his sin; . . . that he had mourned over it with sincere and heartfelt grief, both before and since his suspension; and that he wished to be restored to the communion of the church."[110] Apparently the tenor of Jacoby's confession did not convince those elders who had witnessed a less than penitent demeanor, and concluded that "Mr. Jacoby, in the judgement of the session, appears to be penitent, and they hope he may have been accepted and pardoned by the great head of the church, who alone can tell what is in the hearts of the children of men; but, such was the position, which he sustained in the church and the Sabbath school, that they think the evidence of his repentance should be so completed and finished, as to satisfy, in some good degree, the brotherhood, from whose communion he has been excluded. This can only be done by an humble, prayerful and unostentatious conversation: therefore, they are of the opinion, that it would be premature, and not for the edification of Mr. Jacoby or the brethren, to restore him at this time to church fellowship."[111] In February 1844, Jacoby again requested the session to restore him to the full communion of the church; when they finally consented, he immediately asked that his membership be transferred to another congregation.[112]

Rankin is Reviewed

A. T. Rankin had been in Fort Wayne for nearly five

years when a local newspaper published an extensive analysis of his ministerial style and pulpit personality:

> Our present pastor, Mr. R., is a brother of the celebrated abolitionist of Ohio of that name, who has probably done more than any other individual to render slavery unpopular in the West. Our pastor is likewise an abolitionist, strong and ardent in his feelings of opposition to the institution of slavery and bold and independent in the expression of his views on this delicate subject.
>
> He has a fine head according to the principles of phrenology and a countenance that indicates energy and decision rather than sullenness and benignity. In point of intent he deservedly stands high, but he is not, I apprehend, destined ever to be very popular as a preacher, or eminently successful in winning souls to Christ. You cannot hear him preach many times, without feeling that he has mistaken his vocation. Nature intended him for a lawyer, and his reputation would have been higher had he not done violence to her intentions. His mind is strictly a legal one: keen, clear, discriminating. He can refute and split hairs, and draw distinctions in a manner that would have given him a high rank among special pleaders. In debate he is always ready, ingenious and forcible; but, as a preacher, he seems to lack feeling, sympathy, heart. He labors under the great mistake of supposing that sinners are to be convicted of sin, and brought to embrace the terms of the gospel, by argument! Everything is to be effected by the cogency of his logic . . . . In his anxiety to prove everything, he not unfrequently spends much time in proving positions that are sufficiently clear in their very propositions. Argument is his forte. He imagines that he can overcome error, and make converts by the force and accuracy of his reasoning and without any appeal to the feelings and affections. So inveterate is his habit in this respect, that his addresses on funeral occasions even, are chiefly argumentative . . . to prove that providence does not afflict without cause, nor punish but for good.[113]

The anonymous author was a pietist who judged preachers by their skill in "winning souls to Christ" and had little appreciation for those qualities of mind which excited Hugh McCulloch to praise Rankin as "the best preacher I have heard in the West—concise in argument, clear and correct in language."[114] The writer elaborated on the critique:

> I would not have you understand, however, that Mr. R. is never eloquent, or that his eloquence is only the eloquence of argument. He is powerful in denouncing the judgements of God upon his impenitent hearers. It might be said that he is eloquent in denunciation . . . . There is no tenderness in his discourses. The love of the Saviour, the compassion and kindness of the Father, are subjects which he rarely touches. But, in holding up before his hearers the errors of the law, in describing the vengeance of the Almighty and the suffering of the damned, he is powerfully eloquent. He seems to speak as though these subjects were congenial to his mind. In touching upon them, his language becomes more than usually vigorous, his gestures more than usually energetic. His eye flashes, his lips are compressed, and I cannot at such times, for the life of me, escape the impression that he would like to be the instrument by which the vials of divine wrath should be poured upon the heads of the unconverted. This, however, is, I presume, not the case, as he has the reputation of being an amiable man.

The essayist made no mention of the lectures which Rankin delivered attacking Catholicism, or the challenge to public debate which he issued to the Reverend Michael E. Shawe, a visiting lecturer at St. Augustine's Church.[115] Most Protestants of that era considered such confrontations to be the expected duty of their ministers. The writer did comment, however, on Rankin's particular style in the conduct of worship: "In his public services, the Bible is never read. There is one consideration, however, that reconciles me to this omission. His manner of reading is perfectly intolerable. He murders his hymns in reading them, and it is perhaps well enough that he does not commit the same violence upon the sacred volume. As a general thing, his sermons and prayers are too long. He generally preaches a full hour . . . . In prayer he is not gifted. In this exercise, as in some others, he appears to lack feeling: it is cold, formal, and dull. There is not, apparently, with him that going out of the heart toward his Maker, that deep reverence, that earnest supplication, that humble submission, connected with that spirit of lofty confidence in the mercy and kindness of the Almighty."

Rankin's skills in public debate, especially his talent in finding the chink in his opponent's armor, led the writer to judge him as less than kind: "Mr. R. is a bold and independent thinker, and yet he is not at all liberal towards those who differ with him. Contending himself for the largest exercise of private opinion, he does not appear willing to extend to others the same right that he claims for himsel . . . . A man who is not to be driven by fear or favor from the advocacy of what he considers truth and justice, he is, nevertheless, intolerant and uncharitable. Had he been a Protestant in the days of Queen Mary, he would have been a martyr; had he been a Catholic in Spain during the existence of the inquisition, he would doubtless have been an inquisitor." The author balanced this judgment with the observation that Rankin was always friendly, never pretentious, and, in his earnest advocacy of those causes he felt called to advance — especially temperance and abolition — he was always a gentleman. "I think you will like him. He is courteous and unassuming in his manners, easy and affable in his intercourse with this fellow men. In the discharge of parochial duties he does not assume any special sanctity of character nor obtrude the subject of religion upon those who are not disposed to consider it. He is a man of decided talents, and will make his influence felt in any community in which he may be placed."[116] Such a profile created quite a stir; never before, or after, had a Fort Wayne clergyman been so candidly described in print. In his next article, the author reported that Rankin was "rather flattered than displeased . . . . Like most of his brethren in the church, he would rather be distinguished for vigor of intellect than for humble piety . . . . His more intimate friends contend he is not intolerant . . . . He loves the man while he denounces the opinion."[117]

The Rankin-Steevens Debates

Formal lectures and spirited debates were, at that time, one of the principle public entertainments on the western frontier. Deprived of theatrical or musical presentations, and not yet on the circuit of the travelling shows (which arrived with the railroads in the late 1850s), Fort Wayne citizens attended public lectures and debates on all sorts of subjects—and the more controversial the better. One local resident who enjoyed refuting most of what Rankin advocated was William W. Steevens, the English schoolmaster who had previously taught in the Presbyterian school, and now, with his wife, operated the Fort Wayne Selected Classical and Commercial Academy.[118] Steevens was a Biblical literalist who delighted in depreciating most of Rankin's moral platform; in early 1843, he placed a provocative advertisement in the local newspapers:

> The citizens of Fort Wayne are respectfully informed that W. W. Steevens will (by divine permission) review the lecture delivered on last Thursday evening by the Rev. A. T. Rankin on The Final Resurrection . . . on which occasion it will be proven by Holy Scripture: first, that the resurrection of the righteous will precede that of the wicked; second, that, to assert that the Greek word "ANASTASIS" means a spiritual resurrection, is pronounced a heresy by no less than apostolic authority.[119]

The writer who had reviewed Rankin's style also revealed some of Steeven's thinking: "He holds that domestic slavery was established by the Almighty, and defends the peculiar institutions of our southern states with all the zeal . . . of a Calhoun . . . . [He] is an avowed and fearless opponent of . . . [temperance] associations, contending that they are tyrannical in their operation and, in their principles, at variance with the Word of God; that wine was given . . . as a blessing; that the free use of beer in his native country is attended with the most beneficial results upon the health and happiness of the people, and that distilled liquors are, in many cases, a necessary and healthful stimulant[120] . . . . [He] denies the correctness of astronomy as taught by Newton and others . . . because their opinions are not corroborated by the oracles of truth."[121] Steevens, however, was no match for the master debater, Rankin. The reviewer concluded: "Mr. R. is concise, clear and logical. Mr. S. is diffuse, not always intelligible, and rarely argumentative."[122]

"Pecuniary and Domestic Concerns"

Rankin had arrived in Fort Wayne at the beginning of a severe depression; five years later the general economic situation had measurably improved, but his congregation still owed him almost two-year's salary. When First Presbyterian Church was given a farm by David Hughes in 1842, it seemed that its sale might assist the church's debt; the congregation, however, discovered that, although it could easily receive gifts of money, it could not take title to land without a corporation being formed. The elders immediately petitioned the Indiana Legislature which, on January 25, 1843, passed a special bill to incorporate the church. The congregation then elected five trustees as its corporate officers,[123] who went before a notary public, as required by law, to be sworn into office. At their first meeting, Samuel Hanna was elected president, John Hill treasurer, and Allen Hamilton, secretary. Until this time, the elders on the session had cared for all the affairs of the church; now, the new Board of Trustees assumed responsibility for the congregation's material property and finances, and the Session focused its attention on such spiritual matters as worship, education, evangelism, temperance, and missions. Conflict between the boards was minimized by electing two of the new trustees, Samuel Hanna and John Cochrane, as elders.

The new trustees faced an immediate challenge: the church coffers were empty and Rankin still was owed a year and a half's salary. After hiring a sexton at the rate of a dollar a week,[124] the trustees requested that the pastor announce a special offering to defray the expenses of "lightery, fuel and sexton." Then, in order to produce sufficient income for church maintenance, the officers organized the rental of pews by holding an auction, offering "in the popular middle tier, eight choice seats to be rented at not less than seven dollars each; four of what is termed second choice seats, at not less than four dollars; and six of what is termed third rate seats, not less than three dollars each."[125]

This pew rental system persisted in most Protestant churches well into the twentieth century. A certain number of pews were always reserved as "free seats" for visitors, the poor, and the pastor's family, but members were expected to pay their pew rents and sit in their own places. When a new church was built in nineteenth-century Fort Wayne, the officers would first estimate the cost of the building, divide the sum by the number of seats, and then auction the lot to raise the amount needed. A newly purchased pew, however, was not exempt from annual levies determined by the trustees.

After arranging for a more regular source of income to maintain their facility, the officers sought means to pay Rankin his back salary; by April 1843, however, they still owed him two hundred dollars on his 1842 stipend. Then, on August 24, Rankin submitted his resignation to the congregation, explaining: "My pecuniary and domestic concerns are in such a condition as to require immediate attention and, as I have the prospect of employment in another . . . field of labor, after mature consideration, I have concluded that the interest of this church, as well as my own, would be promoted by a separation." Understanding very well the "pecuniary" cause of the resignation, the elders resolved "that it be suggested to the trustees that proper means be immediately adopted to collect funds . . . to meet the indebtedness of the church for his past services."[126] The deep affection and appreciation of the congregation for their pastor was formally expressed by the elders: "We would record his goodness and mercy in advancing the interest of our branch of Zion. . . our church having increased more than sixfold in as many years and, up to the present time, enjoying harmony and having good prospect of further enlargement."[127]

Rankin's allusion to "domestic concerns" referred to the unsettled state of his family after the death of his wife in 1841, following the birth of their fourth child. His mother-in-law[128] had then come to care for the family, but this was not a permanent solution, and Rankin had found no new wife and mother for his children in the area. His congregation had worried about their pastor's family and now hoped that his new situation might prove more fruitful in providing for their needs. After serving for a while in northern Indiana for the Home Mission Board of the Old School Presbyterians, Rankin went to Monroe County, New York, where he soon remarried.[129] When the news of Rankin's marriage reached Fort Wayne, Elizabeth Wines wrote to Susan Williams: "I do most heartily, with you and the rest of our friends, rejoice that he is once more settled. I wish him great happiness . . . . I was glad the children had a mother."[130]

Rankin left the First Presbyterian Church a much stronger and more mature congregation than when he had arrived six years before. His loyalty to the Old School side of the Presbyterian Church had strengthened the church's position with that branch; his active support of the temperance platform had given the local movement significant impetus; and his fearless advocacy of the antislavery cause had kept church members from drifting into benign silence on an issue that many congregations believed was too divisive to be advocated. Under Alexander T. Rankin's leadership, Fort Wayne Presbyterians became increasingly respected for their successful blend of evangelical piety and moral reform.[131]

Allen Wiley rests on his journey to Fort Wayne.

[Original Illustration by Kenneth B. Dutton]

3
Methodists

"The congregation [at Fort Wayne] appeared very intelligent, displayed a better taste in their dress than is usually seen in this country, and were also very genteel. I felt as though I had got back to New England."

Charles H. Titus, 1843

Methodists were the fourth religious group—after Catholics, Baptists, and Presbyterians—to conduct worship services in the newly laid out town of Fort Wayne. Their missionary policy of appointing lay preachers and establishing circuits of preaching stations enabled the Methodist Episcopal Church to organize congregations quickly in almost every new settlement in the West. An unschooled and itinerant leadership, however, had weaknesses, and Methodism in Fort Wayne, although planted early, was slow to develop to its full maturity and strength. After two decades of steady growth, it finally became firmly rooted, and then flourished to become one of the prominent denominations in the community, distinguished for its evangelical zeal and social conscience.

The Early Visitors

The names of the first itinerant Methodist preachers to visit Fort Wayne are not recorded.[1] During the late 1820s, the denomination did not find a community of Methodists strong enough in size or conviction to warrant sending a resident pastor to organize a congregation, and none of the existing records suggests that Fort Wayne was on a regular circuit during this time. In 1828, Allen Hamilton wrote to the American Home Missionary Society, "The Methodist Church have had ministers to visit this place; they were not encour-

aged, as the generality [greatest part] of the inhabitants wish a minister of regular acquirements."[2]

Hamilton, in this letter, was acting as spokesman for a group of Fort Wayne residents who wanted to secure a Protestant minister for their growing community. In his next sentence he diplomatically avoided speaking of the Methodist clergy's lack of formal education by saying, "I cannot say I have any prepossessions in favor of the tenets of any denomination. I am, however, convinced none would be so useful as a minister from the Presbyterian Church, in as much as they are generally better educated."[3] There were no college graduates among any of the Indiana Methodist clergy during the 1820s and there was no clamor for them, because of a strong denominational prejudice against college-bred ministers. The Methodist *Discipline* of 1784 advised preachers never to allow education to interfere with soul-saving: "If you can do but one, let your studies alone. We ought to throw by all the libraries in the world, rather than be guilty of the loss of one soul." The influential Peter Cartwright declared that formal education stunted a preacher's growth, like "lettuce growing under the shade of a peach tree." Another Methodist leader accused theological seminaries of turning out "learned dunces and second and third-rate preachers." Thomas A. Goodwin, the first college graduate to join the Indiana Conference, stated that his presiding elders were so fearful of exhibiting any favor to a college man that, on several occasions, he was demoted for no other reason than being a college graduate. Goodwin was finally driven from the active ministry by the jealousy and prejudice against college graduates, and intolerance toward a learned clergy continued for decades in spite of the Methodist Episcopal Church's success in establishing schools and colleges.[4]

Fort Wayne Methodists had just such an untutored, unordained, licensed preacher[5] residing among them. James Holman had come from Boston in 1824 and settled outside of town along the north bank of the St. Mary's River, where he built a cabin and farmed for a living. In this cabin Holman "kept up regular Sabbath preaching for several years . . . [and] formed a class of five members,"[6] his wife, brother, sister-in-law, and a single woman. On occasion they welcomed a preacher from some distant circuit, such as Holman's brother William, the Reverend John Strange, and the Reverend Stephen R. Beggs, who visited Fort Wayne in 1829. William Warren Sweet, the preeminent historian of Indiana Methodism, described a cabin quarterly meeting, when visiting preachers attracted a large gathering:

> There were few churches in those early days and quarterly meetings were held at private cabins, and on those occasions they would be crowded with strangers. When bedtime came the "sisterhood" took the beds and the men would "pile down on the floor by the dozen," and with feet extended to the fire, would sleep soundly until the morning.
>
> Let us picture this . . . frontier preacher, clad in ill fitting, homespun preacher garb—for there was a well recognized preacher garb then as now—as he conducts the preaching in one of these rude cabins on a quarterly meeting occasion. He places his chair before him as his pulpit, and begins to read a hymn . . . After the singing of the hymn, comes the prayer . . . and then follows the sermon on the text.[7]

Presiding Elder John Strange

Most circuit riders in those early days traveled considerable distances. Beggs's charge encompassed a one-hundred-fifty-mile circuit along the Wabash River, southwest of Logansport: "[In] 1829, I was sent to the Crawfordsville Circuit with Brother Strange as presiding elder.[8] I was alone on the circuit, which embraced the following towns: Crawfordsville and Lafayette, from thence to Delphi and Logansport, once out to Fort Wayne, and back to Attica, then down to [old] Portland and Covington." The rural preaching points on any circuit outnumbered these urban ones, so that the minister regularly preached between five to seven times

a week. In 1828, Beggs had itinerated in the Richmond area and reported, "This was a four weeks' circuit, and in it I preached nearly every day and often twice a day."[9]

Most Methodist preachers were effective, a few were eloquent, but none on the frontier could surpass the powerful pulpit style of Beggs's presiding elder, the Reverend John Strange who had preached in Fort Wayne in the late 1820s. James Holman's brother Joseph—who claimed to be the first Methodist to settle in Fort Wayne, when he arrived in

Joseph Holman
[Drawing by B. F. Griswold, 1917]

September 1823 to serve as Receiver of Public Monies—remembered Strange as "a very eccentric man."[10] When asked where he learned to preach, Strange replied that his Alma Mater was:

> . . . Brush college, more ancient though less pretentious than Yale or Harvard or Princeton. Here I graduated and I love her memory still. Her academic groves are the boundless forests and prairies of these western wilds; the Pierian springs are the gushing fountains from rocks and mountain vastnesses; her Arcadian groves and Orphic songs are the wild woods, and the birds of every color and every song, relieved now and then with the bass hootings of the night owl and the weird treble of the whip-poor-will; her curriculum is the philosophy of nature and the mysteries of redemption; her library is the word of God, the discipline and the hymn book, supplemented

with trees and brooks and stones, all of which are full of wisdom and sermons and speeches; and her parchments of literary honors are the horse and saddle-bags.[11]

The presence of circuit riders in Fort Wayne in late 1829 was noted by Charles Furman, who had come to survey the field for the Presbyterians. He reported to his mission society: "There are a few Methodists, tho' no church of any kind exists here . . . . The Methodist circuit riders have not been here since the first Sabbath after my arrival. One got drunk and ran away; the other has never made his appearance."[12]

The Fort Wayne Mission

The fall of 1830 marks the beginning of a more organized Methodist effort at the headwaters of the Maumee River. On October 6, the Illinois Conference "resolved that Fort Wayne and its vicinity be . . . constituted a station to be denominated the Fort Wayne Mission" in the Madison district.[13] The Reverend Nehemiah B. Griffith, who had just completed a year's tour of the White Lick circuit, was placed in charge. Griffith was a native of New York and had moved to Ohio with his family at the age of eighteen. In 1822, he entered the ministry and distinguished himself as a "very successful preacher." His biographer stated that "he preached the doctrines of the Bible so practically and experimentally. . . and with such an unction, that his ministry was generally attended with extensive revivals of religion."[14] At Fort Wayne, Griffith was fortunate to have a schoolhouse available for meetings; in South Bend, where he was sent the following year, his congregation met in the barroom of a tavern provided by its Catholic owner.[15]

As Griffith left for his next appointment to the north, the Reverend Richard S. Robinson assumed the Fort Wayne circuit for the year 1831. The local Presbyterian minister was grateful for Robinson's assistance in the community's effort to limit the inflow of whiskey among the canal laborers, and wrote, "Mr. Robinson, a pious and worthy Methodist brother, has engaged heart and hand in this work." Joseph Holman remembered him as "a good young man."[16]

The presiding elder of the Madison district was the Reverend Allen Wiley, one of the early founders of the Methodist Episcopal Church in Indiana[17] and a guiding force in the development of Methodism in Fort Wayne during the early 1830s. An admirer of Wiley remembered his account of a journey to Fort Wayne accompanied by Robinson:

> In 1831, Fort Wayne was included in Madison District. There was a large wilderness, uninhabited save by savage Indians and wild beasts, lying between the settlement on the Upper Whitewater

and Fort Wayne, requiring the presiding elder each round to lie out one night in the woods. Wiley would take off his saddle, and construct a bed out of his saddle and saddle-blanket, tie his horse's bridle around his waist, and get what rest he could with the wolves howling around him.

During one of his visits to Fort Wayne, this year, he was accompanied by R. S. Robinson, and during their stay they held a series of meetings in the Masonic Hall, which exerted a salutary and powerful influence on the minds of the people. Wiley preached in the morning and Robinson at night for several days in succession; and it was Wiley's opinion, if the meetings had continued a few days longer, that nearly the whole community would have professed religion; but the preachers had to leave to attend a camp meeting in Wayne County. Wiley often remarked that he never thought of their leaving Fort Wayne when they did, without feelings of regret.[18]

Camp Meetings

Camp meetings were a Methodist specialty. Each circuit conducted its own meeting annually during the spring or summer months, and invited the preachers from neighboring circuits to participate. John Dawson remembered "a camp meeting, the first, perhaps, ever held by the Methodists in this county, on the site of Lindenwood Cemetery, near a spring of water, on the north side."[19] These extended religious gatherings were great social events in the life of the frontier, and for many rural people they functioned as an annual vacation, when people traveled to the campground and camped out for the duration of the event. In no other form of ministry were the Methodist clergy more successful in adding converts to the church than through their vigorous exhortations at the camp meetings.

It was not unusual for some converts to express their religious enthusiasm in a heightened emotional state. Allen Wiley described a camp meeting held in 1831 on the Wayne circuit where some converts were overcome with uncontrollable laughter, which continued unabated for hours. Not all those attending were amused by what grew to be disruptive to the camp meeting; finally one minister suggested that those who were giddy[20] "should not invite the exercise," and that those who were mocking "should not doubt the sincerity of their brethren, for they could not help seeing that the thing was involuntary when once commenced."[21] Methodists celebrated this special form of religious expression, in the face of derisive remarks by Quakers, Episcopalians, or Catholics, by singing a favorite camp meeting chorus entitled "The Methodist":

The World, the Devil, and Tom Paine,
Have try'd their force, but all in vain.
They can't prevail; the reason is,
The Lord defends the Methodist.

They pray, they sing, they preach the best,
And do the Devil most molest;
If Satan had his vicious way,
He'd kill and damn them all today.

They are despised by Satan's train,
Because they shout and preach so plain;
I'm bound to march in endless bliss,
And die a shouting Methodist.[22]

The Itinerant Clergy

In the fall of 1832, the newly created Indiana Conference assigned the Fort Wayne mission to a new Missionary District and named the Reverend Boyd Phelps to its charge. The following year, however—when the new district was dissolved and Allen Wiley returned to the Madison district—the Conference failed to name a minister for Fort Wayne. Appointments of Methodist ministers were always made each fall at the end of the Conference, and most clergymen were transferred to a new post every year. This unique system of itineracy was rooted in the convictions of its founder, John Wesley, who enjoyed traveling and believed that limiting a minister's stay at any one post was best for all concerned. He wrote: "I know, were I myself to preach one whole year in one place, I should preach both myself and most of my congregation asleep. Nor can I believe it was ever the will of our Lord that any congregation should have one teacher only. We have found by a long and constant experience that a frequent change of preachers is best. This preacher has one talent, that another. No one whom I ever yet knew had all the talents which are needful for beginning, continuing, and perfecting the work of grace in a whole congregation."[23]

Francis Asbury, the father of American Methodism, believed strongly in Wesley's principle of itineracy and, in the colonies, strove to perfect his plan for a "circulation of preachers, to avoid partiality and popularity."[24] The efficient operation of this system, however, required a centralized authority to make appointments and a firm discipline to which each minister subscribed. As a result, American Methodism adopted a strong connectional polity with an "all-for-one and one-for-all" philosophy. *The Methodist Magazine* in 1843 explained this aspect of Methodism to new converts: "That grand feature by which the polity of the Methodist Episcopal Church is characterized—that feature to which the others are in a great degree subordinate, and that feature which constitutes the main difference between ourselves and other evangelical denominations—is *an itinerating ministry*. From this arrangement flows the necessity of episcopacy, of conferences, of the office of presiding elders—and, hence, is perpetuated the unity of the church itself . . . . This is Methodism."[25]

The purpose of the itineracy system was to provide fresh challenges to the pastors and fresh sermons for the people; it also freed preachers from depending on the favor of the people for their employment, and thereby allowed a more independent and prophetic voice from its pulpits; and it avoided long vacancies, experienced by churches with the "call" system, by promptly providing a new minister to all Methodist congregations in need. On the negative side, the itineracy provided little continuity in congregational leadership, and traveling ministers were somewhat limited in their awareness of the social problems of any one town and thus unable to offer sustained community leadership; also, the system did not encourage its circuit riders to marry, and, when permission to marry was granted, the minister was separated from his family most of the time. In comparison with the more settled clergy of other churches in Fort Wayne, these twelve-month pastors left behind few church records and gradually, over the years, became fading shadows in the memories of the people.

The Itinerant Congregation

Whenever the circuit rider arrived in town during the decade of the 1830s, Fort Wayne Methodists gathered for worship in a variety of places. Between 1831 and 1833, the new Masonic Hall was shared with the Presbyterians.[26] Alfred S. Johns, who had established the city's first saddlery business in 1837, wrote that the congregation also met in the "little brick schoolhouse,[27] until the gable end of the house fell in and was abandoned; then [at] a carpenter's shop (on Saturday eves the male members would go and clean the shop and carry in the benches made of slabs); when the owner sold it and moved west, we occupied a cabinet shop; then we occupied the old courthouse until it became dangerous."[28] These facilities, however, were not always available on a regular basis; Eliza Hamilton, who arrived in town in 1832, remembered "that one Sabbath the entire congregation visited four different places before they found one suitable."[29]

It was during the pastorate of the Reverend Freeman Farnsworth in 1834 that the congregation determined to remedy its Sabbath wanderings. The Presbyterians were already making plans to erect a frame meeting house on Berry Street, and the Catholics had purchased some lumber in hopes of building a church. Simon Edsall, one of the leading Methodists in town, approached the Ewing brothers, who provided a lot on the condition that the congregation build a church on it.[30] A subscription was circulated and nearly $1000 was pledged;[31] then, in 1835, under the leadership of their new minister, the Reverend James S.

Allen County's first courthouse — built in 1831 and torn down in 1841 — was sometimes used by Presbyterians, Methodists, and Lutherans for Sunday worship.
[Drawing by B. F. Griswold, 1917]

Harrison, a modest frame structure was begun and partially enclosed. The project, however, was started precipitately and soon stalled for lack of funds. A second financial effort added the roof; then, when money ran short the second time, the congregation wearied of the project. John Dawson wrote that, when he arrived in Fort Wayne in 1838, "A large, unfinished, dilapidated Methodist Church stood near the corner of Ewing and Main streets."[32] By that time the country was languishing in a deep depression, so that the congregation had no immediate hope of raising new building funds. Dawson remembered, "The year 1839 at Fort Wayne was characterized by the prostration of the credit of the state . . . that year made times still harder than in 1837-8, as we well recollect."[33] The unfinished church building soon became an eyesore; William S. Edsall proposed to the church trustees that, "if they would move the old church . . . building, as it was on the lot adjoining his . . . he would give them one hundred dollars . . . . Finally the church building was sold to Mr. W. G. Ewing and moved off from the lot and Mr. Edsell gave his note."[34]

The Quarterly Meetings

In 1836, the Methodist Episcopal Church in Indiana had added to its strength 2616 new members, a ten-percent increase.[35] At the annual Conference, the circuits reported an awakening interest among the population in religious matters. The Reverend Richard Hargrave, presiding elder of the LaPorte District in which the Fort Wayne Mission was now located, wrote, "The cause is marching forward through much opposition in this far North-west."[36] One of Hargrave's duties as presiding elder was to officiate at the quarterly meetings of the congregations in his district. In 1836, Fort Wayne Methodists had secured for their September quarterly meeting the new Presbyterian Church and invited the Presbyterians to attend. Two young women, Susan Man and Alida Hubbell, teachers in the Presbyterian school, attended the service; Miss Man wrote home about the experience: "Yesterday the Methodists held their quarterly meeting in our new church. The elder preached and tried so hard to be eloquent and to show his learning that Alida and I could with difficulty keep from laughing. If he had preached a plain practical sermon, we would not have smiled, but, when he tried so hard to be learned and eloquent, we could but smile at his ignorance."[37]

One of the occasional visitors to Methodist meetings was Hugh McCulloch, the Unitarian-leaning bank cashier, who was then courting Susan Man. When Hargrave preached in Fort Wayne the previous year, McCulloch asked him if Unitarians were admitted to the Methodist communion. The presiding elder replied coldly that "they are not. The ban is strong between us."[38] McCulloch continued to worship with the Methodists until the fall of 1837 when the new pastor of the Presbyterian Church, the Reverend Alexander T. Rankin, arrived. An admirer of good speakers, McCulloch at first alternated between the Presbyterian and Methodist preachers; finally, he made his choice and wrote to his fiancée: "I have just returned from hearing Mr. Ball preach. After hearing Mr. Rankin, I feel but little interest in the sermons of Mr. B."[39]

The Stationed Preacher

McCulloch was referring to the Reverend Stephen R. Ball, the first ordained Methodist minister to settle in Fort Wayne. Methodism at this time was changing its character with the appointment of more stationed preachers. The new challenge to an old circuit rider, when appointed to a settled pastorate, was to preach a different sermon three times a week to the same people, instead of one sermon repeated to a variety of congregations over a period of two to four weeks. Not every self-taught circuit rider had that capability. In addition, the pastoral dimension of the localized ministry was much more demanding, as the expectations of local congregations were increasingly focusing on calling, teaching, organization, and fund raising. Some itinerants balked at the new trend and went farther west to open up new pioneer circuits—but not Stephen Ball: he liked Fort Wayne, and was so admired by his people that they determined to have him appointed as their stationed preacher.[40] Alfred S. Johns recollected, "In the fall of 1836 the Rev. S. R. Ball was sent here and traveled this circuit one year . . . . [His] circuit extended from Fort Wayne to South Bend, then to Logansport, and back to Fort Wayne; it took him two weeks to make this round. . . . At the expiration of [this year], the members of the

Richard Hargrave
[Courtesy of DePauw University Archives]

church and many citizens petitioned Conference to send him back as a stationed preacher, pledging themselves to support him. Conference granted our request and he came back as a stationed minister, to the great rejoicing of everybody." At that time, all Methodist ministers were allotted the same salary: two hundred dollars a year, plus an allowance of sixteen to twenty-four dollars for each child under the age of fourteen, and traveling expenses. On this modest stipend, Ball moved into a double frame house adjoining the Johns's residence, and a door was opened through the common wall between the dwellings to unite the two front parlors. "The preacher stood and preached to the people in both rooms,"

the men sitting on one side and women on the other, as required by the Methodist Discipline.[41]

The strong traditions of the Conference prevented Ball's appointment for a third year in Fort Wayne. Realizing that his health would not endure the rigors of circuit-riding, he declined another ministerial appointment. He was a potter by trade and, by the end of 1837, had established a pottery in town.[42] He continued, however, to be active in the Methodist ministry, preaching regularly at vacant situations and serving as distributing agent for the Allen County Bible Society.[43] In spite of Hugh McCulloch's judgment, Ball had many admirers as a preacher; one resident wrote to a local newspaper that no other minister in town was as fearless in denouncing sin: "On Sunday evening last I had the pleasure of listening to the Rev. Mr. Ball, and he is the first minister of the Gospel that I have heard come out boldly against the nuisance of ball alleys, groggeries, and resorts of licentiousness . . . . The ministers of our holy religion seem to be afraid of preaching against licentiousness . . . .What reason do they give? . . . Why forsooth, they are afraid it will shock 'female modesty!' "[44]

The First Methodist Church

Following Ball were the appointments of the Reverend James Robe in 1838, and the Reverend Jacob Colclazer in 1839.[45] During this time the congregation embarked on a reorganization by electing new trustees and stewards,[46] and, in January 1840, established its own Sunday school. Previously, local Methodists had joined with Presbyterians, Baptists, and English Lutherans in supporting the town's original Sabbath School, organized in 1825.[47] Classes were now held in the Johns's and Ball's front parlors until early in 1840, when the new schoolhouse of Alexander McJunkin was rented for Sunday worship. By this time, the financial depression, which had afflicted Indiana for the previous three years, had lightened, and Colclazer encouraged the congregation to try again to build a house of worship. The denomination's *Discipline* set guidelines, specifically requiring that a portion of the pews not be "rented," but remain "free" and available to visitors and the poor: "Let our churches be built plain and decent, and with free seats; but not more expensive than is absolutely unavoidable; otherwise the necessity of raising money will make rich men necessary to us. But if so, we must be dependent on them, yea, and governed by them. And then farewell to Methodist discipline, if not doctrine too."[48]

A new lot was secured at the northeast corner of Berry and Harrison streets and, by the fall of 1840, a frame meeting house was erected to become Fort Wayne's fourth church building—joining the Presbyterian, Catholic, and Lutheran structures. A visiting Methodist schoolteacher—a native of New England—commented on the new facility: "This was the first pewed church I had seen among the Methodists, west of the Alleghenies. It was beautifully and neatly finished. The pews are after the modern plan, without doors. Only about half of them are rented, the rest left free, usually every other one. Upon the top of each pew is a strip of black walnut, wide enough to hold a note book when singing. The pulpit is also made of black walnut, which being highly polished, presents a rich and beautiful appearance." It was not only the church building that impressed the visitor; the congregation compared favorably with those he had seen at Greencastle and Madison: "The congregation appeared very intelligent, displayed a better taste in their dress than is usually seen in

Alfred S. Johns
[Courtesy of Allen County-Fort Wayne Historical Society]

this country, and were also very genteel. I felt as though I had got back to New England . . . . At six p. m. I attempted to preach to the people. A violent thunder storm commenced about the meeting hour, but yet the people flocked out, and the congregation was quite large. They were very attentive, and I felt that I was speaking once more to an eastern congregation."[49]

In the fall of 1840, the Reverend Francis A. Conwell assumed the charge. Alfred S. Johns remembered him: "He was a new convert and thought he was called to preach. Through the influence of friends he was admitted to Conference and sent out to this benighted part of Indiana, considered, at that time, out of all civilization. He was very much surprised on Sunday to see so large and intelligent a congregation before him; he thought he was coming among gamblers and cutthroats. He stayed with us two years and added many to the church."[50] As a consequence of this

growth, the Conference not only appointed Conwell for a second year, but relieved him of much of his rural preaching duties, freeing him to devote more time to his growing city congregation.

The German Methodists

At the end of Conwell's pastorate in late 1841, Fort Wayne was visited by its first German Methodist minister, the Reverend Wilhelm Heinrich Ahrens. At the age of twenty-seven Ahrens had arrived in Cincinnati, Ohio, in the spring of 1839 as part of the great migration of Germans to the mid-western states. Raised a pious Lutheran,[51] he was soon caught up in the fervent Methodism that was spreading in the new German settlements.

Unlike the other German-speaking religious groups—Catholic, Lutheran, Reformed, Jewish, Mennonite, Amish, Dunker, and Brethren—German Methodism was an American-made movement. Its founder was Wilhelm Nast who, at the age of twenty-one, abandoned his theological studies in Blaubeuren, Germany, and, in 1828, journeyed to America.[52] While serving as the librarian and German teacher at the Military Academy at West Point, he was attracted to the piety and discipline of Methodism. After accepting a call as professor of languages at the Lutheran College at Gettysburg, Pennsylvania, he experienced a radical conversion at a local Methodist camp meeting. As a result, he relinquished his position at the Lutheran College and became a probationary member of the Methodist Church. Soon afterwards, he was appointed professor of Greek and Hebrew at Kenyon College at Gambier, Ohio. By mid-1834 Nast had received his local preacher's licence and, in the following year, was appointed by the Ohio Conference to be the first German Missionary of the Methodist Episcopal Church (which in German he called "der Bischöflichen Methodistenkirche"). Immediately he set off for the largest German community in the state, at Cincinnati.

The Methodists of Cincinnati perceived the religious life of that town from a different perspective than did their traditional Catholic and Protestant countrymen. William Nast's son, Albert, wrote:

> In the early thirties. . . there was a great tide of German immigration which settled in the Ohio Valley. Cincinnati was the center of this stream of immigration. In 1830 it had a population of about 30,000 inhabitants of whom about one-third were Germans. The moral and religious condition of this element of that time was deplorable and became a matter of great concern to the church, especially to the Methodist Church, which, at that time, was the strongest in numbers and in influence in Cincinnati. Of these 10,000 Germans, 7,000 were nominal Protestants and 3,000 were Catholics.

Many of these Germans had brought their old-country drinking customs and habits of thought respecting the Sabbath with them. Many of the so-called pastors were irresponsible religious adventurers and the associates of the brewers and saloon keepers, who constituted, for the most part, the official boards of the churches they served. At this time there were in Cincinnati eight German breweries and three distilleries, and the German . . . press, numbering five or six papers, was spitting its venom of hatred and malice *against the Methodists*.[53]

Cincinnati was not an easy field of labor and, after a year's effort, Nast had won only three converts to his cause. His conference then judged that city to be too hard a field for a first-year preacher, and reassigned him to Columbus on a three-hundred-mile circuit. The following year, however, Nast returned to Cincinnati and soon organized the first German Methodist congregation; in 1839, he began publication of *Der Christliche Apologete;* and, by the end of the decade, the movement had raised up twenty preachers.

It was during this time that German Methodism extended its work into Indiana and, in 1840, established its first mission at Lawrenceburg. The work prospered and, the following year, two more missions were begun at New Albany and Fort Wayne.[54] The minister appointed to begin a new work in the three rivers area was William Ahrens. He had been converted to Methodism at a German camp meeting in Cincinnati in the summer of 1839, three months after his arrival. A young man of intelligence, talent, and energy, he soon felt called to preach the gospel to his fellow countrymen. In October 1841, he received his preacher's licence and, soon afterwards, departed for Fort Wayne. On the way he became seriously ill and was delayed in his arrival.[55] Most likely he located his ministry in the new Methodist Church on Berry Street, and soon founded a "class"—the nucleus of a future congregation.

The German Lutherans React

At first, the German-born pastor of the local Lutheran church, the Reverend Friedrich K. D. Wyneken, out of courtesy, allowed some German Methodist circuit-riders to speak to his congregation, but the friendliness quickly faded when some of his parishioners returned from Methodist meetings questioning the completeness of Wyneken's religious experience. The Lutheran was stunned, and wrote: "The preacher finds himself losing the confidence of all. If he is true to his calling. . . he stands there deserted. Some look upon him as a hypocrite because he does not want to enter into the 'new life.' " Wyneken was soon warning other German Lutherans about these incursions; in Germany—

where he had been promoting the cause of German-Lutheran missions in America—he wrote: "The Methodist Episcopal sect . . . is most active . . . . Within the past several years, it has established a mission among the Germans, which it heavily supports, and which, unless the Lord sends help very soon, will certainly wipe out the name of the Lutheran Church in the West . . . . There is hardly a Lutheran or Reformed congregation which does not have to suffer from these swarming pests. Many congregations have been completely scattered by them."[56] When Wyneken's influential pamphlet, *The Distress of the German Lutherans in North America,* was published in America, German Methodists countered his attack on Methodism with their own pamphlet, *Why Have You Become an Apostate?* —accusing Wyneken of being an inquisitorial Jesuit in disguise.[57]

When Wyneken returned from Germany in 1843—newly converted to a strict Lutheran orthodoxy—he was determined to eradicate any shadow of Reformed or Methodist practice in his congregation. As a result, prayer meetings were discontinued, the pulpit was closed to all but those of strict Lutheran convictions, and Holy communion was denied to those of Calvinist or Methodist leanings.[58] Then, when Wyneken resigned his Fort Wayne pastorate in late 1844, this Lutheran animosity towards Methodism was sustained by his hand-picked successor, the Reverend Wilhelm Sihler. The year before he arrived in Fort Wayne, Sihler had published *A Conversation Between Two Lutherans on Methodism,* which was quickly reprinted in pamphlet form, and sold over 12,000 copies in four editions.[59]

The Bethel German M. E. Church

The identities of the German Methodist clergymen who faced the Lutheran opposition in Fort Wayne during this time are not known,[60] but their pastoral leadership was so fruitful that, in 1846, the congregation was able to erect a church on the west side of Harrison Street between Wayne and Washington streets. The new edifice was of brick construction, with a balcony encompassing three sides of the interior, and fenestrated with twenty Palladian windows arranged in two levels. A paid newspaper notice invited the public to its dedication: "The Bethel German M. E. Church will be publicly dedicated to the worship of Almighty God on Sabbath next (29th inst.). Service will be performed in the German Language by the Rev. Wm. Ahrens, Presiding Elder of the German District, both morning and evening. English Service at half past three o'clock p. m. by Rev. John C Bayless. The public is respectfully invited to attend."[61]

The North-Ohio District which Ahrens[62] now supervised was one of new German districts created after a reorganization of the Methodist Church in 1844.[63] English-speaking Methodists in Indiana were proud of their flourishing German-speaking congregations and many had been distressed to learn that German ministers were proposing separate German districts. In October 1843, the Indiana Conference of the Methodist Episcopal Church had resolved "that our delegates to the next general conference . . . are hereby instructed to use their best efforts to prevent our German Missions from being disconnected from our regular work."[64] Nevertheless, when the General Conference of 1844 approved the request of the Indiana Conference to divide their jurisdiction into Northern and Southern divisions, it also approved the creation of the new German districts. Hence, when the English-speaking Methodists at the Berry Street Church became part of the Fort Wayne District of the North Indiana Conference, their German-speaking coreligionists of the Bethel German M. E. congregation—then worshipping in the same facility—were assigned to the Cincinnati German District[65] of the Ohio Conference. As a consequence, when the North Indiana Conference chose Fort Wayne for its organizational meeting in September 1844, the local German Methodist minister could attend only as a guest.

Joseph K. Edgerton's Journal

During this time, Joseph K. Edgerton, a young lawyer and devout Methodist, moved to Fort Wayne.[66] Always faithful in his church attendance, he was soon invited to teach a class in the Methodist Sunday School. Edgerton greatly appreciated good preaching, and sometimes wrote critiques of the Sunday sermons in his journal; occasionally he would pen a summary of some memorable homily. He especially admired the "very good" sermons of the Reverend William C. Anderson at First Presbyterian Church, and the "excellent" preaching of his successor, the Reverend Hugh S. Dickson.[67] Edgerton would sometimes attend three services a Sunday at different churches and then reflect upon them in his diary. His reviews of sermons between July and October 1844 provide a rare glimpse of the variety of preaching that could be heard in Fort Wayne. His earliest comments are on the local Methodist minister, the Reverend Hawley Baxter Beers, who had arrived in the fall of 1843.[68]

July 28, 1844
Today I was at the Methodist Church and heard a very fine sermon and intend going this evening if I can.

August 4, 1844
Last Sunday afternoon I again attended church and heard Rev. H. B. Beers, our Methodist minister, preach a not uninteresting sermon from the remarks of Festus to the great apostle Paul, "Paul, thou art beside thyself; much learning doth make thee mad." It is a great theme for a great mind.

Mr. Bruce treated it sympathetically, but I should like to have its interpretation handled by Dr. Olin.

Today, I have been again at church to hear Mr. Beers preach a practical and earnest sermon. He is not able, but I think him a good and useful man. He called on me last week and I was pleased with him and glad to form his acquaintance.

September 1, 1844
This morning I attended church and heard a sermon from Mr. Harrison of Detroit. It was short, but very sensible, and well delivered. His text was, "Prove all things and hold fast to that

Joseph K. Edgerton
[Courtesy of Allen County-Fort Wayne Historical Society]

which is good." The subject of his sermon was the importance and necessity of a careful examination . . . of the truth of the Christian system, [and] the duty of holding fast to it, when it has once been fully proved. The subject was treated with a good deal of skill and effect . . . .

There is no afternoon service in the churches here, for what cause I know not, but it seems a bad arrangement . . . .

51

In the evening I again attended the Methodist church, but the congregation was disappointed in their expectation of hearing Mr. Harrison, and there was no sermon at all, but a formal, cold, and lifeless prayer meeting that was well calculated to put spirituality asleep.

September 15, 1844

I have just returned from the Methodist Church where I heard a very good sermon from Mr. Boyd,[69] the presiding elder of this district, from the text, "Oh, taste and see that the Lord is good."

September 22, 1844

Today I have been at church and heard a stranger preach . . . . He was a plain, unlettered man, but he made his subjects quite interesting and instructive . . . . In the evening I attended church again . . . [and] heard the same man preach as in the morning.

October 6, 1844

The sermon was presented this morning by a plain and uneducated man. It was very long and very noisy, but, not withstanding, evinced considerable natural talent and sincerity. It was not, however, precisely that kind of sermon which affects me most seriously.

October 13, 1844

Today I have been at church three times. In the morning at the Presbyterian Church where I heard an old Pole preach from the text, "We would see Christ." He is upwards of seventy-two years of age, though having the voice, manner and appearance of a man of about fifty-five. He was a Polish Count and a colonel in the army of Napoleon and has seen two hundred battles. He is now in his old age an intelligent, able, and useful soldier of the Cross, a preacher of the Gospel attached to the Lutheran denomination. His sermon this morning was excellent, well-conceived, well-delivered, plain, practical, and evangelical. I could not but feel my heart drawn out towards the venerable man . . . . What a busy and eventful scene has his life been, and with how much of joy must he look forward to its close and his final reward![70]

The subject . . . was considered under the following heads. 1. What it is to see Christ. 2. In what we see Christ. 3. What is the effect of seeing Christ. 4. Why many do not see Christ. Each of these topics was discussed with much clearness and effect, in the true spirit of the Gospel.

In the afternoon I attended the Methodist Church and heard Bishop Hamline . . . preach.[71] He is an noble looking man and a very able preacher. His sermon was very superior. . . [on] the passage of Scripture which declares "that we should at all times be ready to give a reason of the hope that is in us with meekness and fear." After alluding briefly to the nature of hope, he considered,
1. The hope of the Atheist—he hopes there is no God.
2. The hope of the Deist—his hope is based upon the idea that the Bible is a fiction and not the book of Divinity.
3. The hope of the Universalist—that all men shall be saved.
4. The hope of the Moralist—that an honest life shall save him.
5. The hope of the Speculationist—that his thinking right about religion, that his speculation-orthodoxy, shall save him.
6. The hope of the Procrastinator—of him who is always postponing . . . putting off the conversion of his soul and the giving of his heart to God.
7. The hope of the Formalist—the nice outward and ceremonious Christian.
8. The hope of the Christian—of him who truly loves and serves his God.

Having briefly and very interestingly defined the character of these various classes of hope, or religious hope, the Bishop proceeded to examine the reasons, or to demand from each one representing these various classes, the reasons of his hope—and, in so doing, furnished a brief summary of the arguments against the errors in which those who trust in any other than the Christian hope have fallen—and presented very startling views of the dangers and destination to which any other than the Christian's hope led those who trusted in it.

The manner and the matter of both the morning and afternoon sermon indicated clear heads and pious hearts in both of the ministers to whom I have alluded.

This evening I heard a man named Smith preach at the Methodist Church. His sermon was dull and ordinary. . . . [He] was, I doubt not, a very good and pious man, but not of a very superior order of talent.

The day has been one of great opportunity for religion.

October 20, 1844

This has been a church-going day. I have been at church three times and heard three of the Methodist ministers, now here, preach: one of them this morning at the Presbyterian Church, his name I do not know, but he preached a very good sermon; an elderly man this p. m. at the Methodist Church, of whose name I am also ignorant, but whose sermon was of a very common cast; Presi-

George M. Boyd
[Courtesy of DePauw University Archives]

dent Simpson of Greencastle this evening, and he preached in the demonstration of the spirit and with power.[72] He is a very strong man and the same person . . . [I previously] alluded to as the "plain Indiana man . . . ." The conference closes it session here tomorrow morning.[73]

The North Indiana Conference Organized

This first meeting of the North Indiana Conference was the largest gathering of clergy ever assembled in Fort Wayne.

Unlike all other Protestant denominations at that time, Methodism made no provision for lay representation at its assemblies and, outside of the local parish, all church matters were decided by the clergy.[74] By October 16, 1844, ninety-five pastors, eight presiding elders, two college professors, and two bishops had arrived at Fort Wayne for their opening session. Providing for this assembly, which would stay in session for a full week, was a challenge to the local pastor and his congregation. A delegate from Indianapolis remarked, "Thanks to the management of the smoothfaced, popular presiding elder, G. M. Boyd, and to the sagacious, gentlemanly pastor, H. B. Beers, ample arrangements had been made for the entertainment of the Conference, including the faithful horses that carried the preachers to Ft. Wayne, for, in the language of ancient hospitality, 'there was straw and provender enough and room to lodge in.' "[75] Appreciation was also directed to the host congregation through a newspaper advertisement, expressing "the thanks of the Conference . . . especially to the pastor and members of the First Presbyterian Church who so kindly furnished us their house for the session of the body."[76]

The actions of the previous General Conference on the subject of slavery dominated the docket of the North Indiana Conference. At the General Conferences of 1836 and 1840, the anti-abolitionists of the North had combined with southern delegates to prohibit any discussion of slavery, and this gag-rule prompted a group of abolitionist churchmen in 1843 to withdraw and form the Wesleyan Methodist Church. Then, at the 1844 General Conference—when the delegates voted to suspend from office a Georgia bishop who had married a slaveholding wife—the southern churches seceded to establish the Methodist Episcopal Church, South. In the wake of this schism, the assembled clergy at Fort Wayne felt torn. They would not suggest any change in their *Discipline,* which categorically stated: "We declare that we are as much as ever convinced of the great evil of slavery: therefore no slave holder shall be eligible to any official station in our Church . . . . Our coloured preachers and members shall have all the privileges which are usual to others in the district and quarterly conferences." Shocked, however, by the secession of the southern churches, they muted the antislavery feelings, and said only "That we do, in the fear of God, protest against all efforts, from whatever source proceeding, to divide the Methodist Episcopal Church, and hereby pledge ourselves, to the best of our ability, to heal the wounds of Zion and promote the peace of the Church thus threatened and endangered."[77]

John C. Bayless Appointed

Towards the end of the meeting, Bishop Waugh requested Allen Wiley, who knew Fort Wayne from personal experience, to assist his cabinet in making the ministerial appointments—and the Reverend John C. Bayless was assigned. Bayless had previously served appointments at Jeffersonville, Vincennes, Evansville, and Terre Haute. He was remembered by his colleagues for the stir he created when the Conference assembled at Rockville in 1838:

> Bayless had married a well-to-do young woman at Vincennes just before Conference, and had brought her to Conference on a steamboat . . . .With no fear of tradition before his eyes, he had his wedding suit made by a tailor in the height of fashion. The fact that it was made of store-goods was not of itself to be censured; for. . . a dozen or more others wore store goods; but the style of the clothes gave offense. The pants were "tights" with narrow falls;[78] the coat was "pigeon-tailed"; and the hat of the "stove-pipe" variety, giving the wearer a unique appearance in a body of Methodist preachers in regulation uniform.
>
> This was too much a departure from traditional Methodism to go unrebuked; hence, Samuel C. Cooper offered a resolution that every member of the Conference be required hereafter to wear to Conference straight-breasted or shad-bellied coats, and breeches with broad falls. It passed without a dissenting vote.[79]

Not every member of Fort Wayne's Methodist Church was happy with the newly appointed pastor. Joseph K. Edgerton wrote: "This forenoon I was at the Methodist Church and heard the Rev. Mr. Bayless, the minister of the church recently appointed, and am sorry to say I consider him not calculated to be very useful. He is a man of quite ordinary talents and of no power as a preacher. I was in hopes that the Christian Church here would have been favored with a stronger man; the size, importance, and religious state of the town requires such a man. My inclinations and feelings are linked to the Methodist Church, tho' there is surely [much] among its members which does not coincide with my views." Edgerton persisted but, on succeeding Sundays, wrote that Bayless's sermons were, in turn, "very tedious," "not very interesting," "ordinary. . . not to my edification." Then, with increasing exasperation, he exclaimed, "I cannot force my mind to a liking of this gentleman in his public ministration, tho' I doubt not his intentions are good." Edgerton expressed concern that "the present and limited talent in the Methodist Church in this place, both in its ministry and membership, is begetting for it a feeling of contempt in the other churches," but rejected, for the time being, the impulse of "cutting loose my connection with the Methodist Church." As a result, unless there was a guest preacher at the Methodist Church, Edgerton avoided Bayless, and attended the preaching of Hugh S. Dickson or the Reverend Charles Beecher at the newly organized Second Presbyterian Church.[80]

Bayless also suffered some public criticism as a result of his congregation's conduct in its Fourth of July observances. Independence Day was then the most celebrated holiday on the American calendar. Christmas was seldom observed outside of the home, as most Protestant churches tended to ignore the day. Neither local newspaper in 1845 carried a single line of advertising relating to the season, except for a paid notice inserted by the ladies of the Methodist Church, announcing that their fund-raising fair was to be held on Christmas Eve.[81] There was equally little public notice of New Year's Day, and only in 1837 had public Thanksgiving Day observances been revived by public decree.[82]

A Methodist Fourth of July

In early nineteenth-century America, the Fourth of July was often celebrated by church and Sunday school observances, along with civil celebrations. The precedent for blending the religious and civil observances went back to the early days of the Republic when John Adams, the principal force behind the adoption of the Declaration of Independence, wrote on July 3, 1776, "It ought to be commemorated as the day of deliverance, by solemn acts of devotion to God Almighty. It ought to be solemnized with pomp and parade, with shows, games, sports, guns, bells, bonfires, and illuminations, from one end of the continent to the other, from this time forward for evermore."[83]

By 1840, Fort Wayne had achieved the official status of a city and was increasingly devoted to elaborate Independence Day observances, with political oratory and Sunday school parades as the dominant features. The Sunday schools used the occasion to celebrate their own anniversaries, as well as the nation's, inviting local citizens with military affiliations to lead their processions. In 1841 there were two elaborate parades. The civic celebration was led by a band to the Presbyterian Church, and the order of procession was a careful blending of the sacred and secular, as the ministers, chaplain, and Sabbath school students were alternated with the civic leaders, orator, and Revolutionary War soldiers. After prayer, the reading of the Declaration, and the oration, the body marched to the American House. The second procession was advertised as the "Sunday School Celebration of the Anniversary of Independence" and paraded with band and orator to the Methodist Church under the leadership of the same marshall, Major Samuel Edsall, and finally crossed the "Maumee River to the grove to partake of a collation . . . provided by the gratuitous contributions of the ladies of this city and vicinity."[84]

By 1845, the Sunday school parades had become the

more popular Fourth of July observances and, when a Methodist procession marched too close to the civic celebration, the courthouse orator was outraged. He immediately fired a letter to the Methodist pastor, protesting "the evidently designed indignity shown me yesterday by you and a portion of your congregation . . . in marching your procession immediately in front of the court house (with music, etc.) during the time I was delivering my oration." Bayless passed the protest on to the laymen of his congregation who had arranged their parade. Insults to one's honor, and especially to one's minister's honor, were serious matters, and so, in answer to the testy complaint that the children had spoiled the orator's speech, these Methodists replied through the columns of the weekly press: "Now the truth is that his [the orator's] failure on that occasion was not attributable to the Sabbath School procession marching by, but to the barrenness of his intellect." The orator then responded that Bayless, for making public his complaint, had a "heart destitute of all common principles of courtesy, as well as Christianity." The laymen replied that the orator "would be perfectly at home in a sixpenny monkey show or Negro fandango."[85]

The church seems to have won out over the state; for the next year there was no civic celebration, except within the German community, as the Sabbath school anniversaries continued to flourish. A local editor noted with some displeasure: "Many now deplore the apathy which leads us to neglect this national holiday. Some attribute it to the custom, now becoming too prevalent, of having Sabbath School celebrations on that day. If this should be the reason, and a proper representation of the fact could be made to the managers of the Sabbath Schools, we think they would hereafter avoid any interference with the regular celebration, and hold the Sunday School anniversaries on some more appropriate day."[86]

The Methodist Social Conscience

The editor of the *Times* may have forgotten that the Methodists had also celebrated the fifth anniversary of the founding of their Sabbath School the previous January. The featured speaker was Joseph Edgerton, and the full text of his address was printed on the front page of the *Fort Wayne Sentinel*. At the conclusion of his speech, Edgerton lauded the social conscience of Methodism which, from its beginnings, had sought out the poor and neglected: "The benefits of Sabbath Schools are perhaps most strikingly exhibited in our large cities, where the children of poverty and vice throng the public ways, exhibitions of the shocking depravity to which, even in tender years, ignorance of God may sink the human mind. While these are regarded by many as outcasts and . . . are seldom brought within the influence of our secular schools—the Sabbath School teacher recognizes in them the same origin, the same nature, and the same susceptibility of improvement which distinguish the offspring of the cultivated classes—and among these they love to labor and do good."

Edgerton then invited his audience to imagine the transformation that might occur in the life of some disadvantaged youth through their Sabbath school's outreach: "What an era in the life of this young mind! What a new world dawns upon his darkened understanding! What new hopes and sympathies spring up within his heart! He is among the young, the happy, and the good. The Book of knowledge and of life are together laid open before him. The name of God is heard by him, not in blasphemy and ribaldry, as was once the case, but

William Rockhill
[Drawing by B. F. Griswold, 1917]

in reverence, in prayer, in praise. He learns to read, he learns to think, he learns to pray, and, from that time forth, a soul is saved from death, a new intellect is added . . . . By his simple exhortations and prayers, his parents, perhaps sunken in vice and misery, and others among whom they move, may be raised to the dignity and the happiness of virtue."

The speaker's praise for dedicated Sabbath School teachers, however, was tempered by his judgment that Methodism had done too little in establishing schools: "It is a matter of regret, however, that, while the influence of the Methodist Church is so great, and its position so highly favorable, it has disappointed public expectation, and failed of its duty, and subjected itself to observation and reproach, by not using as strenuous and effectual efforts as it might use in the cause of education. Though it has done much, it is still, in this respect, behind other denominations which are its inferiors in numbers and strength."[87]

The Fort Wayne Female College — soon renamed the Fort Wayne Collegiate Institute and then the Fort Wayne College — dedicated its first building in 1849.
[Drawing by B. F. Griswold, 1917]

Edgerton may have been referring to the Presbyterians who were in the forefront of the English-speaking Protestant congregations in the city in establishing schools and supporting local education—and who were, at that moment, in the process of establishing a female seminary.[88] Certainly his audience was aware that the pastor of St. Augustine's Catholic Church was also preparing to open a girls' school under the direction of the Sisters of Providence, while the pastor of the German Lutheran Church was strengthening that congregation's educational program, as well as enlarging its seminary for Lutheran missionaries.

The Methodist College

Who first proposed the idea is not known, but, by early summer of 1846, Fort Wayne Methodists were making plans to establish the Fort Wayne Female College. Edgerton, newly elected as a church trustee,[89] was named secretary of the organizational meeting which was led by some of the town's leading citizens: Samuel Edsall, Philo Taylor, and William Rockhill[90]—with the strong presence of John C. Bayless and George M. Boyd, the presiding elder. Boyd had previously served as pastor of the Fort Wayne congregation in 1842.[91]

In September 1846, the committee's plans were approved by the North Indiana Conference, which then as-

sumed formal sponsorship of the institution and named five of its members to the school's board of trustees. The Conference also named Bayless as the college's "agent" to raise the funds necessary to commence classes in the fall. Land was secured from William Rockhill, and Fort Wayne citizens responded by contributing over $13,000 to the project. A Presbyterian minister commented that "subscriptions were quite liberal from all denominations."[92] Nine months later, on June 23, 1847, the cornerstone of the Fort Wayne Female College was laid. A local editor remarked:

> This building will be an honor to the place and to the State, as well as to the numerous and respectable body of Christians who are erecting it. In extent, architectural beauty of proportion and finish, and adaptation to the purposes for which it is designed, it will not be excelled by any edifice in the West. It will be 173 feet in length, by 100 deep in the main building, four stories high. Its position is well chosen, being on a slight eminence at the extreme west end of town, directly south of the aqueduct. It will stand directly across the head of Wayne Street, looking down that avenue for more than a mile, and presenting a front at once imposing and magnificent.

> Its cost, we believe, is estimated at about $30,000;

FORT WAYNE COLLEGE
COMMENCEMENT EXERCISES
BY
THE SENIOR CLASS,
FOR APRIL 23rd, 1856.

Order of Exercises.

1. PRAYER.........................
2. LATIN SALUTATORY...................
   Miss Joanna M. Kimberly.
3. ESSAY—EARTHLY FAME.—Shadowy Dreams.....
   Miss Celina E. Johnson.
4. ESSAY—HAPPINESS.—A Life Dream...........
   Miss Laura S. McMaken.
5. ESSAY.—Force of mind and character must rule the world.
   Miss Joanna M. Kimberly.
6. ESSAY.—The days of originality—are past..........
   Miss Frances E. Swinney.
7. ESSAY.—Would you conquer—press on..........
   Miss Jane M. Tam.
8. VALEDICTORY......................
   Miss Celina E. Johnson.
9. DEGREES conferred by the President............
10. BENEDICTION.......................

VOCAL AND PIANO MUSIC,
WILL BE INTERSPERSED WITH
THE EXERCISES.
Fort Wayne, April 23, 1856.

[Daily Times Job Office Print, Fort Wayne, Ind.]

1856 Commencement Program.

FORT WAYNE COLLEGE
EXHIBITION.
FOR APRIL 18th, 1856.
BY THE EL DORADO AND THALONIAN
LITERARY SOCIETIES.

ORDER OF EXERCISES:

1. PRAYER...........................
2. ESSAY.—Our thoughts slumber but never die.............
   Miss Ellen Tam.
3. AN ORATION.—Public Improvements...................
   Jonathan Keller.
4. EL DORADO GEM.—Part First...................
   Edited by Miss Rosalind L. Edsal.
5. EL DORADO GEM.—Part Second...................
   Edited by Miss Hanna E. Heath.
6. DEBATE.—Resolved, That the time usually spent in the study of the Classics could be more advantageously employed in the pursuit of English Literature..............
   Aff....John Colyar.
   Neg. Isaac Bateman.
7. ORATION.—American Civilization................
   John D. Fox.
8. DISCUSSION.—Is Fashion a greater evil to society than Intemperance.
   Aff....Miss Jane M. Brady.
   Neg. Miss Sarah E. Fielding.
9. BENEDICTION......................

VOCAL AND PIANO MUSIC,
WILL BE INTERSPERSED WITH
THE EXERCISES.
Fort Wayne, April 18, 1856.

[Daily Times Job Office Print, Fort Wayne, Ind.]

1856 college students exhibited their knowledge for the public.

Fort Wayne College's "Commencement" and "Exhibition" Programs of 1856
[Courtesy of Allen County-Fort Wayne Historical Society]

but, like all such structures, the reality will, no doubt, outrun the estimate. Great credit is due to the energetic gentlemen who have charge of the financial department of the concern, for the success that has attended their efforts in raising funds; and particularly to the Rev. Mr. Bayless, the Agent to solicit subscriptions. He has labored incessantly for some months, and he has the satisfaction of knowing that he has not labored in vain.[93]

After his year of college fund-raising, Bayless left Fort Wayne, and was afterwards remembered as a minister willing to devote time outside his parish for the benefit of the community. He had joined with Charles Beecher to organize a local committee "to seek out indigent persons . . . and afford them relief"; First Presbyterian Church invited him to serve on the Board of Visitors of its Female Seminary; the Allen County Bible Society asked that he address them at their anniversary meeting; and he was admired for his "very feeling and appropriate" prayers at civic observances.[94]

In spite of the college's unfinished building—which was not completed until 1849—the first classes were inaugurated in the fall of 1847 under the direction of Alexander C. Huestis. Nearly one hundred girls enrolled in the several departments from primary to college. The published curriculum announced courses in Latin, Greek, French, Spanish, grammar, arithmetic, geography, music, drawing, logic, algebra, chemistry, literary criticism and history—for a tuition of $22.50 a year.[95]

College life in Fort Wayne also had its social side; in 1850, a student wrote: "Fort Wayne has been very pleasant this season. The gentlemen are delivering weekly lectures upon different scientific and literary subjects. They are very interesting and improving; I attend *except* when the mud is too deep. There have been a great many parties for this place. I have attended quite a number—one last night at which there were three hundred present . . . . They have sleighing parties every night when there is any snow and sometimes go in the mud. The plank road makes a fine place for sleigh riding .... The telegraph from Toledo... runs through this place so that [we] get all the Eastern news as quick as *lightning.*"[96]

Samuel S. Brenton
[Portrait by Joseph H. Dile, 1868,
Courtesy of Allen County-Fort Wayne Historical Society]

Samuel S. Brenton

During Bayless's year of fund-raising activity, the Berry St. Church was served by the Reverend Samuel S. Brenton. Born in 1810 in Gallatin County, Kentucky, he had entered the ministry at the age of twenty as a circuit rider, serving parishes in southern Indiana. When his health failed in 1834, he became a "local preacher," studied law and was admitted to the bar, and twice was elected as a representative from Hendricks County to the state legislature. At the end of his second term in 1841, his health had sufficiently improved to permit his return to the active ministry. He then served churches at Crawfordsville, Perryville, and Lafayette before his appointment to Fort Wayne in September 1846.

Brenton's ministry in Fort Wayne soon attracted attention when, in mid-January, he held a series of revival meetings. One local newspaper reported: "A protracted meeting at the M. E. Church . . . has been in progress for the last six weeks, and is still progressing. A large number have been awakened to the importance of seeking a more substantial inheritance than the ephemeral enjoyments of time and sense, and the result is a large accession to the church. May the good work go on and spread from church to church, until all shall feel the influence of innovating grace."[97]

Charles Beecher, at Second Presbyterian Church (New School), occasionally reported to his mission secretary on the state of other churches in Fort Wayne. In 1844, he noted his cool reception by "the Methodists, who think the New School are 'stealing their thunder.'" Three years later, however, the growing strength of Methodism prompted him to report, "The Methodists are the prevailing influence here, as probably in the state. Their motto is 'Methodism against the world.' And with this ambition [is] an organization second in efficiency only to the Papal." Beecher was bold to criticize the Methodist discipline which then required converts to remain on probation for six months before becoming church members or receiving Communion, a practice which the Presbyterian pastor believed "emphatically avows that regeneration is no test of communion . . . a most fatal obstacle to the progress of the Gospel."[98] Beecher also parted company with Brenton on the issue of secret societies. The Presbyterian believed that taking secret oaths compromised one's Christian loyalty, a conviction widely held by Methodists and reinforced by the Methodist Conference in 1844 when it advised its ministers not to join the Freemasons or Odd Fellows, believing that it would impair their influence. Two years later, however, the Conference rescinded its ban and, in 1847, Brenton became one of the first clergymen of his denomination to join a secret fraternity when he was initiated into a lodge of Odd Fellows in Fort Wayne.

At about that time, the wife of Brenton's presiding elder died after a long illness; the funeral announcement was typical of the era: "Died of consumption, on Friday morning, June 4th, 1847, Silence Ann, consort of Rev. G. M. Boyd, of this city."[99] Brenton conducted the funeral and then, five months later, officiated at Boyd's remarriage "to Miss Ann Tharp."[100]

At the 1847 Conference, Brenton was named to succeed Boyd as presiding elder of the Fort Wayne district; the following year he was chosen to represent the North Indiana Conference in the General Conference. He was reappointed to district leadership in 1848 but, soon afterwards, suffered a paralytic stroke and lost the use of the right side of his body. He remained bedfast for some time, and later was able to "get about on crutches."[101] The affection of the local Methodists for Brenton was such that they organized a "donation party" in his honor to be held at his home on the evening of Christmas Day 1848.[102] He resigned his eldership at this time and was granted "superannuated" status by the Conference; by May 1849, however, he had recovered sufficiently to be named to the post of Register of the United States Land Office in Fort Wayne.[103]

The Wayne Street Church Established

In the meantime, the Methodist congregation was served by the Reverend Amasa Johnson in 1847 and the Reverend William Wilson, who continued through the Fall of 1850.[104] Wilson arrived in Fort Wayne with a high level of evangelical zeal and, in the space of two months, was conducting a successful revival. A local editor reported, "A protracted meeting has been progressing in the Methodist Church in this city since last Friday a week. We understand that, during the meeting, thirty to forty persons have experienced religion and been added to the church."[105]

Samuel C. Cooper
[Courtesy of DePauw University Archives]

The growth of the Methodist Church during this time precipitated a spate of church building across the country, and it was estimated that, in 1849, twenty-five percent more churches were built than in any preceding year.[106] Fort Wayne Methodists caught this spirit when the Conference decided to divide their congregation and establish a new parish in the western part of town. Alfred S. Johns recalled: "In the fall of 1849, when Elder Cooper[107] returned from Conference, he preached to us, and surprised the congregation very much by announcing that Conference had divided the church, and made Harrison Street the dividing line. All members living west of that street should go into the New

Charge, as he called it, and he would meet all the west members at the College Chapel the following Sunday and organize."[108]

Of a congregation of 217 members, fourteen families—now living in this developing section of town, including former pastors Samuel Brenton and Amasa Johnson[109]—gathered as charter members of the new congregation. Johns wrote: "The meeting was opened with prayer by the elder; Mr. Samuel Stophlet was appointed recording secretary and recorded the names of all the members . . . . The elder appointed the Rev. Samuel Brenton minister in charge and procured the Chapel of the Methodist College to hold service in . . . . At a later meeting a committee was appointed to wait on the trustees of the Berry Street Church about dividing the church property." The following August they were given a lot which they promptly traded for two lots on the northwest corner of Wayne and Broadway streets.[110] A newly elected board of six stewards then named a "building committee. . . to draw up a subscription and collect funds to build a church, thirty-five by fifty feet." By the fall of 1850, the newly named Wayne Street Methodist Episcopal Church was erected and the Reverend Thomas Henry Sinex was appointed to its charge in time to officiate at the dedication. Sinex was a graduate of Asbury College where he had most recently taught Greek while acting as the school's agent.[111]

Soon after the congregation was settled in its new facility, the membership was called upon to return the favor of the use of the chapel by hosting the College's three-day graduation exercises.[112] A local newspaper reported that the event attracted overflow crowds:

> The Wayne Street Church was crowded, during the whole examination, to its utmost capacity, with an interested, intelligent and gratified audience. During the evenings, when orations and addresses were delivered, the house was literally packed full of people, and many went away, who could not gain admittance.
>
> The addresses by the Hon. G. S. Orth, Rev. Mr. Brenton, and Rev. Mr. Sinex, on Monday, Tuesday and Wednesday evenings, were all marked by a high order of intellect . . . chaste in diction, pure in sentiment, sound and elevated in morals, and highly eloquent in pronunciation.
>
> The whole exercises were such as to give high hopes and encouragement to the friends of the infant institution, and to guarantee its future prosperity and usefulness. A collection was taken up on the second evening to assist in finishing the Chapel of the College, which resulted in the receipt of near six-hundred dollars.

In contrast to the perceived perfection on the inside of the church, the editor was irritated by the defects in deportment exhibited outside the church by the children of those attending: "There is one unpleasant circumstance that we regret to have to allude to—that is the gang of ruffianly disorderly boys that was collected around the house during the evening exercises . . . . Their rioting and hubbub were such at times as to disturb the exercises within. Fathers and mothers were sitting inside, in all the dignity of broadcloth and satin, while their boys were on the outside, practicing the incipient steps to the penitentiary, or the gallows. It strikes us forcibly that the church authorities ought to have adopted vigorous measures for the suppression of the tumult outside the house. A night's meditation in the calaboose would benefit some of those precocious youngsters."[113]

Personal Piety and Public Morality

At the same 1849 Conference which created the Wayne Street Church, the delegates heard Bishop Waugh warn of the dangers of some popular amusements which had gradually proliferated in Indiana, "such as dancing parties, theatrical and circus performances, and comical exhibitions. Such amusements we believe to be wholly inconsistent with Christian character, destructive to vital piety."[114] Methodists were not alone in their disapproval of dancing: not only were Presbyterians and Baptists equally opposed, but Fort Wayne's first Catholic priest, Stephen Badin, had condemned dancing twenty years before, and Jesse Hoover, the first Lutheran pastor, had excommunicated members for attending balls. Hence, when the Methodist Conference directed its ministers to admonish those members who danced, and to bring to trial any who persisted—including those who allowed dancing parties in their homes—it was simply reiterating the accepted social morality held by most churches of the day. Methodists, however, persisted longer than the other mainstream denominations in their disapproval of dancing.

The 1849 Conference did not limit its social concerns to matters of personal morality, but was bold to address those issues of human welfare and community betterment which were to be decided at the ballot box. Indiana, at this time, was struggling to establish free schools, and the State Education Society, aware of the influence of the largest religious organization in the state, requested the two Methodist Conferences to appoint representatives to the Society. In advance of a public referendum on the question, these appointed Methodist clergy wrote to each minister to "request that you preach on the subject of common schools at your earliest convenience. It will be remembered that the question of free schools or no free schools for Indiana is to be decided at the ballot box August next, and it is in behalf of the free schools that this request is made."[115] A majority of

Allen County voters supported the referendum and, by the fall of 1853, a public school system had tentatively begun in Fort Wayne.

By the end of 1850, however, the overriding social concern of Methodism focused on the threatened extension of slavery into the proposed territories of the far West. In September of that year, Congress had enacted a strong fugitive slave law along with other compromise measures designed to appease the slave states and prevent a sectional schism. Slavery was now an option for the emerging territories of New Mexico and Utah under the new principles of "popular sovereignty." Many Americans who firmly believed that the abolition of slavery in the South, however moral, would be unconstitutional, were equally convinced that any extension of slavery into the West would be immoral and illegal.

Brenton Runs for Congress

In the forefront of a concerted effort to keep the western states free of slavery were the Society of Friends, New England Congregationalists, New School Presbyterians, and northern Methodists. In Fort Wayne, Samuel Brenton sharpened the debate in early 1851 by declaring his candidacy for Congress as representative from the Tenth Congressional District. He had maintained his affiliation with the Whigs since his election to the Indiana legislature in the late 1830s, and his recent appointment as head of the local Government Land Office reflected his strong ties with that party. Brenton began his campaign for Congress as one of four Whig candidates and, by May, emerged as the sole standard bearer for the office.

In his speeches, Brenton opposed the extension of slavery outside the old South and urged that the western territories be preserved as "free soil"; he also called for "the entire and unconditional repeal of the Fugitive Slave Law, believing it immoral, unnecessary, and uncalled for." Brenton favored protective tariffs, cheaper postal rates, and the abolition of the franking privilege for members of Congress; he also proposed that refused government land be given to the poor. One consistent theme was his assertion that "he was independent of all parties, always thought and acted for himself, and that no party could or should dictate to him."[116]

Brenton was not an easy candidate for the Democratic Party to attack. He was well known and well liked, and did not carry the stigma of political compromise. As a consequence, the principal issue raised by the local Democrats was Brenton's ministerial profession. Thomas Tigar, Democratic editor of the *Sentinel,* pounded on this theme:

[Brenton's] defeat by an overwhelming majority may show him the folly of striving to unite religion and politics—serving God and Mammon . . . . He has doubtless calculated much on the influence the Methodist Church might exercise in his behalf, as he could not hope by any other means to overcome the strong Democratic majority in the district . . . .

We are unwilling to think that any considerable number of Democrats who belong to the Methodist Church can be induced to sacrifice their principles and vote for such a Whig as Mr. Brenton, merely because he is, or has been, a preacher in that denomination; and any attempt to influence their votes on such grounds would have a tendency to array other sects against him, and to disgust the better informed portion of his own church at such an unholy alliance of religion and politics. The people of Indiana are not yet prepared (and we trust will never be) for a union of church and state.[117]

Brenton's supporters defended his clerical status by citing the Democratic clergy who had previously served in Congress.[118] Democrats also raised the issue of Brenton's health—specifically, that he walked with the aid of a crutch: "The Whigs are swallowing Brenton as fast as they can make up their minds to it, crutch and all." "A poor apology for a candidate he is . . . unable to obtain a livelihood in the honorable calling to which he was educated." "The question to be settled, then, is . . . whether the people of this district will be represented by a clergyman—I will not say a worn-out clergyman."[119] Brenton, however, conducted a vigorous campaign, travelling to every community in the district. When the ballots were counted in Allen County, Brenton had gone against the Democratic tide and won 1112 to 1100; in the rest of the district, he won by 425 votes.

In Congress, Brenton worked hard on the issues of federal land distribution, and addressed the House on fine points in the administration of new laws on the assignability of land warrants granted to veterans of military service. In 1852, Brenton fulfilled a campaign promise by challenging the free mailing privileges for Congressmen. When he moved that "the Committee on the Post Office and Post Roads be. . . instructed to inquire into the expediency. . . of repealing all laws now in force granting the franking privilege to Senators and Representatives in Congress," there were "cries of 'I object!' 'I object!' all over the House." Brenton, whose attendance record in Congress was exemplary, was equally distressed by those colleagues who so seldom answered roll calls. As a consequence, he twice introduced a resolution "That the Secretary of the Treasury shall deduct . . . ten dollars for each day the member or Delegate may have been absent from his seat during the sitting of the House of which he is a member, unless such absence was occasioned by his sickness, or the sickness of his family."[120]

In 1852, Brenton was defeated in his bid for reelection in the wake of the disintegration of the Whig party.[121] Soon afterwards, in September, he was named president of the Fort Wayne College.[122] Brenton had given the principal address at the laying of the cornerstone and maintained a continuing interest in the school, serving as secretary of its trustees; he had been tireless in recruiting teachers and obtaining equipment and, in 1847, the Board, in gratitude, established a two-year scholarship for a student of Brenton's choosing. In 1849, he had urged the Board to establish a "male department," which, in a few years, became the Fort Wayne Collegiate Institute; then, a month after Brenton assumed the presidency, these two institutions were formally merged to become the Fort Wayne College.

Brenton, like so many Methodist ministers—as well as frontier physicians and lawyers—was self educated; but, unlike some of his denominational colleagues, he valued education and supported all efforts to establish schools. When invited to address the Allen County Agricultural Society in the fall of 1853, he proposed the founding of an agricultural school: "To make farmers independent, I have this day proposed to educate the mind with direct reference to agricultural pursuits, just as I would educate with reference to professional, mercantile, or mechanical pursuits . . . . I hope the day will soon come when our . . . addresses will all be delivered by some Cincinnatus, directly from the handle of the plow."[123]

Brenton Reelected

In the fall of 1854, Brenton entered the race for his former seat in Congress as a Free Soil candidate. The issue of extending slavery into the West had become increasingly contentious when, in May, Congress had passed the Kansas-Nebraska Act, repealing that section of the Missouri Compromise of 1820 that had barred slavery in those areas of the Louisiana Purchase lying north of the latitude 36° 30′, the southern boundary of Missouri. Brenton's platform addressed the issue, as the *Fort Wayne Times* reported:

The position of Mr. Brenton was clearly defined and, as such, would be largely and enthusiastically sustained by a majority of freeman of the northern states. Recognizing the binding force of the Constitution, its guarantees and compromises, he feels it his duty to use all just means to restore the eighth section of the Missouri Compromise and harmonize the excited state of the country . . . .

On the subject of the admission of new states to the Union . . . he stands pledged to the doctrine —

so lately repudiated by the supporters of the Nebraska-Kansas Bill — of conceding the power to be in Congress to regulate the question of slavery in the territory of the United States, by refusing admission of such with the stain of slavery on it.[124]

Brenton's platform paralleled his denomination's position. At the North Indiana Conference of 1854, the assembled Methodist clergy reasserted their opposition to "the great evil of slavery" in general, the Fugitive Slave Law in particular, and then spoke to the Kansas-Nebraska issue: "We deplore the impolitic course of the late Congress of the United States in the repeal of that part of the Missouri compromise restricting slavery north of 36° 30′, thereby permitting slavery to go into a vast territory from which it had been forever excluded."[125]

Such resolutions stung the Democrats, and the editor of the *Fort Wayne Sentinel,* while skirting the slavery-extension issue, responded by attacking the whole Methodist Church:

> We notice several of the eastern religious papers are mourning over the lamentable dabbling with politics by ministers of religion, and especially by the Methodists in Indiana. If things continue in the same evil way, that church will become a mere electioneering machine. In our own district we see one minister of that church stumping the country as a candidate for Congress, and indulging in every species of trickery and miserable demagoguery, while many of his brethren, instead of seeking to reclaim him from the evil of his ways, are actually aiding and abetting him in his iniquity. Two more in other parts of the state are officers of the infamous Know Nothing associations.
>
> The whole church is becoming demoralized; its usefulness is departing; and it will soon become necessary to its salvation to cut loose from its ambitious preachers and import a supply of pious missionaries to preach the gospel. They appear to forget that Christ expressly said they could not serve two masters—they cannot serve God and Mammon.[126]

The editorial columns of the rival *Fort Wayne Standard* —which was dedicated to the cause of abolition, temperance, and education—took an opposite position on the place of preachers in the political arena. Charles Case, who had recently assumed the position of coeditor, stoutly defended not only the right but the necessity of clergy addressing the pressing moral issues:

> The pro-slavery democracy [Democratic party] have of late evinced a wonderful anxiety for the purity and perpetuity of the church . . . . They seem to have a wonderfully clear idea of the duty of Christians and especially of Christian ministers . . . . No matter what vital principles of morality and natural justice are at stake . . . no matter though God says "all things whatsoever ye would that men should do unto you, do ye even so to them," . . . if any moral question . . . becomes also a political one, the moment it does so, preachers must keep their hands off and their mouths shut . . . .
>
> And if any preacher dare to rebuke wickedness "in high places"—to denounce any measure or law, as glaringly at variance with the morality of that gospel which he loves to preach—why, this is "mistaking his call and falling into a political pool" and "he is unworthy to wear the armor of Jehovah's buckler any longer!" Sin ceases to be sin if a man commits it as a politician, or if the law commands it, and therefore God's ministers have no right to rebuke it as such! Such is the gospel according to pro-slavery democracy . . . .
>
> On such theology, if a minister in his pulpit ventures to remember "those in bonds as bound with them," to proclaim God's will "that the oppressed go free and that ye break every yoke," and to expose any human enactment which nullifies this mandate of Heaven, he is to be denounced as "out of his sphere," as a "hypocrite and imposter."[127]

When the 13,465 ballots of the district were counted that October, Brenton had lost Allen County by 449 votes, but had carried all of the surrounding seven counties for a majority of 1603. When he was enrolled in the thirty-fourth Congress, he assumed the chairmanship of the Committee on Public Lands. At this time, the House was closely divided on the Kansas-Nebraska issue and, as a result, was unable to elect a Speaker. After many days of balloting, Brenton switched his vote from one anti-Nebraska candidate to another, and Horace Greeley—the influential antislavery editor of the *New York Tribune* and supporter of the candidate Brenton had abandoned—chastised him in the columns of his newspaper: "I wish the honest, faithful opponents of slavery extension, who have twice elected Mr. Brenton to Congress on that issue—when, on other political grounds, the district would have gone against him—could have looked down from the gallery while he was making this demonstration . . . . Mr. Brenton has been restive and uneasy for some time." Brenton answered his critic on the floor of the House: "I confess that I have been restive and uneasy for some time at the predicament in which we stand before the country, not in reference to the success or defeat of any particular man, but in reference to the success of the great principle which I came here to represent. With me, principle is everything—men are nothing. I have no favorites." Soon afterwards Greeley apologized, "not because it was unjust, or that the effect was to injure the gentleman, but because it had resulted in exciting a sympathy for Mr. Brenton to which he is not entitled."[128]

Opposition to the Extension of Slavery

Brenton was ardent in his espousal of the "great principle" and rose on the floor of the House to denounce President Buchanan's assertion that "Congress has no power to limit, restrain, or in any manner to impair slavery; but, on the contrary, it is bound to protect and maintain it, not only in the states where it exists, but where ever its flag floats and its jurisdiction is paramount." Brenton replied: "To those of us who have been . . . taught to believe that it [the American flag] proclaimed death to the tyrant and liberty to the captives, it is a strange and startling announcement to hear it proclaimed . . . that this banner is unfurled to the breeze to serve as a guide to the despot, and as a pledge of protection to the oppressor of his brethren."[129]

In a later speech, Brenton presented a carefully reasoned argument that there was no historical precedent allowing the settlers of new territories to introduce the institution of chattel slavery by their own whim. He noted that all former territories created by the Northwest Ordinance, such as Indiana, had abided by the antislavery provisos established by that act and never questioned the accepted principle that only Congress could change its status. Brenton was eloquent in his suggestion that it would be much better to return Kansas to its original native inhabitants than to surrender it to slaveholders:

> Shall the beautiful, lovely, and charming "Kansas," enamored by the love of freedom, and panting for admission into the family circle as the youngest sister of our bright galaxy of independent states, be now welcomed in all her virgin purity? Shall she be permitted to stand in all her pride of loveliness, beauty, and freedom, and, with arms wide-extended, welcome the free sons of free sires from every land and clime to rest in her pure embrace, and bask in her heaven-born smiles, which secure freedom to all her children? Or shall she be compelled to bow her neck to the tyrants yoke? or submit her ruby lips to the polluting kiss of the task-master's fetid breath?

> Mr. Chairman, rather than submit to such degradation, let her plains, her prairies, and her woodland forests, continue to be the free home of the wild denizen of the wilderness. Let the dulcet strains of the timbrel and harp, poured forth by the enamored swain, as he woos his dusky mate by streamlet and brook, break the stillness of dewy eve and quiet morn, rather than the sobs and heartrending groans of a captive race. Let the solemn funeral dirge of the untutored savage break the stillness of the dense forest, and echo over hill and dale, as he chants its solemn lays over the graves of his fathers, rather than have the beauties of civilization marred by the clank of the bondman's chains.

Brenton concluded his speech with a denunciation of the institution of slavery itself:

> Slavery is contrary to the principles of the Declaration of Independence and the Constitution of the United States, and can derive no support or protection from either. Secondly: it is detrimental to the success of the great interests of agriculture, manufacture, and commerce, the freedom of speech and of the press. Thirdly: it is a violation of the principle of natural justice. And finally: it is destructive of the inalienable rights which the Author of our being had given to all the members of the human family . . . .

> Slavery is the result of a triumph of *might over right* —the triumph of the *strong* over the *weak;* and the fearful struggle is now going on, backed by the power of the purse and the sword of the nation.[130]

The "fearful struggle" to which Brenton referred had been precipitated by the large number of proslavery Missourians who had crossed into Kansas to cast ballots and, by this contested election, established a proslavery territorial government. Soon, antislavery guerrilla bands known as Jayhawkers were confronting a proslavery militia; cannon and rifles—some called "Beecher's Bibles" because of the Reverend Henry Ward Beecher's fund-raising activities for the cause—were imported, cities were fortified, men were murdered, armed bands raided other armed bands, cattle were stolen, farm houses were burned, and the city of Lawrence was sacked. The church women of Fort Wayne were especially distressed by these reports of violence in Kansas—nearly ten thousand Hoosiers had settled there[131] — and a local newspaper carried their plea for help: "The ladies of Fort Wayne, who sympathize with the sufferers in Kansas are earnestly invited to meet at Jesse L. Williams to determine some plan by which assistance can be rendered to them in their distressed condition." A fund raising supper was quickly organized and $170 was sent to "Bleeding Kansas."[132]

When Methodists announced their intention to meet in Jackson, Missouri, in 1856, the city fathers "entered a remonstrance against the Northern Methodist Church holding their annual conference in this city." In Fort Wayne, the front page of the *Times* expressed the dismay of many church-going citizens:

> No wonder, then, that the hotspurs and ruffians of slavery should be alarmed; that those who have violated God's law by trampling His image in the dust should tremble at the anticipated presence in their midst of his assembled ambassadors and appointed ministers . . . . Is it not an unextorted self-confession of guilt that these chivalrous Missourians—so skilled and practised in the use of the revolver and bowie knife—should quake and show the white feather in anticipation of the assembling of a few meek and harmless ministers of the Gospel? It is the tribute which vice pays to virtue . . . .

> It remains to be seen how far such threats and menaces will influence the Methodist Conference. We have greatly misjudged the followers of John Wesley if we did not believe them incapable of fear from any human power . . . . They have learned from the teaching of their master to "fear *not* him who can kill the body . . . ."

> That man of God . . . John Wesley, drew from the holy oracles the true idea of freedom and incorporated it as a fundamental article in the constitution and discipline of that branch of the Church of which he was the founder. Methodism is essentially anti-slavery—the Methodist Church is an anti-slavery society as truly as it is a church of God. And wherever its pure and uncorrupted doctrines are preached and prevail over the hearts and consciences of men, there slavery will come to an end. No wonder, then, we repeat, that the cruel and heartless traffickers in the souls and bodies of men should fear and tremble at the promised coming among them of a Methodist Conference.[133]

The slavery-extension issue became increasingly contentious in the Congressional election of 1856 and, coupled with the presidential contest, created a fifty-percent increase of balloting in Brenton's district.[134] Brenton had returned to Fort Wayne that September on a journey which the *Times* reported was only "thirty-four hours in passage . . . the quickest trip yet," and embarked on his briefest campaign yet, now under the banner of the newly founded Republican party. Brenton had become ill during the closing days of the last Congress and was limited in his ability to visit all of his district. The race was close: he again lost Allen County, but succeeded in garnering a slim majority of 710 of the 20,688 votes cast in the district.

Brenton's deteriorating health did not allow him to return for the opening of the Thirty-Fifth Congress. He died in Fort Wayne on March 29, 1857, at the age of forty-six.[135] His Congressional colleagues resolved to "go into mourning, and wear crepe on the left arm for thirty days"; their eulogies were revealing: "He was distinguished for a ready, abundant, vigorous sense, and was bold and enterprising in maintaining whatever he deemed right. Here he was firm; and between wrong and right nothing was ever yielded to calculation or expedience." "Mr. Brenton was modest and retiring almost to a fault; unaffected and unpretending. . . . He had no enemies . . . . Strictly moral and exemplary in his conduct, he was emphatically an honest man—true to his principles, faithful to his friends, and just to all." In Fort Wayne, an editor wrote: "The young would do well to note that his religious bent of mind was the basis of his usefulness, and that . . . he never knew less of his duty to God, but lived a life which reflected much credit on his holy and civil callings, and, as a consequence, made him a better and wiser officer."[136]

Evangelism, Temperance, and Debt

The Wayne Street Church, which Brenton had served as organizing pastor, grew steadily during his congressional career.[137] January was the traditional time for Methodist revivals in Fort Wayne and, in early 1853, a local newspaper reported that "The Methodists . . . are holding a protracted meeting at the Wayne Street Church, and a great revival is in progress. Many conversions have taken place, and many more are needed."[138] Revivals always confronted the sins of the individual and seldom the sins of society—a situation which pleased the local Democratic editor: "Quite a revival is in progress in this city, and we notice by our exchanges that such things are common all through the country. The preachers, having quit preaching politics and taken to the gospel, are now dwelling more on the merits of the blessed, bleeding Savior than on bleeding Kansas, and their labors appear to be crowned with unwonted success."[139]

This newest congregation in town was also the first to organize a railroad excursion for a "Sabbath School Picnic." In July 1858, the leaders of the Wayne Street Church engaged a special train on the Chicago and Pittsburgh Road and extended a general invitation to other Sunday schools in town to join in an outing to Eagle Lake, near Warsaw, Indiana. On the day of departure, over five hundred adults and children arrived at the railroad station, and were welcomed by two brass bands and an engine brightly decorated by the women of the church. Extra cars were added to the train, and the assemblage was serenaded en route by "a large concourse of our Orff Brass Band and Alert Number One Marshall Band."[140]

The Wayne Street Church was also the first church in the city to invite a minister of the African Methodist Episcopal Church to its pulpit. In March 1859, the pastor, the Reverend Lewis Dale, placed an advertisement in a local newspaper announcing that the Reverend William Paul Quinn, Bishop of the local Conference of the African Methodist Episcopal Church from Richmond, Indiana, would preach, and that the "public is respectfully invited to attend."[141] A few African-

The Berry Street Methodist Church (second building) at Berry and Harrison streets, was begun in 1859.
[Courtesy of Allen County Public Library]

American residents had previously belonged to the Berry Street congregation before the local A. M. E. congregation was organized in the mid-1840s; the service was probably the first occasion that white and black residents worshiped together with black leadership in a white church. When Dale's transfer from Fort Wayne was announced, a local editor wrote: "This able and fearless expounder of the Word will be much missed in the city. His example and influence have been salutary. The energetic and faithful manner with which he has grappled with and contended against vice in this city, has won for him the respect and esteem of the virtuous and good. He was an earnest and eloquent champion of the temperance cause .... He has confronted the great evil of using alcoholic drinks . . . with gigantic power . . . and has done more to stay the evils of this deadly vice than all the other pulpits in this city combined."[142]

No denomination was more zealous in the cause of temperance than the Methodists. When the Indiana State Temperance Convention was held in 1852, a Methodist Bishop, E. R. Ames, was elected president. When the state of Maine, in 1851, passed a law forbidding the manufacture or sale of intoxicating beverages except for industrial or medicinal purposes, this statute quickly became the model for proposed prohibition legislation in Indiana, and the Methodist church marshalled its forces to induce the Legislature to enact such a law. In 1853, the Indiana Legislature passed a compromise bill which pleased no one. As a concession to the Methodist Church the legislators forbade the sale of liquor of any sort within two miles of a camp meeting, but allowed the sale, in any quantity, of spirituous liquors for medicinal or sacramental purposes, and refused to classify wine, even if made from whisky, as spirituous. These limited measures were unacceptable to Indiana Methodists—as well as Presbyterians, Baptists, Congregationalists, English Lutherans, and German Reformed—who pressed for the Maine Law. The united witness of the churches bore fruit in the next session of the Legislature and, in the winter of 1854, the lawmakers passed a strong prohibition statute, making the manufacture and sale of all intoxicating beverages illegal. When the law went into effect in June 1855, celebrations were held all over the state; the elation of the temperance forces, however, was short-lived when the Indiana Supreme Court ruled that the prohibitory law was unconstitutional. As a result, the churches' temperance forces abandoned, for a while, their hope of legislating abstinence, and redirected their energies into the traditional arenas of religious education and moral suasion.[143]

While the ministers and stewards of Methodist churches grappled with sin, the trustees of these congregations struggled with debt. At successive meetings of the trustees of the Berry Street Church, measures were sought to manage the accumulated interest on old debts. Emergency funds were often loaned by the individual trustees to pay outstanding bills; then, when these obligations became unmanageable, they canvassed the congregation for debt-retirement contributions. In other times of crisis, the more affluent members would be asked to loan money to the church at three percent interest. Crucial to the financial health of most of Fort Wayne's congregations were the fund raising activities of their women's societies, whose suppers and fairs produced several hundred dollars annually for whatever projects they believed were most pressing, from a bell at the Wayne Street church to a parsonage for the Berry Street congregation.[144]

Debt was no stranger to the trustees of Fort Wayne College. At the 1855 meeting of the North Indiana Conference, the Committee on Education reported that the school

65

was heavily in debt and that its buildings and grounds were exposed to public sale. To remedy the situation, the Conference approved a resolution requesting each of its members to contribute ten dollars over a three-year period. The school survived the crisis but continued for years to struggle for its financial life.[145]

The New Church Buildings

The financial stability of Fort Wayne's churches was not helped by the economic depression which followed the Panic of 1857. After two years, however, enough money had returned into circulation to encourage some of the town's expanding congregations to build larger churches. The Presbyterians and Lutherans had already constructed their second facilities and now the Catholics and Methodists were preparing to build. The German Methodists at Bethel Church had outgrown their modest brick chapel during thirteen years of steady growth and offered it for sale. When the Jewish community purchased it in the spring of 1859 to convert the church into Indiana's first synagogue, the German Methodists were able to secure a larger property and "under the ministerial charge of Rev. Barth . . . erected a neat frame place of worship in the western part of town, near the Wayne Street charge" on the northeast corner of Washington and Fulton streets.[146]

At the same time, the members of the Berry Street Methodist Church determined to erect a new facility on their present property. The preliminary plan was to hire Samuel McElfrick at a fee of twenty-five dollars to design a brick edifice with Gothic windows, with interior dimensions of forty-one by seventy-three feet, for the total cost of eight thousand dollars. Fund raising activities were initiated and a subscription was carried outside the congregation. At the same moment, the officers of Congregation Achduth Vesholom were raising nearly half of their refurbishing expenses through contributions from members of local Christian churches; so, in reciprocal charity, some synagogue members donated to the new Berry Street facility.[147] Then, in May 1859, the editor of the *Times* reported: "The Methodists of this city are removing the old saw mill—Berry Street Church—to the vacant lot west, preparatory to erecting a new edifice . . . . [It] was a large church when built."[148] In August, the cornerstone was laid, and slowly the structure took shape. Three years later, however, the interior was still bare. By this time, the Civil War's spiraling inflation had both deflated the trustees' debt and more than doubled the cost of the new edifice. Finally, the Reverend Reuben Davisson Robinson, president of the College, met with the church officers and successfully challenged them to take up another subscription in order to complete the project, by plastering and painting the walls in fresco, finishing the carpentry work, installing pews, and grading and fencing the property.

With the dedication of these new facilities in the early 1860s, Fort Wayne's three Methodist congregations assumed a prominent place among the churches of the city. The Wayne Street and Berry Street churches represented more English speaking Protestants than any other single denomination in town. The German Methodists were unique among the six German-speaking congregations in Fort Wayne: where the German Lutheran, Catholic, Reformed, and Jewish congregations strove to reproduce old-world traditions in belief and practice, the German Methodists greeted new emigrants with a German-American church, reflecting the dynamic piety of evangelical Methodism on the western frontier. Each of the congregations had developed a comfortable relationship with the middle of the middle class, without losing their special touch with the laboring class. Methodist leaders in Fort Wayne endeavored to be true to their founder's concern for both personal salvation and social justice. As a result, they were more active evangelically and politically than any other religious group; from camp meetings to Congress, Methodists worked hard to save souls from sin and society from folly.

4
Catholics

"This wild hoosierdom"
Bishop John H. Lüers, 1859

Priests of the Catholic Church were the only Christian clergy to visit the three rivers area during the periods of French and British control in the eighteenth century. The community of French traders at Fort Miami was never large, and by the late 1820s, when Protestant American settlers began to dominate the population of Fort Wayne, the French Catholics were a minority without a priest or church. Two decades later, however, when successive waves of emigrants arrived from Europe, a burgeoning Catholic population created two of the dominant congregations of the community: St. Augustine's for French, Irish, and American Catholics, and St. Mary's for German Catholics.

The Visitors: 1722-1822

In the twentieth century, a few writers have suggested that the seventeenth- and eighteenth-century Jesuit missionaries who ministered to those native tribes near the Great Lakes might have also visited the three rivers area. None of the extensive records of the "Black Robes," as these missionaries were called before their expulsion in 1764, tells of a visit and none of the oral tradition of the Miamis hints that a mission was ever established in the area.[1] The only record of a Catholic priest visiting the settlement at Fort Miami during the period of French control was in 1749 when the

Reverend Joseph Pierre de Bonnecamps, professor of hydrography at the Jesuit College at Quebec, stopped briefly on a survey of the western waterways. He was not impressed: "The fort of the Miamis was in very bad condition; most of the palisades were decayed and fallen into ruin. Within there were eight houses—or to speak more correctly, eight miserable huts which only the desire of making money could render endurable. The French there number twenty-two; all of them, even the commandant, had the fever."[2] The priest's stay at the fort was short, and seems not to have included religious services.

When the British wrested control of the region from the French in 1760, the religious character of the area was unaffected: no British settlers were allowed to enter the territory and no missionaries were sent to the Indians. In 1774, the British Parliament passed the Quebec Act, guaranteeing the religious freedom and other privileges of the native French, nearly all of whom were Catholic; this legislation also annexed the Old Northwest to the Province of Quebec, and Miamitown (as the village was called by the British) continued in the jurisdiction of the Diocese of Quebec. The nearest Catholic church was at Detroit; occasionally one of its clergy ventured by pirogue or horseback to the headwaters of the Maumee.

One such priest who made this journey was the Reverend Louis Payet,[3] a native of Montreal who had come to Detroit in 1781. Payet made several trips to the missions at Vincennes,

Louis Payet, a priest from Detroit, listens to Henry Hay and John Kinzie rehearsing their musical accompaniment for Christmas mass, 1789.

[Original Illustration by Kenneth B. Dutton]

Cahokia, and Kaskaskia, and included Miamitown on his itinerary. Henry Hay, an English trader and partisan who kept a journal of his stay at Miamitown, wrote of attending services on December 20, 1789—the earliest account of a Christian clergyman conducting worship in the three rivers area. Hay was especially intrigued by the manner in which the people were called to worship: "The French settlers of this place go to prayers of a Sunday morning and evening at

Cowbells announced Sunday worship to the residents of Miamitown in 1789.
[Original Illustration by Kenneth B. Dutton]

one Mr. Bartelmis [Barthelemes] which is performed by Mr. Payee(*sic*); the people are collected by the ringing of three cow bells, which three boys run about with thro' the village, which makes as much noise as twenty cows would. I went this morning to their prayers, it being Sunday." Hay and his companion, the Scots trader John Kinzie, were amateur musicians who played for the settlement's frequent dances. He wrote that, on Christmas eve, his hostess "asked me to go with her to the midnight mass—and also asked me if I would play the flute which I did. Mr. Kinzie . . . brought his fiddle with him—we found a Frenchman there who played with us." Hay and Kinzie also performed for Christmas morning mass—"being a particular desire of the peoples"—and evening vespers, as well as for Saturday vespers and Sunday mass.[4] Then, after conducting eight services of worship in as many days, Payet traveled on.

Miamitown continued under the jurisdiction of the

Bishop of Quebec until 1789 when the first American diocese was established at Baltimore.[5] When the Diocese of Bardstown, Kentucky, was created in 1808, Indiana was included in its jurisdiction. The distances between the scattered settlements were great and the clergymen were few. As a result, during the next eighteen years, there are only two recorded instances of a priest of this diocese visiting Fort Wayne. In 1815 the Reverend Charles Nerinckx wrote: "Michigan has one priest, Indiana has no priest. Illinois has two priests."[6]

Part of the neglect of the area may have devolved from a lack of clarity in the Roman documents about in whose jurisdiction northern Indiana had been placed. Eventually, in 1832, the Prefect of the Sacred Congregation for the Propagation of the Faith (*Propaganda Fide*) directed that "the Bishops of the western countries should give the exact boundaries of their respective dioceses, in order to avoid confusion in the exercise of their jurisdiction." Bishop Benedict Flaget of Bardstown then wrote to Bishop Edward Fenwick at Cincinnati: "The two states of Illinois and Indiana are entirely by themselves and out of the line of the three dioceses [Bardstown, Cincinnati, and St. Louis]. Shall their administration be divided among the three bishops by which they are surrounded? . . . I think that a part of the eastern and northern line of Indiana could be administered much better by you than by me—I suggest my ideas, and you will determine what you think is best."[7] As a result of the region's undefined status, Catholic clergy rarely visited Fort Wayne during the first three decades of the nineteenth century. In his study of the journeys of Catholic missionaries after 1789, William McNamara concludes: "Northern Indiana apparently was not visited by a clergyman. Perhaps Father [Gabriel] Richard . . . on his way to Detroit in 1798 . . . used the Maumee-Wabash portage . . . . Father [Michael] Levadoux . . . may have traveled the same way."[8]

In April 1822, Isaac McCoy noted in his diary that three priests had arrived in Fort Wayne to "administer the sacrament, &c." to the "French Catholics." The Reverend Gabriel Richard was returning to Detroit after an extended trip, accompanied by the Reverends Francis Badin and Anthony Ganihl; these clergymen had not made Fort Wayne the object of a special trip, but were merely passing through the area on their way to other responsibilities.[9] McCoy made efforts to be friendly and attended Sunday mass with his family—and noted that the sermon "was mainly directed against Baptist sentiments." Undaunted, the Baptist minister invited the Catholic priests to visit his Indian mission school where they took tea together.[10]

Between the rare visits of a priest, some Catholics attended Protestant worship and supported the minister. Charles Furman, a Presbyterian missionary who came to Fort Wayne in the fall of 1829, reported to his mission secretary that "there is a small population of Catholicks (*sic*) here, some of whom attend punctually my preaching . . . .

There are only three or four influential men of that class here who, though they themselves do not attend my preaching, have subscribed to my support."[11]

Stephen T. Badin

In 1784 there were no more than six Catholic churches in the emerging United States;[12] five years later, when Bishop John Carroll took charge of his newly established American diocese, which stretched from the Atlantic Ocean to the Mississippi River, he had only a few priests, and no seminary or other institutions. Word of the critical shortage of Catholic clergy in America soon became known to those priests in France who were victims of the religious persecution instigated by the Revolutionary government. One of several seminarians who were attracted to the challenges of the American frontier was Stephen Theodore Badin. While studying for the priesthood in his native city of Orléans, he fled from the revolution and eventually arrived at Baltimore in 1792. A year later, he became the first priest to be ordained in the United States[13] and located in Kentucky, where he faithfully served for thirty-two years, eventually becoming Vicar General of the Diocese of Bardstown. In the wake of a controversy with Bishop Flaget, Badin returned to France in 1818. The bishop, however, made him his Vicar General in France, and Badin worked to raise money and recruit priests for American missions while serving French parishes. In 1828, Badin's restless spirit led him to return to America, and at the age of sixty he assumed a pastorate at Monroe, Michigan. In the summer of 1830, when he learned that the Potawatomis in the region of the Indiana-Michigan border desired a *Robe Noire* to settle among them, Badin volunteered and set out for the village of Chief Leopold Pokagon. He was pleased to find that the tribe had preserved a warm, although dim, memory of the eighteenth-century Jesuits; as a result, he was quickly able to establish a chapel and a school.[14]

As he labored for his mission, Badin occasionally visited Fort Wayne, remaining some days with the French Catholic community, celebrating mass and officiating at baptisms and weddings. On his first visit, in early June, 1830, he stayed at the home of Francis Comparet, a trader and the leading Catholic layman in the area.[15] The following winter, when he found that his Potawatomi parishioners had left their villages to hunt, Badin used the hiatus to visit Catholics in Chicago and Fort Wayne, and then traveled to Bardstown where he sought financial assistance for his mission from Bishop Flaget. When he arrived in Fort Wayne in January 1831 to "conduct a mission," Badin was requested to baptize Peter David Gibaud and to give the nuptial blessing to the civil marriage of James Avaline and Catherine Comparet, the daughter of his host. Of the six persons participating in the ceremony, only the groom and the best man could sign

their names, as the bride and three witnesses were able only to make their mark in his parish record.[16]

The following winter, when his Potawatomi parishioners were again hunting, Badin traveled to Kentucky to recruit Sisters for his school; on his way he stopped at Fort Wayne to celebrate Christmas mass at the home of Jean Baptiste Béquette, a manufacturer of trinkets for the Indian trade.[17] Then, in the spring, he retraced his steps through Cincinnati and St. Mary's, Ohio, and reached Fort Wayne in early May. Badin noted that transportation was always uncertain, a condition that tried his restless and impatient disposition: "I preached in the [St. Mary's, Ohio] Courthouse in English, having waited ten days for a water convey-

Francis Comparet
[Courtesy of Allen County-Fort Wayne Historical Society]

ance for Ft. Wayne. At last, having bought a horse &c., I took the resolution of going to that place without my company (although the roads were detestable) where I arrived on the 16th, and preached two English sermons also, in the Free-Mason's hall. Mr. [Ghislain] Bohême and [Brother] Nicholas arrived thither by a merchant boat, with our baggage and some provisions, on the 25th."[18]

The Masonic Hall was at that time occupied on Sundays by the Presbyterians and Methodists; Francis Comparet, however—in spite of official Catholic disapproval—was a member of the local Wayne Lodge No. 25 and made the arrangements necessary to accommodate Catholic worship on such short notice.[19] Badin's mention that he had preached in English indicates that the French language was no longer universal among the local Catholic population; the Fort Wayne congregation now blended Americans, Irish, and Germans with the old families of French-Canadian heritage—and if their children attended the local school, the instruction was in English.

Badin's winter visits to Bardstown most likely included a report to the bishop on the condition of religion at Fort

Stephen Theodore Badin
[Courtesy of University of Notre Dame Archives]

Wayne, with a plea from the local Catholics for more regular pastoral care.[20] In late September 1832, the Reverend Laurence Picot,[21] pastor at Vincennes, made a visit, remaining until the middle of October. Picot, however, had not made Fort Wayne the object of his journey; he had come north to make contact with the remnants of the Miamis settled along the Wabash, and to attend a tribal council convened to hear the request of government representatives that the tribe cede some of its land near Fort Wayne for the proposed Wabash and Erie canal. Badin had also been invited to the meeting by Senator John Tipton to urge Chief Richardville to sell the needed land; the older priest remarked that he had "to come gently round the old man without exciting him."[22] At the end of the council, Badin invited Picot to visit his Potawatomi mission.[23]

At the meeting with the Indian commissioners, Badin shared his dream of founding an orphanage for children of all races and denominations on land he had secured near South

Bend, and then enlisted the support of Senator Samuel Hanna, who represented St. Joseph County.[24] Badin's interest in the Potawatomi mission had now slackened, as he realized that the tribe's deportation to the West was imminent. At the end of the year, an assistant priest[25] arrived at Niles which freed Badin to pursue other projects, especially the establishment of his orphanage; as a result, he was not seen again in Fort Wayne until the following winter.

During 1833, the Reverend Ghislain Bohême made an extended visit to the area. This newly ordained priest had spent the previous summer with Badin at his mission, and on his travels through Fort Wayne had learned of the local Catholics' desire for more regular pastoral visits. Bohême's assigned field of service, however, was in northern Ohio and southeastern Michigan, and he therefore needed permission from his bishop at Detroit to make a detour into the area. He reported that there were over two hundred Catholics at Fort Wayne and that, during his Easter visit, thirty-eight had received the sacraments, including "6 or 7 Irishmen—Deus me adjuvet [God help us]." Bohême also noted that the local schoolteacher, Jesse A. Aughinbaugh, in his spare time, had given religious instruction to the Catholic children during the previous six months.[26]

In the fall of 1833, Badin returned to Fort Wayne and found a mobile parish of Irishmen digging the canal west of town. Here he recorded the first Catholic funeral in the area, and poignantly wrote: "On the 23rd of January 1834, I gave Christian burial to Richard Doyle, aged 40 years, a Hibernian from the Diocese of Ferns, who died suddenly the day previous, six miles from this village."[27] In mid-April, Badin prepared to return to the Potawatomi mission and invited Edward F. Colerick,[28] Comparet's business partner, to accompany him. Colerick later reported that his first Indian meal was boiled pigeon, which was served "feathers and all." When he hesitated to partake, Badin told him, "Do not irritate and insult the red men; we might suffer for it. Strip the feathers from the legs and you will find them eatable."[29]

Content for the moment that his mission station was operating satisfactorily under the direction of his assistant, Badin then returned to Fort Wayne in June and stayed for the summer. Two new challenges had brought him to the Maumee-Wabash portage in the summertime: the increasing number of Catholic laborers on the canal line and the need for chapels in the region. He wrote to the new bishop of Cincinnati, John Baptist Purcell, who he hoped might show more interest in northern Indiana than had the bishop of Bardstown: "I must soon go to Fort Wayne, thence to visit the forks of the Wabash, where many Irish and German Catholics have been expecting me, who are employed in digging a canal, and are desirous of building a chapel. Thence I should go to Logansport eighty or ninety miles west of Fort Wayne. I am besides engaged in making a new establishment near this place for an orphan house, and I must begin with erecting a chapel.[30] You may perceive that at the

Stephen T. Badin is greeted by canal laborers.
[Original Illustration by Kenneth B. Dutton]

72

age of 66 I have a sufficient share of toils. I would wish rather to enjoy solitude and retirement, in order to prepare for my last approaching dissolution."[31]

After a summer of riding to the canal workers' camps, Badin (who was still listed on the rolls of the Diocese of Detroit[32]) again wrote to Purcell, requesting him to impress on the bishop-elect of the new Diocese of Indiana the need for clergy in the Fort Wayne area. He prefaced his report with a candid description of the Catholics in the region:

> I will not expatiate on the character of our Catholics. It is known that the lower class of the Irish, such as work on the canals &c. is too fond of drinking . . . that there are very few of the devout sex, and few children among them. The Canadians are lightheaded, lighthearted, light-footed, and very ignorant, having been without a pastor before I came into the backwoods, and being much intermixed with the Indians. The Germans are of much better dispositions, as also the French from Lorraine and Alsace; but a priest familiar with the Dutch language is indeed wanted. As to the Indians, the greater number of Christians are on the borders of Michigan . . . . The character of our Cath[olics] here has been so little respectable in general, that they rather confirm Protest[ant] prejudices . . . . O tempora, O mores![33] [What times, what manners!]
>
> Our resources must lie in the education of youth. The introduction of Germans & German-French will offer also consolations to a resident pastor. Mr. Comparet estimates that the congre[gation] in & about Ft. Wayne must amount to 100 families.[34]

Part of Badin's critical judgment of the Catholic population derived from his own strict standards. He was opposed to drinking and dancing, two of the more popular vehicles of frontier recreation. While he insisted that "dancing was no sin" in itself, he deplored the practice on the frontier as it was usually accompanied by intoxication, and caused significant absence from religious duties—all of which, he said, was a scandal to the Protestants. Often, when jogging home at evening on horseback and hearing the sound of a fiddle, Badin would appear in the midst of the dancing party and announce a catechism lesson or night prayers.[35]

Teaching these peripheral parishioners was especially difficult without religious books. The Presbyterians in Fort Wayne had already established a society for distributing bibles and tracts, but it was not Badin's style to organize the Catholic laity for such enterprises. Instead, he solicited subscriptions to the *Catholic Telegraph* himself, and then sent a plea to Bishop Purcell "for Catholic books, much

wanted in and about Fort Wayne . . . very few have so much as a catechism or a prayer-book." When the books arrived, Francis Comparet was outraged at the cost and threatened to send them back; Badin prevented him, insisting that they were "universally wanting," but then found himself obliged to pay the bill.[36]

All of Badin's itineration was in the Wabash River watershed between Fort Wayne and Logansport; in these towns, as well as in the intermediate communities of Huntington, Wabash, and Peru, he secured lots for future churches. Several factors, however, impeded the erection of any chapel along this eighty-mile section: "Prevailing sickness & mortality, the absence of a pastor & poverty have prevented the forwarding of Church affairs. No time should be lost in forwarding the erection of chapels along the canal line, because as soon as the work is done in one section of the country, the Catholic hands move to another section, and the prospect of such erection diminishes or vanishes. This has been evidenced in Fort Wayne: the timber alone has been procured! There should be two priests riding constantly every week along a line of 80 miles; they should be active, pious, learned, and disinterested, courageous & mortified."[37]

Both the Presbyterians and Methodists in Fort Wayne were preparing to build churches in 1834, and the Presbyterian minister, James Chute, reported that "the Catholics have raised about 600 dollars toward a meetinghouse. They will probably build one this summer. German and Irish Catholics are coming in great numbers."[38] Badin had encouraged the local Catholics to secure land for a chapel during his first winter visit; as a consequence, in July 1831, Francis Comparet, Jean Baptiste Béquette, and John Baptiste Bruno, acting as "Trustees of the Catholic Church," arranged to purchase on contract what is now the southwest quarter of the present Cathedral square.[39] Badin, however, never saw any of the timber transformed into a chapel; in the fall, he journeyed to Cincinnati to consult a physician, and decided to retire: "Being 67 years of age, I feel sensibly that I must prepare for eternity, even if I were not attacked by a carbuncle. The doctor. . . forbids me to ride."[40]

One biographer states that Badin was witty and dynamic, erratic and difficult;[41] in Fort Wayne he was respected for his intelligence, determination, and compassion, responding to anyone in need, including Protestants and outcast Indians. John Bruno remembered Badin's compassionate concern for the family of White Skin, "the last head of the man-eating Indians . . . . They had no friends that I knew of, except Father Badin, a French missionary who frequently visited them and helped them when they were in want."[42] When Hugh McCulloch, a young bank cashier of Unitarian heritage, lay extremely ill, the elderly priest visited him two or three times a week. Years later McCulloch remembered: "He spoke the English language fluently, and I recollect vividly how charmed I was by the tones of his voice, and how he seemed to strengthen me in my contest for life by his description of

Stephen T. Badin interrupts a dance to begin a catechism lesson.
[Original Illustration by Kenneth B. Dutton]

the fortitude he had witnessed of those of his own order under the cruelties to which they had been subjected [during the French Revolution]."[43]

The Diocese of Vincennes

When Badin departed for Cincinnati in September 1834 to begin a new career of nomadic semi-retirement, he hoped that the episcopal neglect in northern Indiana would be reversed when the Rt. Reverend Simon Gabriel Guillaume Bruté de Remur arrived to take charge of the new Diocese of Vincennes. The fifty-five-year-old bishop was a native of

**Simon Gabriel Guillaume Bruté de Remur,
First Bishop of the Diocese of Vincennes**
[Courtesy of University of Notre Dame Archives]

Rennes, France, and had most recently served as superior at Mount St. Mary's Seminary in Emmitsburg, Maryland. No eastern bishop doubted his zeal, but some questioned his suitability as a missionary bishop: he had spent most of his life as a teacher, was not physically strong (Bishop Flaget gave him five years to live), and spoke heavily accented, imperfect English (aggravated by the loss of all his teeth). Badin, who had spent most of his clerical career serving western missions—and had seen many priests falter on the frontier —thought he should instruct the new bishop on the type of clergy he needed:

Much as priests are wanted in your Diocese, it seems to me that it is a lesser evil to have none than to have bad ones. There must be a very particular grace, especially for such as are young or novices in the holy ministry, to live at so remote distances from both the Diocesan Bishop and a confessor. The air breathed in our back-woods is far from being pure. Profound humility, diffidence of one self, the fear of God and divine charity, the love of mortification and disinterest-

Simon Petit Lalumière
[Courtesy of Sisters of Providence Archives]

edness, a competent learning and the spirit of piety are all equally necessary. Some knowledge of the world, and prudence in the world (not the prudence of the world) are also desirable ingredi-ents in the character of a missionary, who must deal with all sorts of people of different nations, of all ages, sexes, conditions, and various dispo-sitions, &c.... If this Divine monition had been always attended to, we would not be desolated as we are by apostate priests.[44]

In November 1834, when Bishop Bruté arrived at his cathedral at Vincennes—which he judged too large, too cold, and in need of plastering—he had but one permanent priest, the Reverend Simon Petit Lalumière, to care for the entire state of Indiana and part of Illinois. A thirty-year-old native of Vincennes, Lalumière had studied at St. Thomas Seminary at Bardstown and was the first American-born priest to serve in Indiana.[45] In the spring of 1835, Bruté sent Lalumière on a tour of the eastern half of the diocese, while he set out to visit the western section—frequently staying at the homes of non-Catholics, and occasionally with clergymen of Protestant denominations: "We were almost always thrown upon the hospitality of Protestants, and we were treated kindly by all . . . . I passed such simple remarks as would make them acquainted with our faith and practices, and remove some of the prejudices which they had acquired from their parents or ministers of the places from which they had come to settle in the West. They listened to what I had to say, and as very few ministers have as yet come to these remote parts, I found that it would be easy to preoccupy the ground. But, alas, we have not the means to do so, nor priests enough to send to the dispersed sheep."[46] After finding so few Catholics in his area of visitation, Bruté was encouraged by Lalumière's report: "M.[47] Lalumière is encircling also the east and north as I did the opposite side—he went from Daviess County through Columbus, Shelbyville, and Abington to Fort Wayne, thence to sweep the canal to Logansport. . . having more of Catholics to assist than I found."[48] The increased numbers of the faithful in the Fort Wayne area, coupled with Badin's departure, precipitated urgent pleas to the bishop: "Mr. Comparet writes me from Fort Wayne that there has been no Mass there for seven months. There are from 600 to 700 Catholics—and from 1,500 to 2,000 along the canal." Bruté knew that Fort Wayne needed a multilingual priest and had already sent a plea to the bishop of Detroit to send him "a priest who speaks German as well as English for Fort Wayne and the canal."[49]

Lalumière arrived at the end of May for a three-week visit in Fort Wayne. Like Badin, he rode the canal line and was soon confronted with the ugly side of religious and political prejudices among the Irish canal workers. News of bloody fights between northern and southern Irishmen in Williamsport, Maryland, and other eastern communities had been reported in the local newspapers; now the ancient feud was erupting in the region between Fort Wayne and Lafayette. As the anniversary of the Battle of the Boyne (July 12, 1690) approached, rumors circulated among both the Catholic and Protestant Irish canal laborers—who were organized in separate work gangs and kept at a distance—that one faction was marching to attack the other: "Throughout 1835 murders were by no means uncommon. Arson was of almost nightly occurrence. Assaults and the driving away of cattle lost the quality of 'news.'"[50] By the first week in July many Irish families left their huts to sleep, without fire, in the woods in fear of being burnt or murdered.[51] By July 10, about three hundred armed Far Ups (Corkonians and Connaught men) gathered at Lagro as two hundred and fifty Far Downs (Ulstermen) advanced towards Wabash to observe the anniversary with a confrontation. The militia at

Fort Wayne, Logansport, and Huntington was quickly mobilized and made a show of force; Lalumière hurried from Fort Wayne to the scene of impending battle and, joining the canal contractor, David Burr, convinced both sides to retire in peace. Such conflicts shocked Bishop Bruté, who induced Bishop John Hughes in 1838 to forbid the Irish immigrants in New York to join those secret societies whose oaths bound them to do battle.[52]

The First Resident Priest

When Lalumière arrived in Fort Wayne he discovered that the Catholics were constructing a church. The Presbyterian minister, whose flock was also erecting a meeting-house, wrote, "The Catholics are building and doubtless will make great efforts in this place."[53] When Bruté later reported on the state of his new diocese, he assumed that the church at Fort Wayne was then finished: "M. Lalumière. . . found more Catholics than I had, and many places ready to receive a priest. In three places they had begun to build churches. At Fort Wayne they had finished one, 60x30 feet, and the congregation numbered 150 families. I was happy to send them the Rev. M. [Felix Matthieu] Ruff from Metz, in France, recently ordained and speaking the three languages, French, English and German. Of the latter there are a good many living there and in the environments."[54]

The church, however, was not finished; like the Presbyterians, the local Catholics over the next two years could build only when money was raised and materials were available.[55] In the spring of 1835, the bishop confessed that he had no funds to assist the project—he was down to his last twenty-five dollars—and was worried that he could not even provide Ruff with the necessary support "for opening his mission in Fort Wayne where I think he will find nothing of altar furnishings, linen, [and] vestments."[56] Bruté, however, had a dream, and when he submitted his diocesan report for the 1836 edition of *The United States Catholic Almanac and Laity's Directory,* he listed at Fort Wayne two parishes and one priest: "St. Joseph's and St. Mary's: Rev. Matthew Ruff."[57]

By the end of his first year in Indiana, the bishop realized that his diocese needed many more missionaries and much more money. Unlike those Protestant denominations that had well organized societies in the East to support their missionaries in the West, the Catholic bishops in the United States had no American organization to provide financial assistance. Bishops in missionary dioceses, such as Vincennes, were responsible to the Sacred Congregation for the Propagation of the Faith, which provided more administrative advice than monetary aid; as a consequence, Bruté had to recruit his own priests and raise his own funds. In pursuit of these objects, he went to Europe, solicited contributions and clergy, and soon returned in mid-1836 with eight priests and eight seminarians.[58] The students were sent to his old seminary in Maryland, and the priests were posted to the areas of greatest need.

Upon his return to Vincennes, Bruté learned that Ruff, who had arrived in Fort Wayne in early August, had abandoned his post in mid-October. What happened in Fort Wayne is not known, but the young cleric soon requested an "exeat [dismission] and English certificate" from Lalumière

Louis Müller
[Courtesy of Diocese of Fort Wayne South Bend Archives]

(who was administering the diocese during Bruté's absence) and then, in mid-winter, departed for Louisiana.[59] Lalumière knew of only one other German whom he could send to Fort Wayne, a young Prussian priest who had recently arrived at Cincinnati, the Reverend James Ferdinand Tervooren, whose questionable reputation had previously led Bruté to refuse him an appointment.[60] Lalumière, however, was desperate and, upon the recommendation of Bishop Frederick Résé, appointed Tervooren to Fort Wayne. He arrived in mid-November—and quit by the first of the year; like his predecessor, Tervooren left Indiana, never to return. With no other German-speaking priest available, Lalumière dispatched the Reverend Jean Claude François to the vacant parish; the French priest was able to visit Fort Wayne for a few weeks in early 1836, and then returned in May to stay the summer.

Bruté still hoped to establish two parishes among the burgeoning Catholic population in the area and therefore

kept François in town to care for the French- and English-speaking Catholics.[61] To care for the Germans, the bishop sent the Reverend Louis Müller, one of the two German-speaking priests he had recently recruited. Müller joined François in August 1836 and, in a joint letter, the two priests asked the bishop when he might visit Fort Wayne and what financial assistance they could expect for their maintenance and the church's completion. Bruté responded with the caring concern of a teacher of seminarians, and the non-committal diplomacy of a bishop who had more demands on his resources than he could possibly fulfill. He lamented that he did not know when he could visit Fort Wayne: "Your poor bishop is but *one* for a diocese as extensive as the third part of France or all Italy—though . . . he would fain be everywhere at once, in Chicago, for instance, at South Bend, and meanwhile not be too long absent from the new Seminary here." He was equally indefinite when he told Müller that his trunk was "still in Pittsburgh . . . on account of the drought of the Ohio," and would only arrive in Fort Wayne when "heaven sends some rain."[62]

Bruté tried hard to encourage his young missionaries, who were now situated a hundred and twenty miles from any experienced pastor or confessor: "Ah! I am so happy to be able to rely on such good priests and true apostles as you are, for all that is still requiring a little patience united to confidence in God . . . . Courage then, thrice courage, and an increase of forbearance and zeal . . . . Oh, how unfortunate are those blind ones who pretend themselves priests without realizing the sacred duties of their noble calling. Well! let them marry and make money, instead of becoming priests." Bruté also assured his new missionaries that it was largely his responsibility to supply the money for the uncompleted church, but again was vague: "With regard to the funds you need for the achievement of the building, it would be impossible for us just now to spare them . . . . Again, I say, let us renew our patience, too happy if we are enabled to roof it for the winter. I think also of having a stove put in. Outside of the two-thousand dollars, you will get all that is requested for your church: the missal, the chalice, etc, etc . . . . At this début of our episcopal career it is not easy for us to know what is most pressing and best to do."[63]

Bruté hoped that the Archbishop of Vienna, the Most Reverend V. Eduard Milde, would be generous in funding missions to the Germans through the patronage of his Leopoldine Society; to advance the cause, the bishop directed Müller and François to write about "the destitution and hopes—the pressing good at present, and the abundant harvest we anticipate for the future. Do not forget to mention the savages, the leader of their tribes—Richardville and Godfroy, the baptisms, etc.—all, in short, that is touching and true."[64] Bruté planned to use these field reports in his request for funds, especially appealing to the archbishop's interest in the welfare of German-speaking immigrants. The plan succeeded, and the Leopoldine Society, at the end of

1836, sent Bruté 8000 florins ($4000).[65]

Bruté was especially sensitive to the poverty of his missionaries, and was careful to assure them that he was not living in luxury at Vincennes: "Your poverty charms me and I would like to be in your place, as M. Müller knows well . . . . Please find a small remittance for personal use at the approach of the winter; employ it for the most pressing . . . as good brothers, and then write to me your need. . . . I am sure you are as well off as we . . . . We have neither wine nor beer: coffee in the morning, pure water at dinner, and tea in the evening."[66]

The bishop's hope for the establishment of two parishes at Fort Wayne evaporated in mid-September, when he was forced to send François to Logansport to dismiss the pastor there and "put an end to those scandals and worthily prepare here the future of our churches."[67] As a result, Müller was left alone at Fort Wayne to care for the English- and French-speaking Catholics, as well as the Germans—all to be blended in one polyglot parish, named St. Mary's.[68] The task was formidable: his French was adequate, but his English was poor.[69] Then, in addition to his duties in Allen County, the bishop—after purchasing a horse for Müller—directed him to serve the Catholics at Huntington, Lagro, and Wabashtown. François immediately complained that he should not have to serve Peru, as he was already responsible for Lafayette, Williamsport, and Marion—and suggested that Müller was not doing his share. The diplomatic bishop apologized, and then explained to François: "My motive in sending you on this line was particularly because I thought you stronger and more acclimated than M. Müller who . . . feels so much his first winter in the northern part of Indiana . . . . Please keep the care of Peru as far as Legros (sic), as I am writing to our friend [Müller] in Fort Wayne . . . . After seeing you both and the Catholics of your places, we can more easily settle the matter . . . . After the Council of Baltimore I intend to come back through Fort Wayne."[70]

Bishop Bruté did not return from Baltimore by way of his northern missions as he had planned, but in June 1837, accompanied by the Reverend Benjamin J. Petit,[71] he visited Fort Wayne. On Sunday, thirty persons were confirmed; then, at the close of three festive days, Müller took the bishop to visit one of the German settlements outside the town.[72] Bruté was impressed by the number of German Catholics pouring into the region and later wrote to the Archbishop of Vienna: "From Fort Wayne, M. Müller tells us that his congregation has doubled during the last two years with mainly German immigrants. He had 600 communions at Easter."[73] Bruté had also been pleased to tell his priests in northern Indiana: "In this year's *Catholic Almanac* [1838] you will find that we are in the Diocese, 21 priests, some seminarians, sisters, etc.; the churches and stations are altogether fifty."[74] None of these new priests, however, was sent to Fort Wayne to help Müller, who was increasingly burdened with pastoral emergencies and reported to Bruté that "sickness has made sad havoc in his quarters—more than forty-five funerals."[75] Many were canal workers whose demise was recorded by Müller: "Another Irishman dead and buried in our ground"; once, in 1838, he made sixteen consecutive entries, "Buried an unknown Irishman [Hibernus ignotus]."[76]

Progress on the church building during this time was slow. John Dawson, writing in 1860, recollected its unfinished condition when he arrived in Fort Wayne on March 6, 1838: "There were in the town in 1838 . . . six preachers of the gospel . . . two houses of worship [Presbyterian and Catholic] and six religious societies . . . . The first glimpse of Fort Wayne was had from an elevated part of the road . . . . The spire of the old Court House, and that of the old Catholic Church, which stood where the Cathedral now is built, were seen . . . . This old Catholic Church, and the pastor's house just behind it, was all the improvement then on the Church property. The Church was not completed for want of funds."[77] The "want of funds" was more a consequence of the depression wrought by the Panic of 1837 than of any disinterest on the part of the Catholic community. The Methodists, at the same time, were equally embarrassed to see their meetinghouse stand half-finished. How much, if any, of the cost of St. Mary's Church was defrayed by European beneficence is not known, but Müller's trustees had borrowed heavily. Bruté warned François not to follow this example at Logansport: "Avoid contracting debt—at Fort Wayne there is $3000; Müller says, 'it is too much!'"[78]

Müller had another problem: he was often seen intoxicated in public, and the Catholic community was scandalized. The local Lutheran pastor, the Reverend Jesse Hoover, told his mission secretary: "The Catholic priest is a conspicuous example of drunkenness and levity to his people and . . . a number of the better sort of Catholics have become completely disgusted."[79] When Müller vanished from Fort Wayne in September 1837, the distressed bishop told François that he had heard Fort Wayne Catholics exclaim that "Mr. Müller has abandoned them!!! These are words more serious for a good missionary than can be understood by honest people!"[80] Müller returned, but his heavy drinking continued, and eventually precipitated a crisis in the spring of 1839. When a flood of complaints deluged the bishop, he determined to take action, and sought the help of François, his faithful confrère at Logansport:

> After the reception of your so alarming letter about Mr. Müller, I have another of Mr. Bermière still more pressing. Mr. Cholerick (sic), the assistant of Mr. Comparet, having gone to Mr. Müller, reports that the latter is daily exposed to the consequences of the exasperation of his enemies who threaten him with the most outrageous public treatment to induce him to leave Fort Wayne.

Read the letter I am writing him; I ordain his absence for a couple of months, and that he avail himself of it to make a retreat at the good Jesuits; meanwhile, his people will have time to calm themselves and look for his return, especially the Germans, unless it be too late—I hope not . . . . I entreat you to act as my Grand Vicar . . . . Go through the canal or in a carriage [to Fort Wayne] in order that he come back thus with you, and from there take the stagecoach—the one . . . as far as Bardstown will cost more than $50, but sacrifices are nothing in a case like this. To make up that money could he not sell his horse? I would furnish him another from here for his return . . . . Warn him to say that he is going to see the Bishop, without speaking of the retreat.

Mr. Müller is extremely obstinate in his ideas, but has much too much faith as not to acquiesce to this Bishop's commands. Mark, will you also, to be faithful to my recommendations and be mindful of the power I give you to act toward him as my Grand Vicar, threatening him with suspension, and supplying it, if necessary; meanwhile informing me at length of his condition, especially with respect to drink. Your charity will support a friend who can yet be so useful, reminding him gently of the beginning of my letter in which part I render full justice to his real zeal and sacrifices.

I enclose a $20 dollar bill, as a first advancement. I am better, but so feeble that I was obliged to dictate these lines. Pray much for your devoted in Christ.[81]

François immediately went to Fort Wayne and relieved Müller of his duties; after an absence of four weeks, however, Müller returned to claim his pastorate. In the meantime, Bruté's feeble health continued to deteriorate and, two weeks after he dictated his instructions for the pastoral crisis at Fort Wayne, the fifty-nine-year-old bishop died. His successor was the Rt. Reverend Célestin René Laurent Guynemer de la Hailandière—also a Breton, as were most of the priests recruited by Bruté—who had most recently served the cathedral parish and neighboring settlements at Vincennes. He was, at the time, in France where Bruté had sent him to recruit clergy and religious, and solicit money and vestments for the growing diocese. Hailandière had previously been named as Bruté's coadjutor with the right of succession, and his consecration as a bishop was quickly arranged in Paris for mid-August.

Upon his return to Vincennes in November, the new bishop immediately "received denunciations about the priest at Fort Wayne." At first Hailandière thought Müller only "guilty of some 'vivacities,'" and sent a priest to investigate. The report, however, recommended Müller's "withdrawal," and so the bishop appointed the Reverend Julien Benoit to the parish.[82] Müller remained in Fort Wayne until Benoit arrived on April 16, 1840, and then introduced him to the congregation before departing in May.

Julien Benoit
[Courtesy of Sisters of Providence Archives]

Julien Benoit Appointed Pastor

Benoit was one of the few non-Breton clerics whom Bruté had brought to America in 1836. Born in the mountain village of Septmoncel in 1808 of well-to-do parents, he was a precocious student, completing his studies for the priesthood before he was old enough to be ordained. At the age of twenty-one, and still a deacon, he began teaching at a small seminary; his talent was recognized and two years later he was called to a professorial chair at the Grand Seminary at Lyons. It was here in 1835 that Benoit met Simon Bruté who had come to the school to interest young clerics in the challenges of the western American frontier. Benoit was impressed with the bishop and opened his apartment for Bruté's two-week stay in the city. When the young teacher offered his services as a missionary, the bishop responded (in words often repeated by Benoit): "You are a spoiled child; you will never do for missions in America; you are accustomed to all comforts; you have such a beautiful position, but in America I can offer you nothing but corn bread and bacon, and not enough of that. There will be many a night when you will have no shelter, many a night when you will have no bed, many a day and night when you will have to be on horseback through the wilderness." Benoit responded, "If you can do it, why cannot I . . . a young man, be able to do it?"[83]

Benoit spent his first year in America studying English at St. Mary's Seminary in Baltimore; he later confessed that, when he arrived in America, he was very homesick "in a strange country, the language of which I did not know."[84] After his ordination in April 1837, Bruté sent him to serve mission stations in southern Indiana, mostly along the Ohio River.[85] He next served several canal towns near Chicago including Lockport and Joliet "where he lost six to seven hundred in the epidemic raging there." After a three months' rest in New Orleans to restore his health, he was reassigned to southern Indiana. Bruté wrote proudly of Benoit, "None of my priests has had more success in reuniting Protestants to the church."[86]

When he arrived in Fort Wayne, Benoit found a frame church, 35 by 65 feet, "rudely built, not plastered, with rough boards for benches," and a debt of $4367.[87] The original name of the church had died with Bruté; it was most likely Benoit, the former seminary professor, who suggested the theologian, St. Augustine, as the new patron saint. The new pastor made the church's completion and the elimination of debt his immediate priority, a goal more easily achieved now that the local economy was rapidly recovering from the recent depression. Benoit was also able to challenge the pride of the local Catholics, who in the last year had observed the energetic examples of the German Lutherans and Methodists who were each completing new church buildings.

Bruté soon sent to Benoit a German-speaking assistant, the Reverend Joseph de Mutzig Hamion, who had been recruited from the Diocese of Strasbourg. The priests' parish initially extended into several counties: Benoit wrote that they had "to attend La Gro, Huntington, Columbia City, Warsaw, Goshen, Avilla, New France, New Haven, Besancon, Hessen-Cassel and Decatur."[88] In later years Benoit spoke of the traveling required in so large a parish; Bishop Joseph Dwenger recollected, "Father Benoit very often would say mass in Fort Wayne, and then in the same morning ride to Huntington or Decatur, and there say mass, of course fasting, preaching and attending to all the work. I very often heard him say, 'If we had a sick call, if it was only twenty miles, we thought it but a moderate distance, and did not think it a great hardship. But, when it was sixty, seventy

or eighty miles, when we had to be out day and night—then it was really hard.' "[89]

Benoit's initial homesickness had not abated. In 1839, he had told Bruté he wished to resign his American mission and return to France. The bishop, who had a premonition

Edward Sorin
[Courtesy of University of Notre Dame Archives]

about his own imminent death, refused to release Benoit, and then extracted from the unhappy priest a reluctant promise to continue. Benoit later paraphrased the bishop's plea, "Do not let me go into the presence of God with the guilt of having allowed you to return to your beloved France from the face of so much work that is to be done in the New World."[90] Soon after Bishop Hailandière returned to Vincennes in late 1839, he received a letter from Archbishop Anthony Blanc of New Orleans[91] telling him of Benoit's discontent: Blanc considered Benoit to be one of the finest missionary priests he knew and wished to offer him a position in his diocese if Hailandière consented. Hailandière replied, "I like what you have told me about Benoit. I believe we should try every means to keep this best priest in America. I will talk to Benoit, and if he persists in wanting to return to France, I will tell him what you offer. But you should not count on him; he is now at Fort Wayne with an assistant, and seems quite satisfied."[92]

Confident in Benoit's renewed commitment, Hailandière then honored the priest's request to visit his family, and in the fall of 1841 he departed for France, leaving the parish in Hamion's care. The young assistant, however, was suffering from pulmonary consumption. In early October, he was visited by the Reverend Edward Sorin and six Brothers of the Congregation of Holy Cross, who were traveling on the canal at the end of a long journey from France to Vincennes. Sorin wrote that he found "the good Mr. Hammion (sic)

Francis Joseph Rudolf
[Courtesy of University of Notre Dame Archives]

dying."[93] When his condition worsened in April 1842, Hamion was carried by canal boat to be with the nearest priest at Logansport, where he died.[94] In May, the Reverend Augustin Martin was sent to care for St. Augustine's until Benoit's return in mid-July; then the Reverend Francis Joseph Rudolf, an Alsatian cleric who had accompanied Benoit back to Fort Wayne, assumed responsibility for the German-speaking parishioners.[95]

Michael Shawe's Lectures

In the summer of 1842, Benoit announced to the residents of Fort Wayne that he had again arranged a series of lectures by the one priest of the diocese whose native tongue was English. The Reverend Michael Edgar Evelyn Gordon Shawe—who was reputed to have served as a British officer

at Waterloo—had come to America with Bruté in 1836 and was now a popular apologist for his church's faith and traditions. Shawe had first lectured in Fort Wayne two years before, and his presence was especially appreciated by those immigrant Catholics who were feeling the hostility of a nativism that was raising fears that a strong Roman Church would threaten American liberties. As an Englishman, Shawe well understood those Protestant denominations whose history had begun with a sharp, and sometimes persecuted, break with the Catholic Church; Benoit, on the other hand, had never experienced this Protestant dynamic in post-revolutionary France, where most attacks on the Catholic church had come from agnostic rationalists.

Shawe's eloquence attracted Protestants. The local German Lutheran pastor, the Reverend Friedrich K. D. Wyneken, had been so impressed with Shawe when he heard him in 1840 that, when the minister returned to Germany, he told his friends: "Capable emissaries are sent out to explain the nature of the Roman Church to the people. I myself, in a distant city in Indiana, heard such a speaker, who with great skill and popularity for three consecutive weeks, with few interruptions, gave such talks in a packed church to a public consisting of English-speaking people for all denominations, and excited almost the whole city, so that the subject was discussed back and forth in the streets, in inns, and boutiques."[96]

When Shawe returned to Fort Wayne in August 1842, his lectures again attracted a large audience, with many non-Catholics in attendance. His manner was gracious, his logic was forceful, and the over-all effect was persuasive. Not all Protestants, however, were pleased that a Catholic priest would make such a positive impression and, before Shawe arrived, a few began to pressure the Reverend Alexander T. Rankin, pastor of the First Presbyterian Church, to challenge the lecturer to a debate. Rankin, who had often been called upon to defend the causes of abolition and temperance, was a powerful orator and skilled debater. The Presbyterian's written invitation to Shawe to share the platform in a public forum—not an uncommon occurrence[97]—was declined by the priest; then, when some misunderstanding developed about the terms of the invitation and the reasons for refusal, Rankin released their correspondence to the local newspapers. The minister had proposed that Shawe's lectures should be the subject of the debate, asserting that, in fairness, a Protestant should be granted an opportunity to question and respond to several points which the Catholic had alleged:

> That Protestants are dependent on the Roman Catholic Church to tell what is [the] bible, and what the bible means;
> That the bible is imperfect, as to its books [and] is unsafe as a rule of faith and manners, when taken alone;
> That the Roman Catholic rule of faith is perfect,

safe and infallible;

That she alone has authority from the great head of the church to expound the scripture to the nations;

That she is the church of Christ, universal, united, holy, infallible, and the mother of all churches;

That her notion of transubstantiation, purgatory, indulgences, auricular confession, remission of sins, supererogation, image worship, and celibacy of the clergy are accordant with reason and scripture.[98]

Rankin had recently demolished, in public debate, a local schoolmaster who had challenged the minister to defend his views on slavery, temperance, Freemasonry, and resurrection.[99] Shawe's refusal to debate Rankin was, therefore, interpreted by many in the community to be motivated by fear—fear of both Rankin's reputation and Protestant principles. Any public figures in nineteenth-century America who declined to debate their ideas were liable to be judged cowards—much as eighteenth-century mores led men to defend their honor in duels. Rankin had thrown down the gauntlet, and some in the Catholic community now called upon Benoit to uphold their honor. Although a few sensational debates between Catholic and Protestant clergy had occurred in the 1830s—Bishop John Hughes of New York had debated the Reverend John Breckinridge (Presbyterian) and Bishop John Purcell of Cincinnati debated the Reverend Alexander Campbell (Disciples)—the Catholic Church in the ensuing decades avoided public controversy.

At first, Benoit said that he would permit the debate, in order to dispel the accusations of cowardice, but reasserted his distaste for public confrontation: "The office of the Christian ministry is to announce the truths of religion and not to dispute about them. The very idea of discussion supposes the matter to be discussed a matter of doubt and opinion, but as we Catholics have no doubt whatsoever of the verity of our tenets, we have no motive for debating them."[100] Shawe, however, did not want to debate, and told Rankin, that he "will not suffer himself for a moment to be considered as a polemical gladiator, a character of all others most uncongenial with that of a minister of the gospel."[101] Rankin then mounted the platform alone and delivered a series of rebuttal lectures, which attracted more attention than admiration: one local editor commented, "Politics, elections, vetoes, and all that sort of thing have given way to religion. . . . His [Rankin's] lectures we believe have been highly satisfactory to his Protestant hearers, but we are much inclined to doubt whether they have been listened to with as much pleasure and profit, and appeared as convincing to those who differ with him, as Mr. Shawe's were."[102]

The matter was not settled when Shawe left town, but continued in the columns of the *Fort Wayne Sentinel* for more than a month. Rankin declared that his attack on "their

wincing show. . . has reached its mark," judged Shawe "as stamped with the brand of cowardice," and called Benoit "a blackguard . . . . A man so low and vulgar. . . and so far destitute of all sense of decency and courtesy is undeserving of notice."[103] Benoit's last word on the subject was terse: "I was not raised among fish women; and market hall expressions, so familiar in the anti-catholic minister, have been totally unknown to me to the present day."[104]

A year later, when Shawe returned to lecture, Rankin had moved on, and no other Protestant clergyman in the next two decades showed the slightest interest in instigating any public confrontation with Julien Benoit; the Reverend Charles Beecher of the Second Presbyterian Church—the most intellectual of the local ministers—told his mission secretary, "Benoit is as sharp as a brier, and a perfect Jesuit."[105] In comparison with other communities of that era, Fort Wayne was relatively tolerant; one Protestant who attended Shawe's 1843 lectures expressed the feelings of most, "If he does not make converts, he has removed many strong prejudices heretofore existing against the church of which he is so able an advocate."[106]

Some of the Protestants who respected the priests' reticence to debate church doctrine were distressed by the Catholic clergy's silence on such moral issues as slavery and temperance. In Fort Wayne, while ministers of the Presbyterian, Methodist, and Baptist churches were echoing their denominations' opposition to any extension of slavery into the new territories of the West, Julien Benoit and his fellow clerics remained as uncommitted on the subject as were their bishops at the First Plenary Council at Baltimore.

Controversy about Catholicism, however, took a more sensational turn when the local newspapers reported the trial in Evansville of a young Alsatian priest, the Reverend Roman Weinzoepflen, who was charged with attacking a woman in the confessional. Eventually sentenced to the state prison in Jeffersonville in 1844, he was pardoned a year later through the efforts of the many Protestants, as well as Catholics, who were convinced of the cleric's innocence.[107] In the wake of the trial, Benoit prepared for publication a long letter asserting that the priest had been the victim of an anti-catholic plot:

This is another striking example of the fairness and charity of Protestant bigotry with respect to their Christian brethren—the Catholics. Let them go on. We are not dismayed. Truth is powerful and it will prevail. We have been Maria Monkised, Slokumised, Browleeised, Brackenridgedised, and Campbellised. The sword has been unsheathed against our breasts, and incendiary fire has burnt our establishment to ashes. Have we been stopped on our onward way? Do not our ranks fill up in a wonderful manner? Behold, in 1790 but a few thousand of Catholics were settled here and . . . the number of priests [were] twenty; and now . . . upwards of six hundred priests are busily engaged in the work of ministry, and instead of counting by the thousands of Catholics the time is not far when we will have a reckoning of millions.[108]

There was an optimism in Benoit's words which reflected the hope that Protestants in America, when distanced from old European prejudices, would see the Catholic Church as attractive, vital, and true. Archbishop John Hughes declared to his flock at St. Patrick's Cathedral in New York City: "The object we hope to accomplish in time, is to convert all Pagan nations, and all Protestant nations . . . . Everybody should know that we have for our mission to convert the world—including the inhabitants of the United States,—the people of the cities, and the people of the country, the officers of the navy and marines, commanders of the army, the Legislatures, the Senate, the Cabinet, the President, and all!"[109] Initially, Edward Sorin saw this to be a primary mission of the school he had recently established on the site of Badin's abandoned orphanage at Notre-Dame-du-Lac. The *Catholic News-Letter* in 1846 optimistically told its readers that thousands of Protestants had already converted to Catholicism: "From one extreme of the Union to the other, numbers, fatigued with their researches for the truth through the labyrinthal mazes of Protestant error, are flocking to the one fold of the one shepherd, convinced that in the Catholic Church alone can be found the precious jewel they have sought, the true faith. Thousands are at this moment imitating their noble example, and there is not a city, not a town, not a village in the land, that does not count within its limits converts to the Catholic faith."[110]

The Brothers of Holy Cross

Benoit knew that if he were to be successful in fulfilling this mission, he would need teachers—and, in 1843, lamented to a colleague: "I can do nothing without schools."[111] For a decade, since Jesse A. Aughinbaugh left schoolteaching for the tanning business, there had been no organized Catholic instruction in Fort Wayne, and the parish children were left to attend one of several private schools in town, all of which had some Protestant affiliation. Both the Presbyterians and German Lutherans had established schools, and two former pastors, Alexander McJunkin and William W. Steevens, had each opened private academies. Benoit hoped that two religious orders recently established in Indiana, the Brothers of Holy Cross at Notre-Dame-du-Lac near South Bend and the Sisters of Providence at St. Mary's-of-the-Woods near Terre Haute, would provide the faculty for his school.

In late 1843, the Holy Cross Brothers were able to send

Brother Joseph (Charles Rother) to Fort Wayne, enabling Benoit to announce the opening of St. Augustine's Institute.[112] Next, Brother John (Frederick Steber) was appointed to the school; he soon felt himself overwhelmed by his pupils and told his superior, Edward Sorin: "I do not feel

Brother Basil (Timothy O'Neil)
[Courtesy of University of Notre Dame Archives]

very well in my place here, and I believe I mentioned the reason why, last time I wrote. How is it possible, my dear father, that I can learn anything when my mind is continually harassed with so many children of both sexes? I am sure you will be aware of the many, many difficulties that arise from that. I will however do my best; I can do no more . . . . I have removed to the house below the school which has been bought by Mr. Benoit. The room I occupy together with the son of the Chief is a very good one."[113]

Teaching children of "both sexes" was outside the traditions of the Holy Cross Brothers in France, where they taught only boys, and may have been the reason that the order chose not to appoint instructors for the fall term. Benoit, however, was determined to reopen his school, and hired a devout Catholic layman, William B. Walter of Emmitsburg, Maryland, as its new principal.[114] The twenty-nine-year-old schoolmaster had studied at Mount St. Mary's College in Emmitsburg, where he trained in "Classic and Mathematical studies. . . [as well as] Drawing, Painting, and Ornamental Writing."[115] In the fall of 1844, assisted by Joseph Graff, who taught German, Walter opened the school in a former carpenter shop and offered a basic curriculum with optional classes in French, German, drawing and painting. He also established a night school for older students, and advertised a supply of "Catholic books, German Testaments, Instruction and Prayer Books . . . at the School House on Clinton, east of the Catholic Church."[116] By the fall of 1845, the school's enrollment had grown to eighty-four students, of whom fifty-four were boys, including four Protestants.

Walter was remembered as a strict disciplinarian, and one young pupil's resistance became the stuff of local legend; Julia Baker Stapleford recollected her mother's tales of Walter's harshness: "He had a stick of wood that had been split leaving sharp edges that the pupils were made to kneel on when they did not have their lessons. My mother was kept after school and supposed to kneel on this sharp wood, but Helen Peltier beckoned to her to come on. Mother replied that she could not go as she would be punished, but Helen Peltier insisted and mother followed. Then Helen told mother to run ahead of her and if Mr. Walter came after her, she would take care of him. The three ran, and going through a tomato patch she picked up a rotten tomato and threw it, striking the teacher square in the face."[117]

When a separate girls' school was established in the fall of 1846, Walter continued teaching the boys. Benoit, however, wanted his schools operated by religious orders and induced Sorin to send an instructor, Brother Basil (Timothy O'Neil), to teach in the new male division. At the end of the spring term in 1847, Walter was relieved of his position and the boys' school was placed under Brother Basil's direction, with Brother Emanuel (Anthony Wopperman) teaching German and music.[118]

Benoit kept a watchful eye on the Brothers and reported any problems to Sorin, and did not hesitate to request the removal of an unpromising instructor: "I have given to your Reverence time enough, it seems to me, to prepare a teacher for Ft. Wayne. The one we have, at present, for some cause or another, has became odious to our Catholic community, and I will have to change him." Occasionally, Benoit would counsel a Brother who was tempted to abandon his vows of poverty, chastity, and obedience: "I begin to hope he [Brother Thomas (James Donoghoe)] will not forsake his vocation. I do all I can to make him perceive the nothingness of the glittering dust that blinds his eyes."[119] Then, in 1850, the boys' school was deserted by both its principal and teacher. Sorin reported to his superior in France, "Bro. Basil . . . a man of gloomy and variable character—threw off the yoke of his profession and departed incognito, no one knows where . . . . Bro. Emanuel, who taught the German class at Fort Wayne . . . retired . . . . The cause seems to have been . . . the needs of an aged mother who had no support but him."[120] After 1851, the boys' school at St. Augustine's disappears from the records; then, in 1859, Benoit reawakened the order's interest, and Sorin soon reported to his superior

that the school was "reopened in Fort Wayne . . . where the community was established in 1844."[121]

The Sisters of Providence

Benoit's hopes for establishing a girls' school in Fort Wayne rested on the willingness of Mother Theodore (Anne Thérèse Guérin), superior of the Sisters of Providence, to staff the school. The order had been invited by Hailandière

Mother Theodore (Anne Thérèse Guérin)
[Courtesy of Providence Archives]

in 1839 to establish a mission in Indiana and had soon built a novitiate and academy at St. Mary-of-the-Woods in Vigo County. Relationships between the bishop and the mother superior, however, became increasingly strained, and Hailandière ordered Benoit not to communicate with the order. At the same time, the bishop's arbitrary and abrasive leadership caused many of the priests recruited by Bruté to seek dismissal to other dioceses; by 1842, most of the clerics who had served at Fort Wayne, including Bohême, Müller, and François, had left Indiana.[122] Benoit himself wrote to Archbishop Blanc at New Orleans about relocating in his diocese, and Mother Theodore sought a way to escape from Indiana and the bishop's "double mind and his cold heart."[123] Bishop Jean Stephen Bazin, who succeeded Hailandière, said he was "pious as an angel," but also "distrustful, suspicious, and stubborn."[124] Finally, in 1845, when the clerical rebellion became unmanageable, the beleaguered bishop went to Rome and offered his resignation; when it was refused, Hailandière interpreted the declination as an official endorsement of his policies. The accusations of "arbitrariness, caprice, and scandals," however, became more shrill; Hailandière was especially distressed that the "complaints coming from Cincinnati against me . . . have [gone to] France. This time they charge me with a scandalous affair with a woman or a sister."[125] In 1847, when Hailandière again resigned, Rome quickly accepted and named Bazin to the office.

It was in the midst of this diocesan turmoil that Benoit struggled to establish his schools. Hailandière had decided that none of the mission gifts which he regularly received from Europe would be spent for schools at Fort Wayne; instead, most of the donations were spent on his cathedral and auxiliary facilities. As a result, with the promise of only $600 from Mother Theodore toward the estimated cost of $4000 to build and furnish a school and convent, Benoit was left to his own devices. He was, however, amazingly resourceful and, more than any other Indiana clergyman, found ways to develop significant funding for his church projects and favorite charities. Benoit often reflected that, before he came to Fort Wayne, he had received only sixty-three dollars during his first two and a half years of service in Indiana; as a consequence, he said, "My business talents had to be developed; I had to see how to keep from starvation."[126] The business he chose was that upon which most fortunes were built in Fort Wayne at that time: land speculation. His talent for this enterprise was formidable and, over the next thirty years, he acquired significant wealth. His initial land purchases were for a parsonage and schools; in July 1843 he reported, "I have just bought four lots at my own expense on which is the house which I am occupying. I am also in the market for two other lots with a house for the Brothers. Next week I will begin to build a brick house for the Sisters."[127]

The girls' school and convent were under construction by May 1844. Then, in 1845, Hailandière softened slightly to permit Benoit to "write to Terre Haute."[128] By November, the enterprising pastor was able to report to Mother Theodore that he now could provide for her sisters "the best built house in the diocese, large enough for forty boarders; two hundred dollars, or at most three hundred, for furnishings; a garden of two acres, all worth about eight thousand dollars. I would like to meet your conditions stated in your letter of last year, but, as I am already burdened with a considerable debt, I cannot contract any new obligations."[129] Mother Theodore's "conditions" were assurances of adequate financial support for the teachers; she had previously seen her sisters near starvation at other schools in southern Indiana and was determined to do better in Fort Wayne. Both she and Benoit had appealed to Hailandière for "some crumbs from the Episcopal table"[130] but were rebuffed; finally, on faith, Mother Theodore decided to bring three sisters to Fort Wayne and open St. Augustine's Academy.[131] Benoit assured her of his unconditional support: "Your difficulties with His Lordship [Hailandière] rendered very precarious, on your own avowal, your continued existence in Indiana. This is now no longer the case. You are really *our Sisters,* and be convinced I will treat you as such. On your part begin by praying for me."[132]

Sister Caroline (Ann O'Dell)
[Courtesy of Sisters of Providence Archives]

Traveling by stagecoach from Terre Haute to Covington and by canal boat to Fort Wayne, Mother Theodore and Sister Basilide (Josephine Sénéschal)[133] escorted the three teachers to their new mission. When the sisters stepped ashore at the landing in the first week of September 1846, the Angelus sounded from the steeple bell that Benoit had brought from France four years before.[134] A covered wagon then transported the sisters and their baggage up the Piqua Road (Calhoun Street) to their new home on the southeast corner at Jefferson Street, where they were ensconced in their newly carpeted and curtained quarters on the second floor. On the first level they found their classrooms, in the basement were the kitchen and bake ovens, and outside were a cow and calf grazing on the two-acre meadow.

The teachers were young and had trained at the order's school at St. Mary-of-the-Woods. Sister Mary Magdalen (born Augusta Linck in Evansville) had begun her novitiate four years before and was now to be superior; Sister Caroline (born Ann O'Dell in Mount Pleasant) was the music teacher; and Sister Catherine (born Catherine Eisen in Germany) was to instruct the youngest girls. An advertisement in the local papers soon announced the opening of "St. Augustine's Academy of the Sisters of Providence":

> The government of the Institution will be mild, and at the same time firm . . . . As the members of the Institution profess the Catholic religion, the exercises of religious worship will be Catholic; but members of every other religious denomination will be received. It will only be required that they assist with propriety at the public duties of religion . . . . Only parents and guardians may visit, and they only on Thursdays . . . . Letters written to the young ladies, or by them, are perused previously to their being forwarded.[135]

Just as the school was about to open, Benoit decided that he must leave Fort Wayne temporarily to accompany the Miami Indians on their journey from their historic lands to a reservation in Kansas.[136] The tribe had exhausted all hope of delaying their departure and now insisted that Benoit be with them on their exodus. Benoit had been a special friend and advocate of the Miamis, and they trusted him to look after their best interests; the presence of a priest, they believed, would insure their fair treatment and safe passage. When, however, Benoit requested Hailandière's permission to accompany the tribe, the bishop refused; and it was only through pressure from other quarters that he finally relented and directed the Reverend Louis Neyron—the only priest from the band of twenty-one recruited by Bruté now left in the diocese—to substitute at Fort Wayne.[137] In late October 1846, Benoit boarded a canal boat for the long trip to the reservation in Kansas. After remaining there two weeks with the tribe, Benoit hurried back to Fort Wayne; anxious about his new school, he traveled by stagecoach, day and night, for nine days straight.[138]

Upon his return he found the academy flourishing with sixty pupils enrolled. Benoit was elated and told Sorin, "The Sisters are doing beyond my most sanguine expectations."[139] When the winter term commenced, he reported, "Our sisters have ninety pupils and are very much loved. I am now working to prepare a dwelling for some Brothers."[140] Then, on the anniversary of its opening, Benoit exclaimed, "Our schools are succeeding marvelously. Fort Wayne now possesses four Sisters[141] and two Brothers, and the Sisters' school is pronounced by the press of the vicinity the best in the state."[142] As the enrollment grew—eventually reaching one hundred and fifty pupils—Benoit, in 1849, built a bigger school, converting the original facility into a convent and residence for boarding students. From the outset, the academy was self-supporting. Mother Theodore set the tuition fees: "Catholics pay two dollars per quarter, of eleven weeks each. Protestants, three, four, five and even six, according to the studies they pursue . . . . The children provide the wood for the winter."[143] As a result of a steady enrollment of Protestants, the academy "was soon able to contribute to the upkeep of less prosperous houses, and remained for many years the most flourishing and successful of the missions of the Sisters of Providence."[144]

Edward M. Faller
[Courtesy of University of Notre Dame Archives]

The German Catholics

Between 1844 and 1847, the coeducational and bilingual St. Augustine's Institute evolved into four schools—boys' and girls', German and English—administered by two religious orders and located in three buildings. Just as the Brothers and Sisters insisted on separating the boys and girls, the parents insisted on separating the languages. Fort Wayne's German community, of which at least a third was Catholic, had now grown to a significant size, and the influx of new immigrants was expected to continue in the coming years.[145] Some German Catholics had always felt themselves to be aliens in a parish dominated by French, Irish, and American parishioners; then, as their numbers increased, so did their desire for their own parish. Three German Protestant congregations had already erected church buildings—St. Paul's

German Lutheran, St. John's German Reformed, and Bethel German Methodist—and the German Jews were organizing a congregation; most German Catholics wanted no less for themselves.

Swept along with these separatist sentiments was the Reverend Edward M. Faller, the German-speaking assistant priest who had come to St. Augustine's in October 1846.[146] Faller was twenty-two years of age, an Alsatian from Barr, France, who had studied in Strasbourg before emigrating with his family to America in 1840. At the age of sixteen he had enrolled in Bruté's seminary at Vincennes where he studied under the Reverend John Corbe for the next six years.[147] After his ordination in July 1846—which required a dispensation, as he had not yet attained the required age of twenty-five[148]—Faller briefly served a mission in Lanesville before being sent to Benoit.

At Fort Wayne, the young priest found thirty German Catholic families eager to build their own schoolhouse, orphanage, and church. He soon established a church council,[149] organized a school society (*Deutscher Römisch Catholischer St. Josephs-Schulvereins*),[150] erected a frame school house and meeting hall on Calhoun Street adjacent to the church, and purchased lots on the southeast corner of Jefferson and Clinton streets for the site of their future church building. As Benoit had no available cash to defray any of the $1,700 cost of the property, four church families mortgaged their farms to guarantee the funds.[151] Then, in 1848, as various factions in the developing parish attempted to initiate different projects at the same time, including the founding of a parish orphanage,[152] church finances were strained and congregational unity was fractured. When Faller and Benoit were unable to reconcile the disputants, a plea for help was sent to Vincennes; Bishop Bazin had died in April, and so the diocesan administrator, the Reverend Jacques Marie Maurice Landes d'Aussac de St. Palais, came to Fort Wayne and successfully negotiated a settlement of the differences,[153] and work on the church was recommenced.

A local editor, after praising several of the new Protestant edifices in town, concluded, "but the handsomest situation in the whole City is owned by the Catholics, and when they shall have built their new Church, they can justly boast of the most beautiful place in the State."[154] A brick church 32 by 64 feet was gradually erected, as well as a small one-story residence for the pastor, behind which their schoolhouse was soon relocated. Finally, in November 1849, the congregation, led by Faller and Benoit, moved in a solemn procession from St. Augustine's Church to their new facility. The celebrated Jesuit missionary, the Reverend Francis X. Weninger, who had been conducting a week-long mission for the congregation, then dedicated the church "to the service of God under the tutelage of Mary," and named it *Der Mutter-Gottes Kirche*, The Mother of God Church.[155] English speaking residents of Fort Wayne, however, seldom used this title, and usually spoke of the "German Catholic Church" or "St. Mary's Church."

The Cholera Epidemic

Work on the church had been interrupted in August 1849, when a devastating cholera epidemic struck Fort Wayne. The German population seemed to suffer most; Charles Beecher reported: "Our place has been the scene of considerable suffering. Early apprehensions induced preparations to meet the cholera, and yet it came as if nothing had happened. Citizens talked of cutting the canal, or draining off the boats. But the cholera did not come by water. It fell like a bomb shell upon the S. E. part of town, and scattered death and dismay, as by explosion through a particular quarter. Afterwards, it extended itself quite capriciously into other parts of town, and then disappeared. Sixty or seventy deaths were attributed to this Scourge. The principal scope of operation was among Germans."[156]

The citizens of Fort Wayne had watched the inexorable march of the disease up the Mississippi and Ohio rivers, and by mid-July knew that 3905 had died at Cincinnati and 117 at Dayton. When the first cases appeared in Fort Wayne, Benoit offered St. Augustine's Academy as a temporary hospital and the services of the Sisters of Providence as nurses. On July 23, he reported to Mother Theodore: "We are no longer in suspense. The cholera has reached Fort Wayne, and I will officiate in a few hours at the funeral of its first victim. All your daughters . . . are determined not to abandon their post in the moment of danger. This devotedness, this sacrifice is noble and generous. I rejoice in it, my Mother, and it will be registered, I hope, in the book of life . . . . lift your hands toward heaven, very dear Mother, while we are struggling, and if we are called to consummate our

Louis Peltier, Undertaker

sacrifice, say *Deo gratias* with all your heart, for a beautiful crown is prepared for the martyr of charity."[157]

Friday, August 2, was appointed as a day of fasting and prayer for the cessation of the epidemic. A few weeks later, forty-five victims had been "buried in the Protestant burying ground and fifteen in the Catholic."[158] The town's undertaker, Louis Peltier, built most of the coffins. One resident recollected that they "were rough affairs, made hurriedly and from any kind of lumber that could be gotten. The lids were nailed down with heavy wrought iron nails, and the coffins were hauled to the cemetery on ordinary farm wagons . . . . It was the custom for the chief mourner to walk directly after the wagon that bore the body, no difference how far the place of burial was from the house . . . [or] whether the other mourners rode or not."[159]

The Sisters, who had forgone their summer retreat at St. Mary-of-the-Woods, worked hard under the leadership of their new Alsatian superior, Sister Marie Joseph (Josephine Yvonne Pardeillan);[160] Benoit told Mother Theodore, "I loved to see this good Sister among the sick. She seemed a mother with her children, and I am persuaded that not a shadow of fear penetrated her mind. In her noble footsteps Sister Celestia [Sophia Kennedy] walked with a gay heart and seemed to breathe at ease only when she was among the sufferers . . . . As for Sister Lawrence [Julienne Cheminant], she has no fear of fire itself. She is a soldier without fear and beyond reproach."[161] Such devoted service was noted by a local editor: "The praiseworthy, philanthropic, and truly Christian conduct of the Sisters of Providence, whose kind and indefatigable care of the patients in their hospital is best proved by the success which had blessed their labors. They have had in all 21 patients (6 died, 12 discharged, 3 remain)."[162] Then, in early October, the epidemic ceased as suddenly as it had commenced; Charles Beecher, who had been "attacked with cholera in the first stages, but recovered," observed, "Since the disease left, the city has forgotten altogether that there was ever such a thing—and business roars loud."[163]

The cholera, however, returned to Fort Wayne in 1852 and 1854, again killing with frightening suddenness. "One poor Frenchman," Benoit wrote, "newly arrived from Europe, was attacked yesterday morning along with his two infants, and all three of them are in the cemetery today." Sister Lawrence, who again nursed the sick in the epidemic of 1854, succumbed; Benoit, who had been at her sickbed, said the convent's cook and housekeeper was a "victim of her zeal and charity. . . a real martyrdom."[164]

Badin and St. Palais Return

In the aftermath of the epidemic of 1849, Fort Wayne Catholics entertained two distinguished clergymen: their first priest, Stephen Badin, and their new bishop, "Mr. Saint Palace" as he was called by most Americans.[165] Ever since he left Fort Wayne in 1834, the restless Badin had spent his retirement in perpetual motion, itinerating throughout Kentucky, Ohio, Indiana, and Illinois, visiting old friends and assisting needy parishes. During his six-month visit in Fort Wayne, the eighty-year old Badin—who never doubted the correctness of his judgments—climbed high into St.

Augustine's steeple and attempted to chop out the decorativ latticework surrounding the belfry. At the sound of Badin' attack, Benoit ran outside and shouted a protest, to which th old priest replied, "Don't you want your bell to be heard And if you do, why do you crib up the sound with thes painted boards?"[166] Benoit tactfully but firmly persuade Badin to abandon his project, and then locked up the tools

Stephen T. Badin, at Eighty Years of Age
[Courtesy of University of Notre Dame Archives]

In late December 1849, Bishop de St. Palais, who had assumed the episcopate soon after his mediation at the German parish, arrived in Fort Wayne to find an enthusiastic welcome organized by the local Catholic community. A local editor reported: "Our Catholic fellow-citizens were considerably elated yesterday by the arrival of their Bishop in town. We learn that he will remain here during the holidays. Quite a cavalcade of carriages and horsemen met him some miles distant to escort him into town. In the evening the bells of their churches were ringing merrily, and much hilarity and good feeling prevailed."[167] Bishop de St. Palais visited both parishes, administered confirmation, and then presented a gift of $500 to the Mother of God Church.[168] This was to be one of the last substantial gifts received by a Fort Wayne parish from the diocese. Contributions from European mission societies were now directed farther west, and de St. Palais was now dependent on Indiana churches to support his diocesan institutions; as a consequence, in 1850, he inaugurated special Easter and Christmas collections to finance his seminary, orphanage, and other special projects.

Benoit's Sojourn in Louisiana

In early 1852, because of a painful misunderstanding with Bishop de St. Palais, who had just left for Europe, Benoit resolved to leave Indiana, and then asked his old

Jacques Marie Maurice Landes d'Aussac de St. Palais, Third Bishop of the Diocese of Vincennes
[Courtesy of Notre Dame Archives]

friend and admirer, Archbishop Blanc of New Orleans, to give him a position in his diocese. The unhappy priest told the prelate only that his doctors "have advised a less rigorous climate than that of Indiana" and that he hoped to find a "little resting place" where he might serve as a "pastor, assistant, chaplain, or anything you see fit."[169] A friend, who had previously escaped from Hailandière to Blanc, told the archbishop that Benoit was "the best of the Indiana clergy .. he absolutely wants to leave the area."[170] Blanc, who had once offered Benoit a position when he yearned to return to France, consented. As Bishop de St. Palais was still in Europe, Benoit requested his dismission from the Reverend John Corbe, the diocesan administrator. Corbe was reluctant, but Benoit was adamant; he wished to go, he said, "because of a troubled conscience," and then threatened "to return to private life if refused."[171] Corbe finally consented, and then searched for a replacement at Fort Wayne. Benoit cared very much that a competent pastor be assigned to St. Augustine's, and when Corbe suggested a priest accused of "drunkenness," Benoit was incensed: "I will not leave to

such religious the care of a community where I have worked for years, and where there are seven Sisters of Providence of St. Mary's-of-the-Woods."[172] He eventually departed in late November, leaving Faller to care for St. Augustine's along with St. Mary's, and arrived in New Orleans in mid-January. Benoit had told Mother Theodore that his "first days of liberty would be dedicated to solitude. I do not rejoice. I am feeling a sense of profound loss, and throw myself on the mercy of God . . . . to prepare for the completion of my life's course. I count on your prayers."[173]

St. Augustine's new pastor was the Reverend August Bessonies; like Benoit, he had been recruited by Bruté and had begun his ministry in southern Indiana. (At one pastorate he was appointed as the local postmaster by President Polk.) During most of 1852 Bessonies had been in France and did not begin his duties in Fort Wayne until March 1853. The new priest was energetic: he judged St. Augustine's rectory to be inadequate and soon built a brick pastoral residence at Lewis and Calhoun streets, to which he personally contributed two hundred dollars; next, at the growing community of French Catholics at Besancon (named for that French city from which many had emigrated) he directed the people in the building of St. Louis Church, and then led the people at Leo likewise to begin construction.

When Bishop de St. Palais returned to Vincennes and learned that Benoit was gone, he determined to recall the defector to Indiana. After formally revoking Corbe's dismission, the bishop, pleading that his diocese was "too poor in priests to lose one," directed Benoit—who was then serving a church at St. Michael, Louisiana—to return to Vincennes, allowing Blanc first to find a replacement. Benoit said he felt himself "between two fires": "It is true I do not like St. Michael, but I like returning to Indiana even less." Benoit's experience at his Louisiana church had been frustrating: he especially deplored his Creole parishioners' "indifference" toward the faith. He later told Blanc: "I was glad to have [in Louisiana] more ample means of existence and to be delivered from the burden of my own maintenance, something I have born continually since entering the mission of Vincennes. But I am more comfortable in my poverty [at Fort Wayne], surrounded by warmhearted Irishmen . . . . If I tell these Celts to come to services, they come, and if, when in danger of death they do not have the church's blessing, it is never because of impiety or despair."[174]

Upon his return to Fort Wayne at the end of December 1853, Benoit commiserated with Bessonies: as a prodigal, he had returned without joy, and now his brother was departing with regret. In fact, Bessonies was so distressed to be summarily pulled away from St. Augustine's that he complained bitterly to Archbishop Purcell of his "treatment" by de St. Palais.[175] Also, Benoit's attitude was not helped by his frail health: soon after he resumed his position in Fort Wayne, he experienced a "serious and prolonged illness"; he had probably contracted malaria in Louisiana and, during the next two years, "suffered from fevers" as well as "rheumatism."[176] Then a more severe blow to his spirits was dealt by a lawsuit accusing him of defrauding the orphan children of Francis Lafontaine. The Miami chief had died in 1847, and Benoit had been named administrator of the estate valued at $3800. He later reported to Archbishop Purcell:

> Along with several prominent citizens . . . I took stock in the proposed Pittsburgh, Fort Wayne and Chicago Railway—$1200 for myself and $3800 for the orphans—with the authorization of the judge of the [Huntington County] probate court, who unfortunately fell sick and never signed the

August Bessonies
[Courtesy of University of Notre Dame Archives]

decrees of that session of the court. I then left Fort Wayne for New Orleans, and when called back by Bishop St. Palais, was sued for $3800 by the Administrator "De bonis non," who would not accept the railroad stock. The decree of the court was unsigned and I could not raise the money. I plan to keep the case before the court until the youngest Lafontaine is of age, when the children will release me, since they understand the matter. I have been so advised by their guardian, John Roche, and they were also advised by the judge of the court.[177]

Anti-Catholic Feeling in the 1850s

After the establishment of the German Catholic Church, the remaining congregation at St. Augustine's was increasingly composed of French and Irish immigrants. In 1850 Germans constituted 62 percent of the foreign-born in Allen County, of whom about a third were Catholic;[178] French "émigrés" represented 14 percent of the aliens, a majority of whom were Catholic; the Irish were 11 percent of the total, most all of whom were Catholic.[179] Many of the new French who had arrived in considerable numbers during the early 1840s, had settled north of town in Perry and Washington Township; most were from eastern France, Franche Comté, Alsace, and Lorraine, and did not identify with the old families of French-Canadian heritage. Since his arrival in 1840, Benoit had ministered to these French Catholics at their principal French settlements at Besancon and Académie (initially named "the French Settlement at Pinchon" and later termed "New France"—*Nouveau Gaul* or *Nouvelle France*). At the same time, French Protestant émigrés—who came from the same regions of France as their Catholic neighbors—were being shepherded by the Reverend Jacob Bossard, a Swiss-born pastor at St. John's German Reformed Church, and the rural Protestants were being served by French missionaries sponsored by the Presbyterians. In the early 1850s, an area in the south end of Fort Wayne became known as French Town,[180] and by the end of the decade these French residents had founded the Lafayette Benevolent Society (*Societé de Beinfaisance Lafayette de Fort Wayne, Indiana*). The organization's stated purpose was charitable, but its dominant interest was French language and culture; the Articles of Association, therefore, stated that "religion and politics" were to be avoided in discussions, as Catholics were generally Democrats and Protestants were Republicans.[181]

Julien Benoit seems to have encouraged some expressions of French culture in St. Augustine's parish life. The wedding of Adeline LaCroix and Laurence Rennau was described by Susan Man McCulloch, the bride's former schoolteacher: "We went to Mr. Comparet's house where we joined the wedding party, then attended them to the Catholic church where they were married, then returned and spent the day . . . . About sixty were there. After dinner the bride led off the country dance . . . . She is a graceful little French girl, a beautiful dancer . . . in her white satin bodice, lawn skirt and pearl ornaments . . . . They tried to have everything in old-fashioned French style."[182]

A growing number of the new emigrants in St. Augustine's parish were Irish. Unlike the German and French Catholics, who easily joined with their Lutheran, Reformed, Methodist, and Jewish countrymen to form ethnic cultural societies, the Irish Catholics could find no common ground on which to join with the smaller group of Irish Protestants. By 1859, Irish Catholics had organized the St. Patrick's School Socity and were raising funds to implement its purpose: "We ducate the orphan. A good, moral education is the founda-ion of happiness—the watchtower of society, peace, liberty, quality, justice and freedom." At the society's St. Patrick's Day celebration, Irish politics was the predictable theme, nd one of the visiting Irish-born priests, in his address on The Inherent Rights of Man," excoriated the "British gov-rnment . . . for its oppression of Catholic Ireland."[183]

John Dawson
[Drawing by B. F. Griswold, 1917]

It was during this period of increasing Catholic immigra-on and ethnic identification that John W. Dawson, the ublisher of the *Fort Wayne Times,* began to echo the anti-nmigrant and anti-Catholic prejudices of the nativist Ameri-an or Know-Nothing Party in the columns of his weekly ewspaper. The rival *Sentinel* soon warned its readers that "secret organization" of Know-Nothings had been orga-ized in Fort Wayne, and that among the planks in its American Crusade" platform were the following: "A war o the hilt on Romanism . . . . The amplest protection to rotestant interests . . . . Hostility to all Papal influences . . . Eternal enmity to all who attempt to carry out the rinciples of a foreign Church or State . . . . The sending back f all foreign paupers landed on our shores."[184] By the end f 1853, Dawson was receiving angry letters from Fort Vayne Catholics protesting his publication of "lies and orgeries"; one indignant Catholic publicly confronted

Dawson, "How dare you thus insult the Catholic community . . . . We have until now lived here in peace with regard to religious matters. Do you intend to acquire the unenviable notoriety of creating religious animosity? . . . Is this right? . . . Is this American?" Dawson's response to the outcry was an impassioned declaration that he would continue to expose the "hideous features of Popery." When his anti-Catholic diatribes became increasingly vitriolic in early 1854, the town's "daguerreotype artist," Archibald McDonald, be-came so enraged that he physically assaulted the editor.[185]

The publisher's attack on the Catholic Church was fired by a political, not religious, animus. Although he called himself a Protestant, the editor was not affiliated with any local church. His secular faith usually centered on the Whig Party, which was now disintegrating; his animosities most often focused on the Democratic Party—which had attracted a large number of immigrant voters, many of whom were Catholic, and had thus became the dominant power in Fort Wayne politics. Dawson revealed the partisan roots of his anti-Catholicism when he wrote: "Col. Swinney, overseer of the poor, informs us that the County Asylum is literally overrun with Irish paupers, and that during . . . one month . . . he had turned away more than 200 Irish Mickeys who have applied for admission or aid. This is the class of men who in warm weather live by little exertion &c., are driven to the polls like cattle to a market, disenfranchise American citizens virtually by their vote, pay no taxes, not even a poll or road tax, render nothing for the support of the law, and yet are supplied at the expense of honest, hard working men. This is one of the beauties of Catholicism."[186]

Without doubt, some citizens privately shared Dawson's prejudices, but few would join in his public denunciation of Catholicism. The editor finally abandoned the Know-Noth-ings during the election of 1856, and joined the newly organized Republican Party—and lost interest in the anti-Catholic cause. Fort Wayne voters, he had discovered, were not easily aroused by religious bigotry; when someone offered for sale, at a Presbyterian fair, dolls dressed as Catholic sisters with caricatured faces, there were no buy-ers.[187] One local Protestant expressed the feelings of many: "In my opinion, there is more reason to apprehend that the Catholics may be deprived of their just rights in the United States, than that our people will ever be brought under the control of the Roman See."[188] The community had been ethnically diverse and religiously pluralistic since the fort was decommissioned in 1819, and the oldest families in town, such as the Comparets, were Catholic. Although most of the Irish were Catholic, it was Irish Protestant immigrants, such as Allen Hamilton and Hugh Dickson, the Presbyterian minister, who led the community in 1847 to raise funds for the victims of the Irish potato famine. In the mid-1850s, when other areas of the country were allowing religious bias to influence their politics, Fort Wayne elected the president of the Jewish synagogue, Frederick Nirdlinger, as township trustee; a Catholic schoolmaster, William B. Walter, to the city council; and a Methodist minister, Samuel Brenton, to Congress.

Certainly one contributing factor enhancing this mutual respect among Catholics, Protestants, and Jews was the example of Benoit, who always maintained good relations with the non-Catholic community. His speculations in real estate put him in frequent contact with many of the businessmen of the community, the majority of whom were Protestant. Hence, none were surprised that Benoit would invite a Protestant layman, such as Hugh McCulloch, a prominent lawyer, judge, banker, and trustee of Second Presbyterian Church, to deliver the commencement address at St. Augustine's Female Seminary (as the school was now popularly called); as a consequence, these Protestant leaders usually responded generously when Benoit appealed for contributions to his pet building projects.

The Diocese of Fort Wayne

In 1855, Bishop de St. Palais proposed to his fellow bishops, gathered for the first Provincial Council meeting at Cincinnati,[189] that the Diocese of Vincennes be divided. He estimated (incorrectly) that there were now 40,000 Catholics settled in the northern half of Indiana above the National Road, and that this region would experience significant growth in the near future. When asked to name the diocesan seat, he suggested Fort Wayne, but allowed that it could be Lafayette. The Council chose Fort Wayne and forwarded their petition to Rome.

The bishops then suggested candidates for bishop of Fort Wayne. Archbishop Purcell placed Benoit's name at the head of a list of nominees forwarded to the Sacred Congregation of Faith; second on the list was his protégé, the Reverend John Henry Lüers.[190] Bishop George A. Carrell of Covington informed Rome that he "favored the nomination of J. Benoit," and spoke of him "in the highest terms"; Bishop M. J. Spaulding of Louisville, however, preferred Lüers over Benoit. Bishop de St. Palais, who had publicly stated that Benoit was the only priest in Indiana suitable for the office, privately declared that Benoit's previous defection to New Orleans rendered him totally unacceptable. Lüers, the compromise candidate—who had served the same congregation in Cincinnati since his ordination twelve years before, and who had never served on a diocesan staff or in an Indiana church—was selected. Another factor which may have influenced the naming of a German instead of a French bishop was the recent petition of German-speaking priests to Rome, complaining that, "in the appointment to the more important and lucrative parishes, the bishop [de St. Palais] favored the French and Irish priests."[191]

The new bishop had been born near Münster in Westphalia, Germany, in 1819; when he was thirteen his family emigrated to America and settled on a farm near Piqua, Ohio. Two years later, when Bishop Purcell visited his parish, Lüers told him that he aspired to the priesthood, and the prelate soon enrolled him at the Lazarist seminary of

John Henry Luers, First Bishop of the Diocese of Fort Wayne
[Courtesy of University of Notre Dame Archives]

St. Francis Xavier in Brown County, Ohio. Lüers's biographer wrote that the young seminarian "did not possess what would be called a quick or brilliant mind, but. . . a profound mind."[192] Upon his ordination in 1846, he was sent to the parish of St. Joseph in Cincinnati, where he built a church and school. On January 10, 1858, at the cathedral in Cincinnati, he was consecrated to the episcopate by Purcell. Bishop de St. Palais attended; Benoit did not. He was busy in Fort Wayne raising funds for a cathedral.

On February 18, Lüers arrived, alone and unannounced with traveling bag in hand, at the door of Benoit's residence. On Sunday he preached to both congregations, which he described as "quite large and acceptable."[193] Then, during the next two weeks, he began visiting his parishes; he was not impressed and told Purcell:

> Most of the congregations are small and poor, and have been of late years very much neglected. The number of Catholics in this diocese has been very much overrated; I really do not believe that they exceed 15 - 18,000. The Bishop of Vincennes has

been very kind to me and Very Rev. Mr. Benoit is doing all the good in his power.

There is one thing evident to me, which I have not as yet communicated to anyone, except to you now. It is this: Fort Wayne is rather a poor place for a Bishop to accomplish much; for this a good large congregation is necessary. Indianapolis ought to be the seat for Northern Indiana; it is the capitol for the state and has a fine English congregation, besides good church property. Fort Wayne has some 10 - 11,000 inhabitants, without any good prospect of getting much larger; I really cannot see what has made it grow so much as it has. The English congregation is not large and, with some individual exceptions, poor. *Two thirds are farmers* residing from 2 to 8 miles in the country. The whole number of baptisms, railroads and all, last year was 135 . . . . There is nothing here but a good lot and residence; and the subscription towards erection of a new church would not certainly exceed $5000. The rest would have to come from other sources, if there are any; and suppose I receive some aid in the beginning, it might be spent in Indianapolis more profitably. If the Bishop of Vincennes would give up Indianapolis, I would give him, if he should desire it, Crawfordsville.[194]

In his next report, Lüers continued his critique of the diocese, complaining that "the best land has long since been entered; it is high and in the hand of anti-Catholics. There is no coal . . . hence no factories, and there never will be. All the congregations, with few exceptions indeed, have scarcely any church property to build on." Not one word in his four-page letter contained an optimistic opinion or hopeful observation; no parish was praised, no clergyman was commended: "The priests were allowed to do as they pleased, drink, give scandal, pocket the money, and in some instances spread it in the most unworthy manner, buying rings and chains for girls!!" Even St. Augustine's development seemed tenuous: "Two thirds of the congregation resides from 2 to 12 miles in the country around, and hence many do not often come to church at all, and, as their farms extend, will want churches among them, and thus cut up this present congregation into 2 or 3. According to Very Rev. Mr. Benoit's estimate there are some 100 French, and 10 - 15 German families in it; the rest speak the English language. The Sunday collections average from $3 to $4 . . . . Lafayette has a much better and wealthier congregation, but no church property."[195]

When the Bishop of Vincennes declined to cede Indianapolis to Fort Wayne, Lüers's attention turned to Lafayette, where he told Catholic businessmen that he would move the diocesan seat to their city, if a suitable site was secured for the erection of a cathedral, episcopal residence, school, convent, and hospital. A plot of land near the center of town was chosen, but the proposal died when the city council, in a close vote, refused to allocate funds to purchase the property.[196] When the news reached Fort Wayne that the bishop wanted to move to Lafayette, Lüers's popularity plummeted; he later admitted that "the jealousy of the 2 places is such that, if I had stayed much longer [in Lafayette] the usual contributions from here would entirely have stopped."[197]

For over two years, Lüers's obsession with relocation dominated his reports to Archbishop Purcell. No counsel from his superior—who pointed out Lüers's "weaknesses" and advised more "caution"—lessened his preoccupation with finding another site. Eighteen months after he arrived in Fort Wayne, Lüers confessed to Purcell: "Ever since I came into this wild hoosierdom I have been more or less severely assailed with temptation against the *10th or last* commandment. Not longer than a few days ago, I again experienced another quite severe assault . . . . I now again come to see if you have not a *really efficacious* remedy against this truly dangerous malady. . . . I said to myself: 'Could I but only obtain Toledo for my seat instead of this place, how well would I be off, and what a fine, little diocese I would have, and then no one would hear the least word of discontent from me any more.' " Lüers then continued for four pages, alternately damning Fort Wayne—"an old place and biggotted *(sic)* . . . wages are scarce and much lower . . . unproductive soil . . . taxes high" — and praising Toledo —"such a fine location . . . the size of the place . . . the Catholic population is over 5000 . . . Besides I like the place!" He then begged Purcell to detach northwestern Ohio from his archdiocese and cede it to his bishopric. The archbishop's adamant refusal failed to persuade Lüers to abandon his fixed idea, and six months later he complained to the bishop of Detroit that Fort Wayne was a "poor place for a Bishop," and fervently hoped that Purcell would "induce B[isho]p Rappe to give Toledo." Lüers's aversion to Fort Wayne also prompted him to ask Purcell to trade him to another diocese, suggesting an exchange of sees with Bishop George Carrell "who has been made odious to his flock by some unworthy priests whom he had to send away." The archbishop never budged, and Lüers never moved.[198]

Whether Lüers's dissatisfaction came from envy, unfulfilled ego needs, fear of failure, or other factors is difficult to determine; what is clear is that he had become a lonely, anxious, and unhappy man. As a parish priest in Cincinnati he had experienced the appreciation of a caring congregation and the support of his clerical colleagues; now, as a bishop in a foreign land, he was alone, without old friends or professional peers—and he soon became anxious and depressed. Only two months after he arrived in Fort Wayne, he lamented, "Really, I never had so many real difficulties to contend with during my whole life, as during the few months since I have left Cincinnati, without any prospect of diminution. The future is dark indeed!!"[199]

Part of the bishop's unhappiness stemmed from his negative reaction to Benoit's personal popularity, community contacts, financial resources, and sharp mind. Lüers told Purcell that when he "came to Fort Wayne, a new cathedral was needed . . . but no funds could be had from

The second Mother of God Church (*Der Mutter-Gottes Kirche*) — **called St. Mary's German Catholic Church by the English-speaking population** — **was erected in 1858 on the southeast corner of Jefferson and Clinton streets.**
[Courtesy of Allen County-Fort Wayne Historical Society]

people in Fort Wayne . . . . Benoit, however, said that he had friends in the South and would collect funds there . . . which induced me to retain Benoit—and my hands have been tied ever since."[200] The older, wiser, wealthier, and well-liked Benoit could appear intimidating. It was not Benoit's style to kowtow to bishops: a close friend had warned Archbishop Blanc of Benoit's "small fault . . . he is not discreet"; Bishop Dwenger, at Benoit's funeral, said, "The worst we can say is that his frank candor, his truthfulness, sometimes hurt."[201]

Benoit may have offended Lüers when he advised him "to reconcile himself to being bishop of Fort Wayne, lest he lose the esteem of his flock."[202] Hence, when Purcell nominated Benoit to become Bishop of Mobile and coadjutor of New Orleans, Lüers was elated and informed the archbishop that Benoit had just "made a profit of $12,000 to $15,000 in speculating in lots, which the diocese would get if he were appointed"—and then added, "but he is rather old."[203]

Lüers had named the forty-nine-year-old priest as his Vicar General, and Benoit tried to get along. He found it difficult, however, when he learned that Lüers wanted him to leave, and told Sorin, "I am in the way, and they do everything they can to disgust me and force me to go. I have been offered already a better place; but, before leaving, I will witness their maneuvers a little longer and laugh to scorn such mean and degrading policy."[204] Benoit was in no way intimidated by Lüers and would never retreat from any situation where he knew he was right; to surrender would only make his parishioners the victims of the bishop's pique, and might indefinitely stall the completion of his church. After two years with the bishop, Benoit told Archbishop Blanc that Lüers was "far from having conquered hearts," and, "no doubt, regards me as an obstacle. I will remove that obstacle as soon as the church is finished and return to you [in Louisiana] if you permit me to. However, I live in peace with my bishop."[205]

Two New Churches

Benoit's campaign to build a new church was not endorsed by Lüers, who complained bitterly that its size would be burdensome: "The . . . taxes, repairs, and debt of the new church, which *against my express will and consent* has been built so *unnecessarily large* for the place, will swallow up all the revenue and more too, and leave me nothing except constant trouble."[206] Neither the petulance of the bishop nor the poverty of his parishioners, however, could deter Benoit from building in Fort Wayne the largest church yet erected in Indiana.

Part of Benoit's desire to construct such a grand edifice was no doubt stimulated by the announcement in 1857 that the German Catholic congregation would soon erect a new brick church, 66 by 133 feet, crowned with a 165 foot steeple.[207] It was the third building project for the growing congregation in nine years; in 1854, they had erected a school and convent on the south-west corner of Jefferson and Lafayette streets.[208] Before construction on the new church had begun, however, Edward Faller was transferred to another parish[209] and was succeeded by the Reverend Joseph Weutz. On June 26, 1858, Bishop Lüers, assisted by the new pastor, laid the "foundation stone" of what was to be, by far, the largest church in town. Fifteen months later, the *Sentinel* reported that the edifice was "beyond question the most magnificent church in the state . . . of very large size and exceedingly lofty. The roof is arched or groined, supported by massive pillars, and painted to resemble stone; the walls are frescoed in a masterly style, and the imitations of cornices, arches and other projections are so admirably done as almost to deceive the beholder into the belief that they are real." The final cost of construction was nearly $30,000;

The Cathedral of the Immaculate Conception, on South Calhoun Street near West Jefferson Street, was dedicated in 1860.
[Courtesy of Allen County Public Library]

then, when a "very large and costly organ [$3000]" and "two large bells" were installed, the debt on the new Mother of God Church became almost unmanageable.[210]

While construction on the new German church was under way, Benoit announced that an even larger St. Augustine's Church—80 by 180 feet, with two spires—would be erected. The estimated cost of $50,000 was formidable, and Benoit had calculated that only a fraction of the sum could be raised in his own parish. As the local German Catholics were already over-committed and the bishop would not ask other parishes in the diocese to contribute, Benoit turned to local Protestant businessmen for contributions. In January 1859, he wrote to Sorin, "It is very seldom I remain at home, even for one day, now; I am constantly going out and collecting for the grand church we

intend to build this year."[211] The editor of the *Fort Wayne Sentinel* was impressed and urged Protestants and Jews to contribute to the "magnificent cathedral . . . . The members of that church do not often call on other denominations for aid but, on this occasion, they need outside assistance; and, as they design erecting a building which will add so much to our city, they have a just claim to the help of all citizens."[212] Even the erstwhile Catholic-baiter, John W. Dawson, seemed enthusiastic when reporting on the proposed cathedral, "the dimensions of which will exceed anything of the kind in Indiana. . . . Rev. Julian Benoit is the mover in the matter and we presume will be the main director, with ample efficiency."[213]

In late January 1859, Benoit left "for the South on a begging expedition."[214] Archbishop Blanc had given him permission to solicit contributions in the Archdiocese of New Orleans[215] and, to aid his cause, arranged for Benoit to preach the Lenten sermons, in his native tongue, at the Cathedral of St. Louis. The prelate also served as a sympathetic counsellor to the priest's difficulties with Lüers. When Benoit returned in late spring from the most French and Catholic region in America, he wrote to Blanc that his journey was "as agreeable as it could be, surrounded by Yankees and Protestants," and then reported, "Bishop Lüers has increased in humility and patience during my absence, but not in popularity. . . . I do not know what the future holds for me. If the bishop stays in Fort Wayne, I cannot. But where would I go? I will never find a father like the one I left at New Orleans."[216]

Construction on the new cathedral was scheduled to begin on Trinity Sunday at an elaborate corner-stone celebration. Paid advertisements in the local press announced that, on June 19, 1859, the "public was invited to be present and participate in the ceremony. . . . Archbishop Purcell of Cincinnati and several other bishops and clergymen will be present."[217] Purcell, during his visit to Fort Wayne, was especially impressed with the affection shown to Benoit by local Catholics and later commented on "how well-liked he was by the old citizens."[218]

Before he had left on his southern journey, Benoit had given his building committee[219] a thousand dollars in order to begin work on the church foundation—as soon as the original St. Augustine's church was moved to the east side of the block facing Clinton Street. Benoit then assured Lüers that "the church will be built without incurring any debt, with the aid of Catholics and Protestant friends."[220] A church fair netted $2600, and $18,000 was subscribed by residents of Fort Wayne (of which $14,000 was eventually paid). As most of these were promissory notes, Benoit was initially short of cash; in July he said that he was "having trouble finding means to pay the laborers—money is so scarce. If the contract was not so binding, I would write a new letter of demand, but I know it would be useless."[221]

Benoit obtained the funds—probably from his personal

investments—and kept the contractors working. Then, as the walls rose, so did Benoit's spirits; in November he told Sorin, who had not visited Fort Wayne since the cornerstone ceremony, "It will be the biggest, most beautiful church in Indiana." A month later he wrote, "I am still at Fort Wayne, and who knows where I shall be next week, next month, next year? One thing is certain—the Cathedral is covered, and with slate, *if you please.* It is one of the finest churches in the West. Come here, take a good peep at it, and contradict if you dare."[222] By May 1860, the church was plastered and by mid-summer the interior was finished, ready to receive the organ ($3000), main altar ($1200), pulpit ($1000), bishop's throne ($700), and Parisian candlesticks (4500 francs). A local editor, touring the nearly completed structure, noted that its "towers . . . can be seen ten miles off in nearly every direction," and wrote of the "gorgeous colors" of the "magnificent stained glass" in the fourteen 28-foot Gothic windows. Not yet in place was the sanctuary window: "It will contain a representation of the Immaculate Virgin in a luminous cloud of glory, surrounded by angels and with many Christian emblems encircling it. This is being painted in France, and will be one of the most beautiful specimens of the art ever seen in this country."[223] On the recesses of the middle arches were frescoes of the twelve Apostles; among the figures rendered on the sanctuary walls was the first canonized saint of the western hemisphere, Rose of Lima and the recently beatified Mariana of Jesus (The "Lily of Quito").

When the Cathedral was dedicated to the Immaculate Conception in early December 1860,[224] the final cost of the building and furnishings totaled $63,000. In his sermon, Lüers acknowledged "the tact and energy of Father Benoit, to whom we are chiefly indebted for the speedy erection of the Cathedral."[225] Benoit had done it all: he was the co-architect with Thomas Lau (the carpentry contractor) and had carefully supervised the construction; he had traveled to commission most of the special appointments and had personally raised $46,400 from donors at New Orleans and elsewhere. Most likely the greatest portion of this grand sum had come from his own purse.

In thirty years, from the arrival of Theodore Badin to the erection of the city's two largest churches, the Catholic community of Fort Wayne had grown to impressive size and significant influence. Catholic schools were judged among the best in town, and the Catholic clergy and religious were respected for their energetic leadership and personal piety. The internal issues of ethnic identity among the American, German, French, and Irish Catholics were being managed constructively, and the external pressures from the Know-Nothings were easily absorbed by the goodwill already earned in the non-Catholic community.

Epilogue

Julien Benoit continued to serve as pastor of the cathedral until his death in 1885, establishing the longest tenure of any of Fort Wayne's clergy during the nineteenth century. During most of these forty-four years he continued to buy and sell land; anticipating the inflationary pressures of war, "he made some prudent, and, in some instances, rather venturesome investments and speculations in real estate about the opening of the late Civil War" from which "grew his handsome fortune."[226] There is no evidence, however, that Benoit spent any of the profits on himself; in fact, his pastoral residence in 1853 was so humble that Bessonies felt the need to replace it. Year after year, Benoit gave his money to the Church and the poor. Only a fraction of his charities, however, was known, such as fifty pairs of wooden sabots to the Sisters of Providence, $14,000 of the $16,000 cost of a new episcopal residence, $2000 to St. Joseph Hospital, and $5000 to Mother Theodore for a new school. Sorin wrote that, when he was beginning at Notre-Dame-du-Lac, he obtained "a loan for 10,000 francs, which was secured by the pastor of Fort Wayne, Mr. J. Benoit";[227] forty-five years later, in 1890, Sorin told some admirers that Benoit, "a great friend of Notre Dame, came to its aid financially several times. . . . It is not me you should thank, but Father Benoit who has done so much for Notre Dame."[228] When Benoit made an extended pilgrimage to Rome in late 1865, he discovered that his reputation as an entrepreneur and philanthropist had preceded him, and at one of his audiences with Pope Pius IX, the pontiff inquired of him "how the priests in the United States made their living."[229]

During his thirteen-month stay in Europe, Benoit was offered the position of Vicar General in his native diocese of St. Claude, but he chose to return to the parish in which he had invested so much of his spiritual and material gifts. Neither time nor distance, however, had mellowed his relationship with Lüers, and the bishop never ceased complaining about the situation at Fort Wayne. He alleged that his Vicar General "thinks all would have been right if he were bishop of Fort Wayne . . . . Now nothing is right in Benoit's eyes," and then begged Purcell to give him the Diocese of Detroit and Benoit the Diocese of Fort Wayne. "Then he would not feel that he has been slighted, which he has no doubt been feeling all along."[230]

When Lüers died of apoplexy on a visit to Cleveland in 1871, Benoit's name was again among the top three candidates. He quickly declined, citing his age among other impediments; he also knew that Rome would favor a bishop who could speak German.[231] As the acting diocesan administrator, Benoit made a full report to Rome on the financial condition of the diocese. Cardinal Prefect Alexander Barnabo then told Archbishop Purcell that "the condition of the diocese, especially as regards to finances, seems very bad."[232] Part of the fiscal problem, according to Benoit, was caused by Lüers's use of diocesan money for personal investments: "Bishop John Lüers had borrowed $8000 from the St. Aloysius Orphan Society and had given a mortgage on his cathedral to secure the amount. The money obtained was not used for the cathedral, but was spent for private speculations."[233]

In 1883, when he was invested with the title of monsignor, Benoit's health had begun to fail; he told a friend, "I go down nevertheless gradually, and I will soon be on the brink of the graves. It matters not how soon, provided I will be prepared to die a good, Christian and sacerdotal death."[234] In November 1884, Benoit was stricken with cancer of the throat. When told that his condition was terminal, he replied, "If Providence desires to take me by the throat, then God's will be done."[235] Immediately, he began to liquidate his assets and distribute the proceeds; at the end, when Bishop Joseph Dwenger came to his bedside, the priest confessed, "Well, bishop, I came into the world with nothing, and I want to go out of it with nothing. I have about disposed of all I had, and you will likely find that you will be obliged to pay my funeral expenses."[236]

Benoit's funeral was attended by a throng of admirers, including many prominent Protestant friends: seated in places of honor near the casket were the minister of the First Baptist Church, the Reverend Stephen A. Northrup, and the venerable Jesse Williams, chief engineer for the canal and elder of the First Presbyterian Church. A few days before his death on January 28, 1885, former congressman and Episcopal vestryman, Joseph K. Edgerton, expressed the feelings of most citizens in a letter to Benoit: "Your blameless life of faithful well doing as a Priest of the Church and a citizen has been an example, which in its clear and steady light, has given instruction and strength to all who have known you."[237]

5
German and English Lutherans

"Some of our people are from Prussia, and others from every part of Germany and the Netherlands, with different prejudices and apprehensions of Christian propriety and lawful duty. It . . . requires a good deal of discretion to mold this heterogeneous mass into one harmonious American Christian Church."

Jesse Hoover, 1838

Few Lutherans settled in Fort Wayne during the 1820s. John Siebold, a German-born laborer who arrived in 1822, may have been the first of his faith to settle in the county.[1] One of the first American-born Lutherans to come to Fort Wayne was Henry Rudisill, whose business and religious interests combined to encourage Germans—especially German Lutherans—to come to the area. Rudisill, a twenty-eight-year-old native of Lancaster County, Pennsylvania, had been raised in the Lutheran church of that region which used the "Pennsylvania Dutch" dialect in worship. At the time of his arrival in 1829, the only regular religious services in Fort Wayne were conducted by the Presbyterians. As Henry, his wife Elizabeth, and their three children were equally comfortable in English, they attended, and, in 1831, Henry pledged five dollars to support the salary of the new Presbyterian pastor.[2]

Rudisill had been sent to Fort Wayne to oversee the landholdings of his employer, John Barr. When he attempted to hire men to clear land, he discovered that local labor was both scarce and expensive; Rudisill immediately suggested that Barr "hire some Germans from Germany and send them out to me. German emigrants are frequently arriving in Baltimore and would be glad of such an opportunity. You can hire them much lower than the Americans and I think they are more to be depended on. You can hire a good stout young man for sixty or ninety dollars a year. If you could get whole families it would be better. . . . Their women are good in corn fields . . . . They are more industrious and temperate than our Americans."[3]

Two weeks later, Rudisill renewed his request, and became more specific: "I would prefer the Württembergers, as they are the most industrious and temperate."[4] Rudisill also knew that most Württembergers were Lutheran; in addition, he requested both the Lutheran Mission Committee in Philadelphia and the Immigration Commission in Baltimore to direct migrating German Protestants to Fort Wayne.[5] During the next few years, a number of German-speaking settlers came to Fort Wayne; then, when the first link of the Wabash and Erie Canal opened in the summer of 1835, hundreds of native-born Germans—and a few German-speaking Swiss —began to arrive. These immigrants were from all regions of Germany, and reflected that country's pluralistic response to the sixteenth-century Lutheran, Calvinist, and Anabaptist reformers, as well as to the Catholic Counter Reformation. Although most of Fort Wayne's first German immigrants were either Catholic or Lutheran, there were also a substantial number of Calvinists and Zwinglians (who called themselves Reformed), and a few Jews.

The First Pastor, Jesse Hoover

By the end of that first summer's migration, Rudisill realized that a German-speaking Protestant pastor was needed.

As there were no Lutheran clergymen in all of northern Indiana, he appealed to his home synod and placed a notice in an eastern German language newspaper, and received a response from the Reverend Jesse Hoover, pastor of a Lutheran church in Woodstock, Virginia. Hoover was also a Pennsylvania German, born in Dover, York County; three years before, he had been graduated from Gettysburg Seminary where he had expressed interest in serving as a mission-

Henry Rudisill
[Courtesy of Allen County Public Library]

ary; before assuming his Virginia pastorate, he had taught for a year at a private school in Hagerstown, Maryland. Rudisill urged Hoover to visit Fort Wayne; when the twenty-six-year-old minister arrived in July 1836, he was taken on a ten-day whirlwind tour of Allen and Adams counties to preach and visit among the Germans. The people liked this "short, thick-set . . . genial . . . man of great energy" and pressed him to return with his family and settle in the area. A seminary classmate wrote: "Brother Hoover received his license, perhaps from the Synod of Maryland, before he started for the West . . . . None of our men had gone so far West as Fort Wayne."[6]

During Hoover's visit, it became apparent that his future flock lacked the financial resources to support him fully, and, as he was not under any formal missionary appointment by his synod, he could not expect a supplemental stipend from his denomination. Determined to fulfill his calling as a

missionary, he decided to support his family by teaching school in Fort Wayne; in August, however, when he returned with his wife and infant son, he discovered that two young Presbyterian school teachers, Susan Man and Alida Hubbell, had recently arrived from the East and had opened a school of their own. Samuel Hanna and Allen Hamilton, who had recruited the women, then proposed that the three combine their resources to open a tuition academy, under Hoover's principalship, in the lower level of the partially completed First Presbyterian Church. Susan Man wrote to her mother: "It will be much easier for us than an independent school. We have a beautiful room . . . . The whole basement story of the church is fitted up with oaken desks and walls painted for a black board . . . . Next Monday we commence with Mr. Hoover in the academy."[7]

The new "Fort Wayne Seminary," under nominal Presbyterian sponsorship, was non-sectarian, but provided some religious education. Man had previously noted: "Half of our scholars are Catholics, but they make no objection to reading and learning a verse in the Testament every morning . . . . We have about forty scholars, some of them as old as I am, and they keep us very busy. Mr. Hoover. . . a Lutheran minister . . . is an excellent man. He opens the school and closes it with prayer. After prayer we take our scholars into our own room and teach them until it is time to close. They leave Mr. Hoover with a curtsy, and some of them are getting quite graceful."[8]

To supplement his marginal salary, Hoover supplied the vacant pulpit at the Presbyterian Church. Fort Wayne's first resident minister, the Reverend James Chute, had died the previous December, and the congregation was experiencing difficulty in securing satisfactory substitutes. Few of these visiting preachers measured up to Dartmouth-educated Chute or the quality of clergy to which the young schoolteachers were accustomed in the East. Man told her New York friends: "If you were to hear the preaching we do, you would ever afterward feel contented with the poorest preacher I ever heard in Plattsburg. The ministers who come here are such as never could be supported in the East." Jesse Hoover, however, was the single exception: "Mr. Hoover, the Lutheran minister, preaches excellent sermons, and we are therefore poorly prepared to listen to such poor ones."[9] Years later Susan remembered the crowds of Germans who came to town to hear "Herr Pastor Huber" preach in their own language:

Men and women would walk in on Sundays, even eight and sometimes twelve miles to hear him preach; he preached in English to all denominations in the morning. When the English congregation was dismissed, we would see the Germans in their native dress pouring in, in crowds . . . . One morning, a German was seen leaving a load of wood at Mr. Hoover's door; the man threw off his best coat and proceeded to cut and split the wood; when that was completed and piled up, a middle-aged German woman—dressed in black with a white kerchief pinned over her bosom and a quilted cap trimmed with black lace—walked up to the door; the man nodded and knocked on the door; he asked to see Mr. Hoover; he pulled a license out of his pocket, handed it to the preacher, saying at the same time, "we wants to get married." They were soon joined in the bands of matrimony and left together.[10]

By early 1837, Hoover decided that his German congregation was sufficiently developed to celebrate its first Communion. All who desired to partake were obliged to gather on Saturday, January 14, "for the purpose of confessing their sins before God, and requesting the privilege of celebrating the sufferings and death of their Lord and Master, Jesus Christ." At Sunday worship, sixty-three individuals received the sacrament. The service was a simple celebration with scripture, sermon, hymns, prayers, and communion. The pastor wore no special vestments, there were no candles, and the communion bread was the common loaf of the people. The pews were rough boards laid over wooden blocks fashioned by Rudisill and others. As hymnbooks were scarce, the pastor usually "lined out" each verse during the singing, without instrumental accompaniment. During his first year in Fort Wayne, Hoover preached to this congregation solely in German; during the next year, however, he gave occasional messages in English—and kept the church records in English—believing this would help his foreign-born members to become American Lutherans. Hoover did not schedule another celebration of the sacrament until the fall when, on Saturday, October 14, at the preparatory service, he formally organized his scattered parish as a Lutheran church, the first to be founded in northern Indiana. Their first act was to adopt, by unanimous vote, the "Formula for the Discipline of the Evangelical Lutheran Church"; then, according to this Discipline, the adult male members elected Adam Wefel and Henry Dreher as elders, and Henry Rudisill and Conrad Nill as deacons, who constituted the church council, with the pastor as president.[11]

These officers and members were able to provide only a third of their pastor's minimum financial requirements, leaving Hoover still dependent on his other teaching and preaching positions. Apparently the Presbyterian elders paid Hoover promptly for his preaching; the school trustees, however, did not. Susan Man had expressed some initial hesitancy at the subsistence salary they had been offered, and was angry when the teachers were not paid: "The trustees have not paid us for the last session yet. It was due last November . . . . They engaged to pay us $250 for ten months and, at the end of five months, backed out of their bargain, and have not paid us yet, although it was to be paid in

advance. They are the most inefficient set that ever I saw, and, if it were not for the children, I would leave tomorrow. They have been two years building the church and it is not finished yet, not even plastered. The Court House has cost about six thousand dollars and never will be completed. The bare walls stand, with here and there a brick out, and in complete ruin . . . . They say the new bank . . . will be ready next fall, but I do not believe a word."[12]

These financial arrears in the operation of the school may have prompted Jesse Hoover's disassociation with the enterprise. In April, the *Fort Wayne Sentinel* announced: "The third term of the school in Fort Wayne under the superintendence of Miss Hubbell and Miss Man will commence on Monday the 24th of the present month."[13] In order to feed his growing family, Hoover moved into a house next to the Presbyterian Church, and his wife, Mary Catherine, took boarders. The young schoolteachers moved in and welcomed the high level of dinner conversation at the pastor's home. Susan was especially grateful for Hoover's informal art lessons, and wrote: "Mr. Hoover understands drawing and he has taught me some things . . . on mathematical perspective."[14]

When the Presbyterians, in September, installed the Reverend Alexander T. Rankin as their minister, Hoover's stipend as supply preacher ceased. He then decided to open his own school; other school teachers, however, had recently arrived in town, prompting Man to comment: "There are three teachers . . . just commencing three opposition schools. If they think it a very profitable business, they will find themselves mistaken."[15] Hoover hoped to hold his classes in the little schoolhouse—a building avoided by any who could find other accommodations—but failed to enroll enough students. He told Man, who was then at her parents' home preparing for her wedding to Hugh McCulloch: "I had commenced teaching in the brick schoolhouse, but have discontinued for want of such patronage as I thought would justify me in spending my time in school. By refusing to take up school in Smoky Retreat as principal, I have thrown myself out of employ as teacher."[16]

Hoover now devoted all his energies to his pastoral work and, in spite of growth, felt discouraged: "I am still trying to preach in my old-fashioned style. My congregation is increasing. They number about one hundred communing members. We are making preparation to build a church next spring. Judge Hanna has given us a lot and, Deo Volente, by next year at this time, we will have our new church completed. At present, I preach in the brick schoolhouse . . . . There is no more indication of a revival of religion here than there was twelve months ago. I am almost despairing of Fort Wayne."[17]

Hoover's loss of both his preaching and teaching income was exacerbated by the financial Panic of 1837. Hoover noted the depression's effect on the number of marriages he performed in Fort Wayne: "The young people seem to be too cautious these 'hard times' to plunge themselves into all the cares and felicities of wedded life."[18] Then, in November, a second "care and felicity" was born into the Hoover family. During this time, the Hoovers had little more to eat than cornmeal which had been hammered out on a block of wood, and, since they had no oven, the cornbread was baked on a board in the open fireplace.[19]

The American Home Missionary Society Provides Aid

The Presbyterians, who had developed a deep affection for their interim minister, were distressed that neither the local Lutherans nor their eastern synods had provided even minimal support for their intrepid missionary. As a result, they petitioned their own agency of support, the American Home Missionary Society. Alexander T. Rankin and Smalwood Noel, clerk of the Presbyterian session, most likely drafted the request and then sought the endorsement of the other Protestant clergymen in town, the Reverend Steven R. Ball, circuit preacher of the Methodist Episcopal Church, and the Reverend William Corbin, pastor of the Baptist Church.

We, the undersigned citizens of Fort Wayne, do respectfully solicit of your truly evangelical society, a missionary appropriation to enable the Rev. Mr. Jesse Hoover of the Evangelical Lutheran Church to continue his gospel labors with the German population of this place and adjacent country. . . . From an acquaintance of about eighteen months, Mr. Hoover has the confidence of the community as a pious man and one whose desire and aim is to do good; but his pecuniary circumstances are such as to make him entirely dependant on the church for his support. This is a dear place to live in, every article of subsistence being very high.

The petitioners then described the present, and anticipated, size of the German community in the surrounding area—and revealed some anti-Catholic feelings:

The Protestant German population is about three hundred and their number is continually increasing—two or three hundred more are expected in the spring; these people are generally poor, but industrious; many of them have a small piece of land in the green woods, and it is with much difficulty that they can maintain their families until they can make comfortable improvements. Add to this that there is a large number of Roman Catholic Germans—some of whom attend his church—and it is believed that he will be useful

to some of the members of that corrupt and unchristian church.

There is a Lutheran church organized in Fort Wayne of about eighty or ninety communicants [and] another to be organized in a few days up the St. Mary's river about fifteen miles from this place. He has frequent calls to preach in other parts of this and the adjacent counties; and he is the only minister in these parts from whom they can "hear in their own tongues, wherein they were born, the wonderful words of God."[20]

The letter was sent to the Reverend Samuel Lowry, the regional representative for the American Home Missionary Society, who attached his committee's enthusiastic endorsement: "Br. Thomson, in particular, who has had some personal acquaintance with Mr. Hoover, speaks in strong terms of the undoubted excellence of the man, and the importance of the object. He is the only man in all that region that can reach the German population." The Society acted promptly, and Hoover received his commission as their missionary—dated back to July 18, 1837—and a draft for $150.[21]

The American Home Missionary Society expected that Hoover, like all its commissioned clergy, would labor full-time to establish congregations in such promising locations as could grow to support themselves. He was also to establish Sabbath schools, temperance societies, and missionary associations, distribute Bibles and tracts, and strive to improve the moral tenor of the communities. The Society also required its ministers to submit quarterly reports to its secretaries in New York City, who would then remit to the missionary a draft for the stipend due.[22] Hoover's first report reviewed his progress from the date of his commission in mid-1837 to the end of his quarter on March 19, 1838:

Having preached every alternate Lord's day in the town of Fort Wayne, I organized a church, the "First Evangelical Lutheran Church in Fort Wayne," on the 14th of October, 1837. It consists of seventy members; some of these live eight miles from town. All of these had certificates of church membership in Germany except one who was received on a profession of faith. The greater number of them are hopefully pious and manifest their faith by their works . . . .

We have not, however, been without our difficulties. Some of our people are from Prussia, and others from every part of Germany and the Netherlands,[23] with different prejudices and apprehensions of Christian propriety and lawful duty. It is easy to conceive that it requires a good deal of discretion to mold this heterogeneous mass into one harmonious American Christian Church. But, by the grace of God, I have some prospect of succeeding to a very considerable extent.[24]

Church Discipline

Hoover's first challenge in creating an "American Church" was in persuading his German parishoners to abide by the stricter American Lutheran ban on dancing and drinking: "I have a pious, enlightened church council, who feel the importance of maintaining a proper standard of piety and discipline from every communicant . . . . We have been under the necessity of suspending one of our members, and two or three more I fear will have to be suspended or expelled—these still persist in attending Catholic dances. I say 'Catholic' because there are no Protestants here who give balls since the suspension from church privileges spoken of above. These dances, which are the haunts of almost all kind of vice, exert a very pernicious influence on a large portion of the German population of this place."[25]

A Lutheran missionary who traveled through northern Indiana in mid-1836 was shocked by the prevalence of dancing on the western frontier:

> Frolicking is a vice which prevails much in this state. Balls, cotillion-parties, &c., are very frequent. To these bacchanalian feasts old and young, men, women and children resort. Mothers, I am told, go with their infants on their arms, lay them down for a while, and dance with merriment around the altar of their father—their god—the devil . . . . Gatherings are kept in some villages along the Wabash with much regularity . . . . The whole live-long night are they heard thumping on the floor, too drunk to dance. In the morning the streets are filled with drunken men, and perhaps the chambers with drunken women.

> These parties are the destruction of the youthful part of the community. They create luxury, indolence and wastefulness; they discourage industry and thriftiness. It is to be regretted that, in many parts of our land, these gatherings are supported and encouraged by Christians, who hold them in miniature or with a better name when they call them religious parties, or social meetings for spending an evening in friendly intercourse, when it is spending an evening in idle talk, courtship and spending money for luxuries which might have been thrown into the Lord's treasury.[26]

The disciplinary action taken by Hoover's church council was common to most American Protestant churches at that time, for such bodies often functioned as "the moral courts of the frontier."[27] Hoover noted that some immigrant Lutherans avoided formal church censure by attending, but not joining, their church: "There are a number of Protestants here, mostly persons without families, who have thus far refused to become members of the church, because our discipline does not correspond with the ideas they had formed of the liberty they want to enjoy in this country."[28]

The Adams County Church; Hoover's Sudden Death

Hoover also reported to the Missionary Society on his efforts to minister to the many new immigrants who were carving farms out of the forests. His most successful rural mission was among those Germans who had settled south of Fort Wayne in Adams County. He wrote: "On the eleventh of March, I organized a church in the northern part of Adams County (the county next south of Allen) of twenty-three members. This little church is in a flourishing condition. They have kept up a prayer meeting regularly since the latter part of last summer. There I expect to have a flourishing Sunday school this summer . . . . We have not yet commenced building churches. This we will have to do before long. There is a great number of Germans expected this summer. At present, the Fort Wayne Church worships in a school house, and the Friedens Kirche (Church) in Adams county worships in a cabin."[29]

In a letter to a seminary classmate, Hoover shared his feelings about his mission in Fort Wayne: "I am laboring here to build up a church, but it is hard work. I have a few good, substantial members; but many who call themselves Lutherans are a disgrace to our church, and I do not know what the result of my labors will be . . . . I sometimes think of giving up the work and returning to the East; but, as I came out here to raise the standard of Lutheranism, by the help of God, I'll do it."[30]

And Hoover did it. Few other areas in northern Indiana attracted as many German immigrants as did Allen and Adams counties, and part of the attraction was the existence of the only Lutheran parishes in that part of the state. Hoover planned to establish other congregations: "I purpose, if life and health are spared, to visit other sections of the country this summer." But his health failed, and Hoover died suddenly on May 24, 1838, at the age of twenty-eight. Susan Man McCulloch wrote: "My old friend, Mr. Hoover, died a week last Thursday from a determination of the blood to the head and lung. His loss is felt very deeply by us all, but particularly his German congregation. They were so much attached to him."[31]

A seminary classmate, the Reverend John G. Morris, with whom he had corresponded, later wrote: "When the

General Synod met at Fort Wayne in 1864, I was there, and I went out to the cemetery and found a neat tombstone erected by the congregation over his remains: 'To the memory of Rev. Jesse Hoover, Pastor of the Lutheran Congregation of Fort Wayne' . . . . I could not but admire the courage and moral heroism that had led him to make the sacrifice that he had to make . . . . 'Servant of God, well done.'" [32] At the fiftieth anniversary of the founding of the congregation, charter members fondly remembered Hoover as "a man of deep conviction, a pastor of whom it could be said, 'I believe—therefore do I speak.' " [33]

Soon after Hoover's funeral, the church officers wrote to the Mission Committee of the Pennsylvania Synod for assistance in securing a bilingual pastor. They also asked the American Home Missionary Society to aid Hoover's family: "His wife and two orphan children are left without their natural protector. . . . If it is consistent with your mode of business to send Mr. Hoover's widow a draft for the last quarter of the year, it will be thankfully received by her." In the meantime, the officers struggled to conduct Sunday services themselves: "At the close of [Sabbath] school the congregation assembles and have a sermon read to them and an exhortation by one of the elders. The Sabbath school instruction is given in both the English and German languages, many of our young people being in a short time able to read the English language, the desire and necessity of acquiring it is very great. The same plan is pursued by the congregation in Adams County, fifteen miles south of Fort Wayne." The elders, however, had been unsuccessful in their attempts to secure a bilingual pastor: "We have written to another man in the south part of this state who preaches in both languages. He could only, however, supply us by making another vacancy, and the support we can provide, we know, is not sufficient. Those only who have experienced them can know the difficulties, expense, and privations attending our emigration and location in the Wilderness." [34]

Friedrich K. D. Wyneken Arrives

There was, at that time, a critical shortage of German-speaking ministers available to serve the needs of all the new German communities in the western settlements; clergymen who were bilingual, as was Hoover, were even rarer. At about the moment that the appeal from Fort Wayne was mailed, Friedrich Konrad Dietrich Wyneken, a twenty-eight-year-old clergyman from Germany, appeared before the Pennsylvania Synod's Mission Committee, eager to serve immigrant Germans in America. The Synod quickly commissioned him to go to Indiana "to gather the scattered Protestants into congregations." [35] The use of the word "Protestant," instead of "Lutheran," was deliberate on the part of American Lutherans as they endorsed the principles of the Prussian Church Union of 1830 which united Lutheran and Reformed into one church.

Wyneken had been born near Verden in Hannover, Germany, in 1810 —the son of a Lutheran pastor—and, like three of his six brothers, had studied theology at Göttigen and Halle. After serving for a few years as a private tutor, he was attracted by a call for missionaries to the spiritually destitute German immigrants in America. He sailed for Baltimore in the summer of 1838 and tramped its streets, searching for a Lutheran pastor. Some friendly Germans invited him to a religious meeting where he was asked to lead in prayer. During his prayer the congregation began to respond audibly with shouts of "Amen! Amen!" At the close of the service the leader asked the somewhat mystified visitor, "Well,

**Friedrich Konrad Dietrich Wyneken,
at the Age of Thirty-two**
[Reprinted from R. F. Rehmer,
Lutheran Pioneers in Indiana, 1972, p. 14]

Brother Wyneken, how did you like it?" Discovering that he had attended a prayer meeting of the United Brethren in Christ, Wyneken responded, "I do not know whether it is of God or the devil. It is certainly not Lutheran!" Wyneken's reply would later become his primary test for any congregation's faith and practice: "Is it Lutheran?" [36]

For several weeks after his arrival in Baltimore, Wyneken preached at St. Paul's Lutheran Church during the illness of the pastor. Then, when his appointment by the Pennsylvania Synod was effected, he traveled by train to Pittsburgh, by canal boat to Zelienople, and on horseback across Ohio, where he encountered scattered communities of Germans who begged him to stay with them. His arrival in northeastern Indiana at the end of summer in 1838 was not the result of careful navigation; the new missionary had simply bought a horse in eastern Ohio and headed west; eventually he traveled up the valley of the St. Mary's River into Adams County.

His reception in Indiana was initially cool. The first settler he met in the woods near Decatur was immediately suspicious of Wyneken's inquiry about Germans. Apparently a few "tramp preachers"—defrocked German clergy or itinerants posing as pastors—had previously swindled the immigrants, so the man told Wyneken of two German homes ahead: the first of a man who was very ill, and the next of a rich trader. The settler then watched to see at which house he would first knock. Wyneken went to the house of sickness, but again was met with unfriendly suspicion. The woman of the home responded to his pastoral inquiry by

Karl Friedrich Buuck
[Reprinted from G. E. Hageman,
Friedrich Konrad Dietrich Wyneken, 1926, p. 16]

asserting that he should have stayed home in Germany. Wyneken persisted in his concern and eventually persuaded the woman to allow him to pray with her husband.[37] Finally, convinced of his sincerity, the woman directed Wyneken to the home of Karl Friedrich Buuck, an elder in the Friedheim Church which Jesse Hoover had founded two years before.[38] After visiting among the Germans of the Decatur area for a short while, Wyneken arrived in Fort Wayne in the last week of September 1838. He wrote to a friend with whom he had sailed from Germany: "Eight days ago I arrived in Fort Wayne. Here, as well as in two neighboring settlements, I

have already preached five times, baptized children, and read burial services. And now these people want me to stay . . . . I advised the vestry of the church here to write to the committee of their church-body about this. Tomorrow I intend to continue my journey, and I expect to return in four weeks to receive the answer. I am ready to do the Lord's will, and I shall leave it to Him to direct the hearts of the members of the committee as He sees fit."[39]

Wyneken had no intention of serving an organized congregation. He believed that he was called to be a missionary and was thereby under appointment, not to the churched, but to the unchurched, of whose needs he had read in missionary letters published in Germany. Accordingly, in early October, he left Fort Wayne and embarked on a six-weeks mission itineration, traveling as far north as Michigan and south to Crawfordsville. He again encountered unfriendliness and suspicion in many of the German settlements, and was especially frustrated that so few would assist him by telling others that religious services were to be held:

> On one occasion—after I had traveled through a pouring rain in search of a settlement in the far West of which I had heard—I met, towards noon, a man with a gun under his arm. He was a German. I told him of my call as a missionary by the Pennsylvania Synod and that I was willing to preach in the neighborhood. The man expressed his delight at the prospect of hearing a German Lutheran preacher after seven years. He was pleased, also, on account of his children, who had not yet been baptized. But, when I asked him to inform his neighbors in the backwoods, the hunter—who had just come out of the woods— said that it was too wet in the woods. When I tried to urge him, he said that he had no time, though the next house was hardly a half hour's distance off the road.

> He directed me to a house down the road. A mother with six or seven children, big and little, came to the door: the same expression of delight, the same request by me, and the same result. A hundred steps farther on I found her husband chopping wood. I rode over to him, but he hardly looked up from his work and had just as little time. And, because I could find no one to direct me, I had to pass up a whole settlement which for seven years had been without Word or Sacrament.

> A native of Hamburg, whom I found busy at the front of his house, calmly left me standing in the rain and went into his house muttering only, "Is that so?" when I told him why I had come. In a

town on the Wabash Canal, on a Sunday after-noon, I had to round up the men in a saloon after a lengthy argument, although the majority of them, as long as they had been in America, had not heard a German sermon and understood no English.[40]

Released by the Synod and Supported by the A. H. M. S.

When Wyneken returned to Fort Wayne, he found that the petition of the Fort Wayne Lutherans had been approved by the Mission Committee: they agreed to release him from his commission as a missionary, with the understanding that he would care for both the Fort Wayne and Decatur congregations, as well as minister to the neighboring settlements. In assuming these settled pastorates, however, he would no longer receive financial aid from the denomination; his support was now the responsibility of those who sought his pastoral services.

Wyneken boarded with Henry Rudisill and lived at the same subsistence level as did his Presbyterian counterpart, Alexander T. Rankin, who reported that, after the Panic of 1837, "money had disappeared."[41] As no funds were to be appropriated by eastern Lutherans to support these first congregations on the northern Indiana frontier, the local church council immediately appealed to the American Home Missionary Society to support Wyneken as it had Hoover. Shortly after Hoover's death, Alexander Rankin had written to the Mission Society, requesting their assistance in finding a suitable minister; then, when Wyneken came onto the scene and was eventually convinced to accept the call of the people, the Presbyterian pastor immediately notified the Society that the German Lutherans would be requesting aid for their new minister.[42] Before approving the grant, however, the Society sought Rankin's opinion of Wyneken; his judgement was enthusiastic:

> I think Mr. Wynnican *(sic)* is in every way fitted to take the place of Mr. Hoover with a single exception. Mr. Hoover could preach well in English; Mr. Wynnican cannot. But, as a German preacher, he is, I have been informed by some of his people, equal, if not superior, to Mr. Hoover. Of course his influence will, in a great measure, be confined to the Germans. He is learning the English language. I think him decid-edly pious and evangelical . . . . The church is evangelical and would not settle any other kind of a man . . . . Mr. Wynnican is very labourous, and desirous to bring his people up to the proper Christian standard.
> They are generally united in him. The only objection I have heard against him is, I think, in

his favour. Some of them wish to commune in the church and have the privilege of going to balls. He thinks no church members should attend such amusements. Of course some think he is too rigid. . . . His field of labour is arduous and affords him little pecuniary recommendations. But for his desire to do good, he must have left it before now. He says he does not need much. His own language the other day to me was, "If I had only as much as would pay mine board, and py me a horse, and get me mine coat to keep me warm dis winter, 'twould do."[43]

What kind of coat Wyneken wore that winter was not recorded, but how he got his yellow trousers became a legend. Wyneken was more conservative in his theology than in his dress. He saved his one black suit for formal occasions but usually wore jeans,[44] like his parishioners, and often preached with patches on his knees. At a store in Decatur, the Catholic proprietor, who had occasionally been chided by Wyneken for his intemperance, noticed the pastor, in frayed trousers, examining a piece of yellow English leather. When asked if he liked it, Wyneken replied that he had no money. The storekeeper then offered the goods as a gift, but Wyneken declined, explaining that, if he accepted the gift, he could no longer admonish his drinking. The man laughed, gave the pastor the cloth, and told him to scold him as much as he liked. Wyneken immediately took the material to a local tailor and was thereafter seen everywhere in his favorite yellow breeches. Not everyone, however, was as pleased with the new trousers as was their owner. The deacons of the Friedheim congregation were scandalized, not only by the bright color that so pleased Wyneken, but also by the character of the donor, whom they suspected of enjoying a little joke by making the Lutheran minister an object of Catholic charity. They quickly loaded a wagon with corn and dumped it in front of the store in payment. The matter, however, was not settled. Deacon Ernst Voss felt the congregation should assist their pastor in buying an appro-priate suit and eventually collected forty dollars; Wyneken, however, promptly gave the money to a destitute widow. Undaunted, Voss then plotted with a tailor to make a proper pair of pants and, by a ruse, got Wyneken to try them on; in the process, the yellow trousers vanished.[45]

In the summer of 1839, a German missionary sent by the Pennsylvania Synod visited Wyneken in Fort Wayne and wrote:

> I greeted Brother Wyneken . . . riding into the village from his home to instruct the children. He lives with a miller, Mr. Rudisill, about a mile west of the village. I accompanied him on his visit to one of his congregations in Adams County, where he taught school for three days and preached in

the forenoon, while I preached in the afternoon. The people seem to cling to him and hold him in very affectionate regard . . . . His manner in dealing with these people is very plain and simple . . . . He has in mind to introduce some church discipline in order to bring about at least a semblance of order, and to change the rough and coarse behavior of the many Germans who want to join his church.

He is in favor of sending German schoolteachers here . . . . He wishes to return to Germany in order to secure more [missionary] candidates, at least six of whom could be placed in the territory which he has visited, if they would be content with clothing and food. Brother Wyneken, however, does not even know whether he has that. But the fact he has nothing does not worry him. He is content when he receives something, but also when he gets nothing. He has put me greatly to shame by his life of faith.[46]

The "church discipline" which Wyneken devised to "change the rough and coarse behavior" of prospective members was read to the congregation on April 24, 1839. It emphasized the fruits, rather than the formulation, of faith; what had been implied was now required, and each member was expected:

> To separate and remain pure from the world and not compromise with it in any way;
> To shun gross vices (Gal. 5:19) and walk as an honorable person before God, at home, and in public;
> To abandon the frivolity and foolishness of the world with its lust and desires, such as dances, games, and idle leisure—in brief, to abandon all worldly life (Eph. 5:4-9) and act as children of the light (II Cor. 7:1);
> To watch themselves, and watch over others, as well;
> To use the word and the sacrament frequently;
> To exclude from the community whoever is bad (I Cor. 5:11)—everyone who, after having been warned and asked to change, will not, until he has repented.
> Furthermore, members of other communities and strangers should not be turned away from the Holy Communion; but, of those people living in town or the surrounding areas, only those should be allowed to participate who intend to become members of the community.
> And only those whose faith and lifestyle have been first examined should be admitted into the

congregation.[47]

On October 3, 1839, Wyneken received his commission from the American Home Missionary Society, with a six months retroactive stipend. In his first quarterly report (in German) he described his scattered parish: "I preach alternately [at Fort Wayne and Adams County], twice on a Sabbath but, as there are families too far distant from either of these churches to be able to attend regularly, I often preach in their neighborhoods on weekdays . . . . There are also two places, one of them nineteen and the other thirty-six miles distant from this, at which I preach at stated times on weekdays." Wyneken, the former teacher, gave special attention to the education of the young: "In addition to the Sunday Schools, I have established schools for instruction three times a week. Our reading book in these schools is the Bible, which we read in course . . . . The instruction of candidates for confirmation is an additional labor. I examine the Sunday School scholars every month . . . . The greatest pleasure I find is in instructing the young, and many of them are inquiring after the Lord. Thus, I hope that they may be instruments in His hand to convert their aged parents."[48]

Disappointment and Discouragement

Wyneken did not find the parents flocking to his services, nor did he find many of his worshippers filled with the sort of evangelical piety he wanted: "In my family visitations I find earnest desires after information about divine things and, in the life of the members, there is more outward respect for religion, and more consistency of conduct with their profession. True, this is not conversion; nevertheless, I look upon it as a preparation for a better state of things . . . . However, there remains much to be lamented, for the congregations are still far from being Christians. The obstacles in the way are great. Free evangelical Christianity in Germany is seldom found. They have, as, you know, explained away so much of it that there is but little left."[49] Three months later, Wyneken was even more discouraged by the character of his people: "The greatest portion of these people never witnessed or heard of such a thing as living faith in Germany. They come here to earn their bread in the sweat of their brow; they bring with them their heathenish opinions and customs and think that surfeiting, drunkenness, and worldly idolatry are no ways detrimental to their salvation." Wyneken's initial attempts to establish a temperance society were largely ignored: "I have been conversing with many upon the subject of temperance so that I might have some to support me when I addressed them publicly. I think I could get eight to join the pledge."[50]

Most of the Fort Wayne parish, however, supported his leadership in the building of a church on the west side of Barr Street at Lewis Street. The modest frame structure, twenty-four by forty feet, was commenced in the summer of 1839, and the congregation began to worship in the unfinished facility in the fall; with the onset of winter, however, they were forced to move to a heated building at the corner of Barr and Jefferson streets.[51]

During this cold weather, Wyneken headed north on another missionary trip, planning to visit South Bend, Elkhart, and Mottville. On the first day out of Fort Wayne, in early January 1840, his horse went lame, forcing him to walk the frozen road, while leading the animal; then, two miles beyond Elkhart, he became too ill to continue. By the time he had returned to Fort Wayne, Wyneken had accepted the reality that his field was too large for one missionary, and wrote to the editor of *Die Lutherische Kirchenzeitung* in Pittsburgh: "The occasional attacks and skirmishes on the field of the devil, I fear, are practically worthless. We must get a firm hold and wrest the country step by step from the devil and place outposts on the boundaries. If we have not sufficient warriors of Christ in this country, then I am convinced that a strong appeal to the brethren in Germany, especially to the mission societies there (for the consistories cannot supply us with the kind of men that we want), will bring us enough recruits to fill the ranks."[52] Wyneken then wrote a twelve-page report to the General Mission Society of the Synod of Pennsylvania and concluded with an impassioned plea: "O that the Lord might blow the spirit of life upon the dead ones of our church . . . . How else could it be possible that a denomination so strong—and in many parts so rich, as the Lutheran—could behold thousands of their brethren in the West, sleeping upon the brink of eternal death, without being moved. . . to rescue them from this lamentable condition. If each congregation should contribute but $3 annually for the support of missionaries, much under the blessing of the Lord could be accomplished."[53]

Wyneken, during this time, seems to have been struggling with two conflicting emotions: on one side, he felt overwhelmed with the enormity of his task and yearned to leave for a more physically manageable and spiritually satisfying parish; on the other, he was constrained by a strong sense of duty to fulfill his responsibilities as a faithful missionary. His solution was not simple: "If it is the Lord's will, I hope to get an evangelical minister in my place so that I can go to Germany next fall to find some able young ministers to bring with me to America. I shall then go farther west to find a field of labor and to gather a congregation of those who have resolved to flee from the wrath to come."[54]

Recruiting Missionaries in Germany

Wyneken had continued to correspond with mission-minded friends in Germany, and had persuaded some Lutherans in Bremen to organize a society dedicated to recruiting missionaries for America. As a result, in May

1840, he welcomed a teacher from Bremen, Friedrich Wilhelm Husmann, who assisted in the school recently organized in Fort Wayne.[55] Then, when there was no word that other

Friedrich Wilhelm Husmann
[Reprinted from G. E. Hageman,
Friedrich Konrad Dietrich Wyneken, 1926, p. 32]

Marie Sophie Wilhelmine Buuck,
F. K. D. Wyneken's Wife
[Reprinted from G. E. Hageman,
Friedrich Konrad Dietrich Wyneken, 1926, p. 32]

missionaries might embark, Wyneken decided that he must now go to Germany to do the recruiting himself. Support for this project attracted attention in both the General Synod and the Synod of the West (which Wyneken had recently joined), and efforts were made to secure interim pastors for his Indiana parishes. Finally, a year later in May 1841, the Reverend Friedrich Knape arrived to care for the Adams

County Lutherans; then, in June, the Reverend Georg Jensen assumed interim responsibilty for the Fort Wayne congregation.[56] Wyneken was now free to depart. At the end of August, he married Marie Sophie Wilhelmine Buuck, a daughter of "Father" Buuck, who had built for Wyneken a cabin for his overnight stays in Adams County. The newlyweds journeyed east for their honeymoon and, in October, under the sponsorship of the mission committee of the General Synod, embarked from Philadelphia for Germany.[57]

Wyneken hoped that his sojourn in that country would cure a throat ailment which had increasingly curtailed his activities, and immediately consulted a competent physician. Then, after experiencing some improvement, he set out on his mission. As his family was prominent in church and governmental circles, doors were opened for the pastor from America; the thirty-one-year-old minister, who had left his homeland as an unknown tutor, was now a missionary hero. Wyneken's letters, which had been printed in church publications, had made his name familiar to many German Lutherans; more than anything else, these epistles had awakened Lutherans in Germany to a more active concern for the spiritual needs of their coreligionists in America.

Wyneken's enthusiasm and organizing ability soon united the various Lutheran missionary societies in a common cause to save their fellow Germans from those "sectarian influences" which, he warned, were running rampant in America. His lectures in Germany repeatedly emphasized the many spiritual perils that existed in the new world to seduce Lutherans from their true faith. He excoriated Catholics and Calvinists, but warned that Methodists were the most dangerous enemy. A young student, who later became a missionary, wrote about the electrifying experience of attending one of Wyneken's meetings:

> When I reached the school hall, I already found it crowded to the doors . . . . At eight o'clock Wyneken appeared . . . . All listened with rapt attention to his vivid descriptions of American Church life and of his missionary work . . . . He gave attention to the activities of the Methodists. The most brilliant part of his lecture was his description of a camp meeting. When he reached the moment when the individuals are invited to come to the mourners' bench,[58] Wyneken suddenly approached those in the audience who were sitting or standing immediately in front of him, seized their hands and asked them, "Don't you want to be converted too." I can still picture in my mind how some of them stared at the speaker in surprise, and how they drew back, fearing that an actual Methodist conversion was to take place . . . .

At the close of his address, as he pleaded for aid for the forsaken people of our faith, he assailed the numerous [ministerial] candidates of Germany who waited eight or ten years for a charge, while across the seas hungry souls were perishing in the wilderness.[59]

Wyneken's antipathy towards Methodism was a new development, precipitated by the establishment of German Methodist missions in Indiana in 1840, and the arrival in Fort Wayne of a dynamic circuit minister of that persuasion, the Reverend Wilhelm Heinrich Ahrens.[60] At first, Wyneken welcomed the German Methodist preachers and opened his pulpit to them. Then, when some of his own parishioners were converted in Methodist revivals, he sounded a note of alarm: "With what monstrous swiftness the Methodist spirit had soured and infected almost all of Christendom! . . . In all parts of the world, it is striving to undermine the existing fellowships. Everywhere societies have been and are constantly being formed which work in this spirit, to awaken and spread 'in the name of the Christian life.' Meanwhile, they destroy church life with the help of erected chapels, hired preachers, evangelists, colporteurs, and treatises; they seek to win for themselves the faithful who do not recognize the church or despise it; or they seek to alienate them from the existing congregations and then attempt to assign them to their nearby chapels."[61]

Wyneken Adopts the "Old Lutheran" Doctrine and Liturgy

At the same time that Wyneken was so dramatically challenging his German audiences' beliefs, his own theology was undergoing a significant revision. Soon after he had arrived, he had sought the assistance of the Reverend J. K. Wilhelm Löhe in Bavaria, who quickly became an enthusiastic supporter of the American mission enterprise and helped Wyneken publish his influential pamphlet, *The Distress of the German Lutherans in North America*. Löhe, in turn, persuaded Wyneken to adopt his more orthodox doctrinal standards and to embrace the old Catholic liturgical traditions of the sixteenth-century Lutheran church. Under Löhe's influence, Wyneken developed a strong conviction that American Lutheranism had lost the true faith of its founder, and only by reinstituting the old confessional and liturgical Lutheranism could his church resist the new challenges of an aggressive American sectarianism.

Although the Reformed faith of Calvin and Zwingli had influenced German Protestantism from the earliest years of the Reformation, Wyneken now allied himself with the growing cadre of purists who were determined to eradicate all non-Lutheran incursions. He denounced the General Synod in America as Reformed in theology, Methodist in practice, and Lutheran in name only. Especially, he condemned their endorsement of a union of Lutheran and Reformed churches in America. He described Gettysburg Theological Seminary—which was financially aided by German Lutherans (and from which Jesse Hoover had been graduated)—as a serpent seeking to destroy the faith.[62]

Wyneken remained in Europe for two years. During his absence, the Fort Wayne congregation divided into two factions: one desired to retain Jensen as their pastor; the other, led by Rudisill and the teacher, Husmann, remained loyal to Wyneken. Jensen realized his situation was untenable and soon accepted a call to Pittsburgh, leaving Husmann to care for the flock until Wyneken returned at the end of the summer of 1843. Upon resuming his pastorate, Wyneken's first act was to purge from the congregation all Methodist and Reformed elements, against which he had inveighed so vehemently in Germany. His aim was to institute Lutheran formalism in worship and emphasize Lutheran doctrine in his sermons. Only like-minded Lutheran pastors were now permitted as guest preachers. Prayer meetings—a traditional part of American Lutheran church life, begun by Hoover and nurtured by Wyneken—were now discontinued, and private confession was introduced. A crucifix was installed above the altar. His former evangelical emphasis, which praised the personal experience of salvation, was now suppressed. Wyneken's membership rules—which, in 1839, defined the ideal Church member as a person of piety and morality—had not required the affirmation of doctrinal statements; now, he insisted that the Augsburg Confession and other symbolic books of historic Lutheranism be affirmed as primary standards for church membership. Where Hoover had successfully blended the smaller number of Swiss and German Reformed with the Lutheran majority, Wyneken now directed an uncompromising diatribe against all aspects of Reformed faith and practice. Finally, when he declared that all members of the Reformed tradition who held to the Heidelberg Catechism were excluded from Holy Communion, seventy parishioners determined to form their own congregation. They requested that the church council allow them to worship temporarily in the church facility they had helped to build, but Wyneken opposed them, arguing that they were a heretical sect which Lutherans could not, in good conscience, assist. Immediately, the Presbyterians— English speaking cousins of the same Reformed heritage— offered their meetinghouse, and the German Evangelical Reformed Church of St. John was established.[63]

Besides these German and Swiss Reformed, there were other church members equally disturbed by their pastor's new zeal for old Lutheranism, especially those Pennsylvania Germans in sympathy with the traditions and style of American Lutheranism as represented by Jesse Hoover, Gettysburg Seminary, and the Synod of the West. Leading this disenchanted group was Henry Rudisill who, as the acknowledged leader of the German community, had kept the majority of the congregation loyal to its absent pastor. As Wyneken

was without other like-minded clergy to support his position, he invited the Synod of the West to meet in Fort Wayne in October 1844.[64] He then prompted Rudisill to bring charges against him, hoping by this strategy to have the Synod convert to his position and affirm his theology. After Rudisill and others of the Fort Wayne congregation presented their objections, Wyneken mounted his defense in a two-hour speech, first in German and then in English. The Synod took no action and no American-born Lutheran minister was converted to Wyneken's position.[65]

These were not Wyneken's only critics, however. Methodists were also aroused by the pamphlet he had published in Germany condemning revivalism in general and Methodists in specific. Their counterattack was in a pamphlet whose title asked Wyneken, "Why Have You Become an Apostate?" They accused him of being a Romanist, a Jesuit in disguise by creating an inquisition—a serious charge at that time, when American nativism was doubly suspicious of foreign subversion. In Fort Wayne, the Bethel German Methodist Episcopal Church, which had been organized just before Wyneken had left for Germany, flourished amid this controversy and soon built a brick meetinghouse on Harrison Street.[66]

In December 1844, Wyneken suddenly resigned his Fort Wayne pastorate to accept the call of St. Paul's Lutheran Church in Baltimore to occupy the same pulpit in which he had preached his first sermon in America, seven years before. His inaugural message in Baltimore was the same as he had preached in Fort Wayne upon his return from Germany: he ordered the immediate elimination of all Reformed elements and denied communion to those who would not conform; immediately eighty members walked out to organize a Reformed church. Because he wore a black cassock and made the sign of the cross, other Lutheran pastors in that city called him an "Alt-Lutheraner" and a Jesuit who would lead the church back to the pope. Then, when he attacked fraternal lodges—the Red Men, Odd Fellows, and Masons—more of his congregation departed to find a more congenial pastor. The church, however, flourished by attracting those German Lutherans who appreciated the distinctive character of their confessional and liturgical heritage.[67]

Wilhelm Sihler Elected Pastor

Before Wyneken left for Baltimore, he had recommended as his successor the Reverend Wilhelm Sihler, who had come from Germany the previous year to Pomeroy, Ohio. Born in 1801, the son of a Prussian army officer, Sihler had entered military service at fifteen and later attended the War College in Berlin. After resigning his commission, he attended the University of Berlin and became a zealous exponent of German nationalism and confessional

Lutheranism. Sihler became convinced that the Lutheran Church was the only true church of God, and said that his

Wilhelm Sihler
[Courtesy of St. Paul's Lutheran Church]

studies of the symbolical books of Lutheranism aroused in him a hatred for Catholicism and a contempt for church union. He was categorically opposed to the Prussian Union of 1817, by which Friedrich Wilhelm III had combined the Lutheran and Reformed into one state church. In 1843, he read Wyneken's pamphlet, *The Distress of the German Lutherans in North America,* and felt its urgent plea to be God's call for his service in America. His decision was in no way romantic, but religious; he later confessed he had no interest in the American people and had no sympathy for their political order, as he believed that the leaders of the American revolution were criminals in the sight of God, and that the Declaration of Independence was a misguided product of deistic rationalism.[68]

In Pomeroy, Sihler succeeded in driving out the Reformed element from his congregation of miners and farmers, and firmly established confessional Lutheranism. In Fort Wayne, as his predecessor had already cleaned house, Sihler had no initial problems, except for language: Wyneken had been fluent in low German, but Sihler, as a Silesian, was unable to converse in the dialects of the Westphalians and Hannoverians, who made up three-fourths of the congregation.[69]

A Seminary and a Synod is Founded

The new pastor arrived in Fort Wayne on July 15, 1845, and relieved Friedrich W. Husmann, who had served the congregation during the interim.[70] As a bachelor, Sihler took quarters in the parsonage with two students Wyneken had been training for frontier missionary service.[71] He enthusiastically embraced the cause of educating missionaries and, in 1846, his correspondence with Pastor Löhe in Neuendettelsau resulted in the transplanting of his practical seminary for emergency helpers (Nothelfers) from Bavaria to Fort Wayne. Löhe realized that Sihler had the best education of any of the German Lutheran pastors he knew in America,[72] and that Fort Wayne was well situated to both the Indian mission field and the developing western areas.[73] A four-room house was rented as a dormitory for the first eleven students and their tutor;[74] instruction was held in the three-room parsonage. Sihler served as administrator of the school and taught as he was able. In the first nine years of its existence, only one student was American-born; eighty-eight students came from Germany, of which seventy-two successfully completed the course of study and entered the ministry or became parish teachers.[75]

Sihler had kept in close contact with other Old Lutherans, and journeyed to St. Louis in May 1846 to meet with the Reverend C. F. W. Walther and others to discuss the creation of a conservative synod. At the meeting, the Reverend J. Adam Ernst suggested that Sihler consider for marriage a young woman of his congregation, "fit to be a pastor's wife, of Christian mind, of good understanding and a 'soft quiet spirit'—very homeloving and used to work." At the conclusion of the conference, Sihler journeyed with his matchmaker by canal boat and coach to Neuendettelsau, Ohio, and was taken to meet seventeen-year-old Susanna Kern at her parents' farm. When she came in from the fields, Sihler expressed his satisfaction—although he later said that "she would hardly have inspired an artist." He immediately proposed marriage and then arranged for their wedding on the following day. In spite of an age difference of twenty-seven years, the match was a good one; a few years later, on his fiftieth birthday, Sihler wrote, "My deeply, beloved, darling Susanna! . . . You are the one whom the true and merciful God . . . has joined unto me as my dear, faithful partner—friend, mother, and governess of our children—the sweetest sister in Christ, a nurse, a comforter, and an intercessor."[76]

Within a week, the newlyweds were back in Fort Wayne. Sihler immediately convened a meeting of the congregation and persuaded them to leave the Synod of the West and adopt the new Evangelical Lutheran Constitution as proposed at the St. Louis meeting.[77] Sihler then made preparations for an historic meeting of sympathetic German-born clergy to be held at Fort Wayne in July.[78] Friedrich W. Husmann, who was then serving three congregations south of Fort Wayne[79]

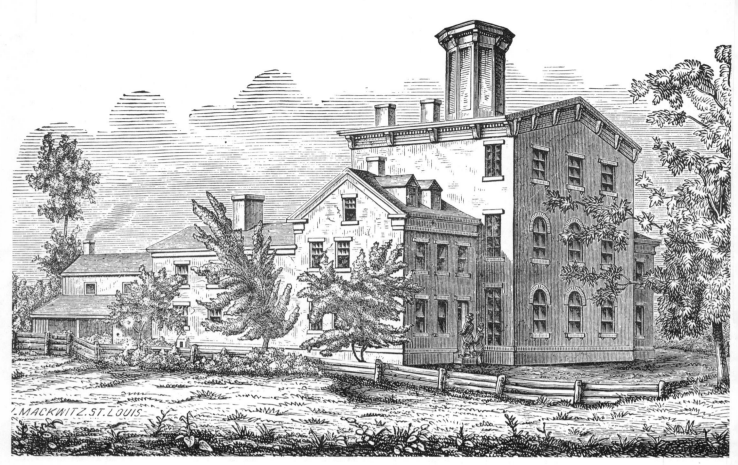

The German Lutheran Seminary
[Reprinted from G. E. Hageman, *Friedrich Konrad Dietrich Wyneken*, 1926, p. 46]

as a licentiate of the Pennsylvania Ministerium, decided to attend, and was sharply questioned by the assembled pastors on the orthodoxy of his beliefs. He noted in his diary: "On Monday, July 6, I rode to Fort Wayne to attend the Pastoral Conference there. Pastors had arrived from various areas. Pastor Walther from St. Louis served as chairman. When upon being asked, I gave the explanation that I was a licensed candidate of the German Evangelical Lutheran Ministerium of Pennsylvania, and that I had come only in this capacity to participate in this conference. Some objections were raised, in particular because the conference seemed to have doubts about the orthodoxy of that Ministerium. Finally I was accepted as an advisory member."[80]

A basic doctrinal formula was agreed upon, which led, the next year, to the formal organization in Chicago of the "German Evangelical Lutheran Synod of Missouri, Ohio, and Other States," with Sihler as vice-president. In 1849, this newest Lutheran denomination in America, dedicated to preserving the Old Lutheranism of Germany, held its third annual assembly in Fort Wayne and officially received Löhe's seminary into their Synod. In transferring his school, Löhe stipulated that "the sole medium of instruction in the

seminary be, and unalterably remain, the German language."[81]

The English Lutherans Withdraw

Soon after he had arrived in America, Sihler had broken with the Ohio Synod, partly over the issue of language. His cultural chauvinism had put him in the forefront of an effort to make German the sole language of theological instruction in American Lutheran seminaries. He failed in Ohio, but never compromised his conviction that Lutheranism needed no other vocabulary than Luther's. He was determined that only the German language and literature should prevail among his countrymen in America, until they developed their own German-American literature. His unwillingness to allow English in the church and school in Fort Wayne[82] soon caused the second splintering of the congregation. Pennsylvania-born Henry Rudisill was the leader of those members who wanted more English for their children. Failing to convince Sihler that the model of bilingual instruction instituted ten years before by Jesse Hoover was best for the

112

development of their children, the group withdrew and, on March 22, 1846, formed the English Lutheran Church of the Holy Trinity.[83]

The Rudisill gristmill fronted on the present Spy Run Avenue.
[Drawing by B. F. Griswold, 1917]

On that same day, an English language service was being conducted at the recently established St. Paul Lutheran Church in Marion Township, a few miles south of Fort Wayne. Husmann, the organizing pastor of this congregation, wrote: "After my sermon, there was an English service by the Honorable Albach, licensed candidate of the English Evangelical Lutheran District of the Synod of Ohio, who has been stationed in Fort Wayne since November of last year, and previously preached in this church three times."[84] This newly arrived clergyman was J. William Albaugh (he had anglicized his name after arriving from Germany as a youth), a graduate of Pennsylvania College, Gettysburg, in 1841 and Gettysburg Seminary the following year. In 1845, he was licensed—although not ordained—as a missionary by the English District of the Joint Synod of Ohio and posted to Butler, Indiana (thirty miles north of Fort Wayne). From here he itinerated to the surrounding communities of English-speaking Lutherans in the upper Maumee and Wabash River valleys, a circuit of more than a hundred miles from Defiance County, Ohio, to Wabash County, Indiana. In November 1845, he moved to make Fort Wayne the hub of his mission, and was soon invited to teach English at the seminary.[85]

It is possible that Rudisill himself, when he perceived that Sihler was incapable of preaching or teaching in English, had petitioned the Synod to establish an English language mission in the area; no doubt he expected that, when Albaugh was in Fort Wayne, he would preach in the Lutheran Church at a time scheduled by the pastor. Sihler,

however, had already broken with the Ohio Synod over the language issue and was increasingly critical of the practices of the American Lutheran Church and seems to have been unwilling to arrange for the Synod's English missionary to conduct services in his church. Sihler's inflexiblity created the immediate need for an alternate place of worship for English services, and precipitated Rudisill's decision to separate from St. Paul's.

This parting from the German congregation—unlike the experience of the Reformed—was, on the surface, amicable: preliminary meetings of the English Lutherans were held at the Barr Street church and the German congregation voted some financial assistance.[86] Rudisill was a diplomat and had no interest in alienating any of the many Germans who patronized his mills and supported his leadership in the Democratic party,[87] and Sihler knew that, if he attacked Rudisill, he would split his congregation. (Years later Rudisill would be fondly remembered by the oldest German Lutherans as one who always had "an open heart and an open hand" for needy immigrants.)[88] There was, however, more to the separation than language. Rudisill had supported Wyneken for as long as Wyneken remained sympathetic with the American Lutheran Church, but when Wyneken returned from Germany determined to bring the Fort Wayne congregation into the Old Lutheran fold, Rudisill publicly opposed him.[89] Also, Wyneken's and Sihler's new orthodoxy had led them to oppose membership in fraternal orders, and Rudisill—who had joined the Free and Accepted Masons in Ohio many years before—had been a member of the local Wayne Lodge No. 25 since January 1830.[90] The issues of doctrine, liturgy, and language were substantial; if Sihler was determined to turn his congregation back to sixteenth-century German Lutheranism, Rudisill was equally determined to restore his remnant to nineteenth-century American Lutheranism.[91]

English Lutherans Buy the Presbyterian Meetinghouse

At the English congregation's initial meeting, "a formula for discipline was read, which—after some amendments by a committee appointed to examine it—was, during the following weeks, signed by a number of brethren." These charter members then gathered on April 19 to elect Samuel Cutshall and Emanuel Rudisill, elders, and Henry Rudisill and Charles Ruch, deacons; after their induction into office, the new officers convened as a church council, elected Rudisill as president, and directed him to head a committee "to inquire on what terms the Presbyterian Church or a vacant lot can be purchased."[92] This forty-foot square frame church had special memories for these English Lutherans, for it was here that their founding pastor, Jesse Hoover, preached each Sunday during his twelve months as interim minister for the Presbyterians. Negotiations with the Presbyterians, who had already laid the cornerstone for a larger brick facility, proceeded swiftly and, on the first of August, an agreement between the two boards was effected. The Presbyterian trustees agreed to sell the building and bell,[93] pulpit and pews (everything except the stoves, lamps and blinds) for the sum of eight hundred dollars, of which three hundred dollars was to be paid in twenty-five hundred feet of hewed timber, and one hundred dollars to be paid in hay, flour, cordwood, and lumber in black walnut, poplar and oak. The Lutheran officers then gave their personal notes for the four hundred dollar balance, of which half was payable January 1848 and the remainder a year later.[94] In turn, the Presbyterians granted the English Lutherans the "use of the church for public worship from three 'till five o'clock on Sabbath afternoons and at such other times as will not interfere with the exercises of our own congregation."[95]

On August 2, the day after the church council concluded the purchase agreement, the congregation elected J. William Albaugh as its pastor. Most likely, Albaugh was expected by his district to continue serving the other English Lutherans in his three-county mission field, so that the Fort Wayne congregation could only expect Sunday preaching once every three to six weeks.[96] This circuit-rider system, which was successful in keeping scattered communities of faith alive, was handicapped in nourishing these groups into self-sustaining congregations. Fort Wayne Methodists, whose congregation had been founded by circuit-riders, eagerly abandoned their participation in the itinerant ministry in 1837 by securing a resident pastor; and the American Home Missionary Society—which had supported both Hoover and Wyneken—did not allow its missionaries to dilute their energies in far-flung fields, believing that permanent congregations were best established by resident ministers. The wisdom of the Society's policy was demonstrated by Fort Wayne's English Lutherans: without a resident pastor and unable to gather regularly for services, they were hard pressed to attract many new members.

During 1847, the embryonic parish added eight communicants to its fellowship, about half of whom were products of the pastor's confirmation class, lifting the total membership to twenty-five—of whom eleven were Rudisills. By mid-1848, however, the congregation's growth stalled, and no additional members joined the church during the next two years. Curiously, the Allen County marriage records show that Albaugh officiated at no weddings in the area after April 1848; and when Henry Rudisill's daughters, Martha and Elizabeth, planned their weddings for September and December 1849 respectively, the family requested the Reverend J. G. Riheldaffer, minister of the First Presbyterian Church to officiate on both occasions.[97] Possibly, as Albaugh developed new preaching stations, the established missions were, of necessity, visited less often. By any measure, the church was not active, and the local newspapers—which regularly announced the special activities of Catholics, Pres-

byterians, Methodists, Baptists, and Episcopalians—made no mention of Trinity English Lutheran Church during the decade of the forties. The congregation, however, kept its identity, worshipped as it was able, and maintained its meeting house.

Alexander S. Bartholomew
[Courtesy of Archives of the Evangelical Lutheran Church in America]

The Pastorates of Bartholomew and Ruthrauff

In 1849, the district finally ordained Albaugh, who, at the end of the year, resigned to accept the pastorate of Trinity Lutheran Church in Carrollton, Ohio.[98] The Ohio District next sent to its English-mission field twenty-five-year-old Alexander S. Bartholomew. The newly licensed candidate for ordination arrived in Fort Wayne in the fall of 1850 with his wife Sarah and son William, and was duly elected pastor of the congregation on November 4.[99] Two married couples then presented themselves for membership and requested baptism for their children—six in one family and ten in the other. Bartholomew soon announced a confirmation class for girls, and in September, nine confirmands joined the congregation. His labors at other preaching points were equally fruitful, and in February 1851, he organized the Zion Evangelical Lutheran Church at Walnut Ridge in Springfield Township. Then, in 1855, the English District, which supported the Fort Wayne mission, seceded from the Joint Synod of Ohio.[100] Bartholomew remained loyal to the mother synod but funding for his work was disrupted, and, on April 28, 1856, he resigned.[101] His ministry at Fort Wayne had encouraged congregational growth and, at the time he left, the English Lutherans had more than doubled their membership.

The church council next turned to the newly organized Evangelical Lutheran Synod of Northern Indiana for assisance. At the synod's second convention at Albion in September 1856, it was resolved to "sustain, in part at least, a missionary in Ft. Wayne, Indiana . . . [and] recommend Rev. D. Smith as a suitable person to take charge. . . [with] entire confidence in [his] prudence, zeal, and fidelity."[102] Smith was an enthusiastic proponent of the revivalistic spirit—then growing among American Lutherans—and reported that at his revivals, "Sinners have been converted, and Christians revived and encouraged."[103] This embryonic synod, with only nine ministers and four licentiates, did not itself have the two hundred dollars to fund the Fort Wayne mission and therefore made its resolution contingent upon support from the Home Missionary Society of the General Synod. These good intentions, however, did not bear fruit, and so, without pastoral leadership, the Fort Wayne congregation during the following three years became dormant. When a local newspaper published a "Directory of Churches" in 1858, it noted that the English Lutherans had "no settled pastor" and listed no schedule of Sunday worship;[104] the parish record book also reveals that no elections for church officers were held in 1857 through 1859. When Henry Rudisill died in February 1858, the family again turned to the Presbyterians and the Reverend John M. Lowrie conducted the funeral service.

The English Lutherans were not the only Protestants in Fort Wayne without a pastor, and the empty pulpits prompted a local poet to comment:

Our city has been styled the city of churches,
But now, alas! we are left in the lurches.
Houses of worship, we have a full dozen;
Why haven't we pastors? We can tell the reason.
The "devil" thinks piety's at a discount,
When of *l'argent* the churches can't raise the
    amount
To get a fine preacher from some eastern city
That'll fill all the pews, "'cause he's pretty and
witty."[105]

Finally, in early 1859, the Reverend William Patton Ruthrauff "was induced to take charge of [the] mission at Fort Wayne."[106] The new pastor was a native of Green Castle, Pennsylvania, attended Pennsylvania College, Gettysburg, and was graduated with honors from Jefferson College, Canonsburg; for the previous six years he had served the "Evangelical Congregation" (later Holy Trinity) in Canton, Ohio.

Ruthrauff was the congregation's first full-time, ordained minister with previous pastoral experience, and Fort Wayne quickly became aware of his presence. Upon his arrival the local newspapers announced: "Rev. W. P. Ruthrauff will preach his introductory sermon in the English Lutheran Church of this city on Sabbath next: 'Ministerial Responsibility,' 10:30 a. m.; 'Duties of the Church to the Ministry,' 2:30 p. m."[107] Not long afterwards, he addressed a letter to St. Paul's Church suggesting they cooperate as sister Lutheran congregations; the German congregation considered the matter at a voter's meeting and resolved that "Trinity English Lutheran Church was not a sister congregation."[108]

The English-speaking Protestant churches in town, however, felt otherwise, and Ruthrauff was invited to deliver the message at their annual community Thanksgiving Day service. John W. Dawson, a local editor, publicly fretted about the sort of sermon which might be preached in the wake of John Brown's recent attack at Harper's Ferry: "Tomorrow is Thanksgiving Day in many of the northern states and, as there are many fanatics among those who preach the Gospel, it would astonish the world if the prayers to be offered up in crazy sympathy for the treason of John Brown could be all told. Verily, *treason* has a daintiness for bigots . . . . These prayers will be regretted ere ten years roll around."[109] Few Lutheran ministers were in the vanguard of the abolitionist movement, and Ruthrauff was no exception.[110] His Thanksgiving message, which was expected to touch on some aspect of national morality, pleased Dawson who reported that the Lutheran preacher "delivered . . . a practical discourse on the demagogical aspect of our times."[111]

Ruthrauff was ambitious for his new congregation and led them to envision a future parsonage, a church library, and eventually a new church building. All of this required ambitious fund raising, and the English Lutherans, who had for years supported other church's fairs and suppers, now mounted their own effort, a Christmas Festival. By mid-December 1859, the local newspapers carried the parish's advertisements for a "Kris-Kindel Festival" at Colerick's Hall "at which those devoted friends of the little folks— Santa Claus and Kriss Kringle—will be in attendance. The hall will be illuminated and decorated with evergreens and Christmas trees . . . with music, singing, etc."[112] The event produced $150 for the parsonage fund; then, two months later, the proceeds from a public "lecture on Jerusalem . . . by the Rev. D. Gaver [were] devoted to the purchase of a library for the English Evangelical Lutheran Church."[113]

In the summer of 1860, Ruthrauff was named chairman of the community Fourth of July Sunday School Celebration. When it was decided to dispense with the usual parade to the picnic grove and engage omnibuses with a five cent fare, Peter Bailey, a prominent Episcopal vestryman, objected: "A Fourth of July celebration without a procession is like an American flag without stars."[114]

By Easter 1861, Ruthrauff had doubled the size of the congregation, with the addition of sixty new members.[115] As a result, the parish was soon making plans to build a larger church; a lot on the southeast corner of Wayne and Clinton streets was purchased, the cornerstone for the Gothic-style brick structure was laid on July 29, 1863, and the edifice was dedicated eight months later. In a few short years, the English Lutherans had vigorously responded to Ruthrauff's leadership and transformed their identity from a part-time, family congregation to a mainstream American Lutheran Church, capable of ministering to both the increasing number of its eastern adherents moving into the area, as well as to a new generation of young people who were leaving the German Lutheran Churches for an English-speaking congregation.[116]

Trinity English Lutheran Church (second building) at Wayne and Clinton streets, was dedicated in 1864.
[Courtesy of Allen County Public Library]

St. Paul's: A New Name and a New Church

Three days after the English Lutherans had first gathered to choose a name for their new congregation, Sihler's trustees met to devise a new title for their now all-German parish, and legally changed its designation to the German Evangelical Lutheran St. Paul's Church *(Der Deutsche Evangelische-*

Lutherische St. Pauls-Gemeinde).[117] The issue of language continued to be contentious in all German speaking congregations, until America's declaration of war on Germany in 1917 made the public use of German instantly unpopular. By 1848, five German speaking congregations had been established in Fort Wayne: Lutheran, Catholic, Methodist, Reformed, and Jewish. Those congregations which insisted on speaking only German in church and school became increasingly dependent on new arrivals from abroad to fill the empty pews vacated by those young people who had departed to join English speaking congregations.[118] In the 1840s, however, the arrivals far outstripped the departures,[119] so that, by the spring of 1846, the members of St. Paul's Church commenced construction on a larger facility, designed to triple their seating space. The eight-year-old chapel was moved to the rear of the church property to be converted into a school, and a new frame church, sixty-six by forty-four feet, was erected on the site. A local editor reported: "Within a few days the German Lutherans of this city have put up the frame of a large and substantial church that, we understand, is to be finished without delay. The situation of this church is decidedly the finest of any in the city, it being on the high ground in the south part of town, about midway between Calhoun and Barr streets. It will quite overlook the new First Presbyterian Church, and, from its elevated position, its spire, which is to be of a respectable height, will have an imposing appearance. We hope to see it furnished with a good bell, and we know that the enterprise and liberality that will build such a church will not be long without one."[120]

A year later, as the building neared completion, the editor noted that "the Lutherans have the tallest steeple and—when finished, we think—the largest church; but they have need of it, for they have a very large congregation."[121] St. Paul's new church bells, however, soon became a source of contention in the congregation and confusion in the community. On July 4, 1854, when some members of the congregation rang the bells to celebrate Independence Day, as was the custom in "American" congregations, they were rebuked by the pastor and church council. For three months the bell-ringing issue dominated St. Paul's congregational and council meetings, as a vocal minority defended their action as patriotic and suggested that the pastors and officers were less than American in their political sentiments. To some in the English-speaking community, such accusations reinforced a nativist suspicion of foreigners.

In the fall, Sihler and his council realized that they must make a public statement on the issue, and purchased two columns in both weekly newspapers to publish their "Vindication of the German Lutheran Church of Fort Wayne." Before making their defense, they acknowledged that "misunderstandings of some members of our congregation" had led many in the community to believe that they: "Had publicly declared the government of the United States to be usurped authority and, therefore, it ought to be restored to the supremacy of the crown of Great Britain . . . . Are opposed to any celebration of the Fourth of July and have preached against it several weeks previous to the observance . . . . Preach against a republican, and in favor of a monarchal, government, and consequently against the liberty of the

St. Paul's German Evangelical Lutheran Church (second building), on Barr Street at Lewis Street, was begun in 1846.

[Courtesy of St. Paul's Lutheran Church]

country. . . . Reject the Declaration of Independence."[122]

The pastor and his council refuted each of these allegations and, in the process, made some theological observations: "Though, from a Christian point of view, we cannot consider the insurrection . . . as the good and gracious will of God," they did feel that they should accept the American Revolution, "as it was e. g. with the Germans, about fifty years ago, when God submitted them, on account of their infidelity, to the usurpation of Napoleon." They praised "the glorious freedom which the church is enjoying here," but criticized the absence of controls: "In Germany there is too much ruling, and here, too little." On the issue of bell-ringing, Sihler and his officers were understanding but adamant: "We understand that a part of our fellow-citizens were offended, because we, as a congregation, reproved certain persons, who rang the bells of our church on the Fourth of July, without authority. But Christian order required such a reprehension . . . . Those members who rang

them, or caused them to be rung, encroached upon the rights of the other members . . . in our congregation who had conscientious scruples as to whether the ringing of the bells on the Fourth of July was such an adiaphorous (indifferent) matter that either might be done or not, without sin."[123] When a few "pro-ringing" members of the congregation continued their protest in print, Sihler and his council excommunicated them.[124]

Most Fort Wayne residents believed that their German neighbors—whether Catholic, Protestant or Jewish—were good citizens. A decade before, the local German society's celebration of the Fourth had prompted a local editor to write: "The Germans here never neglect to celebrate the Fourth. The native-born citizens seldom take the trouble to get up a celebration, but content themselves . . . with a Sunday School celebration."[125] Sihler's "Vindication," however, had not convinced everyone that the German Lutherans were appropriately loyal, for, at the next celebration of the Fourth of July, one citizen noted that "some in our midst are of the opinion that they are semi-Roman [Catholic] in their views of our American Government."[126] Convinced that this judgement was unwarranted, the sympathetic resident reported to a local newspaper on the activities of the St. Paul's congregation at its 1855 Independence Day observance:

At 9 o'clock A. M. a procession was formed at their church, which marched to the German Lutheran Theological Seminary, east of the city, where a truly sumptuous feast was prepared in the beautiful grove of the institution. Suitable hymns were sung on the way, and the American flag was waved by the cooling breeze of the most pleasant Fourth we ever spent.

After the multitude was seated and an appropriate hymn sung, an excellent extempore address was delivered by the Rev. Prof. A. Crämer,[127] at the close of which a few verses more were sung, and the Sunday-school children[128] of the church, to the number of two hundred, were soon seated at the tables. . . . During the whole repast, some eight or ten students of the institution, led by Pastor Föhlinger,[129] delighted us with instrumental music. After ample justice was done to the tables, the company, in little groups, found refreshing, innocent amusement in athletic and other exercises. The agility of Pastor Föhlinger, in particular, attracted our attention.

Although we could understand but little of the German language, yet we must say, we never spent a pleasanter Fourth, nor could we wish to. Everything was done, "in decency and order."

117

The interior of St. Paul's German Evangelical Lutheran Church (second building) was finished in 1847.
[Courtesy of St. Paul's Lutheran Church]

No boxing, drunkenness, or swearing could be seen or heard.[130]

The German Lutherans were now celebrating the Fourth of July exactly as were their Methodist and Presbyterian neighbors with parades, picnics, and speeches—but omitting the customary reading of the Declaration of Independence. Most traditional German religious holidays were observed, and, in September, the people of St. Paul's Church turned out to mark the day when, three centuries before, Lutheranism was given permanent legal status in Germany. A local newspaper reported that "Wednesday the 26th [of September 1855] is the 300th anniversary of the Peace of Augsburg (Westphalia), a day regarded with peculiar interest by the German Lutheran Church in the Old and New Worlds . . . . It is the custom of the Lutheran Church to observe this day as a period of thanksgiving. There will be a service in the different congregations of the district on Tuesday morning and afternoon. And, on Wednesday, the congregations of the city and county will unite in a social festival at their college grounds near this city."[131]

The common suspicion that German Lutherans were semi-Roman Catholic was reinforced by their liturgical worship and traditional symbolism. The Old Lutheran liturgy, introduced by Wyneken in 1843, had been amplified by Sihler when the new church facility allowed a more liturgical service. When an American Lutheran from Philadelphia visited St. Paul's on a Sunday morning, he was surprised by the style of worship and reported his experience to the *Lutheran Observer*:

The edifice is a large and commodious building with galleries, and was filled with worshippers in every nook and corner. The church is surmounted by a cross. The first thing that attracted my attention on entering, was the gilt crucifix with a gilt image of Christ suspended upon it, erected in front of the pulpit; on either side was an angel and, in addition to this, a candlestick with a candle in each, resembling wax.

The minister who officiated on the occasion was, as I learned afterwards, a theological student (the regular pastor being absent). His habit consisted of a black gown, with what might, perhaps, be termed a white cravat—after the Episcopal style. He introduced the exercises by turning and bowing to the image and offering up a short invocation; then, turning round, he read the gospel of the day; turning again to the image and bowing before it, he offered up the first prayer; he then, while the congregation was singing, retired into the small apartment adjoining the altar and pulpit. . . . In a short time, he again appeared at the altar, read the epistle of the day, then again retreated into the aforementioned apartment whilst the

Christian Hochstetter
[Courtesy of St. John Evangelical Lutheran Church]

congregation sung a few verses; he then ascended the pulpit and delivered a short harangue on religious tolerance. At the close, he offered up the Lord's prayer, during which some person near the door tolled the bell, and, whilst the congregation again sung, he descended from the pulpit and disappeared in the closet, and, at the close of the hymn, once more appeared before the crucifix and the image with his back to the congregation in the attitude of prayer. On beholding these things, it occurred to me that I must have entered a Catholic Church.[132]

St. John's German Lutheran Church Formed

Not every German Lutheran who migrated to Fort Wayne was enthusiastic about this liturgy. In the early 1850s, recent emigrants from southern Germany attended St. Paul's, but resisted joining because of "the pastor's liturgical practices

A. Kleinegees
[Courtesy of St. John Evangelical Lutheran Church]

in divine worship and the strictness of church doctrine . . . . A serious controversy arose in the congregation on the subject, and, at that time, there were strong, stormy meetings."[133] The dissidents were finally given an ultimatum: join the church or leave. They left and, during summer of 1852, organized a new Lutheran congregation under the leadership of "a preacher who was a baptized Jew by the name of A. Strauss."[134] When Strauss's leadership was deemed unhelpful, a plea for an ordained minister was posted to a Pastor Barth in Calw, Germany, who nominated the Reverend Christian Hochstetter, a recent graduate of the University of Tübingen, then serving in Königen. After an exchange of letters, Hochstetter offered his services, and the membership—only able to offer a salary of $200 a year—gratefully accepted. When the time of his arrival approached in the summer of 1853, the people arranged that every canal boat docking at Fort Wayne was met, until their new pastor finally stepped ashore on August 11. Hochstetter conducted his first Sunday service in a one-story frame church, 20 by 35 feet, which the people had recently erected near the southeast corner of Van Buren and Washington streets.[135]

St. John's German Evangelical Lutheran Church (first building) was erected near the southeast corner of Van Buren and Washington Streets in 1853.
[Courtesy of St. John Evangelical Lutheran Church]

Hochstetter was kept busy with the tasks of beginning a new church: a confirmation class was organized; plans for a school were initiated and a teacher was hired; a melodeon, brought from Germany, was installed; on October 2, a constitution was adopted naming their congregation "The German Evangelical Lutheran St. John's Congregation of Fort Wayne and Vicinity"[136] *(Der Deutsche Evangelische-Lutherische St. Johannis-Gemeinde zu Fort Wayne)* ; a second church lot was purchased (adding to the $300 debt on the first lot); and, in the spring, Hochstetter traveled to Bucyrus, Ohio, to attend the meeting of the Northern District of the Synod of Ohio, and brought St. John's into its jurisdiction.

The new congregation—sometimes called the Second German Lutheran Church—attracted new members and, on Good Friday 1854, at the first service of Holy Communion, fifty-one members received the sacrament. Hochstetter's success in Fort Wayne did not go unnoticed; a year after his arrival he accepted another position, but delayed his departure until October 1, when his successor, the Reverend A. Kleinegees, was installed.

During Kleinegees's three-year pastorate, debts were paid, a parsonage was erected, and the church rules were enforced. One member who was summoned before the church council for an infraction of church discipline sent word that he would not appear before them on the appointed Sunday, stating that he intended to swear freely at the officers and could only do so in good conscience on week-days. The strict enforcement of church rules did not please

all of the members and a few left.[137] Additional dissention surfaced when no member would serve as sexton—for $20 a year —to heat the church on Sunday mornings; by default Kleinegees assumed the task, and some members complained to the synod that their preacher left the chancel during divine worship to tend the stove.

Kleinegees was sensitive to the hard feelings which still persisted in both German Lutheran congregations over the circumstances of their withdrawal. St. Paul's parishioners felt that the dissidents had partaken freely of their fellowship and sacraments, while secretly plotting to establish their own church; St. John's members felt that their concerns about the ceremonial liturgy were not heard, and that their motives were misunderstood. These old issues were now exacerbated by a migration of dissatisfied German Lutherans back and forth between the two churches. Kleinegees believed that something should be done to create harmony between the parishes and made an overture to St. Paul's. In the fall of 1854, the parent congregation considered Kleinegees letter; their first reaction was harsh, judging St. John's to be a prodigal who should repent and return: "St. Paul's cannot acknowledge this congregation to be a validly existing church; St. Paul's is willing to prove its position from the Word of God. If the aforesaid group should repent and make amends, St. Paul's would see what could be done in the mutual relations."[138] This letter was withheld, and in December the congregation voted to meet with the members of St. John's Church. Throughout 1855 representatives of the two congregations conferred; St. Paul's insisted that a reconciliation depended on St. John's confession of wrong-doing in the past and a promise to receive no St. Paul's members in the future. Finally, on March 9, 1856, an accord was signed, and the people of St. John's confessed: "We have sinned against St. Paul's Church —where at first we had been Communion guests, although later denied permission—by not asking for a formal release from the congregation (according to standard procedure), which would have

C. Baumann
[Courtesy of St. John Evangelical Lutheran Church]

allowed the congregation to accept the situation more mildly and without anger, and encouraged them to assist and take part in building a second congregation."[139] The second article stipulated that neither congregation would accept any of the other's parishioners who wished to transfer simply because "that member dislikes the confessions, ceremonies, or pastor." The accord was signed by only twenty-six of the St. John's voting members; an equal number abstained, and some of these left the church. When Kleinegees felt that his vision of harmony between the congregations was realized, he resigned his position to assume a pastorate in Freedom, Michigan, in September 1857.

During the fall and winter, St. John's was served by the Reverend A. Herzberger, who was paid two dollars for a Sunday service, out of which he was to pay his travel expenses. Then, in March 1858, the Reverend Hugo B. Kuhn arrived, and the church began to grow—both by restoring former members and attracting new emigrants—and numbered sixty male voting members by mid-summer. The increasing number of children in the parish challenged

St. John's limited facilities, as the pastor was now teaching some of the students in his study. As St. Paul's parish school was also in need of more space, the officers of St. John's offered to donate their church building to be used for a joint schoolhouse, if the money that St. Paul's was planning to spend for a new school was given to St. John's to build a new church. St. Paul's was unenthusiastic, and St. John's then made plans to erect its own school.

St. John's German Evangelical Lutheran Church (second building) was dedicated in 1862.
[Courtesy of St. John Evangelical Lutheran Church]

In early 1859, relations between the two churches became more fragile when the year-old protocol restricting membership migration was rescinded by the smaller congregation. Probably, St. John's felt it could not afford to turn away new members; publicly it stated that they did not wish any persons to attend the "cold, unceremonial service at St. John's if they do not like it," and that such a policy was contrary to the rules of the synod.[140] Relations with the Ohio Synod, however, had also deteriorated and, in August of that year, St. John's left its jurisdiction.

When Kuhn resigned in the fall of 1860, the congregation sought a new pastor from the Pittsburgh Synod (General Council), to which it had applied for membership. On April 12, 1861, the Reverend C. Baumann was installed as pastor; immediately he led the people in the building of a new church. The brick edifice, dedicated in October 1862, was of a simple Georgian style, measuring fifty by eighty feet, with a steeple topped by an angelic weathervane.

With a new church building, St. John's finally emerged from a decade of growing pains to became a viable German Lutheran congregation—somewhat closer to the American

121

Protestant mainstream than St. Paul's. As the third German-heritage congregation to break away from St. Paul's Church (along with St. John's German Reformed and Trinity English Lutheran) it presented a moderate theological position, a modest liturgy, while preserving German language and culture—and thereby attracted many German Lutheran immigrants.

Wilhelm Sihler Continues at St. Paul's

Pastor Sihler and most of the St. Paul's congregation were unfazed by these developments. Now that the dissidents had left, the parish was more at peace to preserve its confessional posture, high liturgy, and German language, in fellowship with other congregations of their synod. In such matters as church discipline and dogmatics, parish organization, and school development, Sihler was a strong and fearless leader. As synod vice-president and Central District president, he visited numerous congregations, exercising a "rather rigid supervision." His style in questioning congregations and pastors bordered on the inquisitorial, requiring ministers to submit their most recent sermons for examination. In his biography, Sihler implies that every effort was made not to hurt the pastor or teacher who was being visited, but a "responsible elderly churchman" in Fort Wayne reported that Sihler was "particularly outspoken when he visited the schools. The teacher's work was bitterly criticized in the presence of the children."[141]

Sihler did not possess his predecessor's personal charm or pulpit eloquence; by his own admission, he lacked Wyneken's "gift to touch the heart and soul" and his sermons were usually didactic and dogmatic.[142] He preached as he believed, and declared: "Pretty sermons and illustrations, shining fireworks and impressions are no substitute for God's Word."[143] Much of his preaching was "against" something: "Against Life Insurance," "Against the Dance," "Against the Lodges," "Against Drunkenness," "God's Purpose in the Chicago Fire."[144]

As a father, Sihler always commanded his children and never requested them; he forced his unwilling and tearful eighteen-year-old daughter, Marie, to marry a widower with several children.[145] He had strong ideas of male preeminence and believed in that form of democracy where only male adults were permitted to vote in congregational meetings. During worship, men and women were required to sit in segregated parts of the church. Sihler went so far as to forbid young men from escorting young women to church, so that it became customary for unmarried couples to walk together to within a few blocks of the church and then go apart to enter separately.

All this occurred during the era which saw the emergence of the woman's rights movement in America. In 1847, local Presbyterians had affirmed the right of women to vote at congregational meetings, and Fort Wayne Methodists were establishing a college for women—but Sihler would have none of it. He condemned women who were studying for professions at Ann Arbor,[146] just as he excoriated the "modern women who, instead of rearing children, sit in a rocker, play a little piano, embroider, read a light novel—preferably romance—sing love songs, chat with frivolous girl friends about dress, games, young men, concerts or theater and cosmetics. Their first idolatry is primping and slaving to fashions."[147]

Just as he dismissed the woman's rights movement as misguided and dangerous, Sihler also attacked the abolitionist movement as unscriptural. His views paralleled those of C. W. F. Walther, then the president of the Synod, who had adopted a states' rights position (which he said was analogous to the German federation of states) and supported the right of settlers to establish slavery in the new territories in the West. Walther tried to be discreet in his support of slaveholding, but Sihler boldly attacked the abolitionists and published four articles in *Der Lutheraner*, stoutly defending slavery as warranted by the Scriptures.[148] Both Walther and Sihler were sympathetic with the political ideology of the Democratic party,[149] and Walther compared what he called the "Republican rabble" of Abraham Lincoln's party to the political liberals and social radicals of the German revolution of 1848. As a result, the "forty-eighters"—those Germans who fled to America after their unsuccessful uprising for democratic government—did not find a congenial home in the Missouri Synod or feel welcomed by Wilhelm Sihler. A few settled in Fort Wayne and, in 1849, the local German Society dedicated their Fourth of July celebration to the revolutionaries, whose democratic and romantic ideals had caught the imagination of many admiring Americans.[150] Sihler, however, was so outraged by the extreme views of a few German radicals, that he judged all of the forty-eighters to be agents of the devil—and expressed his strong feelings in the Fort Wayne newspapers:

> Since the year 1848 . . . Germans emigrate to this country. . . who are imbued with the most infidel, immoral and anarchal principles of the mad European revolutionists; and those demagogues are carrying on their machinations against legitimate authority and social order in language which very few of our fellow-citizens would read without shuddering.

> They promulgate a dissolute liberty and push democracy to extreme radicalism. Some of their journals are the vilest that can be imagined, and some of their association avow doctrines the most horrible . . . . They not only deny God, but also declare themselves openly, in the most hostile and malicious manner, against every moral prin-

Wilhelm Sihler poses with students at the parish school
[Courtesy of St. Paul's Lutheran Church]

ciple of the civil commonwealth, and carry on their war against the peace of nations and social order to an alarming extent.

For instance, they contend against the right of marriage, against the possession of personal property, against the government that protects our persons and property, and in general against all discipline, morals and due subordination to authority and law, and would be willing to establish—through the influence of their father, the devil—a red republic in which they would be the blood-tyrants and terrorists according to the example of a Danton, Marat and Robespierre.[151]

Sihler never sidestepped the controversial issues, but, with his reflexive conservatism, he could never ally himself with the crusading movements of social reform. He tended to romanticize the past and see modern political and social change to be portents of a dark future. More than most immigrant pastors, Sihler was suspicious of American culture and declared: "[T]his land is confessedly a land of humbugs, in many respects a large house of fools with only the roof missing."[152]

Sihler was not, however, without social sympathies; his many private charities revealed a genuine concern for ministering to human need. He wrote with moral earnestness on many questions of political and ethical philosophy and was eager to mold public opinion,[153] but, for all of his energy and organizing abilities, he was predictably conservative and

consistently negative, regularly coming down on the losing side of many issues. As a churchman, he was a phenomenal organizer; as a battler for Old Lutheranism, he was one of the most polemic of his generation, attacking his perceived enemies with a passion that could seldom be ignored.

When he resigned his pastorate in 1885, he wrote to the congregation from a sickbed: "It is because of God's grace that I can assure you with good conscience that, in all those [forty] years, I never had in mind to gain money, honor, or a life of pleasure through you. But, instead of that, I had in mind God's glory and your eternal salvation through my whole ministry.... I ask every one of you, whom I may have insulted with words in years gone by, for forgiveness from the bottom of my heart, in Christ's name." Pastor Sauer remembered Sihler as a man who "carried, under an external rough shell, the sweet core of a heart full of love for his whole congregation."[154]

Fort Wayne's first Lutheran leaders, Henry Rudisill and Jesse Hoover, had hoped to create on the western frontier an inclusive and broad-based congregation of German-speaking Protestants who would gradually incorporate English into their church life. Friedrich Wyneken, however, eventually supplanted this native Lutheranism with an infusion of old world orthodoxy, liturgy, and language. Wilhelm Sihler, in turn, carefully cultivated Wyneken's theological seedbed and diligently weeded out any threatening incursions of American culture, laboring long and hard for the cause of Old Lutheranism in the Missouri Synod. As a result of a sustained zeal for missionary education, confessional theology, liturgical formalism, and the German language, St.

Paul's Church and the German Lutheran Seminary achieved national prominence for its contributions to conservative Lutheran churchmanship.

Wilhelm Sihler, in His Later Years
[Courtesy of St. Paul's Lutheran Church]

Jesse Hoover's plaint, however, was prophetic: there were many "difficulties" in ministering to people "from every part of Germany. . . with different prejudices and apprehensions," and no leader found it possible to "mold this heterogeneous mass into one harmonious church."[155] In a dozen years after its founding, the First Evangelical Lutheran Church of Fort Wayne had divided into four congregations: St. John's German Reformed; St. Paul's German Lutheran, Missouri Synod; Trinity English Lutheran; and St. John's German Lutheran, Ohio Synod. Each new congregation was created in response to larger issues of theology, liturgy, language, and tradition which were developing in America and Germany—issues which continued to be significant to many Lutherans into the twentieth century.

6
Baptists

"There is in the non-slaveholding states a large society of the so called regular Baptists, who . . . disown slavery and all its Heaven-daring practices."
Daniel W. Burroughs, 1855

The first Protestant church to be established in Indiana was Baptist, and the first Protestant clergyman to visit Fort Wayne was of this pioneer denomination.[1] This early presence, however, lacked permanence, and Fort Wayne Baptists were relatively slow in developing a viable church fellowship.

The Early Visitors

When General Anthony Wayne and his army of 3,500 arrived at the headwaters of the Maumee in 1794, they were accompanied by their Baptist chaplain, the Reverend David Jones.[2] Twenty years earlier Jones had embarked on a largely unsuccessful mission to the Shawnee and Delaware Indians in the Northwest Territory; during the Revolutionary War he had served for four years as a chaplain under Wayne. Then, in 1794, when Wayne was ordered into the Northwest Territory against the Indians, he requested that Jones again serve as his chaplain. When the army arrived at the site of the the future Fort Wayne, one of Wayne's officers, Capt. John Cooke, noted in his diary that on Sunday, September 21, "We attended divine service. The sermon was delivered by Rev. David Jones, chaplain. Mr. Jones chose for his text, Romans 8:31: 'But what shall we then say to these things? If God is for us, who can be against us?' This was the first time the army had been called together for the purpose of attending divine service since I joined it." Attendance at Sunday worship in Wayne's army does not appear to have been a matter of choice; Cooke wrote that, when the

commander determined to hold a service, the troops were ordered to assemble, and stood in formation: "At ten o'clock the church call was beat. The troops fell in and marched by platoons out of the square to the front of the garrison, where a discourse on Romans 13:1 was delivered by Mr. Jones, chaplain."[3] These were the first English-speaking religious services to be conducted in the area, as well as the first by a Protestant minister.

The presence of a Baptist missionary in Fort Wayne between 1820 and 1822 did little to encourage the new settlers of Baptist persuasion. Isaac McCoy's energies were focused on the needs of the Indians, and the French and American residents were not invited to affiliate with his fledgling congregation. During the next fifteen years, local Baptists attended whatever Protestant services were available; in 1829, the new Presbyterian pastor reported that there were, among the local residents, "a few Baptists, all of whom are very friendly to me and constantly attend my preaching."[4] Baptists continued to worship with the Presbyterian congregation after its formal organization in 1831; one settler later recalled: "Presbyterians, Methodists, and Baptists worshipped together, their respective ministers preaching on alternate Sabbaths."[5]

A Plea for a Preacher

It was not until the mid-1830s that Fort Wayne Baptists could persuade a preacher of their denomination to visit the area. When Indiana Baptists created a state-wide General Association in 1833, local Baptists immediately petitioned its president, Jesse L. Holman, to direct a preacher to the three rivers area. Holman had served as a judge of the Indiana Supreme Court and was an ardent abolitionist and hardworking churchman. In 1830, he was elected a vice president of the American Sunday School Union; the fol-

David Jones
[Courtesy of Franklin College Library]

lowing year he organized an Indiana Bible Society; three years later he was ordained to the Baptist ministry. Holman occasionally visited Fort Wayne where his daughter, Emerine (Mrs. Allen Hamilton) was active in the Presbyterian congregation. The hope of the Fort Wayne Baptists was that one of the seven new missionaries recently sent to Indiana by the newly established American Baptist Home Missionary Society would make regular visits to the area.

The author of the plea to Holman was Ann Turner, one of Isaac McCoy's first Miami converts; she was fondly remembered as a lady "of refinement and piety"[6] and in whose home "religious service was first held here."[7] In the absence of a Baptist fellowship, Turner had become a charter member of the First Presbyterian Church in 1831, and was faithful in her participation; in her heart, however, she remained a Baptist and yearned for the arrival of a Baptist preacher in Fort Wayne. Of this hope she wrote Holman:

We rejoice that our conduct has met with your approbation; we knew the almost inseparable barrier between our own denomination and the Presbyterian Church; we did not wish to incur the displeasure of our own church, but thought, however rigid they might be, that they would, in our situation, make all the allowance that we wished.

We rejoice at the prosperity of Zion, and hope the day is dawning when the watchmen thereof shall see eye to eye. We still insist upon a Baptist preacher. Why cannot the Home Missionary Society supply us? We wish one well furnished unto every good work, a workman that needeth not to be ashamed. We wish you to make our wants known and use your influence in procuring us a minister well recommended, of known piety and talents, and some experience in the ministry. We will get what we can towards his support, but I have no idea that we can get anything like a competency. We shall be anxious to hear from you on this subject . . . . We should be glad to see you in this place . . . . Your children are well.[8]

A Congregation Is Organized

To what "inseparable barrier" and "allowance" the writer refers is difficult to ascertain, but her hope for a Baptist Home Missionary was unfulfilled. Ann Turner died the following year and there is no record of a Baptist preacher visiting Fort Wayne until 1835 and 1836 when the "Reverends Robert Tisdale, Enos French, and J. L. Moore, preached . . . occasionally."[9] Finally, in early 1837—when the Presbyterians were assembling regularly in their new meetinghouse and the Methodists were laboring to build their own facility—the local Baptists felt that it was time to organize themselves as a congregation. On January 14, under the leadership of the Reverend Robert Tisdale—a native of Virginia who had recently settled in Adams County—invitations were sent out to other Baptist clergy to gather as an ecclesiastical council at the First Presbyterian Church on Saturday, April 15, 1837, for the purpose of organizing a church in Fort Wayne. On the appointed day, with the Reverend J. L. Moore acting as moderator, assisted by Tisdale and the Reverend Eli Fry, the First Regular Baptist Church of Fort Wayne was constituted with ten members who presented letters of dismission from other Baptist churches. On the next day, at Sunday worship, the congregation heard Moore preach and then received "the right hand of fellowship" from Fry and Tisdale. Preaching services continued, and during the ensuing days the congregation gathered at a nearby riverside (or canal bank) to witness the baptism by immersion of six new converts.[10] Tisdale later reflected on this beginning in Fort Wayne: "With the exception of the labors of Elder[11] I. McCoy, missionary to the Indians for a while in Fort Wayne, I was the first Baptist minister that ever labored in this section of Indiana . . . . The country was very new, without roads or bridges, and very little feed for my horse . . . . The first church which was constituted here under my feeble efforts, was formed in Fort Wayne in 1837."[12]

Jesse L. Holman
[Courtesy of Franklin College Library]

No practice of the new congregation was as distinctive among the other churches of Fort Wayne as believer baptism by immersion. All of the churches established in Fort Wayne before 1860[13]—Presbyterian, Methodist, Catholic, Lutheran, German Reformed, and Episcopal—ordinarily administered their sacrament of baptism to infants as well as adult converts by "sprinkling"; all claiming the name Baptist, however, would administer their ordinance to believers only by immersion. The pioneer Baptists in Indiana knew nothing of baptistries inside their meeting houses; most congregations, however, knew of occasions when the ice on a mill pond was broken to conduct a baptism.

Soon after the converts were received into the new Baptist fellowship, the visiting clergy departed. The little band then met as they were able in members' homes for Sunday worship, while individual members continued to attend the union Sunday school. Occasionally, if a visiting minister was in town on Sunday, the congregation gathered to worship in the schoolhouse. In February 1837, they had written to Jesse Holman, requesting an "able minister." He suggested that they first seek financial support from the unchurched in the community; the members immediately made inquiries and reported that "several who are not members of any denomination . . . say they would be willing to support such a man, if he is liked."[14] Finally, on December 6, 1837, the Reverend William Corbin arrived in Fort Wayne, having recently served churches in Logansport and Crooked Creek. A twenty-three-year-old native of Cazenovia, New York, Corbin had been converted and baptized at the age of seventeen, and two years later was granted a licence to preach. During his one-year pastorate in Fort Wayne, he endorsed a petition initiated by the Presbyterians seeking aid for the local German Lutheran pastor, Jesse Hoover, testifying to his qualifications and great need of a German language ministry in the area.[15] A few residents responded to the young preacher's ministry and, in the cold of January and February 1838, Corbin baptized three new members into the faith. Later that year, the First Baptist Church was officially received into the Tippecanoe Baptist Association—along with two other new congregations at LaFayette and Crawfordsville—swelling the total membership of the association's eleven churches to 310.[16]

By the end of 1838, Corbin had departed.[17] Robert Tisdale, however, did not forget the spiritual needs of the congregation he had organized, and labored to arrange a "protracted meeting" for them in the early summer of 1839. Customarily, protracted meetings in most Indiana Baptist congregations were held annually and were anticipated as a high point in the congregation's spiritual life. In form, the meetings were much like regular Sunday services but extended over a number of days which heightened the emotional intensity. Penitent individuals were encouraged to discuss their religious feelings with the congregation, and, if unsatisfied with the completeness of the person's quest for salvation, the membership would continue its prayers and exhortations for the candidate. John F. Cady writes: "Withal, there was much of weeping, rejoicing, handshaking, and fellowship. Successful revivals were times long to be remembered . . . [and] became deeply embedded in the traditions of the church."[18] In order to organize a protracted meeting in Fort Wayne, Tisdale advertised the event in *The Regular Baptist Messenger*:

Adams County, Indiana, March 16, 1839
Dear Brethren: The Fort Wayne Regular Baptist Church being destitute of a pastor, and wishing to have a protracted meeting to commence on Thursday the 27th of June next, at 2 o'clock P. M., and by order of the church I am requested to take measures to engage ministers to attend; . . . I avail

myself of this method to accomplish that object.

Therefore the following Brethren are earnestly and affectionately invited to attend the above contemplated meeting; viz: J. L. Holman, William Reese, T. Hill, Jr., A. R. Hinkley, G. Minor, William Corbin, Geo. C. Chandler, William M. Pratt, and T. W. Haynes. The above time was concluded on as it will include the fifth Sunday in the month, and of course will not interfere with any regular monthly meeting.

Dear Brethren, as there is great need of ministerial aid in the above mentioned church, it is hoped that you will attend without fail; and no appointment will be published until we have the promise of ministers to attend . . . . Be sure to come prepared to continue as long as the interest of the meeting may require it.[19]

Tisdale had taken charge of the congregation beginning April 20, 1839.[20] (Most likely he maintained his residence in Adams County and visited Fort Wayne as he was able.) If his protracted meeting was ever held in Fort Wayne, it brought no converts into the church.[21] The growth of Baptist churches in Indiana during this time was impeded by several causes. The first emanated from those Baptists of strict Calvinist persuasion who argued that any attempt to convert the heathen was a denial of God's eternal election of some to eternal salvation and others to eternal damnation. The result was a vigorous campaign by some Old School Predestinarian Baptists and Primitive Baptists to frustrate any plans to send missionaries, either to the Indians or settlers.[22] These ideas, in turn, made some Baptists suspicious of any preacher who would work for money; one itinerant pastor wrote: "It is hard to be called by professed Baptists a Gospel Speculator, laboring for the fleece and not for the flock."[23] Compounding this problem was the inherent weakness of the regional associations which had little power to raise funds or to appoint missionaries; a Methodist bishop had unquestioned authority to send a minister to a new settlement, but Baptists, by conviction, were opposed to any hint of ecclesiastical authority beyond the local congregation. In addition, the Panic of 1837 precipitated a financial depression in Indiana which significantly dried up contributions to the missionary enterprise and consequently stalled church growth until after 1840.

In the late 1830s, the local German Lutheran pastor, the Reverend Friedrich Wyneken, observed another problem afflicting the Baptist community: along with the variety of Protestant persuasions was the proliferation of different Baptist societies—Separate Baptists, United Baptists, Free Will Baptists, Predestinarian Baptists, General Baptists, Regular Baptists, Particular Baptists, Primitive Baptists, Seventh Day Baptists, and German Baptists (Dunkers). He told his supporters in Germany: "How great is the number of sects in North America! . . . . An old Baptist preacher, who preached in the English-speaking neighborhood of my parish, complained bitterly to me that his listeners consisted, as far as he could count at the moment, of members of fifteen different religious communities. His predecessor, he added, had counted nineteen. And how many listeners do you think he had? They consisted of, at best, sixteen to twenty households who lived within a radius of four or five English miles."[24]

The First Resident Pastors

In 1840, the General Association in Indiana was finally able to appoint a full time agent to direct a Baptist church extension program; as a result, twenty preachers volunteered for one to three months' service that year and succeeded in organizing twelve new churches. Along with this new impetus, the Home Mission Society—besides supporting a dozen eastern missionaries in selected areas of Indiana—now offered financial assistance to "destitute" congregations. The Fort Wayne Baptists applied and, in 1841, received $150 for the partial support of the Reverend William Cox, a young licentiate who had begun his work at Fort Wayne in October 1840, and was subsequently ordained in December.[25] Along with William Corbin, Cox was a leader in forming the new Huntington Baptist Association—into which he brought his new congregation—and served as its first clerk.[26] Like his predecessors, Cox remained at Fort Wayne for a year and then moved on.

In October 1841, the Reverend William Gildersleeve was elected pastor of the church, and settled in the community with his wife and children.[27] Gildersleeve was energetic and effective; in the first six months of 1842, the membership of the congregation more than doubled when fifty members were added to the congregation—two thirds of whom received baptism. During this time, he led the congregation in adopting the New Hampshire Confession of Faith as their Articles of Faith. This statement (which had been adopted by the Huntington Association the year before) appealed to those northern Indiana congregations whose membership had New England roots; it moderated the controversial issues of election and predestination—which had so animated the ultra-Calvinistic, anti-mission Baptists in southern Indiana—and presented a clear and positive affirmation of Baptist beliefs. The congregation also adopted Rules of Decorum for their monthly meetings, as well as a Church Covenant. The Covenant declared both the purpose of their fellowship and the responsibilities of individual members:

That we will exercise a mutual care, as members

one of another, to promote the growth of the body in Christian knowledge, holiness, and comfort . . . .

That we will cheerfully contribute of our property for the support of the poor, and for the maintenance of a faithful ministry of the gospel among us . . . .

That we will . . . religiously train up our children, and those under our care, with a view to the service of the Christ and the enjoyment of heaven . . . .

That we will walk circumspectly in the world, that we may win their souls . . . .

That we will frequently exhort, and if occasion shall require, admonish one another, according to Matthew 18th, in the spirit of meekness — considering ourselves, lest we also be tempted; and that, as in baptism, we have been buried with Christ and raised again, so there is on us a special obligation thenceforth to walk in newness of life.[28]

In all congregations during this period, the financial and property matters of the congregation were normally handled by elected trustees; in the Baptist Church, however, all other affairs of the church were decided at covenant meetings, held in the meetinghouse on the first Saturday of the month. Most meetings were "opened in the usual way of singing, reading, and prayer"; then, after the "Brethren and Sisters related their feelings and the dealings of the Lord with them . . . the door of the church was opened to receive all who wished to become members." Those who "gave in" their letters from other Baptist churches would be invited to speak, and those who came as candidates for baptism were required to "relate their Christian experience." Any member could bring charges of moral transgression against another, and the meeting might be asked to "exclude" a member for "continual habits of intemperance and disorderly conduct."[29]

A Meetinghouse Is Erected

In the winter of 1841-1842, covenant meetings and Sunday worship were held in Alexander McJunkin's schoolhouse; the increased size of the congregation, as well as the rental fee, soon induced the congregation to build its own meetinghouse. Samuel Hanna (in whose store they had first met for Sunday School) was approached, and donated a lot on Clay Hill.[30] One of the first meetings in the modest frame structure was of an Ecclesiastical Council convened on Saturday, June 18, 1842, in conjunction with the congregation's annual protracted meeting, for the purpose of examining William R. Combs, a candidate for ordination. Combs, a twenty-eight-year-old native of Philadelphia, was

a licensed Baptist preacher who had united with the congregation in 1839. Ordinations were significant events in the life of a congregation, and invitations were sent to all

The First Regular Baptist Church of Fort Wayne erected its first meetinghouse on East Washington Street in 1842; six years later the building was moved to the west side of Clinton Street between Wayne and Berry streets.
[Drawing from a Description by Mrs. Robert Renfrew, Courtesy of First Baptist Church]

neighboring Baptist churches with whom they were in fellowship. In response, delegates arrived representing congregations at Concord, Huntington, Jeffersonville, and Orland, as well as New Carlisle and St. Mary's, Ohio, and Reading, Michigan. The Council elected Gildersleeve as moderator, and then "called upon Brother Combs . . . for a relation of his Christian experience, his call to the ministry, [and] his views of Biblical theology." On the next day, Sunday, the congregation gathered for worship under the leadership of the visiting clergy and, with "sermon . . . consecrating prayer . . . charge, and right hand of fellowship," Combs was ordained; he then closed the service by leading in the final hymn (without instrument or choir) and pronouncing the benediction.[31]

After his ordination, Combs was invited to preach at occasional evening services and, in the absence of the pastor, to supply the pulpit and conduct baptisms. A year later, he enrolled at the seminary at Georgetown College, Kentucky, in preparation for a life-long career in the ministry.[32] Unlike many Indiana Baptists—and most Methodists—Fort Wayne Baptists had no prejudice against an educated clergy, and were equally pleased to commend their pastor's son, William C. Gildersleeve, to the Ohio Education Society for assistance "in order to prepare for the ministry."[33] In contrast to the traditions of Presbyterians, Lutherans, Episcopalians, Reformed, and Roman Catholics—where candidates pursued their theological education before ordination—Baptists often certified a preacher's gifts and call to the ministry by ordination, and then encouraged formal education.

After a fifteen-month pastorate, Gildersleeve resigned. He was then in debt to both the congregation and individuals, and formally requested forgiveness of these financial obligations; the congregation said it could not: "that, in our embarrassed condition, duty to legal creditors of this church forbid our gratuitously assuming a debt of 75 to 100 dollars upon the request of our late pastor."[34] The church's financial embarrassment came from unpaid bills on the new meeting house and past due rent for the McJunkin schoolhouse. The congregation then resolved "that every member shall pay to the trustees of the church the sum of 371/2 cents every month to liquidate the debts on the meeting house."[35] The Baptists were not the only church in town struggling with finances at that time: the minister at First Presbyterian Church, the Reverend Alexander T. Rankin, was owed over a year's back salary and was about to resign his position for "pecuniary and domestic concerns."[36]

Church Discipline

William Combs exercised his new ministerial office during February 1843, until the arrival of the Reverend James H. Dunlap in March. Dunlap had served the Jeffersonville Baptist Church and was well known to the Fort Wayne congregation: he had assisted at their recent protracted meeting and had preached at Combs's ordination. At the Covenant meeting at which Dunlap was "called to labour with the church," the congregation also voted to exclude Mr. and Mrs. Henry Stifflebeam and her mother "for absconding and joining the Mormons."[37] There is no record of Mormon activity in Fort Wayne during this period; the local newspapers, however, were full of news about the burgeoning Latter Day Saints settlement in Nauvoo, Illinois, which, since its founding in 1839, had become the largest city in that state with a population of 20,000. Fort Wayne's first Mormon family most likely left town to join the thousands of new converts in a pilgrimage they believed was the "gathering of Israel to the Land of Zion." One local Protestant wrote that "Mormonism is, at present, increasing more rapidly, I believe, than Romanism."[38]

The exclusion of members grew to be the principal business transacted at covenant meetings during Dunlap's pastorate. As a decreasing number of new members were received, an increasing number of old members were accused of immorality or heresy: in twelve months only one person was baptized while seventeen were excluded. Typical charges were: a disorderly walk; using spirituous liquors; gambling; unchristianlike character; holding to the doctrine of the Freewill Baptists; lying; communing with other denominations; and living in adultery. Those who sought to avoid the increasingly contentious atmosphere at church were cited for non-attendance, and excluded. At a meeting in mid-1845, the clerk wrote: "Found a very unpleasant state of feeling in the Church." The Reverend Charles Beecher, minister of the Second Presbyterian Church,

declared that "the Baptists are dead."[39] These many self-inflicted wounds in the body of the church were slow to heal; years later, a member wrote: "During this period, severe trials came upon the church and serious troubles arose among the membership, which were never fully healed until death removed all parties concerned."[40] During these difficulties, Dunlap somewhat unwillingly accepted a second year's appointment, and finally escaped from his contentious congregation in the spring of 1845.

The Reverend George Sleeper, who had been pastor of the Huntington Baptist Church for the previous three years, next occupied the pulpit; after a few months with the congregation, however, he declined to continue.[41] The congregation—whose membership had dropped from 85 to 61 during the purge—was deeply discouraged and, in their annual report to the association, told of "enduring a continual scene of trials during the past year. . . . that the ways of Zion mourn because so few come up to her solemn feasts."[42]

Then, in May 1846, the congregation called the Reverend H. D. Mason[43] to the pastorate; the terms were "for compensation of three hundred dollars, if the church can raise it; if not [he] will take what they can."[44] Mason brought healing and new direction to the congregation; one member remembered that "by his earnestness, new life was infused into the work of the church and a new inspiration was given all along the line."[45] One theme which interested the new minister was Christian union, and, when serving as moderator of the annual Association meeting, he was asked to express his views in their circular letter. Some months later, he announced through the local newspapers that he would "present, in a short course of lectures, a plan of truly Catholic Union for Christians."[46] His remarks expressed the conviction that union could be achieved only through exclusion:

> The most ill-informed Romanist knows that unity is one of the characteristics of the church, and upon this, bases his strongest objection to Protestantism. The evils of divisions are apparent to all, and are deeply regretted by every Christian . . . .
>
> The principle cause of divisions in faith are the following: pharisaical formality and legality; antinomian indolence; infidel nonessentialism; hierarchical usurpation, and a blind idolatry from the people; ignorance of the word of God, and the substitution of human tradition and human wisdom; a reliance on the faith of others. Divisions in feeling are . . . to be ascribed to covetousness, sometimes to stubbornness, and often to prejudice . . . .
>
> The commands of the Gospel . . . require a perfect union of mind and judgement. The claims of God upon Christians to be thus united are also clearly

implied .... We have reason to expect this union will take place among all Christians ... and that the conversion of the world will follow this event ....

This work will be effected when the Churches of Christ shut the door against unconverted members. As this union is only to take place among believers, all others should be kept out of the church .... This will be effected when churches carry out efficiently the discipline of the Gospel, and exclude all unworthy members from their fellowship.[47]

During Mason's tenure, the congregation decided to move the meetinghouse to a more central location and secured a lot on the west side of Clinton Street between Wayne and Berry streets; then, in the summer of 1848, the frame structure was jacked up, placed on skids, and pulled by teams of horses to its new site. Charles Beecher noted the move in a report to his mission secretary: "The Baptists have obtained a more central location for their house (a small frame) which they have lately moved. Their minister, Mr. Mason, tho' strict close-communion, is otherwise kind, liberal and cooperative. Perhaps he means to proselyte me. He is quite attentive."[48]

Missions, Abolition, and Temperance

After a two-year pastorate, Mason resigned, and was followed by the Reverend S. B. Searl. Under his leadership the congregation responded to their denomination's call to assist in its world-wide mission enterprise, and resolved to "occupy the first Sabbath evening of every month [in a] concert of prayer for the heathen and those who do not enjoy the privilege of the Gospel."[49] Other issues regularly brought to the attention of the membership by their delegates to association meetings were slavery and temperance. A year before, the Huntington Association had declared:

Whereas, we consider American Slavery a great political and moral evil, endangering our very existence as a nation, and hindering the prevalence of the Gospel, therefore, Resolved, that we recommend to our brethren of this Association to give the suffering Slave a place in their sympathy and prayers; and also, that they express as far as practicable to the slave-holder their disapprobation of the sin of Slavery, relying on Divine power, by moral means alone, to overthrow this great evil.
Resolved: That the cause of Temperance is identified with the cause of Christ, that this Asso-

ciation regard the practice of manufacturing, vending, or drinking intoxicating liquors (except when prescribed as a medicine) to be a moral evil, and as such should be discountenanced by the Church.[50]

In late summer of 1848, Searl became ill and left for New York.[51] The congregation then invited the Reverend Daniel W. Burroughs to "supply the church until we can get a pastor ... at the rate of $200 dollars a year," of which only one hundred dollars was actually raised.[52] Burroughs was a forty-year-old native of Vermont, who had opened a book store in Fort Wayne; active in community affairs, he had been elected to the first city Board of Health in 1842 and soon afterwards became the town's Sealer of Weights and Measures. He was also one of the community's most vocal proponents of temperance, universal education, abolition, and equal rights. When he established a local newspaper, *The Standard,* to advocate these moral reforms, the editor of the rival *Fort Wayne Times* accused Burroughs of being "a rank abolitionist, a real amalgamationist .... He is in favor of equal rights to all mankind, which ... signifies the Negro race."[53] He was also active in the underground railroad— assisting escaped slaves on their flight to freedom—and his antislavery speeches and editorials sometimes provoked opposition. One resident remembered that "the 'egging' of his newspaper office and the murmurs of the crowd had no terrors for him."[54]

There is no record of his formal affiliation with the local Baptist church, but, as an ordained Baptist clergyman, he was an active member of the Huntington Association. In 1849, he served on the Association's committee on resolutions which declared: "That slaveholding, or holding as a slave one of the human family, is a sin against God, humanity and nature; therefore, we will in no wise countenance either, but will bear our testimony against these as against other sins."[55] Burroughs was especially sensitive to the divisions among Baptists on the issue of slavery and carefully explained to the people of Fort Wayne: "There is in the non-slaveholding states a large society of the so-called regular Baptists, who have separated themselves from ... such ... as fellowship slavery. ... They disown slavery and all its Heaven-daring practices."[56]

During Burroughs's interim pastorate, the news of the California gold strike excited the city, and, in early 1849, a newspaper reported: "The California fever is raging very severely in this place, and a large number of new cases are daily reported .... The complaint will doubtless carry off some of our best citizens."[57] One of the first to depart in the gold rush was a church trustee, A. B. Miller. Most Indiana congregations experienced a regular turnover of members: some immigrants became unhappy with frontier life and returned to the East; others were restless types who left for Iowa and Kansas when these new lands were opened, and then went on to Oregon and California. When a migrating clergyman spoke at the church in 1849, an enthusiastic editor wrote: "The Rev. Mr. Davis, pastor of the Canon Street Baptist Church in the City of New York, preached in the Baptist Church of our city last Sunday. It is hoped that he may be induced to remain with us, for surely the services of such men are much needed in the West."[58] The preacher, however, was not persuaded and moved on.

Finally, in July 1850, the church succeeded in calling the Reverend John H. Meeson, who was under appointment by the Home Mission Board. Since 1841 the congregation had received annually some financial aid from the Board;[59] now, with their promise to pay half the cost, the people agreed to raise the new pastor's salary to three hundred dollars a year. The membership—which was not in the habit of fulfilling their salary obligations and still owed Burroughs eighty dollars for his past services—made an effort. Subscriptions were circulated to pay off the cost of the lot and to support the pastor's stipend; then, following the example of the other congregations, the women of the church held a public supper to liquidate the debt on the church.

Under Meeson's influence, worship became slightly more formal as the congregation resolved to stand for hymn singing and to have communion once a month. He also attempted to interpret Baptist beliefs to the community through Sunday afternoon and evening lectures on such subjects as "The Origin and History of the Baptists" and "Will there be any 'Restoration' after the Judgement?"[60] Meeson's two years in Fort Wayne were fruitful; one member later wrote: "His ministry was one of great power, and Zion put on new life, for God was with her and the Spirit seemed to find ready access to many hearts. A revival of great power followed."[61]

Meeson delivered his farewell sermon on May 8, 1852— with the congregation still owing him back salary—and, for the next twelve months, the church was without pastoral leadership. Finally, realizing that they must offer more than a subsistence wage, the congregation called the Reverend Ulrich Butler Miller at a salary of five hundred dollars. Miller was described as "a man of more than ordinary force in the pulpit,"[62] and was active in the community.

Ministry at the Gallows

One of the assumed responsibilities of Fort Wayne clergy was to visit the local jail, offering to the inmates religious instruction with a strong emphasis on repentance. When two convicted murderers were sentenced to be hanged on May 3, 1855, U. B. Miller joined the pastor of the Second Presbyterian Church, the Reverend Eleroy Curtis, and the new president of the Methodist College, the Reverend Reuben D. Robinson, in ministering to the prisoners. On the day after the public execution, the *Fort Wayne Times,* in a special edition, reported on the work of the ministers:

During their confinement and since their conviction, these two prisoners have manifested a very different temper and disposition. Madden at once abandoned all hope of pardon, expressed his willingness and cheerful acquiescence in the justice of his doom, and seemed to set about in earnest sincerity to prepare for the fate that awaited him in this life, and the still more awful and solemn retribution of the life to come. He received with a cheerful and thankful heart the religious instruction imparted to him by the clergy of this city and other friends of humanity. He confessed his guilt and the many sins of his life,

Ulrich Butler Miller
[Courtesy of First Baptist Church]

and seemed deeply penitent over his misspent and wasted existence. And we may charitably hope that his penitence has been availing with Him, who gave his life a ransom for us all, and pardoned even the thief and murderer on the cross.

Keefer, on the contrary, clung to the hope of life and, contrary to all advice, relied upon the chances of executive clemency till within a few days

.... But, during the last few days, and when all hope of pardon had fled, his spirit has been broken; the strong man, with no moral forces to sustain him, has became a trembling child; he who but a few days ago, with blinded conscience and hardened heart, seemed insensible to human punishments, has now, under the awakening influence and dread of impending and inevitable death, thrown himself in almost the helplessness of despair upon the much abused mercy of Him "whose mercy endureth forever" and who came to save even the chief of sinners ....

At eight o'clock most of the clergy of the city, and the friends and relatives of the condemned, assembled at the jail. Religious exercises of a solemn and affecting character were observed, in which the prisoners took part with deep feeling and propriety. They seemed resigned to their fate, and expressed a readiness and preparation for death. Madden said he was happy.

Shortly after, the more public religious exercises commenced in the jail by reading and singing the beautiful hymn commencing, "There is a fountain filled with blood, Drawn from Immanuel's veins." The Rev. Mr. Curtis then read a portion of the 23d chapter of Luke, from the 32d to the 43d verses inclusive. The Rev. Mr. Robinson then offered up a prayer, and was followed by the Rev. Mr. Miller with the hymn commencing, "When I can read my title clear." The Rev. Mr. Curtis closed the religious exercises with prayer ....

Madden took a very friendly leave of the ladies of the sheriff's family, bidding farewell to each, and saying in conclusion, "I hope to meet you all in heaven." To his friends Keefer said, "All is well with me," and earnestly exhorted them to prepare for death .... While the sheriff was fastening the rope around around the neck of each, they made various exclamations: "I feel that I am going to heaven," &c. Keefer's last saying was, "Into thy hands, O God, I commit my spirit."[63]

It may be assumed that, on the following Sunday, some preachers in Fort Wayne used the public hanging as an object lesson for their hearers. The editor of the *Times*, however, saw the event as an object lesson for the local religious leaders.

Will the Sabbath School teacher learn from the instruction of this day an added lesson of the importance of his vocation, and be more earnest and faithful in gathering the lambs into that fold, where they will be sheltered and secured from the power of those temptations whose bitter fruits have signalized this day as one of sorrow, if not of mourning, for all true hearts. Will the minister of Christ, he who is the heaven appointed teacher of men, receive any new instructions and impulses to duty, like his master, to think and care more for the "lost sheep," the outcasts of society, for those who, though they may be alienated from the sympathies of men, may yet be dear to the heart of God, because they have been purchased by the blood of redemption. If much of the time that is spent in prisons with the felon after conviction, was spent in the "highways and hedges," many of the now abandoned might be saved from the felon's fate and felon's dreadful end.

If many who style themselves the people of God, instead of turning up their pious noses and shrinking in mock and affected horror from contact with what they term the wicked, would part with some of their hypocrisy and, in genuine Christian humility, imitate the Savior's example in "going about doing good," their example would not only be more consistent, but their efforts more useful, and their Master and the cause of religion be more honored by their bearing the name of the one, and professing the other.[64]

Chronic Financial Problems

Miller was the first Baptist minister to remain in Fort Wayne for more than two years; during his third year, however, the Home Mission Society discontinued all aid to Indiana churches, as they redirected their limited resources to the new settlements in Kansas and Nebraska. The Society's one hundred and fifty dollar supplement to Miller's salary was more than the congregation could cover; eventually, the members decided: "On account of the necessary means not easily being raised for the support of our minister, we therefore feel the propriety of releasing him half his time from our church."[65] Miller tried to establish a singing school in Fort Wayne to supplement his reduced income, but, when the response was insufficient, he resigned.

The struggle of Fort Wayne Baptists to fund an adaquate ministerial stipend had been experienced by most of the town's emerging congregations; some church members, however, would not fault themselves but projected the problem onto the minister, complaining of the cost. In response to those people who were unwilling to contribute appropriately to their clergyman's maintenance, one local editor wrote: "Some people talk a great deal about ministers, and the cost of keeping them, paying their house rent, table

**The First Baptist Church (second building),
Dedicated in 1868**
[Courtesy of First Baptist Church]

expenses, and other items of salary. Did such croakers ever think it cost thirty-five millions of dollars to pay the salaries of American lawyers; and twelve millions of dollars are spent annually to keep our criminals, and ten millions of dollars to keep the dogs in the midst of us alive, while only six millions of dollars are spent annually to keep six thousand ministers in the United States. These are facts."[66]

The Reverend Cyrus W. Rees, a young bachelor who had just been graduated from Kalamazoo College, assumed the pastorate in September 1856; a few months later, a local newspaper reported: "The Rev. Rees of the Baptist Church in this city, returned with his new bride last week and resumed his pastoral duties."[67] Rees was a dynamic evangelist and, during the following year, over sixty new members were added to the membership — the majority by baptism. After fourteen months, he "tendered his resignation . . . on account of a bronchial affection of the throat."[68]

The decade of the fifties closed during the pastorate of the Reverend Stephen Wilkens; a member recalled that he "strongly impressed his hearers with his quaint way of putting gospel truths. He served the church for two and a half years with great satisfaction."[69]

By 1860, Fort Wayne Baptists had evolved from a small subsidized band of pioneers into a self-sufficient urban congregation whose evangelical zeal had made it one of the community's fastest growing churches. It was a radically democratic congregation which shunned all symbols of aristocracy or establishment—eschewing the pew rental traditions of the Presbyterians and Episcopalians—and extended a warm welcome to persons of every social station. Along with the Methodists and New School Presbyterians, Fort Wayne Baptists were on the leading edge of moral reform and were especially vocal on the contentious issue of temperance and abolition; they attacked sin with persistence and loved the sinner with persuasion.

7
Episcopalians

"We are not yet old enough for a society of this kind. In other words, there are not people enough in this county who are constitutionally fitted to be Episcopalians."
"A. B.," 1842

The Protestant Episcopal Church was the last of the mainline denominations to establish parishes in Indiana. By the time Fort Wayne was laid out in 1823, the Roman Catholics, Presbyterians, Congregationalists, Methodists, Baptists, and Lutherans had developed flourishing congregations in southern Indiana; but it was not until 1835, when the Right Reverend David Jackson Kemper was consecrated as its first missionary bishop, that any formal activity by the Episcopal Church was instituted in the state.

Kemper was a native of Pleasant Valley, New York, and had been graduated from Columbia College in 1809 as valedictorian of his class. After theological studies and ordination, he began his ministry as an assistant to Bishop White of Philadelphia, a position he held for twenty years; during this time he undertook missionary trips to western Pennsylvania, Virginia, and Ohio. In 1831, Kemper assumed a rectorship in Norwalk, Connecticut; three years later, at the age of forty-five, he made his first journey to the Northwest, visiting the Indian Mission near Green Bay, Wisconsin. With his elevation to the episcopate the following year as the church's first "missionary bishop," he assumed oversight of the new Diocese of Missouri and Indiana, popularly known as "The Northwest." Kemper said he began his labors in Indiana with but one youthful missionary, and that not a brick, stone, or log had been laid toward the erection of a place of worship.[1]

During the fall of 1837, he made an extensive itineration throughout northern Indiana, accompanied by by the Reverend Samuel Roswell Johnson, missionary at Lafayette. Kemper wrote that in Fort Wayne they "received many civilities from several of its inhabitants—three of whom accompanied us for a mile or two" on a crowded canal boat. "Everything on board was comparatively rude. For instance: at dinner there was not more than half enough tumblers .... At night we were arranged in the following order. In one apartment Mr. J[ohnson] was in one corner; I in another; Mr. Hoover, a German [Lutheran] clergyman, in a third; while the fourth was occupied by the cook and a little girl about twelve years old. A man and his wife were in the middle on the floor. Another apartment, which was likewise the barroom, was occupied by the rest of the men."[2]

The enthusiasm of the little band of Episcopalians in Fort Wayne encouraged the bishop; two years later, when he acquired more missionaries, he appointed one to Fort Wayne. Kemper was determined to refute Bishop Philander Chase, who had declared a few years before that Indiana was forever lost to the Church; Kemper wrote: "We trust, through Divine grace, to prove, in the course of a few years, that if Indiana was ever lost to the Church, she is regained."[3]

Christ Church Organized by Benjamin Hutchins

Fort Wayne's first Episcopal minister was the Reverend

Benjamin Hutchins, a graduate of the University of Pennsylvania and General Theological Seminary. In 1838, at the age of thirty-four, he had come from the East with his wife to assume a mission parish at Albion, Illinois. Complaining that he was unable to find suitable housing, he quit his post after three weeks.[4] At his next appointment in Vincennes, Indiana, he soon found himself at odds with the congregation and, after five month's service, abruptly departed. As he

D. Jackson Kemper
[Courtesy of Trinity Episcopal Church]

awaited the bishop's next assignment, his wife and infant daughter returned to Philadelphia. Kemper wrote to Hutchins's father that his son was "ignorant of the world" and had fallen into debt; the bishop, however, did express confidence in his "purity and devotion,"[5] and sent him to organize a parish in Fort Wayne.

Hutchins arrived by stagecoach[6] in Fort Wayne on May 15, 1839, accompanied by his ever-present father, Henry.[7] His first report lamented a paucity of Episcopalians: "We have seen Mr. Moon, Dr. Huxford, Mr. Bellamy, and have heard of a Dr. Beecher; and these persons seem to constitute, so far as we have yet ascertained, the sum total of the Episcopal Church . . . . I shall commence my ministrations here on Sunday next (Whitsunday) in tent and tabernacle style, officiating in the forenoon in an academy building[8] and in the afternoon in the Presbyterian Church. I may also officiate again the ensuing Sunday wherever I can procure a place."[9]

Hutchins was not pleased to have been posted to Fort

Wayne and immediately told his bishop: "[A]t Maumee City [Ohio]. . . I found much encouragement for my ministrations and a strong inducement to remain and, had it not been for my appointment at Fort Wayne (and the place being in another diocese), should most assured have done so . . . . It will take some days or weeks for me to acquire any correct idea of my prospects of usefulness; indeed, according to present impressions, Maumee City seems far more deserving of ministerial or missionary attention than my allotted place."[10]

By the third week in May, a few other local residents had responded positively to the announcement that an Episcopal Church was about to be established. Plans were quickly devised to elect a vestry and adopt the name of Christ Church. The congregation was formally organized on May 27, 1839, by calling a general meeting of prominent men of Fort Wayne in the Academy building. Samuel Hanna and

The Academy Building, a schoolhouse built by Alexander McJunkin in 1838, was rented for Sunday worship by Episcopalians in 1839 and 1842, Methodists in 1840, and Baptists in 1841. In 1853, the facility was leased by the newly organized public school board and became the first "free" school in Fort Wayne.
[Drawing by B. F. Griswold, 1917]

Allen Hamilton, both active in the Presbyterian Church, were in attendance and Hamilton was called upon to chair the meeting. Elected as vestrymen were Thomas Broom, William L. Moon, James Hutchinson, Samuel Stophlet, and Merchant W. Huxford.[11] Membership in the congregation was, for the time being, loosely defined: Moon had not been baptized and Huxford had not been confirmed, but neither had many other members of the fledgling congregation.

Confirmation required a bishop, and Hutchins was bold in chiding Kemper: "I cannot forbear reminding you that much time has elapsed since your last . . . and only visit to this place.

Merchant D. Huxford, Fort Wayne's first mayor, was warden of Christ Episopal Church.
[Courtesy of Trinity Episcopal Church]

. . . You left behind a promise of coming again within a year. . . . People have large expectations . . . . Your promise and your protracted absence are distinctly remembered."[12]

Then, after only two Sundays of services, Hutchins boarded a canal boat with his father, bluntly informing Kemper that he was "going to Logansport, Terre Haute, [and] Vincennes on a visit of inquiry whether one of the other vacant missionary stations in the diocese might not prove a more eligible field of duty for me than Fort Wayne."[13] This journey, however, brought no invitations for his services. Hutchins then lingered in Cincinnati until the last week in June when a letter from Kemper arrived, sending him back to Fort Wayne. Still unreconciled to his appointment, Hutchins continued to complain about being consigned to so remote an area to which he would not bring his family: "Had I been transferred to Vincennes, I should have gone with my father to Philadelphia to bring out my wife and child but, under existing circumstances, and having been long enough already absent from my mission spot, I shall return there forthwith and alone."[14]

Hutchins's dislike of Fort Wayne and his new congrega-

tion became apparent to his parishioners, and the distaste soon became mutual. The vestry likewise became alienated in its affections and, in August, the officers tabled a motion "to raise funds for the support of public worship."[15] By November, church attendance had declined; in addition, the vestrymen felt their missionary had not properly consulted them about parish decisions. Hutchins's appointment by the bishop was for a year, and so he hoped that "the vestry generally and others, who have withholden themselves and their families from public worship and the sacraments, [will] bear with the imperfections of their present missionary now that they know he will not be long with them."[16] The vestry replied: "We consider any further effort on our part towards continuing . . . the services of our church here decidedly unavailing, from the prejudices that exist against you."[17]

Hutchins wrote to Kemper, who was also the rector of Christ Church in St. Louis, begging him to make an episcopal visit to Fort Wayne on the pretext of confirming six adult candidates and thereby resolve the controversy. The missionary was aware that his present troubles might reach an unsympathetic episcopal ear and reminded Kemper: "To break up housekeeping at once, part with my furniture at a sacrifice, and take my flight in winter will just throw me as much open to your reproof and censure as did a similar scene last summer at Vincennes, on somewhat similar grounds."[18] Kemper replied that Hutchins should "Preach, if you can, in the town or neighborhood until spring, as it is now too late to travel with your family and your cow; I will continue your salary until spring opens, when you return to Philadelphia."[19] Rejected and discouraged, Hutchins soon departed,[20] but wrote to Kemper from Philadelphia that he had left behind a band of Episcopalians who deserved the bishop's attention: "From the Sunday School [in Fort Wayne] I received no harsh resolutions requiring me to remove . . . . I cheered up the hearts of Miss Margaret Forsyth, Mrs. Bellamy and others by intimating that . . . you might be successful in turning the steps of some graduate of General Theological Seminary that way."[21] Kemper was happy to be rid of "the worthless and most eccentric Mr. Hutchins," as well as "old Harry, the father, almost as queer as Ben." The bishop's sympathy was with the disillusioned Episcopalians in Fort Wayne: "Poor, well-meaning, fear-minded, but crazy, Mr. Hutchins did here as much harm as good."[22]

The Dormant Years: 1840-1843

In July 1840, Kemper journeyed by canal to Fort Wayne for his first visit in three years. He did not find Indiana's packet boats overly comfortable and wrote that "the meals were pretty good, the bedding was very bad," the weather "excessively hot," the "water shallow and stagnant," the boat "leaking" and "often aground," along with "rain, mosquitoes, [and] plenty of water snakes."[23] When Kemper arrived at Fort Wayne he found "the tavern full; there had been a political meeting [and] the payments by the state Treasurer had brought many people together." The bishop lodged with the Huxfords, and was informed that he was scheduled to conduct Sunday morning, afternoon, and evening services[24] at First Presbyterian Church, whose pastor was away on summer vacation. Kemper was pleased with the "good attendance" and that the Episcopalians had participated with the proper "responses, to some extent." After the morning service, he "dined at [the] Moons'," noting that "neither he nor his wife have been baptized"; following afternoon worship he "took tea at [the] Brooms'" and later commented: "He and his wife [are] from Yorkshire, illiterate, a wagonmaker, the only male communicant here. He has the records of the church, well prepared by Mr. Hutchins."[25] Kemper had planned to baptize the children of the Huxfords and Nelsons of the disbanded congregation that Sunday, but found them unprepared: "The parents, on reading the service, were alarmed and determined to part from the ordinance."[26]

On Monday morning, the bishop discovered that the mail boat had already departed and that he was stranded in Fort Wayne. Failing to find a wagon ride to Logansport or Goshen, he submitted to more socializing, this time with the Presbyterians. He was impressed with Allen Hamilton, whom he described as "one of the richest men of the place—originally from Ireland—and but lately joined the Presbyterian Church," and was surprised by Fort Wayne's culinary style when the Hamiltons "put fresh fish and stewed chicken on my plate at the same time." Kemper also admired the home of Mr. and Mrs. Marshall S. Wines, a canal contractor and elder in the Presbyterian Church, whose home was "out of town, very pleasantly situated."[27] When he finally embarked, Kemper was again subject to the vagaries of canal travel; he wrote that, on the packet boat out of Fort Wayne, there were "some hard characters on board—one singing Smith's hymns, [an] Indian chomper, swearing, gambling, [and] mosquitoes; [it was] poor sleeping, for I was bit frequently... [we were] sometimes aground... [I] could get nothing but canal water to wash in."[28]

The people of Fort Wayne, however, had created a good impression; he noted in his diary: "Prospects [are] good here," and then wondered, "Will [the Reverend Mr.] Young suit?" Kemper, however, sent no missionary to Fort Wayne during the next four years.[29] The occasional visit of a neighboring clergyman, such as the Reverend George Fiske of St. Paul's Church in Richmond, helped to keep the Anglican spark alive; in October 1842, the local newspapers announced that Fiske would conduct "Divine Worship... at Mr. McJunkin's schoolroom."[30] These sporadic services, however, did not develop into a continuing congregation, and a local citizen observed: "We are not yet old enough for a society of this kind. In other words, there are not people enough in this county, who are constitutionally fitted to be Episcopalians, to support a preacher of this denomination."[31]

Peter Bailey Organizes a New Parish

Kemper returned to Fort Wayne in July 1843, and still made no move to reconstitute the dormant parish. Apparently, he was waiting for a more determined leadership to develop among Fort Wayne Episcopalians before sending

Peter P. Bailey
[Courtesy of Allen County-Fort Wayne Historical Society]

another missionary. Then, in October 1843, Peter P. Bailey, a dedicated churchman from New York City, arrived in town to establish a hardware store and, finding no worship in Fort Wayne according to his tradition, led the local Episcopalians in organizing a parish and electing a vestry. Sunday services, led by lay readers, were conducted in the courthouse, usually by Bailey or Lucien Ferry. If Bailey officiated, one hymn would invariably be "I Would Not Live Always"; if Ferry led in worship, the congregation might sing his favorite, "A

Charge to Keep Have I."[32] Bailey later wrote: "So anxious were we to have all our people out to our services that, on wet days, I would send my horse and wagon around to bring certain families to church, and this so often that the wagon was called the parish wagon."[33]

A Sunday school[34] was also organized in the same courthouse room, which always required an early Sunday morning preparation. Bailey remembered: "It was a tiresome undertaking, for the room was always unfit for use on

Lucien P. Ferry
[Drawing by B. F. Griswold, 1917]

Sunday morning and we had to sweep and clean it regularly before we could hold our Sunday school in it. We then had our church services. But that work was always done by some three or four of us, viz., Ellis Worthington . . . Isaac Kiersted . . . [and] R. M. Lyon."[35]

Convinced that their embryonic congregation could only flourish with clerical leadership, the group petitioned the bishop for assistance. After several urgent letters from Fort Wayne, Kemper offered the position to the Reverend Benjamin Halsted.[36] Thirty-three years of age, a native of New York and graduate of Bristol College and Virginia Theological Seminary, Halsted had recently served as a missionary at New Harmony, Indiana. He conducted his first service in Fort Wayne in the courthouse on May 12, 1844; two weeks later, they erased the memory of the short-lived Christ Church of 1839 with the selection of a new name, Trinity Church, and the election of a new vestry.[37] On July 7, at the parish's first celebration of the Eucharist, seventeen mem-

bers received Holy Communion at the hand of their new "minister of the parish";[38] the offering was $3.56.

In August, the bishop arrived in town, still unreconciled to traveling on the canal which he considered "slow and very uncertain—and very destitute of comfort." Fort Wayne and Trinity Church, however, pleased him: "This place has greatly improved since I first knew it, and I consider the prospects of the church quite encouraging." Kemper was also impressed by Mrs. Halsted, "a nice little woman, an excellent, economical house-keeper, and quite a lady."[39]

One of Halsted's first projects with the vestry was to address the issue of religious ignorance in the congregation: "We have reason to fear the vitality of religion is mournfully wanting, and of the distinctive features of the Church they are lamentably, if not wholly, ignorant."[40] The vestry's initial approach to the problem was to establish a parish library. By the end of 1845 the project had caught the attention of a local editor who reported, "We were yesterday politely invited to inspect a small but valuable selection of

Benjamin Halsted
[Courtesy of Trinity Episcopal Church]

books that form the nucleus of a parish library for the Episcopal church of this city. . . intended for free circulation. . . . At present they may be found at Mr. Bailey's store."[41]

Religious Debates and Party Politics

The new rector not only confronted religious ignorance in the parish, but attacked religious error in the community. In the fall of 1844, he challenged a Universalist minister, the Reverend Erasmus Manford, to a public debate. Manford, a New England cleric, was editor of the *Christian Teacher* and lectured throughout Indiana on Universalism. The Reverend

Ann Halsted (Mrs. Benjamin)
[Courtesy of Trinity Episcopal Church]

Charles Beecher of the Second Presbyterian Church complained that the Universalist minister had commenced preaching in the courthouse on Sundays without consulting either of the Episcopal or Presbyterian pastors who regularly conducted worship there;[42] Halsted's irritation focused more on that doctrine of the Universalists which declared that all humanity would eventually be saved by God and that none would suffer everlasting punishment. On the public platform, he may have quoted from the *Articles of Religion* of the Protestant Episcopal Church which affirmed that "Predestination to life is the everlasting purpose of God."[43] The two days of debate attracted considerable attention, and Manford noted that "the assemblies were large."[44]

Halsted seemed constitutionally prone to instigate public confrontations against supposed heresy. Three years before, he had joined in a denunciation of Robert Dale Owen's community at New Harmony and sent to the *Epis-*

copal Recorder an article condemning the "Hypocrisy an Intolerance . . . [of] Atheistic Owenism."[45] The publicatio of this harsh criticism in a nationally distributed organ of th Episcopal church, with the endorsement of one of its clergy men, precipitated a town meeting in New Harmony where unanimous populace issued a formal statement to the Epis copal Church in defense of their community's faith an morals. As a result, Halsted's ministry in New Harmony ha been brought to a standstill.[46]

In Fort Wayne, during the fall of 1844, when the electio campaign was heating up, the interim minister of the Firs Presbyterian Church, the Reverend William C. Anderson called on Peter Bailey at his place of business on a Monda morning to inquire if he had attended a Whig politica meeting on the Sabbath. The pastor said he knew that severa prominent members of his congregation, as well as leadin Methodists, had been seen there, but wanted to know if an Episcopalians were present. At that moment the Episcopa minister entered the store and the Presbyterian then aske him more pointedly: "Now Mr. Halsted, was not Mr. Baile at that meeting?" Bailey later recalled:

> Mr. Halsted straitened himself and with much animation said, "No, sir; he was not there, for he knows better. I read to him the ten commandments every Sunday, by which he learns to keep holy the Sabbath Day." Dr. Anderson was so pleased by this answer that he repeated it to his friends all over the city, much to their amusement, so that, in a day or so after this, Mr. Halsted received a note from Major [Samuel] Edsall, a prominent Democrat and Methodist, and the owner of the large flouring mill on the west side of the town, which in substance read thus,

> "Dear Sir: With this note I send this barrel of flour to the minister who reads to his people the Ten Commandments every Sunday, which keeps them from attending political meetings on that sacred day."[47]

This religious sensitivity to the Whigs' electioneering on Sunday was exploited by the Democrats. The editor of the staunchly Democratic *Fort Wayne Sentinel,* Thomas Tigar— whose wife, the daughter of an Episcopal clergyman, was active in the local parish and whose children were among the first to be baptized in the Episcopal Church—editorialized: "We were informed that a leading Whig in this place—a member of a church, too—offered a resolution at the Clay Club, appointing committees to wait upon every voter. . . the day before the election. Our election is held on Monday; consequentially the Whig missionaries will have to perform their duty on the Sabbath! . . . This seems wrong to the Democrats."[48]

As the minister of the First Presbyterian Church was wary of the competition from political parties, the Episcopal rector was sensitive to any competition from the fledgling Second Presbyterian Church. Charles Beecher, pastor of this newest congregation in town, was aware of the perceived rivalry and, in September 1844, wrote that he had experienced "the dislike of the Episcopalians, even weaker than we, who think that, if it were not for us, they would have a chance."[49] By December, however, Beecher wrote that the feelings had faded and that "opposition is nearly imperceptible. The Episcopals are becoming high in their exclusiveness in proportion as they get low in efficiency. There is perfect cordiality in social matters but less community in

Benjamin Halsted's endorsement of a patent medicine was published in Fort Wayne in 1853.

worship. They cannot be considered even as rivals any longer . . . [and] have proposed to give us two services every Sunday—they retaining the forenoon only."[50]

Beecher's "low efficiency" charge may have focused on the rector, for criticism of Halsted had begun to surface in the parish. One of Halsted's parishioners described him as a "quiet, grave man, of slow utterance, and abrupt speech . . . . He had no gifts but earnestness, zeal, and devotion to the Master's service."[51] The bishop, during his annual visit to the parish in August 1845, noted the dissatisfaction: "Mr. Halsted is devoted, but alas, he is not popular. He has a few choice spirits to sustain him, but even they think how much could be done by another clergyman."[52] When Kemper next met Halsted at a neighboring parish in October,

he learned that his Fort Wayne missionary had been asked to resign. The bishop had recently experienced this same kind of pastoral crisis at Bloomington, and his distress was poured out in a letter to a friend: "The manner in which my mission has been cut down has agonized and stupefied me, and a week or two of calm reflection (which I cannot obtain on a visitation) will be necessary before I can decide upon the best plan to be adopted . . . . Are Fort Wayne or Bloomington to be abandoned?"[53] In December 1845, Halsted formally tendered his resignation to the vestry, stating "that dissatisfaction exists on the part of members of the parish towards me, which must hinder my usefulness and retard the growth and prosperity of the Church in this place."[54] Halsted remained with the parish through the following Easter and then went back to Mishawaka.[55]

Kemper assured Halsted of his continued support, and then suggested that he soften his ministerial manner: "In your purity, devotedness, and orthodoxy, I have perfect confidence. Perhaps, at times, you are rather abrupt—perhaps your opposition to little things is sometimes too decided—perhaps by reflection and care you might improve the severity of your manners. I have often thought that, if it could always be deeply impressed on my mind that my great duty is to win souls to Christ, my influence would increase and I would never offend."[56]

Bishop Kemper was also beset with conflict at the diocesan level. When the Indiana Convention had met in June, 1844, there was criticism from the evangelical wing of the church that the bishop's High Churchmanship was leading his clergy too close to Rome. Kemper was hurt and angry: "[R]eviling accusations are on every tongue and we are rapidly advancing in the high privilege of being persecuted, because we boldly, though I trust in meekness, maintain the faith as it was once delivered to the Saints."[57] Later, in 1846, he was specifically charged with promoting his High Church ideals in such a manner that contributions to domestic missions were falling off. Kemper responded by requesting his Indiana clergy to write to the missions' secretary and testify to his evangelical sermons and lack of party spirit.[58]

The attack on Kemper in 1844 was only a prelude to the conflict witnessed at the denomination's General Convention in October of that year. Peter Bailey attended its sessions in Philadelphia and lamented: "The whole system of the church from its founder down to the present day has been overhauled and exhibited to our view. Romanism, Puseyism, low churchism and many other isms from candles and flowers on the communion table, high mass and the Sovereignty of the Pope, down to Calvinistic doctrines and open infidelity have been brought to light and urged upon. . . this Convention." Bailey was not without his own opinions, and especially rejected "the offensive doctrines of the Oxford school,"[59] which sought a return of Anglicanism to the High Church ideals of the late seventeenth century.

A New Church and a New Rector

During the ensuing vacancy at Trinity Church, two vestrymen left the community; Peter Bailey noted that their departure "leaves us in quite a lonely state, as they were both very active men in the sense of the church." Bailey, however, was not discouraged, but directed the interests of the membership towards the building of a church: "Within the month past I have obtained a subscription of about $1700 from our citizens here for an Episcopal Church .... I am not without hopes of raising the amount to twenty-five hundred dollars before August .... It is to be built of brick and in the gothic order; we want to get the building enclosed this fall and finished next spring, which will place us in much better circumstances and will offer more inducement for a good clergymen of the right stamp to come and make his abode with us."[60] When Kemper visited the indefatigable Bailey in May 1846, his optimism for the future of the Fort Wayne congregation was restored: "Bailey is not discouraged; he is a well read and consistent chairman; [he] has opened a subscription for a church ... is writing a clergyman, is in good spirits, [and] has lay-reading every Sunday morning."[61]

That year, William Rockhill offered the congregation two lots in his new addition, if it could raise one thousand dollars toward the construction of the proposed chapel. Apparently the location of these gift lots did not appeal to everyone in the parish for, in July 1847, the vestry purchased a new site from Samuel Hanna. Then, when the architect's proposed design and fee was deemed too expensive, Bishop Kemper offered to send to Peter Bailey a "cheap church plan [soon] to be published in New York."[62] Construction was again delayed and, in August, Charles Beecher—whose congregation was now worshipping in their new church— wrote: "The Episcopalians, who commenced with us and occupied the court house alternately, still worship there, if at all, numbering not over thirty or forty, and without any curate."[63]

The vestry had begun its search for a new rector even before Halsted departed but, during the next two years, it was turned down by half a dozen clergymen. Then, in the spring of 1848, the officers raised the salary from $400 to $500 a year, and the Reverend Henry P. Powers, rector of St. Luke's Church at Ypsilanti, Michigan, accepted their invitation "to the charge of the Church ... for two or three months ... with a view of becoming rector, if mutually agreeable at the expiration at that time."[64] Powers, a fifty-one-year-old native of Vermont, arrived on April 4 and preached in the courthouse on the following Sunday. Peter Bailey was pleased: "We have heard his first sermon and like him much."[65] The following week, a public notice announced

that "Episcopal Services will be held in the basement of the 1st Presbyterian Church on Sunday morning at 11 o'clock and in the afternoon at 3:30 o'clock by the Rev. H. P. Powers."[66] He so impressed the people of the parish that three weeks later, the vestrymen voted to waive the trial period and tendered him a call to the rectorship. They further assured him that, if any of the two hundred dollars from the denomination's mission society were not forthcoming to their "mission station," they would make up the difference.[6...]

When Powers arrived, the congregation was anticipating the completion of their first house of worship. Bailey's hope that a gothic brick church would be built in one year had been compromised; after a two-year struggle, a small frame chapel, costing one thousand dollars, was finally erected on the southeast corner of Berry and Harrison streets. When the new facility was first occupied for worship in August, the vestry proudly advertised: "The Rev. Mr. Powers will preach in the Chapel on the Rite of Confirmation or laying on of hands."[68] Soon after this, Powers terminated his ministry in spite of the bishop's directive: "Do not think of leaving Fort Wayne until you have a successor on the spot."[6...] Powers judged that, in the presence of four other English-speaking congregations in Fort Wayne, the parish of twenty-eight families would struggle; at the Annual Convention, he told Kemper: "The congregations have been respectable and attentive; and though the ground seems to be preoccupied, I can scarcely doubt that, by great perseverance and care, the Church may eventually be placed upon a permanent footing in Fort Wayne."[70]

Joseph Large Arrives

The little congregation had now been two and a half years without a minister, yet had succeeded in building a church and had continued to hold Sunday services with lay reading. Then, in the first week in October, Bishop Kemper visited Fort Wayne[71] and suggested that they invite the Reverend Joseph S. Large of the Diocese of Michigan. The vestry immediately wrote:

Our parish is small, but we have the hopes of a respectable sized congregation when we shall be favored with one to administer to us in holy things. We have a small church furnished and paid for. We have just placed in the church a fine toned organ of 4 stops which is also paid for. We have no embarrassments, being out of debt.

The population of our city is about 5,000 and constantly increasing. We cannot doubt of the rapid growth of the church under the efforts of an active and zealous Missionary of the Cross. From your place here is about a two days travel at an expense of about $5.00. As we are without services and are most anxious to have the vacancy filled before close of navigation, may we ask for an immediate reply, or will you at once, in receipt of this, come up and see us for a few Sundays before deciding.[72]

Joseph S. Large
[Courtesy of Trinity Episcopal Church]

Large packed up and was in Fort Wayne before the third week in November. Like his predecessors, Large was an Easterner, born in Buckingham Township in Bucks County, Pennsylvania in 1811, and raised in the comfort of a family estate where fox hunting was a pastime. He had taught school for a while in Buckingham before commencing his theological studies; in 1841, he was ordained a deacon and a few years later was serving a parish in Marne, Michigan. The summer before he arrived in Fort Wayne, he had married Caroline H. Cuming, the twenty-four-year-old daughter of a clergy colleague.

Large seems to have been worth waiting for. In a matter of months the little chapel was overflowing and additional seats were installed in front of the altar. The rental of pews, which they called "slips," had gone so well that the vestry raised the rector's salary a hundred dollars. Then, in the spring, they approved plans to enlarge the chapel with a new transept, chancel, and vestry. A special feature of the addition was three stained glass windows, some of the first

in any Protestant church in town.[73] A local newspaper, commenting on the financial success of the Episcopal women's fund-raising supper, noted that the proceeds would "be devoted to the enlargement of their chapel which, since the settlement here of their talented and popular minister, Rev. Mr. Large, has become altogether too small to accommodate the rapidly increasing congregation."[74]

The church wardens and vestrymen formally invited the bishop of the recently established Diocese of Indiana, the Right Reverend George Upfold, to officiate at the consecration of their enlarged edifice on May 23, 1850.[75] He had just been consecrated to his new office in December 1849. Fifteen years before, when serving as rector of Trinity Church in Pittsburgh, he had entertained Jackson Kemper, who was then on his first episcopal journey to the West; Upfold had invited him to preach and succeeded in raising $150 for his mission. Indiana's new bishop had been born in Surrey, England, in 1796 and, at the age of six, emigrated with his parents to New York. He had first studied medicine, then switched to theology, and was ordained to the ministry in 1818. Upfold was an intense, devout churchman who admired E. B. Pusey, but rejected much of the Oxford Movement. He deplored most liturgical innovations and, in 1857, refused to authorize for his diocese those changes recently approved by General Convention. He also condemned the "novel and objectionable . . . decoration of the church with flowers on Easter Sunday," and declared, "I will not visit or officiate in any parish where this floral display is attempted." Publicly, Upfold appeared plain and dignified, sometimes aloof, and occasionally imperious. Privately, his family and close friends enjoyed him as a genial man with the facility for seeing a humorous side in events, which served him well during attacks of progressively debilitating arthritis.[76]

The original Diocese of the Northwest, which had grown to include the states of Michigan, Kansas, Nebraska, Iowa, Minnesota, and Wisconsin, was now divided; Indiana had its own diocesan bishop, as Jackson Kemper, its founding missionary bishop, had chosen to serve the church farther west.[77] Upfold's duties in Indiana, however, were only defined as part time, and, until 1854, he also served as rector of St. John's Church in Lafayette. Unfortunately, Upfold was not blessed with that missionary temperament and vigorous constitution which had so energized Kemper; his health was fragile and he disliked the traveling required of a bishop. Kemper was a widower who easily spent long periods away from home, but Upfold was seldom happy when separated from his family. Once he wrote to his daughter: "I am glad to learn there is a prospect of having, when I reach home, a substantial dinner, a thing which I have had only twice since I left Fort Wayne. Pickles, sweetmeats, cookies, and tea, are the usual articles provided, morning, noon, and night. If there is any meat, it is done to death, all the juices evaporated in the cooking and covered up with melted lard. Then the beds are inconvenient—sometimes feather, sometimes corn husks with the cobs left in, sometimes straw, sometimes spring mattresses with the springs dilapidated and worn."[78]

The initial excitement surrounding the bishop's consecration of Trinity Church's enlarged facilities eventually cooled, and the congregation gradually settled back into a more routine parish life. In mid-1851, Joseph K. Edgerton,

George Upfold
[Courtesy of Trinity Episcopal Church]

a former member of the Wayne Street Methodist church who had recently been elected to the vestry, commented on this lassitude: "I was at church today twice and heard very good, practical, evangelical sermons from Mr. Large—tho' men, better than he, preached of late. Somehow, he does not seem to be able to stir up people to a sense of religious duty. His stated congregation seems very indifferent on religious subjects and declines to attend church but when it is convenient."[79]

Large was a good speaker and had been chosen to inaugurate a local series of "Scientific Lectures," addressing his audience on "The Evidences of Revealed Religion."[80] He was also an energetic leader, and his people's lethargy, of which Edgerton complained, may have frustrated his creative spirit. The Women's Sewing Society responded to his challenge to build a parsonage and, during their Christmas fair in 1850, had dedicated their receipts of $190 to the project;[81] but, as no other funds were forthcoming, the best that the vestry could do was to offer to loan him the women's

money, interest free, toward building his own home.[82] September 1851, Large determined to establish a day school for boys. Upfold had encouraged his clergy to establish schools "to supplement their meager incomes," and had often recommended such establishments to his diocese.[8] The vestry was amenable and gave Large permission "t fence off forty feet of the south part of the church lot and erec a schoolhouse thereon." Like the parsonage proposal, th vestry offered no financial support for the school and re solved that the small frame building would be "subject t removal by sixty days notice given by the vestry."[84] Larg then engaged Joseph Jenks to carry the principal teachin responsibilities. The school continued until Large resigne his Fort Wayne rectorship in September 1854, ostensibl because of his wife's health, and departed for what appeare to be a more exciting ministry in gold-rush California.

Caleb A. Bruce and Eugene C. Pattison

The Reverend Caleb Alexander Bruce assumed th rectorship of Trinity Church in November 1854. Born i 1818 at Duanesburg, New York, Bruce had begun his min istry in the Methodist Church and had recently served congregation of that denomination in Kalamazoo, Michi gan.[85] At the age of twenty he had married sixteen year-ol Mary Sortore; before the couple arrived in Fort Wayne the had already lost several children in infancy.

No church records were preserved during the years 1852 to 1857; as a result, very little is known about his ministry or that of his successor. Only when Trinity Church and its rector were reviewed by an anonymous "Church-goer" during the Christmas season of 1854, is there a glimpse, albeit distorted, of the parish during that time. The visitor's comments first focused on the Christmas decorations arranged in the nave and chancel: "On entering we felt that it has been truly said, 'There is but one step from the sublime to the ridiculous.' Whence those chaplets of evergreens? those little Gothic windows enshrouded with the same? those deep festoons over the preacher's head, terminating in an ill-shaped cross? Surely we might imagine our Divine Master exclaiming, 'My house shall be a called the house of prayer, but you have made it a child's play house.' Away with these Romanish trappings, dear friends . . . and the real insignificance of your temple might escape criticism."

The visitor, who seemed more sensitive to style than substance, next turned his attention to the officiating clergyman, and found fault with his ministerial manner: "The organ sounds and Mr. Bruce, with a rather quick, unclerical step, crosses the dais to the reading desk, and commences reading the beautiful liturgy of the Church of England . . . . We should be apt to imagine him betrayed into the performance of a task for which he had neither taste nor inclination—he reads hurriedly and lacks emphasis . . . . Mr. Bruce appears to labor under great inconvenience as it regards light. The unmeaning colored window behind him only serves to 'Teach light to counterfeit a gloom' rather than throw any on the books of the preacher."

"Church-goer," who claimed to be a lapsed Episcopalian, concluded his review of the aesthetics of Anglican worship with some negative comments on the chancel arrangements: "We are sorry to see the little organ so unhappily placed, which, together with its being out of tune, produces but a poor effect; but we suppose the construction of the church admits of no other, unless, indeed, the desk and pulpit were removed further forward, in which case the preacher would have the benefit of the two side windows, and the organ and choir (being placed behind him) would have the benefit of the one above. And now gentle reader . . . for having meddled with matters which may not appear to concern us. . . we might yet be able to remove a stumbling block from our brother, or cast a light on his path and, in so doing, we conceive we have performed our mission."[86]

The next edition of the *Times* contained a surprising gentle response, probably composed by Bailey, although signed, according to the custom, with an anonymous initial. "Church-goer" was politely invited to return again, but next time to turn his attention to matters of faith—and to worship

> . . . God in His own house and not Mr. Bruce's or Mr. Edwards' or Mr. Beecher's or Mr. Chaplin's[87] or any other preacher of greater or less celebrity . . . . But really, sir, you are too sad a stranger to the church to attempt a criticism of the reading of its solemn service, or to appreciate the beauty of its Christmas dress . . . . Trinity Church, Fort Wayne . . . has had no rich patroon to endow it with grounds or money, but owes its foundation, rise, and progress to the affectionate and devoted attachment of a very few, firm, and most worthy friends and members, who have given liberally of the means they possessed.
>
> Adieu, my dear sir; I hope you will attend the Episcopal church as often as you have opportunity; and I have a firm conviction that, if you will take your prayer book and reverently unite in the services, you will soon truly feel more love and veneration for its solemn and sublime liturgy than you ever fancied in your most poetically inspired moments.[88]

In early 1856, Bruce accepted a call to Trinity Church in Michigan City, Indiana.[89] In the spring, the vestry invited the Reverend Eugene C. Pattison to visit Fort Wayne; on May 3, 1856 he preached his trial sermon and was then invited to assume the rectorship of the parish. Pattison, at the

age of twenty-five, was the youngest clergyman to lead Trinity parish. He had been ordained a deacon the year before by Jackson Kemper and had served his deaconate in Indianapolis. Undoubtedly Pattison had been nominated to the vestry by Bishop Upfold, who had already scheduled the young clergyman's ordination for June 4.

Pattison was the first rector of Trinity Church to have received his theological education at Nashotah House in Wisconsin. In 1840, a few students at General Theological Seminary in New York City, who had heard Jackson Kemper's call for "self-denying men, willing to go. . . and endure every species of hardship for the sake of Christ and His Church,"[90] vowed to go to the Northwest to work under the bishop, organizing themselves as a "Society of Protestant Monks" to live together in a religious house under a superior. With the continued support of Kemper, this semi-monastic brotherhood, under the influence of the tractarian wing of the Oxford Movement, established its house at Nashotah, Wisconsin, and, by 1845, saw its first graduate ordained. Pattison was an Easterner, born in New Rochelle, New York, and therefore must have made a strong commitment to Anglo-Catholic theology and worship to journey to Wisconsin for his theological education.

Republicans and Democrats in the Pews

In early June 1857, Trinity Church was host to the annual Convention of the Diocese of Indiana, meeting for the first time in Fort Wayne. Thomas Tigar wrote an editorial praising the Episcopal Church for refusing to comment on the contentious social issues of the day:

> The Episcopal Convention for the Diocese of Indiana was in session in this city the present week. Bishop Upfold and nearly all the clergy of the diocese and several lay members were in attendance. As this church confines itself exclusively to religious matters, the business of the convention was speedily and pleasantly transacted, without any of that discord and wrangling which has been characteristic of similar convocations of other churches, where slavery, temperance, and other party questions, in a great measure, monopolize the attention and destroy all Christian feelings among its members. The Episcopal Church, in this respect, sets a very worthy example, which others would do well to follow.[91]

It is doubtful that Tigar's commendation of the Episcopal Church was prompted by any deep devotion to the parish in which he rented a pew but had never formally joined.[92] He was an ardent supporter of the Democratic Party and therefore aimed his remarks at recent Methodist and Presbyterian assemblies which had vigorously attacked slavery and advocated temperance, causes toward which his party was decidedly unenthusiastic.

Tigar, however, did not represent the opinions of all local Episcopalians on these "party questions." Peter Bailey, founder, patron, and senior warden of the parish, had become an ardent Republican and began to make plans in 1857 to establish a weekly newspaper reflecting the progressive politics and social ideals of that new party. On May 5, 1858, the first edition was published and contained substantially more religious news than had ever been seen in any other Fort Wayne newspaper. Not every Republican however, wished to read church news, and one citizen complained: "I took up a paper the other day ... *The Fort Wayne Republican*. Now ... I am a real Republican .... But I read and read, and found nothing but Trinity Church and slang against the Fort Wayne *Times*." [93] Allen Hamilton, who had recently joined the Democratic Party was incensed by Bailey's Republican editorials and filed an affidavit stating: "We have a Republican editor here who pretends to be an Episcopalian, who reads prayers and sermons on Sunday and lies the balance of the week—the meanest man and the greatest liar we ever had in the county." [94]

Peter Bailey's leadership in the parish was tested in the fall of 1857 when the finances of the congregation fell into such arrears that Pattison was owed over two hundred dollars in back salary and Joseph S. Large was still unpaid for the services he had conducted during the previous summer. Bailey proposed that the vestrymen personally collect the delinquent pew rents; they agreed and assigned the debtors, carefully giving the name of Thomas Tigar to someone other than Bailey.

On April 5, 1858, Pattison resigned his rectorship "on account of feeble health" [95] and asked the vestry to act upon his request immediately. He was not the first Episcopal clergyman in the diocese to resign for reasons of physical infirmity, and Bishop Upfold, himself in poor health, later wrote: "During this period, great hindrance in the work of building up the Church in the diocese had been caused by the frequent removal of clergymen to other dioceses, and some of the very best and most reliable and useful from failing health. This has given me much embarrassment in the prosecution of my labours, as well as seriously retarding the growth of the several parishes." [96]

In early summer, when the vestry failed to interest a Cincinnati clergyman in the rectorship, Bishop Upfold nominated the Reverend James Runcie of Evansville, then serving as chaplain to the state prison. The officers, however, "unanimously agreed ... that, in his present situation, ... the Rev. Mr. Runcie occupied a field in which his labors promised more fruit ... and therefore the vestry deemed it most prudent not to extend to him a call to the rectorship." [97] During August and September, the vestry proceeded to elect, in turn, three clergymen, each of whom declined. Finally, in

October, the congregation was informed that a potential rector was on his way, and Bailey's newspaper reported that the "Reverend Stephen H. Battin, of Cooperstown, New York, officiated in Trinity Church... last Sunday and, at the request of the vestry, will officiate next Sunday." [98] Two weeks later it was announced that Battin had "received a call to the rectorship... and entered on the discharge of its duties." [99]

Stephen H. Battin
[Courtesy of Trinity Episcopal Church]

Rector, Schoolmaster, and Insurance Agent

Battin was forty-four years old, a graduate of General Theological Seminary, and had served in the Episcopal Church for the previous sixteen years, most recently at Christ Church in Cooperstown, New York. [100] He arrived in Fort Wayne with his daughter Kate and, with her assistance, soon opened a school "for young ladies at his residence on Wayne near Harrison Street ... [for] boarding scholars as well as day scholars." [101] Battin had an entrepreneurial spirit and became the first Fort Wayne clergyman to serve as a life insurance representative; in early 1860, a local newspaper announced: "Rev. Stephen H. Battin, of this place, is agent for the N. Y. Life Insurance Co., the accumulated capital of which is $1,595,901.56." [102]

Battin appears to have begun well as Trinity's rector and,

by the end of his first year, eight new families were added to the parish. By the middle of his fifth year, however, the vestry had become dissatisfied with his ministry and two of the officers informed the rector of their judgement. Battin was hurt and responded to the wardens and vestrymen with deep emotion:

> In severing one of the most sacred of earthly ties, I have taken some time to deliberate. It is no easy matter, especially at so short notice, for a clergyman to break up and move to another, perhaps a distant parish; and, when my rent and debts are paid and furniture packed, there will be little left of my salary to carry me away.
>
> During my rectorship of almost five years, I have never asked for a week's vacation. I did hope to obtain the superintendency of our city schools,[103] but conclude it will be better for myself and the interest of the church to remove as soon as possible.
>
> In view of the above,
>   First: I desire five or six weeks leave of absence;
>   Second: [I] will hand in my resignation "to take effect at the end of my fifth year," the very day my salary is paid; and
>   Third: [I] desire the vestry to grant me a further indulgence of an amount sufficient to remove my family and effects to their home in the East.[104]

On July 6, the vestry accepted Battin's resignation,[105] effective August 1, noting that they would owe him $384.50 for his salary through September, in the face of a cash balance of $24 in their treasury and the hope of only $127 from outstanding pew rents. Seven days later Peter Bailey proposed a solution to their double problem of a vacant pulpit and empty treasury: "that Rev. Jos. S. Large be called to the rectorship of Trinity Parish at a salary of $1000 per annum."[106] After the few years in California, Large had returned to the region to assume the rectorship of St. John's Church in Louisville, Kentucky; he was now fifty-three years of age.

A New Church With an Old Rector

Apparently the vestry wanted to build a new church and had come to the conclusion that Battin was not the man to lead the parish in such an ambitious undertaking. Between 1848 and 1850, Joseph Large had successfully led them through the fund-raising efforts for the enlargement of their

chapel and had personally donated a stained glass window. He was also remembered as a popular leader and, under his former rectorship, the congregation had grown; now the

Trinity Episcopal Church (second building), on the southwest corner of Berry and Fulton streets, was dedicated in 1866.

[Courtesy of Allen County Public Library]

vestry was convinced that what he had done for them before, he would do again. As a consequence of this reasoning, the officers called a meeting of the parish in September 1863, and presented their plans. The people responded positively and, in order to support Large's proposed salary of $1000—which reflected the inflationary pressures of the war—voted to raise their pew rents by 33 1/3 percent. Next they appointed a committee to investigate the availability of suitable lots for the location of their new church building. Then, in October, when they received word that the bishop had certified Large to officiate in the diocese, the vestry moved quickly to purchase a new church site at the southwest corner of Berry and Fulton streets, at a cost of $3000;

and, when Large arrived in December, the officers engaged "C. C. Miller, Esq., as architect of the church Building."[107]

The alacrity with which the project was begun was soon slowed by the more difficult business of raising the necessary $21,000. It was not until the fall of 1865 that the church's walls were up; then, when the construction stalled for lack of funds, the vestry appealed to the Women's Sewing Society for a loan of $2400 from their Parsonage Fund. This organization had worked hard for over a decade in pursuit of their dream of a new parsonage, and were not about to see it lost to the vestry's deficit financing. The women therefore required the men to give them a note at 10 percent interest, with a signed assurance that, when the pews in the new church were sold, their note would be paid off with the initial receipts.[108]

When the first services of divine worship were conducted in the new edifice on September 9, 1866, the public was awed by its Indiana limestone walls, imported English windows, and elaborately detailed arches. The new Trinity Church was the first English-Gothic house of worship erected in Fort Wayne and was judged as one of the finest examples of this style in the region.

By the early 1860s, the Episcopal Church in Indiana claimed 1,500 members. Trinity Church in Fort Wayne had arrived late and grew slowly, yet it gradually developed into one of the more significant parishes in the city. During its first three decades the congregation was tenacious for its survival and faithful to its traditions. Because the parish had been founded by strong lay leaders without clerical help, the people tended to be hard on their rectors: of its first seven ministers, four had been asked to leave, including Joseph S. Large in 1872.[109] Unlike the Lutherans who had split on theology, the Catholics who divided on language, the Presbyterians who separated on church program, and the Quakers who parted on the slavery issue, the Episcopalians maintained a strong unity. To many people, this was appealing, and a local poet expressed the admiration of many residents with these lines:

> The dear old Episcopalian Church,
> Her ways all pleasant lie,
> Like placid streams that fertilize
> When noisier ones are dry.[110]

8
Women's Societies

"When man can give to God a ransom for the soul of woman, then, and not 'till then, is it his privilege to control the mind of woman, and limit the sphere of action that results from an enlightened mental culture."
"T" (Mary F. Thomas, M. D.), 1856.

The development of women's societies in Protestant churches and Jewish synagogues was a remarkable phenomenon of the early nineteenth century; by 1860 more American women belonged to religious groups affiliated with congregations than to all other women's organizations combined. In Fort Wayne, these societies were a vital part of many women's spiritual and social life. The activities of the groups developed leadership and organization skills, and gave many women the confidence to assert themselves in public life. With a focused spiritual and ethical emphasis, most women's societies stimulated an energetic concern for moral reform, especially in the causes of temperance, abolition, and woman's rights.

A variety of forces had merged to make these religious societies the most popular and powerful women's organizations in America. Protestant women had responded in great numbers to their churches' declaration that they had "a prodigious influence, and consequent responsibility, in the great work of regenerating a world lying in wickedness." Lydia Maria Child noted, in 1837, that many women, by responding to this challenge, had found that their "sympathies and thoughts" had become "active, and enlarged from beyond the bounds of the hearth and nursery." It was also in "the zeal and strength of newly exercised freedom"[1] that women took up the cause of the new foreign missionary enterprise, with a special concern for the emancipation of their overseas sisters from the most oppressive features of

certain Asian and African cultures. Historian Dorothy C. Bass notes that "the evangelicals [were] the first agitators of the woman question: religious reform was the largest and most important extrafamilial activity of middle-class women in this [antebellum] period, and it became the arena in which many of the tensions surrounding their role in the modernizing and expanding society surfaced."[2]

Early Societies

The earliest record of Fort Wayne women actively working in any sort of organization besides the church and Sunday school is of a Tract Society which was established by the Presbyterians in 1832 to distribute religious literature to the unchurched. Normally, the society met once a month to plan their next itinerations; occasionally, the mission was "discontinued for want of tracts" while the members labored to raise the necessary funds "to prosecute the work." The women's zeal carried them into rural areas, where they recruited other like-minded women to the cause; their pastor, the Reverend James Chute, reported: "By the aid of a pious female in Huntington, about 25 miles distance, we have a prospect of extending the work."[3]

In 1833, Fort Wayne's first women's organization of record, a "female prayer meeting," was gathered from the Presbyterian congregation and dedicated itself to minister to the poor. Chute noted that the founders of this new organization were "a few who seem willing 'to come up to the help of the Low against the Mighty.'"[4] Later, when the congregation was erecting the town's first meetinghouse, the women of the parish organized the Female Sewing Society. Susan Man, who taught school in the church's lower level, reported: "Next Saturday we are going to have a female prayer meeting . . . and the ladies are about forming a sewing society

Eliza Taylor Hanna (Mrs. Samuel) helped organize the First Presbyterian Church's Women's Society.
[Engraving by Finlay and Conn for the American Historical Society]

for the benefit of the unfinished church. After that is finished they will work for other benevolent objects." The young school teacher later noted that there was a great demand for their handiwork: "I have been making little shoes and sell them before they are completed."[5]

Fund Raising

The church women seldom handed over the proceeds of their handiwork sales to the male church officers to spend as they wished; ordinarily, a women's society chose some specific project, such as a Sunday school library or steeple bell, and then carefully saw that it was completed to their specifications. When the Presbyterian Sewing Society, in 1837, discovered that an item to be installed in their new house of worship was constructed contrary to their expecta-tions, the president, Miss Sally C. Vance, refused to pay the bill because the trustees had failed to "make the pulpit circular."[6]

Methodist and Episcopal women became active in the 1840s. Early in the decade, a group of Methodist women organized a fair and were the first to schedule their event on Christmas Eve. (During this period, no English-speaking Protestant Church in Fort Wayne conducted special services on December 24.) Soon after the establishment of their parish, Episcopal women began sewing and selling for their proposed church edifice. Sarah Huxford recollected: "A few months after the organization of the church, the ladies formed a society to help raise funds to build a place of worship. We did sewing for anyone who wanted it. All our work was done in the society by the ladies' hands; we had no sewing machines . . . . [We] met every 2 weeks at some one of the members' homes [and] always had supper (and a good one too) . . . . [At] one fair—I was treasurer—we took in one night over $400 . . . . We held annual fairs for many years after the organization of the Church and the funds we raised helped largely to build the first building."[7] In June 1860, the Episcopal women mounted an elaborate Strawberry Festival for the benefit of the Sunday School, which featured "fancy costumes of the time of Charles II . . . a large Camera Lucida [with] a beautiful series of dissolving views . . . Professor Strubey's String and Brass Bands," as well as "strawberries, ice cream, fancy articles, and bouquets."[8]

It was not until the 1850s that the Baptist, English Lutheran, Catholic, and Jewish women began fund-raising. The Baptist society served large public suppers to reduce the debt on their church; at the end of the decade, the women of Trinity English Lutheran Church sponsored elaborate "Kris Kindel" festivals. On St. Patrick's Day in 1859, a group of Roman Catholic women from St. Augustine's parish organized a fair and supper sponsored by their St. Patrick's School Society in order to assist needy pupils with their parochial school tuition. A local editor reported that more than a thousand local citizens attended, of which 700 to 800 partook of the supper: "All sects, creeds, and parties were fully and fairly represented, and all met and parted with kindness and Christian good feeling."[9] A few months later, the "Ladies of the Thiriza Association" of Achduth Vesholom Synagogue were publicly commended for their efforts in decorating their newly refurbished facility, by "raising funds . . . purchasing drapery and furniture . . . and the tasty manner in which they have arranged it."[10]

Some parishes never sponsored fund-raising activities. There is no record of any German-speaking congregation (Lutheran, Catholic, Methodist, Reformed, and Jewish) raising money by a public event. Congregational expenses at St. Paul's German Lutheran Church were usually defrayed by assessments, and single women were expected to contribute as much as men, "at least 5 cents every Sunday in the collection (*Klingelbeutel*)." [11] One Protestant parish, the

Second Presbyterian Church, decided not to hold fairs; in 1846, one member lamented: "The ladies are trying to raise money in the Society to send for a carpet in spring for the whole church . . . . I do not know whether we shall have a fair or not. Some of our gentlemen are very much opposed to them."[12]

Susan Man McCulloch (Mrs. Hugh) came to Fort Wayne in 1836 to teach school and soon became active in the town's first women's society.
[Courtesy of Allen County-Fort Wayne Historical Society]

George W. Wood, editor of the *Times,* questioned the propriety of the fairs: "We doubt the morality of receiving . . . three times as much for articles, offered for sale, as they are worth . . . . [W]e regard Fairs of religious societies to raise money for Church purposes as a sort of pious swindling."[13] After announcing a church strawberry festival, he admonished his readers: "Let him remember, when he goes, to be *just* before generous, and if the tailor or seamstress, or landlord or laundress, be unpaid, to exercise his justice and then give freely to the Lord and 'lend to the poor.' "[14]

All of the fairs, festivals, and suppers were held away from the church premises: a few were in private homes; most were in a hall or store downtown. When money was needed faster than the ladies could sew, they served public suppers. Usually, the proceeds from these events were quickly disbursed; occasionally, a women's society chose a

large project, such as the building of a parsonage, and accumulated a considerable sum of money. The trustees of the First Presbyterian, Berry St. Methodist, and Trinity Episcopal congregations occasionally negotiated emergency loans from their women's societies, and usually paid them as much as 10 percent interest.

The Commitment to Missions

Only a portion of the activities of the Protestant women's societies were directed towards raising funds for their local church buildings and parsonages; an equal effort was made

Eleanore Guin Comparet (Mrs. Francis) was a leader in the French-speaking Catholic community.
[Courtesy of Allen County-Fort Wayne Historical Society]

in behalf of their denomination's missionary enterprise. These endeavors, however, seldom attracted public attention. Many citizens considered it their civic duty to support any local congregation's efforts to erect a new house of worship, and Protestants, Catholics, and Jews contributed to each other's building projects. No congregation, however, asked the general populace to contribute to their clergyman's salary or denominational program. A rare exception to this tradition occurred when the young girls of a local "Juvenile Missionary Society" offered their handiwork for sale, and announced: "The proceeds of sale to go for the aid of missions."[15]

Most women's societies worked hard to support their missionaries, and many members made personal sacrifices for the cause. Early in the century, the first of the "Female Cent Societies" had been organized in eastern congregations; by 1839, there were 680 "Ladies Associations" collecting funds for the interdenominational American Board of Foreign Missions.[16] Much of this money came directly from the labor of the members: the egg, butter, and rag money was theirs to spend as they chose, and thousands of Protestant women chose the cause of foreign missions.

Many saw this work to be women's work for women: church women supporting female missionaries who labored for the betterment of their illiterate and downtrodden sisters around the world.[17] Ellen C. Parsons, one of the first historians of the woman's missionary movement, paid public tribute in 1893 to those pioneer women's societies of the first half of the nineteenth century: "This was the era of the universal sewing-society and the home missionary box. Before railroads, in the days of canal-boats, when postage was twenty-five cents and purchasing by sample through the mail was yet uninvented. . . oh, then, great was the Box! . . . . No small contribution of sympathy, constancy and substantial aid did a generation of women put into those boxes."[18]

Susan Creighton Williams (Mrs. Jesse) was a leader in the Missionary Circle of the First Presbyterian Church.
[Courtesy of Allen County-Fort Wayne Historical Society]

Jesse Williams, Fort Wayne's first church historian, in 1860 was awed by the labors of the women of First Presbyterian Church in raising funds for both their local church and distant missions: "The Ladies Missionary Circle . . . was instituted at an early period. Many are the instances in which the families of missionaries laboring in the destitute surroundings, have been essentially relieved through their unobtrusive labors. The ladies of the church have also contributed through this agency, first and last, near two thousand dollars towards erecting and furnishing the [second] church building."[19]

Not every citizen of Fort Wayne was enamored by the amount of local energy and money that was spent on the peoples of distant lands. When one critic complained that "charity begins at home," the Reverend Charles Beecher responded that "charity *begins* but does not *end* at home."[20] When editor John Dawson learned that a "poor woman residing in the suburbs of this city died, leaving an infant four months old, and four other children," he vented his nativistic spleen on the local women's missionary circles: "Where are all the societies for propagating the Gospel amongst the Heathen? and where are all the kindhearted and charitable people? We call upon them to provide for our own indigent and unfortunate women and children, before they make any more flannel jackets for the little Hindoo Niggers."[21]

Local Charity

The work of charity among the poor was considered to be the special calling of women, not that the work was demeaning for men, but because women were judged to be more fully endowed with the gifts of sympathy and charity. In the early nineteenth century, a new concept of the male and female natures had come to be accepted: men were considered to be physically and mentally superior; women were judged to be morally and emotionally superior. The Reverend John M. Lowrie of the First Presbyterian Church taught this view: "Man has his strength, woman has hers; man his weaknesses, and woman hers; and they are all the better adapted to be mutual helpers, because they are not alike."[22] The belief that women were more fully endowed by their Creator with a heightened sense of morality and a deeper feeling of charity was a forceful stimulus to many women to exercise their gifts in human service. Joseph K. Edgerton, a young lawyer, called attention to the new church woman's spirit of evangelical charity in his speech at the local Methodist church:

Let us observe, by way of illustration, a female Sabbath School teacher on one of her missions of mercy to the low and degraded poor. She may be humble in life—herself destitute of wealth and friends and of many of those casual advantages upon which so many value themselves—but she feels within her breast the strong sympathies of a human heart, refined and elevated by piety. She loves to do good to her race—not for money, not for the applause of men, but because she has been made happy in the possession of the religion of the Gospel and earnestly desires that others may be also happy in it.

She goes from her humble home; she shuns the thoroughfares where the wealthy and the worldly love to display their fine equipages and rich attire and all those costly adornments "which make the poor man's humiliation proud." She seeks the haunts of poverty and vice; conscious of rectitude within, she fears no evil from without. She goes from door to door 'till, by her earnest, heartfelt appeals, she has persuaded some one, ignorant, and forsaken child to become an inmate of her school.

Thro' her efforts, aided by. . . others likeminded with herself, she frees him from his filth and rags, and, in cleanliness and comfortable garments, he takes his seat for the first time in the Sabbath School . . . . The glories of ambition and of worldly power, pale before the mild lustre of such examples of Christian virtue.[23]

Many church women of Fort Wayne worked as hard for the poor in their community as they did for the needy overseas, and, by 1840, had organized the Fort Wayne Female Benevolent Society.[24] During the first decade of its

The Hedekin House, on the east side of Barr Street between Columbia and Main streets, was built in 1844.
[Drawing by B. F. Griswold, 1917]

existence, the work was principally financed by the offerings collected at the annual Union Thanksgiving Day service held at one of the Protestant churches, and local residents were encouraged to "contribute liberally" to this "annual collection for the poor of the city."[25]

When additional funds were required, the women served suppers. As no church buildings were equipped with kitchens or dining facilities, the affairs were held in such places as the "Saloon of the Hedekin House"; in 1847, patrons were charged twenty-five cents and requested to bring "food

donations."[26] When the temperature dropped to -21 degrees in January 1856, the Female Benevolent Society arranged for an emergency benefit supper at Colerick's Hall. John Dawson, who had expressed concern for the welfare of the town's needy in the cold weather, praised the women and encouraged the men: "The ladies—God bless that heart which, during all the mutations of things, has beat true to His first and Holy impartings—have moved in the matter, and tomorrow night at the Hall ask our sex to their aid. It is an appeal from God's best gift. Will it be unheeded? Gentlemen of Fort Wayne, these ladies come to you as angels ministering to the race; they have yielded to you the control of the purse, and now, when they would ask you to tithe your loose means to alleviate age and want, will you, because you are fat with wealth, 'hold back this pittance!' "[27]

Ticket sales, as reported by the Society's secretary, Alida Hubbell Taylor, brought in $480,[28] but the net profit fell short of the funds needed for the winter emergency. Immediately the women announced that ten days hence they would hold a "Calico Dress Ball" for the benefit of the needy. When the arrangements committee changed the site of the event from Colerick's Hall to the Rockhill House, a large number of sponsors—including Henry Rudisill, D. F. Comparet, S. H. Shoaff, James Hoagland, John Bass, T. W. Swinney, and several young Hannas—declared that the Rockhill would be inappropriately expensive, "thus depriving the poor of an amount from $100 to $150."[29] This, however, was "but one objection"; some were not comfortable in an atmosphere of dancing and drinking, especially the Methodists, Baptists, Presbyterians, and English Lutherans whose discipline disapproved. As a consequence, two competing affairs were scheduled for the same hour.

The dissenters renamed their event the "People's Calico Dress Ball" and advertised, "the festivity is intended to illustrate the sentiment of *true charity* and, at the same time, to furnish an occasion of pleasure and enjoyment to all who may attend. . . . Refreshments . . . [will be] sandwiches and coffee . . . . Ladies are respectfully requested to appear in plain calico dress, and which dresses they are invited to send in the next day, to be donated to the poor. Admission $2."[30] The rival committee, who had made their event "by invitation only," attempted to counter "the impression that the Rockhill House party is to be an aristocratic affair, designed to keep the poorer classes of our community from participating in the party," and hoped that "the paper ball war will end after the party is over and the calico distributed, and we shall all meet again on the broad platform of common benevolence."[31]

About three hundred men and women attended, about equally divided between the two parties; the People's Ball, however, raised more money. A few months later, the president and treasurer of the Benevolent Society, Louisa E. Sturgis and Mary J. Randall, reported that the women had distributed over four hundred dollars for "groceries, rent, wood, medicines, flour and meal, articles of clothing, shoes, bedding, and 183 yards of flannel and linsey. Ninety-two families have been relieved, including those of fifty-six widows." The officers concluded their financial report with a comment for their critics: "In order to relieve the Society from the charge of favoritism and sectarianism which is often brought against it, the Ladies would say that nearly all

The Rockhill House, on the southwest corner of Main Street and Broadway, was opened as a hotel in 1854. In 1869 it became St. Joseph's Hospital.
[Drawing by B. F. Griswold, 1917]

the families assisted are foreigners and most of them Catholics. The distress and poverty of many of their families have been brought on by intemperance."[32]

Temperance

The experience of assisting those women and children who had become the innocent victims of "intemperance" turned many Fort Wayne women into ardent supporters of prohibition and, in 1854, a concerned group organized their own Female Temperance Meetings. (Between 1790 and 1840, Americans drank more alcoholic beverages—nearly half a pint per man a day—than in any other time in the nation's history; in 1830 the annual per capita consumption exceeded five gallons, nearly triple the rate in the twentieth century. By 1880, however, the national rate of alcohol consumption had declined to less than two gallons per capita, a change wrought almost entirely by the efforts of the temperance movement.)[33]

A local ordinance forbidding the sale of alcoholic beverages on the Sabbath—"except to travellers and in case of sickness"—had been enacted in 1836, largely through the efforts of the Presbyterian and Methodist ministers and the total-temperance society that they had organized. In 1851,

when the state of Maine passed a law prohibiting the manufacture and sale of alcohol, Indiana's prohibition advocates were strongly encouraged, and the state's many local temperance societies began petitioning their legislators to enact a similar measure. The lobbying in Fort Wayne for state-wide prohibition was led by Samuel Hanna, the chairman of the county temperance society. Apparently there was no place for women in the leadership of the society, and so they determined to organize their own meetings. When some in the community criticized these women for speaking out on their own, one of the leaders, under the pseudonym of "Fidelia," responded that women had not only a right but a duty to influence public opinion on the issues of moral reform:

> Female temperance meetings are common over the civilized world, and have been opposed only by pedants and pretended conservators of the public good . . . . It might answer for a Mohammedan who believes that women were created without souls, consequently destitute of moral faculties; but such sentiments should not be as much as named among Christians . . . . Only the high minded and benevolent can nobly dare to suffer in a worthy cause . . . . The temperance question . . . is a moral reform, and must be decided by moral feeling . . . . She can mould opinion which, after all, makes our laws . . . . The ladies of Fort Wayne should feel much encouraged in their efforts to get up a female temperance organization, and while they "labor and wait" they should remember, "Woe to you when all men speak well of you."[34]

In early 1855, the Indiana legislature passed a strong statute making the manufacture and sale of all intoxicating beverages illegal. Less than a majority of the citizens of Fort Wayne, however, endorsed this legislation; consequently, when news of the new prohibitory law reached the town, an anti-prohibition rally was organized. "There was a torchlight procession which passed the residence of John Hough, Jr., Jesse L. Williams and other prominent temperance men, and the members gave three groans for each of those gentlemen. Afterwards, the procession . . . dug a large grave [where] they buried their lost liberties in the shape of a keg of whiskey . . . . But . . . many of the saloonkeepers refused to close up. This aroused indignation in the bosoms of the prohibitionists, who got up a popular excitement, held a series of public meetings, and finally raised a large fund to be used in the prosecution of the law . . . . and the result was that in a short time there was scarcely a place in Fort Wayne where a glass of liquor could be obtained."[35] The editor of the *Sentinel,* who had not supported the legislation, was impressed by the results of its enforcement: "Our streets seem to be unusually quiet and still as a consequence . . . much good may be derived from its passage and a large amount of crime and suffering be prevented through its means."[36]

A week after the passage of the prohibitory law, Fort Wayne welcomed one of several women lecturers who would visit the city by means of the new railroads. One listener commented: "Miss Lucretia Wright spoke in this City last week on three different nights on the subject of Temperance and a Prohibitory Law, to very crowded houses. She is not only an eloquent, but impressive Lecturer, and we trust and believe that she left an influence lasting as time. Never was the hall so densely crowded as on those occasions. A little more of female influence in this city might make the men more independent, and less fearful of loosing a 'shilling or two' in business, or a rum-seeking voter or two at the election."[37] A local church woman wrote that the speaker left town "carrying with her the prayers of the friends of temperance, that success may attend her worthy efforts in behalf of the poor victims of the rum traffic."[38] A male resident called for more women to enter the public debate on community betterment: "We need more of the female character brought to bear on this and many other reforms . . . . Woman is half the moral creation and she ought to bear her proportion of moral duties and responsibilities."[39]

The state-wide prohibitory law went into effect in June 1855, and many Fort Wayne women joined in the celebration with the satisfaction that they had made a significant contribution to the cause. When the Indiana Supreme Court, the following year, declared that the new statute was unconstitutional, the women's temperance movement did not disband, but redoubled their energies in the areas of moral suasion and education. Not all Indiana women, however, were content to fight the problems of alcohol abuse through peaceful persuasion. A Fort Wayne newspaper, in 1856, reported that the church women of Princeton, Indiana, had marched on the town's reopened taverns, then called "groceries": "A large number of ladies met at the Methodist Church this evening equipped with axes and hatchets, and from there went and destroyed five groceries, entirely destroying the contents of each. Great excitement prevails."[40]

Woman's Rights

The temperance cause was the gate through which most women first entered the political arena; once there, other issues of moral reform became apparent, especially chattel slavery and woman's rights.[41] Emerine Holman Hamilton, a leader among the women at First Presbyterian Church, had followed this path; her granddaughter, Alice Hamilton, remembered her as "an ardent advocate of the temperance movement and, chiefly through it, of woman's suffrage."[42]

In the mid-1840s, some Indiana women had attempted to induce the General Assembly to abolish legislative divorces

and to allow women absolute control of their own property; the *Fort Wayne Sentinel* observed that men who wished to shed their wives could receive legislative divorces without a hearing, a procedure it deemed to be "a monumental unfairness to women."[43] At a state constitutional convention assembled in Indianapolis in 1851, these inequities were debated. The leading advocate of a proposal to protect the property rights of women by constitutional guarantees was Robert Dale Owen;[44] a principal opponent was William Steele Holman who, in a speech of twelve pages, blasted the cause of woman's rights. Holman was the younger brother of Emerine Hamilton, who had successfully led the women of First Presbyterian Church in 1847 to secure full voting rights in the congregation. A few days after his anti-woman's rights speech, Holman addressed the convention in a different tone and, somewhat chastened, presented a petition signed by one hundred women of his own county requesting that the convention adopt the proposition he had so vehemently opposed. When the convention adjourned, however, the status of woman's rights in Indiana remained unchanged.[45]

In Indianapolis, a group of women who had worked for this cause publicly expressed their gratitude to the minority of "high-minded gentlemen delegates in the Constitutional Convention, who favored the adoption of the motion securing to the married women of Indiana independent rights of property." These women, however, in a desire to disassociate themselves from a more radical group who sought political as well as property rights, expressed their disapproval of "the efforts of those of our sex who desire to enter the political arena—to contend with men at the ballot box, or sit in our public councils."[46] In Fort Wayne, more than a few women appeared to side with the radicals, and when men attempted to justify women's inequalities, these women's feelings on both property and voting rights boiled over into the pages of the *Weekly Times*. Their spokesperson, who wrote under the pen name "Eliza," was articulate: "We ask not for seats in legislative halls, nor to be heard in the councils of the nation; but we protest against being coerced into submission to laws, unjust and oppressive, without a voice in making them. It was this kind of oppression that caused an infant country to revolt, and seek its independence. Men now boast of their republican and happy institutions, but in respect to women they are oppressive and unjust. The right to exercise the elective franchise, and hold property, as naturally belongs to women as to men."[47]

The issue of woman's rights was now a lively subject of discussion in Fort Wayne, and some women were increasingly angered by the patronizing pronouncements of male acquaintances. "Eliza," in the first of two articles, spoke directly to these men:

It is strange yet true, that there are some whose minds are so contracted, as to suppose that fe-

155

males have no right to the enjoyment of anything, save that of performing acts of vassalage to those who style themselves their superiors. They assign to woman certain prescribed limits, as her sphere of action, beyond which she must not venture. And if perchance she should dare to assert her privileges, and take measures to maintain them, she is assailed by *gentlemen* as trespassing upon forbidden ground, and assuming prerogatives which do not belong to her, and which she is incapable of maintaining . . . . Such views in relation to females were prevalent in the benighted and barbarous ages, with which they should have passed away, and not to be advocated now in the nineteenth century, in the broad blaze of truth and knowledge . . . . Females certainly have a higher vocation, than filling the office of slaves—than yielding servile obedience to the opposite sex.

"Eliza" illustrated her critique by relating a conversation with a *"refined and sentimental young gentleman"* whose "ideas of females seem to be that they are only qualified for the most menial offices, and can possess no dignity of mind or nobleness of soul, which is so characteristic of the stronger sex. Possessing the true spirit of woman, I deem it my duty to defend my sex against such low scurrility and vile insinuations. We would advise the *gentleman* to pause and reflect ere he fabricates any more invectives to hurl at the female sex. All history proves that women are endowed with talents not inferior to those of men."[48]

The use of a pseudonym was the expected literary convention; most of the local woman's rights advocates in Fort Wayne, however, would have known the author's identity—as well as the content of her articles before they were published. "Eliza" was most likely Beulah C. "Mary" Ninde, who had just returned from the organizational meeting of the Woman's Rights Association of Indiana, convened in October 1851 at a church in Dublin, Wayne County. Ninde was a twenty-two-year-old native of Newport, Winchester County, who, the year before, had married a young lawyer, Lindley M. Ninde, and moved to Fort Wayne. Both were "birth-right" Quakers (her father, Daniel C. Puckett, was a prominent minister in the Indiana Yearly Meeting of Anti-Slavery Friends) and shared reform sentiments on abolition, temperance, and woman's rights. In the absence of a Friends Meeting in Fort Wayne, the young couple became "zealous members of the Presbyterian Church."[49]

Beulah Ninde corresponded with a Presbyterian minister, the Reverend John Witherspoon Scott, principal of the Oxford Female Institute in Oxford, Ohio. Scott had encouraged her literary gifts as a student and now welcomed her contributions of prose and poetry to *The Philalethian*, a monthly woman's journal published at the school. Soon after she had settled in Fort Wayne, Scott told Ninde: "I am . . . glad that you are one of the ladies who can find time from the drudging of mean household affairs to study Latin and cultivate the muses, &c."[50]

Dr. Mary Frame Thomas

The call for a convention of Indiana women (the first state association to be organized[51] after the 1848 national woman's rights convention assembled at Seneca Falls) was issued at an antislavery meeting held in Greensboro, Henry County. Amanda M. Way, an active agent in the "Underground Railroad" (soon to become a licensed preacher in the Methodist Church), introduced a resolution which compared two conditions of involuntary servitude in America: "The women of our land are being oppressed and degraded by the laws and customs of our country, and are in but little better condition than chattel slaves."[52] Ninde affixed her name to the new Association's constitution, which encouraged "the organization of District societies throughout the State."[53] Then, upon her return to Fort Wayne, she most likely met with Mary F. Thomas to discuss the formation of a local woman's rights society. Thomas, who had signed the call for the convention, was unable to attend but had addressed the delegates through a letter (probably delivered personally by Ninde) which "urged all those who believe in woman's rights to be firm and outspoken. She encouraged young ladies to enter the trades and professions, to fit themselves in some way for pecuniary independence." Thomas concluded her remarks with a personal note: "Although a wife, mother, and housekeeper, with all that that means, I am studying medicine, and expect to practice, if I live."[54] A thirty-five-year-old Quaker, Thomas's first interest in woman's rights had been stirred by Lucretia Mott in an address at the Friend's Yearly Meeting in Salem, Ohio, in 1845.[55] Her husband, Owen, was a physician who had brought his wife and three young daughters to Fort Wayne in 1849 to open a medical practice. Once settled in Aboite Township, Mary Thomas began her study of medicine, resolving that her family should not "suffer any comforts a wife and mother owed them." In a letter to a friend, she allowed that managing both vocations required "the most vigorous discipline of my mind and systematic arrangement of time."[56]

Thomas's professional preoccupations prevented her from attending the second Woman's Rights Association meeting at Richmond in the fall of 1852, and again she sent a letter which was "listened to with great interest."[57] In September 1853, after arranging for her children's care (and having sewn steadily to provide her family with clothing for six months) she journeyed to Philadelphia to enroll in the first session of the female department of the Penn Medical University in Philadelphia where her half sister was demonstrator in anatomy. Her studies, however, were cut short by the news of her oldest daughter's illness. Again unable to attend the 1853 annual state convention, she sent a letter; her leadership in the cause of woman's rights was admired and, in absentia, the delegates elected her a vice-president of the Association. In the winter of 1853-54, Thomas traveled to Cleveland to attend medical lectures at Western Reserve College where her husband was completing his medical degree; upon their return to Fort Wayne in the spring of 1854, they opened a joint practice, advertising in the local newspapers: "Drs. Owen and Mary F. Thomas: Office . . . over Foellinger's Shoe Store."[58]

Thomas wrote that she found in Fort Wayne "much opposition and prejudice" to a woman physician, "often from those of our own sex, who have been so long dependant on men that they judge all women by themselves, and doubt the capacity of any for a more enlarged sphere of action." In the face of such prejudice, it was Thomas's religious faith that gave her hope for the future: "Yet, by the eye of faith, through perseverance and toil, success is visible in the glimmering of the future; God's hand is guiding the work, and it must succeed, and it is ours in faith and patience to bear cheerfully whatever conflicts may cross our pathway in our endeavours to hasten the day when woman shall fill the station assigned her by our common father, as the co-worker with man in all that is good and grand and noble."[59]

Thomas limited her medical practice to "Obstetrics, Diseases of Women and Children, and General Practice among Females," and believed that there was a great need for more of her sex to enter this field. She was especially distressed by the unethical deportment of some of Fort Wayne's physicians, and expressed her strong feelings in a letter to the *Fort Wayne Jeffersonian:* "For proof of this we need not travel out of our own city. It is well known that there are men in the profession whose moral characters totally unfit them for the responsible situation they would aim to fill . . . The introduction of competent women as practitioners . . . will elevate the standard of professional morality, and save the lives of thousands from untimely graves, who would suffer, rather than outrage the most sacred feeling of woman's nature, by submitting to the unhallowed officiation of male physicians."[60]

Thomas was an a strong advocate of women's vocational education and led her own children in that direction. When her oldest daughter, Laura, died in March 1855, she sent a memorial to the editor of *The Lily:* "She was a young and joyous spirit, not yet fourteen years of age . . . . She had been learning the printing business, several months previous to her death . . . . She was devoted to her business, and looked forward to the time when she should be able to make it the means of doing good to her fellow-creatures . . . . Her young mind was awake to the necessity of women acquiring knowledge of business to render themselves independent."[61] When a business school opened in Fort Wayne in 1856, Thomas was quick to advertise its benefits for women in the pages of *The Lily* (then published in Richmond, Indiana): "There is also one [Institute] in Fort Wayne, Mr. C. J. Dietrich, Principal, where ladies are instructed in a full mercantile course, preparing them for book-keeping . . . . Here is an opportunity for ladies to fit themselves for an employment at once lucrative and useful, and one well adapted to women."[62]

Throughout her medical career, Thomas never lost sight of those ideals of moral reform that united church women: abolition, woman's rights, and temperance. After meeting in Richmond with a group of the "many women laboring for the right," she declared: "These faithful ones shall have their reward when the jubilee of freedom shall sound through the land—when the slave shall stand forth in his manhood—when *woman* can raise her unshackled arm and use her unfettered mind—when the children of the redeemed inebriate shall 'rise up and call him blessed'—then will they feel that they have not labored in vain; nor need they wait till then, for every day's discharge of duty brings its reward."[63]

In early 1856, Thomas resumed her studies at Penn Medical College and, in July, was awarded the degree of Doctor of Medicine. The following month, she and her husband moved their family to Richmond (they judged Fort Wayne's schools to be inadequate) where they united with the Methodist Church.[64] In October, she was elected president of the state Woman's Rights Association. Her friend, "Mary" Ninde, was likewise elected to the Committee on Arrangements and, at the next convention, to the Executive Committee. When Thomas addressed the Association in 1857, she said: "Although I have not enjoyed the privilege of attending the annual meetings, owing to my many cares, I have not been an idler in the vineyard. By my example, as well as my words, I have tried to teach women to be more self-reliant, and to prepare themselves for larger and more varied spheres of activity."[65] In 1858, Thomas was editing *The Lily,* "devoted to Temperance and the Elevation of Woman."[66] The following year she was one of a delegation of three women chosen by the Association to address a joint session of the Indiana General Assembly on the subject of woman's rights. "Dr. Thomas read the petition signed by over one thousand residents of Indiana, and urged the Legislature to pass laws giving equal property rights to married women,[67] and to take the necessary steps to so amend the Constitution of the State as to secure to all women the right of suffrage. She claimed these rights on the ground of absolute justice, as well as the highest expediency, pointing out clearly the evils that flow from class legislation." Some legislators responded with ridicule for the women and their cause; their views prevailed and the Assembly voted "that legislation on this subject is inexpedient at this time."[68] A *Cincinnati Daily Gazette* reporter judged that the General

Assembly's behavior was "a farce" and "the most disgraceful affair he ever saw in which ladies were concerned."[69]

Some Men Help; Others Harass

If a large majority of the all-male legislators was opposed to redressing women's legal inequities, then it may be

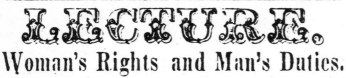

LECTURE.
Woman's Rights and Man's Duties.

Mrs. M. F. Emerson will deliver a Lecture on the above subjects at the Baptist Meeting House in this city on Thursday (17th) evening at half past seven o'clock. Admitance 15 cts. General attendance is solicited.

The first publicly advertised lecture in Fort Wayne on the subject of Woman's Rights was held at the Baptist Church in 1854.

assumed that most of the male population in Fort Wayne were of a similar disposition. A significant minority, however, was emerging: some men were simply disturbed that a daughter might be divorced through the machinations of a local politician, or that a surviving widow might lose her inheritance to a fortune hunter; a growing number of men in Fort Wayne, however, clearly understood that the root issue was male power, and said so publicly: "There seems to be a very watchful eye over the doings of the gentler sex . . . . Some have thought it is because of what Paul had occasion to say in a barbarous age; or . . . that old mother Eve *happened* to be mistaken or deceived in regard to a certain matter, before father Adam. But there is another reason more important than either of these, and I fear it is *the* reason, viz. that, was woman to transcend her present allotted sphere, it might interfere somewhat with the pursuits and avocations of men. But it has occurred to a few minds, at least, that there are various occupations, now monopolized by men, that would be more appropriately filled by women . . . . [W]oman has too long been hampered by the false notions of society."[70]

A number of these male advocates of female rights soon brought pressure on the local Young Men's Literary Society[71] to include a leader of the woman's movement in their lecture series, and, in the fall of 1855, it was announced that Lucy Stone would deliver three lectures. Stone was not the first woman to speak in Fort Wayne on the subject: the previous year a lecture entitled "Woman's Rights and Man's Duties" had been given by Mrs. M. F. Emerson—an event

most likely sponsored by the local woman's rights association.[72] Stone, however, was the first woman to speak under the aegis of the popular and prestigious Men's Literary Society. Fort Wayne women usually outnumbered the men in attendance at the Society's programs, which had prompted one man to say, "We are almost inclined to think they are the *Literati* of Fort Wayne."[73]

In order to encourage a larger male attendance at Stone's lectures, an editor wrote: "Her talents as a lecturer, the novelty of the occasion, and lastly, though not least, her Bloomer costume will not fail to draw a crowded house."[74] Bloomer costumes were first seen in Fort Wayne in the summer of 1851, an event noted in the *Fort Wayne Times*. "Two young women promenaded our streets yesterday with short dresses and wide (or Turkish) trousers. The new style looked exceedingly well and is bound to prevail."[75] Many men saw the costume to be both modest and practical; one Fort Wayne resident, who called himself "The Old Bachelor," wrote to Amelia Bloomer:

> Females, too long . . . have been slaves to the opinion of the opposite sex. Along our streets can be daily seen what I would term *Butterfly Ladies;* one half of their heads and bosoms bared to the gaze of *man*. Why is it that females will so expose themselves? Is it not to please that portion of creation, that are so called 'Lords?' . . . In the good days of old . . . our mothers did not go half-naked. Nor did they wear long dresses—or in other words foot-traps! Ah, no, in those days women loved to walk active, and use their hands for a better purpose than holding up *long dresses* . . . . I would that all girls had sense enough to wear short dresses . . . in a few words, wear the *Bloomer costume*.[76]

Bloomers had already drawn a large crowd in Fort Wayne; in May 1854, it was reported that "a country school teacher . . . an innocent and respectable female choosing to enter our city on business . . . [was] hooted at and gazed at, insulted by men who are not better than a *swell mob,* [and] followed by a bevy of vicious boys."[77] The editor was distressed that the "becoming pair of *trousseau* and a neat dress falling slightly below the knee," which had been "repeatedly seen on our streets and at every mountebank exhibition had in our city," should cause such a stir; he suspected that those men who had behaved with such "incivility" had been "captivated" by the female "foot and ankle," and had misjudged the woman's character.[78]

Lucy Stone Lectures

Lucy Stone arrived at Colerick's Hall in a Bloomer

costume—which she "complimented" as "more sensible than the present style"[79]—and was greeted by an overflow crowd who had paid enough in admissions to erase the Literary Society's accumulated deficit. Stone had been speaking throughout the country since her graduation from Oberlin College in 1847—the first woman of Massachusetts to earn such a degree. Her earliest lectures were under the sponsorship of the American Anti-Slavery Society and she often compared the inferior status of the American woman with the African-American. Stone wrote that she was not infrequently "hindered by the falsehoods and misrepresentations of the press" on her tours: "After one of my lectures in Indiana, the morning paper reported that I was found in the

Colerick's Hall, on the north side of Columbia Street between Clinton and Barr streets, was built in 1853 and served for many years as Fort Wayne's only theater.
[Drawing by B. F. Griswold, 1917]

bar-room, smoking a cigar and swearing like a trooper." Lecturing on such controversial subjects as abolition and woman's rights required both courage and wit; when a man threw a prayer book, hitting her head, she observed that only a man without a good argument would stoop to such a low one.[80] After helping to organize the first national woman's rights convention in 1850 (where her speech converted Susan B. Anthony to the cause), Stone lectured solely on the subject of woman's rights. She avoided the florid rhetoric so common on the podium, and her clear, strong voice projected a sincerity and natural eloquence that moved her listeners;[81] Elizabeth Cady Stanton said, "Lucy Stone was the first person by whom the heart of the American public was deeply

stirred on the woman question." Her lectures attracted large audiences, and in three years she had earned $7000; she also had attracted Henry Browne Blackwell, a Cincinnati hardware merchant and abolitionist, whom she married in 1855.[82]

Stone's lectures in Fort Wayne followed her regular format. Her first, on the "Social and Industrial Disabilities of Woman," was judged by one man to be "an able clear and argumentative appeal in favor of women enjoying an equality of social privilege, and having the right to follow any pursuit which their abilities and inclinations may prompt them to."[83] Another reported: "She . . . enlarged upon the proper sphere of woman, maintaining that capacity alone was the limit of sphere; that every woman should be allowed that position in social and political matters which her talents and capability allow her to hold. She said, whatever is fit to do at all can be done . . . as well by woman as by man if they are able to do it. She remarked at some length upon the injustice done towards women in the remuneration they received for their services, and gave as examples the teachers and needle-women throughout our country. She also gave instances of women in the U. S. who were earning for themselves not only a bare subsistence but handsome fortunes by being engaged in occupations which were considered as unfit for females to follow."[84]

Stone's second lecture on "The Legal and Political Disabilities of Woman" was deemed by one reporter to be "an able vindication of the rights of her sex to a more equal participation in the rights of self government than the lords of creation have hitherto accorded them." On the subject of discriminatory laws, the reporter came away totally convinced: "As to the legal disabilities woman labors under, there can be no doubt but the present system is an outrage on common sense and a disgrace to the age"; on the issue of suffrage, however, he was not as sure: "As to the political rights—the right of voting and holding office—there will of course be many who disagree with her views, but none can deny the ability with which she sustains her positions."[85]

In her final lecture on the "Scriptural Position of Woman," Stone confronted the traditional interpretations of scripture with her own Biblical scholarship. As a young woman she had suspected that those passages in the English Bible that touched on the status of women—which many believed proved that women should assume a subordinate status—were unsupported in their original texts, and so she mastered both Biblical Greek and Hebrew at college. In her closing address, Stone explained her own exegesis of the first chapters of Genesis and portions of the Pauline epistles. The audience was impressed, and one man concluded: "This lady is an able, clear minded, eloquent, and forcible lecturer, of modest and unpretending manner, and affords in herself the strongest evidence that her claims for the equality of the sexes are well founded. We consider her lectures the best that have ever been delivered here."[86]

Changing Attitudes

The percentage of women who supported the woman's rights movement in the mid-1850s is difficult to determine, but the number had become sufficiently large that retailers began using the subject to attract attention to their products. In 1854, an advertisement in the *Sentinel,* under the headline "Woman's Rights," stated, "It is an undeniable fact that the rights of women, by your existing Laws, are unprotected and abused. It has also recently been discovered that women have a right to protect their Glossy Ringlets. This can be done by using Emerson's American Hair Restorative."[87]

Only one Fort Wayne man chose to attack Stone's lectures publicly, and his long (one hundred and forty column inches), rambling essay was published by the *Daily Times* in four installments. Several women immediately responded to its anonymous author, "R. S." (whom they dubbed "Rather Shallow"), and each reasoned from a religious perspective: "It is evident to the unprejudiced investigator, that our common Father has given to each that versatility of talent that best fit them for their several duties, and they are alike accountable to *Him,* not one to the other; when man can give to God a ransom for the soul of woman, then, *and not 'till then,* is it his privilege to control the mind of woman, and limit the sphere of action that results from an enlightened mental culture."[88] Another respondent, "Lizzie B.," couched her critique in the language of a Biblical chronicle:

And it came to pass . . . that the people wondered among themselves and said . . . "Now, therefore, let us inquire into this matter, if, peradventure, there be wrong between us and the women, that it may be put away." But others said, "Not so; lest when there be equal rights and privileges extended to woman, she shall take it into her head, to leave off the frivolities of fashion, and seek after wisdom and truth, so that those who now delight in balls, parties and such pastimes, will find no more pleasure therein, but strive to benefit their race by every consistent means, even if it be by holding office and going to Congress in the performance of those duties much better than we sometimes do, and there be found among us no more excuse for grumbling and complaint and we be constrained to hold our peace.

And moreover, there be other evils which will come from this thing; for none will be found any more who will consent to be beaten by drunken husbands, but the liquor will be put away from this people, so that we cannot so much as get a drop to burn our cooling tongues . . . . For the multitudes of homeless laboring women will see the wrong which hath been done unto them, and the voice of their cry shall come up after this wise: 'Our necks are under persecution; we labor and have no rest. Our fathers have sinned and are not; and we have borne their iniquities. We gat our bread with the peril of our lives, because of the custom of the country.' (Lam. 5: 5, 7, 9) . . . . 'Woe unto them that decree unrighteous decrees, and that write grievousness which they have prescribed; to turn aside the needy from judgement, and to take away the right from the poor of my people, that widows may be their prey, and that they may rob the fatherless!' " (Isaiah 10: 1, 2.)[89]

A large segment of Fort Wayne's English-speaking population responded to Stone's lectures with an understanding that had considerably matured since 1851, when several items deprecating the woman's rights convention had been published in the *Fort Wayne Times*.[90] The Reverend Jonathan Edwards of First Presbyterian Church, who had once mocked the "harangues and resolves of our Woman's Rights Conventions,"[91] had been succeeded by Dr. John M. Lowrie, who taught that woman was created equal with man.[92] The pastor of the Second Presbyterian Church, the Reverend Eleroy Curtis, also expounded a theology of equality, which was amplified in a lecture series "addressed particularly to young ladies. . . Bible Portraits of Women . . . or what the Gospel has done for women."[93]

A Fort Wayne clergyman in the 1850s who openly opposed the woman's rights movement (as he also opposed abolition) was Dr. Wilhelm Sihler of St. Paul's German Lutheran Church; his stout defense of the Teutonic tradition of limiting women to children, church, and kitchen *(Kinder, Kirche, und Küche),* however, did not deter his daughter Elizabeth, who became a professor at Mount Holyoke College, from strongly supporting woman's equality.[94] The only other Fort Wayne clergyman to publicly condemn the woman's rights movement was the rector of Trinity Episcopal Church, the Reverend Joseph Large, who "took a very decided stand against the whole movement. . . with great energy and force; but, in the opinion of many he was somewhat ultra in his position. This called out a great deal of criticism in essays and reviews; in numerous editorials and reviews; in allusions in the late female Suffrage Convention; in the effusions of verse-writers, all of whom have been down on the Reverend gentleman."[95] Between 1849 and 1854 Large had been highly esteemed by his congregation, and was invited to the rectorship again in the early 1860s; his uncompromising ideas of male superiority, however, made his continued ministry in Fort Wayne untenable, and the vestry demanded his resignation, citing "a want of that congeniality of feeling that should exist between a rector and the members of his parish."[96]

In the Reformers' Wake

During the first half of the 1850s, every woman lecturer who came to Fort Wayne, such as Wright, Emerson, and Stone, brought an urgent message of moral reform on such issues as temperance, abolition, and woman's rights; by the end of the decade, however, another group of women, entertainers, from the famous to the infamous, followed the reformers' trail on the popular lecture circuits. In early 1860, Sarah Jane Clarke Lippincott, "better known by her *nom de plume* 'Grace Greenwood,'" spoke on "The Heroic in Common Life." Greenwood was a facile and popular writer whose works reflected, rather than challenged, the values of her day; in Fort Wayne, her remarks were much more concerned with woman's role than with her rights, and

Lola Montez in 1847
[Courtesy of Schloss Nymphenburg Gallery]

encouraged her audience "to be reconciled with our positions in life."[97] A month later (following a lecture by Horace Greeley) Lola Montez came to town to speak on "Fashion." Montez was an Irish-born dancer, actress, and adventuress who had once been the mistress of King Ludwig I of Bavaria; more recently she had experienced a religious conversion

and was admired for her generosity and charity. In Fort Wayne, she was judged "a fair and witty lecturer" whose address was "delivered with a great deal of vivacity, and abounded with many happy and humorous illustrations of the absurdities to which people will go in order to follow the fashion. Montez was decidedly in favor of hoops when worn in moderation, and asserted many ladies had prematurely shortened their lives by an excessive indulgence in petticoats." She also chided those men in the audience "who make so much ado over the periphery of a ladies dress, and had them scrutinize more closely whether the flowing drapery of a female dress is not more graceful . . . than their own ungainly pipestem apologies for legs encased in pantaloons as tight as eelskins."[98]

The "flowing drapery" of the new hoop skirts had already provoked controversy in some of the more conservative denominations: the *Fort Wayne Republican* reported that, at an Ohio camp meeting, a bishop of the Church of the United Brethren had recently "forbade anyone with hoops on to partake of the sacrament. . . . The warning was heeded, and rings, breast pins, artificials and hoops came off—some of the latter being used to kindle fires."[99] In Fort Wayne, a man who attended a wedding at the Episcopal Church noted that the church "was well filled; yet it could have held more . . . if some of the young ladies had spread out their manners and kindness as well as they did their hoops."[100]

The lengthening parade of women in the lecture halls made it increasingly difficult for many persons to maintain the fiction that women were intellectually inferior to men. In addition, the success of women's leadership in the crusades for moral reform, so warmly applauded by those men who labored for temperance and abolition, did much to promote the principles of woman's equality. As a result, the men and women in Fort Wayne joined forces to merge the interests of the men's and women's temperance societies into the total abstinence Washington Lodge of the Independent Order of Good Templars, the first secret society established in Indiana with equal privileges for men and women. Among the first projects proposed to the Good Templars was a more adequate supply of potable water: "A very large share of the beer and ale which is drunk in this city is taken to quench the thirst, because water, pure and cool, can only be obtained with difficulty . . . . We would respectfully suggest to this benevolent society that they make the abundant supply of *good* water one of their special aims."[101]

Among the first officers of the Good Templars were three women: Beulah C. Ninde, Eliza J. Allen, and Imogene Smith.[102] Ninde had continued to represent Fort Wayne women at the annual meetings of the Indiana Woman's rights Association until the outbreak of the Civil War, when the formal activities of the state society were suspended. In 1869, when the Association proposed the resumption of their state-wide conventions, those representatives from Fort Wayne who signed the call were "Beulah C. Ninde" and

"Hon. L. N. Ninde."[103] Upon her return from the state meeting, Mrs. Ninde led in the reorganization of Allen County Woman's Rights Association; under her leadership as president, the local Association soon made plans to hold its own three-day convention in March 1871.[104] Encouraged by an attendance of sixty men and women, they then invited the state Association to schedule its annual convention at Fort Wayne in May 1874. In attendance at this meeting were some of the foremost leaders in the Woman Suffrage movement, Frances Willard and Susan B. Anthony, who were entertained by Emerine Hamilton, now a wealthy widow and significant contributor to the woman's movement.[105]

At the beginning of the decade of the 1860s, the strength of the woman's movement in Fort Wayne, as in most communities across the nation, remained in the women's religious societies: the sewing circles, Dorcas groups, missionary bands, temperance societies, benevolent associations, and prayer groups. By this time, many woman's societies had significantly increased in size, affluence, and power, and were now affiliated with the new regional and national associations of women within their denominations. In the 1860s and 70s, almost all local missionary societies' funds were being funnelled through these national woman's missionary organizations, which increasingly supported only women missionaries. In spite of the emergence of the national woman's organizations for moral reform, such as the Women's Christian Temperance Union, more American women belonged to congregational religious societies than to all of the reform groups combined. After their family, the religious societies were for most women their agency of mutual support, their vehicle for human service, their reinforcer of personal worth as a woman, their interpreter of the issues of moral reform at home and abroad, and the door through which they entered the public arena in pursuit of social change.

9
New School Presbyterians

"I have come to divide your church."
Henry Ward Beecher, 1844.

During the six-year pastorate of the Reverend Alexander T. Rankin, Fort Wayne Presbyterians had successfully kept their distance from the controversy which had divided their denomination into the Old School and New School factions. Sometime after 1837, the membership of First Presbyterian Church had quietly joined the Old School side of the denomination's schism and continued to be comfortable with this more conservative wing represented by Princeton Theological Seminary and Hanover College. The New School branch, however, with its inspiration from New England schools and Wabash College, had won the allegiance of the nearby Presbyterian churches in Lima (Howe) and Huntington; then, when Rankin resigned in the fall of 1843, the Fort Wayne congregation was judged by some New Schoolers as an open field for missionary activity.

The Vacant Pulpit Attracts New School Attention

When Samuel Merrill, president of the State Bank, visited Fort Wayne on business in October 1843 and learned that Alexander T. Rankin was about to depart for a new position, he took action. As an ardent advocate of New School Presbyterianism, Merrill saw this vacant Old School pulpit as an inviting prize to be captured for his side. Immediately he wrote to his brother, David, then serving a church in Vermont:

This church is now without a pastor. Mr. Rankin has been dismissed[1] and is to leave within a few days. It is numbered with the Old School, yet the leaven of the New is so strong that they only hope to keep together by getting a pastor in principle with the New, but willing to go with the Old.

They have applied to Mr. Stephenson of Troy... but it is not decided whether he is to come or not. This is now a fine town with at least 2500 inhabitants and growing rapidly. There ought to be a first rate man here, yet the people have not been in the habit of *paying* their pastor or contributing to religious purposes. I wish you were here and I think you would suit very well; yet, at your age, it will not do to make experiments.[2]

It may have been Merrill who reported the news of the Fort Wayne opportunity to his pastor, the Reverend Henry Ward Beecher of the Second Presbyterian Church in Indianapolis. Beecher was then thirty-one years of age and had come to Indianapolis in 1839 after serving a congregation of twenty souls in Lawrenceburg. He was a son of the Reverend Lyman Beecher, who had become one of the most influential clergyman in the West after settling in Cincinnati in 1832. A native New Englander, Henry had attended Amherst College and Lane Theological Seminary. His gifts, however, were not in scholarship but oratory and he was destined to become the most well-known, influential, and controversial American preacher in the mid-nineteenth century. John Hay was later to aver that Beecher was "the greatest preacher the world has seen since St. Paul preached on Mar's Hill." By 1844, he had gained a wider reputation through the publication of *Seven Lectures to Young Men,* a series of dramatic exhortations to Christian virtue in the face of temptation and vice on the western frontier.

Henry Ward Beecher in the 1850s
[Courtesy of Second Presbyterian Church, Indianapolis]

Church politics and polemics were not Beecher's first love, but the future career of his younger brother, Charles, then in his final year at Lane Theological Seminary, was of deep concern to him. Henry, therefore, saw the vacant pulpit in Fort Wayne not only as a prize to be captured for the New School, but as a position to be occupied by his brother. Charles, however, would not be graduated from seminary until the following spring, so Henry was forced to wait.

In the meantime, First Presbyterian Church's invitation to the Reverend John M. Stephenson of Troy, Ohio, was declined; then, in January, they were refused by the Reverend Hugh S. Dickson of Bardstown, Kentucky. With the pulpit still unfilled by the spring of 1844, Henry Ward Beecher made his plans. Rumors of his intentions reached Fort Wayne and immediately the congregation sent a distress call to the Reverend William Caldwell Anderson, professor

of rhetoric and belle lettres at Hanover College, whose faculty was solidly Old School. Dr. Anderson was forty years of age, a graduate of Washington and Jefferson College who had been in Pittsburgh before coming to Indiana to serve the Presbyterian Church at New Albany. Recently, he had suffered from a throat ailment[3] which made his lecturing increasingly difficult. As a consequence, he declined a formal call to the pastorate of First Presbyterian Church, but consented to assist in the emergency.[4] Understanding well the vulnerability of the vacant pulpit with Beecher about to pounce, and seeking some respite from his daily lectures, Anderson resigned his professorship and arrived in Fort Wayne on Sunday, April 14, 1844, and immediately took charge of the church.

Henry Ward Beecher Arrives

The following Saturday, Beecher arrived in Fort Wayne and went directly to the home of Jesse L. Williams, chief engineer for the canal system and a respected elder on the session of First Presbyterian Church. Williams later recollected:

> The Rev. Henry Ward Beecher reached Fort Wayne in the mud-spattered condition of the outward man. Hitching his horse, he hastened to my house and said to Mrs. Williams (being myself absent), "I have come to divide your church." Just then, favoring providences became manifest. Rev. W. C. Anderson comes to the front; . . . [he] had reached Fort Wayne just six days before Mr. Beecher, neither one knowing the plans or whereabouts of the other. There was this difference between them, however, that the former had come upon the regular call of the church. He had already preached one sermon, thus acquiring control of the pulpit.
>
> Dr. Anderson, on the Sabbath morning, invited Mr. Beecher to occupy the pulpit with him and take part in the services. But, in the afternoon, Mr. Beecher commenced his two weeks' preaching in the old court house . . . . Dr. Anderson was a man of mark fully equal to the emergency and entirely comprehended the situation. He preached with great power . . . .
>
> In a town of two thousand, the presence of two such ministers . . . [in] contest . . . became at once the absorbing topic. Farmers visiting the town heard the street conversation and carried into the country exaggerated reports of the supposed conflict.[5]

164

Anderson's invitation to Beecher to assist in Sunday worship was the required courtesy of the day, but it also made clear who was pastor of the church. Beecher could not refuse without appearing rude; after the amenities had been exchanged, however, he began his campaign in earnest and, during the next three weeks was "preaching daily and visiting families of the church."[6] When the smoke finally cleared, a total of five women and one man of the congregation of one hundred and thirty-nine communicants had been persuaded to join the New School.

A member of First Presbyterian Church later commented: "The church had grown in numbers and strength and was dwelling in peace and quiet. They did not wish to be divided. The men and women prayed against Mr. Beechers's division movements. And it seems their prayers were stronger than all his 'two weeks thundering.'[7] Mr. B., with his geniality and broad sympathies, was out of place in such efforts. His genius does not run in that direction. That was perhaps his first and last attempt in the dividing of churches. It was, however . . . a notable failure."[8]

Beecher had miscalculated the mood of the people: the congregation was united and had no faction or party spirit to exploit; Anderson was an able representative of the Old School; and few of the fine points of the tedious controversy were of real interest to Fort Wayne Presbyterians. If, in other parts of the country, the Old School was soft on the slavery issue, certainly their last pastor, A. T. Rankin, could put most Indiana New Schoolers in the shadows with his abolitionist zeal. To the average Presbyterian on the frontier, the theological dispute seemed only to be playing with words; Presbyterian historian L. C. Rudolph concluded: "Distinguishing the two in doctrine was a hair's breadth business. It was mostly a matter of specialized vocabulary, a difference of phraseology and mode of illustration. The three points of an Old School sermon might vary from those of a New School sermon if the sermon was on a controversial doctrine, but even then the conclusion and the invitation were the same."[9]

Towards the end of his two-week preaching mission in the courthouse, Henry arranged for his brother Charles to preach. Some of those attending, upon learning that Henry would not deliver the principal message, began to move towards the door. Charles immediately rose and announced to the assembly: "Those who have come to worship Henry Ward Beecher, may now depart; those who have come to worship Almighty God will, of course, remain."[10] The next day Henry departed for Indianapolis; Charles felt overwhelmed and wrote: "Never having had any ministerial charge, I found myself suddenly, as my brother said, 'not *placed,* but *pitched* into the middle of the hardest field in all Indiana.' "[11]

Second Presbyterian Church Is Organized

The six New School converts applied for and were granted letters of dismission from First Presbyterian Church. Then, on Saturday May 4, 1844, combined with six others whom Beecher had convinced, the fledgling congregation invited Charles Beecher to serve as their Stated Supply[12] for one year. The next day at worship, under their new pastor's leadership, they were formally organized as the Second[13] Presbyterian Church of Fort Wayne. The keystone of Henry Ward Beecher's plan was now in place: his brother Charles had a pastorate and the flag of New School Presbyterianism had been planted in Fort Wayne.

Two of the members to leave First Church and join Second were Susan Man McCulloch and Alida Hubbell Taylor, who had come to Fort Wayne eight years before as teachers at the school established in the church. Susan's defection was more for personal than theological reasons. She had attended the Hartford Female Seminary in Connecticut, established by the Beechers' sister, Catharine. Here she listened to letters from Harriet Beecher read to her class and, on occasion, heard the father, Lyman Beecher, preach when he visited the town.[14]

Susan's husband Hugh, who had been an admirer of A. T. Rankin, accompanied his wife in her transfer. He was subsequently elected a trustee of the infant congregation, and, although never formally joining this or any other church, became a great admirer of Henry Ward Beecher. Whenever McCulloch visited Indianapolis on business, he attended Second Presbyterian Church and, over the years, maintained contact. In his autobiography, he fondly described Beecher:

> He was not only the most popular, but the most influential preacher this country has ever produced . . . . His sermons, both in style and topics, were quite different from those which had been heard from Presbyterian pulpits . . . . It was religion, not theology that was preached by Mr. Beecher. Christianity was, in his estimation, the moral purifier of the world . . . a system of which love was the corner-stone, and active benevolence, unselfish efforts for the well-being of others, and personal purity were the legitimate results.

> He was frequently in my house . . . . To me he was an open book . . . . His vitality was immense, his jollity at times irrepressible . . . . I recollect how he sang and shouted as we rode through the woods together, how admirably he mimicked preachers who seemed to think that sanctimonious countenances and whining tones were the indications of zealous faith. To Mr. Beecher,

religion was joyousness, Christianity the currency by which men were to be made not only better but happier.[15]

Charles Beecher Begins His Pastorate

Henry's brother, Charles, projected quite a different personality. Much more the scholar, he had acquired a working knowledge of eight languages by the time he was graduated, near the top of his class, from Bowdoin College. He was a good athlete and had been president of his college gymnasium society. A talented musician, he possessed a fine singing voice, played the violin,[16] and was an accomplished organist. At the age of nineteen Charles completed his college studies and was immediately enrolled in Lane Theological Seminary. "I went to college too young. Father was in a hurry to get us all through and into the ministry."[17] At Lane, his unsuccessful effort to accept the tenets of Jonathan Edward's *Freedom of the Will* drove him to despair and extinguished his interest in pursuing further theological studies.

To the distress of his father, Charles determined to become an organist and church musician. After studying and teaching music for a few years in Cincinnati, he traveled to New Orleans where he served as organist in a Presbyterian Church, while working full time as a clerk in a cotton brokerage. During this time he married Sarah Coffin and their first child was born. It was also in New Orleans that he began to collect material on slavery for his sister Harriet, including data on the Simon Legree of real life, to be used in her book, *Uncle Tom's Cabin*.[18]

When his brother Henry was called to Second Presbyterian Church in Indianapolis, Charles was invited to take charge of the music in the congregation. Soon, through his experiences in teaching a Sunday School class, he regained sufficient faith to renew his call to the ministry. There he also developed a preaching style distinct from those of his father and brothers. In narrative sermons Charles could move his listeners to tears as he touched the deep feelings of the Biblical characters. One hearer long remembered "the pathos and beauty beyond anything"[19] in a series of sermons on the Virgin and the Son.

Such individuality of style could have its pitfalls, however. In September, at a meeting of his presbytery at Noblesville, Henry heard that Charles was having trouble in Fort Wayne. Apparently Old School tongues were circulating a rumor that the new pastor of the Second Presbyterian Church leaned towards Unitarianism. Henry's immediate fear was that newly arrived Congregationalists might shy away from Charles. As a consequence, he wrote to his father: "If the stream from the East begins to go wrong, it will be difficult to check it, since strangers will be told [by Old Schoolers], 'all who have come from Congregational Churches have gone with us.' We shall be cut off for

supplies, defeated, and Charles, leaving with stigma of Unitarianism fastened upon him, will go away . . . . It seems to me that everything depends on his succeeding in this enterprise."[20] Henry also encouraged his father to write to Charles and, if possible, to visit Fort Wayne. Then Henry penned Charles some practical advice: "Preach little doctrine, except what is of mouldy orthodoxy . . . . Take hold of the most practical subjects; popularize your sermons. I do not ask you to change yourself; but, for a time, while captious critics are lurking, adapt your mode as to insure that you shall be rightly understood."[21]

Charles, however, had already attracted many of the independent-thinking and liberal-minded Protestants in Fort Wayne who admired his intellectual gifts, wide-ranging interests and solid scholarship. In his first report to the American Home Missionary Society, whose support had been quickly secured, Charles confessed: "Many of the congregation, and some of my warmest friends, are Unitarians from New England. Others are skeptical, others Universalist. In short, I am much like David in the mountains: plenty of lawless characters. This, of course, affords means of misrepresentation to the ill disposed. These people have been thrown off by ultra-high Calvinistic and Old School influences and are becoming regular and attentive listeners. And, as I have the misfortune to be, at any rate, rather original, I am, of course, represented as anything but sound in the faith."[22]

Charles knew that the rumor about his unorthodoxy was not the only reason that First Presbyterian Church was retaining its members and experiencing growth. Anderson was an able pulpiteer and attracted visitors from other congregations. A Methodist who visited First Presbyterian Church was sufficiently impressed to record in his diary that Anderson preached a "very good sermon."[23] Under their interim pastor's leadership, the congregation was now awakened from a sleepy complacency to an alert activism. Beecher acknowledged Anderson's proficiency: "They have thrown in their ablest leader in the state, Mr. Anderson, plausible, affable, travelled, sagacious, crafty, eminently skillful . . . . The Session, rich, aristocratic, and formerly idle, are now . . . kept vigilant and active. Every new arrival visited, courted, told that they are New School in sentiment, and we Unitarian . . . . They do nothing openly, invidiously. All is civil, polished. Even those reports of heresy, etc., are so covertly conveyed that their origin does not appear."[24]

In October, Charles met with his father and brothers, William and Henry, at a meeting of the New School Synod in Indianapolis; one action of the assembly was to divide the Logansport Presbytery to create the new Presbytery of Fort Wayne. Second Presbyterian Church now became the hub of this new judicatory, which included the congregations of Lima (Howe), Goshen, Salem Center, Elkhart, and Huntington. When the inaugural meeting of the new presbytery was scheduled for Friday, November 8, 1844, in Fort Wayne,

Charles Beecher requested that his ordination be included on the docket.

Lyman Beecher Visits Fort Wayne

The service of ordination was a memorable one. The candidate's father had accepted Charles's invitation to participate and then conduct a series of meetings in the courthouse following the ordination.[25] At the age of seventy, Lyman Beecher left his home in Walnut Hills, outside Cincinnati, and traveled alone by canal boat to St. Mary's, Ohio, arriving at sunset on Friday. As Charles's ordination was scheduled for the next evening, he immediately hired a horse and then found a man who would guide him for the first fifteen miles of the journey to Fort Wayne. Dr. Beecher recalled:

At 10 o'clock [moonrise] we took to our saddles—and well it was he went with me, for sure enough I never could have found the way—deep in woods half the time, leg-deep in mud, and stumps, and logs, and sometimes black sloughs, and places where we had to turn off the track and make a circuit of a mile through the woods on the right and then come back and just strike the path, and diverge a mile on the left. We must have made as much as eight miles additional in these crossings.

At last, between two and three o'clock at night, we came out of the worst of it onto a tolerable western road and, as there was a little village there, I thanked my guide and told him I would not trouble him to go farther; so he stopped to lodge in the village. As for me, I felt lively and brisk, and the moon shone clear, and I thought I would just hold on the rest of the night. About daybreak, I got into the town of Willshire, where I slept two hours, took breakfast, and then went on. At 3 o'clock I came within eleven miles of Fort Wayne, and really, I did feel tired—almost worn out. I don't know but I had gone beyond the mark. I stopped an hour for dinner, and jogged on. Soon a young man overtook me, and company and talk revived me, and seemed to revive my horse too, for he pricked up and, the first I knew, we came right into Fort Wayne. It was five o'clock, and I had traveled, as I reckon, with all the windings and turnings, about seventy-two miles since 10 o'clock the evening before. [26]

Hugh McCulloch remembered Dr. Beecher's arrival at their house that Saturday afternoon: "He was covered from foot to head with mud, but was far from being exhausted by his long and tiresome ride. Immediately after his arrival, he asked if he could have some whiskey to 'rub himself down with!' as he said. The whiskey was sent to his room and, soon after, he joined the family, apparently as fresh as if he had been resting for hours."[27]

Lyman Beecher had been a New England Congregationalist who became widely known in the East as a revivalist, battling Unitarianism, Catholicism, rationalism, and the liquor traffic. In 1832, he turned his attention to the evangelization of the West and accepted the call of the Second Presbyterian Church in Cincinnati and later the presidency of Lane Theological Seminary in nearby Walnut Hills. His famous lecture in 1835, "A Plea for the West," captivated audiences throughout the East by coupling the spiritual needs of the frontier with the patriot's pride and the nativist's fear, as he asked, "What is to be done to educate the millions, which in twenty years, Europe will pour out on us?"[28]

Hugh McCulloch fondly remembered Lyman's visits to his home in Fort Wayne, especially the delight he took in hunting in the neighboring woods, and wrote: "It did not take me long to discover that . . . he abounded in sympathy, in geniality, in good-will for everybody . . . . Dr. Beecher had the reputation for being the father of more brains than any other man in the country . . . . His six sons and four daughters were very unlike in talents and in their leading characteristics; but there was not an ordinary one among them."[29]

Henry Ward Beecher was also delayed in his journey to the ordination and, upon his arrival, hurried off to meet with some persons who were to unite with the congregation. McCulloch recalled: "The meeting was in a private house, and the room was well filled, as it was expected that Mr. Beecher would be present, and if present, that he would speak. He did not disappoint them. After some business . . . Mr. Beecher arose, read a few passages from the New Testament, and made an address in language so beautiful and appropriate, in a voice so tender and affectionate, that all present were spellbound, and when he closed there was not a dry eye except his own in the room."[30]

On the appointed Saturday, November 9, the Fort Wayne Presbytery (New School), consisting of three ministers and one elder, gathered to hear a sermon delivered by Lyman Beecher and then proceeded to organize their new judicatory. Charles's request for ordination was soon taken up and the candidate was subsequently examined in his knowledge of theology. Then, after a trial sermon on the subject of faith, "it was resolved to proceed with the ordination exercises at candlelighting"[31] in the courthouse. Susan McCulloch described the ceremony:

The ordination was very affecting. Henry Beecher preached from the text contained in I Corinthians 2:2, which was the same text that Charles Beecher preached from when we settled him, though they did not know what the other was going to preach

167

Lyman Beecher and his children, ca. 1855: *(bottom row, left to right)* **Isabella, Catherine, Lyman, Mary, and Harriet;** *(top row)* **Thomas, William, Edward, Charles, and Henry.**
[Courtesy of Radcliffe College Library]

from. Mr. [Thomas] Anderson from Huntington made the prayer after the right hand of fellowship, and the Venerable Dr. Beecher gave the charge. He commenced thus,

"Twenty-eight years ago, my son, your mother (now a saint in heaven) committed you to my arms to bear you from her sight forever, exclaiming 'what will become of you poor child?' She gave you her blessing and consecrated you to God, and said to me, 'I desire all my sons to be ministers of Christ'.... One [George Beecher] had gone to meet her there; the others are, thanks be to God, ministers of him."

You may suppose, there was not a dry eye in the house. We feel very happy in having such a minister.[32]

Lyman Beecher had made his reputation in the East as a revivalist and was determined to do his best to augment the five-month-old congregation by holding a protracted meeting. Joined by Henry, they gathered every morning and evening in the courthouse for nearly three weeks, but the response was thin. Charles wrote: "Tho' we were enlarged and cheered and strengthened, yet the revival we had prayed for came not."[33] One devout Methodist who attended Charles's ordination and the suceeding services was Joseph J. Edgerton, a young lawyer who had recently arrived in Fort Wayne from New York City. He commented in his diary that Dr. Lyman Beecher "was less interesting and less earnest and impressive than his son, Henry Beecher," whom he described as

... a young man of brilliant and powerful mind, and apparently of deep and earnest piety. I like him very much .... On Friday evening [November 15, 1844] I heard Mr. Beecher preach from the text "Strive to enter in at the straight gate; for many, I say unto you, shall like to enter in but shall not be able." He took somewhat of a new view of this passage and preached from it with much ability and power. He is a man, it seems to me, deeply impressed with the magnitude of his calling and who constantly strives to discharge his duty in it.

He took occasion from his text to show the probability that a majority of those now impenitent would be lost, not from an inadequacy of the means provided by God for their salvation, but from their own evil inclination, passions, associations, and habits. He displayed the fallacy of the hopes of those, who living impenitent, yet expected to enter into heaven, the powerful disappointment that would await them when . . . [they] seek to enter in, but would not be able. Mr. Beecher's meetings do not seem to have been very well attended. I regret it. This town requires a strong manifestation of the power and grace of God in converting souls. It is almost lifeless in religion and, so far as my observation has extended, I have seen no cases of what I consider fervent piety or deep devotion among the churches.[34]

Edgerton's judgement of Fort Wayne as "almost lifeless in religion" may have been justified for, at the end of this extraordinary effort by the Beechers, who preached morning and evening for nearly three weeks, only nine persons had been converted to join the little flock. But many others, like Edgerton, who did not choose to unite with Second Presbyterian Church, were nevertheless deeply moved by the ministers' earnest preaching. Even the independent-minded Hugh McCulloch had been touched, and declared that he had now begun "to feel there is something in being a Christian."[35] Fort Wayne residents had never before seen such concerted efforts expended to found a church as they witnessed in the combined energies of the three Beechers.

Building the Church

On the final day of these protracted meetings, a subscription was circulated to raise funds for a church building. Worship in the courthouse was shared with recently organized Trinity Episcopal Church which occupied the facility on Sunday mornings. Charles Beecher was especially sensitive to the problem of attracting visitors to services which could only be scheduled on Sunday afternoons. A member of Second Presbyterian Church in Indianapolis, who was visiting the McCullochs, lamented in a letter to her family: "Sunday morning has come again, beamed brightly upon us and, while you are listening to the words of life falling from the lips of Mr. [Henry Ward] Beecher, I am waiting patiently

at home until this afternoon, when I too will be permitted to enjoy that blessing. They do not have preaching here but once a day, as they have to hold meeting in the Court House and the Episcopalians have it in the morning."[36]

Not only were members of the congregation and regular attenders solicited, but prominent citizens, who might consider it their civic duty to help erect a new church in town, were also invited to contribute. Leading the list of subscribers with a pledge of two hundred dollars was Alexander H. Ewing of an old Fort Wayne fur trading family, followed by

The Second Presbyterian Church (first building) was erected on the south side of Berry Street between Webster and Ewing streets in 1846.

[Original Illustration by Robert D. Parker]

Dr. Charles E. Sturgis, a physician active in the Democratic party, Royal W. Taylor, a merchant from Vermont, Capt. Asa Fairfield, who operated the first boat on the Wabash and Erie Canal, as well as William Rockhill and Hugh McCulloch.[37] None of these men had formally joined the congregation.[38] Their pledges of support however, along with other sources, were insufficient, so the pastor made an extended trip to Lafayette, Terre Haute, Indianapolis, and Cincinnati, and personally raised five hundred dollars towards the total cost of $2537 for the new structure. Beecher's excitement for the project was evident when he wrote to the Home Missionary Society: "Our new church progresses and will be the most beautiful little church in the state. The spire terminates in a cross, much to the surprise of some Hoosiers. But I tell them it is my most significant declaration of war against the Romish Church and presently they will find it so."[39]

On February 22, 1846, the new facility—described by Beecher as "a handsome New England frame church, fifty-five feet by thirty-six"—was dedicated.[40] A proud member wrote: "The church is completely finished from the cross on the point of the spire to the door steps [and] painted white outside and inside . . . . The pulpit is Gothic. The curtain

Olive and Asa Fairfield
[Courtesy of Allen County-Fort Wayne Historical Society]

behind the pulpit in the Gothic arch is crimson damask and the cushion for the Bible crimson velvet . . . . The ten large windows were curtained with white cotton. (We will have blinds in the Spring.) Oh how comfortable everything looked after being so long in that dirty court house."[41]

A local newspaper reported that "this church is not extravagant and gorgeous; but it is finished to the driving of the last nail and is as 'neat as a pin'. For all the essential purposes it is just as good as the Trinity in New York or St. Peter's at Rome." In a separate column an editorial lamented the carelessness of tobacco chewers in church: "Will not the trustees of the 2nd Presbyterian Church, which is to be dedicated tomorrow. . . before the floors have been defiled with . . . 'tobacco filth,' establish so wholesome a regulation [to ban spitting]; and then let the man be marked who would first violate it."[42]

Charles Beecher's Controversial Sermon

At the dedication of the new building Charles Beecher delivered two discourses entitled "The Bible a Sufficient Creed," and declared that

. . . liberty of opinion in our theological seminaries is a mere form. To say nothing of the thumb-screw of criticism by which every original mind is tortured into negative propriety, the whole boasted liberty of the student consists in a choice of chains . . . whether he will wear the Presbyterian handcuffs or the Methodist, Baptist, Episcopal or other Evangelical handcuffs. Hence it has secretly come to pass that the ministers themselves dare not study their Bibles . . . . There is something criminal in saying anything new. It is shocking to utter words that have not the mould of age upon them . . . .

I know not what others may say, but if ever I shrink from declaring that the Bible, the whole Bible and nothing but the Bible is the perfect and thorough furniture of the Christian minister and the Christian church, then may my right hand forget her cunning and my tongue cleave unto the roof of my mouth.[43]

These sermons constituted a public declaration by the pastor of the faith of this New School congregation and, thereby, created a stir. Susan McCulloch reflected on the impact of Beecher's address on the non-members attending the dedication, and said: "[I]f they read their Bibles, they would know what our belief was and the principles that we professed to act upon, but if they went to judging . . . according to any creed or confession except the Bible they would not know what to make of us. There were a great many long faces among the Methodists, Episcopalians and O[ld] S[chool] but I think now they will know what we profess."[44] The officers of Second Church,[45] however, were so pleased with their pastor's doctrinal exposition that they published the dedicatory sermons at their own expense for general distribution. The men well understood the controversial ground on which their minister stood and thus wrote to Beecher: "You will of course expect the censure of those who deliberately regard the Bible as an insufficient 'rule of faith,' but we cannot believe that the great mass of Protestants, if properly enlightened, would be prepared to sustain systems, which insidiously but effectively undermine the authority of the Bible, by a virtual denial of its claims."[46]

For Methodists and Episcopalians,[47] Beecher's position undermined the authority of the ancient Nicene and Apostles' Creeds; for Lutherans, his critique also challenged their adherence to the Augsburg Confession. Presbyterians—like their Reformed and Lutheran cousins—were a confessional church, and required their ministers, elders and deacons, to affirm in their ordination vows that the Westminster Confession of Faith contained the system of doctrine as taught in the scriptures. Beecher, however, argued that to make any creed or confession "a test . . . is the apostasy we have to fear."[48]

Beecher's officers had been prophetic, for censure was soon to come from his denominational colleagues. At the spring meeting of his New School presbytery, when the young pastor was unfortunately absent, a committee was appointed to confer with him concerning "erroneous sentiments published by him in two recent sermons, endeavoring to reclaim him."[49] Hugh McCulloch commented: "I apprehend that there is as little liberty among Christians as among politicians. The man who dares to think differently from his party in political matters, and to give utterance to his opinions, is denounced as a traitor and treated as a criminal."[50] In September the committee of Presbytery reported that Beecher was "confirmed in the sentiments taught in his sermons . . . and he wishes to remain in connection with the Presbytery." The gathered ministers and elders then accepted the committee's judgement "that, while we would by no means abandon the great Protestant doctrine that the Bible is the only infallible and sufficient rule of faith and practice . . . we regret the course which Brother Beecher had taken . . . . Many of the views . . . are a total misapprehension of the views and practices of the Presbyterian Church with which he is connected . . . . The whole subject of creeds and confessions, and the use we make of them, is set in its appropriate light by the Constitution of our church."[51] The presbytery took no further action, and the report was sent with its minutes to the synod where it had to be signed by the new moderator, Henry Ward Beecher.

Charles Beecher viewed the Presbyterian schism as an impediment to the church's mission and refused to serve as a theological swordsman for his denomination: "The division of O[ld] & N[ew] S[chool], wherever the blame lies, is a perfect millstone about the neck of evangelical piety. It is something that annihilates revival."[52] His congregation, however, had an insatiable appetite for polemics: "'Beecher,' I have heard myself addressed of a Sunday morning, 'Beecher you must *put in your best licks today!*' 'You must *knock the socks* off those Old School folks!' And so they stood by to see me fight. Fight? For what? For Christ? They never dreamed of that; they wanted to hear what I had to say for *New School.* Now I had nothing particular to say for New School . . . . I *didn't,* and told them so. 'Well,' said they, 'What did you come up here for?' "[53]

The Pastor, Teacher, and Musician

Charles Beecher never became a spellbinding preacher as was his brother Henry, but he outshone his brother as a pastor.[54] Those who had not seen him since his seminary days were impressed by his spiritual growth in Fort Wayne. A young acquaintance from Indianapolis commented, "I think he is much changed; his feelings are softened and he now thinks and acts as a devoted Christian."[55]

As a pastor, he understood the dynamics of congregational life with a sure instinct that created a rich educational, musical, and devotional program. Religious education in his Sabbath School utilized the new memorization method in which each member committed five verses of scripture to memory and then allowed the rest of the class to correct their recitation. The school's enrollment never climbed much above fifty scholars, and there is no clear picture of how the classes were divided according to age, gender, or learning ability. Vital to the school was a library, and Beecher labored long and hard to develop a collection of nearly three hundred volumes at a cost of thirty dollars.[56]

Beecher never forgot that he was officially titled a missionary and, as such, he developed four preaching points in the country, often conducting services there on Sunday morning and returning to Fort Wayne in time for the mid-afternoon service in the court house. He also founded two Sunday schools in these unpopulated areas, but quickly turned these classes over to laymen who went out into the country each Sunday to instruct their pupils, often in a rural schoolhouse: "Mr. Tilden, a young man of mine, walks 15-20 miles every Sunday. He has two Sab. Sch.—& about 50 pupils—Solemn. Steady. & Eager. He teaches them music."[57]

Beecher viewed his Fort Wayne congregation as a seed-bed of Christian piety which would nurture the best of faith and morals, a fellowship of Christians who were to be in the world, but not of its worldliness. After three years, he wrote: "There is more disengagement from the world. The church is better able to feel her own identity. We read no new novels, go to no more parties. We visit each other more and are more bent on spiritual progress."[58] Especially innovative was his Thursday evening inquirers' class which he subtly transformed into an opportunity for leadership training and congregational fellowship. He said of this experiment, "Especially we get acquainted and get bashful people talking in meeting before they know it. So I never let on that they are 'speaking in meeting.' If I should, they would hold their tongue. They are like the Irishman's pig, who went steadily enough to Cork because his driver had persuaded him the road led the other way."[59]

Music, especially church music, was Beecher's special passion and he was extraordinarily talented as a teacher. As a youth he had studied with the eminent Lowell Mason, who directed the music in Lyman Beecher's church and was then considered the country's leading church musician. Soon after he arrived in Fort Wayne, his former choir members and friends in Second Presbyterian Church, Indianapolis, sent him a viol.[60] The bass-viol was then commonly used to accompany singing, and was the first musical instrument (after the pitch pipe) allowed into New England Churches.[61] As no piano or organ was available in the local courthouse for Sunday worship, this viol, played by Beecher or someone instructed by him, supported either the hymn melody or the bass line of the anthem. Beecher occasionally accompanied his choir on the violin;[62] soon after the new church was dedicated, however, he was playing on a new seraphine (melodeon), personally selected by Mason in New York City.[63]

In the fall of 1844, Beecher announced a series of vocal classes and was overwhelmed with the large response of townspeople who wished to improve their singing skills. The following year a newspaper editorialized:

> We are gratified to learn that the Rev. Charles Beecher has again announced his school for instruction in vocal music. It will be held at the Court House on Tuesday and Thursday evenings of each week at the moderate charge of $1.50 per series of twenty-five lessons. Mr. Beecher is a perfect master of the science of music and, as a practical singer, he probably has no equal in the Western Country. His method of instruction is elementary and inductive; no better opportunity need be desired of learning that polite accomplishment then by attending Mr. Beecher's school.[64]

Five years later, Beecher's classes were still overflowing with students eager to learn from his acclaimed talents. He saw his music teaching to be an integral part of his ministry and thus reported to the Missionary Society: "The 'Experiment' in teaching music has, in part, proved successful. The School numbered 50 at the first evening and rapidly rose to 130 . . . . I expect to more than double my choir . . . . An interesting feature in the class is the alto division of boys and girls—some twenty or thirty little folks who learn as fast as the best of the old ones, and some faster. I shall thus bring several of the young children right into the choir. I lead the choir myself . . . . It is close by my pulpit. Most of my singers are pious. It is *sacred* music and I look on it as a means of grace."[65]

Most probably the fee for the vocal classes was designed by Beecher to create in the student an attitude of serious participation, as well as to cover the cost of the music supplies. If there was any profit, it did not add measurably to the marginal salary provided by the congregation and augmented by funds from the Missionary Society. Beecher's admirers, keenly aware of how much he contributed to the community out of the treasure of this talents, determined to assist him by organizing a "donation party," inviting the general public to visit Beecher's home with gifts.[66] The response must have been overwhelming, for the minister and his wife immediately responded through the pages of the weekly newspaper: "Mr. and Mrs. Beecher would express their acknowledgements to their friends . . . for the many gifts presented on that occasion. May these favors, which we are unable to requite, be recompensed to the generous donors at the Resurrection of the Just."[67] Not to be outdone in expressing affection for their pastor, the Methodists soon organized a donation party for their minister—and soon donation parties became annual events.

The one area in which Beecher had some self doubt was his ability to organize and lead the women of the parish. He lamented that "nine of the ladies of my Church, and those the most influential, have unconverted husbands . . . and . . . are kept much under worldly influence. Against this I hardly know how to operate." He was distressed at "tossing of the head, at turnings up of the head," and in exasperation exclaimed, "Women are monstrous hard subjects. I'd rather meet an army of men than a squadron of spinsters and virgins. But, by the help of the Lord, I trust I shall succeed. At any rate, if I do not get the ladies of the church in harness, I shall seek some other field of labor, for the church will not be blessed."[68]

These women of the congregation were not without their own criticisms of their minister. Julia Merrill, who was an admirer of Charles when he directed the music program in his brother's congregation in Indianapolis, visited Fort Wayne in 1845 and reported, "Mr. Beecher is pretty well liked here, though not so much as I expected. The truth is they find too much fault with him. Some think he is conceited, that he tries to show too often that he is *Dr. Beecher's* son. Others say he preaches too plain, that no man ever did succeed that preaches *the Bible*. [Some say] he has not enough tact, etc., etc., etc. He seems to be common property and every[one] that pleases picks at him. He does not hear all that is said, or I should think he would become disheartened . . . . All unite in loving Mrs. Beecher [and] think she is goodness personified."[69]

Social Issues:
Lodges, Racism, Temperance, Politics, and Poverty

In Beecher's attempt to shield his flock from the distractions of the world, he preached against the newly organized lodge of Odd Fellows, warning his men to avoid its fellowship.[70] The editor of the *Sentinel* took umbrage at Beecher's statements about the fraternal order and, after printing a heart-rending tale of charity by an Old Fellows Lodge for the widow of a member, concluded: "It sounds bad to hear any Christian minister preach *against* the secrets of such an order."[71] Another new fraternity Beecher frowned upon was the Sons of Temperance, a national organization dedicated to the cause of sobriety. Beecher lumped both these societies together with the dangers of infidelity, universalism, and politics. When the Sons of Temperance published a sharp denial of a rumor that they initiated black members, Beecher commented publicly: "From the anxiety manifested . . . to remove the impression that Colored people are, or can, be

Sons of Temperance, I presume there must be some reason, supposed to be a good one, on which their exclusion from the benefits of the order is based. I would respectfully request any brother of that order, who may be able, to tell us what that reason is. At present, tho' I can conceive of reasons enough, I can not conceive of a single *good* one."[72]

The Sons of Temperance were quick to reply to Beecher's query, but, instead of presenting their rationale, turned the question back on him: "Why are colored people, for example, not received into social society generally? Why are they not found among the Presbyteries, Synods, and Conferences of our churches? Why do we not meet them on the platform of social equality in our family circles? Are there any *'good* reasons' for excluding them from these?"[73] Beecher responded that, whereas the lodge had legislated against black membership, "the colored man, who gives good evidence of piety, is not forbidden by our legislation to unite with our Churches, and sit with us in perfect social equality at the Lord's table .... Nay, if it were known that any session had ventured to exclude from the Lord's table a pious family, for no other reason than their color—that session would be liable to be proceeded against . . . for a violation of Christian duty and fellowship." Beecher then concluded:

> The real reason why people of color are not more frequently found in our churches, and Presbyteries, and why they do not more freely move in good society, is owing, in part, to a deep and silent sense of wrong and injurious treatment received at our hand .... Deprived of their vote in some states, and of testifying on oath, and subjected to various disadvantages, they are really forced down into a species of *low caste* like what prevails in India, a phenomenon at war with the Gospel we profess, and disgraceful to our free institutions.
> . . .
>
> Christ said, "I was hungry, I was thirsty, naked, sick, in prison, a stranger—and ye ministered not unto me; inasmuch as ye did it not to one of the least of these my brethren, ye did it not to me." Now the African is a stranger—and in distress. . . . He has long suffered under great disadvantage. The mere gratification of an unreasonable caste spirit, a silly prejudice of color . . . is bad . . . and worthless .... It is unkind—ungenerous— unchristian—and without apology.[74]

By mid 1847, it was reported that Fort Wayne now had "one Masonic Lodge, . . . two Odd Fellows Lodges, one Sons of Temperance, one Fathers of Temperance and Friends of Literature, and. . . a Lodge of Cadets of Temperance."[75] Beecher voiced the suspicion of many churchmen that the new lodges' espousal of a moral cause, such as temperance, was only window dressing to divert attention from the societies' secret and exclusive character. Protestant clergy were active in supporting most temperance groups but, when politicians began to use these lodges for partisan purposes,[76] the ministers demurred. As the old temperance society was nearing collapse in the face of the new lodges, Beecher saw his local congregation to be the more effective temperance organization. None of the new groups, however, seemed to hinder the proliferation of taverns; Beecher noted sadly, "There are 35 grog-shops here to 3500 people."[77]

The cause of temperance was endorsed by all of the churches, both Catholic and Protestant, English and German speaking; each denomination, however, differed on the degree of censure which should be laid on their offending members. Beecher's presbytery took the most severe position by declaring that "Dram-drinking, dram-selling, dram-giving, or the signing of petitions for retailing intoxicating liquors, or the furnishing of materials for the manufacture of the same, are crimes which require church discipline."[78] New School Presbyterians, however, seldom condemned intemperance without also indicting the institution of slavery, and so the Fort Wayne Presbytery, in the same breath, also declared that "Slavery is a great sin, opposed to the word of God and contrary to the rights of man; that slavery in the church should be a subject of discipline the same as any other crime." On these resolutions Beecher made public comment: "I would simply remark, that I would have proposed one more, 'Resolved, that the disenfranchisement of the free people of color as practised in the state of Indiana is a *crime* analogous to that of slavery.' "[79] His conviction that slaveholding was criminal was expressed in his reply to a member of the pulpit committee of a Congregational church in Washington, D. C. (where slavery was legal) that, if he became their pastor, he would "make slaveholding a test of membership and of communion."[80]

Beecher commented on every social issue of moral consequence—temperance, abolition, elections, poverty, Indians—and, if possible, took appropriate action. When the poor of the community were without medical care, food and shelter, Beecher and the local Methodist minister, John S. Bayless, organized a committee to meet these needs. The committee was not designed to sit passively and receive requests but was commissioned by the ministers to "seek out indigent persons and persons in distress, in this vicinity and afford them relief." They advertised: "Persons in the city or county acquainted with families or individuals in distress are requested to give information to any member of the . . . committee."[81] The community's newly awakened concern for the indigent spread to the Board of County Commissioners, who then employed Dr. Charles Schmits "to give medical attendance and medicine to all persons who have or may become paupers."[82]

A religious concern for the poor and the needy was well

appreciated by the general populace, but any minister who criticized the root causes of the poverty in the established political, social, or economic institutions was liable to be denounced a "meddler." Many Presbyterian, Baptist, and Methodist clergymen delivered pre-election day sermons; when the Whigs lost the local election, Beecher's sermon was judged by the editor of the *Fort Wayne Times* to have contributed to their defeat:

> When our minsters of the Gospel so far forget themselves as to turn their churches into political arenas, it is high time they should be taught to earn their bread in some more legitimate manner. We are eternally harping upon poor priest-ridden Europe, and yet allow our own preachers here in democratic America to preach from newspapers instead of the Bible—we care not how much gentlemen of the cloth talk of nation and state affairs in the streets (or Groceries), but we do think that they are descending far below their high calling when they suffer private feelings, or political bias, to get the better of their Christian meekness, and then, like frozen snakes warmed into life, bite the hand that has cherished and sustained them.
>
> All we remember of the aforesaid sermon is comprised in the words below, to wit: "Some politicians can give donations to churches and Irish relief, even if they have to cheat the Indians out of it." Now if we should ask any boy in our streets of 10 years old, who he thought was meant by that dig under the fifth rib, we will bet our old fiddle he would say unhesitatingly, W[illiam] G. Ewing .... But the above extract is but a shadow of the merits of his discourse. He talked all the time of politicians—swearing, drinking, gambling and licentious politicians—just as if the people of this town could not discriminate between good and bad men, as well as he! If we were a preacher, rather then preach such a sermon as that, we would earn our bread by fiddling in a Grog Shop.[83]

Beecher responded by submitting to the newspaper his sermon notes, which the editor then printed. These published remarks do not support the allegation that Beecher had indirectly attacked the Whig candidate for Congress from the pulpit, but it is clear that Beecher had held before his congregation the highest moral standards for office seekers, and urged Christians not to vote for any who were profane, licentious, intemperate, Sabbath breakers, duellists, or slaveholders.[84] The Whigs were sensitive to charges that Ewing's firm had held slaves in Missouri, and traded deceit-

fully with the Indians in the new reservations west of the Mississippi River.[85] Richard Chute, son of the minister who organized First Presbyterian Church, came to Ewing's defense, differentiating him from "the low, depraved, and desperate whiskey seller on the frontier, who setting all laws civil and humane, at defiance, continue to furnish the border tribes with the deadly poison that is so silently, but swiftly, working their destruction."[86]

The Author

There was in Charles Beecher the emerging form of a frontier Renaissance man: he was a musician, an athlete, and a scholar of wide ranging interest. He was counted a good speaker by his listeners[87] and a challenging teacher who prepared informative lectures on a variety of current topics from temperance to Judaism.[88] When civic leaders organized a lecture series, Beecher was invited to give the first address, and spoke on geology. A series of Sunday evening talks was eventually prepared for publication, possibly with the encouragement of his sister, Harriet Beecher Stowe. Beecher entitled his work *The Incarnation; or Pictures of the Virgin and Her Son.* Harriet prefaced the two hundred page volume with an introductory essay, inviting the reader of traditional religious works to be open to the imaginative style of the author as he expands on the Biblical narrative:

> There may be some who, at first, would feel a prejudice against this species of composition, as so blending together outlines of truth and fiction as to spread a doubtful hue of romance over the whole. They wish to know that what they are reading is true. They dislike to have their sympathies enlisted and their feelings carried away by what, after all, may never have happened.
>
> To such we would suggest the idea, that no human being ever reads a narrative without some image and conception of what they read; and that the blank, cold, vague, misty images of an uninstructed mind are no more like the truth than the conceptions of a vivid imagination chastened and guided by accurate knowledge of typographical and historic details respecting these distant scenes and events.
>
> So, though incidents may be inserted into the narrative which, though probable by historic verisimilitude, are still confessedly conjectural; yet these are more like truth than a blank, void of any incident whatever; because *some* incident confessedly did occur over and above what is scripturally recorded, and there is, therefore, a large

and legitimate field for a combined imagination and critical ingenuity to fill up chasms in the most skillful and probable manner.

A local reviewer of the book, who had often heard Beecher lecture, wrote:

> The style and manner of the work are strongly characterized by the peculiarities of the author in the pulpit—they are *sui generis*—paragraphic, ejaculatory—in short, eminently "Beecheronian." Possessing a most luxuriant and vivid imagination, he clothes—loads to redundancy—at times, almost smothers—his ideas in the most gorgeous drapery of words, until they become obscure, and one loses sight of the subject in admiration of its adornment. Thus he is always brilliant, often beautiful, but, not infrequently, sweeps away to the very outer verge of philological propriety.[89]

An admirer of his sermons and lectures once said of Beecher: "He has the most beautiful, practical and well-cultivated imagination of anyone I ever saw."[90] His style shows some influence of the best of the early Victorian poets, and yet he writes with a fresh creativity, blending the Biblical narrative with both historical and mythological allusions. In the first chapter he introduces the subject of the advent of Christ with dramatic parallels to the classical world:

> And while Elijah bowed in Carmel before the still small voice, Homer was weaving his tuneful tale of gods and goddesses Olympian.
>
> And while the constellation of the captivity throws a far ray athwart the pagan chaos, Philosophy sends Thales to light, at Babylon, the earliest Ionic taper.
>
> Pythagoras also kindles there his Italic torch, and lends a borrowed ray to Plato.
>
> Anon, while Ezra and Nehemiah are closing the annals of sacred revelation, Herodotus starts from fabulous somnambulism to begin authentic history, and wends his way inquiring to old Babylon.
>
> And when Malachi is closing revealed religion, devout Paganism commands a Socrates, a Plato, a Confucius to originate theology.
>
> Yes, while the mighty orbs of inspiration, conscious of the coming sun, and paling before the dawn, withdraw their shining, upward at once she soars to classic zenith with all her lesser lights. Now first she bids the world believe, history, science, religion, poetry, and art are born. Haughty Alexander she employs as her schoolmaster to teach barbarian lips to whisper Greek. Then furtively she scatters all abroad in her domain the stolen rays of Hebrew fire, gleaming from the Alexandrine scroll. And thus, with old tradition, scripture cross-light, and new-born classic genius, she bathes the dreamy nations with a chilly star-light, and calls it day. The sleeping millions stir and sigh as dawn approaches, in troubled slumber. We hear them moaning in their dreams, calling to one another in restless presage of the breaking of day, "It is contained," they whisper all over the benighted orb, "in the fates that at this very time the East shall prevail, and some one who shall come out of Judea obtain the empire of the world!"
>
> "Haste!" we hear one cry, "thou mighty offspring of Jove! hasten thine appearing;" while the tremulous earth, sea, and heaven exult in the impending era.
>
> So, perchance, on darking plains of Bethlehem, the shepherds scanned the faintly-kindling east, and began to augur day. Yet twilight, chill, and cheerless, clothed the silent fields.
>
> But, as on their astonished vision a dazzling Shekinah burst through azure empyrean, and harmonies ineffable charmed the ear, bringing morning all surpassing down around them, so through moral empyrean, upon chill and cheerless human thought and feeling, burst with rapturous light and melody the all-outvying dawn of Messianic love.[91]

Return to the East

By 1850, Beecher's congregation, which had grown eightfold since his arrival in Fort Wayne, now realized that their popular pastor, with a much wider reputation, was a treasure not to be lost. As a result, they requested the presbytery to change his status from that of a stated supply to an installed pastor. On June 4, the service of installation was held in Second Church; soon afterwards Charles and his wife Sarah, with their young children, left Fort Wayne to visit relatives in the East. Immediately their families pressured them to remain. For a while Charles talked of returning to Indiana, but the recurrence of Sarah's malarial symptoms, contracted in New Orleans, made him reluctant to stay longer in the West. He resigned his pastorate on August 30.

Charles Beecher had been taken for granted by his people while he was with them and was sorely missed when he did not return. Twenty-five years later a member of the congregation looked back on his ministry in Fort Wayne and wrote:

> Mr. Beecher was a zealous worker in the Redeemer's cause. This being his first charge, he confined himself very closely to his studies and

gave the congregation much food for thought and investigation; and his peculiar manner of presenting Gospel truths invariably elicited the attention of his audience, so that much of the seed of truth that was dropped yielded fruit in the salvation of souls. The six years of his labor showed a result of an increase from twelve to one hundred and two members. The house we now worship in was built the first years of this ministry and much of the financial help was obtained through his exertion.[92]

There were few Presbyterian ministers in the West who could follow Charles Beecher as pastor of Second Presbyterian Church without suffering unfavorable comparisons. During the next two years the congregation listened in turn to the Reverends Isaac W. Taylor, David C. Blood, and John W. Ray,[93] but, as none of them engendered an enthusiastic response from the membership, each departed after six months' labor. The resulting lack of pastoral leadership caused the congregation's once strong fellowship to deteriorate. In February 1852, with a hint of desperation, Hugh McCulloch wrote to Charles Beecher, urging him to visit his former parish:

Scarcely a day has past, since you left Fort Wayne, that I have not lamented the necessity, real or supposed, that led you to break off your connection with our little society and interrupted a personal intercourse, the value and happiness of which I did not properly estimate until your departure. There are very few persons who seem to differ to a greater degree in temperament, style of thought, habits and opinions than Charles Beecher and myself, and yet I do not recollect any man with whom I have become acquainted that I value so highly or whose society is to me half so congenial . . . .

The Society in which you take so deep an interest, as you doubtless are aware, still remains without a pastor and the prospects of obtaining one who will unite our decadent material is by no means encouraging. Christians, although they may be members and elders even of the same church and doubtless love each other very tenderly, are not very charitable in their estimate of each other's conduct and character nor very lenient towards each other faults. Will it not be possible for you to obtain a furlough of a month or two to visit us next summer? Such a visit would be very grateful to your friends personally and might be very serviceable to the Society.[94]

In March, Susan McCulloch visited the Beechers in Newark, New Jersey, where Charles had revitalized the moribund Free Presbyterian Church, eventually persuading the congregation to affiliate with an association of Congregational Churches in New York and Brooklyn.[95] When she asked him to come back to Second Church, he replied that "if he were to return to Fort Wayne, he would change our church from Presbyterian to Congregational in the shortest possible time, for such churches in the West do so much better than Presbyterian." But Charles Beecher never returned; Susan sadly reported: "They had almost made up their minds to go to Fort Wayne when they were all taken down and have now given it up as an impossibility . . . on account of health. They are likewise too poor to move as they are in debt where they are."[96]

If Charles Beecher had visited Fort Wayne in the summer of 1852, he would have been pleased to hear Hugh McCulloch's address to the graduating class of St. Augustine's Academy, a local girl's school established by the Sisters of Providence. Although McCulloch had said that there were few persons with whom he differed more in thought and opinions than his former pastor, the bank president's remarks on the worship of wealth (he later became Comptroller of Currency and Secretary of the Treasury) were pure Beecher:

I fear that the present tendency of things—the governing influence of the age, is anything but humanizing—that our power over matter, and the triumphs we are achieving with it, are not only shutting our eyes to the ideal and the spiritual, but creating a kind of personal self-reliance and independence, which disregards our true relation to our fellow-man. and renders us oblivious of our allegiance to our Creator . . . .

Again, the present age is not only distinguished for its advancement in the practical sciences, but also, and still more, for its love of gold . . . . The love of gain, conspicuous in every age, is now predominant. The almighty dollar is not only the object of individual idolatry, but it is the governing power of the age. It controls the destiny of nations—the policy of kings. It covers guilt as with a mantle—sanctifies crime—is the apologist of baseness. It blinds the eye—corrupts the understanding—hardens the heart. One loves it because it administers to his passions—another, because it stands in the place of respectability—another, because it gives him power—and another, for itself, alone; while all strive for its acquisition, as though it were the source of all good. The great tide of human passion is flowing in the channel of gain. I apprehend there never was an age when wealth was so anxiously sought for and so heartily worshipped as at the present day.[97]

Amzi W. Freeman and Eleroy Curtis

In June 1852, the Second Presbyterian Church succeeded in calling the Reverend Amzi Whitfield Freeman to the pulpit. The thirty-one-year-old New Jersey native had attended the college at Princeton before enrolling at Union Theological Seminary in New York; upon graduation in 1847 he came to Indiana to serve the New School Presbyterian Church at Covington. As the newest minister in Fort Wayne, he was invited to deliver the sermon at the community Thanksgiving Day service. After a traditional enumeration of the "blessings" for which "every creature should be thankful," Freeman reflected on the recent elections: "I cannot recollect anything that can be compared to the extremely vile personal abuse of candidates for office which has filled our papers for many months. If such habits should continue, none but men *without shame* surely will enter the political arena . . . . Let us pray that our hearts may not again be sickened by such a disgraceful prostitution of the freedom of the press."[98]

Freeman tried hard to unite the congregation but was not rewarded by the affection of the congregation, and, after two years, he departed to begin a thirty-year pastorate in Aurora. One member summed up the problem: "The time intervening between Mr. Beecher's resignation and the acceptance of the call by Mr. Freeman were years of great spiritual dearth in the Church, and Mr. Freeman, not having the peculiar gift needed for the condition in which he found the Church, did not succeed in uniting the hearty interest and sympathy of its membership in the work of the Lord."[99]

This period of "spiritual dearth" was finally ended in November 1854, by the arrival of the Reverend Eleroy Curtis, a dynamic preacher and personable pastor from Middlebury, Ohio. Curtis had been born in Vermont in 1819 and came to Ohio with his parents during the migration of New Englanders to that area. At the age of eighteen he left the family farm to enroll in the Huron Institute at Milan, Ohio, where he experienced a religious conversion; he then entered Western Reserve College and Seminary to prepare for the ministry, all the while supporting himself as a school principal. Curtis was talented and energetic, and was recognized as one of the more capable clergymen in Fort Wayne. When some community project needed leadership, Curtis was often called: in 1855, the Protestant clergy asked him to organize their community Thanksgiving service; when two felons were to be hanged, Curtis headed the group of clergy who ministered to the prisoners;[100] when the officers of the Friends of Temperance—such as Samuel Hanna, Jesse Williams, Charles Case, and John Dawson—needed a minister to frame a resolution, they chose Curtis.[101] His strong antislavery speeches, however, provoked the ire of the Democratic editor of the *Sentinel* who lamented the preacher's "Politics in the Pulpit."[102]

Like Beecher, Curtis was a man of wide-ranging interests and broad sympathies: his popular lectures on the new "Ocean Telegraph" were published in the *Fort Wayne Republican;* [103] and when Rabbi Isaac Leeser visited Fort Wayne to assist in the dedication of the new synagogue, Curtis invited him to preach at his church.[104] It was as an evangelist that Curtis made a reputation in his denomination, and in 1857 he conducted a revival "of great power . . . at Fort Wayne."[105] Three years later, in October 1860, Curtis resigned to accept the call of a Congregational Church in Sherburne, New York. An admiring member of Second Presbyterian Church reflected on his pastorate: "By his faithful teachings and his genial Christian influence while ministering with the people of his charge were many hearts in sympathy with him in the service of the Lord; and the bond of union in that service was very reluctantly dissolved between Pastor and people . . . . [He left] this Church much benefited by his six years' faithful service. Sixty-six were added to its membership while he was with us."[106]

In sixteen years the Second Presbyterian Church had grown from a dozen members who first gathered in the court house, to a flourishing congregation of a hundred and fifty members with a pleasant church building. The congregation had brought into its membership many of the Universalists and Congregationalists[107] who came to Fort Wayne—and earned the reputation of being broad in its non-creedal theology, warm in its evangelical piety, and strong in its social conscience.

Epilogue

Several Fort Wayne families, such as the McCullochs, maintained a lifelong correspondence with Charles and Sarah Beecher, and many followed the Beechers' careers as they were occasionally reported in the local newspapers. In September 1850, only a month after he had resigned his pastorate, the Fugitive Slave Law was enacted and Charles's righteous indignation boiled over in a Sunday evening sermon entitled "The Duty of Disobedience to Wicked Laws." He was scathing in his denunciation of the new law, which provided stiff penalties for those aiding runaway slaves or hindering their capture in free states: "It is the monster iniquity of the present age . . . . If a fugitive claim your help on his journey, break the law and help him . . . . Feed him, clothe him, harbor him, by day and by night, and conceal him from his pursuers . . . . If you are summoned to aid in his capture, refuse to obey."[108] This defiant message was published by his church in pamphlet form and widely quoted.

Such militant views, however, were not met with universal approval: on one occasion, a child distributing the pamphlet was threatened with violence, and the local ministerial association in Newark expelled Beecher, not for opposing slavery, but, for advocating disobedience to the law. In Fort Wayne, George Wood of the *Times* wrote: "We have long been a warm friend and admirer of Mr. Beecher, and he has many such here, but we cannot let such language pass without marking it with especial reprehension. . . . It would appear that some of the clergy of the present day do not desire us to go through any gradations. They want us at once to embark in civil war and bloodshed . . . . Truly, we have fallen upon evil times."[109]

Charles soon took a leave of absence from his parish duties to assist his sister Harriet with the manuscript of *Uncle Tom's Cabin* and to accompany her on a trip to England and Scotland. He had recently been rejected as a candidate for a pulpit in Washington, D. C. because of his antislavery views. In spite of ill health Beecher lectured evenings on the Book of Revelation and prepared for publication an essay on symbolic prophesies. His theological mood had become darker when he wrote to Susan McCulloch in Fort Wayne: "Tell [Hugh McCulloch] that the prophesies of my former ministry are being fulfilled. The great crisis of world-convulsion is coming. This sin-sick, delirious world will never know peace, nor sanity, until the foot of the Crucified once more hallows the soil."[110]

After three years in Newark, his brother Edward secured him a position as professor of rhetoric at Knox College,

where he also taught music. At this time he was named music editor of the *Plymouth Collection of Hymns and Tunes,* a work which exerted great influence on church hymnody. He later assumed the pastorate of the Congregational Church in Georgetown, Massachusetts. In 1860, when President Buchanan proclaimed a day of prayer and fasting for all Americans to atone for the "sin of opposing slavery and provoking southern rebellion," Beecher mounted his pulpit to denounce the President and then led his congregation to sign a resolution declaring such politically inspired worship to be "an act of hypocrisy . . . in the highest degree insulting and detestable" and charging Buchanan with "treasonous conspiracy."[111]

In 1863, Beecher was convicted of heresy for espousing a doctrine of the preexistence of souls. His congregation, however, rallied to his support and, the next year, the people of Georgetown elected him to represent them in the Massachusetts legislature. A few years later another conference of Congregational ministers rescinded the verdict and restored his ecclesiastical standing. After the trial, Charles published his major work, *Redeemer and Redeemed: An Investigation of the Atonement and of Eternal Judgement.*

In 1870, at the urging of Harriet, Charles and Sarah moved to Newport, Florida, where he preached among the poor Negro freedman and served as superintendent of public instruction for the state of Florida. He returned to his congregation in Georgetown and later preached in Wysox, Pennsylvania, until his retirement at the age of seventy-eight. His athleticism persisted; in 1900 he ice-skated with his grandson at the age of eighty-six, the year of his death.

10
Old School and Associate Reformed Presbyterians

"They not only pay their minister now, but they are putting up a splendid church—and they have all become workies."
Susan Man McCulloch, 1845

Henry Ward Beecher's theological assault on the First Presbyterian Church did more to strengthen the congregation than had any previous event in its twelve-year history. The membership, which had become complacent, was sharply challenged to define its identity and defend its integrity. In the presence of a second Presbyterian congregation, Old School members now became active in courting new arrivals to town, and were soon talking about establishing a parish school and erecting a new church.

Hugh Sheridan Dickson Arrives

William C. Anderson had continued as interim pastor until the newly elected minister, the Reverend Hugh Sheridan Dickson, arrived from Bardstown, Kentucky, in the early fall of 1844. A thirty-one-year-old native of County Down, Ireland, Dickson brought a decisive style of leadership to both church and community during his three-year tenure at First Presbyterian Church.[1] The two Presbyterian clergymen now in Fort Wayne were exemplars of the subtle differences which had divided the denomination: Hugh Dickson, with his Scotch-Irish roots and Princeton Theological Seminary education, was typical of the more conservative Old School; Charles Beecher, in contrast, had an English-American background and was trained in the more liberal New England theology of the New School. More-

over, Beecher was not greatly interested in the denominational disagreement. Church politics and controversy, however, were Dickson's food and drink; soon after his arrival, he sided with a faction in the local German Reformed congregation and persuaded them to affiliate with the Old School Presbyterians.[2]

At the first meeting of the newly organized Presbytery of Fort Wayne (Old School)—which chose to meet on New Year's Day 1845 in First Presbyterian Church—Dickson presented his letter of dismission from the Presbytery of Louisville (which had ordained him eighteen months before). Then, as was the custom, he was "examined as to his views in Theology and, his examination being sustained, was received as a member of this Presbytery."[3] Dickson's talents were quickly perceived, and he was immediately elected Stated Clerk of the Presbytery; then, he and Elder Samuel Hanna were chosen commissioners to the annual meeting of the Presbyterian General Assembly to be held in Philadelphia; the following year he was elected moderator of the Presbytery.

Hugh Dickson was an immediate success as a preacher and lecturer. Joseph K. Edgerton was so impressed that he wrote in his diary: "This evening I heard Mr. Dickson preach a most admirable sermon from the parable of the prodigal son. The sermons of this young gentleman are excellent, plain and clear in language, logical and accurate in their arrangement, and sufficiently practical. They show the efforts of a well-informed, disciplined and pious mind, anxious to do good in his high vocation. I always hear him with pleasure."4 Equal praise came from Elizabeth Wines, who had temporarily moved from Fort Wayne to Springfield, Indiana, and very much missed her church and minister. She wrote to Susan Williams: "Mr. Rucker from Indianapolis . . . is considered a great preacher here but, if they could only hear our Mr. Dickson, they would not look

Hugh Sheridan Dickson
[Courtesy of First Presbyterian Church of Fort Wayne]

on him as so great a man. How I long to hear him again. When you write again, give all the particulars . . . how his lectures to the youth took, if the church increased, if it is in prosperous condition . . . . I also attended Mr. Quillet's church [and] liked him well, but none like our beloved Mr. Dickson."5

Dickson was energetic in developing the congregation; forty-two persons were received into the membership before the Presbytery was able to assemble a quorum to install him formally as pastor of First Church. With an enlarged membership and the challenge of another Presbyterian church in town, the congregation determined to build a larger house of worship. A former member who had defected to the New School Presbyterians at Second Church wrote: "Sometimes I think that the Lord planted our church here on purpose to stir up the old one for they have done wonders since. They

not only pay their minister now but they are putting up a splendid church and they have all become *workies*."6

Governor Bigger's Leadership

The subscription drive for the new facility was led by former Governor Samuel Bigger, who had moved to Fort Wayne in 1843 to practice law, after his defeat for re-election that year. Bigger had been active in a Presbyterian Church in Indianapolis where he served on the Session and directed the choir; he possessed a fine voice and played the violin capably. Bigger may well have been defeated in his bid for re-election by the influence of the Methodist Episcopal Church, which counted more registered voters in Indiana than any other single denomination. He had previously opposed some legislation which resulted in the establishment of Asbury College (later Depauw University) and was rumored to have said that the Methodist Church did not need an educated clergy, that an ignorant one was better suited to the capacity of its membership. His gubernatorial opponent, James Whitcomb, was a Methodist and was solidly supported by his co-religionists. Methodist Bishop Edward. R. Ames said in 1846: "It was the Amen corner of the Methodist Church that defeated Gov. Bigger, and I had a hand in the work."7

The sensitivity of the Methodists went beyond Bigger's alleged quip. Presbyterians were accused of monopolizing the state seminary at Bloomington where the faculty of four professors were all Presbyterian ministers, a situation repeated on other campuses in the West at that time. Of the first fourteen colleges established west of the Alleghenies between 1780 and 1829, eight were founded by Presbyterians, one by Episcopalians, one by Baptists and the remaining four by state legislatures; and each of the state colleges, as in Indiana, was begun under strong Presbyterian influence. In Indiana, Vincennes University was started by the Reverend Samuel Scott, the first resident Presbyterian pastor in the territory. Hanover Academy was founded by the Presbyterians in 1827 and chartered as a college in 1834; a theological Seminary was also organized at Hanover in reaction to Lane Seminary in Cincinnati. In Crawfordsville, five Presbyterian ministers established the Wabash Manual Labor College and Teacher's Seminary in 1833, which later become Wabash College.

In reaction, the Methodists petitioned the legislature to appoint a Methodist minister to the faculty at Bloomington. An Indianapolis attorney wrote: "Two [Methodist] ministers who were written to on the subject replied that there was no one in the Conference whom they could safely recommend for the station. Upon faith of the statement, Bigger (who was then a member of the legislature) moved to lay the memorial on the table with the simple remark that there was no minister in the State of that denomination qualified to fill the place of the professor. This charge has slept until Whitcomb the loco[foco] candidate for Gov. waked it up & has bruited it all over the state with all the improvements & additions that an artful demagogue was capable of making to it."[8]

Bigger's move to Fort Wayne may have been influenced, in part, by the fact that Presbyterians were strong there and were mostly Whigs.[9] This fact was no doubt impressed upon

Samuel Bigger
[Drawing by B. F. Griswold, 1917]

him by Fort Wayne's foremost booster, Samuel Hanna, who had served as a fellow Whig in the Indiana legislature during Bigger's term as governor. Bigger soon became active in the Fort Wayne community and was often asked to chair civic meetings. He seemed especially interested in education and served as a sponsor of A. J. Bennett's Select School and, at the time of his death in 1846 at the age of 44, was superintendent of his church's Sunday School.

An Organ Is Installed

Bigger, an enthusiastic church musician, was probably instrumental in inducing the Presbyterians to bring an organ into the church. No American Congregational or Presbyterian church in the seventeenth or eighteenth centuries allowed an organ in worship; by the early nineteenth century,

however, an increasing number of these congregations in the East had installed instruments. Pipe organs were expensive and churches in the West were far from organ builders and tuners, so, when a reed organ maker came to Fort Wayne in 1845, one of his instruments was installed in First Presbyterian Church on a trial basis. The event prompted a local editor to comment:

> The congregation at the O. S. Presbyterian church, was delighted last Sunday with the thrilling and magnificent music of the choir. It is always excellent, but on this occasion it so far excelled itself as to be a subject of general remark, and few we believe, understood the cause. We attended in the evening and, not having heard of the additional attraction, were enchanted with the power and pathos of the music (albeit, we have no cultivated musical ear). We have no hesitation in saying that the overture was one of the most splendid performances we ever listened to. The secret of the superior music, however, lay in the fact that the choir had procured a *Seraphim,*[10] which was played by Miss [Amelia E.] Sykes, the junior preceptress of the Female Seminary. We learned that the instrument is only taken on trial, but we know that wealthy and respectable congregation will never dispense with it.[11]

The editor's enthusiasm for the organ playing at First Presbyterian Church was a marked change from his critique of the music in another congregation: "Much opposition exists to the choirs of some of the churches in this city, and parties are becoming arrayed upon that question. The opponents in one of them we believe have about succeeded in abolishing the choir and substituting the family organ. The instrument plays rather out of tune, and out of time, but then the music is excruciating."[12]

Presbyterians Found a Female Seminary

In the fall of 1845, the congregation decided to sponsor a "Seminary for Young Ladies . . . at the house east of the Presbyterian Church," and invited Mrs. Lydia A. Sykes to serve as the principal teacher.[13] The style of the school, in its standards and discipline, was described in detail in a newspaper advertisement: "The government is parental and kind, but decided and firm, enforced by reason and affection, sustained by the Bible, and administered in such manner as will inculcate the important lesson in self-government."[14] The curriculum was comprehensive, and a decided challenge to the usual ideas of young women's education as taught in the academy of the Reverend and Mrs. William W. Steevens,[15] who advertised that their Ladies Department taught the "usual branches of a polite and useful education: French, Piano Forte, and Ornamental Needlework."[16] In contrast, Mrs. Sykes's young ladies could study

> Reading, Orthography, Writing, Arithmetic, Geography, English Grammar, History, Ancient and Modern, but especially of our own country, Watts on the Mind, Antiquities, Composition, Natural History, Natural Philosophy, Physiology, Political Science, Botany, Chemistry, Astronomy, Geometry, Algebra, Rhetoric, Intellectual and Moral Philosophy, Criticism, Logic, Evidences of Christianity, Analogy of Natural and Revealed Religion, and Music. When requested, instruction will be given in needlework &c. A short time will be devoted to Calisthenic exercises, adapted to promote health and graceful motion . . . . Instruction in guitar or piano . . . Drawing, painting or French.[17]

In order to broaden the school's base of support, the church established a Board of Visitors of religious and civic leaders representing most of the English-speaking congregations, including the ministers of the Methodist, Episcopal, and New School Presbyterian churches. It was the intention of the congregation to make this a permanent institution, but Mrs. Sykes's failing health forced her to resign after eighteen months. She was succeeded by the Reverend James Greer,[18] who had previously served the Presbyterian church in LaPorte. By the summer of 1847, for unknown reasons, the church-sponsored school expired and Greer announced that he was opening "on his own responsibility. . . The Fort Wayne Academy: English, Classical, and Mathematical," and offering classes in the "English, Latin, Greek, French and Hebrew Language."[19]

A New Church Building Is Planned

In October 1845, the Old School Presbyterians were ready to break ground for a new house of worship to be erected on the southeast corner of Clinton and Berry streets. A local newspaper's account of the ceremony was quickly sold out and then reprinted the following week:

> On Monday at 3 o'clock, P. M . . . . the ceremony of laying the cornerstone of the new First Presbyterian Church at Fort Wayne was . . . opened by an impressive and solemn invocation by the Rev. Mr. Dickson, pastor of the church . . . . A Hymn was then sung by the choir. A brief but comprehensive history of Fort Wayne was then read by Judge Hanna, by whom it was prepared, followed by another of the First Presbyterian Church, from

its organization, by James H. Robinson, Esq., after which were deposited in a leaden box . . . a copy of the Bible; a Hymn Book; the Presbyterian Confession of Faith; the Histories of the town and the church that had been previously read; a specimen of each of the coins of the United States and various other articles . . . . A brief extemporaneous address was pronounced by the Rev. Mr. Dickson.

> This church, when completed, will be worthy of the wealthy and respectable Society that is erecting it, and an ornament to the deity . . . . It will be 55 by 80 feet, of suitable height and proportions, with a spire about 150 feet high, and is estimated to cost from $6,000 to $10,000. This edifice will be no temporary affair—it is intended, not only for the present time, but for posterity.[20]

The ambitions of the congregation to establish a school and build a new church were not followed by sufficient contributions to sustain the efforts. In addition, the church still owed William C. Anderson $103 on his salary, and was equally delinquent on a significant portion of Dickson's stipend. And there were other unpaid bills. At the annual meeting of the membership, Dickson proposed that all creditors of the church cancel their accounts and that cash contributions be made immediately to pay off the debts. Then, to demonstrate his seriousness, Dickson himself gave $50 to the church. The sexton immediately gave $28; then, one by one, Samuel Hanna, Allen Hamilton, Jesse Williams, Jonas Townley, James Robinson, John Cochrane, and Samuel Bigger followed their pastor's example and paid off the church's debt of nearly six hundred dollars.

In January 1846, on the eve of the church trustees' reorganization meeting, Dickson wrote a chiding challenge to the officers, whom he saw to be as inept in managing the financial matters of the congregation as they were competent in caring for their own business affairs. In his campaign against deficit financing he pleaded:

> First: No debt should be allowed to remain against the church for another week. If our people are not now able and willing to meet them they never will be, and the longer they continue the greater will be the difficulty of discharging them, added to the dishonesty and disgrace.
> Second: No new obligation should be assumed unless you have the means of discharging it. I am sorry that churches so seldom act upon the plain principles of morality as laid down in the Gospel. This is the case with all corporations, but surely the Church of Christ should set an example of promptness and strict integrity in all her business

transactions.[21]

The trustees gathered in the office of Samuel Hanna and, as their only item of business, addressed the issue of securing a more regular income for their minister. By the end of the meeting they resolved to "proceed immediately to raise a subscription for a pastor's salary," and named B. H. Tower, J. Hough, Jr., and S. C. Evans[22] as collectors of the funds.

Members Disciplined for Dancing

Dickson's strong leadership style was also directed towards church discipline and personal morality when he appointed Elders John Cochrane and Jesse Williams to frame a policy statement on church attendance and dancing; in 1847 their recommendations became the standard for all church members:

> Whereas it is the solemn judgement of the Session of this church, that private, social, or public dancing parties or public balls, are opposed to the spirit of Christianity, incompatible with the duties it requires, and utterly inconsistent with the Christian profession; as they tend to inflame the passions, and unfit those who are in the habit of attending them for the right performance of Christian duties; and because they bring reproach on the cause of religion, and wound the feelings of Christ's devoted followers; therefore, resolved, that the members of this church be affectionately warned not to attend, countenance, or allow such parties or balls to be held in their houses, under any pretense whatever.[23]

In spite of most churches' opposition to dancing, the opportunities to attend balls in Fort Wayne were plentiful. A year after the Presbyterian pronouncement, a local newspaper reported: "The [Fourth of July] celebration was closed by two or three balls at different parts of the city, where the dancing was done up in style, and kept up until nearly morning."[24] One member recalled: "Dancing was forbidden by the Church in early days; nevertheless, we made our first attempts at the homes of Mrs. Hugh McCulloch and Mrs. Watson Wall."[25]

The Mexican War

The sound of dancing in the homes was, for a brief time, drowned out by the noise of soldiers marching in the streets. The Mexican War had begun in the last week of April 1846; by the first week in June a call for volunteers was met in Fort Wayne by the creation of two companies of soldiers. On June 16, with only a few weeks of drilling, the volunteers boarded canal boats to rendezvous with other Indiana units at New Albany. A local editor noted that two ministers were at the embarkation ceremonies: "Patriotic addresses were made and a very feeling and appropriate prayer was offered up by the Rev. Mr. Bayless of the Methodist Episcopal Church of this city. Previous to their departure we noticed the Rev. Mr. Dickson, of the 1st Presbyterian Church, distributing testaments to the volunteers and, we believe, not an individual among them was unsupplied. Many of them appreciated the present very highly."[26]

The pastors and the people in every way supported their fellow citizens who went off to assist the military campaign in Mexico, but the community was divided, as was the nation, on the morality of the enterprise. The war was enthusiastically supported by those expansionists who wished to acquire the Mexican territories of New Mexico, Arizona, and California, as they had Texas. It was also applauded by the southern states who supported President Polk, a slaveholder, and had already seen their influence grow with the admittance of Texas as a slave state. On the other hand, the invasion was strongly opposed by Whigs and abolitionists who feared that all the new territory acquired from Mexico would become slaveholding. And there were other concerned Americans who simply believed that it was immoral to acquire any territory by waging an unjust war. None of the Christian Churches in America would declare that the war was just, and there was much uneasiness about the issue. An editorial in a local Fort Wayne newspaper summed up the feelings of many of the local church people, "It is a miserable, pitiful, pusillanimous war of aggression and conquest against Mexico."[27]

The testaments distributed by Hugh Dickson to the departing troops were no doubt supplied by the Allen County Bible Society. Allen Hamilton was president of this local "Auxiliary" of the American Bible Society. Henry Rudisill and John Hough, Jr. also served as officers along with the predictable presence of those more community-minded Protestant ministers: Dickson, Bayless, and Beecher. A Methodist minster who had settled in Fort Wayne, the Reverend Stephen A. Ball, served as the distributing agent of the Society whose aim was "to secure the exploration, and supply speedily and thoroughly the destitute of the counties of Allen and Adams."[28]

The Appeal for Irish Relief

Two of the leaders of the Bible Society, Allen Hamilton and Hugh Dickson, had been born in Ireland, and when news of a famine in that country reached Fort Wayne in early 1847, they immediately challenged the community to respond with generous contributions for the relief of the millions who were on the edge of starvation.[29] Hamilton had received news of the disaster from his Irish friends and relatives: "Your blood would run cold to see the people observing each other with ravenous looks, crowding into the houses, and not able to leave them with hunger . . . . The murders, burglaries, and noonday robberies are most frightful."[30]

Fund-raising suppers were served, appeals were made from the pulpits, and rallies were held to elicit significant donations. Interestingly—in a town that was sensitive to historic Catholic-Protestant rivalries, and which had seen, a decade before, combat between northern and southern Irish canal workers—the local leaders in the relief effort for Ireland were largely Protestant, and most of these, such as Hamilton, Dickson, and Hugh McCulloch,[31] were Presbyterians.

When a resolution was presented at a public meeting requesting the clergy "to preach sermons and take up collections in their respective churches[32] . . . . Rev. Mr. Dickson, warmly seconded this motion, as it would give all an opportunity of showing how much they were sorry for the appalling distress now existing in Ireland. He related an anecdote of a humane Frenchman who, when a crowd of sympathizers were expressing their sorrow for an accident which had befallen an unfortunate poor man, asked 'how much' each one was sorry; he was sorry $10, and invited the others to follow his example, by relieving the distressed man to the amount of their sorrow. Mr. D. in conclusion, remarked that he was 'sorry' $10, which sum he handed to the Secretary. Mr. D. H. Colerick[33] responded, and said he was 'sorry' to the full amount of what he had in his pocket, and would continue 'sorry' as long as the distress lasted, and he handed in $60.00. Major Edsall was sorry $20.00, which was twice as much as he had been sorry when he put his name on the subscription . . . . Upwards of $100 were contributed at the meeting."[34]

Presbyterians and the Press

By the mid 1840s, both of the local newspapers, the *Fort Wayne Times* and the *Fort Wayne Sentinel,* were regularly reporting activities of the local churches: new buildings and schools, fund-raising and fairs, lectures and classes, protracted meetings and visiting clergy were often in the news. If a funeral was newsworthy, such as the death of the pioneer tailor, John Edsall, it was reported in detail:

In 1843 he experienced religion, and joined the Presbyterian Church, of which he continued a sincere and consistent member to the day of his death—dying in the firm belief that his sins were forgiven. His death was very sudden. He was attacked on Monday with a severe constipation of the bowels which in a few hours terminated his existence . . . . We never witnessed a larger attendance at a funeral. The Presbyterian Church was crowded with citizens of all ranks and classes—not drawn together by the music of the military, or the imposing appearance of the aprons, badges and insignia, for he was not the member of any society—but by the spontaneous impulse of long cultivated friendship. An impressive discourse was delivered by the Rev. Mr. Dickson from Proverbs, 14th chap. 32nd v.—"the Wicked is driven away in his wickedness; but the righteous hath hope in death." [35]

It was not unusual at funerals or civic celebrations to invite a prominent layman to offer a prayer; and, in an era when the public admired good orators, some aspiring Daniel Websters adorned their prayers with florid rhetoric. A local editor commented on these persons "of ardent temperament and glowing piety. . . . This class of men (pure and excellent, too, in the main) are prone to give loose to their imaginations to exuberant outbreaks of pious ejaculation, in a style highly ornate and metaphorical."[36]

Such prayers could continue for as long as twenty minutes and it was expected that any proper public oration would last at least an hour. Sermons and prayers in church were of the same extended duration and some worshippers found other things to do during a long service. A repeated complaint, expressed in letters to the editor, was directed at whispering and other distracting behavior: "It is an every day occurrence to see, in at least one of the churches in this city, a little *clique* of would be exclusives, seated in a conspicuous place, a little *above* the balance of the congregation, during the time of service, talking, laughing, cracking jokes, writing *bon mots* to be passed from hand to hand, pinching each other until the pinchee is made to squeal . . . . If I am compelled to witness them again, as I do not choose to leave the church of my choice on their account, I shall just jot down the names of the conspicuous actors in these disgraceful actions and ask you to publish them."[37]

A Presbyterian took pen in hand to echo the same concern: "There are those. . . regular attendants upon divine worship . . . who are shamefully guilty of this . . . outrageous and abominable practice [of whispering in church] . . . greatly annoying those who wish to direct their thoughts to the contemplation of high and holy things." Aware that the writer was a member of the First Presbyterian Church, the editor displayed a little of his own prejudice when he commented: "These exhibitions of indecorum, strange as it may seem, are most prevalent among those who are of high standing in society, and who occupy *high places* in the church."[38]

The readiness of the editor of the weekly *Fort Wayne Times and People's Press* to moralize about members of First Presbyterian Church was evident in his review of that congregation's Ladies' Fair in February 1847. Church fairs had become a regular part of community life: the women of most Protestant congregations would sew, knit, bake, and otherwise create a variety of wares for sale, the proceeds of which would assist in furnishing their church edifice or in aiding a missionary enterprise. On Christmas Eve 1846, the fair presented by the ladies of the Methodist Episcopal Church was reviewed with nothing but praise by the editor: "This splendid exhibition came off on Christmas Eve . . . and it really exceeded the highest expectations . . . . We cannot now . . . do it justice; but it is no exaggeration to say that a more rich, splendid and fanciful display of articles was never before made in this city, or got up with better taste, and with finer effect; . . . their sales which we are happy to hear, reached about $450. Well done. That is worth trying again."[39]

When the women of the First Presbyterian Church held their fair in February, the reviewer at first seemed equally effusive in his praise:

> The fancy and ornamental articles, prepared chiefly by the Ladies of the Society reflected credit upon their industry and skill. Fair faces presided at different tables, and were as successful as usual in commanding the admiration and opening the hearts and pockets of the rougher sex. That man must have had a tight hold upon his purse, who did not find the change rapidly leaving it, when the fairest and most interesting of our Ladies (and they have not their superiors in this wide world) were inviting them to the purchase of articles so captivating to the eye and gratifying to the taste. The whole affair . . . resulted in the receipt of about five hundred and fifty dollars.

The editor's gallantry in complimenting the ladies lasted for a paragraph, and was followed by an attack on the ethics of church fairs in general:

> We must say that we doubt the morality of influences by which young men, out of a spirit of pride, and to escape the appearance of meanness before those whose good opinion they desire, are induced to spend more money than their circumstances will justify. We doubt the morality of receiving, at any time and for any purpose, three times as much for articles, offered for sale, as they are worth . . . . We cannot refrain from saying that we regard Fairs of religious societies to raise money for Church purposes, as a sort of pious swindling, and we are of the opinion that every Church which resorts to them, loses more in Christian character than it gains in money.[40]

Evidently many local citizens were offended by the

editor's wholesale condemnation of fairs in the wake of the Presbyterian effort, but none was more incensed than Hugh Dickson who, under the cover of the pseudonym of "Vindex," penned a sharp reply to the editor's "ungentlemanly and abusive attack upon the ladies of the 1st Presbyterian Church" and sent it to the rival newspaper. The offending editor, George W. Wood of the *Fort Wayne Times,* responded in a

George W. Wood, publisher of the Fort Wayne Times, was twice elected mayor of Fort Wayne.
[Drawing by B. F. Griswold, 1917]

long and defensive article and attacked the editor of the *Fort Wayne Sentinel,* Thomas Tigar, for printing "in his last paper, over the signature of 'Vindex,' a communication as silly and uncalled for as it was malicious." Dickson then reminded Wood that he had recently praised the Methodist Fair with unqualified superlatives, and asked why "this guardian of public morals was not [then] awake to the evils of Fairs?" The pastor then chastised Wood for publicly insulting ladies, and noted that "a member of the Missouri legislature was lately expelled for insulting a lady in the street, and the House declared, in their resolution, that his conduct rendered him unfit to associate with gentlemen."[41]

Ordinarily Wood might have made peace with Dickson, but he could never forgive him for working through his arch rival, Thomas Tigar. Finally, when the identity of "Vindex" was revealed, Wood attacked Dickson with a fury:

> This community does not yet know the man as they will know him. Innocent and unsuspecting themselves, they know not the rottenness and

185

corruption, the hatred and malignity, the fiend-like bitterness and the 'Vindex'-like spirit, that rage within, but that are concealed by a few smooth, well brushed sacerdotal vestments . . . . And when he sacrilegiously breaks the consecrated bread and pours the wine for pious men and women at the table of the Lord's supper, if any of them should call to mind the fish-market slang . . . and remember its meanness, its mendacity, its bitter malice, and should think its author out of his element in that sacred place—that he would be with more congenial spirits in singing bacchanalian songs with midnight rowdies, or dancing fandangos at a Mexican rancho—he must accuse himself.[42]

By this time, the controversy was the talk of the town; Susan McCulloch wrote to her mother: "At present Mr. Dickson, the old school preacher, is quarrelling with Mr. Wood, the editor, about fairs. *Big business*. I will send you the papers."[43] After two months, however, the exchanges between the two had inflicted emotional wounds, and both men were feeling much more persecuted than vindicated. Wood became somewhat paranoid and complained bitterly: "We are threatened in certain quarters with a loss of patronage . . . . We have been for years the object of a malicious persecution—a persecution unprecedented in virulence and duration."[44]

Dickson Resigns

Dickson was also feeling more isolated. He had told his congregation that Wood's attack on fairs was an attack on them, but most of the members felt this was more their preacher's fight than their own. Unfortunately, Dickson did not realize that, by neglecting to consult either his officers or the women involved in the fair before he sent his "Vindex" letter, he had climbed out on his limb alone. Dickson felt so deeply hurt that, on April 10, 1847, he tendered his resignation as pastor of the church. The elders of the congregation immediately met at Samuel Hanna's office and drafted a reply:

As you state no reasons for the course you have adopted, we hope that circumstances under the Providence of God may arise which will induce you to change your mind and withdraw your resignation. If the recent publications in the "Times and Free *(sic)* Press," in which the Editor has endeavored to traduce your Christian character, has had any influence in causing you to resign your charge, we beg of you to discard all such influences, and be assured that, while we deeply

sympathize with you under any unpleasant feelings you may have to encounter from such an attack upon your Christian character, we nevertheless now, as heretofore, cherish unabated confidence in your piety and zeal in the cause of our common Saviour. You have a strong hold upon the affections of the people of your charge, and unless God in his providence has so plainly marked out your path, as to make it clear to your mind that it is your duty to leave us, we hope you will change your views and remain with us.[45]

At first, Dickson suggested that family pressures had precipitated his resignation: "The truth is, the situation of my family is such as to render my removal from this place in the course of a few years absolutely necessary. It has been anxiously desired by my father-in-law for some time." Then his deeper feelings about the incident surfaced: "It is now with me a matter of doubt, whether the church would not suffer more by my remaining, than by my going. Those late publications to which you refer . . . I cannot think they were aimed so much at me as at the church of which I am pastor. But, if the intention was to injure the church, it will to a great extent, if not entirely, be defeated by my removal, as the prejudices excited in the minds of some is directed exclusively against me."[46]

At a meeting of the congregation, called to act on Dickson's request that the pastoral relationship be dissolved, the members formally expressed to Dickson their regret, assuring him that he "possesses the qualifications, Christian and ministerial character, which, with the blessing of the Holy Ghost and his continued experience in the ministry, will render him a still more useful servant of the Lord in this place, and one under whose ministry we hope to be richly blessed."[47] Unfortunately, they did not fully understand the one thing in the controversy which had so deeply pained Dickson: that his own people had not rallied to his defense when he had stormed the editorial barricades for their honor. Therefore, when the membership at their meeting said absolutely nothing in support of their pastor in the controversy that was still raging, Dickson became more candid:

While I sincerely thank them for the many expressions of affection and attachment which appear in their proceeding, I have felt deeply pained that they could have allowed one to whom they were so sincerely attached, to be repeatedly attacked in the most brutal manner, without even expressing their disapprobation either by words or actions. For, even if it is believed that I erred in the first instance, it was surely an error which a husband or father might have forgiven. So deeply do I feel upon this subject that it would be a relief to me to retire from the public duties of the ministry among you as soon as possible. I cannot continue here longer than the 21st of June, and hope you will take measures immediately to secure the services of a successor.[48]

Dickson moderated his last meeting of the church session on the fourth of July and then journeyed to the East where he enjoyed a long and fruitful ministry. He was a natural leader whose talents were often sought to help organize local activities and his departure left a gap in the ranks of the local clergy. He left First Presbyterian Church much stronger than when he arrived: the membership had increased, a day school had been established, and a new church building was begun.

The Women Gain Voting Rights

The Session next engaged James Greer—who had just moved into Dickson's house—to supply their pulpit until a new minister was called. One of the interim pastor's first tasks was to moderate a special congregational meeting, called to "consider the question of selecting a pastor for the church."[49] The membership quickly declined to invite the nominated candidate, and then proceeded to debate the issue which all were anticipating: voting privileges for women.

Every congregation in Fort Wayne at that time—Catholic, Protestant, and Jewish—defined a voting member as an adult male, and none allowed women to serve on their official boards. All of these parishes, however, had more women members than men, and the women's many activities, from teaching to fund-raising, were vital to the life of any congregation. It was Allen Hamilton who introduced the motion "that the ladies be allowed to vote on the question before the meetings." His wife, Emerine Holman Hamilton, had most likely directed the efforts to mobilize the sentiment of the congregation in favor of allowing women to participate fully in the meetings. Emerine's granddaughter, Alice Hamilton, remembered her as "a tiny person, quick and wiry, and her mind was as quick as her body. She loved reading passionately. . . . Those two valiant crusaders, Frances Willard and Susan B. Anthony, were her personal friends and used to stay at the [Hamilton's] Old House when they came to Fort Wayne. It took a good deal of courage in those days to come out for such causes, especially for woman's suffrage."[50]

The church women's strong feelings on the subject had been clearly communicated to the men of the congregation; as a result, after "an animated discussion," all but one of the men voted to extend the franchise to women. Then, as voting members, the women joined the men to consider the subject of the vacant pastorate and resolved that the Reverend Lowman Hawes "be invited to preach as candidate before the church for the office of Pastor for six months on trial."[51]

Hawes was a twenty-two-year-old Kentuckian who had graduated first in his class at Centre College, and had recently completed his studies for the ministry at Western Theological Seminary in Pittsburgh. His youth and lack of experience did not compare favorably with the dynamic personalities of Dickson and Rankin. Consequently, when the congregation gathered four months later to vote infor-

Emerine Jane Holman Hamilton (Mrs. Allen)
[Courtesy of Allen County-Fort Wayne Historical Society]

mally on whether to extend Hawes's tenure, a minority demurred, and the members then "unanimously agreed that they press the call no farther."[52] The young pastor, although invited to supply the pulpit for another six months, soon departed.[53]

The straw vote on Hawes's candidacy was disrupted by Elder James Robinson, who insisted that a separate tally be taken of men alone, implying that only this enumeration was legal.[54] Apparently, Robinson's remarks on women voters had so deeply offended many in the congregation that Allen Hamilton called for his resignation from the session. Robinson, stung by the rejection of his ideas and the repudiation of his leadership, then took his case to the public arena, where he announced in a paid newspaper notice that he would make available his pamphlet on the "Voluntary Resignation of an Elder in the Presbyterian Church . . . calculated to prevent causes leading to such events in our newly formed churches."[55]

187

Finishing the Church

In June 1848, the congregation finally agreed on a new pastor, the Reverend John Gillin Riheldaffer. A native of Beaver County, Pennsylvania, Riheldaffer, at age thirty, was older than Hawes, but no more experienced, just having been graduated from Princeton Theological Seminary. He arrived with his wife in the fall, and immediately made plans for his ordination on November 15 by the Presbytery of Fort Wayne.

The immediate challenge to the new pastor was the uncompleted church building, the cornerstone of which had been laid four years before. Charles Beecher, a close friend of Riheldaffer, noted that the members "are somewhat inconvenienced in relation to their building, having put up the walls and covered in an edifice of brick, about 75 or 80

The First Presbyterian Church (second building), on the southeast corner of Clinton and Berry streets, was begun in 1845, opened for worship in 1848, and dedicated in 1852.

[Courtesy of First Presbyterian Church of Fort Wayne]

by 40—which now they are embarrassed to finish. And while this is slowly proceeding, they are obliged to rent their own church of the English Lutherans."[56] Finally, the offic-

ers were able to announce in the local press that "the new Presbyterian Church will be opened for religious services on Sunday morning next. Services will commence at 11 o'clock, seats free."[57]

The Presbyterians had not changed their pew rental policy; they were simply postponing the auctioning of four-fifths of the seats until the facility was totally finished.[58] The common Protestant practice of renting pews to members—and charging premium prices for choice locations—was questioned by a local editor just before the church was readied for its first worship service: "A majority of the churches of the present day, construct cheap accommodation in some remote corner for the occupation of the poor . . . providing them with a 'steerage passage to Eternity.' If the Saviour should again appear on earth, soiled and travel worn . . . [he] would be compelled to take a seat in 'the poor man's corner,' for he would be admitted to nowhere else."[59] Hugh McCulloch, a trustee at Second Presbyterian Church, echoed this critique when he told an audience of schoolteachers that the Catholic Church in America was the only Christian denomination where rich and poor could be found worshipping together in the same pews.[60]

The new church still lacked its interior finish and some furnishings, and awaited additional funds to add a cupola, bell, fence, and sidewalk. The needed monies were slowly raised over the next three years through the efforts of the men soliciting subscriptions and the women holding fairs. The trustees declared that "each male of the church [should] consider himself a member of the subscription committee." The women took the building needs one at a time: serving a supper "for enclosing, with a suitable fence, their new church edifice," then holding a fair, "the proceeds of which will be appropriated to the purchase of a new bell for the church."[61] One member who appreciated the women's dedicated service was a trustee who had gone west in 1849 to seek his fortune in the California gold fields; when he gave them a nugget, the women published their acknowledgement in a local newspaper: "The Treasurer of the Fort Wayne Female Sewing Society of the First Presbyterian Church of this city, acknowledges the receipt from Rufus French, Esq., of the beautiful specimen of California gold, weighing over an ounce, as a donation to the Society."[62]

In May 1851, after three years in Fort Wayne, Riheldaffer resigned his pastorate to accept an appointment by the Board of Domestic Missions to organize a congregation in St. Paul, Minnesota; he told the session, "My impression is, this step will promote my own, and the future usefulness of the Church."[63] A year later, he appealed to his former congregation to donate one hundred dollars to the building fund of his new mission parish, explaining, "I am the only minister of our [Old School Presbyterian] Church in the whole territory of Minnesota."[64]

The Associate Reformed Mission

The size and affluence of Fort Wayne's two Presbyterian churches suggested to some Scottish Presbyterians that the area was a potential source of members for their "kirk." In March 1851, the Reverend John Davis Glenn,[65] a minister of the Associate Reformed Presbyterian Church, obtained permission from the First Church officers to hold a worship service in their facility.[66] Glenn's denomination was composed mostly of those Scots and Scotch-Irish whose religious heritage stretched back to the "dissenting" Presbyterians of seventeenth- and eighteenth-century Scotland, known as "Covenanters" and "Seceders."[67] Between 1825 and 1850, twenty-four Associate Reformed Presbyterian churches had been established in Indiana,[68] and several of their members had moved to Fort Wayne and joined local congregations. Only one of these, however, Judge Joseph H. McMaken,[69] chose to leave First Presbyterian Church for the new congregation; to Glenn's distress, a few A. R. P. members who had newly arrived in town ignored his mission and joined the Old School congregation.[70] After his initial sermon at First Presbyterian Church, Glenn conducted services at regular intervals, first at the courthouse and later at Hulburd's schoolhouse.[71] In early 1852, eight families were formally organized into a "vacancy" (as mission congregations were called), and Glenn reported that there were "fair prospects of building up our cause in that growing and important place."[72] In the fall, the "wee kirk" of twenty members received their new "supply," the Reverend James Miller, a fifty-year-old Scot who had begun his ministry as a missionary in the Scottish Highlands and Orkney Islands before immigrating to America. Miller had received his "literary and theological education" in Glasgow, and was described by one colleague as a "man of good education and ability, but slow of speech."[73]

American-born Presbyterians, upon visiting this A. R. P. church, would have noted several distinct differences: the congregation was self-consciously ethnic, preferring an eighteenth-century Scottish style of worship; no organ was allowed and the psalm singing was led by a "precentor." First and foremost, the doctrines of Calvin and Knox were exalted. James Albert Woodburn, an Indiana historian who claimed this heritage, wrote: "Their Sabbath services usually consumed most of the day. They had two long sermons, one in the forenoon and one in the afternoon, with a brief noon intermission. They were long on sermons . . . often . . . an argumentative defense of beliefs. The minister always explained the psalm before it was sung—a critical discourse almost as long as a modern sermon. They were a strict, close-communion church and they zealously barred from their communion all who did not accept their faith, and also all of their own members who by their misconduct or 'neglect of the ordinances' (failing to go to church) or by 'breaking the Sabbath,' had fallen from grace or had lapsed from the standards. They were strict Sabbatarians, and trials before the session were frequent for Sabbath-breaking and not infrequent for over-indulgence in Scotch whisky."[74] In Fort Wayne, the A. R. P. mission was politely ignored by most English-speaking Protestants—who judged the congregation to be clannish and its doctrines to be dour—and, after four thin years, the mission was abandoned.[75]

The Church Dedicated; An Academy Founded

In September 1851, First Presbyterian Church called as their minister the Reverend Jonathan Edwards, who, for the

Jonathan Edwards
[Courtesy of First Presbyterian Church of Fort Wayne]

past three years, had been principal of the Female Seminary in Springfield, Ohio. Edwards was a thirty-four-year-old graduate of Hanover College and its theological seminary at New Albany,[76] whose vocational career had alternated between the pulpit and the schoolroom.

The new pastor found the church building nearly completed, and suggested that the officers invite his alma mater's president, the Reverend Thomas E. Thomas, to deliver the dedicatory sermon on November 14, 1852. The edifice, which had cost $13,500, was at the moment Fort Wayne's outstanding house of worship; Alice Hamilton described it as "a lovely Christopher Wren building of red brick with wide steps up to a white pillared portico."[77]

Edwards's interest in education became manifest when he determined to revive the day school which had been allowed to close after Dickson's departure. Many Old School Presbyterian congregations were, at that time, attempting to establish elementary and secondary schools according to a plan proposed by their Board of Education and endorsed by the General Assembly in 1847. When James Greer, Lowman Hawes, and Samuel Hanna (who had recruited the congregation's first school teachers in 1836) had been asked by the Fort Wayne Presbytery in 1848 to survey the schools in its jurisdiction, they reported that there were about 1500 Presbyterian children enrolled; the quality of the education, however, they judged to be

> . . . insufficient, many of them being kept up but three months in the year—supplied with incompetent teachers—and while the pittance received from the state gives them the name and the character of "Public Schools," the burden of support falls mainly on individuals. Hence many are removing them, and supporting schools at their private expense. Public opinion on the general subject of education is quite encouraging: yet characterized by many mistakes and grievous errors. Our wants then as a presbytery in relation to education are numerous, urgent, immediate wants. The obstacles, which exist at present, to the establishing of Parochial Schools in our bounds are serious, but not unsurmountable.[78]

The fact that two local Presbyterian school teachers, Alexander McJunkin and James Greer, had closed their schools in 1852 probably induced Edwards to suggest that the presbytery assist in establishing an academy in Fort Wayne. At their June meeting, the ministers and elders agreed that a school was needed, but some objected to its location in Fort Wayne, noting that "a large town affords too may inducements to young men to neglect study and form evil habits."[79] In spite of this concern, the body resolved "that the Male and Female High Schools of Fort Wayne, under the care of the Session of the First Presbyterian Church of Fort Wayne . . . be . . . under the care of the Presbytery and recommend them to the Board of Education for appropriations as may be found needed and expedient."[80]

In the fall, Edwards announced the opening of the school "in the Basement Rooms of the 1st Presbyterian Church";[81] presbytery's Committee on Education reported in February 1853 that it "had been in successful operation for one term of fourteen weeks with an average attendance of twenty-five scholars. Recitations in the Scripture and in the catechism

are heard once in each week by the pastor.[82] The session have secured a house which they can occupy comfortably until a suitable house can be erected on the lots already purchased for that purpose."[83] Martha Brandriff Hanna remembered playtime in the primary school with fond affec-

Jacob W. Lanius
[Courtesy of Allen County-Fort Wayne Historical Society]

tion: "We all, little and big, attended school in the basement of the First Presbyterian Church . . . . Our first teacher's name was Miss McFadden. At playtime, we sometimes nearly scared the wits out of the new pupils by our prank of playing ghost in the furnace room. We had playhouses in all the deep-seated windows which the pastor and elders benevolently smiled on [at] the weekly prayer meeting. Occasionally a doll would be left in a pew, but it caused no reprimand."[84]

The school, popularly known as the Presbyterian Academy, was one of more than a hundred primary schools and forty-six academies under the care of local sessions and the denomination's Board of Education.[85] During these early years, the school thrived and soon moved to the larger facility. One resident recalled the "one story frame building, with a hall, cloak room, and two school rooms, separated by folding doors, which on occasion, were thrown open to provide one large assembly room . . . . The class rooms were supplied with good desks and were well lighted and ventilated. The first teachers were Henry McCormick [principal] and Jacob Lanius,[86] both college graduates. George A. Irvin, a graduate of Hanover college . . . who had been in charge of a ladies seminary at Paris, Kentucky, succeeded to the management of the school." One student recollected, "Mr. Irvin was a young Kentuckian, and he was a liberal user of the switch as well as of chewing tobacco."[87]

In the fall of 1853, a common or free school opened in Fort Wayne, but its future seemed uncertain: funding was minimal, public support was divided, classes were held in a rented building, and private school teachers comprised the faculty. More than a few Presbyterians, as well as Methodists and Episcopalians, agreed with their Roman Catholic and German Lutheran neighbors that a common school was potentially a godless school. Soon, in early 1854, Fort Wayne's "free school was subjected to bitter criticism . . . . [It] had taught a non-denominational Protestant morality . . . along with daily prayers and readings from the King James translation of the Bible . . . . All Protestant groups agreed that public schooling did not go far enough to insure a 'good Christian education.' Some religious leaders exerted considerable pressure upon the school trustees to make religious instruction an integral part of the school's program. The trustees refused."[88] Lacking adequate facilities and sufficient funding, the common school failed to reopen in the fall, and no tax supported free public education was available in Fort Wayne until February 1857, when a new schoolhouse—the most expensive built in Indiana—was opened at Washington and Clay streets.

At the same moment, two events conspired to threaten the Presbyterian Academy. One was the onset of a nationwide economic depression, which weakened financial support for most private schools. The other event, as the church reported to the Presbytery, was that their principal teacher, George Irvin, "had been recently chosen superintendent of the Fort Wayne Public Schools, and for this and other reasons, it had been deemed expedient temporarily to suspend the exercises of the Academy."[89] The school later reopened, and continued until 1867 when the property was transferred to the city school board and became the Harmar Street School. By this time, however, the Presbyterians, along with most English-speaking Protestants and Jews in Fort Wayne, were becoming strong advocates of free, public education and never again attempted to organize a parochial school. In the meantime, George Irvin, a deeply religious man who had been elected a ruling elder at First Presbyterian Church, was ordained to the ministry in 1863 and enlisted as a chaplain in the 88th Indiana Volunteer Infantry Regiment.[90]

The Southern Sympathizer Is Attacked

Jonathan Edwards—once described by a local editor as "a man of large ability"[91]—was an excellent preacher and an effective teacher. His lecture to the Men's Literary Society on "Aspects of Society" in early 1855 displayed his erudition, but it also betrayed his conservatism on the issues of slavery and woman's rights:

> It may not be difficult to conceive of certain uses arising out of the continuance of slavery until this time—certain benefits which shall yet enure to our common civilization. Slaveholding, as a vestige of Feudalism, evinces its ancient tendency to promote a high sense of personal independence, a lofty self-respect. It may be that this virtue is not enough cultivated at the North . . . . And the South in our country is honorably distinguished for its high courtesy and chivalrous bearing to woman. Have we at the North nothing of this to learn? ("Much in every way," if we take as testimony the statements of some portion of our northern press, or the harangues and resolves of our Woman's Rights Conventions.)[92]

Edwards was attempting to walk the thin line traced by many Old School Presbyterians by condemning the institution of slavery as sinful without condemning slaveholders as sinners—hoping that, by patience and reasonableness, a rupture with the South might be avoided. Even though he concluded his address with a ringing declaration that there should be "no indefinite extension or perpetuation of Slavery," his suggestion that civilization was enhanced by the institution, as well as his praise of southern chivalry, provoked a scathing attack by local abolitionists. Charles Case, who was elected to Congress in 1857, mocked Edwards's "glorification of American Slavery. . . [and] chivalry."[93] The editor of the *Times* wrote: "Chivalry never was kindness . . . . It is a relic of barbarism . . . 'tis a *refinement* where Christianity seldom enters . . . [and is] widely different from the true courtesy, kindness, affection and religious humanity and benevolence of northern religionists and philanthropists."[94] There is no corresponding record of what Emerine Hamilton and other sympathetic women thought of their pastor's aspersions on the "harangues and resolves" of woman's rights advocates, but Edwards had doubtless alienated an equal number of his parishioners on this subject as well.

A few months later, Edwards announced that he had been named to the presidency of Hanover College and would leave Fort Wayne in mid-summer. The Fort Wayne congregation formally expressed their gratitude for his labors as "a faithful pastor . . . in the strengthening of our beloved congregation . . . in the additions to its membership . . . [and] his zealous efforts in the cause of education . . . so promising of good to our children and to the community."[95] Before he left Fort Wayne, Edwards suggested that the Hanover trustees hire "Lowman C. Hawes, now of Carroll College, Waukegan, Wis. . . . a gifted and accurate scholar, specially in Languages, Ethics, and Philosophy, and well adapted to attack and yet control young men."[96]

John Marshall Lowrie

After twenty-five years, Fort Wayne's oldest continuing congregation had achieved a maturity that could appreciate scholarly gifts in a clergyman; as a result, they persuaded the Reverend John Marshall Lowrie of Lancaster, Ohio, to assume their pastorate. Lowrie was a thirty-nine-year-old native of Pittsburgh, Pennsylvania, who had been graduated

John Marshall Lowrie
[Courtesy of First Presbyterian Church of Fort Wayne]

from Lafayette College and Princeton Theological Seminary, where he had "amused himself by putting some of the plays of Sophocles and Euripides into a metrical translation," and became "profoundly read in Latin theology."[97] In 1856, the Presbyterian Board of Publication published his work, *The Christian in the Church*——the first of more than a dozen volumes that he wrote during the next ten years.

Most of Lowrie's books were adaptations of his popular lectures on Biblical themes delivered in Fort Wayne. Soon after his arrival in the fall of 1856,[98] he announced a series of twelve Sunday evening talks on the Book of Esther—and the following year, a two hundred and seventy-six page volume entitled *Esther and Her Times* was offered for sale by the Presbyterian Publishing House. A local editor noted that these talks "elicited many encomiums"; Lowrie's later

lectures on "The Life and Character of Moses" (published as *The Hebrew Lawgiver*) were judged by a reviewer to be of "extraordinary merit, not only in historic research, but in perspicuity and beauty of diction."[99] As a consequence, Lowrie was launched on a lecture circuit, speaking to many

Harriet Dusenberry Lowrie (Mrs. John)
[Courtesy of First Presbyterian Church of Fort Wayne]

local organizations. His themes were usually biblical and always moral; typical was an address to the Working Men's Institute, gathered on a Friday evening at Colerick's Hall: "Decision of Character: the duties, habits, etc. of the young—their mental and moral culture."[100]

In his second lecture series (and resulting book *Adam and His Times*), Lowrie touched on the subject of woman's place in the order of creation, a theme recently brought into sharp focus in Fort Wayne by the public lectures of Lucy Stone.[101] Although he prefaced his message with an assurance that his theology "accords . . . with that of the old Calvinistic divines," he echoed the sentiments of Matthew Henry: "The woman was made of a rib out of the side of Adam; not out of his head to top him; nor out of his feet to be trampled on by him; but out of his side to be equal with him." Lowrie also spoke of the plight of oppressed women in patriarchal cultures: "Take the world at large, and the bondage of woman . . . is by far the worst social evil of the race. The Bible alone exerts an influence to make woman truly free [and] raises her from her degradation."[102]

Curiously, Lowrie's willingness to address the subject of woman's equality from a biblical perspective did not find parallel expression on the slavery issue. The First Presbyterian pulpit, which two decades before had projected the strong abolitionist sentiments of Alexander Rankin, had

Alice Lowrie
[Courtesy of First Presbyterian Church of Fort Wayne]

gradually become silent on the subject: as the North and South moved inexorably toward a political rupture, most Old School Presbyterians in the North attempted to maintain harmonious relations with their sister congregations in the south by assuming a posture of tolerance. During the decade preceding the Civil War, the minutes of the local Old School Presbytery (in contrast to the New School) recorded no references to slavery or the increasing national tension. Their limited goal of preventing a denominational schism temporarily achieved its aim (the southern New School Presbyterians had separated from their northern brethren in 1857), but, when the Old School Southerners withdrew in 1861 to form the Presbyterian Church in the Confederate States of America, many northern church leaders were ashamed that they had traded their prophetic birthright for a mess of compromising pottage. Lowrie was one of these, and it was not until the war began that he publicly condemned "the viciousness of the [slave] system: politically, as at war with the genius of a free people; financially, as

retarding, rather than advancing, the good of states; and morally, 'as a gross violation of the most precious and sacred rights of human nature.'. . . In his [Lincoln's] words . . . 'If slavery is not wrong, nothing is.' "[103]

Lowrie was a preacher's preacher, and when his Old School presbytery "cordially accepted" the invitation of their New School brethren "to join them in celebrating the Lord's Supper,"[104] he was invited to deliver the sermon. The service was a ceremonial act of peace and reconciliation because Lowrie, with two fellow presbyters, had previously "invaded the New School parish in Huntington, and organized an Old School Second Presbyterian Church there."[105] The celebration, led by both moderators, marked the beginning of a steady movement of the two "sides" towards their formal reunion in 1870.

Lowrie was not a dramatic or stentorian preacher; a colleague later remarked: "Dr. Lowrie was not, as the phrase is now by many understood, an eloquent man. His voice was not good, and he was indifferent to the graces of manner. He was too quiet, too undemonstrative, too sparing of gesture, too meditative to be classed among pulpit orators. Indeed, for very much of what goes under the name of eloquence he could scarcely conceal his contempt."[106] But people flocked to hear him; his sincerity and scholarship, combined with an evangelical earnestness attracted large numbers to his special meetings. In 1858, a local editor noted, "In our city . . . prayer meetings are held at 8 o'clock every morning and every evening at the 1st Presbyterian Church and are largely attended. May much good attend such efforts! There is ample room for reformation here."[107] When Lowrie died of tuberculosis in 1867, the membership had nearly doubled, making it the largest Presbyterian congregation in the Synod of Northern Indiana.

Dickson and Ross Return to Fort Wayne

As the decade of the 1850s drew to a close, Fort Wayne Presbyterians prepared to welcome two former pastors. Hugh Dickson—who had recently been honored by Hamilton College with the degree of Doctor of Divinity after concluding an eleven-year pastorate in Utica, New York—was still popular in his former parish and, in May 1858, occupied the pulpit of First Presbyterian Church, both morning and evening, on two successive Sundays. Peter Bailey, a prominent Episcopal vestryman, reported that "the congregation, on both occasions, was large and attentive. Mr. Dickson appears to have lost nothing . . . since he left here, either in vigor of body or mind."[108] John Ross, who had been invited to serve as chaplain at a reunion of "Old Settlers," visited in 1860. Now seventy-seven-years of age, Fort Wayne's pioneer pastor was presented with a cane fashioned from a beam salvaged from the old fort where he had first conducted worship services thirty-eight years before. Ross's memory

The First Presbyterian Church was remodeled and enlarged in the 1860s.
[Courtesy of First Presbyterian Church of Fort Wayne]

was sharp and his candor was disarming; he recollected that, in the early 1820s, none of pioneer settlements he visited were as irreligious as Fort Wayne: "There was no Sabbath kept there but on the part of a few."[109]

The Sabbath was now kept by many more than "a few" residents of Fort Wayne, and no congregation was more zealous in its observance than the Presbyterians. Moreover, Presbyterians had become leaders in the emerging causes of temperance, education, and women's rights. The congregation was never the city's largest (Catholics, Lutherans, and Methodists were more numerous), but many of its members were among the more influential (if not affluent) leaders in the community—and such interfaith groups as the local Bible Society and Temperance Society were often headed by a member of First Presbyterian Church. By 1860, Old School Presbyterians were judged to be strict on dancing, drinking, and Sabbath observance; timid on the slavery issue; conservative in their reformed theology; progressive in their education philosophy; and radical in extending the vote to women.

11

German and French Reformed

"The German Presbyterians . . . are a fine, honest, well dressed, devout looking people."

Susan Man McCulloch, 1845

"The life among the German Evangelicals is a life of miserable toil and disgust to any generous mind. Mostly stingy and stupid, they are excessively bigoted and narrow in their ideas."

Charles Beecher, 1846

No church organized in Fort Wayne during the 1840s was born amid more pain and passion than the German Evangelical Reformed Congregation of St. John. By the mid-1850s, however, the congregation was effectively ministering to those German and French speaking immigrants from Switzerland, Germany, and France who were loyal to the Reformed heritage of Huldreich Zwingli and John Calvin.[1]

The Reformed Worship with the Lutherans

In the early nineteenth century, the influx of Germans and Swiss into Indiana created a special challenge to the largely Americanized German Reformed congregations of the eastern United States.[2] An Ohio Classis of the Reformed Church had been established in 1820; in 1837, an attempt was made to create a Classis of the West for Indiana and Illinois,[3] but when it dissolved in 1840, German Hoosiers of the Reformed persuasion were on their own.

The pressing problem for the Reformed was the same one experienced by the Lutherans: there were few German-speaking ministers available to send to the new western settlements. Of the thirty-nine German Reformed seminary students in America in 1835, it was reported that only seven or eight could preach in German. As a result, no German Reformed pastor visited Indiana until 1840, when the Reverend Peter Herbruck traveled through Fort Wayne by canal boat on his way from Massilon, Ohio, for a brief stay among the German Reformed in Miami County.[4]

In the early 1830s, the new immigrants found no German-speaking clergy in Fort Wayne—only a resident Presbyterian pastor, a Methodist circuit rider, and a French-born Catholic priest who visited occasionally. By the summer of 1836, however, there had arrived a Catholic priest from Alsace, the Reverend Louis Müller, and a German-speaking Lutheran pastor from Pennsylvania, the Reverend Jesse Hoover. The Pennsylvania Ministerium, from which Hoover came, looked favorably on uniting the Lutheran and Reformed elements in one congregation—and, in Fort Wayne, Hoover welcomed both traditions. Blending the various immigrant groups was a formidable challenge, as each Protestant province of Germany had its own state church: some exclusively Lutheran, some Reformed, and some a blend of both. In his reports to the American Home Missionary Society (which supported his salary), Hoover carefully avoided the designation "Lutheran," understanding that the

Society was primarily a Presbyterian and Congregational organization which aided churches of the Reformed tradition. As a result of the society's expectations and his ministerium's desire to be inclusive, Hoover made no mention of the Lutheran Augsburg Confession or the Reformed Heidelberg Catechism when the German-speaking Protestants of Fort Wayne first celebrated the Lord's Supper in January 1837, or at their formal organization in October as the "First Evangelical Lutheran Church in Fort Wayne."

The Lutherans Exclude the Reformed

For the next seven years the Reformed members—many of whom came from Lienen, Prussia—felt accepted and comfortable in this congregation, until the second pastor, the Reverend Friedrich K. D. Wyneken, returned from a visit to Germany in 1843 as a much stricter Lutheran.[5] His new standards for church membership now insisted on adherence to the Augsburg Confession and the elimination of all elements of the Reformed tradition. When Wyneken announced that only confessional Lutherans could henceforth receive Holy Communion, the Reformed members determined to arrange for their own services, and asked the church officers for permission to worship separately in the meeting-house they had helped to erect. Pastor Wyneken, however, vigorously opposed their request, arguing that they intended to establish a "congregation of false teaching, which Lutherans could not, in good conscience, assist."[6] These newly-orphaned members then turned to the Presbyterians—their English-speaking cousins in the Reformed family—who immediately offered them free use of their house of worship. Because of their nurture in First Presbyterian Church, the members of the new congregation were called "German Presbyterians" by the English speaking residents of Fort Wayne. A local citizen, after attending a funeral service for one of the members, reported: "The funeral was here and the German Presbyterians buried him. They are a fine, honest, well dressed, devout looking people."[7]

A New Congregation Organizes and Builds

With a membership of about seventy, the congregation wrote to Mercersburg Seminary in Pennsylvania for assistance in securing a pastor. Early in the summer of 1844, the Reverend Andrew Carroll[8] arrived and organized the worshippers under the formal name of the "German Evangelical Reformed Congregation of St. John" (*Der Deutsche Evangelische-Reformierte St. Johannis-Gemeinde*). He again asked the Lutheran congregation for permission to worship in the church building which Reformed members had helped to erect, and was again denied on the grounds that the issue was "a matter of principle—that only pure Lutheran

doctrine was permitted."[9] Although the First Presbyterian Church welcomed a continued use of their facilities, the new congregation's trustees[10] soon purchased a site for a church building, and, by January 2, 1845, a simple frame house of worship was erected on the southeast corner of Washington and Webster streets.[11] As was customary, the general populace was invited to contribute toward the new structure

St. John's German Evangelical Reformed Church, on the southeast corner of Washington and Webster streets, was completed in early 1844.

[Courtesy of Grace St. John's United Church of Christ]

and, as usual, the men of prominence and substance pledged: William Rockhill, Allen Hamilton, G. B. Dubois, and Saul Freeman, all of whom belonged to other congregations. Two years later, the congregation topped their facility with a spire; a local newspaper reported: "The German Presbyterians have added a beautiful steeple to their church this Spring and, for beauty of proportion and style of architecture, is not surpassed by any in the city—Mr. Lauer, the able architect is entitled to much praise."[12]

In March 1845, Carroll resigned;[13] the congregation then invited the Reverend John Adam Bayer,[14] who was at

196

the time serving a German Reformed congregation in Dansville, New York, where he had already experienced some sharp conflict between conservative Lutherans and traditional Reformed. Bayer said that, at various times in New York, he had been called a Methodist, a Universalist, and a Socinian, in spite of his avowed loyalty to the Heidelberg Catechism as the confessional standard of his church.[15]

When Bayer arrived in April 1845, it became apparent that the little congregation lacked the financial resources to support a minister with a growing family—his wife was soon to give birth to twins. At the suggestion of the Presbyterians, correspondence was initiated to the American Home Missionary Society for financial assistance.[16] In the appeal to the Society, the officers of St. John's Church expressed their strong feelings about the circumstances of their expulsion from their original congregation, two years before:

> Some ten or twelve years ago, German emigrants began to settle in and around Fort Wayne; a German Christian society was formed as soon as possible without any reference to the Lutheran or Reformed creed; they wanted the Gospel of Jesus Christ preached. The clergy of the Lutheran church had charge of this growing congregation hitherto. About two years ago sectarianism awoke from its sleep in the society and spiritual tyranny was made use of by those whose duty it was to preach Christ crucified. Without mentioning all the cunning and the Jesuitical tricks resorted to, we merely will say that the Lutheran Romish creed of the Lord's Supper was intended to be forced upon us; without full faith in this creed, we were pronounced unworthy to appear at the Lord's table; faith without works was proclaimed the gate to salvation; the Augsburger confession was set even above the Word of God; instead of pronouncing God's readiness to forgive the repenting sinner, Christ's servant (?) pretended to do it himself and our children were secretly led astray from our Saviour before we almost got aware of it and burdened with human inventions.

> We honestly confess, we could not stand it any longer; our God and Saviour and our own conscience called loud on us to oppose such unchristian proceedings, and so we were told to go where we please, if we could not submit; we were driven out the meeting house, which we helped to build, and even not allowed the use of it at the time not occupied by the ultra-Lutherans. And thus, you see, we were forced to separate ourselves. In reliance on God we commenced building a house for divine worship and we have succeeded so far that we hold already our reli-

> gious meeting in it. There are some twenty families and from 70 to 80 communicants in our little flock. We gave a call to the Revd. John A. Bayer as minister of regular standing in the German Reformed Church; he accepted the call and moved among us two months ago; he has a family and now we see we cannot give him support sufficient for himself and family. By great effort we could raise not more than $180 for the first year, some of which cannot be collected, as we think. We therefore petition the A. H. M. Society for assistance without which we must give up and become like scattered sheep in the wilderness, for we cannot understand preaching in the English language. However, we trust in God; he was so far with our little flock and he certainly will not forsake us in the future. The Society connected itself with the German Reformed Synod.[17]

Letters of endorsement were written by the Reverend Hugh S. Dickson of the First Presbyterian Church and by an elder of that congregation, James H. Robinson, who had recently moved from Newark, New Jersey, where he had become personally acquainted with the Reverend Charles Hall, the corresponding secretary of the Society. The Missionary Society immediately sought the opinion the Reverend Charles Beecher, pastor of the Second Presbyterian Church (New School) in Fort Wayne, which had received aid from the Society since its organization the previous year. Beecher had been out of town on a two-month fund-raising tour for his new church building when the request was sent, but was pleased to give his unqualified support. He also felt it necessary to make a few comments on the German Lutheran Church and its new pastor, Wilhelm Sihler: "As to the importance of the case, I can only say that there is a body of some 500 Germans *called* Lutherans, but who (excepting about 80 who constitute the church in question) are being quickly and blindly conducted into the open arms of Her Holiness, the Mother Church of Rome. And this man [Bayer] is the only man who in their own language can lift up the voice and rescue them."[18]

The Missionary Society also wondered why Dickson, of the Old School wing of the Presbyterian Church, would write to them, as their General Assembly had condemned the work of independent, interdenominational mission boards, and had directed their congregations to support only Presbyterian enterprises. The Society knew the First Presbyterian Church well, for it had assisted the congregation from 1830 to 1840; now the Society supported only New School Presbyterian congregations, such as Beecher's church, whose General Assembly had endorsed its multi-denominational ministry.

Beecher, who was far from a church politician, wanted to believe the best of his Presbyterian colleague, Hugh Dickson,

197

and therefore tried to assure the Society that the Reformed congregation was not involved in the denomination's division:

I called on Bro. Bayer and he told me that he had received assistance before from Am. H. M. S. . . . He is connected with the Erie Classis and . . . has no connection with the O[ld] S[chool] Pres[byterian] Ch[urch], more than with the New . . . . [H]e was entirely unaware of the existence of the [Presbyterian] Assembly's board or that the parties did not both support the same body . . . . The lot was bought of Hanna, one of the elders in the O. S. Church and this naturally introduced him to that class of people . . . . Mr. Dickson appeared to be friendly and consented to sign his application.

I called on Bro. Dickson . . . [and] asked him how it happened that he did not recommend him [Bayer] to the Assembly's board. He replied that, by their constitution, they were prohibited from assisting any other Churches but of their own connection . . . . The reason [the] application was not made to me, was that I was then absent for some two months and that circumstances had not thrown them acquainted with me or mine . . . . Whatever designs the Old School heads may have had (and they are crafty) I acquit Dickson of any evil purpose, and, even if it were otherwise, the case is clear. He [Bayer] is not Old School nor can he be identified with them, and, if I cannot secure his cordial friendship, it will be my fault.[19]

The Rural Missions

The Missionary Society approved the request for Bayer's support retroactive to the date of his arrival and included in his commission the charge to serve, not only as pastor of the Fort Wayne congregation, but also as missionary to all Reformed Germans in the surrounding areas. In his first quarterly report, Bayer wrote:

The greatest part of the congregation lives in the country around the town; on this account we made a beginning with two regular meetings on weekdays 4 miles south and north from the town; I always have to go afoot to the meetings; how I shall stand it in the winter I do not know. . . . The greatest part of my time is spent in visiting the sick and the families of the congregation. 300 mile I have travelled around in the country hunting up the lost sheep in the wilderness. In Whitley County I met with a family which had not heard the Gospel preached for eight years. There is a large field for German missionaries in the north part of Indiana.[20]

By the end of the year Bayer had extended his mission labors even farther afield: "From time to time I visit Wells county about 30 miles from here; there are two new German settlements on both sides of the Wabash river, chiefly people of the German Reformed denomination, between 20 and 30 families; and 12 miles from there in Adams County is another settlement from 12 to 18 families . . . . What hinders me from going oftener there is: I have no horse and am not able to buy one."[21]

By the spring of 1846, Bayer had established another mission outpost in Springfield Township where he preached in both German and English. He had now stretched his footpath ministry to the limit and was frustrated that he could not respond to the requests of the Germans in DeKalb County who were without a pastor. He sadly noted the immigrants' poverty: a typical offering at one settlement produced fifty cents for mission work, and in the winter some people did not go to church because they were without shoes.

Bayer was especially distressed by the steady stream of denunciations coming from the Lutheran pulpit: "A shocking opposition I have to contend with: Dr. Sihler . . . speaks against prayer meetings, Bible classes, tracts, Sunday schools—and nobody but a Lutheran of the old stamp can be saved!! Br. Beecher does think this would work in my favour by and by. . . . I know mere formalities of religion cannot satisfy the soul for a great length of time. . . . But the party prejudice runs indeed very high and has blinded the poor people . . . . There is already forbodings of discord in their own rank and one family had left lately and attends our meetings."[22]

The Pastoral Controversy

Unfortunately, this external opposition from the German Lutheran Church was soon overshadowed by internal dissention at St. John's. Bayer was a native-born German who had married an American and was comfortable with the piety of the German Reformed Church in the eastern United States. Compared with many of the Reformed and Lutheran ministers in Germany, Bayer was more evangelical and a stronger advocate of temperance. He reported that his "congregation consists entirely of emigrants from Germany where the church is under the control of the government and, consequently, very little attention is paid to the religion of the heart . . . . It is very difficult to approach the Germans in regard to the cause of temperance; it requires the serpent's cunning. In the pulpit you may expose this sin in all its abominations, but to ask them to sign the pledge of abstinence, that would be signing away their liberty, and they are in a free country... and they begin to look upon you as the enemy."[23]

Bayer's zeal for the purity of the church led him to recommend that certain "gamblers and drunkards... be cast out of the church";[24] he was, however, rebuffed by his elders, he said, because the accused were contributors to the minister's salary. Bayer argued that they should be expelled anyway and that he would endure the reduction in salary, but his officers would not act against them. Bayer, at the same time, with equal stubbornness, refused a request by his officers to conduct catechism classes for all the children twelve to fifteen years of age and confirm them as members of the church at Easter. Bayer explained that "the children could not read with the exception of one, who has taken hold already of her Saviour; I declared myself ready to catechize her and to take her into the church. The same time we had no catechisms and could not get any. I explained the case over and over to them, but in vain; at last I told them I would not do it—for God and Jesus, [and] my own conscience likewise, were against such a religion of a mere outward form, and I sooner would stop preaching amongst them than do such unchristian business. They raised an excitement against me and voted me out of the congregation by this false information: 'I never would catechize young folks.' "[25]

A Presbyterian Steps In

Into the middle of this dispute came Hugh Dickson, not to mediate but to capture the congregation for the Old School Presbyterians. When Dickson first arrived in town at the end of the summer of 1844, the German Reformed congregation had already joined the Ohio Synod of the German Reformed church and was preparing to move out of First Presbyterian Church into their own structure. Then, when the embryonic congregation applied for aid to the American Home Missionary Society, Dickson felt threatened. Only a year before, Henry Ward Beecher had come to town under the banner of the the New School wing and had broken off a splinter from the Old School congregation to establish Second Presbyterian Church and then installed his brother, Charles, as pastor.[26] Dickson was now determined that no new victories were to be won by the New School. Hence, when he learned of Bayer's troubles in the St. John congregation, Dickson offered him conditional help: join the Old School Presbyterians and receive financial aid from its General Assembly Mission Board. Bayer reported that when he declined to change his affiliation, "Dickson advised me to leave."[27]

The members of St. John's were about equally divided on the issue of Bayer's tenure. Dickson had brazenly attended the congregational meeting at which the subject was first to be voted on; when the dissenters were unable to muster a majority, Dickson advised them to circulate a petition addressed to the Missionary Society expressing their desire for continued support, but not for this minister. He then volunteered to deliver their petition personally to the Society's offices in New York City when he attended the meeting of the Old School General Assembly in the beginning of summer.

Charles Beecher was shocked at Dickson's blatant interference with the internal affairs of the German Reformed congregation, and offered the Society his reevaluation of the situation in Fort Wayne:

> It is probable Mr. Dickson will wait on you while East and lay before you the paper to which Bro. Bayer refers. I have not conversed with Mr. D. on this subject lately and do not clearly see how his conduct is to be defended. For a political partizan, it might seem proper, or at least to be expected. For a Christian minister, I know not what to call it.... The majority of the legal voters, and they the Christian part, are satisfied with Bayer. The factious, drunken, antichristian part, always the most active in such cases, have gathered every name they could, in or out, pious or impious, voter or not voter, drunken or sober, men that never saw the inside of that Ch[urc]h. And that paper, thus signed, Bro. Dickson proposes to lay before you. If he had not put himself at the head of that faction, the disturbance would ere this have subsided.[28]

Bayer saw clearly that he could not unite the badly divided congregation, and so, on May 1, 1846, he discontinued his ministry in Fort Wayne and concentrated on the congregations he had established in Springfield Township and Huntington County.[29] Charles Beecher's sympathy for Bayer—who was now without an adequate income to support his family—prompted him to project blame for the sad affair on the German character of the congregation:

> The life among the German Evangelicals is a life of miserable toil and disgust to any generous mind. Mostly stingy and stupid, they are excessively bigoted and narrow in their ideas. While intoxicated with the idea of "liberty" and a "free country," they are no more free than slaves, except with the freedom to behave in all ways unseemly. Coming from a country where the church is a state institution, they regard membership as a matter like citizenship, the privileges of a certain age and degree of knowledge; hence evangelical piety is very low among them and ambition high. Attempting, therefore, to accomplish many contradictory objects, to be rich and religious, free yet old-fashioned, well organized

and numerous and powerful, yet without paying their minister, except as they would pay a meanest day laborer. In one word, to be American, yet Dutch, they present to a mind of any refinement, a material upon which to operate, the most disheartening, the most wearisome of which it is possible to conceive.

In contrast, Beecher praised Bayer as "a gentleman of liberal education, polished manners, (altho not personally prepossessing) and delicate and generous sentiments . . . . He is thoroughly spiritual in all his aims . . . one of the most unworldly and self-sacrificing laborers I ever saw."[30]

Altermatt Fails

The leaders of the rebellion against Bayer were careful in their search for a new pastor to select one who would neither chastise their drinking nor take the confirmation of children too seriously. Hugh Dickson only wanted a minister who would join the Old School Presbytery and bring St. John's into his denominational fold. And so, in the person of the Reverend E. B. Altermatt, everyone's desires were fulfilled—but in a manner that was judged either to be a cruel joke or a just punishment. Dickson was, no doubt, pleased to introduce the new German Reformed pastor to the Old School Presbytery. He would have been ecstatic when, on September 28, 1847, the request of St. John's Church to unite with the Presbytery was unanimously approved,[31] but in July, Dickson left Fort Wayne in the wake of his own controversy.[32]

Altermatt had been a pastor in Germany before coming directly to Fort Wayne and was content to confirm the children without much study or evidence of spirituality. He was also happy to forego all temperance sermons, as he drank heavily and often appeared inebriated in public. Soon Altermatt was cited to appear before the Fort Wayne Presbytery on charges of "falsehood and intoxication."[33] St. John's dismissed him in May 1848; the Presbytery, unable to make Altermatt appear before them to answer the charges, eventually deposed him from the ministry in 1852.

Bossard Succeeds

The members of St. John's were now determined to use more caution in calling their next pastor and therefore sought the counsel of Dr. Schneck, of Chambersburg, Pennsylvania, editor of the Reformed Church weekly newspaper, *Reformierte Kirchenzeitung*. Upon his recommendation, correspondence was initiated with Johann Jacob Bossard, a thirty-year-old native of Basel, Switzerland, who had come to the Reformed Seminary in Mercersburg, Pennsylvania,

the year before to prepare himself for a ministry in America. Bossard was a scholar: in 1841, he had earned the degree of Doctor of Philosophy and Philology at the University of Basel in ancient and classical languages; during his year at Mercersburg Seminary he served as a language instructor while studying English.[34]

In late May 1848, the candidate was licensed to preach by the Classis of Maryland; in early June, he arrived in Fort

Johann Jacob Bossard
[Courtesy of Grace St. John's United Church of Christ]

Wayne and made plans to be ordained. According to the practice of churches of the Reformed tradition, Bossard, a licentiate, could not be ordained until he received a call from a congregation. Therefore, at the ordination service, Elder Siebold of St. John's first presented to the moderator of the Old School Presbytery the formal call of the church members; the body then convened for "the laying on of the hands of the presbytery."[35] The service was necessarily conducted in English, with the charge given to the people of St. John's by the new interim pastor at First Presbyterian Church and local school teacher, the Reverend James Greer. In spite of Dickson's conniving, the affiliation of St. John's Church with the Old School Presbyterians was truly helpful to the struggling congregation. With no other German Reformed pastors for miles around, the fellowship and encouragement of the nearby Presbyterian ministers and members, as well as the financial aid from their General Assembly Mission Board, provided the necessary support for St. John's first years of growth. In addition, the Presbytery for several years maintained an intinerant minister to visit the scattered settlements of German Reformed in the surrounding counties.[36]

Jacob Bossard, although possessed with a somewhat eccentric personality, was an excellent preacher and hard-working pastor. His scholarship in classical and biblical languages was thoroughly European, but his theology, like Bayer's, reflected an American piety; he insisted on the same high standards of temperance held by Bayer and most Protestant congregations in Fort Wayne. Bossard kept the church records in English, and signed his name "James," not "Jacob"; he well understood that the young people of the congregation could only be kept loyal if the English language was equally acceptable in both church and school.

The French Congregation

The new pastor's name, a blend of the German "Jacob" and French "Bossard," so common in his native Switzerland, reflected an ethnic duality which had begun to emerge in his congregation in the late 1840s. After the failed European Revolution of 1848, a number of immigrants came to Fort Wayne—some from Germany, and more than a few from France.[37] Between 1848 and 1853, there was in France a conscientious effort by the French government, as well as land speculators, to encourage people to emigrate to America. The *Fort Wayne Times,* in September 1848, reported: "Agents of the French Government have arrived in the United States for the purpose of purchasing a tract of land on which to colonize a portion of the insurgents of June."[38]

Most of the French émigrés were from eastern France, where the Protestant Church was strongest. Although there were some Lutherans, the French Protestants were mostly Reformed from the Franche Comté, whose ancestors had escaped the sixteenth-century persecution that had precipitated the Huguenot migrations. Along with these French Protestants, some French-speaking Swiss Reformed from the neighboring canton of Berne also migrated into Indiana at this time. In Allen County, two major French settlements were established. The earliest was Académie, at first called the "French Settlement of Pichon" and later named "New France" (Nouveau Gaul or Nouvelle France); the second was Besancon, a namesake of that prominent city in eastern France from which so many had emigrated. Arcola also had a cluster of French families. In Fort Wayne, an area in the south end of the city became known as Frenchtown in the 1850s.[39]

French names appeared early on St. John's rolls. One of the charter members of the church, Philip Bachelier, was elected an elder in 1852. Two other French speaking families who joined the congregation were Brey and Dothage,

but only a few of the arriving French-speaking Protestants formally united with the German congregation. When Bossard saw that these Swiss and French emigrants were unable to appreciate either the German or English services in

John L. Klein
[Courtesy of Grace St. John's United Church of Christ]

town, he began to conduct regular worship in French—and carefully kept the records of these members in the French language.[40] Then, in February 1854, when he was about to conclude his ministry in Fort Wayne, he polled these worshippers to determine their interest in forming a French language Presbyterian Church, and reported to his session that ten families "have declared that they will support French preaching."[41]

Bossard took this petition to his Old School Presbytery, which in turn endorsed their request to their Board of Domestic Missions. The following year, the Reverend Peter Niel,[42] a former French Catholic priest, arrived in Fort Wayne and began ministering to the French Reformed in the city and the country, where the larger number had settled. By 1857, it was reported to the presbytery that a congregation had been organized at Vera Cruz, consisting of twenty-two families. The parish had erected a parsonage and a house of worship, and owed only $200; attendance at Sunday worship ranged upwards of seventy-five, including eight Roman Catholics. When a commission of presbytery visited the church, it was ascertained that there were in the congregation at least fourteen "thrifty families," each of whom owned from forty to a hundred acres of land, who should be able to support part of Niel's salary, which was then augmented by the Board of Domestic Missions.[43]

Benz and Klein

In 1854, Bossard was called to a pastorate in Sheboygan, Wisconsin; he later became one of the founders of Mission House College and taught there until his death. The church was next served by a young seminary graduate, the Reverend H. Benz, who departed after less than a year's service.[44] Finally, the Reverend John L. Klein, who was serving his first charge at the Black Swamp congregation near Freemont, Ohio, accepted the congregation's invitation. A native of Germany, the twenty-six-year-old minister arrived in Fort Wayne in September 1846 to begin a thirteen-year pastorate.[45] One of his first endeavors was to lead the people of St. John's to reaffiliate with the German Reformed Church of America, as that denomination's strength and organization was now established in Indiana. On January 17, 1856, at a meeting of the St. Joseph's Classis at Fairfield Centre, the congregation presented a letter of dismission from the Fort Wayne Presbytery (Old School) and, "after an examination of the papers and some explanatory remarks, the congregation was received by the Classis, and a committee appointed

with authority to receive the Rev. J. H. Klein, as soon as he presents a dismission from the Tiffin Classis, and to install him over the congregation as pastor."[46] The following year, the congregation felt itself fully restored to its Reformed roots when Klein was named as a delegate to the German Reformed Synod meeting at Carrolton, Ohio.

Klein next challenged the congregation to build a schoolhouse: in 1859 a structure, 24 by 36 by 12 feet, was erected on an adjoining lot and soon filled with seventy-five scholars.[47] The congregation of 118 members sensed its new maturity when it was able to host a meeting of its Synod, and to arrange for many of the visiting German Reformed ministers to preach in neighboring Protestant churches. St. John's close identification with the Presbyterians was still evident, however, when a local newspaper editor mistakenly described the assembly of sixty ministers and elders as the "Synod of the German Reformed Presbyterian Church of Indiana, Ohio and Adjacent States."[48]

The establishment of a strong German Reformed church—the first in Indiana—helped to make Fort Wayne increasingly attractive to the new arrivals from Germany and France. Its nurture of the French-speaking Protestants during the height of their emigration was unique, for no other congregation in the area was so equipped to minister in their language. In the next decade, St. John's developed into a strong parish by effectively welcoming the new arrivals from Switzerland and Germany and caring for the rising generation of youth in its parochial school.[49]

12
African Methodists (A. M. E.)

"Though denied in some things the full enjoyment of liberty and the pursuit of happiness at present, which are awarded to the whites, yet we are determined to use all lawful means, and to continue in so doing, until we shall be allowed the full privileges of American citizens; for our forefathers fought, bled, and died, to secure for us and to us those things, in common with other citizen soldiers, in the Revolutionary War."

"The Colored People of this City,"
July 10, 1849

As the Presbyterian, Catholic, Methodist, and Baptist churches in Fort Wayne were founded, African-Americans were accepted at worship, but never invited to positions of leadership. As a result, a small but growing black community established their own African Methodist Episcopal church as soon as they were able. This congregation, closely affiliated with other A. M. E. churches throughout the state, provided the spiritual resources and moral framework to support a small group of black residents who were increasingly beset by laws designed to exclude them and programs initiated to deport them.

The Multi-Racial Congregation and School

When the Baptist missionary, Isaac McCoy, formally organized Fort Wayne's first church on April 3, 1822, its membership was more racially integrated than would be any future congregation established in town during the nineteenth century. Affixed to the constitution of this new church were the names of eight missionaries, two Native American women, and "Jesse Cox, a black man."[1] Most likely Cox was not a new convert, for McCoy makes no reference to his baptism, as he does of the Indian women. Cox may have been the father of the "one Negro" boy enrolled in the mission school.[2]

African-Americans had been a part of the earliest history of Fort Wayne: some arrived as captives of the Indians; others came as slaves. Although slavery was strictly forbidden by the Ordinance of 1787 creating the Northwest Territory, William Wells worked his farm in Fort Wayne with several slaves he had brought from Kentucky.[3] Even a commandant at the Fort held slaves,[4] and during treaty negotiations with the Miami tribe, the American government gave a slave to Chief Little Turtle to reward his cooperation. Other African-Americans arrived in the three rivers area as servants of early explorers and traders; a few were soldiers stationed at the Fort; most simply came to seek their livelihood on the frontier.[5] Although the census of 1820 did not identify any "Negroes" or "Mulattoes" as residing in Fort Wayne, Isaac McCoy, in his journal, made several references to African-Americans in the village, indicating that blacks were already living in the area at that time.[6] When the land around Fort Wayne was first offered for sale in 1823, at least two local black residents made arrangements to purchase lots.[7] In the 1830 census, the first black land owner in Fort Wayne, Benjamin Harris, was enumerated; during the following decade, however, the constituency of the African-American community in the village becomes more difficult to determine. When John W. Dawson, in 1872, reminisced about the Fort Wayne of 1838, he remembered only "Burrell Reed, bootblack, town crier and factotum—the only Negro in town—the merry, loud-laughing Reed whom all knew . . . obliging and honest."[8]

Early Legal Barriers

In April 1842, the "merry" and "honest" Reed was summoned before the local court, charged with failure to post a five-hundred-dollar bond, required by Indiana law of all blacks entering the state to settle after 1831. The charge was serious; if Reed was unable to post the bond, then the overseers of the poor could hire him out to their profit for a period of six months. The statute, designed to limit black immigration, was only sporadically enforced in Indiana.[9] Its proponents argued that the law would prevent an influx of old or infirm freed slaves who might burden the welfare budgets of township trustees. In Allen County, the charges against Reed were initiated by the zeal of the newly elected overseers of the poor[10] to fulfill their campaign promises to exert stringent economies. Before serving warrants on local black residents, the overseers had charged Chief Richardville with bringing a blind Indian woman into Wayne Township, thereby creating a potential liability to the taxpayers. Burrell Reed was able to post the five-hundred-dollar bond—a sum greater than any local minister's annual salary—and may have been helped by his many friends, both black and white. Identical summons were also served on five other black men including Henry Canada and James Canada.[11] The latter two brothers contested the charges, engaged legal counsel, produced witnesses and, as a result, were not required to post bond. It is possible that the Canadas had resided in Fort Wayne before 1831 (perhaps related to the Canada family reported in the 1820 census) and had recently returned to Fort Wayne after some years of absence—to which their witnesses testified. Henry Canada was one of the more prominent black residents in Fort Wayne, the proprietor of a prosperous plastering business.[12]

The African Methodist Episcopal Church

Methodist churches in Indiana were required to report to their annual conference the number of their "colored members"; as a result, the earliest record of a black resident

formally joining a Fort Wayne congregation is at the Methodist church in 1842.[13] It is possible that a family named Hudson had joined the First Presbyterian Church in 1836, and that blacks attended the Baptist congregation after it was organized in 1837, but there is no early evidence of black worshippers at the Catholic, Episcopal, or English Lutheran churches.

Methodists were the most numerous among blacks moving into Indiana, just as they were among whites. In the early 1840s, the Methodists were divided on the slavery issue: in the General Conferences of 1836 and 1840, the anti-abolitionist conservatives of the North had combined with southern delegates to impose a gag rule on the church, prohibiting discussion of slavery in all Methodist conferences. This led to the withdrawal in 1843 of the more determined abolitionists to form the Wesleyan Methodist church. Then, in 1845, when a Georgia bishop was suspended for marrying a slaveholding wife, Methodists in the slavery states seceded to form the Methodist Episcopal Church, South, of which 30 percent were African-Americans.

By the end of the 1840s, the strength of black Methodism in Indiana had shifted into the African Methodist Episcopal Church, which had been founded in Philadelphia by the Reverend Richard Allen in 1816 in reaction to attempts to segregate blacks in Methodist worship. On October 2, 1840, the Indiana Conference of the A. M. E. Church was organized at Blue River in Rush County, Indiana, with twenty-one preachers representing 1168 members.[14] Gradually eight circuits were laid out to serve forty-nine places of worship throughout the state; as a result, the membership of blacks in the predominantly white Methodist churches in Indiana declined from a high of 442 in 1839 to only 138 in 1851.[15]

William Paul Quinn

The outstanding missionary of the A. M. E. Church in Indiana during this formative period was the Reverend William Paul Quinn. Born in Calcutta, India, raised a Hindu, converted by English Quaker missionaries, he immigrated to America when his father disowned him for his commitment to Christianity. At first befriended by Hicksite Quakers, he later became a dedicated Methodist. When his dark skin impeded his acceptance as a Methodist preacher, he affiliated with the A. M. E. Church and became that fledgling denomination's first missionary in Indiana and Illinois; between 1840 and 1844 he held seventeen camp meetings, established forty-seven churches, fifty Sunday schools, and forty temperance societies. Quinn continued to serve in Indiana after he was elected a bishop in 1844, and was especially active around Richmond, Indiana, where the largest A. M. E. congregation in the state developed under his leadership.[16] Exactly what role Quinn played in the organization of the A. M. E. congregation in Fort Wayne is not known; later, however, in his capacity as bishop, he visited the city.

In 1844, Quinn journeyed to Pittsburgh for the Seventh Annual Conference the A. M. E. Church and described to the eastern delegates his western mission field:

William Paul Quinn
[Courtesy of Coy D. Robbins]

The number of colored inhabitants in the states of Indiana and Illinois is 18,000 . . . . Our people in these states are chiefly employed in agricultural pursuits, and are rapidly improving themselves by cultivation of the ground, from which they make, under the providence of God, a good living for themselves and families, and sustain churches and schools in a manner truly surprising. Although many of them, within the last ten or fifteen years, broke away from the fetters of slavery and settled with their families in these states, yet, by the dint of industry, they are not only supporting their families, schools and churches, but many of them are also acquiring wealth amid opposing laws and chilling prejudice. There is, however, a very good state of feeling evinced toward our people by the more enlightened part of the white community in these states. There are many useful mechanics among them, such as shoemakers, blacksmiths and carpenters. They have, in a word, every constituent principle among them, when suitably composed, to make them a great and good people.[17]

Quinn's reputation as an abolitionist preacher was well remembered by a clergy colleague, the Reverend Benjamin Tanner:

The writer had often heard him preach when it was absolutely dangerous to be either in the house or out of it; when the greater portion of his audience were either "mobcrats" or "lewd fellows of the baser sort"; and when the "Amens" and "Hallelujahs" came louder from the children of the wicked one than from the children of light. The principal cause of all this persecution was the inveterate hatred toward the Abolitionists; and it is passing strange that, in those days, some colored people were found entertaining the same hatred for Abolitionists as their white fellow-citizens. It was a very common expression among some of the colored people to say, "I would go and hear this great Paul Quinn preach if I thought he would say nothing about Abolition; it is something we colored folks have nothing to do with, and it only makes it worse for us to be stirring it up all the time." It is due the Bishop to say that he acted very judiciously with the whole subject, and the colored people were much indebted to his manner of procedure for the comparative peace they enjoyed. The idea of the Bishop being an Abolitionist originated from his preaching so often from his favorite text, and which at times was so very appropriate, to wit, "I have surely seen the afflictions of my people."[18]

Fort Wayne Placed on a Circuit

Who first gathered Fort Wayne's black congregation in worship is not known. The people may have come together at the urging of zealous laymen who had attended one of Quinn's camp meetings; possibly Quinn himself founded the congregation on one of his itinerations; or perhaps a traveling preacher from the A. M. E. Ohio Conference organized the first services. As Fort Wayne was near the Ohio border, the denomination's Ohio and Western Conference assumed initial responsibility for the fledgling congregation, and the Conference minutes of 1845 show Fort Wayne on the Carthagena Circuit, between Van Wert, Ohio and Eel River, Indiana.[19] No black clergyman could count on a safe journey as he traveled, a reality impressed on Fort Wayne residents when they read in a local newspaper that another black minister was reported missing: "Rev. Mr. Cartwright, pastor of the Third Baptist Church (coloured) in Zanesville, Ohio, left his charge several months ago to preach a funeral sermon of a brother minister. . . in St. Louis. He has not since been heard from, and fears are entertained

The Trustees of the African Methodist Episcopal Church of Fort Wayne — Willis W. Elliot, Henry H. Canada, and George W. Fisher — purchase land at public auction in 1849; observing the transaction *(left)* **is their pastor, George Nelson Black.**

[Original Illustration by Kenneth B. Dutton]

that he has been kidnapped, and sold down the river. The church of which he is pastor will be very thankful for any intelligence respecting him."[20]

In spite of the perils, these ministers persevered and were very effective; one circuit rider later recollected: "The years 1848, '49 and '50 were the palmy years in the Indiana [A. M. E.] Conference, containing more traveling preachers those three years than at any other time."[21] It was during this period that the Fort Wayne African Methodist Episcopal Church was formally organized. Also, at this time, it appears that black members of the local M. E. church transferred their affiliation to the new A. M. E. Church; after 1848 no blacks were reported as members of the white M. E. congregation.[22]

A. M. E. Trustees Purchase Land

On May 16, 1849, three prominent black residents of Fort Wayne purchased, at public auction at the Allen County courthouse door, a lot located on the south side of Jefferson Street between Hanna and Francis streets.[23] Title to the property was granted to Willis W. Elliot, Henry H. Canada, and George W. Fisher. These three men, who outbid others at the sale by paying its appraised value, were leaders in the African Methodist Episcopal Church of Fort Wayne. Elliot, a thirty-eight-year-old native of North Carolina, owned two barber shops in town; Fisher, was a twenty-four-year-old lather from Ohio. When the three men finally received the deed to the property, it failed to identify them as church trustees; as a result, their property was subject to the same tax and inheritance laws as any other city lot. Their bishop probably advised them that they were required to operate under the rules of the Indiana District of the A. M. E. Church, which, in 1843, decreed that "no church should be suffered to be built among us until a deed, according to our Discipline, be first procured, or a title bond is obtained for double the value of the ground on which the church is built."[24] The congregation may have elected Elliot, Canada, and Fisher as trustees of the church at that time to take title to the land. In order to change the deed, the property then was momentarily sold to a "straw man," the Reverend George Nelson Black, a prosperous, thirty-four-year-old local blacksmith who served as the congregation's pastor;[25] immediately the three church officers repurchased it, and the lot's ownership was officially recorded as the "Trustees of the African Methodist Episcopal Church of Fort Wayne and State of Indiana."[26]

It does not appear that any building was erected on the property, and there is no evidence that it was used as a cemetery. In December 1853, the church trustees sold the lot for the same price they had purchased it. No church records have survived during this period, but traces of the activities of the church trustees appear occasionally in the county records. In 1858, a mechanic's lien in the amount of two hundred dollars was brought against the A. M. E. officers, hinting that some sort of building project had been undertaken. In another court appearance in 1863, the trustees successfully proved that an alleged debt had long ago been repaid.[27]

The Colonization Movement

The Methodist Episcopal Church during this time had alienated itself from its remaining black members by endorsing a nation-wide campaign to urge African-Americans to emigrate to Liberia.[28] This movement had its origins at the beginning of the nineteenth century among those British and American abolitionists who believed that the repatriation of freed slaves to Africa was the best solution to the problems of dismantling the institution of slavery. In 1820, Isaac McCoy naively imagined that the black residents of Fort Wayne would welcome the opportunity to immigrate to the land of their ancestors. The missionary assumed that his students of European and Indian heritage would remain in America, each contributing to the common good, but, of that lone black scholar, "we hoped [he] would one day find his way to Liberia, Africa."[29] One Fort Wayne citizen expressed the hope that the African-American colonists would transform the "dark continent": "Africa's children, now in our refined happy America, may yet return to their native, sunny clime carrying with them civilization, learning and refinement; so that Ethiopia may yet stretch out her hands, and Africa—trodden, oppressed Africa—may yet take her stand among the nations of the earth, and rejoice in the results which have grown out of her bondage among us."[30] By mid-century, however, an increasing number of segregationists were also endorsing the voluntary expatriation of African-Americans to Liberia; among these was Indiana's governor, Joseph A. Wright, who promoted the colonization movement in "this great struggle for the separation of the black man from the white."[31] Many white antislavery church members, however, agreed with the Reverend Alexander T. Rankin of the First Presbyterian Church who denounced the colonization movement as a "true yoke-fellow" of slavery.[32] The overwhelming majority of free American and Canadian blacks were strongly opposed to the idea of emigrating to the continent from which their ancestors had been taken a century or more before, and resisted the colonization movement by every means available.

There were, however, a few blacks in Indiana who saw no hope for freedom and equality in America and therefore decided to join in this effort to create a new African nation of African-Americans governed by and for people of African heritage. One of them was William W. Findlay of Covington, Indiana, a leader in the African Methodist Episcopal Church. In April 1849, he addressed an "Appeal to the Colored People of Indiana":

Dear Friends: The writer being a colored man . . . it has long been an inquiry with me, how can our race be elevated? *How can colored men be made truly independent?* After much anxious and painful inquiry, I have concluded that, to be truly independent, we must enjoy rights and privileges as *broad* and as *liberal* as those enjoyed by the white citizens of the United States. In other words, have the right of electing our law-makers and our magistrates; and all the offices of State should be accessible to our color; and not only so, but we should be free to move in such circles of society as we may be entitled to by our moral worth, character and talents; and likewise free to form alliance with those classes of society. Those, in my humble opinion, are the rights and privileges *we must possess* before we can be *independent.*

But now let us inquire in candor, do . . . colored men in the most liberal of the northern States enjoy such independence? You all know that they do not—the sad reverse is the case. And will the time soon come in the history of American society, when the colored man will be permitted to enjoy such independence—independence, not only in civil things, but independence in all the more delicate matters of social equality? I must honestly confess I think not. And further, I am bold to confess that anything short of the above described independence will not satisfy me, nor should anything short satisfy the man of an independent spirit.

But such independence we cannot obtain in the United States; therefore I will seek it outside the United States. *I will seek it where I know I can find it,* and that is in the Republic of Liberia, which is the only Christian republic where the colored man can find a quiet and secure home. Nor do I act dishonorably in thus escaping from civil and social oppression, for I am only doing what thousands of the first and best settlers of the United States did, and I think it an honor to follow their example in seeking liberty, though like them I be compelled to seek it in a wilderness. And the object of this appeal is to invite you who love true independence, and are willing to endure some toil to obtain it, to go with us to that land of liberty, where we may likewise aid in the elevation and enlightenment of our whole race, *which duty is more obligatory on us,* than upon the white race, many of whom are willing to *sacrifice* their lives and property in the work of converting Africa.

Findlay had probably debated the issue with African-Americans before, because he anticipated several objections. To those detractors he presented a religious view of future race relations in America:

Some of you may blame us for not staying in this land and contending for all the above rights of man. Our answer to all such complaints is this: we believe that civil slavery in this land will be abolished by Divine Providence without the co-operation of the free colored man; he requires not our aid in this work—he can and will, in his own way, sweep slavery from the civil institutions of America. But I honestly doubt where it is the will or order of Providence to grant us perfect social equality with the white race at this time; nor am I disposed to strive or quarrel with them for this favor, but would follow the example of Abraham, who disliked the strife that had sprung up between him and Lot, and religiously proposed separation as a remedy for the quarrel, and a means of perpetuating peace; for doubtless God has given this land to them. Acting from the above religious and honorable views, we confidently expect that God will bless us in our movements.

Findlay concluded by urging Indiana African-Americans to join him to settle in the Free Republic of Liberia:

It is the design of the writer and some of his friends to go out to Liberia about the month of October or November next, and it is desirable to have as many emigrants from Indiana as we can muster. Liberia holds out many attractions for the man of color, but the greatest is that of liberty and independence. Thousands have gone from this land to that, and all who have been industrious have done well, many of them are becoming wealthy, but what is best, *they are all free!* Come, let us go and cast our lot in with them and be free likewise. If any of you have been cherishing the spirit of independence and long for such freedom as the free Republic of Liberia offers, and if you desire a passage to that land, just let your wishes be known to the Agent of the American Colonization Society in this State. Address Rev. J. Mitchell at Indianapolis, who will be pleased to book your name as an emigrant and procure for you a passage out, and send you all the information that you may want. No time should be lost; *act now,* act for yourselves, your children and your race.[33]

Fort Wayne's African-Americans Reject Colonization

In Fort Wayne, Findlay's appeal and the recruitment efforts of the American Colonization Society in Indiana prompted the leaders of the A. M. E. Church to call a meeting to discuss this controversial issue. The gathering was moderated by their pastor, George N. Black. As a result of the meeting, a bold statement was issued by Fort Wayne's black community condemning the colonization campaign:

City of Fort Wayne, Indiana,
July 10, 1849

At a meeting of the Colored People of this City, held on the 16th inst., to take into consideration the merits of an appeal made to the Colored People of Indiana by William W. Findlay, urging them, if they would enjoy social, civil and political privileges, and be truly independent, to colonize in Liberia;—in answer to said Appeal, it was Resolved:

1. That the enjoyment of life, liberty, and the pursuit of happiness belongs to us as an inalienable right from our Creator, in common with all mankind.

2. Though denied in some things the full enjoyment of liberty and the pursuit of happiness at present, which are awarded to the whites, yet we are determined to use all lawful means, and to continue in so doing, until we shall be allowed the full privileges of American citizens; for our forefathers fought, bled, and died, to secure for us and to us those things, in common with other citizen soldiers, in the Revolutionary War.

3. That, because we are at present denied some of these rights in this State, we should not abandon the hope of attaining justice for ourselves and our posterity, when already the leaven of justice is beginning to show its perfect work in some of the Eastern States; and in some of the Western, though not yet arrived to a state of maturity, is so far improved as to assure us that patience and perseverance are only needed on our part; and, if we should at such a time flee our country, forsake the graves of our fathers, desert the places of our birth and the scenes of our childhood, we should show ourselves unworthy of the enjoyment of those things now withheld from us.

4. That the Prince of Slavery and Slaveholding never sprung upon the American people a more sure and destructive scheme for the annihilation of the Free Colored People of this land, than the scheme of colonization in Africa. It never designed to do any thing for our benefit but to destroy. Let it speak for itself: "The moral, intellectual, and political improvement of the people of color within the United States are objects foreign to the powers of this society." (Address of American Colonization Society to its Auxiliaries, *African Repository,* vii. 291.)

5. That, since the Colonization Society has sent forth to the world this broad declaration, we feel insulted when asked to emigrate to Liberia; and, when a colored man becomes the tool of such a society or, on his own responsibility, advocates colonization, we look upon him as recreant to the best good of his race.

6. That, while we will labor to elevate our race and secure to them the enjoyment of equal civil and political privileges with the whites, we feel bound to labor to prevent our people from colonizing in Liberia; for every one that leaves this county for that American Golgotha weakens our hands and throws obstacles in our way that are hard to be overcome.

7. That a copy of the foregoing preamble and resolutions be forwarded by the Clerk to the Editor of the *Bugle,* published in Salem, Ohio, with the request that he will publish the same in that paper.

Done by order of the meeting.

George N. Black, *Moderator*
George Fisher, *Clerk* [34]

This strong statement by Fort Wayne's black community was published in its entirety in the *Anti-Slavery Bugle,* which had a wide circulation throughout Ohio and Indiana. (Fort Wayne newspapers, which tacitly supported colonization, did not publish it.) The Colonization Society, however, was stung by the Fort Wayne manifesto's accusation that their organization had no real interest in the betterment of African-Americans; then, fearing its effect on their recruitment efforts in Indiana, they attempted a rebuttal.[35] The determined resistance of the leaders of the Fort Wayne A. M. E. Church to colonization, however, was damaging, and the movement in Indiana began to stall. A Fort Wayne resident noted: "The black population are incredulous in regard to Liberia; they look upon the whole scheme of colonization with distrust, advocated, as it is . . . by those who are not their friends . . . . It is more repulsive to them than the snows of

Canada, or the sugar plantations of the South."[36]

The Underground Railroad

There is no record of any Fort Wayne resident ever volunteering to emigrate to Liberia, but most likely some local citizens did volunteer to assist escaped slaves to emigrate to Canada. The first account of "conductors" leading "passengers" on an "underground railroad" through the three rivers area told of a group of Quakers from Richmond, who arrived at Fort Wayne with their "train" on October 10, 1829. Frederick Hoover, one of the conductors, later wrote of the incident in language inspired by the Biblical account of the exodus of Hebrew slaves from Egypt:

> Now it came to pass that in the first year of the reign of John [Quincy Adams], who was governor of the United provinces and territories of North America, that the Ethiopians in the province of Kentucky were sore vexed by reason of their taskmasters, and they lifted up their eyes toward the land of Indiana, which lieth toward the north country, over the great River Ohio .... Now Indiana is a land flowing with milk and honey, and they said, "Therefore, let us flee thither; peradventure the people of the land will deal kindly with us and deliver us out of the hands of the oppressor." So the people gat them away by stealth and fled into the land of Indiana and gat them possessions in the land. Howbeit, they were sought by the Negro-hunters .... The children of Ethiopia said, therefore, to one another, "Wot ye not that if we tarry in this land we shall be spoiled of our possessions; let us, therefore, make ready and flee even unto the land of Canada."

The group then journeyed north under the protection of the Quakers and came to the outskirts of Fort Wayne. Fearing that the community was populated by "men of Belial" who would "evil entreat them," the conductors left their passengers hidden and entered the town to confer with "the chief men of the city," who gave them permission to travel through the village if they "would not turn to the right hand nor to the left—and if they took anything from thence they would give them pieces of silver."[37] Passing safely past the wary populace, the fugitives continued their journey through Defiance, Ohio, and Monroe, Michigan, and arrived in Detroit for a final ferry to Windsor, Ontario.

No one knows how many fugitive slaves were assisted by Hoosiers on their flight through Indiana to freedom in Canada; few records were kept and most were deliberately destroyed after the passage of the Fugitive Slave Law in 1850. Estimates vary widely; probably four thousand former slaves were guided across the state to safety.[38] Fort Wayne was a crossroads for two minor routes. One was the towpath of the Wabash and Erie Canal. Occasionally, hardy male fugitives—able to travel without a conductor—would be guided to the towpath in the southwestern part of the state and instructed to follow the canal upstream to its summit at Fort Wayne and then downstream to Lake Erie.[39] Travel was usually under cover of darkness, with "stations" located at appropriate locations along the line for food and rest during the daylight hours.[40] Addison Coffin, a "conductor" on the "line" wrote in 1844, that "the Wabash line was in good running order and passengers very frequent."[41] A second route—the "splinter line" used by Frederick Hoover—came north from Richmond through Winchester and Bluffton to Fort Wayne and then forked, one track continuing north through Auburn and the other turning west towards Toledo, Detroit, and Canada.[42] No fugitive slaves were apprehended in Fort Wayne, but the events surrounding their capture in other areas of the state were widely reported in the local newspapers.[43]

If there was a white leader of Fort Wayne's underground railroad operatives during the late 1830s and early 1840s, it was most likely the Reverend Alexander T. Rankin, pastor of the First Presbyterian Church, a founder of the Indiana Anti-Slavery Society, and brother of the Reverend John Rankin, who assisted escaping slaves at Ripley, Ohio. In the mid-1840s and 1850s, the Reverend Daniel W. Burroughs, a local Baptist preacher who was a bookseller and publisher of *The Standard,* "was active in the 'underground railroad' system of the time."[44] Burroughs's antislavery editorials and speeches brought upon him many threats of personal injury; an admiring editor of the *Sentinel* later wrote: "Mr. Burroughs was as brave as a soldier."[45]

"The Odious Black Law"

The racial prejudice which attacked abolitionists and promoted colonization also worked for exclusion. The idea was not new: in Ohio, laws were passed in 1804 and 1807 to discourage blacks from settling within its borders and, in 1819, Illinois passed a Black Law to restrict immigration. The presenting issue in Indiana focused on the statutes of slave states prohibiting free blacks from settling within their borders and requiring that emancipated slaves leave the state or be re-enslaved. A Tennessee law forbade the emancipation of slaves unless they were immediately transported out of the state.[46] By 1850, a tide of fear and prejudice had risen to such a level as to make the exclusion of blacks a principal question at the constitutional convention which had assembled in Indianapolis. Article Thirteen of the proposed constitution stated: "No Negro or mulatto shall come into, or settle in the State, after the adoption of this Constitution." In addition, fines were established for those who employed illegal black immigrants or encouraged their settlement, and the revenue from the fines was to be used to assist in transporting legal Indiana black residents to Africa.

Allen Hamilton, a Whig delegate from Fort Wayne to the state constitutional convention, published an appeal to the voters of his district asking them to advise him on "a provision in our new constitution prohibiting persons of color from emigrating hereafter to the state. It is argued that . . . slaveholding states will all enact stringent laws to get clear of all free persons of color within their states; that, as a border state, we will be overrun by the worn out slaves of adjoining states who are set free . . . unless we, like Illinois, take strong measures to prevent it . . . . I am at a loss to know what our people desire on this subject. I have strong feelings of sympathy for this oppressed and downtrodden race. I, however, desire to conform my actions to the wishes of those I represent."[47]

One reply, signed "Mechanic," was printed in the Whig newspaper and reflected the serious tone of the moral debate:

> This subject is one of great magnitude . . . bearing on humanity, morals, religion, and state policy . . . . If the unhallowed institutions of slavery shall . . . require the inhuman state policy of driving from their soil their unfortunate fellow beings, who . . . have been degraded to slavery and served as long in degradation as the conscience of the master allows—shall we, by constitutional law, station a soldiery with pointed bayonets on our State borders, to stab the breast of the poor Negro, while he is fleeing from the pursuing "Blood Hounds" at his heels, or lashes on his back . . . because, forsooth! his God made him black and a human master freed him from bondage!
>
> What shall be done with this class of our population? . . . It will not do to say, "let them go to other states," for the same spirit that refuses them an asylum in one state, may reject them in another. . . . The question is a clear one to me, that our state convention ought not to incorporate in the new constitution a prohibition against a Negro population. Humanity, with all it kindred sympathies, calls aloud to our delegates, to leave to the legislature the future regulating of this question.
>
> Indiana, it is to be hoped, will not subject herself to be the object of future reproach, and the scorn of the civilized world by enactments so repugnant to the honest sense of mankind . . . . But spare us! spare us now! and spare posterity! the mortifying legacy that so inhuman a provision, as the one proposed, was ever incorporated in the Constitution of Indiana.[48]

Allen Hamilton was not moved by this or similar pleas

for tolerance and, in spite of the Whig's strong opposition to the measure, became his party's only convention delegate to vote for exclusion. Few local Democrats were distressed about the issue and one of their leaders declared that the measure "is deemed necessary. . . to prevent the state from being overrun with a worthless and degraded people, the off-scourings of the slave states."[49] Allen County then voted, in the state-wide referendum on the issue, to forbid black immigration by a margin of 85 percent.[50] In 1851, the new constitution, with its black exclusion provision, was adopted; then, at the next session of the General Assembly, "An Act to Enforce the Thirteenth Article of the Constitution" was passed. The immediate impact of this new punitive legislation on the black residents in Fort Wayne was to require them to register, in effect, as resident aliens. In an editorial in the *Fort Wayne Times and People's Press,* John W. Dawson wrote: "We would call the attention of colored people to the advertisement of the County Clerk in another column, touching the law in regard to them. We loath and abhor the cruel and oppressive laws that bear so heavily upon these people and, if we had the power, would strike them from existence; but, as they are the laws of the state, and likely to continue so, those concerned should make the best of them. Under the circumstance, a compliance with the notice will be a decided benefit to those who were here at the specified time. It will cost them nothing."[51]

Then, in the summer of 1855, the same editor lamented the fact that Fort Wayne had "the dishonour of producing the first fruits of the odious black law":

> Ten days ago, James P. Brown, a citizen of Ohio, travelling westward, stopped in this city and was detained here on business a few days. This person belongs to that proscribed and hated race on whose skin God's sun has imprinted a darker hue than our own. All unconscious of wrong, the stranger was awaiting the time when he should pursue his journey through our State to a distant destination. Suddenly he was seized and dragged as a criminal before a magistrate, for violating the constitution and law of Indiana which makes it a penal offence for a negro or mulatto to come into or settle in the state. Yet a man was found, degraded enough, and with enough of the spirit of the hyena, to hunt down this inoffending man and, as a vile informer, subject him to the penalties of a law that would shame the tyranny of Austria or the oppression of Turkey. . . . To compare him with his victim, would be an insult to the despised race to which his victim belongs. And yet there are such in this community. . . ready and willing to ensnare the innocent, and treat God's unoffending freemen as felons, because an atrocious law had made a man guilty for wearing

a black skin, when he has no power to make it white.[52]

The magistrate fined Brown the minimum penalty of ten dollars; in default of payment he was jailed. Why the fine was not paid is not known, for Brown was not without friends in Fort Wayne. The local black community "showed deep

Charles Case
[Courtesy of Allen County Public Library]

interest in the case . . . not only in their sympathy for Brown . . . but . . . by their . . . anxious watching . . . and numerous and constant attendance on the trial."[53] It is possible that neither Brown nor his friends wished to contribute ten dollars to the state's colonization fund. Two prominent attorneys, Charles Case and Lindley M. Ninde,[54] quickly volunteered their legal services. Case was an ardent abolitionist: in 1837, he had proposed immediate abolition in the District of Columbia; in 1842 he successfully defended a fugitive slave; later, he edited an abolitionist and free-soil newspaper in Bryan, Ohio. In 1850, he moved to Fort Wayne, took an active part in the political campaign growing out of the repeal of the Missouri Compromise, and was named editor of the abolitionist, free-soil, and free public education newspaper, *The Standard*.[55] As Brown's defense lawyer, Case immediately secured his client's release on a writ of habeus corpus. Then, at the hearing before Judge James W. Borden, Case argued that the prosecution had

entirely failed to prove an essential point: "The state designates two classes of persons and only two, who are prohibited from coming into the State, viz: *Negroes* and *Mulattoes*, and, being a highly penal statute, every word and sentence of

Lindley M. Ninde
[Courtesy of Allen County Public Library]

it must be strictly construed . . . . Adopting this rule, only a full-blooded African or his descendant, and a half-blood— half white and half black-blooded—are excluded by the statute; and, when a prosecution is instituted under it, the State must prove what she alleges, viz: in this case, that the accused is a *Mulatto*. She has utterly failed to make such proof." After rebuttal by the prosecuting attorney and a summation by defense counselor Ninde, the judge rendered his verdict: "The state, having failed to prove Brown to be a Mulatto or Negro, he must be discharged. Ordered accordingly."

Dawson concluded his report on the incident on a religious note: "After his discharge, Brown took the first eastern train of cars for his home in Ohio. He thought, doubtless, of his unhappy lot in life, and of the sad hope of his doomed and hunted race: that in Africa they had been the prey of *civilized* nations; that in America they have been the victims of *Christian* laws and *Christian* institutions. But let him hope and remember there is a God in the heavens, and that His power is on earth, and that it will work mightily for those who are in bonds. Yes, let him hope, for He who is the sovereign

212

of all worlds, is pledged, in the eternal principles of his moral government, to break every yoke and let the *oppressed* go free."[56]

James W. Borden
[Drawing by B. F. Griswold, 1917]

Fort Wayne Clergy Divided on Slavery

Was this sermonette by Dawson an echo of some strong convictions he had recently heard pronounced from pulpits in Fort Wayne? Very few sermons from mid-nineteenth-century Fort Wayne survive and these are mostly messages preached on the the occasion of some civic observance, such as Thanksgiving or Independence Day. In the eighteen-fifties, the bold abolitionist preaching of the previous decade by Alexander T. Rankin of First Presbyterian Church and Charles Beecher of the Second Presbyterian Church had become weaker and more tentative in the pulpits of their successors. In 1855, the Reverend Jonathan Edwards of the First Presbyterian Church was sharply criticized by Charles Case who mocked the minister's naive view of southern culture and slavery; with tongue in cheek, the lawyer hoped that Edward's listeners "were not all so charmed with the beautiful and beneficial operations and results of the slave system as to be led to emigrate to the sunny climes of the South, where they may enjoy the fulness of civilization, which they but part enjoy in these northern climes."[57]

The Reverend Amzi W. Freeman of Second Presbyterian Church declared to the assembled community on Thanksgiving Day 1852 that there were some things in America "which should *humble* us. We should bow our heads in the dust that, in such a land as this, 3,000,000 of our fellow men should be held in the chains of servitude; and, especially, that so little has been done during the past year for their improvement and emancipation." Like many of those who abhorred slavery, Freeman did not believe that instant abolition was a "practicable or merciful" solution to the problem; on the other hand, he held the widespread fear that the South would continue to do little or nothing to dismantle their institution of slavery. He carefully reasoned, "The fact of slavery, as it concerns the present generation, is not so much a sin, in our opinion, as the disposition to perpetuate it . . . . If the people of the South refuse . . . the problem of righteousness will work itself out with terrible vengeance in our time. There is an aspiration for human freedom at the present time, throughout the world . . . and . . . significant signs of a struggle for rights . . . . It were sin for us to return thanks today without remembering with sympathy . . . those that are bound in our midst."[58]

The only Fort Wayne minister to argue that the institution of slavery was warranted by the Scriptures was the Reverend Wilhelm Sihler, pastor of St. Paul's German Lutheran Church. Sihler developed a line of reasoning parallel to the mind of the leader of the Missouri Synod, Dr. C. W. F. Walther, who declared that the Scriptures were not opposed to slavery. Walther was pleased to publish four articles written by Sihler, which stoutly defended the institution of slavery as biblically based.[59]

Another European-born clergyman who supported slavery was Isaac Mayer Wise who, in 1859, became the first ordained rabbi to visit Fort Wayne. Wise was increasingly influential among Fort Wayne Jews in the late 1860s and 1870s but, during and immediately after the Civil War, the members of Achduth Vesholom Synagogue were more attracted to the Reform theology of Rabbi David Einhorn, who had violently denounced Wise as an anti-abolitionist and a copperhead.

Roman Catholic clergy in Fort Wayne maintained a neutral silence on the slavery issue during the 1840s and 1850s. If the Reverend Julien Benoit at St. Augustine's Church had any strong convictions on the subject, none were expressed in his correspondence or public statements. Like his clerical colleagues in the diocese, he was as uncommitted on the issue as were the Catholic bishops at the First Plenary Council at Baltimore.

The Episcopal rectors in Fort Wayne were equally silent on the subject as were most of the clergy in the Diocese of Indiana. Their bishop, however, the Rt. Reverend George Upfold, was more outspoken, and publicly opposed emancipation and the antislavery platform of Abraham Lincoln.

Baptists in Fort Wayne were sensitive to the fact that the largest percentage of southern slaveholders were Baptist and that many Americans believed Baptists to be soft on the slavery issue. The Reverend Daniel W. Burroughs, who had occupied the pulpit of the local Baptist Church in 1849 and 1850, declared: "We are Baptist and have no hesitation in saying so, but we claim the right of disowning those who do such wickedness; and more, we claim the right to denounce the so-called religion that tolerates, yea, that gives vitality to such a damning practice. But let not your wrath expend its full force on the Baptist denomination. They are not alone in this Heaven-daring wickedness. Other denominations are practicing and tolerating the same things."[60]

Antislavery Clergy Attacked in the Democratic Press

No sermons of the Methodist clergy in Fort Wayne during this era have survived, but it may be assumed that they honored their denomination's Discipline which urged "the extirpation of the evil of slavery."[61] The president of the Fort Wayne Methodist College, the Reverend Samuel Brenton, was elected to congress in 1851 as a Whig, in 1854 and 1856 as a Free Soil candidate. He opposed slavery on moral principle and campaigned against it as unfair competition to the small farmer, and these views were influential in his denomination.[62] At election time, the local Democrats not only attacked their clergyman-congressman, but criticized Methodists in general; the Democratic editor of the *Fort Wayne Sentinel* deplored the "lamentable dabbling with politics by ministers of religion, and especially by the Methodists in Indiana."[63] Dabbling with politics was a code word for pulpit denunciations of the Fugitive Slave Law and any proposed extension of slavery into the new territories in the West.[64]

Charles Case, however, spoke out to defend those local clergy who preached on the slavery issue by mocking what he called the "Gospel of Hunkerism," a narrow theology he believed would restrict preachers to a few pious platitudes: "On such theology, if a minister in his pulpit ventures to 'remember those in bonds as bound with them,' to proclaim God's will 'that the oppressed go free and that ye break every yoke,' and to impose any human enactment which nullifies this mandate of Heaven, he is to be denounced as 'out of his sphere,' as a 'hypocrite and impostor.' "[65] When Case was nominated to fill Brenton's seat in Congress in 1857, Thomas Tigar, the "hunkerous" editor of the *Sentinel,* attacked the candidate's liberal views on black Americans: "Case . . . not only contends that they [African-Americans] are citizens, but wishes to place them on a level, socially, and politically, with himself. Those who share his views and feel themselves on a level with the 'cullid pussons' will of course vote for Mr. Case. Those who think differently will vote for Mr. [James] Worden."[66] Tigar attempted to make the status of African-Americans a central issue in the election and warned the voters: "A member of Congress is to be elected,

and the character of the district to be determined—whether it is to be ranked with the fanatics of the Western Reserve and New England, as an advocate of the odious doctrine of Negro equality. . . or whether it will take its place on the Democratic platform and maintains the doctrine of the superiority of the white race."[67] Case won the election, but not Allen County.[68]

When the pastor of the Second Presbyterian Church, the Reverend Eleroy Curtis, at a community Thanksgiving service in 1856, took issue with the anti-abolitionist and racist sentiments of the local Democratic party, Tigar blasted the preacher, who he said, "desecrated the pulpit and insulted his hearers by launching for a miserable tirade of falsehood and abuse against the democratic party. A man who is so destitute of Christianity as to pursue such an unwarrantable course . . . is far better adapted for a bar-room slangwhanger than for a minister of the gospel."[69] Then, when some clergy commented unfavorably on the Dred Scott decision, Tigar took them to task as well: "They have worn bleeding Kansas to tatters, and now take up Dred Scott in preference to 'Christ and him crucified,' which in the better days of the church . . . used to be the theme of pulpit eloquence and ministerial endeavors."[70]

Some of the best sermons with a religious perspective on the slavery issue were presented by local laymen. A learned exposition of the biblical passages that touched on slavery filled three columns on the front page of the *Fort Wayne Times* in 1854. Its anonymous author, who signed with the traditional pen name, concluded: "In vain do we look for the justification of slavery, either in the law or the gospel. We may quote the 'immortal Greeks' to our hearts content, or even the Romans; but theirs was only a one-sided liberty— liberty for myself and slavery for others—the very antipodes of liberty—a word they did not understand . . . . Slavery is a blot upon the present civilization."[71]

One "lay preacher" whose strong convictions on the slavery issue were heard in Fort Wayne was Harriet Beecher Stowe.[72] Her novel, *Uncle Tom's Cabin,* published in 1852, had a powerful influence in mobilizing American sentiment against the evils of slavery and the Fugitive Law of 1850. In 1855, a popular dramatic adaptation of the novel came to Fort Wayne and played for five nights.[73] A reviewer encouraged local citizens to attend: "This drama exceeds in interest anything now produced upon the stage. The plot and incidents of the story address themselves to all the strong, tender, and better feelings on man's nature . . . . It is one of those exhibitions of the sternly and solemnly truthful, that makes man reason as well as feel, and leaves them better and more thoughtful for the seeing."[74]

The suasive power of this dramatic story about the plight of plantation slaves was such that it prompted a local Southern sympathizer to attempt a rebuttal. Writing under the pseudonym "Civis" he asserted: "Whatever slavery may have been a half century since, the artistic pictures of it drawn by Mrs. Stowe in *Uncle Tom's Cabin* . . . [are] no where in the South, at this day, and for a score of years preceding, can be found the revolting practices and degrading effects of the institution as depicted by Northern fanatics in their stump, *bunkum* speeches and wishy-washy novels . . . . The condition of the Southern Negroes is *entirely* superior to the condition of the same classes in the North."[75]

More Restrictive Legislation

If any of Fort Wayne's black community attended performances of *Uncle Tom's Cabin* at the new Odeon Theater, they would have been required to sit in the gallery. Indiana laws offered nothing close to equality to its black residents and, in the decade of the fifties, additional legislation was enacted for restriction and exclusion. In 1853, a law provided that "no person having one-eighth or more of Negro blood shall be permitted to testify as a witness in any cause in which any white person is a party in interest."[76] Hence, when the trustees of the African Methodist Episcopal Church in Fort Wayne appeared in courts to defend the interests of their congregation in litigation brought by a white person, they would have been limited in their ability to testify. The legislature also decreed in 1853 that "Negroes or mulattoes shall not . . . derive any of the benefits of the common schools of the state."[77] Although exempted from school taxes, black residents did contribute to the support of the all-white schools through the payment of fines, escheats, and forfeitures. Isaac H. Julian, corresponding editor of the *Fort Wayne Standard,* was invited by the Indiana Yearly Meeting of the Anti-Slavery Friends, to prepare for them a summary of "Legislation of Indiana Respecting Colored People." To these abolitionist Quakers, who had withdrawn from the main body of their society in the 1840s, he concluded:

That a great 'sovereign State,' while holding the colored man as an 'outside barbarian,' alien to all the rights and sympathies of humanity —registering him like cattle—refusing him a voice in public affairs— denying the protection of its laws to his person and property—and shutting him out from all the avenues of education and progress— should at the same time filch from him a portion of his hard-earned pittance for its own exclusive benefit—nay, worse—to aid in the sustenance of the very measures taken for his oppression—is certainly the superlative of all comparative decrees of meanness!

Such are the Black Laws of Indiana. We have not spoken . . . of that other law . . . often more terrible and irresistible than express legislative enactments—we mean public sentiment. The colored people also suffer severely from this unwritten code. Under its rule, they are constantly subject to insult and annoyance in traveling and the other daily avocations of life, are practically excluded from all social privileges, and even from the Christian communion . . . . Verily, our first work of repentance, of reform, lies within our own borders— even at our very doorstep. May the spread of liberal education and of the spirit of Christianity hasten our preparation for it![78]

Methodists Invite the A. M. E. Bishop

At this time, the Wayne Street Methodist Church in Fort Wayne became a bridge between the black and white churches by inviting Bishop William Paul Quinn to preach at a special mid-week worship service on March 30, 1859. Quinn, who resided in Richmond, was now the Senior Bishop in the African Methodist Episcopal Church. The program was well advertised in the local newspapers and emphasized that the general public was invited to attend.[79] Quinn thus became the first clergyman of that denomination to preach in any white congregation in Fort Wayne.[80] It is possible that the Wayne Street church was already providing space for the local A. M. E. congregation to worship whenever a guest preacher came to town.

During the 1860s, a majority of the local black community continued to be organized around their A. M. E. congregation but, because of the their small numbers,[81] were unable to support a full time minister or secure a church building. By 1869, however, the congregation exhibited sufficient potential that a resident pastor was assigned, the Reverend Nixon Jordan, "a laborer by trade and minister of the gospel."[82] Worship was held at Hafner's Hall, a place ordinarily used for athletic events. When St. John's German Reformed Church determined to build a larger house of worship on its property, the A. M. E. officers[83] purchased the twenty-four-year-old frame church and moved it down Jefferson Street to a lot donated by Emerine Holman Hamilton, widow of Allen Hamilton.[84] This modest edifice was then renamed "Turner Chapel A. M. E. Church" in honor of the Reverend Henry McNeil Turner, a black chaplain who served in the Tenth Calvary, United States Army, during the Civil War, and later as a bishop in the A. M. E. Church.

At the end of the decade, the zeal of the black community in providing for their church and educating their children evoked admiration from their white neighbors, prompting a local editor to write: "As a city, we have comparatively less negroes than any city we know of; but we venture to say of those few, they are more black, put on more style, their hair is more frizzed, and they carry more Sunday School books of a Sunday afternoon than any other equal number of 'black lilies' in the State."[85]

13
Orthodox and Reform Jews

"We, who like so many other immigrants from Europe, have come to these happy shores in order to find a refuge from European tyranny . . . and feel deprived of the consolation of our Religion . . . have bound ourselves hereby to help each other in all of life's adversities."
Preamble to the Constitution of the "Society for Visiting the Sick and Burying the Dead," 1848.

In 1848, the first Jewish congregation to be established in Indiana was organized by German Jews in Fort Wayne. In one respect they were only one more German-speaking religious group— with German Catholics, Lutherans, Reformed, and Methodists—struggling with the initial problems of finding an acceptable place for worship and a suitable spiritual leader. With rare exceptions, Fort Wayne welcomed their new Jewish settlers, patronized their businesses, contributed to their synagogue, and elected them to public office.

John Jacob Hayes: Indian Agent

The first mention of a Jew living in the three rivers area is found in the journal of a British officer, Captain Thomas Morris, who, in 1764, narrowly escaped being burned at the stake by hostile Indians. When he arrived at the relative safety of Fort Miami, he was befriended by "Mr. Levi, a Jew trader."[1]

Levi's identity has not been determined. Better known is John Jacob Hayes, who, in 1820, was appointed as the local Indian agent. Born in New York City in 1770, the son of a

Tory who fled to Canada during the Revolutionary War, Hayes began his career in the Indian trade as a clerk in a Canadian trading house. In 1793, he settled at Cahokia, Illinois, where he served in a variety of government positions until his appointment to Fort Wayne. One of Hayes's first tasks as Indian agent was to renew the agency's permission to the Reverend Isaac McCoy, the Baptist missionary who had recently opened a school in the old fort, to house the Indian students in the former barracks. Hayes later regretted his open-house policy when the forty unsupervised children raced through his offices, damaging government property and disrupting the work of the agency.[2]

Hayes was never happy in Fort Wayne and departed after three years, partly because he had left his family in Cahokia, a seventeen-day overland journey. In 1801, he had married Marie Louise Brouillet in Vincennes; although his three daughters were raised in the Christian faith, he does not seem to have abandoned his Jewish heritage.[3] His life-long friend, Governor John Reynolds of Illinois, testified that Hayes was a man of "moral and honest character, and that his morality throughout his life was exemplary. He was not a member of any Christian Church, but observed the precepts contained in the word, with due respect and devotion."[4]

The Pack-Merchants

Only a few American-born Jews of English or Dutch heritage, such as Hayes, came to Indiana in the early years of settlement.[5] The first Jewish visitors to the Fort Wayne area were most likely young German pack-merchants. Their numbers gradually grew to such significance that a local newspaper in the late 1840s called attention to the presence

John Jacob Hayes
[Courtesy of Indiana Jewish Historical Society]

of a band of "itinerant Jew peddlers."[6] Many were from southern Germany where most young Jewish men, traditionally excluded from most trades and professions in Germany, became cattle dealers or peddlers. In a letter to President George Washington, banker Moses Mendelssohn expressed his hope that the American West would be a haven for these itinerant Jewish merchants:

> You would be astonished, most mighty president, at the perseverance of the German Jew if you could witness it. The great, nay, perhaps the greatest part of them, spent almost their whole life on the highway in pursuit of retail business, and the trader consumed for his own person nothing but a herring and a penny loaf; the

nearest brook or well has to supply his drink . . . . Granted that a Jew has at last become possessor of a capital that would suffice to support a family, still he will not be able to marry the woman he loves; . . . he is obliged to acquire protection money . . . and then seeks permission to marry. If he obtains it . . . he has to pay dearly for this permission.[7]

No Jew in Germany could engage in a trade or profession unless he had obtained a "Letter of Protection" from the government and, because of a strict quota system, the applicant might wait for years. In Bavaria, a Jewish youth faced an additional barrier: if he was not a firstborn son, he could not marry until he first obtained a *matrikel,* a registration certificate costing as much as a thousand gulden, and then proved that he followed a "respectable" trade. Peddling and cattle dealing were declared "disreputable." A German wrote in 1839: "The register *[Matrikel]* makes it little short of impossible for young Israelites to set up housekeeping in Bavaria; often their head is adorned with gray hair before they receive the permission to set up house and can, therefore, think of marriage."[8] As a consequence, many Bavarian Jewish youths in their teens and early twenties were attracted to the newly opened American West, where they could work in dignity, live in freedom, and marry young. On August 1, 1847, the first recorded Jewish marriage in Fort Wayne united Abraham Oppenheimer and Emma Eppstein; the local justice of the peace, John B. DuBois, officiated.[9]

In that year there was no organized synagogue in all of Indiana; the nearest congregation was located in Cincinnati. Even if a peddler could walk to Fort Wayne by sundown on Friday, he would find no regular gathering of the Jewish community for Sabbath services; at best, he could hope to be invited by a Jewish family to share their Sabbath meal. Observing the sabbatical and dietary laws of traditional Judaism was especially difficult for the pack-peddler who usually found his best customers located farthest from any settlement. When an itinerant first started out on the road, his pockets often bulged with hard boiled eggs, so that the Cherokee Indians called him *Jew-wedge-du-gish,* meaning "egg-eater." One peddler in Ohio, Abraham Kohn, bartered his wares for corn, vegetables, and eggs in a valiant effort to keep a kosher diet, and lamented the religious poverty of the itinerant Jew: "None of us is able to observe the smallest commandment. Thousands of peddlers wander about America: young, strong men, they waste their strength by carrying heavy loads in the summer's heat; they lose their health in the icy cold of winter. And thus they forget completely their Creator. They no longer put on the phylacteries; they pray neither on working day nor on the Sabbath.

In truth, they have given up their religion for the pack which is on their backs."[10]

For many settlers, the pack-merchant was the first Jew they had ever met. Some expressed awe to be in the presence of a latter-day Old Testament figure; a few displayed prejudice against "Christ-killers"; but most were happy to talk with any visitor with news from other settlements, and especially one who opened a bountiful pack of towels and ribbons, buttons and hairpins, hairbows and bracelets, pins and thread, lace and combs, toothbrushes and toothpicks. The settler usually gave the peddler a bed for the night and, if he awoke on Sunday, might have invited him to attend church. Living in a Gentile culture could be frustrating to the solitary religious Jew. The determined peddler, Kohn, exclaimed: "God in heaven . . . Thou alone knowest my grief when, on the Sabbath's eve, I must retire to my lodging and, on Saturday morning, carry my pack on my back, profaning the holy day. God's gift to his people Israel, I can't live as a Jew. How should I go to church and pray to the 'hanged' Jesus? Better that I be baptized at once, forswear the God of Israel and go to hell . . . . No, by the God of Israel I swear that, if I can't make my living in any other way in this blessed land of freedom and equality, I will return to my mother, brothers, and sisters, and God will help me and give me his aid and blessing in all my ways."[11]

Kohn was one of the strong-willed peddlers who resisted the pervasive temptations to compromise his religious convictions, but many Jewish itinerants became accustomed to visiting churches and became thoroughly assimilated into the nominally Christian culture of the West.[12]

Early Jewish Residents

No synagogues in Indiana were established by itinerant peddlers; all were founded by the settled merchants of the larger towns. Although no Jews are listed in the 1840 census of Allen County, Sigmund Redelsheimer had arrived the year before and soon established a general store on Columbia Street in partnership with Abraham Oppenheimer.[13] Then, in 1844, Isaac Lauferty, at the age of twenty-four, arrived from France[14] to establish a clothing store, and later a private bank. By 1846, the presence of these first Jewish families inspired a local Presbyterian minister, Charles Beecher, to deliver a series of lectures on Judaism: "There are several Jews here," he explained to his mission society headquarters in New York City.[15]

The merchant who became the acknowledged leader of the little Jewish community in Fort Wayne was Frederick Nirdlinger. Born in Hechingen, Germany,[16] he came to America at the age of sixteen and first settled in Chambersburg, Pennsylvania; later, in Fort Wayne,[17] he established a clothing store, the New York Emporium,

which grew to be one of the largest in Indiana. Nirdlinger spoke his Württemberg dialect (German Jews did not know Yiddish, a medieval German dialect written in Hebrew orthography, which served as the common language of east European Jews). As a result, he closely identified with the local German population, and, in 1850, was named a marshal in the elaborate German-American Independence Day cel-

Leaders in Fort Wayne's Jewish community — Frederick Nirdlinger, Sigmund Redelsheimer, Isaac Lauferty, and Abraham Oppenheimer — posed in a photographer's studio as card players.
[Courtesy of Indiana Jewish Historical Society]

ebration. Nirdlinger was equally recognized in the English-speaking community as an effective civic leader: in 1845, he was an organizing member of new Lodge of Odd Fellows; later, he helped to found the Kekionga Guards. Active in the Democratic party, he was elected a township trustee in 1855 and functioned as the overseer of the poor; he was elected again in 1865 and served for two terms. When Stephen A. Douglas, the Democratic candidate opposing Abraham Lincoln for the presidency, came to town in 1860, he rode in Frederick Nirdlinger's carriage.[18]

As a natural leader, Nirdlinger assumed special responsibility for those young Jews who first migrated to Fort Wayne. His home was the largest in the local Jewish community and thus became a meeting place for most of their religious and social gatherings. By 1848, the dozen or so local Jewish families were able to assemble regularly the necessary minyan of at least ten men required to be present in order to conduct the traditional services, as well as officiate at weddings and say Kaddish for the dead. From the beginning, Fort Wayne Jews determined to conduct their services according to the German orthodox tradition. The principal Sabbath service was held on Saturday morning, as the men of the congregation assembled in the large front parlor of the new Nirdlinger residence and the women took their places in a smaller sitting room to the rear.[19]

The Visitation and Burial Society

In October 1848, the Fort Wayne Jewish community took two significant actions: first, they acquired land to be dedicated as a Jewish cemetery[20] and built on it a Metaher-house for preparing the dead for burial;[21] next, they organized a Society for Visiting the Sick and Burying the Dead *(Verein Fur Krankensbesuche Und Todesbestattung)*. A

The Nirdlinger home, on the southeast corner of Main and Harrison streets, served as a synagogue from 1848 to 1856.

[Courtesy of Indiana Jewish Historical Society]

constitution and bylaws for the society was devised and signed by twenty-three men. The preamble, written in excellent German,[22] states poignantly the deep feelings of the immigrants in binding themselves to care for each other in a land so far from their origins:

> We, who like so many other immigrants from Europe, have come to these happy shores in order to find a refuge from European tyranny;
>
> We, who have left our native homes, kinfolk, and everything that was precious and sacred to our youth, realize that, when any calamity visits us, we have left all assistance behind and feel deprived of the consolation of our Religion;
>
> We, the undersigned citizens of Indiana, have bound ourselves hereby to help each other in all of life's adversities, and to pay the last tribute of respect to our members, selecting the name of the Society for Visiting the Sick and Burying the Dead *(Chebrah Bikur Cholem Ukeburath Methim)*.[23]

Nothing in the constitution and bylaws spoke of religious faith or worship, much less dietary laws or Sabbath obser-

vance; these were matters already determined by a German orthodox tradition and generally accepted by all. The initial concern of the "Verein" focused entirely on their religious responsibilities to the sick and the dying, the dead and the bereaved. The trustees were to visit sick members, making calls several times a week. If circumstances required, sick members of the society were to "be cared for free of charge by a good physician under contract to the association." In addition, a sick benefit of two dollars a week was promised to those who were unable to work, but no member was to "receive benefits for illness resulting from immoral living." A death benefit of ten dollars would be paid to the family of the deceased and a burial plot would be furnished by the society without charge. Benefits were to be paid out of a fund to which each male member contributed fifty cents a month. Additional monies were to accumulate from a ten dollar entrance fee—half price for bachelors—and a variety of fines levied for infractions of the rules: a trustee could be fined two dollars for failing to make a sick call within six hours after being notified; a member could be fined for not accepting an office, attending meetings, or serving on a committee. In addition, the members of the society pledged themselves to attend all funerals "properly dressed for the occasion," to provide ten men for a minyan at a funeral, and then to see that a minyan gathered daily during the first week after the death for Shivah at the home of the deceased. The president was also empowered "to give three dollars of the society's money to a worthy Israelite in need."[24]

Jewish-Gentile Relations

Apparently the people of Fort Wayne were well disposed towards the newly established Jewish merchants and were not inclined to impose Sunday blue laws in any discriminatory manner. In 1845, the editor of the *Fort Wayne Times* wrote: "We see it stated that thirteen Jews were recently fined in Cincinnati for keeping their stores open on Sunday. It strikes us that this was not right, especially if they kept their own Sabbath, which is Saturday. . . . The laws of the state should not meddle with the right of conscience."[25] The same newspaper two years later rejoiced at the continued emancipation of the Jews from centuries of European oppression: "No feature in the Christian world is more extraordinary than the disposition which is beginning to appear, after eighteen centuries of oppression and hatred, to extend to Jews the privileges of free citizenship. This has not only been done in our own country, in Great Britain and France, but in Norway orders have been issued from the throne to place them on the same footing of equality as their kindred in France."[26]

The open-minded spirit of the editor of the *Times* was not endorsed by the editor of the *Fort Wayne Sentinel,* Thomas Tigar. In early 1849, a report spread through the rural areas that there was an outbreak of smallpox in Fort Wayne, which frightened many in the country from frequenting the city shops. Tigar immediately took to print to counter what he said was an unfounded rumor and to assure his rural customers that it was safe to patronize Fort Wayne businesses. He also promised vengeance on those who he believed had deliberately circulated the false information:

Thomas Tigar
[Drawing by B. F. Griswold, 1917]

We are informed that the report of smallpox originated and has been circulated chiefly by a band of peddlers who infest this country, palming off on the unwary their damaged and worthless goods at higher prices than good ones could be obtained at any respectable store in the country. They have spread the report with a view of keeping people from coming here to trade, and hope to turn it to their own advantage by selling goods themselves to those who are weak enough to be thus duped.

We would caution the country people to look out for the scoundrels— believe not a word they say, for falsehood comes more natural to them than truth—buy none of their trash, or you will certainly be cheated, for trickery and cheating is what they live by—and above all, keep a strict watch and keep your cupboards and bureaus locked when they are on your premises, for there

is no saying what such men would do if they had the opportunity.

Is there no law on the subject of peddling? . . . Cannot some public spirited citizen of Fort Wayne look into the matter? Anyone who could abate the nuisance and stop the prowling of such sharks would confer a favor on the community.[27]

In the next issues of the *Sentinel* the editor admitted that there were at least two cases of smallpox in Fort Wayne, and that the report on the subject had really been initiated by his own colleagues in neighboring newspapers.[28] The Jewish community, however, was aroused and viewed the editor's statements about peddlers to be more prejudiced against Jews than protective of the populace. F. & J. Nirdlinger[29] immediately cancelled their advertising and subscription to the paper. The editor then revealed more of his prejudice:

The remarks . . . on the conduct of certain peddlers in spreading false reports of the great ravages of the small pox in this place, caused a great excitement among the descendants of Israel, many of whom unfortunately reside here. Why they should be so sensitive on the subject, unless they felt that the remarks properly applied to them, is more than we can conjecture . . . . One firm, the Messrs. Nirdlingers, immediately notified us to discontinue their advertisement and subscription to the paper—a request with which we cheerfully complied, as we have all along entertained some misgivings that the appearance of their advertisement in our columns might be more profitable to them than to our readers . . . . Messrs. Nirdlinger, it appears, are connected with the peddlers,[30] and feel more interest in their success than in the prosperity of the city.[31]

Tigar would not give up on the subject of Jewish peddlers and, in his next edition, suggested that they might be directly responsible for the outbreak of smallpox in town: "We allude to the visits of itinerant Jew peddlers,[32] who are strolling all over the country and who, in addition to laying in their goods at this place, may also, in travelling through Noble County, stop at infected houses . . . . We have as yet not heard of its having actually been thus disseminated, but . . . as a measure of precaution, their visits ought to be discountenanced, and no prudent person should deal with them."[33] Apparently, community leaders confronted Tigar on these baseless allegations, and he was forced to recant: "The report that two or three peddlers were lying sick with the smallpox at a Jewish boarding house in the south part of the city is, we believe, entirely unfounded. The rumor, that some persons in the country had caught the infection from a

Jew peddler, is also we believe, unfounded . . . . Still we feel it our duty to admonish our country friends to be careful how they deal with this class of persons . . . paying higher prices for the worthless and damaged articles they usually vend."[34]

Tigar did not have the last word. His editorial rival, George W. Wood of the *Times,* later took the opportunity to express the warm admiration which so many citizens of Fort Wayne held for their Jewish neighbors by commending to his readers an editorial from the *Cincinnati Gazette:*

For centuries the "children of Israel" have been a "scattered race"— persecuted by nations, denounced by sects, denied citizenship, a home and often life itself . . . . Being the subjects of almost incessant persecution, banished from country to country, and their property confiscated without previous notice, they have for years and years followed those pursuits among "Christians" that enable them to make their worldly possessions immediately available . . . . Even in this country . . . they are found engaged, generally, in the same business . . . where persecution has instructed them . . . to be prepared to "leave" on "short notice."

And among the numerous failures, frauds, and bankruptcies that have occurred, how comparatively few Israelites are among that number? . . . In their monetary dealings, they are seldom chargeable with violations of the word or bond. Again, among the thousands of paupers, beggars, vagrants, and convicts who fill our poorhouses, walk our streets and crowd our asylums, houses of refuge and prisons, how many Jews are to be found? . . . We have never seen one to our knowledge.

We have no Gentile prejudice whatever against the Jews—we have known them long and well, and . . . greatly admire many prominent traits in their character . . . which we should rejoice to see as prominent and universal among Christians.[35]

The First Cantor

During the first two years of its organization, the Fort Wayne Hebrew Society, as it informally called itself, was dependent upon its own male members for whatever leadership was required for Sabbath, holiday, and special services. There was no east-coast Jewish organization dedicated to

establish frontier congregations, nor was there any concerted effort to send rabbis, teachers, and cantors to the West. American Judaism followed the European tradition of giving total independence to local congregations. As a result, there was at this time no "denominational" Jewish religious organization; instead, a considerable number of Jewish voluntary associations had emerged, each dedicated to some aspect of Jewish education or benevolence. In this laissez-faire system of synagogue development, Jewish religious journals became a vital link for the developing congregations of the West. When the Catholics of Fort Wayne needed help, they petitioned the bishop; when Protestants had a vacancy they usually communicated with their denominational headquarters; but when the Jews of Fort Wayne determined to engage a spiritual leader, their only recourse was to write to synagogue leaders in the East and place advertisements in the popular religious journals, such as the *Occident and American Jewish Advocate,* a publication representing their orthodox viewpoint.[36]

By 1850, the Society had secured its first spiritual leader,[37] the Reverend Joseph Salomon, to serve as hazzan or cantor.[38] Nothing is known of his origin, training, or previous employment. Because very few ordained rabbis were available to the new congregations in the West, most of the emerging Indiana Jewish congregations had to be content with trained laymen. In addition to his duties as the leader of congregational worship, Salomon was employed as shochet to slaughter all food animals according to orthodox tradition. He was also to function as mohel to perform all ritual circumcisions. For this he was paid $250 and "admonished not to render Jewish services to any non-Jew here in this area . . . or be fined."[39] One subtle change of language occurred with the arrival of the new hazzan: not only did they call themselves a society *(verein)* but also a congregation *(gemeinde),* "Congregation Chebrah Bikur Cholem Ukeburath Methim."[40]

After the High Holy Days of 1856, the congregation moved from the Nirdlinger residence into a rented hall on the north side of Main Street between Calhoun and Harrison streets;[41] in the process, they adopted a revised constitution which was more specific in matters of worship. Sabbath and holiday services were to be conducted according to the Minhag Fürth, a Hebrew prayer book common to many orthodox German Jews. The new rules detailed both duties and deportment: "It is the duty of all members to attend services at the time stipulated in the Jewish calendar . . . [and] to attend the funerals of deceased members, as well as the Shivah at the house of mourning."[42] The deportment of some younger children at worship had created chronic dissatisfaction, for the new bylaws specifically forbade any child under the age of six from attending services, and parents of children under the age of thirteen were warned that, if their children were disruptive, they would be fined.

The Hebrew School

To provide for their children's religious education, the congregation secured a school room in a building across the street from the Nirdlinger "synagogue"[43] and Salomon was appointed as instructor. His initial responsibilities were to teach the Hebrew language and Jewish doctrine (religionslehre) three times a week. By 1856, the school had grown to the point that the Society felt the need to purchase twenty-five armchairs and a new rug. Initially the school's finances were handled separately from the congregation, with the burden of the rental and upkeep of the schoolroom resting on the parents. Eventually, in 1860, the congregation assumed responsibility for the school and subsidized the tuition of needy pupils.

In the autumn of 1856, a sixty-year-old professional Hebrew teacher, Mayer Eppstein, moved to Fort Wayne with his wife to be near his daughter, Emma, who had married Abraham Oppenheimer.[44] Eppstein, like his son-in-law, was a native of Klein Nördlingen in Württemberg, and had recently retired from a distinguished career in teaching Hebrew and German at a large synagogue school in Hechingen, Germany. A product of the European enlightenment which had opened educational institutions to Jews, Eppstein was graduated with high honors from a school in Eslingen; in 1848, the King of Prussia honored him with two gold medals "in testimony of his ripe and varied scholarship."[45]

Soon after he arrived in Fort Wayne, Eppstein offered classes in the German language to the general population. His talents as a teacher were quickly appreciated and a local editor reported, "He is quite competent."[46] The presence of an experienced German and Hebrew teacher in the congregation of fifteen families did much to raise their aspirations. In February 1857, a proud member reported to the editor of the Occident:

> The necessity of instruction for our children, who frequent the English schools, in religion and the Hebrew and German languages, was long felt and spoken of. But, as the means of carrying out a plan to effect this matter were wanting, people had to remain satisfied with the expression of their pious wishes. Yet behold! on us also was accomplished the Talmudical sentiment, that Heaven will guide man on the way he is desirous of going; for we were unexpectedly enabled to render possible, what had hitherto appeared to be impossible. During the last autumn there arrived here Mr. M. Eppstein, who had conducted with credit a Hebrew and German school as principal teacher in a considerable congregation in Germany.

Shortly before the New Year's festival the board of our congregation requested him to have the kindness to impart to the divine service more solemnity, by delivering a few addresses in the German language. Mr. E. did not alone comply, and made on Genesis xlviii. 8, "Bring the children to me, and I will bless them," an impressive address, in which he endeavored to convince the parents of the necessity to give their children a religious training, but he also kindly stated at the conclusion, that he would himself assume the task of religious teacher if it were desired.

Mr. Eppstein assumed the instruction in religion, German and Hebrew, and a teacher for the English was also appointed,[47] and placed under his superintendence. We entertain the confident hope that the All-merciful will bless our new school with the best success, so that it may produce beautiful blossoms and wholesome fruit, and speedily enjoy the sympathy of Israelites all over the land.[48]

Not all of the Jewish children were as awestruck by their new instructor as were their parents. The minutes of the congregation suggest that the students occasionally exhibited less than pious attitudes toward their studies, and, on one occasion, a teacher became stuck fast in tar which students had spread on the steps.[49] In each of these cases of mischief-making, the parents were fined.

Jewish Preachers

The Jewish community was less enthusiastic about the arrival of another so-called leader, Aaron Bloch. Little is known about this man who came to Fort Wayne in the 1850s, apparently under the sponsorship of a missionary society dedicated to the conversion of Jews to Christianity, and no mention of his mission to the Jews of Fort Wayne is recorded in any of the records or correspondence of the local churches. Apparently Bloch preached without success and, abandoning his mission, established a brokerage office on Columbia Street. On July 2, 1855, he married Kezia Steevens, the daughter of the Reverend William W. Steevens, a local school teacher turned lawyer.[50]

A public altercation involving Bloch was reported in the local newspapers: "A slight collision occurred on Monday between Rev. Mr. Bloch and J. D. Werden, Esq. It appears that Werden had called Bloch (who is a reformed Jew), Shylock, from his frequent buying of notes, city and county orders, etc., which incensed the little man so that he sprang into Werden's face and scratched it like a Kilkenny cat. Mr.

Werden was held and kept from injuring Mr. Bloch."[51] A year later Bloch was convicted of usury and fined $220. A local editor reported that Bloch "bears this little rebuke with very ill grace, especially as there is a probability that the charge and fine will be repeated two or three times. Poor Bloch!"[52] Finally, when Gentiles in Fort Wayne began to avoid his business, just as Jews had shunned his message, Bloch decided to leave. He was so well-known in the community that one newspaper printed a farewell: "Rev. Aaron Bloch, who was a reformed Jew, as he said—who was sent out to Christianize and ameliorate the condition of the Jews[53]—who preached the gospel for a while, and then set up a broker's office in Fort Wayne, and then got fined heavily for taking usury. . . has at length gone from the city, and perhaps will cast anchor in Davenport, Iowa. If we were only allowed, we might say, 'May the Lord's blessing go with him.' "[54]

Bloch was not the only Jewish preacher who wished to address the Fort Wayne Jewish community; a few itinerant German Jews, claiming to be teachers, cantors, or rabbis found their way to the synagogue and expected to be invited to speak and receive the traditional congregational hospitality. Often their credentials were questionable and their message unhelpful. Finally, to protect their people, the officers announced: "No strange minister, who cannot prove that he is employed by any Jewish congregation in America, will be allowed to give a speech in the synagogue."[55]

Isaac Leeser Visits Fort Wayne

The first widely-known Jewish leader to visit the congregation was the Reverend Isaac Leeser, who made a train trip to the West in the spring of 1857 and included Fort Wayne on his itinerary. Leeser was not only the editor of the Occident and American Jewish Advocate but also served as hazzan of the Portuguese Congregation Beth El Emeth in Philadelphia. He had already founded the Jewish Publication Society of America, published the first Hebrew primer for children, translated into English the Sephardi prayer book, and established the first Hebrew high school. His major literary achievement was the first American translation of the Hebrew Bible into English—a work that took him seventeen years to complete and which remained the standard translation for American Jews for the next seventy-five years. Leeser was impressed with the development of the Fort Wayne congregation and reported:

> We were more pleased in this pretty place than in any of our visits to country congregations. The number of families, we do not believe, exceeds fifteen; but they are united, and are thus in possession of what many large communities have not yet acquired. Mr. Isaac Lauferty is president;

and the Rev. Joseph Salomon is hazzan; we heard him officiate on Wednesday evening; he read devoutly and well; and Mr. M. Eppstein, of whom we reported in our April number, had charge of a school, and is zealously and successfully engaged in imparting knowledge in religion and the Hebrew and German languages.

Isaac Leeser
[Courtesy of American Jewish Historical Society]

We were hospitably entertained at the house of Mr. Isaac Wolf, and other gentlemen were ready to receive us with equal friendliness. We spent Wednesday with our friends, and were conveyed by them in the afternoon to see the town; and among other things they showed us the burying ground, which we found in excellent order.

In the evening there was a religious meeting at the [Main Street] Synagogue and, after evening service, we had the pleasure to address men, women and children, nearly the whole of the Jewish population of the city, on Joshua xxiv. 15: "But I and my household—we will serve the Lord," exhorting all to remain steadfast amidst temptation, and to educate their children, by precept and example, that they may also say with justice, that under all circumstances they would remain true to the Lord. After service many came to bid us farewell at the house of Mr. Wolf, and we have to thank Mr. Eppstein for the beautiful and feeling manner in which he responded to our remarks in the Synagogue. We shall not soon forget our visit to Fort Wayne.[56]

The issue of congregational unity, upon which Leeser commented, was present in many Jewish communities. Reform Judaism was gaining strength in the West and those observers of a more orthodox persuasion rejoiced to see Fort Wayne holding out against the liberal tide. A traditional Jew who visited Fort Wayne in 1858, noted with satisfaction that Salomon and Eppstein were following the established forms and exclaimed, "The motto of the Western Israelites seems to be 'onward, rigid orthodoxy, no modern reform.' May our God grant them success."[57] The visitor was equally impressed with the excellence of the reorganized religious school: "I attended the examination of the Hebrew and German school, under the supervision of Mr. Eppstein. The proficiency exhibited by the pupils in their Hebrew and German studies, and the able manner in which they responded to the various questions regarding the observances and tenets of our holy religion, reflect the highest credit on their venerable and talented tutor."[58]

Bar Mitzvah

On March 20, 1858, Albert Nirdlinger,[59] son of the congregation's patron, became the first young man of the religious school to make his Bar Mitzvah. This confirmation was a most significant event in the life of the maturing congregation, and they proudly sent to Isaac Leeser a full report:

It has become our duty to communicate for your highly esteemed journal, which, like the Prophet Elijah on Mount Carmel, has alone, among many others, remained faithful to the Lord, and contends with unyielding truth for His Word and Law, a description of a solemn scene which is well suited for its papers. On last Sabbath, Parshath Vayikra,[60] the son of F. Nirdlinger became Bar Mitsvah [i.e., attained his religious majority at his thirteenth anniversary, literally a son of the commandment].[61] As he was the first Israelitish child that had attained his religious majority since the existence of our school, and as a confirmation in proper form with the confession of faith could not take place, the lad was instructed to celebrate the day in the old fashion.

During Divine service in the morning, at which all the members of our community, both males and females were present, he read the sixth section in a manner both harmonious and grammatically correct, and in a style more beautiful than we had ever heard it before. In the evening, at half past six, we assembled by invitation at the house of Mr. Nirdlinger, where, after the evening service had been read, his son delivered the subjoined speech in the German language with so much feeling and evident emotion, that all were deeply moved, and no eye remained tearless. Mr. Eppstein closed the solemnities with some powerful remarks, taking for his text, Genesis xlvii. 23: "Here have you seed," &c., which confirmed the impression already made on us to such a degree, that we had to join the lad in the remark he had made in his address, that we shall never forget this day and its solemnities.[62]

The speech which the young Nirdlinger presented to the assembled congregation that evening expressed the core beliefs of the Jewish community and succinctly stated the obligations and privileges of Judaism:

I shall from this time forward not alone be accounted as worthy to observe equally with others the ceremonies, the holy precepts which are obligatory on the confessor of the Mosaic religion; but I shall also be bound to fulfill conscientiously the duties I owe to God, to myself, and to my fellow-beings.

I shall be bound to observe the duties toward God, our Creator and Preserver, on which we depend for our temporal and eternal welfare; to acknowledge Him as the sole and only eternal Being; to love Him with all my heart and all my soul; to fulfill His behest revealed through Moses, the greatest of the prophets, and to believe firmly in the promises which He had announced to us.

I shall be bound to observe duties toward myself, to show, by words, and acts, that I am indeed a being created in the image of God, to make holy my body as the temple for the immortal soul which dwells within it, and to guard it against sin and vice.

I shall be bound to fulfill duties toward my fellow-men, to love them all like myself, as my brothers, as children of the same heavenly Father, to endeavor to attract to myself, through my conduct, their love and the esteem of all good and upright men; and to do therefore for all mankind, without distinction of faith, what I might desire that each one might do for me under similar circumstances, and to strive with all my power to remove from every one that evil from which I may desire to be exempt.[63]

Under the guidance of Eppstein, young Albert's statement of duties to God, self, and fellow-beings expressed the
high moral teachings of Judaism to which all Jews, whether
traditional or reform, could assent. No word was spoken to
highlight any of the controversy which was developing
between conservatives and liberals in the West; and nothing
in his affirmation touched on differences between Jews and
Christians. It was a positive declaration of religious faith and
ethics to which most church members in Fort Wayne would
have given a hearty "Amen."

Appeals For Contributions

The congregation did not formally support any organized Jewish charities, nor did they take offerings or otherwise raise funds for any distant Jewish cause. When the
Ahavath Joseph Synagogue in St. Joseph, Michigan, was
destroyed in a fire and appealed to the Fort Wayne congregation for assistance in rebuilding, the officers declined to
help, and directed the petitioners to make a private solicitation. When the plight of transient Jews traveling through
Fort Wayne stressed the funds of the congregation, they
resolved to discontinue further aid.[64] The one continuing
benevolent concern of some members was the distress of the
Jews in Palestine, then under Turkish rule. Isaac Lauferty
zealously collected funds in Fort Wayne for the Palestine
Relief Fund, and persuaded some in the Christian community to contribute. Interest in the Holy Land had always been
high in America; in 1845, a local newspaper reported on a
speech in New York City: "The Reverend Dr. Herschel
delivered an address at the Tabernacle [church] on the
present condition of the Jews in Palestine . . . . A collection
was taken up in aid for the Society for the Melioration of the
Condition of the Jews. There is so much poverty and distress
among the 4000 Jews in Jerusalem They pay for leave to
worship near Mount Moriah without the walls of the city."[65]
In 1849, the same newspaper published a letter from "Rabbis
and a very large number of Hebrews in Jerusalem" who
wrote, "our support from the [European] Society of Holy
Offerings have fallen off dreadfully. . . our condition is
deplorable beyond description."[66] The cause of overseas
Jewish relief also had its detractors, who argued with the
same nativistic logic that had attacked the support Christian
congregations gave to their foreign missions. Isaac Lesser
attempted to balance the controversy: "Fully as we acknowledge the necessity of spending all we have to spare in
America on our own improvement, and hence would dis-
countenance the system of seeking for objects abroad when
so much is left neglected at home; still can we not deny our
sympathy to those of our brothers who linger at the graves of
our ancestors, submitting to hardships innumerable, merely
to tread the soil of Palestine."[67]

A Church Becomes a Synagogue

The Fort Wayne congregation's need for a suitable
synagogue soon overshadowed other calls for charity. Apparently the rented hall was less than ideal; consequently,
Mayer Eppstein challenged the people to start a building
fund. In April 1858, a sign was prominently placed in the
vestibule, "Donations for the Building of a Synagogue."[68] A
visitor noted: "I attended Divine service on Sabbath morning and found the congregation worshipping in two adjoining rooms set apart for that purpose, for I learned that the
congregation . . . are not yet in possession of sufficient funds
to erect a building for Synagogue purposes. There are in Fort
Wayne some fifteen or twenty Jewish families and, for their
earnest zeal in frequenting the house of God with their wives
and little ones, they deserve much commendation."[69]

Early in 1859, the German Methodists[70] offered their
church building for sale. This modest brick structure,
located on the west side of Harrison between Wayne and
Washington streets, was priced at $1200. At the May
meeting of the officers, it was reported that the church could
be purchased for $600 down and the balance in a year. As
only a few hundred dollars had been donated—and as the
officers were unwilling to commit themselves personally—
the matter was tabled. Then, on June 27, when the issue came
to a vote, the board was divided: six, led by Isaac Lauferty,
the vice president, voted against the purchase; but eight,
following the counsel of the president, Frederick Nirdlinger,[71]
voted to buy. Most of the members, except Lauferty, then
rallied with the majority to organize the fund-raising and
plan the remodeling of the edifice. Later, Nirdlinger said:
"No one wishes to impeach Mr. Lauferty's services or
character; but it is notorious that he . . . threw every
impediment in the way to our obtaining the Synagogue."[72]

One of the first steps taken by the officers was to initiate
a general solicitation of the Christian community for contributions. It was traditional for congregations in Fort Wayne
to seek building funds outside of their own fellowship. A
local newspaper editorialized:

> The Hebrew Congregation of Fort Wayne, hav-
> ing purchased the lot and building belonging to
> the German Methodists, situated on Harrison
> Street, are preparing to erect a church for denomi-
> national worship, but find themselves in need of
> a few hundred dollars to accomplish this work;
> and the society, feeling a consciousness in having
> responded liberally to all calls for church, be-
> nevolent, and charitable purposes made on them
> for several years past and, having not even for
> once asked for themselves, they are free to ask
> now a small donation from such as feel able in
> order thereby to complete their contemplated
> new, but humble, place of worship. Who then

that is able when called upon will give?—more we trust than will refuse the reasonable request.[73]

The solicitation was successful and provided a good portion of the total of $3000 needed for the purchase and remodeling. The *Occident* noted: "Their Christian fellow-

Achduth Vesholom Synagogue, on the west side of Harrison Street between Wayne and Washington streets, was dedicated in 1859.

[Courtesy of Indiana Jewish Historical Society]

citizens, indeed, contributed liberally; but still the larger portion will have to be paid out of their own means."[74] A Jewish visitor to Fort Wayne in early August 1859 was impressed:

The leading Israelites have been settled in Fort Wayne from twelve to fifteen years. They have acquired wealth and position and are now seeking to share with their less fortunate brethren the fruits and blessings of their labors . . . . Mr. Isaac Wolf . . . brought me to a neat brick edifice, situated on a retired but elegant street, where, said he, "Henceforth Israel shall have an abiding place, and the God of Abraham a home." Though few in number, the Jews of Fort Wayne have just purchased this little brick church and are speedily converting it into a Synagogue. They have added a story and otherwise enlarged and improved it and, in less than six weeks, expect to dedicate it . . . .

From all I heard and saw in Fort Wayne, I came to the conclusion that our fellow-Israelites were happy, contented, prosperous—as it is possible for them to be in "a strange land among a strange people." One thing struck me as most gratifying

to their character and worth, the readiness with which members of other persuasions came forward when solicited for subscriptions to buy and complete the Synagogue . . . . In no town or city in the West have I found Jews more united, dwelling together in unity, brotherly love, and social happiness, than in Fort Wayne.[75]

The congregation immediately set for themselves the goal of transforming the church into a synagogue by Rosh Hashana, Jewish New Year's Day, which was to begin on September 30. In order to celebrate the High Holy Days in the new facility, they boldly scheduled the dedication ceremonies for the preceding Sabbath, and then invited Isaac Leeser, who had visited the congregation two years before, to conduct the dedicatory ceremonies and deliver two sermons in English. The invitation to Leeser was delivered personally by a committee of the congregation which had journeyed to Philadelphia to purchase gas fixtures and other appointments for the redecoration of the synagogue. Leeser, in turn, promoted the cause of the Fort Wayne synagogue among his people; as a result, Congregation Beth El Emeth lent their silver Torah ornaments for the dedication services, and some of their members made financial contributions.

At this time, the Jewish women of Fort Wayne, who had previously organized themselves as the Thiriza Association, were technically not counted as members of the congregation: they had no vote at congregational meetings; they could not be confirmed, lead in congregational prayer, or be counted in a minyan called to observe Shivah (seven days of mourning); nor could they sit with the men during formal services. The Jewish women, however, were devout and equally excited about the prospects of a new synagogue. They knew that it was a tradition in the neighboring Protestant congregations for the women's societies to assume responsibility for securing funds to furnish the interiors of their houses of worship. The usual money-raising enterprises, however, were not practical that summer: there was insufficient time to organize a fair to sell handicrafts and, as they all kept kosher kitchens, it was inappropriate to serve fund-raising dinners for Gentiles. The women were, however, determined to do their part, so each contributed five dollars to make velvet curtains for the ark, brocade dresses for the Sepharim, and covers for the Torah.

The Synagogue Dedication

The interior of the new synagogue was brilliantly lighted with a new double gas chandelier donated by a member of Isaac Leeser's congregation in Philadelphia. The walls and ceiling were painted "in fresco." A women's gallery, situated on three sides of the building, seated over one hundred persons; the main floor, with the old pews and new carpeting down the center aisle, seated one hundred and thirty. Above the ark (hechal), in white marble with gilt lettering, were the Ten Commandments.[76] The *Fort Wayne Times* reported: "The building is a small structure, but amply large enough for the congregation in this place. The appearance inside is very neat and tasty, and reflects great credit upon those who have carried out its design. It stands due east and west—the pulpit in the east end. This position, we believe, is absolutely necessary for all churches of the Hebrews, as King Solomon's temple was so situated[77]—the first building erected to the worship of the true God. . . . During the service, the whole congregation, as well as the priest, retain their hats on their heads and do not uncover, as do the Christian denominations."[78] Thomas Tigar, the editor of the rival *Sentinel* who had excoriated Jewish peddlers ten years before, was effusive in his praise: "The edifice . . . is one of the neatest places of worship we have seen, highly creditable to the good taste and liberality of our Jewish citizens."[79]

Isaac Leeser described the dedication service in detail: "On Friday, about three o'clock, the afternoon service was read in the old hall used for a Synagogue hitherto and, after a brief interval, all proceeded to the new house which, having been opened about half past three, was filled to its full capacity at four o'clock, with an attentive and expectant audience, many of whom were Christians, including several Protestant clergymen, at which time the exercise commenced as announced in the printed programme."[80] When the procession, led by the bearers of the Law, arrived at the door of their new synagogue, Salomon (who was termed "minister" in the English program) knocked three times and said in Hebrew, "Open for me the gates of righteousness, that I may enter through them to praise the Lord." The doors were then opened and the congregation was lead in seven circuits around the interior as the Cantor led in singing seven psalms. An hour-long dedicatory address was then presented by Leeser in English. Acknowledging the presence of Christian religious leaders, he said that Jews "were not at all jealous of the missionary efforts of those who called themselves Christians, because they knew that they helped to spread abroad a knowledge of the 'old Testament' Scriptures, and a knowledge of the Lord Jehovah."[81] Leeser concluded his remarks by reminding his audience that they were chosen by God: "Always . . . a remnant [of faithful Jews] remained firm and devoted to the cause of their election. Consequently, God's providence stands justified in human reason, even for having chosen the people of Israel as the depository of everlasting truth."[82] The ceremony concluded with the traditional Friday evening service.

Realizing that many of the local community would not be able to attend the Friday afternoon dedicatory service, the officers scheduled a repetition of the service for Saturday morning. Many citizens were proud to learn that this was the first synagogue to be organized in all of Indiana, and few, if any, Christians in Fort Wayne had ever before entered a

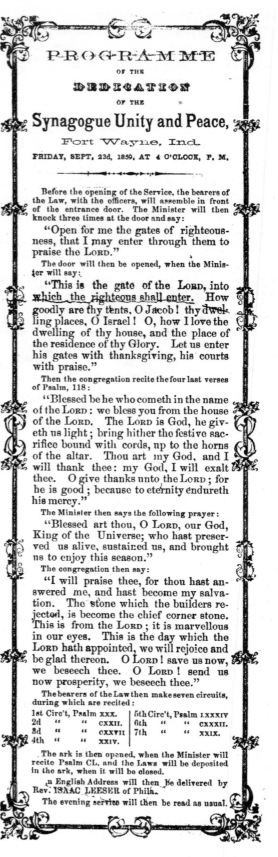

"Programme of the Dedication of the Synagogue Unity and Peace," 1859
[Courtesy of Achduth Vesholom Synagogue]

228

synagogue or heard the Hebrew language spoken in worship. An Episcopal vestryman, Peter Bailey, was impressed and wrote: "We hope that many of our citizens will attend a few times to hear the 'law and testimony' read in what is, most probably, the original language—we mean the language or the dialect closely resembling it, in which Adam and Eve, and the patriarchs and prophets conversed and wrote the inspired words." He also noted some similarities in worship: "The minister [cantor] reading a portion of Scriptures and the congregation answering with another portion, [was] something in the same way as the Episcopalians read the 'Psalter' or Psalms of David. We noticed also that the black silk gown and bands worn by the minister were similar to those worn by the Episcopal clergy and also many of the Presbyterian ministers of the present day."[83]

This second dedicatory service also gave an opportunity for the Jewish visitors to participate more fully; and, although there were only nineteen male members of the Fort Wayne congregation, guests from the surrounding area[84] swelled to forty-five the number of men over the age of thirteen—all of whom were invited to read a portion of the service. At the Saturday service, Leeser delivered a cautionary message, urging the congregation "to remain steadfast and true to the ancestral customs no less than the evident words of the Scriptures, inasmuch as we have no warrant to say that any of our precepts, except those immediately referring to the temple service, depended on time and locality." Then, referring to the increasing presence of Reform Judaism in the West, he warned these frontier Jews of "the danger of the tendency of some modern reformers," and praised "a system conservative of the truths which distinguish our people." Leeser concluded his message with the vision that their corporate faithfulness to traditional Judaism would contribute to the spiritual transformation of all humankind: "Their perseverance will ultimately result in the conversion of the whole world to the one God, which as it were, the folds of the flag round which they rally, will encircle all mankind, while the star which shines above it will shed the light over all the nations of the world."[85]

After Leeser's hour-long sermon in English, Mayer Eppstein rose to present the German address. He first touched on the difficulties which had surrounded them, how they had little hope a year ago of possessing a house of worship; yet "behold! it was so nevertheless." Eppstein concluded that "it was the evident work of God and 'therefore should they all be glad and rejoice therein.'" The congregation s gratitude to God, he insisted, "should be constituted in a diligent observance of divine precepts and a strict adherence to the institutions which they had inherited from their fathers . . . . This was all that they could render unto God, as He could not be recompensed by any act of benevolence which they could bestow on Him; whereas the observance of His precepts would prove that they were worthy to rejoice in the event, which they then celebrated, to

possess a house named Unity and Peace [Achduth Vesholom], the first erected in the name of our God in the state."[86]

Services were also held on Saturday afternoon and evening; then, on Sunday morning, the congregation gathered for Selichoth, the service of preparation for Rosh Hashana, the New Year. On a lighter side, the Jewish young people had arranged a ball on Saturday evening in honor of the dedication and invited their Christian friends to join in the festivities. Leeser attended and reported that "good humor prevailed till a late hour of the night, or rather the following morning, and yet many who had participated in the amusements were present at the meeting for prayer."[87] By the end of Sunday afternoon, Leeser confessed that he was then too fatigued to accept the invitation of the Reverend Eleroy Curtis of the Second Presbyterian Church, as well as several other Protestant ministers, to preach at the evening service. On Monday evening, the congregation met again and resolved to publish their gratitude to all who joined in its celebration: "That the Israelites of Fort Wayne herewith return their sincere thanks to their fellow-citizens of other persuasions for their kind contributions toward the obtainment of their new Synagogue, and their sympathy and participation in the dedication."[88] In the days following, the congregation became aware that many of the Christians who had attended the dedication service had a sincere interest in attending the forthcoming High Holy Day services, and an invitation was soon published: "The Atonement Day among the Jews begins this evening . . . . They fast from 5 a.m. 'till 6 p.m. All who feel so inclined are at liberty to attend the service."[89]

Isaac Mayer Wise Lectures

The news of the dedication of the new synagogue in Fort Wayne did not escape the notice of other Jewish leaders in the West, especially Rabbi Isaac Mayer Wise, who immediately arranged to visit Fort Wayne. Born in Steingrub, Bohemia, and largely self-educated, Wise came to America at the age of twenty-seven with a mission to bring the principles of Reform Judaism, then flowering in Germany, to fruition in the New World. After serving congregations in New York, he went to Cincinnati in 1854 to serve as rabbi of Congregation B'nai Jeshurun and immediately established an English language Jewish newspaper, *The Israelite*. Through its pages, he expounded a liberal Judaism whose rational, ethical, monotheism, he believed, would influence the millions of orthodox Christians in America and convert them, if not literally, at least spiritually, to the universalism of the Reform Jew. Wise's biographer wrote: "This religious universalism, Wise hoped, would ultimately be accepted by all liberal Christians and, if joined with American political liberalism, would sweep over Europe, wipe away traditional Christian beliefs, and create a New Europe . . . .

Wherever this self-constituted apostle to the Jews went, he preached his gospel of inevitable progress and of the improvability of mankind."[90]

On his way to Fort Wayne, Wise visited Lafayette and exclaimed, "Here I saw, the first time, Israelites in the pork-packing business."[91] He had not previously visited in Fort Wayne and knew only from others of its reputation for orthodoxy:

Isaac Mayer Wise
[Courtesy of Indiana Jewish Historical Society]

Let me confess at the start, I had a prejudice against Fort Wayne, on account of the peculiar Orthodoxy of the congregation. This, however, finds its excuse in the fact that Fort Wayne entertained a prejudice against me, on account of my Reform principles. Therefore, I disliked to go to Fort Wayne . . . . I could easily imagine how I was written down in Fort Wayne. I know only two men personally in that whole city. Hence I went to Fort Wayne just to see some of my opponents, something I do not exactly like, but I think it is a moral necessity for every man.

Depict to yourselves my surprise when, on arriving at Fort Wayne, the four first officers of the congregation waited on me in the depot, welcomed me most courteously and conducted me to the splendid residence of the Parnass,[92] Mr. Nirdlinger. Furthermore, depict to yourselves my surprise when I learned that Fort Wayne is not the Orthodox, benighted, and form-worshipping Fort Wayne, but the congregation consists almost exclusively of reasonable, enlightened, and well-intentioning Israelites, led by an old and venerable gentlemen, Rev. Mr. Eppstein, formerly principal teacher of Hechingen, who is himself a man of extensive knowledge and enlightened principles. Depict to yourselves the surprise of the Fort Wayne congregation when it was found out that Isaac M. Wise, of Cincinnati, is not half so much of a heretic as his opponents are of hypocrites. It was a wonder and surprise, but we did not talk about it.

It must be mentioned here, that the seashore [east coast] fashioned Orthodoxy counts two representatives in Fort Wayne. Before I arrived, they, in public meeting, opposed my being invited or permitted to speak in the synagogue, fearing, as my pious opponents did, I might throw out some Reform ideas . . . . One of them is so pious that he never joined a Hebrew congregation till a few months ago, most likely out of godly fear it might not be pious enough for him. The other saint . . . would not visit the synagogue in Fort Wayne, because the carpet on the floor—horror! horror!! horror!!!—looked as though crosses were wrought in it . . . .

In congregational affairs our brethren in Fort Wayne have advanced far beyond the minor congregations of the West. From thirty to forty members, headed by the indefatigable Messrs. Nirdlinger and Wolf, and instructed by the excellent old gentleman, Rev. Mr. Eppstein, have erected a splendid synagogue, which the good ladies furnished with rich curtains, bought and fenced in a burial ground, and keep up as nice a congregation as there is one in the western towns. Rev. Mr. Eppstein preaches occasionally and instructs the rising generation in the religion of Israel. Again, I have been convinced here, how much good one generous man can do, and how susceptible the Israelite everywhere is for the better and holier things. The divine service, conducted by Mr. Solomon, a good old man, minus his fondness of the *Zohar*,[93] is somewhat reformed, viz: the ritual of Württemberg is introduced. I do not like Dr. Mayer's demi-reform; still in Fort Wayne it must be considered quite a reform. . . .

In the evening I delivered a lecture in the synagogue. All the Israelites, except one who dreads the crosses in the carpet, were present. Several Gentile friends were also present, but it was not sufficiently known in the city that a lecture was delivered, hence the audience was not as large as I expected.[94] Next day I roamed about town to see the sights, and left in the evening train for Chicago, glad to have gotten rid of my prejudices.[95]

The New Cantors

In April 1860, Salomon requested a raise in salary. His stipend was probably less than most Protestant clergymen in town. In 1855, he had been forced to borrow $165 from the board at six percent interest; the loan was renewed each year and interest had accumulated. At their next meeting the officers denied Salomon's request and he immediately resigned. Apparently members of the congregation had become irritated with his occasional absence from his duties at meat inspection and once admonished him to "rehearse, on a weekly basis, the chapters of Scripture before they are recited in the synagogue."[96] Salomon's general competence, however, quickly brought an invitation from the Jewish congregation in Lafayette for his services.

In July, the officers recommended that Isaac Rosenthal of Pittsburgh, be engaged as their new cantor, shochet, mohel, and teacher. He arrived with his wife in September and entered into a one-year contract, which stipulated: "The congregation will pay $400; he will receive two cents per fowl in his capacity as shochet, and $5.00 for each circumcision and wedding."[97] Rosenthal was to serve as shochet exclusively with Abraham Wolf, the butcher with whom the congregation had an exclusive agreement to purchase their meat; he would, in turn, receive free meat from Wolf on each market day. The cantor's contract was renewed the following August; then, in October, he was dismissed "because he did not live up to paragraph seven of his contract: 'to live a moral life.'"[98]

In their advertisement for a new hazzan the officers stipulated that "Testimonials must accompany applications. No expenses paid to applicants coming here on trial."[99] By fall, the congregation had elected the Reverend Edward Rubin as their new spiritual leader. Rubin, like Nirdlinger and some others in the congregation, was a native of Hechingen in southern Germany, and had studied in Mayer Eppstein's school. At the age of sixteen he went to Baden as a teacher; later he moved to Alsace where he taught and served a congregation. There is no record of his formal ordination as a rabbi.[100] In 1853, at the age of thirty-five, he came to the United States to lead a congregation in Easton, Pennsylvania. When he responded to Achduth Vesholom's invitation he was serving in Newark, New Jersey. Apparently he traveled to Fort Wayne at his own expense to preach a trial sermon in German and to demonstrate his competence as a shochet. His contract was for one year, with a salary of $300 and the guarantee of at least $100 in fees for his services

Edward Rubin
[Courtesy of Achduth Vesholom Synagogue]

as mohel and shochet; he later supplemented this salary by teaching German in the public high school.

The congregation was very specific about some aspects of his responsibilities: "As a preacher, it is Mr. Rubin's obligation to give a serious sermon, on the first day and the day before the last day of the three main holidays, in the German language . . . . He will also blow the shofar at the New Year's holiday . . . . Mr. Rubin is also obliged to collect all monies owed to the congregation by local members . . . appoint the attendants for the sick as well as guards for the bodies of deceased members . . . inform the women about the sewing of the burial garment . . . see to it that the coffin is made correctly and the burial place dug correctly . . . . On request he shall give eulogies, for which he will receive a fee of two dollars." Finally, to warn against any repetition of his predecessor's behavior, the contract admonished: "He is duty-bound to comport himself decently and with dignity . . . and to observe a religious and virtuous life in his social

231

and personal life."[101]

Rubin worked hard and gained the confidence of the people. After he had established the Emek Baracha Lodge of B'nai B'rith, he began to make changes in worship. A choir was organized with women participating—and the women singers were allowed to sit in the "men's synagogue" on the main floor. Then, to improve the quality of the music, a Melodeon was purchased, lessons for the choir members were mandated, and the congregation was asked to refrain from singing with the hazzan. Next, the Hebrew prayers were shortened and German hymns were added to the service. New rules for order and reverence during worship were established: children under the age of five were excluded; loud praying or singing, as well as private conversations or humming, were discouraged; members were requested to keep the same seats during the entire service; and mourners were admonished not to remove their shoes.[102]

In 1864, the congregation was greatly distressed by an act of vandalism in their cemetery in which several children's gravestones were damaged. A reward was offered for information about the desecration, and the congregation then determined to build a caretaker's cottage on the cemetery premises. The cost of such a house, however, forced the members to restudy the problem, especially in light of the pressing need for a new school house. Finally, the priority of education became paramount. To save money the officers posted a standing ten dollar reward for anyone reporting an intruder in the cemetery, and then renegotiated the contract with the builder to erect a new school house, complete with an apartment for the teacher. They were, however, without the necessary funds to finance the project and appealed to Frederick Nirdlinger for help; he agreed to loan the required money at 10 percent interest.

The Movement Towards Reform

The issue of the cemetery and the school worked to unite the congregation, but the issue of reforming the ritual deeply divided the people. In October 1865, the strong desire of a majority of the members to follow the suggestions of Rubin for significant changes forced a vote. Rubin proposed that they adopt a "native service" with the prayer book of Rabbi David Einhorn, which included more German prayers and hymns in the service. Reinforcing this recommendation was a petition signed by thirty boys and girls of the congregation "requesting reform . . . that German prayers and hymns be added to the service for its enhancement, so that young people . . . understand what and to whom they are praying."[103] Rubin also proposed that they allow the women and children to sit with the men. Thirty-two men, voting with Nirdlinger, supported the reform; twelve, including Isaac Lauferty, opposed the change. Mayer Eppstein, who had previously opposed this style of reform, tendered his resig-

nation and walked out of the meeting.[104] The minority subsequently declared they would not pay their dues until a compromise ritual was instituted.[105] They especially objected to the Einhorn prayer book because, they believed, it diminished belief in the "resurrection of the dead . . . the immortality of the soul . . . the Messiah . . . the restoration of sacrifice . . . and the literal fulfillment of the commandments of the Torah."[106] A few of the traditionalists then expressed their displeasure by stoning Rubin's house.[107]

The reform majority soon notified those who were delinquent[108] in their dues that they would be suspended from the membership, forfeiting their rights to the religious school, shochet, and cemetery. Eight of the dissenters subsequently resigned and held traditional services elsewhere. In February 1866, after purchasing ground for a cemetery, they formally organized themselves as the Fort Wayne Hebrew Congregation Amumath Abothenu (Congregation of the Faith of Our Fathers).[109] Then, in late spring, they placed an advertisement in the *Occident* seeking a hazzan, shochet, mohel, and teacher of Hebrew and German.[110] Isaac Leeser lamented:

> We regret to learn that, owing probably to the influence of the local minister, a Mr. Rubin, ultra-reform measures have lately been adopted. About ten lovers of the ancient order of things petitioned of those in the majority not to proceed to extremes; but their petition remained unheeded, and these, therefore, have resolved to meet in a private house for worship. We are sorely disappointed about Fort Wayne. They promised us something different when we dedicated their Synagogue somewhat more than six years ago; but new influences have since been introduced and, with them, changes and heart-burnings have come as usual. We still hope, against hope, that the majority may reconsider their hasty action, and restore the ancient order, which surely was *reform* enough to satisfy any reasonable mind.[111]

The prayer book, around which the reform took shape, was the work of Rabbi David Einhorn of Baltimore, who had come to prominence through his monthly magazine, *Sinai*. He was an uncompromising reformer who denounced Isaac Mayer Wise's broadly based platform to unite the various tendencies in American Judaism as treachery to the cause of Reform. Einhorn had also violently attacked Wise's anti-abolitionist, pro-copperhead political stance during the civil war, and led his wing of Reform movement to condemn slavery. Wise had also created a prayer book, *Minhag America,* but Rubin, apparently, considered it too much of a compromise with orthodoxy. By contrast, Einhorn's prayer book, *Olat Tamid* (Burnt Offering), was no mere shortening of the traditional liturgy, but a new work written mainly in German.

In the summer of 1866, a succession of informal meetings between the reform and traditional groups were held and, in August, the dissident minority was readmitted into the parent congregation. The negotiated compromises provided that men and women would sit together during services, except on Rosh Hashana and Yom Kippur; no one would be allowed, as an expression of mourning, to remove their shoes in the synagogue; most services would be accompanied by the choir and other music; the German-language Einhorn prayer book would be used for the greater part of congregational worship, but some portion of each service would include the old prayer book, the *Maschsor*; on Succoth, the Feast of Booths, only the prayer leader would be allowed to hold the symbolic palm, myrtle, willow, and citron on the pulpit; and the hazzan would now lead in worship facing the congregation without a prayer shawl, except on the Rosh Hashana and Yom Kippur, when he would face the Holy Ark wearing the shawl.[112]

The pact was then sealed with an election of new officers: Heinrich Redelsheimer of the reform party was elected president and Simon Freiberger of the traditionalists, vice president.[113] Redelsheimer, then assured the reform group of his commitment to their course by introducing a motion that "no additional prayers shall be included into our services from the old orthodox prayer book, but only those that were accepted on August 13, 1866; . . . all requests for further additions shall be considered unconstitutional and must be ignored by the congregation."[114] The motion was passed unanimously and the congregation was once again restored to peace and unity.

By 1872, Congregation Achduth Vesholom had firmed its position in the Reform branch of American Judaism by joining the Board of Delegates of American Israelites. Its membership had grown in sufficient numbers and confidence to erect a new house of worship. Unlike the other German-speaking congregations of Fort Wayne, the people of Achduth Vesholom strongly supported the public schools: in 1864, when the free schools were firmly established, their parochial school was changed to a Sunday religious school with weekday instruction in the early evening hours. Jewish relations with the Christian congregations of Fort Wayne were always exemplary: when the First Presbyterian Church burned, the officers of the Temple opened their facility gratis for Sunday worship. From its earliest days, Fort Wayne's Jewish community contributed significantly to the welfare of the community.

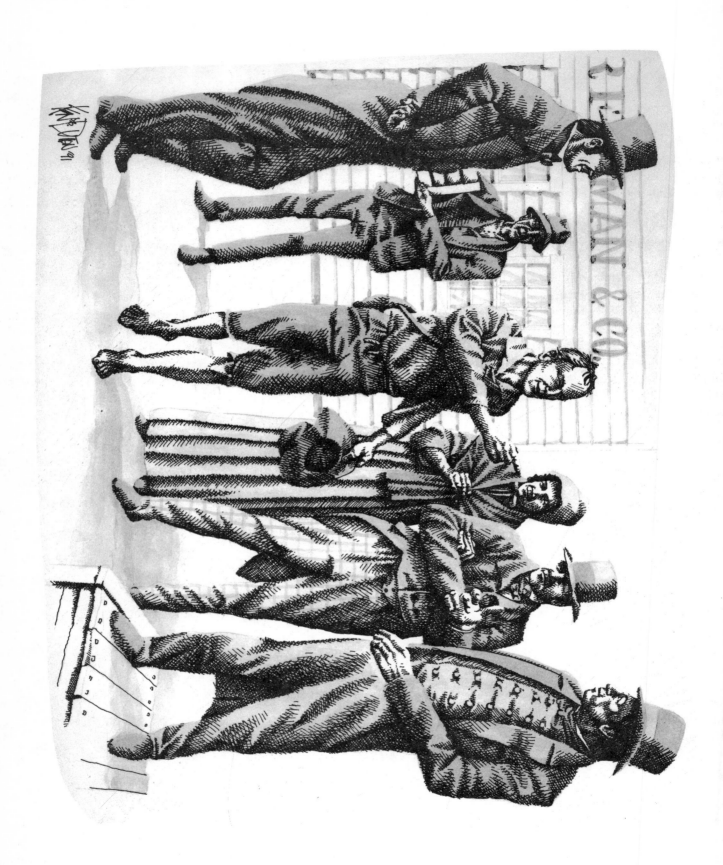

**John Chapman called out, "Here he is, a barefooted primitive Christian clad in coarse raiment,"
in response to Adam Payne's street-corner harangue at Fort Wayne in 1830.**

[Original Illustration by Kenneth B. Dutton]

234

14

Swedenborgians, Universalists, and Christians (Disciples)

By mid-1844, Fort Wayne residents had seen seven Protestant denominations—Presbyterian, Methodist, Lutheran, Baptist, Episcopal, German Reformed, and African Methodist Episcopal—organize six English-speaking and three German-speaking churches; for the next twenty years, however, no other denomination would succeed in establishing a continuing congregation in the city. Three tried—Universalists, Disciples, and Associate Reformed Presbyterian[1]—and each failed; before these denominations arrived, however, one lone missionary of the Church of the New Jerusalem had spent almost two decades in the area announcing "news right fresh from heaven."

The Swedenborgian Church of the New Jerusalem

"News right fresh from Heaven."
John Chapman

Among the many missionaries who came to northeastern Indiana after 1820, only one name, John Chapman—better known as Johnny Appleseed—is widely recognized today. Among the several religious societies that supported the first missionaries in the area, however, the least familiar is the denomination which Chapman so enthusiastically represented, the Church of the New Jerusalem—commonly known as the Swedenborgians. No other religious figure who carried the faith to the Indiana frontier has been so exhaustively researched, and none has suffered more from the accretions of legends. During the century and a half following his death in Fort Wayne, John Chapman has been transformed into a national folk hero—celebrated in poetry, prose, drama, and music, and memorialized by murals, statues, plaques, and parks. As a result, the search for John

Chapman, the man of faith, leads through the cloud of romantic myth surrounding Johnny Appleseed.

"He procures what books he can . . . and lends them."

John Chapman stated that he was "by occupation a gatherer and planter of apple seeds."[2] To his church, however, he was a pioneer sower of the seeds of the Christian faith as interpreted by the Swedish scientist and theologian, Emanuel Swedenborg. In 1817, a Philadelphian wrote to the New Church society in England:

> There is in the western country a very extraordinary missionary for the New Jerusalem. A man has appeared who seems to be almost independent of corporal wants and sufferings. He goes barefooted, can sleep anywhere, in house or out of house, and live upon the coarsest and most scanty fare . . . .

> He procures what books he can of the New Church; travels into the remote settlements, and lends them wherever he can find readers, and sometimes divides a book into two or three parts for more extensive distribution and usefulness. This man for years past has been in the employment of bringing into cultivation, in numberless places in the wilderness, small patches (two or three acres) of ground, and then sowing apple seeds and rearing nurseries. These become valuable as the settlements approximate, and the profits of the whole are intended for the purpose of enabling him to print all the writings of Emanuel Swedenborg and distribute them through the

western settlements of the United States.[3]

Chapman was ten years old[4] in 1784 when the first American lectures on the "Heavenly Doctrines" were delivered in Philadelphia by James Glen. Gradually New Church societies of intense and sometimes distinguished adherents were formed in the major cities on the east coast; by 1817, the fledgling denomination's first General Convention could

This earliest picture of John Chapman is said to have been drawn in the 1850s by an Oberlin College student who had known him.

[Frontispiece in H. S. Knapp,
*History of the Pioneer and
Modern Times of Ashland County, Ohio,* 1863]

report seventeen American societies, with a total of 360 members living in nine states. The most western society represented at the Convention was from "Madison Town, Indiana," which reported "several members."[5]

Sometime during this early period of church development, John Chapman had become an enthusiastic "receiver" of the Swedenborgian revelation and dedicated himself to promulgate its message in his sojourns beyond the Allegheny mountains.[6] Chapman was not alone, however, in bringing the New Church doctrines into the settlements on the western frontier: in 1789, a society was formed in Bedford, Pennsylvania—the first New Church congregation west of the Appalachians; in Ohio, the New Church was planted in Steubenville (1794), in Cincinnati (1811), and

Lebanon (1812).[7] By 1817, a Western Association of the New Jerusalem Church was organized and a few New Church missionaries were traveling throughout Maryland, Pennsylvania, western Virginia, and Ohio. At the foot of the Alleghenies, these preachers abandoned the eastern intellectual style of meeting and quickly adopted the camp meeting style of the Methodist circuit riders. As one New Church historian explained: "Under the stimulus of competition with the evangelical sects, the New Church in the Middle West took on a wholly new emotional and evangelical aspect, better suited to the high-strung pioneer temperament than the intellectualism which prevailed in the Eastern Societies."[8]

"Our doctrines will suit them better than the Old Church."

Chapman first appears in recorded history in 1797 in the upper Allegheny River valley of northwestern Pennsylvania, where he had cleared land for his apple nurseries. Apples were an important multi-purpose staple of the early nineteenth century American larder, and highly valued by pioneer settlers. Unlike most fruits harvested in the fall, apples could be stored through the winter, as well as dried, rendered into apple butter, or pressed into cider—from which both hard cider and vinegar could be made. Chapman gathered his seeds at cider presses and then planted them in the small plots he had previously cleared; later, when his seedlings were sufficiently grown, he called on every new settler to whom he could deliver the trees.

It was on these visits to potential customers that Chapman developed his missionary style. He would first, if possible, perform some neighborly courtesy: "He was one of those characters, very often found in the new country, always ready to lend a helping hand to his neighbors," recalled one settler. "He helped others more than himself."[9] Chapman also related the news from neighboring settlements, and then made known his supply of apple trees. Often he was invited to share in a meal and, sometimes, to spend the night. His gifts as a storyteller were well remembered: "He was a singular character," one pioneer recollected; "I knew him in Venango County, Pennsylvania, nearly sixty years ago, when a child of eight or nine years [ca. 1800]. . . . He was very fond of children and would talk to me a great deal, telling me of the hardships he had endured, of his adventures, and hairbreadth escapes by flood and field—some of them I remember."[10] Chapman's gifts as a storyteller—greatly admired in a region devoid of other entertainments—created an audience; and always, at the appropriate time, he would draw from his tunic a copy of one of Emanuel Swedenborg's works and read from it. If the slightest spark of interest was struck—and if his hosts were literate—Chapman would offer a portion of Swedenborg's writings, which he declared was "news right fresh from Heaven,"[11] promising to return later to exchange their chapters for others. A typical evening with Chapman was related by one pioneer:

> After talking about his nurseries and relating some of his wild wood scenes, encounters with rattlesnakes, bears and wolves, he engaged the conversation and introduced the subject of Swedenborg; at the same time he began to fumble in his bosom and brought forth some three or four old half-worn-out books. As we were fond of reading, we soon grabbed them which pleased Johnny. I could see his eyes twinkle with delight. He was much rejoiced to see us eager to read them.
>
> Johnny partook of a hearty supper and give us a full history of the Seymour family, and block-house scenes, etc. When bedtime arrived, Johnny was invited to turn in, a bed being prepared for his especial accommodation, but Johnny declined the proffered kindness, saying he chose to lay on the hearth by the fire, as he did not expect to sleep in a bed in the next world, so he would not in this.[12]

The author of this letter does not tell how he and his book-hungry siblings reacted to the philosophical speculation and mystical revelation in the Swedenborgian books already available to Chapman in American editions: *Heaven and Hell*, *The True Christian Religion*, *Divine Love and Wisdom*, *Arcana Coelestia* (12 volumes, 8000 pages), *Divine Providence*, *Conjugal Love*, and *the Four Doctrines*. These works were only a fraction of the twenty-nine religious volumes penned by Swedenborg (he had previously written sixty books and papers on scientific subjects). Obtaining a sufficient quantity of these books for distribution was a challenge to Chapman. After 1815, he corresponded regularly with William Schlatter, a wealthy importer and wholesaler of dry goods and leader in the Swedenborgian society in Philadelphia, who, after his conversion in 1814, had determined to publish Swedenborg's writings at his own expense for free distribution. By 1817, Schlatter had sent out over three thousand books in bales of merchandise, mostly to Ohio, Kentucky, Tennessee, Indiana, and Missouri, and was optimistic about the reception of the faith by the western settlers: "I look for a great harvest from that quarter. We may reasonably expect, whenever they do get into an enquiring state, that our doctrines will suit them better than the Old Church, for they are independent, free-minded people, and not disposed to be shackled in religion or politics."[13]

Apparently Schlatter never met Chapman during their years of correspondence; once the Philadelphian wrote to a clergyman in Wheeling: "I have sent some books to Mr. Chapman, do you know him and has he received the Books, he travels about in Ohio and has much to do with appletrees; I am told he is a singular man but greatly in love with the New Church doctrines and takes great pains in disseminating them."[14] Two New Church missionaries who had met Chapman on their itineration through western Pennsylvania and Ohio told Schlatter that they found him to be intelligent, with an absorbing desire to promote the doctrines of the church.[15] Chapman's intelligence always impressed the more literate of his acquaintances; he was remarkably well read, and could speak informally with great feeling on those subjects dear to his heart. In 1816, he was invited to deliver the Fourth of July oration at a celebration in Huron County; as a native of Leominster, Massachusetts, and the son of a veteran of Lexington and Concord, Bunker Hill, and Valley Forge, he must have enthralled his listeners with the tales of the struggle for independence.

"One very extraordinary missionary continues."

To advance his nursery enterprises, Chapman tried to anticipate the future destinations of the westward moving settlers, always his best customers. As a consequence, he moved from Pennsylvania into Ohio, traveling through inner Ohio from Zanesville, Newark, and the Licking River, up into the valleys of the Muskingum River, and across the divide onto the plains along Lake Erie. By the early 1820s, there was a thriving New Church society in Mansfield, Ohio; Chapman, who was honored as the first "receiver" in the area, wrote to Schlatter, requesting that a former Methodist minister, Silas Ensign, be licensed as a lay reader for their group. He also asked Schlatter if he would trade land for books. Chapman, by this time, held lifetime leases on at least 640 acres of prime land, and owned several town lots. Schlatter replied that, although "the society had it not in their power to . . . barter books for land at a fair price . . . . our friends of Cincinnati . . . have lately published some of Emanuel Swedenborg's works and might . . . exchange some for land. I informed you our Book society were indebted to the English society for the books imported, and that we could not on that account barter them but only sell for cash. I hope you will receive that [other] letter. I directed it [to] Richland county, Ohio, it was the only direction I had . . . . I am truly glad to hear the doctrines are spreading in your section of the country, and I make no doubt if you had more books they would increase faster. I informed you in my last I would furnish you with a few of my small works if you would write me by some of your merchants, when they came on this spring."[16]

Chapman's missionary zeal on the western frontier became increasingly known throughout his denomination, and some admirers presented a formal tribute at the New Church's Fifth General Convention in 1822:

One very extraordinary missionary continues to exert, for the spread of Divine Truth, his modest and humble efforts, which would put the most zealous members to the blush. We now allude to Mr. J. Chapman, from whom we are in the habit of hearing frequently. His temporal employment consists in preceding the settlements, and sowing nurseries of fruit trees, which he avows to be pursued for the chief purpose of giving him an opportunity of spreading the Doctrines through the western country.

In his progress, which neither heat or cold, swamps nor mountains, are permitted to arrest, he carries on his back all the New Church publications he can procure, and distributes them wherever opportunity is afforded. So great is his zeal, that he does not hesitate to divide his volumes into parts, and, by repeated calls, enables the reader to peruse the whole in succession.

Having no family, and inured to hardships of every kind, his operations are unceasing. He is now employed in traversing the district between Detroit and the closer settlements of Ohio. What shall be the reward of such an individual, where, as we are told in holy writ, *They that turn many to righteousness shall shine as the stars forever.*[17]

"The exact period is not known."

Sometime in the mid-1820s Chapman made his first journey to northeastern Indiana.[18] The news that the land around Fort Wayne was now platted and soon to be sold was just the sort of information that attracted Chapman to establish nearby nurseries for the future sale of seedlings. One early settler recalled that Chapman "went about seeking the small fractions of land that occurred in the surveys of public lands. There he purchased and later cleared patches, fenced them with brush, and planted apple seeds, which when grown to sufficient size, were bought by the settlers. These fractions became valuable and were bought by owners of adjoining lands."[19] Between 1834 and 1838, Chapman purchased four parcels of land in Milan, Maumee, and Eel River Townships, Allen County,[20] and set out other orchards on leased property.[21] To assist him with his expanding nurseries, and to give him more leisure for his missionary activities, Chapman brought his half-sister and brother-in-law, Persis Chapman and William Broom, and their children—of whom he was exceedingly fond—from Ohio to Indiana. By now, the three rivers area had became the hub of both his secular and religious enterprises.

Soon after *Harper's New Monthly Magazine* published a biographical sketch about Chapman in 1871, John Dawson, a former Fort Wayne editor, inquired of the oldest local residents about the date of Chapman's first visit to Fort Wayne, and concluded that "the exact period is not known. One gentleman, a pioneer of this place, fixes it as early as 1825—others some later; but certain is it, that in 1830, he was seen one autumn day, seated in a section of a hollow tree, which improvised for a boat, laden with apple seeds fresh from the cider presses of a more eastern part of the country, paddling up the Maumee river, and landing at Wayne's fort, at the foot of Main street, Fort Wayne."[22] Although Chapman occasionally traveled by horseback or pirogue, he usually walked, and his destinations were his nurseries and his customers in the country. As a result, he was not often seen by townspeople, unless he needed to purchase supplies or visit the courthouse on a matter of land title. When he landed in downtown Fort Wayne on that day in 1830, he was probably on business. (Chapman had an account at the Hamilton-Taber & Company store; on February 22, 1840, a clerk wrote that "John Appleseed" purchased a "pockett nife.")[23]

"His wardrobe . . . was so scanty that he appeared as a beggar."

Unfortunately, many residents were unable to remember little more about Chapman than his eccentric clothing. Dawson noted: "His wardrobe was on his person—and was so scanty that he appeared as a beggar. His footgear generally consisted of odd shoes—or a shoe and a boot—now and then only one foot covered, the other bare, to chastise it for a transgression, as he declared. His head-gear rarely ever alike for a long time—sometimes a crownless hat, limbered with rough usage, which he often ran his hand through and carried on his arm—sometimes a tin vessel worn on his head, which he used to cook his frugal meals in, and sometimes another hat which had a crown, and which he wore over the first and the tin vessel—and in the crown of which thus rested over the two . . . . But his garb was not always alike, and some have seen him in other garbs and under other circumstances . . . so that some would describe him one way and some another."[24]

Nothing of the New Church doctrine dictated this mode of dress, and certainly no word or example of Emanuel Swedenborg inspired Chapman's innovative habit. Even when Swedenborg was old "there was nothing of the uncouth and unkempt recluse about him. He was meticulous in dress, usually appearing at social functions in black velvet, fine lace, jeweled sword and buckles—a typical eighteenth century aristocrat."[25] Chapman seems to have been a frugal Yankee who simply enjoyed making do with what he had on hand. Although his clothes were eminently economical and practical, they were never helpful to his mission; more than a few people laughed at his costume, some were frightened or repelled and found it difficult to take him or his message seriously.

Chapman's shoeless state, however, is another matter, for bare feet, unlike casual clothes, do not normally aid comfort or practicality. Apparently Chapman had enjoyed going barefooted as a child and, as a result, his feet had become so hard and callused that he could stick a needle through the horny flesh—a feat he occasionally performed to amuse children. As a young man he seemed to have been especially proud of his hardy feet: one western Pennsylvanian wrote that the young Chapman had "walked several miles on the ice barefooted merely to show off his powers of endurance,"[26] and, as early as 1817, the English Swedenborgians were told, "He has actually thawed the ice with his bare feet."[27]

Swedenborg, who was neither a teetotaler nor a vegetarian, was emphatic in his condemnation of ascetic self-denial and insisted that the body is not to be neglected or abused. He taught that it was unnecessary to renounce the world, the flesh, and the devil, but merely to keep them in their proper order. When Chapman said he slept on the floor because there were no beds in heaven, or went unshod because he was punishing a wayward foot (he did not punish other members), he was most likely masking the fact that he simply preferred to sleep and walk that way, and offered these more esoteric answers to stop conversation on the subject—just as he replied to inquiries about his unmarried state by asserting that he was waiting for a wife in heaven. These oblique remarks, however, only reenforced in the popular mind the notion that Chapman was a religious ascetic; his obituary in the *Fort Wayne Sentinel* reiterated this assumption: "He . . . denied himself almost the common necessities of life— not so much perhaps for avarice as from his peculiar notion on religious subjects. He was a follower of Swedenborg and devoutly believed that the more he endured in this world the less he would have to suffer and the greater would be his happiness hereafter—he submitted to every privation with cheerfulness and content, believing that in so doing he was securing snug quarters hereafter."[28]

Chapman, however, never preached asceticism and freely acknowledged his own personal indulgences: snuff, catnip, and an occasional dram of whiskey "to keep him a little warm." He treasured the freedom to do as he wished; and, like most humans of above average intelligence, he usually responded to any prying questions or personal comments about his individualistic life-style with some imaginative and inarguable rationale. When the New Church reported Chapman's death, its lengthy obituary did not suggest that his personal eccentricities were the fulfillment of any Swedenborg doctrine: "The new Church evangelist and 'circulating library' of the wilderness . . . . clad in the simplest raiments, barefooted *par preference,* with an old coffee-

sack for overcoat, and for a hat the tin pot in which he prepared his meals, loaded with bags of apple seeds and packages of Swedenborg's Writings . . . . His greatest delight was the announcement of the glories of the New Jerusalem."[29]

"His voice would rise to the heroic."

To announce these "glories" Chapman sometimes offered his services as a day laborer. James Barnett, one the community's early settlers, said that Chapman often came to Fort Wayne during the fall harvest and that he was "the best hand he hired to husk corn."[30] He was amazingly strong for his 125 pound wiry frame; one Pennsylvanian remarked that, when he assisted the settlers in making clearings, "he could chop as much wood or girdle as many trees in one day as most men could in two."[31] It was not only Chapman's industry, but also his visage and manner that impressed many who met him. One early settler recalled: "His refined features, seen through the gray stubble that covered his face (for he cut his hair and beard with scissors—yet he was not a Nazarite), told of his intelligence. He was serious; his speech was clean, free from slang or profanity. . . . When he would find hearers, he would read to them; inspired by their spirit [Swedenborg's writings], his voice would rise to the heroic. He believed in communication with spirits, a first, second, and third heaven, and marriages in heaven."[32]

Although there is no record of Chapman attending worship services in any "Old Church" meetinghouse, he was attracted to the open air religious meetings. John Dawson wrote: "A certain Adam Payne, who was also an eccentric man, but in a different way, a preacher of a very illiterate kind, who wanted to appear a second Lorenzo Dow,[33] in 1830 came to this city and, standing on a box on the northeast corner of Clinton and Columbia streets, announced himself thus: 'Hear ye! Hear ye! I am now about to scold the devil.'" Payne, who traveled widely in Ohio and Indiana, often concluded his harangues by asking rhetorically: "Where now is a man, who like the primitive Christians, is traveling to heaven barefooted and clad in coarse raiment?" Chapman, earlier that year, had heard Payne's same "scold" in Mansfield, Ohio, and had there responded to his question about the whereabouts of the barefooted Christian by calling out, "Here he is." In Fort Wayne, Chapman "went forward and asked Mr. Payne if he recollected 'the primitive Christian' which he had before seen in Mansfield, Ohio."[34] People enjoyed Chapman's speaking style and testified to his "shrewdness and penetration" in discussion; one admirer said that "in expounding his religion or describing his apples, he was remarkably eloquent, and used excellent language."[35]

John Dawson wanted to correct the impression that Chapman had been an occasional heckler at open-air religious meetings, and wrote: "I have seen him under many

239

circumstances at public meetings, and never heard a disorderly word fall from his lips. In the year 1841, at a camp meeting...on the site of Lindenwood Cemetery...I saw him lying on the ground, near a large tree in good hearing of the pulpit; and I now have a vivid recollection of the earnest attention he gave to the eloquent words of the clergyman, who discoursed of that New Jerusalem, which our hero hoped to reach."[36]

Later in 1841, the New Church inaugurated its first formal missionary effort in northern Indiana when a lay reader, George Field, visited Elkhart, Mishawaka, LaPorte, and Goshen. Soon a New Church Sabbath School with thirty scholars was established at Elkhart; then, on January 2, 1843, the "Association of Readers and Receivers of the Doctrines of the New Jerusalem Church in Michigan and Northern Indiana" was organized, with one of its strongest societies flourishing at Goshen, Indiana.[37] There are no extant records to indicate whether Chapman participated in this Association; if he thought of himself as a member of any New Church society, it would have been in Mansfield, Ohio, where he continued to have business interests.

"A man is as the quality of his love is."

By the 1840s, the writings of Emanuel Swedenborg were attracting widespread attention in intellectual circles. In Europe, the Swedish seer influenced Kant and Goethe, whose *Faust* was said to represent a Swedenborgian world view; Balzac and Coleridge discussed his ideas, and Thomas Carlyle called him "a man of great and indisputable cultivation.... One of the loftiest minds in the realm of the mind." In America, Henry James, whose father was a New Church leader, declared Swedenborg to be the "sanest and most far-reaching intellect this age has known"; Ralph Waldo Emerson called him the "last father of the church," and Bronson Alcott put Swedenborg in his hall of fame along with Plato, Plotinus, and Boehme.

No religious thinker of this era, however, attracted a greater diversity of dissenters from the established denominations: spiritualists claimed him as their patron, as did those in utopian communitarian experiments; the free love movement saw him as blessing their cause, as did those devotees of faddish medical cults, faith healing, and mesmerism. By 1845, Swedenborg meant many things to many minds, and his name and philosophy were invoked by intellectuals and charlatans alike.[38]

In the Fort Wayne area, the gentle spirit of John Chapman had many admirers, but his Church of the New Jerusalem found no converts.[39] Episcopalians had been warned by their bishop, Jackson Kemper, that Swedenborg's ideas in *Conjugal Love* "encouraged licentiousness and were dangerous and immoral" for teaching that a married man might ethically take a mistress.[40] In spite of this "Old Church"

opposition, however, many read the Swedenborgian literature which Chapman extolled and distributed, and some of these, no doubt, became interested. There was, however, no one in the region capable of teaching the Heavenly Doctrines and thereby sustaining an embryonic society. Chapman had always limited his mission to awakening interest in Swedenborg's vision and distributing his books; he was not an organizer, and never remained in any community long enough to nurture a continuing fellowship of receivers.

By 1845, the year of his death,[41] John Chapman had already become a legend. In the memorial tribute presented at the New Church's General Convention in 1847, it was noted that the "Indians looked upon him as a great 'medicine man'"[42] and that the early settlers valued him as a " 'guide, philosopher, and friend'. . . especially during the war of 1812, when he traveled unceasingly, day and night, warning the settlers against the raids of the Indian allies of Great Britain.[43] He thus gained a wide and lasting reputation as a picturesque, eccentric philanthropist, of whom a thousand tales, amusing, pathetic and inspiring, are still being told."[44] The tales that were told seldom focused on Chapman's Swedenborgian beliefs; most illuminated his courage and resourcefulness, his intelligence and wit, and his kindness and generosity.

John Chapman was not remembered for his superficial eccentricities, his scattered orchards, or his Swedenborgian faith; he was remembered for his genuine goodness. Children loved him: "They would help in planting his orchards, while he was telling them about the beauties of the other world, until he left them, enriched by presents of pennies and New Church tracts."[45] His concern for the welfare of animals, even rattlesnakes, was unusual on the western frontier. An early historian of the region stated that Chapman "was the constant and faithful friend of all dumb brutes, reptiles and insects. He made the care and protection of aged and infirm horses his special duty on his rounds. If he saw a settler working a horse that was lame or blind or afflicted in any way, as settlers were frequently compelled to do, he would purchase it at the owner's price and then give it to someone who could afford to treat it gently or turn it loose to end its days in peaceful pasture. Hundreds of reminiscences of his strange and beneficent doings are related by farmers from the Ohio [River] to Lake Michigan."[46]

Dawson wrote that Chapman's "vade mecum was his New Testament and a few volumes . . . by Emanuel Swedenborg."[47] If Swedenborg provided Chapman with a detailed and dazzling vision of life in the hereafter, it was the Sermon on the Mount which provided most of the inspiration for his life-style in Ohio and Indiana. Chapman took seriously, even literally, the admonition: "Take no thought for your life, what ye shall eat, or what ye shall drink; nor yet for your body, what ye shall put on. Is not the life more than meat, and the body more than raiment."[48] The western frontier always had more than its share of ragged eccentrics, but it never had an excess of caring and capable neighbors. John Chapman was both caring and capable. He combined the best of Yankee independence, ingenuity, common sense, and practicality with a deeply religious view of life. He successfully ignored the world's temptations to materialism and consistently remained free from the pretenses of power and pride, always upholding his high ethical standards with the purest spiritual values. He was a shining exemplar of Swedenborg's maxim: "A man is altogether as his love is. . . . If there is with a man the love of God and the love of the neighbor, and consequently the love of goodness and truth, and of what is just and honorable, then—however he may appear in the outward form—he is an angel."[49]

The Swedenborgians have often been dismissed by church historians as a denomination whose message was too esoteric and intellectual to appeal to the settlers on the western frontier. Many of the migrants from the East, however, were very interested in matters intellectual, and many communities, including Fort Wayne, had active literary societies. The presence of a Swedenborgian congregation in Goshen was noted by Charles Beecher[50] soon after he arrived in Fort Wayne, and, when a Swedenborgian minister was appointed chaplain to the Michigan State Prison, it was of sufficient interest to be reported in a Fort Wayne newspaper.[51] The Swedenborgians in Indiana lacked missionaries; when any appeared, however, they always attracted interest, often acquired "receivers," and sometimes established societies.

The Universalists

"The Friends of liberal Christianity, near and abroad, are invited."
Fort Wayne Sentinel, 1857.

When the first regular religious services were held in Fort Wayne in the fall of 1829, several Universalists were in attendance. The young Presbyterian preacher, Charles Furman, reported to his mission board: "There are as many as three or four who say they have thought that the doctrine of universalism might be true, but they do not pretend to maintain their sentiments in my presence; and one, [who] has heretofore been most favourable to the doctrine, and has much influence in the town, has utterly disclaimed the sentiments with which he has been charged. There are no . . . unitarians."[52]

The suspected Universalist of "much influence" was probably Dr. Lewis G. Thompson, a Kentuckian who had come to Fort Wayne in 1827, and was now dividing his time between medicine and politics. Thompson was a popular and respected leader and, in 1829, was elected to the town's first Board of Trustees. Hugh McCulloch, who had been urged by the young physician to settle in Fort Wayne, later wrote:

Lewis G. Thompson was for many years the leading physician of Fort Wayne. He had that instinctive knowledge of diseases which distinguishes the born physician, and without which medical knowledge derived from books is a snare. Belonging to the old allopathic school, he believed in medicine, and gave evidence of his faith by prescriptions which were the reverse of ho-

The Thompson Family, by Horace Rockwell, ca. 1842-1845. The painting depicts Lewis Garrett Thompson and his wife, Ann McFarland Scott Thompson, five of their seven children, and (left) Ann's widowed sister, Eliza Forsythe, holding her daughter Margaret.
[Courtesy of The Newark Museum]

meopathic, but so accurate was his intuition in locating diseases that he was rarely at fault in treating them. I admired Dr. Thompson for his medical skill and for his many noble and manly qualities, but more than all for the conscientiousness and humanity which compelled him to treat with equal carefulness and attention those who were able to pay for his services and those who were not.[53]

Another resident remembered Thompson as "a man of dignified appearance and not easily approached." In 1833, he was elected an associate judge and "was, upon one occasion, asked by a visitor to the courtroom what his initials stood for. 'Why, "Lord God," of course; what do you suppose?' "[54] He was also a man of religious sensibility, and when a subscription was circulated in 1831 seeking financial support for the town's first resident minister, a Presbyterian, Thompson pledged five dollars;[55] apparently he worshipped at First Presbyterian Church, referring to its pastor as "Brother Rankin, our Minister."[56] The physician-politician was never shy to offer an opinion on religion and religious leaders and, in 1833, was sued by a Methodist minister for libel.[57] Thompson was especially critical of the emotional style of preaching favored by a presiding elder of the local Methodist district:

Our Temperance folks are going crazy. Old Brother Burroughs Westlake has been stirring up the monkies (sic) here for the last week. He told them that Capt. Alcohol was an arch old scoundrel; a souse, thief, and murderer, with every other opprobrious epithet he could heap upon his accosted head—and concluded by telling them that any man who would have anything to do with him in any way, or even be caught in his company, had not one drop of American blood in his veins. Now I have always been an advocate for temperance, and for temperance societies properly conducted—yet I must confess, that I anticipate but little good from such excitements, and after having stood their intemperance in language & zeal (all of which I was will[ing] to admit was occasioned by the best of motives) for two or three successive evenings, I could hold in no longer—and I gave them "Jesse"—and promised them "more anon."[58]

"The first sermons on the Restitution ever delivered in that town."

Thompson had not formally united with any local congregation and, in spite of his alleged denials, continued to be interested in Universalism. His coreligionists were small in number and slow to organize. When the denomination's first state convention met in 1837, there were only two Universalist clergymen in all of Indiana. In 1838, with the aid of missionaries from Michigan, small societies were organized at Elkhart and South Bend, but no missionary activity by the Indiana State Convention effectively reached the northern part of the state until after the Civil War. It was only individual ministers, acting on their own initiative or responding to invitations, who kept alive the special message of Universalism. The first of these wide-ranging itinerants to visit Fort Wayne was the Reverend Erasmus Manford, publisher of *The Christian Teacher*. Manford later recollected: "At the earnest solicitation of Dr. Thompson of Fort Wayne, I visited that place, and delivered a series of discourses. These were the first sermons on the Restitution ever delivered in that town. An Episcopal clergyman proposed debating, and we accordingly spent two days in discussion. The assemblies were large, and, I trust, much good was effected. Dr. Thompson was a prominent citizen . . . and an

intellectual and Christian man."[59]

The lectures and debate were held in the fall of 1844[60] at the courthouse where Episcopalians worshipped each Sunday morning and New School Presbyterians in the afternoon. Charles Beecher, the Presbyterian pastor, noted Manford's arrival: "A Universalist minister commenced preaching in the Court H[ouse] without consultation with us, and then

Erasmus Manford
[Frontispiece for Erasmus Manford, *Twenty-five Years in the West*, 1885]

there were three denominations using the same house at once—this however only during the past month."[61]

The Episcopal clergyman who challenged Manford to debate was probably the Reverend Benjamin Halsted, who seemed to enjoy attacking theological error in a public forum: three years before he had joined in a sharp denunciation of the "Hypocrisy and Intolerance. . . [of] Atheistic Owenism" at the New Harmony community in southern Indiana. The debate at Fort Wayne doubtless focused on the one unique tenet of Universalist theology: that all of humankind would eventually be saved by God and none would suffer everlasting punishment, not because of humanity's merit, but because of God's loving and forgiving nature. "Universalists insisted that all men *must* be saved."[62] Halsted's position on the issue was probably predestinarian, for the *Articles of Religion* of the Protestant Episcopal Church in the United States affirmed that "Predestination to life is the everlasting purpose of God, whereby (before the foundations of the world were laid) he hath constantly decreed, by his counsel, secret to us, to deliver from curse and damnation, those whom he hath chosen in Christ out of mankind, and to bring them by Christ to everlasting salvation, as vessels made to honor."[63] Most local Baptists, Presbyterians, and Lutherans would have agreed with the doctrine of divine election; Methodists, however, tended towards Arminianism, holding that, although God wills salvation for all humankind, only those who have repented and received God's grace will be saved. Unitarians tended to be Arminians with more self-confidence, which led one Universalist to comment: "The Universalist thinks God is too good to damn them forever; the Unitarian thinks they are too good to be damned forever."[64]

"A class of minds, ardent, intellectual, skeptical."

Manford's lectures stimulated interest, and a dozen young men soon formed a Bible class. Manford, however, was not interested in organizing congregations, much less serving as a parish pastor.[65] After he left town, the Presbyterian pastor, relieved that his former schedule of worship and Sunday school was now restored, told his mission board: "The Universalists have interfered with the S[unday] S[chool] for some Sab[bath]s back, but are now discontinued. [I] am thankful. They sought collision, a little, but the Lord gave us grace to treat them kindly; and so the thing fell through. A Bible Class of some 12 or 15 young men is connected, which I instruct."[66]

As Beecher assumed the leadership of the class, Manford persuaded the Reverend Benjamin F. Foster, pastor of the Terre Haute Universalist congregation, to visit Fort Wayne. Foster, who was the Grand Secretary of the Order of Odd Fellows in the state and later the state librarian, was described as "the most eminent clergyman of the denomination in Indiana."[67] He seems to have held a modified position on universal salvation: when an evangelist of the Christian Church, H. St. John Van Dake, challenged him to debate the proposition "that liars, thieves, robbers, murderers, assassins, and all other workers of iniquity, who die in willful disobedience to the Gospel of Christ, will be finally holy and happy," Foster responded, "As I do not believe in the salvation of either of these classes, you will excuse me if I decline meeting you upon such an issue."[68] The Terre Haute pastor preached in Fort Wayne "with some degree of regularity during most of the year following."[69] During this time, Universalist services were held "once a month," wrote Charles Beecher: "Numbers of citizens of general intelligence and good character made a demonstration in favor of Universalism; some, because they were Universalists, some infidels, some nothingarians, and all dignified with any religious affair they had seen. A subscription of nearly $1000 was raised and they came near raising a brilliant income."[70]

Then, something happened to terminate Foster's monthly visits; as a consequence, the group increasingly leaned on their Bible class teacher. Although the Presbyterian minister did not espouse the unique tenet of Universalists, he admired their freethinking spirit and cared about their spiritual welfare. Of all the local pastors, Beecher was the most intellectual and scholarly, and had already attracted a disparate following: "Many of the congregation, and some of my warmest friends, are Unitarians from New England. Others are skeptical, others Universalist."[71] Then, when Beecher's controversial sermon, *The Bible a Sufficient Creed,* caused his more conservative colleagues to question his orthodoxy, Fort Wayne Universalists rallied to his support. Beecher wrote:

> All . . . who started the Universalist enterprise . . . got the idea that our little church was persecuted, and they said: "Beecher is a clever fellow and, tho' we don't believe what he preaches quite, yet we want to see fair play and we can't stand by and see him put down." So they subscribed $300 and came to meeting, and then, before they knew it, the Lord had a cord around their hearts, and they became warm personal friends. Some of them, right noble natures, began to love me and I them. . . . Yes, a class of minds, ardent, intellectual, skeptical and utterly beyond the reach of any existing organization came and surrendered themselves to me and were willing to hear the Gospel. Perhaps they thought that, as I had been an infidel, I should have some feeling for them, and not scold them always, and call them hard names, which never does anybody any good. And indeed I did feel for them—and Oh how I have loved those men and labored and prayed for them![72]

With their gift of $300—probably the contributions to their subscription—Fort Wayne's Universalists also gave Beecher their loyalty, and gradually abandoned plans for a separate congregation. Their numbers were still small, and, in 1845, the leadership of their group had been significantly diminished by the sudden death of L. G. Thompson. Universalist preachers continued to be scarce in northern Indiana and the state convention did little to encourage church development. During the next fifteen years, however, a few Universalist preachers, on their own initiative, made brief visits to Fort Wayne, at the rate of about one each year: besides Manford, who returned in 1846 and 1848, there was William J. Chaplin, J. George, Charles Craven, T. C. Eaton, and P. Hathaway.[73] Chaplin, the most active and interested, traveled to Fort Wayne from Kosciusko County, and, in 1850, organized a Universalist congregation of seventeen members at Huntertown.[74] In the 1850s, Fort Wayne was still eyed by some leaders of the denomination as a potential field. One attempt to identify interested residents was made by the Elkhart Association of Universalists who scheduled a meeting at Fort Wayne in September 1857, and then announced in the local newspapers that "The Friends of liberal Christianity, near and abroad, are invited to attend."[75]

No congregation of Universalists was organized in Fort Wayne until 1875.[76] Up to that time, however, the message of Universalism was kept alive mainly by several religious publications, all of which were the independent enterprises of individual church leaders. New journals emerged regularly. When William J. Chaplin came to Fort Wayne in June 1847, he met with J. M. Day, "a citizen of Fort Wayne [who] did some missionary work in the interest of the denomination,"[77] and the two formulated plans to offer a new publication. Soon, the *Fort Wayne Sentinel* announced the "Prospectus of a Religious Journal to be called the *Indiana Religious Inquirer,* a family paper devoted to Theological Discussion, Religious Intelligence, Literature, and General News to be published in Fort Wayne by J. M. Day and W. J. Chaplin."[78] The journal apparently died as quickly as it was conceived; there is no record of its actual publication.

The journals nurtured many of the scattered, unchurched Universalists of northern Indiana and kept alive the spirit of their "liberal Christianity." By the last decade of the nineteenth century, however, the bright promise of Universalism had faded, and each of the four congregations which had been organized at Huntertown, New Haven, Fort Wayne, and Yoder had disbanded.[79] In 1917, a Universalist minister in Anderson reflected on the causes of his denomination's decline: "Every truth may be abused; the acceptance of the negative elements of Universalism without a grasping of its affirmations produced 'anti-hellians' who were often against every policy of denominational expansion and in favor of nothing . . . . Church membership as an essential to future salvation was rejected; church membership as an opportunity to work for present social salvation was rarely visioned. Hence the most prominent Universalists were often not members of their own organization, and their children and grandchildren joined other churches. Add to these the causes of extreme individualism, occasional unwise leadership . . . [and] a theology sometimes more liberal than the pocketbook."[80]

The Christian Church (Disciples of Christ)

"We found the people much more willing to risk their lives in the uncertain chance of war upon the plains of Mexico, than to enlist under the banner of the Prince of Peace, and fight for glory undying, and a crown unfading!"
Elder James M. Mathes, June 1846

In late 1845, the first missionary of the Christian Church (Disciples of Christ) arrived in Fort Wayne and placed a notice in the *Fort Wayne Times:* "Elder Barber of the Christian Church will preach at the School Room of Mr. Steevens in this city on Thursday evening next, December 11."[81] Barber's identity is unknown, but his single visit was the prelude to a conscientious, albeit belated, effort on the part of his denomination to establish a congregation in Fort Wayne. The Christian Church's missionary thrust had been frustrated by its decentralized polity, which shunned strong church associations or ecclesiastical authority.[82] As a consequence, it was not until 1839 that a state-wide meeting of Indiana Disciples[83] was organized; then, six years elapsed before funds were collected to support traveling evangelists—of which two were commissioned to labor for a month in northern Indiana.

Fort Wayne was chosen as the principal target of the mission and, in the spring of 1846, Elders Milton B. Hopkins and James M. Mathes headed north on the canal. Hopkins, twenty-five, had grown up near Rushville, where he now farmed and preached; Mathes, a thirty-seven-year-old Kentuckian who had attended Indiana University, had recently established a religious journal, the *Christian Record,* at Bloomington. He reported that, on May 27, he had left his home

. . . for the purpose of laboring for a season at Fort Wayne, in conjunction with brother M. B. Hopkins, in discussing the great principles of christianity, and endeavoring to establish the cause in that young and rising city; where at present it is but little known. We had chosen this as the most suitable time for such a campaign; taking into consideration the nature of the country, the badness of the roads, &c. But experience proved that the time was badly chosen. His Excellency, Governor Whitcomb, had just made a call upon Indiana for three regiments of volunteers, to march for the Rio Grande; and the whole country was full of excitement. We found the people much more willing to risk their lives in the uncertain chance of war upon the plains of Mexico, than to enlist under the banner of the Prince of Peace, and fight for glory undying, and a crown unfading![84]

Mathes was joined by Hopkins at Lafayette where the missionaries boarded a canal boat bound for Fort Wayne. At

Logansport they "found the war excitement running very high," Mathes reported; "Capt. Tipton had his company of volunteers on parade, and they accepted an invitation . . . to attend the meeting at night; and . . . a large audience having already assembled at the court house, the company marched in to the sound of martial music! I addressed them for an hour. My theme was the 'Christian warfare,' predicated upon the words of Paul to Timothy, 'Fight the good fight of faith, lay hold on eternal life.' " [85]

When Mathes and Hopkins arrived in Fort Wayne on Sunday, June 7, they found the same "unfavorable circum-

James M. Mathes
[Courtesy of Disciples of Christ Historical Society]

stances. The whole community," he lamented, "were electrified with the idea of going to war with Mexico. Two companies of volunteers were raised in Fort Wayne, and organized during the first ten days of our stay among them. And, during that time, our meetings were frequently forgotten, and broken up by 'war meetings'; and even when we were permitted peaceably to meet in the courthouse, which was the only house we could get (except the school house one evening), we were annoyed by the thunder of the cannon, roll of the drum, or the shouting and huzzaing of boys in the streets (except Lord's days)." [86]

After the troops had departed for Cincinnati on June 16,

the evangelists found that the local population had little interest in their message. Mathes suspected that some of the local pastors had conspired against them: "Our cause is very unpopular here. The old Lady, who resides upon the 'scarlet colored beast,' has many children in this place.[87] And some of the little protestant sects seem to entertain equally strong prejudices against us! The 'Missionary Baptists'. . . had been warned against us by their preacher, a Mr. [H. D.] Mason, and not only refused us the use of their meeting house, but no one of them came to hear us during our stay, as we were informed! The Methodist friends were more liberal; for though their preacher, Mr. [John C.] Bayless, is noted for his opposition to us, yet many of them were among our most faithful auditors."[88]

Until their last day in Fort Wayne, the two evangelists had received no converts in response to their earnest efforts, and consoled themselves that "under all the unfavorable circumstances . . . much prejudice was doubtless removed." On Sunday, they "broke bread" with "a small congregation in the city, composed of five members, to wit, brother and sister Griffith from the country; and brother and sister [John] Johnson and sister Demott, in the city." Then, that evening, "a young man of much moral worth came to our room and desired to be immersed, and accordingly we went straightway down to the water and 'buried him in baptism.' Others will no doubt follow his example when brother Hopkins returns. We consider it quite important that the gospel should be sustained in Fort Wayne, on account of the influence it would have on all the regions round about. Fort Wayne is a beautiful young city, and growing up very rapidly . . . . Brother Hopkins will return about the first of September, and finish the work assigned to us by the State Meeting."[89]

"The Gospel of Reformation is as yet but begun in this community."

In October 1846, the State Meeting was sufficiently impressed by the evangelists' report on Fort Wayne's potential that it appointed Elder John Bowman New to the post. As this was their first experience in funding a missionary, the delegates were unsure of what salary should be appropriated; finally, they asked New "to state the amount for which he would serve. He responded $300 was about a fair compensation for an Evangelist, and that Mariah New [his wife] would contribute $50 of that sum herself."[90]

At the age of fifty-three, New was the oldest Protestant clergyman—and the only veteran of the War of 1812—to begin a ministry in Fort Wayne. Born in North Carolina, he had spent his early years in Kentucky, and then moved to Indiana in 1815 to escape the anomalies of a slaveholding society. He said: "I saw that a man in a slave State might possess twice as much property as his slaveholding neighbor; might have four times as good fare on his table; might have eight times as much good sense; and might manifest sixteen times as much honor in his business transactions; and yet the slaveholder would not regard him as his equal. The possession of a few poor, ignorant, debased slaves was a standard of respectability that I was unwilling for myself and my posterity to be measured by."[91]

New was of a rougher cut of homespun than Mathes, who had studied Greek at Bloomington, or Hopkins, who later became the State Superintendent of Public Instruction. A

John Bowman New
[Courtesy of Disciples of Christ Historical Society]

contemporary wrote candidly of New's preaching style: "His mind is well informed, though neither of the highest order nor thoroughly cultivated . . . . In the pulpit, he is an eccentric, yet safe teacher—an earnest and effective exhorter. His gestures are quick, cramped, and rectilinear; and he utters bluntly whatever he thinks, whether it relates to friend or foe. He is mainly argumentative, proving all things and holding *very fast* that which is good. Owing to his highly nervous temperament, he thinks and speaks rapidly; yet he is not always brief; and it need not surprise you if, in his enumeration of topics, he ascend[s] even to *thirteenthly*. True, he very often looks at his elegant watch; but he cares no more for its admonitions than he does for a Confession of Faith."[92]

"I have immersed . . . an Episcopalian preacher."

New, who had been serving congregations in the Greensburg area, arrived in Fort Wayne on November 7, and found that the little band of five had maintained their fellowship (for a time they had been reduced to three, but later welcomed three more). By the end of the month, the evangelist reported that he had "added eight more, making at this time fourteen. We preach four times per week in this place. . . . Our audiences are as good as could be expected, all things considered. We meet in the court house, which is as convenient and comfortable as any meeting house in the city; but not so fine, nor so well calculated to attract the attention of the lovers of this world."[93] Since the Episcopalians had exclusive use of the courthouse on Sunday mornings, the embryonic Christian congregation had to wait until the afternoon for the "breaking of bread," as they termed their weekly observance of the Lord's Supper.

In mid-February 1847, New reported additional progress: "We have had 16 additions to the Church of Christ in this place, 10 by confession and baptism; some from the Baptists, some from the Methodists, some from the Presbyterians. . . . We have had some to immerse every Lord's day for the last four weeks; and we expect to immerse some others next Lord's day. We have meeting every night this week. There is much work to do here."[94] These immersions, during December and January, took place "in the canal, in which the ice was more than a foot thick." New believed that this act of faith impressed the local residents: "The inhabitants became anxious to know more of those people that were everywhere spoken against."[95] Four weeks later he reported ten more immersions with the prospect of "many more. Our audiences are good and very attentive. We preach from 5 to 9 times per week, and teach daily from house to house. We have not had time to leave the city since we came to it, and shall not have time to do so soon."[96] One conversion which attracted attention was that of Edward Hodgkins, a lay reader of the Episcopal Church; New wrote: "I have immersed a schoolteacher in this place who had been an Episcopalian preacher. He has begun to teach the ancient gospel."[97]

New's facility in attracting sheep from other folds was not well received by the shepherds of the established congregations. When a member of the First Presbyterian Church, Sophia Ball, was immersed, the church session removed her name from the rolls without granting a letter of transfer.[98] New reported that the Presbyterian pastor, Hugh S. Dickson, had declared that "I [New] do not believe in a change of heart, nor in the influence of the Holy Spirit, nor in any other regeneration than water alone;[99] but [Mrs. Ball] told [Dickson] that I preach the reverse of that. 'Well,' he said, '[New] did that to deceive the people'; however, I immersed her and her husband and son some 17 years of age, with six others the same day. Mr. Mason, the Baptist preacher, makes about the same false charges against us."[100]

Following the tradition of Methodists, Baptists, and some Presbyterians, New arranged for a protracted meeting to be held "before the fourth Lord's day" in August, to which he invited Elders Love H. Jameson of Indianapolis and Randall Faurot of Auburn; services were held at the court-house on Friday night, Saturday afternoon and evening.[101] Other Protestant churches always arranged that their protracted meetings would conclude with a Sunday communion service, which, in most congregations, was celebrated quarterly;[102] the Christian Church, however, was unique among all Protestant groups in their regular observance of the ordinance each Lord's day.

New's tenure with the "Church of Christ in Fort Wayne"—now fifty members strong—was scheduled to expire at the end of October. The congregation's newly elected elders and deacons, anxious that they would not be without leadership, drafted an urgent appeal to the State Meeting gathered at Greensburg: "The Gospel of Reformation is as yet but begun in this community. The great majority of the people are blindly led away by that spirit of Antichrist which doth already work in creeds, confessions of faith, books of discipline, and other traditions of men, and devices of Satan whereby thousands are lead away captive at his will. . . . To be plain, brethren, we still indispensably need an Evangelist, to carry on the good work, already, through your generosity, begun in Fort Wayne . . . . The field is white for the harvest, all that is lacking is the laborer . . . . Help us, beloved brethren, but a little longer, and rest assured, we will disburse to others, as freely as you have given to us."[103]

"To withhold the ear, appears to be the policy."

The petition of the Fort Wayne congregation was accompanied by their pledge of $150 towards an evangelist's stipend of $300. In response, the Meeting appointed Hiram St. John Van Dake to the post for the coming year, and "then proceeded to raise by contribution and subscription the sum of $150." The delegates were wary of overpaying their missionary, and noted: "The church at Fort Wayne think that they can probably increase their subscription to $200; if they should succeed in this, there will be $50 in the hand of brother Van Dake, to be handed over to the next State Meeting."[104]

Van Dake had been in residence in Union County during the previous two and a half years and his ministry had been limited to the immediate area because of illness. In concern for his health, a friend brought him by horse and buggy to Fort Wayne. Van Dake was surprised by the comparatively undeveloped condition of northeastern Indiana:

Our route much of the way, was not that most

usually travelled . . . . On this side of Richmond, we came though vast quantities of wild or slightly improved lands . . . . We found ever and anon, the hardy pioneer carrying on victorious war with the strength of the forest. The sound of the hammer and the axe disturbed the solitude of the woods, and the lowing of the ox, and neighing of the steed, broke the gloom of the wilderness. Even a few sheep escape the prowlings of the wolf; but in Jay [County], nearly every man we met, on foot, on horseback, or with team, carried his gun!

Since arriving in Fort Wayne, I have found the sheep somewhat scattered, and the prospect is not the most flattering for wholly gathering them into the fold again. We have found some attentive disciples and were affectionately received by a little band . . . . I addressed them a short time, giving then a general view of what, by God's blessing, I expected to advocate among them. In the afternoon, and at night, I preach to small audiences at the Court house . . . . We have two meetings weekly, besides those on the Lord's day. I have received but a very limited hearing. My audiences have been small.[105]

During his first month in the city, Van Dake had received no converts and, like his predecessor, supposed that he was the victim of a conspiracy by the established churches: "The prominent influences of society here are religiously (or irreligiously) against us, and, to withhold the ear, appears to be the policy intended to defeat us. This silence of contempt is of too slender a basis to remain undisturbed, and, by the grace of God, shall be broken."[106] Unlike the Methodists and Baptists who declared that their evangelical outreach was directed primarily toward the unchurched and unconverted, the preachers of the Christian Church directed their message to the active members of other denominations—in the belief that their "Reformation" faith would save these wayward sheep from the errors of creeds, hierarchies, and infant baptism. In the same spirit, the Christian Church in Fort Wayne did not join in the cooperative activities of the local Protestant churches—either in the united worship services at Thanksgiving and Independence Day or in cooperative educational and charitable endeavors.

Van Dake, frustrated because his meetings and messages were largely ignored, determined to break the "silence of contempt" by challenging a Universalist minister to debate, and then placed an advertisement in the local newspapers:

Arrangements have been made, on the part of the Universalists, for Mr. Charles Craven of Indianapolis to debate me. The public may expect, if God wills, the debate [to] commence at the Court

House on the 19th of June at 10 o'clock A. M. and continue for four days.

Prop.[osition]: "The Universalist Gospel (i.e., that all mankind, without exception, shall finally be made holy and happy) is the Gospel of Christ in the New Testament."

H. St. John Van Dake[107]

Most of the local Universalists were now worshipping at Second Presbyterian Church, and the pastor, Charles Beecher, had carefully avoided such public confrontations. Universalist preachers often used public debates as means of spreading their ideas, and most had developed significant expertise. "Universalists prowl forth sharp-set for debate," observed Beecher, "able to trip up the clumsy circuit rider with his year's worth of spiritual provender."[108] The four-day theological joust was not reviewed positively in the local newspapers; one editor concluded: "If ministers would labor more to produce harmony and good feeling among members of their church, they would do a greater amount of good than in separating them in angry discussions."[109]

In comparison with New, Van Dake had brought few converts to the faith. It is possible that most of the potential proselytes from local congregations had already converted, and the supply of new "come-outers," as they were called, was exhausted. It was doubtless a challenge to nurture such a congregation of "scattered sheep," three quarters of which had recently left other denominations. When Van Dake lamented that he was having difficulty in "gathering" New's converts "into the fold again," he came to understand that more than a few "come-outers" were temperamentally predisposed to become dissatisfied with whatever church they joined and, as such, were called "church tramps."

After making an initial report upon his arrival in Fort Wayne, Van Dake was silent, probably because there was little to write about. His year-end report to the State Meeting in September 1848 was brief: the minutes noted only that "no doubt was left, but that much good had been accomplished by his efforts."[110] There was, however, considerable doubt as to whether the Fort Wayne mission should receive additional financial support. At the end of the meeting, it was decided that "the church at Fort Wayne still need assistance; therefore, *Resolved,* that we advise the brethren in Fort

Wayne to co-operate with churches in that vicinity in sustaining an Evangelist to labor among them the ensuing year."[111]

Such advice was difficult to implement; there was no established Christian church within fifty miles, and no evangelist had been appointed to minister in either Allen or the surrounding counties. As a result, the congregation soon disbanded. After 1848, there is no record of any minister of the Christian Church conducting services in Fort Wayne until September 1855, when a local newspaper announced that the "Rev. J. D. Moffett of the Christian Church" was "expected to preach in the Court House . . . on the next Sabbath at 3 o'clock P. M."[112] Moffett's reception must have been discouraging, and his ensuing report on the state of religion in Fort Wayne must have been uncomplimentary, because the next Christian minister who arrived in town had already decided that the city was far from redemption. Elder N. A. Walker, on April 6, 1856, viewed the city from the train station, during a thirty minute stop, and wrote: "I stepped from a new train on the beautiful streets of that commercial, though Christless, benighted, bedrunkened city of Ft. Wayne. I think that the brethren of Indiana would do well to send brethren J. B. New and H. St. John Van Dake[113] both back again to Ft. Wayne, with a reinforcement, if necessary, and try once more . . . to bring down her superstitious walls. What a pity for her destitute thousands, who scarcely know one word of the ancient gospel! But in one half hour the bloodless steeples of the "Old Lady" and her daughters disappeared, and my spirit was quiet within me."[114] Neither New nor Van Dake ever returned to Fort Wayne, and no Christian church was established in the city until 1871.

The demise of the Christian Church in Fort Wayne could have been predicted: unlike every other congregation in the community, they had attempted to organize before there was a large enough core of residents who earnestly desired, and would work for, their own church. Furthermore, the Christian evangelists attempted to attract new members by attacking the beliefs of the other denominations—a strategy which tended to isolate the small fellowship. The effort might have succeeded if the State Meeting had been willing and able to support the mission for a few more years; most of the newly established congregations in Fort Wayne had required a longer period of denominational assistance.

Reflections

"There is among us as much of the true benignant spirit of christianity, as exists in places where the forms of religion are more observed, and the influence of the clergy is more powerful."

"A. B.," 1842

During the period between the establishment of the first French Fort in 1722 and the first sale of land in 1823, no visitor considered the settlement at the headwaters of the Maumee River to be a promising field for religious labor. A Catholic priest described living conditions in the village as hardly "endurable"; a Quaker missionary reported that no one paid the least "respect" to the Sabbath; a Protestant missionary wrote that no place in the West was so "unpromising" as Fort Wayne; and a government surveyor reported that the Indians were the "most christianized" and "least savage" of the local population.[1]

By 1842, the religious tenor of the former trading and military post had been dramatically changed by the influx of new settlers: the American-born migrants from the East and the German, French, and Irish emigrants from Europe. In that year, a New Englander, who had resided in Fort Wayne since its first congregation was organized, reported positively on the state of religion in the community:

We have here our full quota of religious denominations. In the new States, settled as they have been by emigrants from almost every corner of the globe, there is probably a greater variety of religious sects, greater boldness and independence of thought upon religious subjects, than exists in States that have been long settled. In Fort Wayne we have a Presbyterian, Catholic,

Methodist, Baptist and Lutheran society, all of which have regular preachers .... The Presbyterian, Methodist, and Catholic societies are respectable in point of numbers. Their churches are pretty well filled on Sundays and a good degree of interest in religious matters is manifested by our people generally. Our citizens are not as much a church going people as those of New York or New England, but they are by no means a class of infidels and scorners .... [T]here is among the mass of our people who are not members of churches, a deep respect for religion; and, although there is more riding, visiting, and sporting on the Sabbath than would be tolerated in some communities, I am still of the opinion, that there is among us as much of the true benignant spirit of christianity, as exists in places where the forms of religion are more observed, and the influence of the clergy is more powerful.[2]

The "variety of sects" noted by the writer came from both the traditional Anglo-Protestant denominations of the Eastern states—Presbyterian, Methodist, Baptist, and Episcopal—and the established religious communions of Germany, France, Switzerland, and Ireland—Catholic, Lutheran, Reformed, and Jewish. Apparently, the founding of strong traditional denominations insulated the community from an

249

incursion of the new American-born "sects," such as Mormons, Millerites, and Spiritualists.

One significant factor that nurtured such strong and influential congregations was the quality and dedication of the leadership. Almost single-handedly Peter Bailey organized the Episcopal church, as did Henry Rudisill the Lutheran church and Frederick Nirdlinger the Jewish congregation. Other lay persons such as Baptist Ann Turner, Presbyterian Allen Hamilton, and Catholic Francis Comparet persistently petitioned their church leaders to send a pastor to their isolated village.

Equally significant was the dedication of many of the early missionaries—and for those who lacked sufficient dedication, the subsistence salaries and cultural isolation of the frontier hastened their departure. It was solely Isaac McCoy's undaunted determination that created a Baptist mission school for the Indians, and it was his vision and energy alone that sustained its work. Jesse Hoover organized two Lutheran churches in less than two years, without the sponsorship of his denomination and in spite having to teach and preach for the Presbyterians to support his family. Stephen Badin continued to ride horseback to minister to the Catholic laborers along the canal line until, at the age of sixty-six, his health failed. And William Paul Quinn faced formidable obstacles in his pioneering ministry to African-Americans.

All of the preachers confronted the laissez-faire mores of the dissolving frontier. As a result, the local church councils, sessions, and vestries became moral courts for many in the community. Sabbath observance, although not as strictly interpreted as in New England, gradually became the approved norm, and abstinence from alcoholic beverages was soon accepted as an ideal in most Anglo-Protestant churches.

Many preachers confronted public policy as well as personal piety in their sermons, lectures, and debates. No one in Fort Wayne was more outspoken in the antislavery movement than Alexander Rankin, Daniel Burroughs, and Samuel Brenton, and no one was as articulate as Charles Beecher in condemning discrimination against African-Americans.

Some of the clergy, such as James Bossard and John Lowrie, were admired for their scholarship. All of the clergy were expected to be effective teachers of religion, as well as leaders in their congregations' efforts to establish parish schools. Prominent in advancing the cause of education in the community were Julien Benoit, Joseph Salomon, Friedrich Wyneken, and Joseph Large. Not only were most of the early schools founded by the congregations, but the first college, seminary, and orphanage, as well as the three hospitals were established by religious denominations.

In hindsight, the modern reader may feel that there were areas in which the clergy and their congregations were timid. When the Miami Indians were about to be removed from the region, it appears that only a few voices from the local congregations were raised to protest their deportation. Similarly, there is scant record of constructive measures initiated by the religious leaders to bridge the social and political chasm that separated white and black residents. And, despite the fact that Anglo-Protestant church women were the leaders of the emerging woman's rights movement, there is no record of Fort Wayne clergy actively promoting the cause.

Each of Fort Wayne's congregations—Jewish, Catholic, and Protestant—shared a common mission: to gather regularly for worship and instruction, to educate their children in the faith, to provide for their members' spiritual and moral welfare, and to bring converts into their fellowship. Spiritual piety and moral purity were strongly emphasized in every congregation.

The religious congregations, however, indirectly served other purposes: the newcomer found in their society a welcoming fellowship; persons concerned for the disadvantaged worked for foreign missions or local charities; those interested in moral reform used their religious body as a forum to examine the current social issues. Emigrants, anxious to preserve the best of their old world heritage, found strong support in the ethnic congregations. African-Americans valued their church as the only local institution to provide comfort and courage in their struggle against racial prejudice. And many women who had responded to their congregation's call to be of service to the wider community developed leadership skills which soon challenged society's patriarchal establishment.

From a sociological perspective, the congregations were voluntary associations of local people who held common values and shared similar concerns. The congregations, however, always defined themselves from a theological perspective—as a fellowship of believers called by God to faithfulness in worship and service. In antebellum Fort Wayne, an increasing number of the population were attracted to this theological ideal, and the human values and spiritual vision it represented. When a reporter in the 1850s casually described the community as "A City of Churches," the sobriquet caught the imagination of many residents, and for nearly a century and a half it has been a persistent image of how Fort Wayne would like to envision itself.

Appendix
Clergy and Religious at Fort Wayne: 1749 - 1860

African Methodist Episcopal

William Paul Quinn: missionary, 1840 to 1844; bishop, 1844 to his death in 1873..

African Methodist Episcopal Church of Fort Wayne (est. 1845).

George Nelson Black: pastor, mid-1840s to late 1850s.

Baptist

Occasional Preachers: 1835 - 1837.

Robert Tisdale
Enos French
J. L. Moore
Eli Fry

Fort Wayne Regular Baptist Church (est. 1837).

William Corbin: December 1837 to October 1838.
Robert Tisdale: April 1839 to March 1840.
William Cox: October 1840 to September 1841.
William Gildersleeve: October 1841 to January 1843.
William Combs (supply): February and March 1843.
James H. Dunlap: March 1843 to March 1845.
George Sleeper: October 1845 to December 1845.
H. D. Mason: May 1846 to January 1848.
S. B. Searl: February 1848 to September 1848.
Daniel W. Burroughs: September 1848 to July 1850.
John D. Meeson: July 1850 to May 1852.
Ulrich Butler Miller: June 1853 to September 1855.
Cyrus W. Rees: September 1856 to November 1857.
Stephen Wilkins: September 1858 to August 1860.

Catholic

Joseph Pierre de Bonnecamps, S. J. (Quebec, Diocese of Quebec): 1749.

Early Missionary Priests.

Louis Payet (Detroit, Diocese of Quebec): December 1789.
Gabriel Richard (Diocese of Detroit): April 1822.
Francis Badin (Diocese of Detroit): April 1822.
Anthony Ganihl (Diocese of Bardstown): April 1822.
Stephen Theodore Badin (Diocese of Detroit); June 1830; January-February, May, and December 1831; May and December 1832; January, October, and December 1833; January, February, April, June, and September 1834.
Laurence Picot (Diocese of Bardstown): September to October 1832.
Ghislain Bohême (Diocese of Detroit): April (Easter) 1833.

Missionary Priests of the Diocese of Vincennes.

Simon Petit Lalumière: May to June 1835.
Felix Matthieu Ruff: August to October 1835.
James Ferdinand Tervooren: November to December 1835.
Jean Claude François: January, February, and May to August 1836; June 1839.

Pastors of the original parish, which was successively named [Old] St. Mary's (1836), St. Augustine's (1840), and Immaculate Conception Cathedral (1859).

Louis Müller: August 1836 to April 1840.
Julien Benoit: April 1840 to November 1852; December 1854 to his death, 26 January 1885.
August Bessonies: March 1853 to January 1854.

Assistant Pastors at St. Augustine's Church (German-speaking Alsatians).

Joseph de Mutzig Hamion: September 1840 to his death, April 1842.
Francis Joseph Rudolf: August 1842 to November 1844.
Alphonse Munschina: January 1845 to February 1846

Anthony Carius: April to June 1846.
Edward Faller: October 1846 to November 1849.

Pastors of Mother of God (St. Mary's) German Church (est. 1849).

Edward M. Faller: November 1849 to 1857.
Joseph Weutz: 1857 to 1872.

Sisters of Providence at St. Augustine's Academy (est. 1846).

Arrival date (usually September) and number of years at Fort Wayne.

Sr. Mary Magdalen (Augusta Linck), superior: 1846 (3 yrs.).
Sr. Caroline (Ann O'Dell): 1846 (2 yrs.).
Sr. Catherine* (Walburga Eisen): 1846 (3 yrs.).
Sr. Marie Thérèse (Marie Françoise Delahaye): 1847 (1 yr.).
Sr. Gabriella (Mrs. Anne O'Neill Moore): 1848 (9 yrs.).
Sr. Philomene (Mary Doyle): 1848 (1 yr.).
Sr. Marie Joseph* (Josephine Yvonne Pardeillan), superior: 1849 to her death, 17 March 1851.
Sr. Mary Celestia (Sophia Kennedy): 1849 (9 yrs.); 1859 (2 yrs.).
Sr. Lawrence (Julienne Cheminant): 1849 to her death, 20 August 1854.
Sr. Martina* (Johanna Lehner): 1849 (1 yr.).
Sr. Clotilde (Mary De Lille): 1849 (3 yrs.); 1856 (3 yrs.).
Sr. Felicité* (Margaret Melchior): 1850 (4 yrs.).
Sr. St. Vincent Ferrer+ (Victoire Gagé), superior: 1851 (7 yrs.).
Sr. Alphonse* (Caroline Brutscher): 1851 (1 yr.).
Sr. Mary Xavier+ (Françoise Louise Lerée): 1852 (1 yr.).
Sr. Louise (Mary Malone): 1852 (1 yr.); 1859 (3 yrs.)
Sr. Isidore (Mary Thralls): 1853 (2 yrs): 1857 (1 yr.); 1859 (2 yrs.).
Sr. Melanie (Theresa Frances Cambron): 1853 (2 yrs.).
Sr. Elizabeth (Theresa McNeil): 1854 (2 yrs.).
Sr. Norbert (Mary Kelley): 1854 (1 yr.).
Sr. Rose Ann (Mary Koch): 1855 (3 yrs.).
Sr. Veronique (Margaret Smith): 1855 (6 yrs.).
Sr. Mary Jane (Justine Herman): 1855 (2 yrs.).
Sr. Mary Thomas (Elizabeth Hiler): 1857 (4 yrs.).
Sr. Mary Theodore (Mary Theresa Le Touze), superior: 1858 (3 yrs.).
Sr. Mary Pauline (Emma Michael): 1858 (1 yr.).
Sr. Dominic (Mary McLaughlin): 1858 (1 yr.).
Sr. Athanasius (Margaret Fogarty): 1860 (1 yr.).

Sisters of Providence at St. Mary's German School (est. Aug. 1854).

Sister Catherine* (Walburga Eisen): 1854 (7 yrs.).
Sr. (St.) Edward* (Magdalena Marendt): 1854 (6 yrs).

Sr. Maria* (Caroline Vicaire): 1856 (2 yrs).
Sr. Mary Ursula* (Eliza Fearn): 1858 (4 yrs.).
German-speaking
+*One of the original six Sisters to come to America.*

Holy Cross Brothers at St. Augustine's School (est. 1843).

Br. Joseph (Charles Rother): 1843.
Br. John (Frederick Steber): 1844.
Br. Basil (Timothy O'Neil), director: fall 1847.
Br. Emanuel (Anthony Wopperman): 1847 to 1848.
Br. Benedict (Patrick Fitzpatrick): fall of 1848.
Br. Thomas (James Donoghoe): 1850 to 1851.
(During the mid-1850s the Brothers discontinued serving the school.)
Br. Bernadine (Francis Ryan), director: 1859.
Br. Stanislaus (Manasses Kane): 1860.

Episcopal Visits, Diocese of Vincennes (est. 1834).

Simon Gabriel Guillaume Bruté de Remur: June 1837.
Jacques Marie Maurice Landes D'Aussac de St. Palais: December 1849.

Bishop of the Diocese of Fort Wayne (est. 1857).

John Henry Lüers: in residence at Fort Wayne, February 1858 to his death, 29 June 1871.

Christian (Disciples of Christ)

Church of Christ in Fort Wayne (est. 1846; dissolved 1848).

Elder Barber: December 1845.
Milton B. Hopkins: June 1846; June 1848.
James Madison Mathes: June and September 1846.
John Bowman New: November 1846 to October 1847.
Love H. Jameson: assisted at a protracted meeting, August 1847.
Randall Faurot: assisted at a protracted meeting, August 1847.
Hiram St. John Van Dake: November 1847 to October 1848.
J. D. Moffett: September 1855.

Episcopal

Christ Episcopal Church (est. 1839; dissolved 1840).

Benjamin Hutchins: May 1839 to January 1840.

Trinity Episcopal Church (est. 1844).

Benjamin Halsted: May 1844 to April 1846.
Henry P. Powers: April 1848 to August 1848.
Joseph S. Large: November 1848 to September 1854; August 1863 to March 1872.

Caleb Alexander Bruce: November 1854 to October 1855.

Eugene C. Pattison: June 1856 to April 1858.

Stephen H. Battin: October 1858 to August 1863.

Episcopal Visits:

David Jackson Kemper: August 1837, July 1840, July 1843, August 1844, August 1845, May 1846, July 1847, October 1848.

George Upfold: May 1850; 3rd Sunday after Easter in 1851 and 1852; 4th Sunday after Easter in 1853; 28 April 1854; 14 February 1855; 5-8 October 1855; 20-24 November 1856 (Thanksgiving); 30 May to 6 June 1857 (Diocesan Convention); 24 to 26 April 1858; 10 and 11 April 1859; 25 and 26 June 1959; 26 to 29 May 1860; 13 to 17 March 1861; 15 to 19 August 1861; 11 to 16 December 1861; 1 May 1862; 18 to 24 April 1863; 25 September 1863; 30 March to 1 April 1864; 15 to 18 April 1864.

Jewish

Achduth Vesholom Congregation (est. 1848 as "The Society for Visiting and Burying the Dead").

Joseph Salomon: 1850 to May 1860.

Isaac Rosenthal: September 1860 to October 1861.

Edward Rubin: September 1862 to his death, 20 May 1881.

Lutheran

First Evangelical Lutheran Church in Fort Wayne (est. 1837).

Jesse Hoover: July 1836 to his death, 23 May 1838.

Friedrich Konrad Dietrich Wyneken: October 1838 to December 1844.

Georg Jensen, interim pastor: August 1841 to 1842

Friedrich Wilhelm Husmann, interim pastor: 1842 to fall 1843.

On 25 March 1846 the name of the congregation was changed to:

The German Evangelical Lutheran St. Paul's Church *(Der Deutsche Evangelische-Lutherische St. Pauls-Gemeinde).*

Wilhelm Sihler: July 1845 to his death, 27 October 1885.

Vicars *(Vikar oder Hilfsprediger)* **at St. Paul's Church.**

Ernst Ludwig Hermann Kühn: 1852 to 1853.

Friedrich Föhlinger: June 1853 to late 1857.

Martin Stephan: 1858 to 1860.

Julius C. Renz: 1860-1861.

The English Lutheran Church of the Holy Trinity (est. 1846).

J. William Albaugh: August 1846 to December 1849.

Alexander S. Bartholomew: November 1850 to April 1856.

William Patton Ruthrauff: February 1859 to May 1867.

The German Evangelical Lutheran St. John's Congregation of Fort Wayne and Vicinity *(Der Deutsche Evangelische-Lutherische St. Johannis-Gemeinde zu Fort Wayne)* (est. 1853).

A. Strauss: September 1852 to unknown date.

Christian Hochstetter: August 1853 to September 1854.

A. Kleinegees: October 1854 to September 1857.

Hugo B. Kuhn: March 1858 to October 1860.

Methodist Episcopal

Berry Street M. E. Church (est. ca. 1830; successively called the Maumee Mission, Fort Wayne Mission, Fort Wayne Station, and the Eastern Charge; appointments were for one year and concluded in the fall of the year listed.)

Stephen R. Beggs : 1829.

Nehemiah B. Griffith: 1830.

Richard S. Robinson : 1831.

Boyd Phelps: 1832.

Freeman Farnsworth: 1834.

James S. Harrison: 1835.

Stephen R. Ball: 1836 and 1837.

James T. Robe: 1838.

Jacob Colclazer: 1839.

Francis A. Conwell: 1840 and 1841.

George Milton Boyd: 1842.

Hawley Baxter Beers: 1843.

John C. Bayless: 1844 and 1845.

Samuel Brenton: 1846.

Amasa Johnson: 1847.

William Wilson: 1848 and 1849.

Henry Clark Benson: 1850.

Milton Mahin: 1851.

Charles W. Miller: 1852 and 1853 .

J. D. G. Pettijohn: 1854 and 1855.

Lawson W. Monson: 1856.

John H. Hull: 1857.

Almon Greenman: 1858.

Valentine M. Beamer: 1859 and 1860.

Wayne Street M. E. Church (est. 1849).

Samuel Brenton: 1849.

Thomas Henry Sinex: 1850.

Reuben Davisson Robinson: 1851.

F. A. Hardin: 1852.

James Armstrong Beswick: 1853.

Hawley Baxter Beers: 1854.
Asahel S. Kinnan: 1855-56.
Francis Asbury Sale: 1857.
Lewis Dale: 1858.
Charles Martindale: 1859-60.

Bethel German Methodist Episcopal Church (est. 1841).
(Appointments were for one year; the names of most pastors are unknown.)
Heinrich Wilhelm (William) Ahrens: 1841.
Karl Schelper: ca. 1843-44.
John H. Barth: 1859.
Friedrich Albert Hoff: ca. 1862-1863.

Presiding Elders for Fort Wayne.
John Strange: 1818-29, Madison District.
Allen Wiley: 1830-31, Madison District.
James Armstrong: 1832-33, Missionary District.
Richard Hargrave: 1834-37, LaPorte District.
George M. Beswick: 1838-41, Logansport District.
Burroughs Westlake: 1842, Fort Wayne District .
George M. Boyd : 1843-46, Fort Wayne District.
Samuel Brenton : 1847-48, Fort Wayne District.
Samuel C. Cooper: 1849-50-51, Fort Wayne District.
H. N. Barnes: 1852-53, Fort Wayne District.
D. F. Stright: 1854-55-56-57, Fort Wayne District.
G. C. Beeks: 1858-59-60-61, Fort Wayne District.
Heinrich Wilhelm (William) Ahrens: 1846-? North-Ohio German District.
Georg A. Breunig: 1855-1859, Northern Indiana German District.

Presidents of Fort Wayne College (est. 1846; opened, fall 1847; successively called Fort Wayne Female College, Fort Wayne Collegiate Institute, and the Methodist College).
A. C. Huestis: September 1847 to May 1848.
G. H. Rounds: 1848 to 30 July 1849.
Cyrus Nutt: 1849 to 3 September 1850.
A. C. Huestis, acting president: 1850 to 19 April 1852.
S. T. Gillette: 1852 to 24 September 1852.
Samuel Brenton: 1853 to 4 August 1855.
Reuben Davisson Robinson: 1855 to 18 December 1866.

Agents of Fort Wayne College
John C. Bayless: 1846.
J. H. Bruce: 1847.
Samuel C. Cooper: 1848.
Amasa Johnson: 1848.
Ancil Beach: 1849.
Amasa Johnson: 1850.
J. G. D. Pettijohn: 1850.
O. V. Lemon: 1851-52-53-54.
Lawson W. Monson: 1852.

Jesse Sparks: 1853.
Josiah Jackson Cooper: 1855.

Presbyterian

Early Visitors
Matthew Wallace: 1812 (chaplain with Gen. William Henry Harrison).
John Ross: five visits between 1822 to 1826.

First Presbyterian Church (est. 1831).
Charles Furman: November 1829 to May 1830.
James Chute: June 1831 to his death, 28 December 1835.
Daniel Jones (interim pastor): January to July 1836.
Jesse Hoover (Lutheran pulpit supply): August 1836 to August 1837.
Alexander Taylor Rankin: September 1837 to September 1843.
William Caldwell Anderson (interim pastor): May to September 1844.
Hugh Sheridan Dickson: September 1844 to July 1847.
Lowman C. Hawes (candidate on trial): November 1847 to April 1848.
John Gillin Riheldaffer: October 1848 to May 1851.
Jonathan Edwards: September 1851 to June 1855.
John Marshall Lowrie: October 1856 to his death on September 26, 1867.

Second Presbyterian Church (est. 1844).
Henry Ward Beecher: April 1844.
Charles Beecher: May 1844 to August 1850.
Isaac W. Taylor (temporary supply): fall 1850 through winter 1851.
David C. Blood (stated supply): spring through summer 1851.
John W. Ray (temporary supply): fall 1851 through winter 1852.
Amzi Whitfield Freeman: June 1852 to May 1854.
Eleroy Curtis: November 1854 to October 1860.

Associate Reformed Presbyterian Mission (est. 1852; dissolved 1856).
John Davis Glenn: March 1851 to January 1852.
James Miller: September 1852 to January 1854.
John R. McCalister: February 1854 to October 1855.

Reformed

German Evangelical Reformed Congregation of St. John. (est. 1844). *(Der Deutsche Evangelische-Reformierte St. Johannis-Gemeinde).*
Andrew Carroll: June 1844 to March 1845.

John Adam Bayer: April 1845 to May 1846.

E. B. Altermatt: fall 1846 to May 1848.

Johann Jacob (James) Bossard: June 1848 to May 1854.

H. Benz: June 1854 to May 1855.

John H. Klien: September 1855 to May 1868.

Swedenborgian

John Chapman: Missionary, 1825 to 1845.

Universalist

Erasmus Manford (Terre Haute): November 1844, November 1846, November 1848.

Benjamin F. Foster (Terre Haute): occasionally in 1845.

J. George: June 1846.

Charles Craven (Indianapolis): June 1848.

William J. Chaplin (Kosciusko County): June 1847, January 1849, January 1851, (?) 1855, June and September 1857.

P. Hathaway: January 1849.

T. C. Eaton: February and March 1859.

J. M. Day: "A citizen of Fort Wayne [who] did some missionary work in the interest of the denomination."

Notes

Notes

Abbreviation used in the notes of this book are
AHMS — American Home Missionary Society Letters
UNDA — University of Notre Dame Archives
SMWA — St. Mary-of-the-Woods Archives

Introduction

[1] *Fort Wayne Times*, 24 June 1852.

[2] Michael C. Hawfield, "Religion and the Origins of Fort Wayne." Paper presented at the Spring History Conference of the Indiana Historical Society, May 5-6, 1989, at Clifty Falls State Park, Indiana.

Chapter 1

[1] See Francis Parkman, *LaSalle and the Discovery of the Great West* (Boston: Little, Brown & Co., 1904).

[2] Otho Winger, *The Last of the Miamis* (North Manchester, Indiana, 1935), 3.

[3] B. J. Griswold, *The Pictorial History of Fort Wayne, Indiana,* 2 vols. (Chicago: Robert O. Law Company, 1917), 1: 27.

[4] Mary B. Brown, *History of the Sisters of Providence of Saint Mary-of-the-Woods,* (New York: Benziger Brothers, Inc., 1949), 545.

[5] W. Vernon Kinietz, *The Indians of the Western Great Lakes, 1615-1760* (Ann Arbor: University of Michigan Press, 1940), 69, 137.

[6] Bert Anson, *The Miami Indians* (Norman, Okla.: University of Oklahoma Press, 1970), 24.

[7] *The Journals and Indian Paintings of George Winter, 1837-39* (Indianapolis: Indiana Historical Society, 1948), 177, caption Plate 27.

[8] Vaudreuil to Council of Marine, 22 October 1722, Archives of the Province of Quebec, Canada, cited in Charles Poinsatte, *Outpost in the Wilderness: Fort Wayne, 1708-1828* (Fort Wayne, Ind.: Allen County-Fort Wayne Historical Society, 1976), 6.

[9] In the Quebec Act of 1774, the British Parliament annexed the Old Northwest to the Province of Quebec and guaranteed the religious freedom and other privileges of the native French, nearly all of whom were Catholic. As a consequence, Miamitown came under the jurisdiction of the Diocese of Quebec, and the clergy at Detroit visited the village occasionally. See chapter "Catholics."

[10] Charles Poinsatte, *Outpost in the Wilderness: Fort Wayne, 1708-1828,* 13.

[11] William Wells, at the age of twelve, had been kidnapped by a band of Miamis and adopted by Little Turtle's tribe. He had married Anaquah, Little Turtle's sister; upon her death, he married Sweet Breeze (Manwangopath), the chief's daughter. Wells willingly fought with the Miamis against the Americans, but later became a scout for General Anthony Wayne. At Little Turtle's request, Wells was appointed resident interpreter at Miamitown. He was killed in 1812 by Potawatomis while attempting to rescue women and children from the siege at Fort Dearborn.

[12] Gerald T. Hopkins, *A Mission to the Indians from the Indian Committee of the Baltimore Yearly Meeting to Fort Wayne in 1804, Written at the Time, with an Appendix, compiled in 1862, by Martha E. Tyson* (Philadelphia: T. Ellwood Zell, 1862), 171.

[13] John Johnston, Memorandum for the Committee of Friends from Baltimore, May 26, 1808, Records of the Office of the Secretary of War, National Archives, Washington, D. C., cited in Paul Woehrmann, *At the Headwaters of the Maumee: A History of the Forts of Fort Wayne* (Indianapolis: Indiana Historical Society, 1971), 138. The "factor"

was appointed the federal government to administer the "Indian factory" where trade goods were stored, the Indian trade was managed, and the annuities were distributed.

[14] Little Turtle, as a result of his first visit to the East in 1797, had received two plows from Philadelphia Quakers, which he said, "now need repair; we have nobody among us that can mend them." *Ibid.*, 166, 167.

[15] Jacob Piatt Dunn, *Indiana and Indianans* (Chicago: American Historical Society, 1919), 74.

[16] Gerald T. Hopkins, *A Mission to the Indians,* 4.

[17] *Ibid.,* 47-48.

[18] John Johnston, who was appointed factor for the Indian Department at Fort Wayne in 1802 and agent in 1809, wrote that, during his ten years of service, "There was not a Protestant clergyman of any denomination that performed divine service at the post." Letter of John Johnston, November 1859, quoted in J. L. Williams, *Historical Sketch of the First Presbyterian Church, Fort Wayne, Indiana* (Fort Wayne: John Dawson, printer, 1860), 11.

[19] Gerald T. Hopkins, *A Mission to the Indians,* 48, 49, 51, 57, 59, 60.

[20] *Ibid.,* 74-77. This address was published by the Indian Committee at Baltimore in 1804 and also appeared in the newspapers of the period.

[21] *Ibid.,* 80-83.

[22] *Ibid.,* 86-87.

[23] *Ibid.,* 88-90.

[24] *Ibid.,* 182.

[25] The Baltimore Society of Friends made two additional efforts to minister to the Native Americans in the Fort Wayne area. In 1806, Secretary of War Dearborn instructed Captain Whipple, commander of the fort, and William Wells, the Indian agent, to give appropriate assistance to a Maryland Quaker, Mrs. Catherine Shaw, who planned to teach domestic arts in the "Indian County, on the Upper Waters of the Wabash." There is no record that she ever came to the area. The most successful mission of the Baltimore Quakers was directed by William Kirk who worked among the Miami and Shawnee between 1806 and 1809. For the story of William Wells's hand in frustrating Kirk's attempt to establish his mission at Fort Wayne see Paul Woehrmann, *At the Headwaters of the Maumee: A History of the Forts of Fort Wayne,* 119-136.

[26] Calvin Young, *Little Turtle* (Indianapolis: Sentinel Printing Co., 1917), 175.

[27] Jesse L. Williams, *Historical Sketch of the First Presbyterian Church, Fort Wayne, Indiana ,* 8.

[28] Riley to Tiffin, 14 November 1820, quoted in T. B. Helm, *History of Wabash County, Indiana* (Chicago: Kingman Bros., 1885), 78.

[29] Isaac McCoy, *History of Baptist Indian Missions: Embracing Remarks on the Former and Present Condition of the Aboriginal Tribes; Their Settlement Within the Indian Territory and Their Future Prospects* (Washington: William M. Morrison, 1840), 92.

[30] Ben. F. Keith, *History of Maria Creek Church* (Vincennes, Ind.: A. V. Crotts & Co., 1889), 8.

[31] *The Latter Day Luminary, I,* 44-45, quoted in John F. Cady, *The Origin and Development of the Missionary Baptist Church in Indiana* (Berne, Ind.: The Berne Witness Co., 1942), 86.

[32] William Turner became Indian agent in 1820 and died in 1821.

[33] Isaac McCoy, History of Baptist Indian Missions, 67, 68.

[34] The American Colonization Society was founded in 1816 to encourage repatriated slaves to settle in their ancestral homelands. The first freed American slaves arrived in Liberia in 1822.

[35] Isaac McCoy, *History of Baptist Indian Missions,* 75, 76.

[36] *Ibid.,* 111.

[37] Joseph Lancaster, an early nineteenth-century English Quaker schoolmaster and pioneer of popular education on a voluntary basis, was the father of undenominational religious teaching.

[38] "Journal of Thomas Scattergood Teas" in *Indiana as Seen by Early Travelers,* Harlow Lindley, ed. (Indianapolis, 1916), 98.

[39] Isaac McCoy, *History of Baptist Missions,* 85,

[40] *Ibid.,* 86, 89, 90. 92.

[41] *Ibid.,* 103, 106.

[42] See Paul Hutton, "William Wells: Frontier Scout and Indian Agent," in *Indiana Magazine of History,* vol. 24, no. 3 (September 1978), 183.

[43] Ann Turner, in a letter to a cousin, spoke highly of McCoy's ministry; her relative replied, "I am glad that you have the privilege of Brother McCoy's company and instruction; it is a great thing to have such an example of piety." Ann I. Wells to Ann Turner, 21 October 1821, Wells Papers, Allen County-Fort Wayne Historical Society, Fort Wayne, Indiana.

[44] Isaac McCoy, *History of Baptist Missions,* 76, 77.

[45] *Ibid.,* 77. McCoy probably composed the hymn; a decade before, "he experienced a temporary infatuation for authorship, especially in the line of poetry, for which he had some talent." Walter M. Wyeth, *Isaac McCoy: A Memorial* (Philadelphia: W. N. Wyeth, 1895), 12.

[46] Isaac McCoy, *History of Baptist Missions,* 77, 78.

[47] *Ibid.,* 94.

[48] *Ibid.,* 133. See chapter "Catholics" for details about these priests.

49 *Ibid.,* 123-125.

50 *Ibid.,* 126, 127.

51 *Ibid.,* 143, 144.

52 *Ibid.,* 145-151. The commission was dated July 16, 1822.

53 *Ibid.,* 156.

54 *Ibid.,* 87.

55 Ten years later, Timothy S. Smith published *Missionary Abominations Unmasked or a View of the Carey Mission* (South Bend, Ind.: Beacon, 1833) alleging: "[N]ot withstanding the ostensible object of Mr. McCoy's was to teach the Indians a knowledge of Christianity, the secret motive and the one which appears to have governed his whole course of conduct was to gather together 'money.'" Smith's identity is unknown and the truth of his charges has not been substantiated.

56 Isaac McCoy, *Periodical Account of Baptist Missions Within the Indian Territory for the Year Ending December 31, 1836, Published by Isaac M'Coy, Shawanoe Baptist Mission House, Indian Territory,* 33.

57 After establishing the Carey Mission (and encouraging the Thomas Mission to the Ottowas near Grand Rapids in 1826), McCoy was commissioned by the government to explore the Indian Territory west of the Mississippi in preparation for the settlement of the eastern Indians on reservations. When Andrew Jackson appointed him surveyor of the Territory, the McCoys moved to Fayette, 170 miles west of St. Louis. In 1832, he was called to Washington where he arranged a new treaty, and then returned with more missionaries. In 1834, he was again summoned to assist in the reorganization of Indian affairs and continued these trips to Washington until the legislation he personally penned, organizing the Indian Territory, was approved by Congress; McCoy then visited all the Indian tribes and secured their approval. He purchased a printing press in 1835 and published the first newspaper in the Shawnee language. In 1842, his denomination named him corresponding secretary of their newly established department of Indian Missions at Louisville, Kentucky. He died there in 1846. For more on the Baptist mission in the Indian Territory, see the biography of his missionary niece by Calvin McCormick, The *Memoir of Miss Eliza McCoy* (Dallas, Texas: published by the author, 1892).

58 Richardville, a Catholic who was more politic than pious, was probably criticized for sending his son to the Baptist school, and may therefore have desired to silence his critics by stating a future policy of non-participation.

59 Between 1830 and 1834, the Reverend Stephen T. Badin, who was operating a mission to the Potawatomis near Niles, Michigan, occasionally visited Fort Wayne; when he came to Fort Wayne in the summer of 1834, his ministry focused on the canal workers, not the Indians. See chapter "Catholics."

60 Benedict Flaget to the Societé de Paris-Lyon, 1 November 1828, *Annales de la Propogation de la Foi, 1822-1844,* 3: 191, quoted in William McNamara, *The Catholic Church on the Northern Indiana Frontier, 1789-1844* (Washington, D. C.: Catholic University, 1931), 10.

61 Hugh McCulloch, *Men and Measures of Half a Century* (New York: C. Scribner's Sons, 1888), 110.

62 Mary B. Brown, *History of the Sisters of Providence,* 545.

63 Hugh McCulloch, *Men and Measures of Half a Century,* 110.

64 The south half of Cathedral Square was then used as a cemetery. All bodies were later removed except Richardville's.

65 *Biographical Sketch of the Rt. Rev. Julian Benoit. . . by a Clergyman of the Episcopal Household* (Fort Wayne: J. J. Joquel, 1885), 9.

66 Hugh McCulloch, *Men and Measures of Half a Century,* 102.

67 William G. Ewing to John Tipton, 3 February 1830, *The John Tipton Papers,* Nellie A. Robertson and Dorothy Riker, eds., 3 vols. *(Indiana Historical Collections,* Indianapolis: Indiana Historical Commission, 1942), 2: 245. William G. Ewing had a "notorious reputation for selfishness." Mark E. Neely, Jr., "'Perfidious Whig Rascals': A Businessman Runs for Congress in Fort Wayne, 1847," *Old Fort News,* vol. 44, no 1 (1981), 19.

68 *Catholic Telegraph,* 14 July 1832.

69 Logan Esarey, *A History of Indiana* (Boston: Harcourt Brace & Co., 1905), 330. Timothy Howard, *A History of St. Joseph County, Indiana* (Chicago: Lewis Publishing Co., 1907), 711.

70 See Ray Allen Billington, *Westward Expansion: A History of the American Frontier* (New York: The Macmillan Company, 1914) and Francis Paul Prucha, *American Indian Policy in the Formative Years: The Indian Trade and Intercourse Acts, 1770-1834* (Cambridge, Mass.: Harvard University Press, 1962).

71 Isaac McCoy, *History of Baptist Missions,* 124.

72 See Irving McKee, *The Trail of Death* (Indianapolis: Indiana Historical Society, 1941). Petit died from an illness contracted on the march.

73 Charles Blanchard, ed., *History of the Catholic Church in Indiana,* 2 vols. (Logansport, Ind.: A. W. Bowen & Co., 1898), 1: 195.

74 Chief Richardville's family, Francis Slocum's family, and some of Metocinyah's band were permitted to remain in Indiana. *U. S. Statutes at Large,* 6: 942.

75 *Fort Wayne Sentinel,* 26 September 1846.

76 B. J. Griswold (quoting Edward F. Colerick), *Pictorial History of Fort Wayne,* 1: 378.

77 *Ibid.,* (quoting John W. Dawson), 1: 379.

78 Bert Anson, *The Miami Indians,* 225.

79 *Fort Wayne Times,* 14 March 1846.

80 *Ibid.,* signed "M, 5 February 1846." A tradition of modesty encouraged writers to sign such compositions with an anonymous initial.

81 *Fort Wayne Sentinel,* 3 October 1846.

82 *Ibid.,* 10 October 1846.

83 Alfred J. Vaughn, Osage Subagency to Thomas H. Harvey, St. Louis, 12 November 1846; Thomas H. Harvey, St. Louis to William Medill, Washington, 26 November and 13 December 1846, Letters to the Office of Indian Affairs, National Archives. See Bert Anson, The Miami Indians, 227.

84 Fort Wayne S*entinel,* 10 October 1846.

85 Bert Anson, *The Miami Indians,* 238.

86 See chapter "Catholics" for details of Benoit's real estate activity.

87 Mary B. Brown, *History of the Sisters of Providence,* 547.

88 Hugh McCulloch, *Men and Measures of Half a Century,* 103.

Chapter 2

1 "Father" was an informal title affectionately bestowed on venerable Protestant clergy in the early nineteenth century; Catholic and Episcopal clergy were then commonly addressed as "Mister," seldom, if ever, as "Father." Until the 1960s, when a significant number of women were entering the ministry, "Fathers and Brethren" was the traditional form of address to all assemblies of the Presbyterian Church.

2 Hanford A. Edson, *Contributions to the Early History of the Presbyterian Church in Indiana, Together with Biographical Notices of the Pioneer Ministers* (Cincinnati: Winona Publishing Co., 1898), 150. J. L. Williams, *Historical Sketch of First Presbyterian Church, Fort Wayne, Indiana* (Fort Wayne, Ind.: John Dawson, 1860), 13. A "destitution" was a community without a church or minister.

3 Joseph P. Moore, *History of the Churches in Fort Wayne Presbytery: To which is added Biographical Sketches of deceased Ministers* (Swan, Indiana: manuscript, 20 July 1876), Presbyterian Historical Society, Philadelphia, Pa., 74.

4 J. L. Williams, *Historical Sketch of First Presbyterian Church, Fort Wayne, Indiana,* 14, 15. Ross's letter was dated November 26, 1859, and was in reply to Jesse L. Williams's inquiry. Williams published his *Historical Sketch* the next year on the occasion of the Old Settlers' Reunion on the Fourth of July. Ross returned to Fort Wayne for the event and was named honorary chaplain to the Settlers. In 1824, Ross accepted the call of the Presbyterian Church in Richmond, Indiana. When he died at the age of ninety-three years, he was the oldest minister of his denomination.

5 Born in 1774, Wallace was graduated from the College of New Jersey (Princeton) and, in 1799, was one of the first Presbyterian ministers to serve in Ohio. In 1802, he became pastor of First Presbyterian Church in Cincinnati, later serving congregations in Springfield and Hamilton; he died in Terre Haute, Indiana, in 1854. *Encyclopedia of the Presbyterian Church in the United States of America,* Alfred Nevin, ed. (Philadelphia: Presbyterian Publishing Co., 1884), 980. James McClune, *History of the Presbyterian Church in the Forks of Brandywine, Chester County, Pa., From A. D. 1735 to A. D. 1885 With Biographical Sketches of the Deceased Pastors of the Church* (Philadelphia: J. B. Lippincott Co., 1885), 121, 122.

6 Major Josiah H. Vose was the last commandant of Fort Wayne, serving from May 1817 to April 1819. He and his wife were members of the Park Street Congregational Church in Boston. He later assisted the Presbyterian mission near his command at Fort Touson, Indian (Choctow) Territory from 1832-1840. His son, the Reverend Gardiner Vose, became professor of rhetoric at Amherst College. Letters of John Johnston, November 1859, and C. Kinsbury, 23 February 1860, cited in J. L. Williams, *Historical Sketch of the First Presbyterian Church, Fort Wayne, Indiana,* 11, 12, 26, 27.

7 Five great waves of Scotch-Irish emigrants came to America in the eighteenth century; at the end of the twentieth century they were the largest "minority" in the United States, after the English.

8 Paul W. Wehr, *James Hanna* (Fort Wayne: Fort Wayne Public Library, 1971), 15, 20, 54.

9 The American Sunday School Union, *Sixth Annual Report,* Philadelphia, May 1830, quoted in G. L Hartman, *A School for God's People: A History of the Sunday School Movement in Indiana* (Indianapolis: Central Publishing Company, Inc., 1980), 4.

10 Isaac Reed, *The Christian Traveler in Five Parts including Nine Years and Eighteen Thousand Miles* (New York: J. and J. Harper, 1828), 86-88. The Reverend John George Pfrimmer may have founded a Sunday school at Corydon, Indiana, in 1814. See Grover L. Hartman, *A School for God's People: A History of the Sunday School Movement in Indiana,* 8.

[11] J. L. Williams, *Historical Sketch of First Presbyterian Church, Fort Wayne,* 22.

[12] Hamilton had been born in County Tyrone, Ireland, in 1798. His father was an attorney who served as deputy clerk for the crown; when his health and fortunes failed, his fifteen-year-old son's dream of a law career was dashed. Determined that his fortunes were elsewhere, Hamilton secured passage on the cheapest boat to Quebec in 1817. After serving a term as clerk in Philadelphia, he journeyed west to Aurora, Indiana, where he learned something of the land business. At the urging of Samuel C. Vance, the first registrar of land titles, and Joseph Holman, the receiver of public money, Hamilton came to Fort Wayne. See Allen C. Wetmore, *Allen Hamilton: Evolution of a Frontier Capitalist* (Ball State University, Muncie, Ind.: dissertation, 1974).

[13] Allen Hamilton to Absalom Peters, 10 December 1828, AHMS.

[14] Ibid.

[15] On November 15, 1829, Furman signed the county marriage register: "Charles E. Furman, a regularly licensed minister of the Gospel." *Marriage Register,* Allen County Courthouse, Fort Wayne, Indiana.

[16] "In theory, the A. H. M. S. commissioners in Indiana, supported by Presbyterian and Congregational funds, might have been expected to aid and produce both Presbyterian and Congregational churches. In fact, most of the A. H. M. S. missionaries in Indiana related themselves to the presbyteries, and the large majority of the churches aided or founded in Indiana were Presbyterian." L. C. Rudolph, W. W. Wimberly, and Thomas W. Clayton, *Indiana Letters: Abstracts of Letters from Missionaries on the Indiana Frontier to the American Home Missionary Society, 1824-1893,* 3 vols. (Ann Arbor, Michigan: University Microfilms International, 1979), 1: 6.

[17] This schoolhouse, the first in Fort Wayne and called the "County Seminary," was built in 1825 on the west side of Calhoun Street, north of Water [Superior] Street. George W. Brackenridge recollected that, in 1830, "There were only two public buildings in the town. One was the schoolhouse, brick, about eighteen by twenty feet square, windows in front and west, large chimney in east end. One window on the northeast corner overlooked the river . . . . The furniture was very simple—benches without backs. Writing desks were boards pinned to the wall. It served for a number of years." *Fort Wayne News Sentinel,* 22 January 1883, reprinted in *Reminiscences of Old Fort Wayne,* compiled by L. C. Woodworth et al., comps., (Fort Wayne, Ind.: Fort Wayne Public Library, 1906), n. p.

[18] Charles E. Furman to Absalom Peters, 19 February 1830, AHMS.

[19] Ibid., 15 May 1830.

[20] Joseph M. Wilson, *Presbyterian Historical Almanac and Annual Remembrancer of the Church for 1867, Vol. 9* (Philadelphia: Joseph M. Wilson, 1867), 305.

[21] L. C. Rudolph, *Hoosier Zion* (New Haven: Yale University Press, 1963), 116.

[22] Charles E. Furman to Absalom Peters, 19 February 1830, AHMS. Charles Edwin Furman (born December 13, 1801, died June 10, 1880) went on to serve churches in Hamilton, Ont., Rochester, N. Y., Victor, N. Y., and Medina, N. Y. Upon retirement he returned to his wife's hometown of Rochester, N. Y., and published two books and poetry. Hamilton College conferred on him the degree of Doctor of Divinity in 1878. *Auburn Theological Seminary: General Biographical Catalogue, 1818-1918* (Auburn, N. Y.: Auburn Seminary Press, 1918), 33.

[23] *In Memoriam: Rev. James Chute* (Fort Wayne, Ind.: 1874), 2, 3. Chute's success as a teacher caught the attention of a group of philanthropists in Cincinnati who sent him to Hartford, Connecticut, to study under Dr. Thomas H. Gallaudet with the aim of establishing a school for the deaf. Upon the death of the principal benefactor, however, the project dissolved and Chute returned to resume teaching.

[24] *First Presbyt. Church Session Record No. 2: July 1, 1831 to April 20, 1845,* First Presbyterian Church Archives, Fort Wayne, Indiana.

[25] B. J. Griswold, *The Pictorial History of Fort Wayne, Indiana,* 2 vols. (Chicago: Robert O. Law Company, 1917), 1: 247, 273, 274, 295, 596. The other charter members of the First Presbyterian Church were Sally Vance, Ann Griggs, Eliza Hood, Jane Clinger, and Elizabeth Stinson. For details of Ann Turner's and Rebecca Hackley's relation to the Baptists, see chapters "Mission to the Miamis" and "Baptists."

[26] Hugh McCulloch to Eunice Hardy, 14 December 1833, Connie Hurni Collection, Hicksville, Ohio.

[27] *Fort Wayne Daily News,* 23 January 1880.

[28] James Chute to Absalom Peters, 20 September 1831, AHMS.

[29] Smalwood Noel to Absalom Peters, September 1831, AHMS.

[30] James Chute to Absalom Peters, 20 September 1831, AHMS.

[31] *In Memoriam: Rev. James Chute,* 3.

[32] Susan McCulloch wrote: "Mr. Hamilton lost a fine interesting little boy about 18 months old last week. He fell backwards into a tub of hot water just as his father was going to take him up and carry him out of the kitchen. They are in deep affliction. This is the fourth child they have lost out of five. . . . He united with the Presbyterian Church last Sabbath and appears to be an altered man." Susan McCulloch to Maria Halsey, 6 May 1840, McCulloch Papers, Lilly Li-

brary, Bloomington, Indiana.

33 *Ibid.,* 27 November 1836.

34 Chute "lived on the Maumee Road, this side of the Lutheran College," (near the present Chute St. and Maumee Ave). *Reminiscences of Oliver Jefferds* (1812-1900), Allen County Historical Society.

35 James Chute to Absalom Peters, 7 April 1832, AHMS.

36 Ibid., 12 December 1831, 27 January 1834. In Washington Township, Chute held the first religious meetings in the homes of Thomas Hatfield and David Archer; in St. Joseph Township, Christian Parker opened his residence to the early Presbyterian ministers; and in Perry Township, services were conducted in a cabin near Huntertown. T. B. Helm, *History of Allen County, Indiana* (Chicago: Kingman Brothers, 1880), 168, 173, 178. Chute was also requested by his presbytery "to visit Fort Defiance, about 50 miles down the Maumee." James Chute to Absolom Peters, 8 July 1835, AHMS.

37 The women's interest in promoting this work was noted by Chute: "By the aid of a pious female in Huntington, about 25 miles distance, we have prospect of extending the work." Ibid., 27 January 1834.

38 Ibid., 12 March 1832.

39 Chute reported 145 members in 1833. Ibid., 20 March 1833.

40 Ibid., 12 December 1831, 12 March 1832.

41 W. J. Rorabaugh, *The Alcoholic Republic, An American Tradition* (New York: Oxford University Press, 1979), 8.

42 Hugh McCulloch to Eunice Hardy, 17 August 1833, Connie Hurni Collection, Hicksville, Ohio.

43 James Chute to Absalom Peters, 12 December 1831, 12 March 1832, 13 June 1832, AHMS.

44 Ibid., 13 September 1832, 6 July 1833.

45 Hugh McCulloch to Eunice Hardy, 17 August 1833, Connie Hurni Collection, Hicksville, Ohio.

46 James Chute to Absalom Peters, 13 September 1832, 6 July 1833.

47 Williams's wife, Susan, was a Presbyterian. Hugh McCulloch to Eunice Hardy, 14 December 1833, Connie Hurni Collection, Hicksville, Ohio.

48 Hugh McCulloch, *Men and Measures of Half a Century* (New York: C. Scribner's Sons, 1880), 107.

49 James Chute to Absalom Peters, 17 December 1832 and 27 January 1834, AHMS. A German laborer, who came to the area in 1834, remembered his job selling whiskey to the canal workers: "I went to the feeder dam [at Fort Wayne]. . . . There were two brothers, both born in America but spoke German, who said I could stay with them—and that I could get $25 a month for only selling whiskey to the laborers, and to register them when they came to eat. . . . He said that his

brother was an alcoholic, so I got the job. I had to care for 125 men. I had my job for two and a half months. . . . I left Fortwein *(sic)* with disgust because the friends of our group had died there." Gottfried Weber, *Buch,* translated by Antonius Holtmann (Cincinnati: 1877), 12, original held by the Igel family, Engler, Ohio.

50 Hugh McCulloch, *Men and Measures of Half a Century*, 107.

51 D. W. Moffatt (funeral sermon), *Fort Wayne Sentinel,* 24 November 1880. Hugh McCulloch wrote that "Mrs. Wines is one of the best singers I ever heard. . . . [She and Mrs. Williams] are examples of industry and ingenuity. They rise about 4 o'clock and have breakfast before day." Hugh McCulloch to Eunice Hardy, 14 December 1833, Connie Hurni Collection, Hicksville, Ohio.

52 James Chute to Absalom Peters, 12 September 1833, AHMS. Martha Hewes Chute died on August 18, 1833, at the age of thirty-eight, and was buried at the Chute homestead on Maumee Road.

53 John W. Dawson, *Dawson's Daily Times,* 24 July 1860.

54 Robertson, Robert S., *History of the Maumee River Basin, Allen County, Indiana* [vol. 2 of *History of the Maumee River Basin from the Earliest Account to Its Organization into Counties,* edited by Charles Elihu Slocum] (Indianapolis: Bowen and Slocum, 1905), 2: 522-524.

55 J. L. Williams, *Historical Sketch of First Presbyterian Church, Fort Wayne,* 18, 28.

56 James Chute to Absalom Peters, 17 March 1835, AHMS.

57 Smalwood Noel to Absalom Peters, 18 September 1833, AHMS.

58 "Brother Morrell and wife. . . on their way to the St. Joseph Country" and "Brother Samuel Lowry, agent." James Chute to Absalom Peters, 27 January 1834 and 26 September 1834, AHMS.

59 *In Memoriam: Rev. James Chute,* 4.

60 James Chute to Absalom Peters, 26 September 1834, AHMS. Ann Wells Turner, in whose home the mid-week prayer meeting was held, died July 27, 1834.

61 Ibid., 12 December 1835.

62 *In Memoriam: Rev. James Chute,* 5. Sometime after 1838, James and Martha Chute's remains were reinterred in the Broadway Cemetery; when the neglected graveyard became a park in 1886, they were removed to Lindenwood Cemetery, section G, lot 130.

63 *Ibid.* Mary Chute later moved to Crawfordsville, Indiana, for the benefit of her children's education; she died there in 1862.

64 J. L. Williams, *Historical Sketch of First Presbyterian Church, Fort Wayne, Indiana,* 20.

65 Joseph W. Wilson, *The Presbyterian Historical Almanac and Annual Remembrancer of the Church for 1867, vol. 9,* 304-306.

66 Daniel Jones to Absalom Peters, 27 October 1836, February 1837, 26 April 1837, AHMS. In 1840, Jones was serving churches in Illinois; three years later he went to Keokuk, Iowa; in 1847, he returned to Fort Wayne, where his son Silas C. Jones lived, purchased land and built a house. In 1848, he "supplied the pulpit of Charles Beecher for several Sabbaths" at the Second Presbyterian Church; in early 1849, he was serving as an A. H. M. S. missionary to "eight preaching places over fifty miles in Allen and Whitley County" (including the newly organized congregations at Flat Rock and Troy); by mid-1849, he had departed for California. In 1854, he was in Michigan; without employment in 1859, he lectured on astronomy with a magic lantern; in November 1861, he settled with his family on a farm near Fort Wayne where he died December 12, 1863. He was married four times and had nine children. Joseph W. Wilson, *The Presbyterian Historical Almanac and Annual Remembrancer of the Church for 1867, vol. 9,* 304-306; Daniel Jones to Charles Hall, 9 February 1849 and 5 March 1848, AHMS; James H. Robinson to Charles Hall, 20 June 1848, AHMS.

67 For the story of Jesse Hoover in Fort Wayne, see chapter "Lutherans."

68 Proceedings of the Detroit Presbytery, meeting at Pontiac, Mich., 6 July 1837, printed in the *Michigan Observer,* quoted in letter of Hugh McCulloch to Susan Man, 29 September 1837, McCulloch Papers.

69 Hugh McCulloch to Susan Man, 29 September 1837, McCulloch Papers.

70 George W. Brackenridge in the *Fort Wayne News Sentinel,* 22 January 1883, reprinted in *Reminiscences of Old Fort Wayne,* L. C. Woodworth et al., comps., n. p.

71 B. J. Griswold, *The Pictorial History of Fort Wayne,* 1: 341. The following year McJunkin built his own school house on the east side of Lafayette Street between Berry and Wayne Streets, and for many years was the most prominent school teacher in the city. He soon married and became a leader in the community, serving on the Common Council in 1848 and 1849, and as treasurer of school districts No. 1 and No. 2 in 1852. McJunkin closed his school in 1852 to became treasurer of the Pittsburgh, Fort Wayne, and Chicago Railroad. His schoolhouse was occasionally used by the Episcopalians, Methodists, and Baptists before they built churches; in 1853, the school trustees leased the facility to open, in the "east end," the city's first "free school."

72 Charles R. Poinsatte, *Fort Wayne During the Canal Era 1828-1855* (Indianapolis: Indiana Historical Bureau, 1969), 152.

73 Hugh McCulloch to Susan Man, 19 September 1837, McCulloch Papers.

74 Ibid., 26 November 1837. William Lloyd Garrison was editor of the *Liberator,* which advocated the immediate emancipation of slaves and opposed the scheme of African colonization; Garrison also attacked war, alcoholic liquors and tobacco, freemasonry, capital punishment, and imprisonment for debt.

75 Ibid., 7 December 1837.

76 Susan Man, Plattsburg, New York, to Hugh McCulloch, 29 January 1838, McCulloch Papers. Susan also complained about the preaching in Plattsburg: "Mr. Newton is so dull that I have no patience to hear him. . . . If Alida [Hubbell] and myself were in Fort Wayne this winter we should take some comforts in going to church and hearing a good sermon." When she returned to Fort Wayne, she was not disappointed and said of Rankin, "We have an excellent minister who preaches interesting sermons." Susan Man McCulloch to Marie Halsey, 21 February 1839, McCulloch Papers.

77 Alexander T. Rankin was born December 4, 1803; he married Mary Merriweather Lowry in 1829.

78 John Rankin, *Life of Rev. John Rankin: Written by Himself in his Eightieth Year* (1873), Western Reserve Historical Society, Cleveland, Ohio (typescript copy), 59-60.

79 *Philanthropist* (Cincinnati, Ohio), 25 February 1837; reprinted in the *Friend of Man* (Utica, New York), 29 March 1837.

80 *Proceedings of the Indiana Convention, Assembled to Organize a State Anti-Slavery Society, held in Milton,Wayne Co., September 12th, 1838* (Cincinnati: Samuel A. Alley, 1838), 7, 10.

81 Jesse Hoover to Susan Man, 11 November 1837, McCulloch Papers.

82 *Fort Wayne Sentinel,* 19 August 1843.

83 Alexander T. Rankin to Milton Badger, 4 September 1838, AHMS.

84 See chapter "Lutherans" for Rankin's activities in behalf of Lutheran pastors.

85 Alexander T. Rankin to Milton Badger, 29 February 1840, AHMS.

86 An "interesting time" was when a heightened "interest" in religious matters became manifest.

87 Alexander T. Rankin to Milton Badger, 31 March 1840, AHMS.

88 Claims that the Catholic Church was Fort Wayne's first completed religious facility are not supported by the testimony of any early resident: John S. Irwin writes of "the Presbyterian Church—the first church edifice in the city"; George W. Brackenridge states, "The first church erected

and completed was the Presbyterian." See *Fort Wayne News Sentinel,* January 22, 1883; T. B. Helm, *History of Allen County, Indiana,* 93; and Thomas J. Cramton, "The First Church Building in Fort Wayne," *Old Fort Bulletin* (Fort Wayne: Allen County-Fort Wayne Historical Society, January-February 1976).

89 Susan Man to Mary Hawkins, 27 October 1836, McCulloch Papers.

90 Jesse Hoover to Susan Man, 10 November 1837, McCulloch Papers.

91 In 1842, the county grand jury reported: "The courthouse itself is comparatively a heap of ruins. . . . The only place in the county that can be obtained to hold court is a [Presbyterian] church used for religious worship, the privilege of which was granted with reluctance and is now about to be refused." B. J. Griswold, *Pictorial History of Fort Wayne, Indiana,* 1: 355.

92 George W. Brackenridge in the *Fort Wayne News Sentinel,* 22 January 1883, reprinted in *Reminiscences of Old Fort Wayne,* L. C. Woodworth et al., comps., n. p.

93 Alexander T. Rankin to Milton Badger, 29 February 1840, AHMS.

94 Ibid., 3 September 1840.

95 *Minutes of the General Assembly of the Presbyterian Church, 1837,* 442.

96 See chapter: "New School Presbyterians"

97 John Rankin wrote that their mother "felt that dancing was a sinful practice. . . opposed the use of whiskey and tobacco, and she zealously spoke against Free Masonry. Her opposition to these evils made a lasting impression." John Rankin, *Life of Rev. John Rankin: Written by Himself in his Eightieth Year* (1873), 4.

98 Signed "P. M. Mills," *Fort Wayne Sentinel,* 10 April 1841.

99 "A. B." (pseud.), "Letters From Indiana - No. IV," *Fort Wayne Sentinel,* 14 May 1842. This was the fourth of seven essays signed "A. B"; the unknown author, originally from the East, had lived in Fort Wayne for ten years and was an acknowledged church attender.

In Dayton, Ohio, Rankin had observed that "the Masonic fraternity have taken in their heads that abolition is connected with anti-masonry. . . . [but] many of this body are zealous advocates of anti-slavery." *Philanthropist* (Cincinnati, Ohio), 25 February 1837; reprinted in the *Friend of Man* (Utica, New York), 29 March 1837.

100 Alexander T. Rankin to Milton Badger, 7 April 1839, AHMS.

101 Ibid., 15 February 1838.

102 *Fort Wayne Sentinel,* 10 April 1841.

103 *First Presbyt. Church Session Record No. 2: July 1, 1831 to April 20, 1845,* 9 February 1839.

104 *Ibid.,* 20 November 1841.

105 Farrand was appointed by the session as an assistant to the new chorister, O. W. Jeffords, "for improvement in singing." *Ibid.,* 22 June 1839.

106 Noel was a convinced teetotaler: when his daughter, Sarah, was married, "a troop of boys came about the house . . . and gave them a chevaree . . . but they were temperance people and, therefore, did not give them a treat." Susan Man to Marie Halsey, 27 November 1836, McCulloch Papers.

107 *First Presbyt. Church Session Record No. 2: July 1, 1831 to April 20, 1845,* 20 November 1841.

108 *The Constitution of the Presbyterian Church in the United State of America,* "Form of Government," ch. 13, iv, 5; ch. 14, xii, 6 (Utica, New York: William Williams, 1822), 367, 379.

109 *First Presbyt. Church Session Record No. 2: July 1, 1831 to April 20, 1845,* 15 February 1843.

110 *Ibid,* 3 April 1843

111 *Ibid.,* 4 April 1843,

112 *Ibid.,* 9 and 12 February 1844.

113 "A. B." (pseud.), "Letters from Indiana - No. III," *Fort Wayne Sentinel,* 30 April 1842. This was the third in the series of seven articles, and touched on the state of religion in Fort Wayne; the anonymous author mentioned no other clergyman by name.

114 Charles Poinsatte, in *Fort Wayne During the Canal Era,* suggests Hugh McCulloch as the author of "Letters From Indiana." McCulloch was an admirer of Rankin's rationalistic style, and it is doubtful that he would ever have used such pious, evangelical phrases as "winning souls to Christ" and "the love of the Saviour." Compare A. B.'s essay with McCulloch's description of Henry Ward Beecher in *Men and Measures of Half a Century.*

115 See chapter "Catholics" for details of Rankin's challenge.

116 "A. B." (pseud.), "Letters from Indiana - No. III," *Fort Wayne Sentinel,* 30 April 1842.

117 "A. B." (pseud.), "Letters From Indiana - No. IV," *Fort Wayne Sentinel,* 14 May 1842.

118 Steevens was born in England in 1800 and came to America in 1832; the following year his daughter Kezia was born in New York; the family moved to Fort Wayne in late 1836 or early 1837. By the late 1850s, "Humpy" Steevens had discontinued teaching to form a law partnership with W. S. Smith, and in 1859 was named a Justice of the Peace. His last residence in Fort Wayne, according to the 1867 *City Directory,* was at a boarding house; there is no local obituary.

119 *Fort Wayne Sentinel,* 14 January 1843. Rankin and Steevens had previously debated "on the 'Wine Question.'" *Ibid* 10 July 1841.

120 Steevens wrote to his sister in England: "All America is crazy on the *cold water* system—they are so *intemperately* intemperate that they count it a sin for a man to drink a glass of beer with his dinner—and in their misguided zeal are consigning many a nursing mother to a premature grave." William W. Steevens to "little sister Mary," 3 May 1844, William W. Steevens Letters, Allen County-Fort Wayne Historical Society, Fort Wayne, Indiana.

121 "A. B." (pseud.), "Letters from Indiana - No. III," *Fort Wayne Sentinel,* 30 April 1842.

122 "A. B." (pseud.), "Letters From Indiana - No. IV," *Fort Wayne Sentinel,* 14 May 1842.

123 The first trustees were Samuel Hanna, Charles E. Sturgis, Allen Hamilton, John E. Hill, and John Cochran.

124 Duties for the sexton, Aaron Mershon, were later detailed by the trustees: "The sexton shall ring the bell at all meetings, twice when there is preaching and once for all other meetings and whenever an alarm of fire is given. It shall be his duty to scrub the church once a quarter and always on Friday preceding the communion Sabbath; to sweep and dust the church every Saturday. It shall be his duty to fill, clean and light the lamps when necessary and attend the fires and see that the house is comfortable, the wood to be furnished in the basement, ready for burning. He is to be allowed extra for scrubbing the house." *First Presbty. Church Trustees Record No.1: Apr. 12, 1843 to Dec. 22, 1868,* 12 December 1845, First Presbyterian Church Archives, Fort Wayne, Indiana.

125 *First Presbyt. Church Trustees Record No.1: Apr. 12, 1843 to Dec. 22, 1868,* 12 April 1843.

126 By the end of October, 1843 Rankin had received only half of the two hundred dollars still owed him.

127 *First Presbyt. Church Session Record No. 2: July 1, 1831 to April 20, 1845,* 24 August 1843.

128 Julia Doak Lowry was the daughter of the Reverend John Montgomery and the widow of the Reverend Adam Lowrie.

129 Rankin's second wife was Mrs. Annie Burt Smith; she died October 1865. He married Annie P. Kelly of Buffalo, New York, in 1872; she died in 1873.

130 Elizabeth Wines (Mrs. Marshall), Springfield, Indiana, to Susan C. Williams (Mrs. Jesse), Fort Wayne, 19 February 1845, Allen County-Fort Wayne Historical Society. Rankin's brother, John, wrote: "I am pleased to hear of your happy circumstance." John Rankin to A. T. Rankin, 25 December 1845, *Antislavery Papers,* Clements Library, Ann Arbor, Michigan.

131 In 1860 Rankin was sent to Colorado by the Presbyterian (Old School) Home Mission Board; in Denver, there was later erected a monument inscribed: "The Reverend Alexander Taylor Rankin organized the first church (Presbyterian) in Denver on September 5, 1860." Rankin's zeal for the cause of abolition led him to speak at many Civil War meetings; a letter to his youngest son, serving in the Union Army, was published and widely distributed. After the war he served churches in Buffalo and Baltimore. In 1878, Tusculum College conferred on him the degree of Doctor of Divinity. At the age of seventy-eight he returned to Fort Wayne in the fall of 1881 for the observance of the fiftieth anniversary of the founding of the First Presbyterian Church. While attending this celebration he was invited to preach at Hanging Rock in Lawrence County, Ohio, where he remained until the fall of 1884, when he contracted malaria while helping during the great flood of that year. He died at his daughter's home in Baltimore on April 20, 1885, and was buried in Buffalo, New York. *Diary of Alexander T. Rankin,* State Historical Society of Colorado, Denver; Andrew E. Murray, *The Skyline Synod; Presbyterianism in Colorado and Utah* (Denver: Golden Bell Press, 1971), 48-52; Mary Burt Rankin, *A. T. Rankin* (manuscript, 1957), Chapman House, Ripley, Ohio.

Chapter 3

1 B. J. Griswold erroneously asserts (and Poinsatte reasserts) that the Reverend James B. Finley, a Methodist missionary to the Wyandott tribe in Ohio, visited "the village [Fort Wayne] during the period of the distribution of the annuities to the savages" in 1819; Finley's autobiography, however, makes no mention of his ever visiting this area, and Griswold's citation from the book is mistakenly attributed to Fort Wayne. Compare James B. Finley, *Life Among the Indians* (Cincinnati: Cranston & Curts, 1857), 518-519, with B. J. Griswold, *The Pictorial History of Fort Wayne, Indiana* (Chicago: Robert O. Law Company, 1917), 1: 248, and Charles Poinsatte, *Outpost in the Wilderness: Fort Wayne, 1706-1828* (Fort Wayne: Allen County-Fort Wayne Historical Society, 1976), 85.

2 Allen Hamilton to Absalom Peters, 10 December 1828, AHMS. These early Methodist ministers mentioned by Hamilton may have been "local" or lay preachers from neighboring townships: "In the Maumee settlement in Adams township . . . services were conducted by Reuben Nickerson, of the Methodist Episcopal church, in 1828, and he was followed by Rev. James B. Austin." Robert S. Robertson, *Valley of the Upper Maumee River* (Madison, Wis.: Brant & Fuller, 1889), 1: 457.

3 Allen Hamilton to Absalom Peters, 10 December 1828, AHMS.

4 *The Doctrines and Discipline of the Methodist Epis-*

copal Church (New York: T. Mason and G. Lane, 1836), 55. William Warren Sweet, *Methodism in American History* (New York: Abingdon Press, l933, rev. 1953), 221. Goodwin kept his convictions and utilized his education as editor of a newspaper dedicated to "fight the saloon and slavery."

5 "Licensed preachers" or "exhorters" were neither under the appointive power of the bishop nor a member of the conference; they functioned primarily as laymen and could not serve beyond their local mission area. As a licensed preacher, Holman was authorized to officiate at weddings and funerals.

6 Joseph Holman, in a letter quoted by A. S. Johns in his *Sketch of Early Methodism in Fort Wayne* (Fort Wayne, Indiana: 30 August 1901), 5, Allen County-Fort Wayne Historical Society.

7 William Warren Sweet, *Circuit-Rider Days in Indiana* (Indianapolis: W. K. Stewart Co., 1916), 22, 23.

8 The Presiding Elder was a minister in charge of the several circuits and stations constituting a District, later termed District Superintendent.

9 Stephen R. Beggs, *Pages from the Early History of the West and Northwest* (Cincinnati: Methodist Book Concern, 1868), 81, 208, quoted in Earl L. Carvin, "The Methodist Church in Fort Wayne, Indiana," in *History of the First Wayne Street United Methodist Church, Fort Wayne, Indiana* (Fort Wayne Public Library Pamphlet, 1975), 5. Portland was then an important trading center situated between Attica and Covington.

10 Joseph Holman, a letter quoted by A. S. Johns in *Sketch of Early Methodism in Fort Wayne,* 5.

11 John C. Smith, *Early Methodism in Indiana* (Indianapolis: J. M. Olcott, 1879), 38-39. Strange, a native of Virginia, was born in 1789; he ministered in Ohio for thirteen years and, in 1824, came to Indiana; he died in 1833.

12 Charles Furman to Absalom Peters, 19 February 1830, AHMS. Furman had arrived November 13, 1829.

13 Journal of the Illinois Conference of the Methodist Episcopal Church, 6 October 1830, cited in W. W. Sweet, *Religion on the American Frontier* (Chicago: University of Chicago Press, 1946), vol. 4, quoted in *History of the First Wayne Street United Methodist Church,* 4.

14 F. C. Holliday, *Indiana Methodism* (Cincinnati: Hitchcock and Walden, 1873), 112.

15 Frederick A. Norwood, *History of the North Indiana Conference, 1917-1956,* vol. 2 (Winona Lake, Indiana: Light and Life Press, 1957), 23. Griffith died in St. Joseph County, August 22, 1834.

16 James Chute to Absalom Peters, 12 March 1832, AHMS; A. S. Johns, *Sketch of Early Methodism in Fort Wayne,* 6.

17 Born in 1789, Wiley was baptized at the age of

twenty-three; in 1811, he was given a permit to "exhort" and two years later he received a local preacher's licence. In 1818, Wiley was appointed to the Whitewater charge; in 1828, he was named presiding elder of the new Madison District, which included the old Whitewater circuit and extended north to Fort Wayne. He died in Vevey, Indiana, in 1848.

18 F. C. Holliday, *Indiana Methodism,* 76. See F. C. Holliday, *Life and Times of Allen Wiley, A.M.* (Cincinnati: S. Swormstedt & A. Poe, 1853), 62.

19 *Fort Wayne Sentinel,* 21 and 23 October 1871.

20 The root of "giddy" is the Old English "goddy," meaning "God possessed;" "enthusiastic" is from the Greek "en theos," meaning "in God."

21 *Western Christian Advocate,* 20 October 1846.

22 Seth Mead, comp., *Hymns and Spiritual Songs* (Richmond, 1807), hymn 107.

23 *The Letters of the Rev. John Wesley, A. M.,* John Telford, ed. (London: Epworth Press, 1931), quoted in E. Dale Dunlap, *The System of Itineracy in American Methodism* (typescript), DePauw University Archives, Greencastle, Indiana, 5.

24 *The Journal and Letters of Francis Asbury,* Elmer T. Clark, J. Manning Potts, and Jacob L. Payton, ed. (Nashville: Abingdon Press, 1958), 1: 16.

25 *The Methodist Magazine,* vol. 25 (1843), 278, cited in James David Lynn, *The Concept of Ministry in the Methodist Episcopal Church, 1784-1844* (Ann Arbor: University Microfilms, 1973), 223.

26 James Chute to Absalom Peters, 12 December 1831, AHMS.

27 Joseph Holman wrote: "Soon after I came here I was appointed a school trustee, and proceeded to collect monies to build a school house . . . with the understanding that all orthodox preachers of whatever denomination should have privilege of preaching there, when not interfering with school hours." A. S. Johns, *Sketch of Early Methodism in Fort Wayne,* 6.

28 *Ibid.,* 2.

29 A. Marine, "Methodist Episcopal Church," in T. B. Helm, *History of Allen County* (Chicago: Kingman Brothers, 1880), 96.

30 W. G. Ewing to William Hood, 15 April 1834, Allen County-Fort Wayne Historical Society. Ewing noted that the congregation also planned to use part of the land as a cemetery and commented, "I should like to see a Church . . . its erection will add to the beauty of our. . . property." He also suggested that the terms might be a "lease for 99 years"; apparently that land reverted to the Ewings after the failure of the project.

31 James Chute to Absalom Peters, 14 March, 8 July

1835, AHMS.

32 *Fort Wayne Daily Sentinel,* 15 March 1872.

33 *Dawson's Daily Times,* 24 July 1860.

34 *Trustee Minute Book of the M. E. Church, March 24, 1846-February 7, 1870,* 32, Allen County-Fort Wayne Historical Society, Fort Wayne, Indiana.

35 William Warren Sweet, *Circuit Rider Days in Indiana,* 67.

36 *Western Christian Advocate,* 22 July 1836.

37 Susan Man to Mrs. Frederick Halsey, 19 September 1836, McCulloch Papers, Lilly Library, Bloomington, Indiana. Hargrave, a native of North Carolina, was born in 1803, licensed to preach in 1821, served in Indiana all of his life, and died in 1879. He was remembered by one colleague as a strong preacher: "We visited a man in a jail at Springfield . . . . [On] the day the man was hanged, in November, 1826, Hargrave stood and delivered the greatest exhortation I ever heard, to the thousands of people then assembled." After 1827, Hargrave was "often . . . in one of his blue moods . . . he could not help it . . . he was dyspeptic." Joseph Tarkington, *Autobiography, Written in 1887* (Cincinnati: Curts & Jennings, 1899), 108

38 R. Hargrave to Hugh McCulloch, 13 April 1835, McCulloch Papers.

39 Hugh McCulloch to Susan Man, 12 November 1837, McCulloch Papers.

40 "These station appointments were much coveted by Methodist preachers. Indeed it was almost as much an honor to receive a station appointment as it was to be made a presiding elder over an entire district." Elizabeth K. Nottingham, *Methodism and the Frontier: Indiana Proving Ground* (New York: Columbia University Press, 1941), 75.

41 A. S. Johns, *Sketch of Early Methodism in Fort Wayne,* 3, 8; *The Doctrines and Discipline of the Methodist Episcopal Church* (New York: T. Mason and G. Lane, 1836), 156. Johns lists the members of the congregation in 1837 as Mr. and Mrs. Robert Brackenridge, Mr. and Mrs. Oliver Fairfield, Mr. and Mrs Henry Work, Mr. and Mrs. Joseph Bushey, Mrs. Samuel Edsall, Mrs. John P. Watters, Miss Eliza Hamilton, Mrs. Stapleford and her children Thomas, Edward, Mary, and Elizabeth.

42 B. J. Griswold, *The Pictorial History of Fort Wayne, Indiana,* 339. John W. Dawson recollected: "Near the northeast corner of Harrison and Main [were] a few small shanties, among which was the pottery of Reverend Stephen R. Ball of the Methodist Church." *Fort Wayne Daily Sentinel,* 23 March 1872.

43 *Fort Wayne Times,* 29 November 1844.

44 *Ibid.,* 17 May 1845.

45 Colclazer was born in Washington, D. C., in 1813; in 1836, he was licensed to preach by the Reverend Richard Hargrave; he served the Berry Street Church in 1874, and died at Kendallville in 1885. *Minutes of the North Indiana Conference, 1886,* 68.

46 Methodism recognized "ten classes of officers: Bishops, presiding elders, elders, deacons, local preachers, exhorters, class-leaders, stewards, Sunday-school superintendents, and trustees." Appendix to the *Catechism of the Methodist Episcopal Church, No. 1* (New York: Hunt and Easton, 1884), 32.

47 A. S. Johns, *Sketch of Early Methodism in Fort Wayne,* 3. Jesse Williams wrote: "The first Sabbath School in this place was organized in 1825, by James Hanna, an elder in the church of Dayton, then on a visit to his children residing here. For some years all Protestant denominations united in the work. In 1840, the Methodists and Lutherans, and in 1842, the Baptists established separate schools in connection with their respective churches." The school met in the First Presbyterian Church, then the only English-speaking Protestant church in town. *Historical Sketch of the First Presbyterian Church, Fort Wayne Indiana* (Fort Wayne: John W. Dawson, 1860), 23.

48 *The Doctrines and Discipline of the Methodist Episcopal Church* (New York: T. Mason and G. Lane, 1836), 155.

49 Charles H. Titus, *Travel Journal: 1843,* Henry E. Huntington Library, San Marino, California (Manuscript HM 29181). See "Through Indiana by Stagecoach and Canal Boat: The 1843 Travel Journal of Charles Titus," edited by George P. Clark, *Indiana Magazine of History,* vol. 85 (September 1989), 229.

50 A. S. Johns, *Sketch of Early Methodism in Fort Wayne,* 9.

51 Ahrens was born November 18, 1811, in Drackenburg, Hannover, which he described as a "village on the banks of the Weser." Adam Miller, *Experience of German Methodist Preachers* (Cincinnati: Methodist Book Concern, 1859), 105.

52 Nast was born in Stuttgart, Germany, June 15, 1807, and was educated at the local Latin School and later at Vaihingen an der Erz.

53 Albert J. Nast, *Souvenir of the Ninetieth Anniversary of the Organization of German Methodism* (Cincinnati: Nast Memorial Church, 4-9 September 1928), 14.

54 *Minutes of the Annual Conferences of the Methodist Episcopal Church for the Years 1839-1840 to 1841-1842* (New York: T. Mason and G. Lane, 1840 et. al.). Because the Indiana Conference minutes make no mention of the Fort Wayne German Mission after 1841, W. W. Sweet (in *Circuit Rider Days in Indiana,* 81) mistakenly concluded that it had been abandoned. After 1841, the German appointments for Fort Wayne were reported to the new Cincinnati German

District, and published annually in the Ohio Conference minutes. (Charles Poinsatte, in *Fort Wayne During the Canal Era*, 161, repeats Sweet's error.)

55 *Deutscher Kalender für das Jahr 1902 . . . der Central Deutschen Konferenz der Bischöflichen Methodistenkirche* (Cincinnati: Jennings and Pyne, 1902), 95, "Memoiren."

56 F. K. D. Wyneken, *Die Noth der Deutschen Lutheraner in Nordamerika,* first published in *Zeitschrift fuer Protestantismus und Kirche* (Erlangen: 1843); reprinted in Pittsburgh, Pa. (1844). S. Edgar Schmidt, trans., *The Distress of the German Lutherans in North America,* edited by R. F. Rehmer (Fort Wayne: Concordia Theological Seminary Press, 1982), 32, 34, 38, 51.

57 G. E. Hageman, *Friedrich Konrad Dietrich Wyneken: Pioneer Lutheran Missionary of the Nineteenth Century,* in the series *Men and Missions, III,* L. Fuerbringer, ed. (St. Louis: Concordia Publishing House, 1926), 44.

58 H. G. Sauer and J. W. Miller, *Geschichte der Deutschen Ev.-Luth. St. Pauls-Gemeinde zu Fort Wayne, Ind., vom Jahre 1837 bis zum Jahre 1912* (St. Louis: Concordia Publishing House, 1887 and 1912), 28.

59 Wilhelm Sihler, *Gespräche zwischen zwie Lutheranern über den Methodismus,* 4th ed. (St. Louis: M. C. Barthel, 1878); English edition: *A Conversation Between Two Lutherans on Methodism* (St. Louis: Publishing House of the Evangelical Lutheran Church of Mo., Ohio and other States, 1877). For an analysis of Sihler on Methodism see Lewis W. Spitz, *Life in Two Worlds: Biography of William Sihler* (St. Louis: Concordia Publishing House, 1968), 164-171.

60 The Reverend Karl Schelper may have served during this time. Born in Bovington, Hannover, he immigrated with his wife in 1836, settled in Wheeling, West Virginia, and served congregations in Dayton and Madison before coming to Fort Wayne. He retired to New Albany, Indiana, and died September 4, 1865. C. Golder, John H. Horst, J. G. Schaal, *Geschichte der Zentral Deutschen Konferenz, Einschiesslich der Unsangsgeschichte des deutschen Methodismus* (Cincinnati: Jenning & Graham, 1907), 267; Julie M. Overton, *The Ministers and Churches of the Central German Conference (Methodist)* (Thomson, Ill.: Heritage House, 1975), 38.

61 Signed "L. Muhlfinger," *Fort Wayne Times,* 28 November 1846.

62 Ahrens had served at Louisville (1842), Cincinnati (1843-45), and Pittsburgh (1846) until his appointment as presiding elder in the fall of 1846. He later ministered to churches in Ohio, Kentucky, and Indianapolis. Ahrens established the Christian Relief Association, began the German Tract Association, and was the principle founder of an orphanage in Berea, Ohio. He died at the age of eighty-nine.

Among his publications were *Der Universal-Konflikt swischen Gut and Böse* (Cincinnati: 1902); *Die Taufe in Lichte de Bibel* (Cincinnati: 1869); and *Beetrachtungen über die biblische Geschichte* (Cincinnati: 1852). *Deutscher Kalender für das Jahr 1902 . . . der Central Deutschen Konferenz der Bischöflichen Methodistenkirche,* "Memoiren," 95,

63 The first three German Districts were "Cincinnati" (which in 1844 encompassed Fort Wayne); "Pittsburgh," in the Ohio Conference; and "St. Louis," in the Missouri Conference. Separate German conferences were established in 1864. See Paul F. Douglass, *The Story of German Methodism: Biography of an Immigrant Soul* (Cincinnati: Methodist Book Concern, 1939).

64 "Minutes of the Indiana Conference 1832-1844," cited in William W. Sweet, *Circuit Rider Days in Indiana,* 2: 315.

65 Fort Wayne German Methodists were in the Cincinnati District until the fall of 1846, when the North-Ohio District was established.

66 Joseph K. Edgerton was born in Vergennes, Vermont, in 1818; he was admitted to the bar of New York City, moved to Fort Wayne in the spring of 1844, and joined in a law partnership with Samuel Bigger, and later Charles Case. Edgerton became a large landowner, was named president of the Fort Wayne and Chicago Railroad in 1857, and was elected to Congress in 1862; later he established the Fort Wayne Steel Plow Works and was President of the Fort Wayne Medical College.

67 Joseph K. Edgerton, *Private Journal No. 3, Commenced October 27, 1843,* summer 1844 and 22 December 1844, 170, 248, Allen County Public Library, Fort Wayne, Indiana.

68 Beers was born on Long Island, New York, in 1810, was licensed to preach in 1836, and served the Wayne Street Church in 1854; he died at Goshen, Indiana in 1873. *Minutes of the North Indiana Conference, 1874,* 54.

69 George Milton Boyd had served as pastor of the local congregation in 1842. Born in 1814 in Lewis County, Kentucky, he was licensed to preach at the age of twenty; he served as presiding elder of the Fort Wayne District from 1843 to 1846; Boyd died in Valparaiso, Indiana, in 1890. *Minutes of the North Indiana Conference, 1890.*

70 The "old Pole" was the Reverend John Jacob Lehmanowsky. See William A. Sadtler, *Under Two Captains* (Philadelphia: General Council Press, 1902), 218.

71 Bishop Hamline was traveling with his wife in a two-horse wagon from Detroit to Cincinnati, and had arranged to visit in Fort Wayne during the Conference. Joseph Tarkington, *Autobiography,* 144.

72 When Simpson next returned to preach at the Meth-

odist Church, a local editor wrote, "All who wish for a 'feast of reason and eloquence' will hear him, of course. He is emphatically one of the great men of the day." *Fort Wayne Times,* 11 July 1846.

73 Joseph K. Edgerton, "Private Journal No. 3," July to October 1844, 173-225.

74 In 1830, Methodists protesting the exclusion of laymen from the Conferences withdrew to form the Methodist Protestant Church, which enfranchised "white, lay, male members . . . [of] twenty-one years." *Constitution and Discipline of the Methodist Protestant Church* (Baltimore: Book Committee of the Methodist Protestant Church, 1853), 29. A Methodist Protestant Church in New Haven, Indiana, was dedicated on November 7, 1858. At the 1856 M. E. General Conference, a resolution to allow lay members some share in governance of the church was defeated; at the 1856 North Indiana Conference, limited lay participation on the Committee on Finance was approved.

75 J. L. Smith, *Indiana Methodism* (Valparaiso, 1892), 114.

76 *Fort Wayne Sentinel,* 25 October 1844.

77 *The Doctrines and Discipline of the Methodist Episcopal Church* (New York: T. Mason and G. Lane, 1836), 188. Herrick and Sweet, *A History of the North Indiana Conference,* vol. 1 (Indianapolis: W. K. Stewart Company, 1917), 8. See *Western Christian Advocate,* 29 November 1844.

78 A "whole fall" was a flap extending across the front to side seams; a "narrow fall" was a smaller, central flap, similar to sailor pants.

79 Thomas A. Goodwin, in his "Introduction" to Joseph Tarkington, *Autobiography,* 16. Goodwin concluded, "[B]ut more and more, from that [time] on, preachers dressed as they pleased, so that the cut of the coat or pants is no longer a distinguishing badge of a Methodist preacher."

80 Joseph K. Edgerton, "Private Journal No. 3," 10 November and 22 December 1844, 21 December 1845. Edgerton resigned from the Board of Trustees of the Berry Street Methodist Church in 1849 and was elected a vestryman of Trinity Episcopal Church in 1851.

81 The fair was held "at the store on Columbia Street, lately occupied by T. D. Lewis." *Fort Wayne Times,* 4 December 1846.

82 John W. Dawson recollected that, in 1838, "the most important days of the year were New Year, Fourth of July, Indian Payment Day, and Christmas." *Dawson's Daily Times,* 7 July 1860.

83 John Adams to Abigail Adams, 3 July 1776.

84 *Fort Wayne Sentinel,* June 26, 1841. The American House was a hotel on Columbia Street, erected in 1836.

85 *Fort Wayne Times,* 12, 19, and 26 July 1845.

86 *Fort Wayne Sentinel,* 11 July 1846.

87 "An Address: Delivered at the anniversary celebration of the Methodist Episcopal Sabbath School in the City of Fort Wayne, Jan. 27, 1845. By Joseph K. Edgerton." *Fort Wayne Times,* 8 March 1845.

88 *Fort Wayne Sentinel,* 4 October 1845.

89 *Trustee Minute Book of the M. E. Church, March 24, 1846-February 7, 1870,* 7 April 1846, 13.

90 Also consenting to serve on committees were Benjamin Mason, George Johnson, G. Hartman, W. G. Ewing, and Thomas Hamilton.

91 *Fort Wayne Times,* 26 July 1846.

92 Charles Beecher to Milton Badger, 3 May 1848, AHMS.

93 *Fort Wayne Times,* 19 June 1847.

94 *Ibid.,* 13 April 1845; *Fort Wayne Sentinel,* 4 October 1845; *Fort Wayne Times,* 28 March 1845 and 20 June 1846. After Bayless, the College Agents were J. H. Bruce (1847), S. C. Cooper and Amasa Johnson (1848), Ancil Beach (1849), Amasa Johnson and J. G. D. Pettijohn (1850), O. V. Lemon (1851), Lawson W. Monson and O. V. Lemon (1852), O. V. Lemon and Jesse Sparks (1853), O. V. Lemon (1854), and Josiah Jackson Cooper (1855). Bayless was appointed to the Central Charge, Indianapolis in 1849; the following year he withdrew from the conference "under an evil report."

95 *Fort Wayne Times,* 17 June 1847. See William Ringenberg, "Fort Wayne Methodist College," *Old Fort News,* vol. 35, no. 3 (1972).

96 Maria Hubbell to Cousin Helen, February 14, 1850, Maria Hubbell Collection, Indiana State Library, Indianapolis, Indiana.

97 *Fort Wayne Times,* 6 March 1847.

98 Charles Beecher to Milton Badger, 18 September 1844 and 19 July 1847, AHMS.

99 *Fort Wayne Sentinel,* 6 June 1847.

100 *Fort Wayne Times,* 28 October 1847.

101 A. S. Johns, *Sketch of Early Methodism in Fort Wayne,* 10.

102 *Fort Wayne Sentinel,* 16 December 1848.

103 Brenton's obituary, *Fort Wayne Times,* 2 April 1857.

104 Wilson was born in Belfast, Ireland, in 1812; at the age of twenty-one, he was converted at a camp meeting under the preaching of Richard Hargrave; active for fifty-four years (his last charge was at Bluffton in 1873), he died in 1893. *Minutes of the North Indiana Conference, 1893,* 74.

105 *Fort Wayne Times,* 14 December 1848.

106 H. N. Herrick and William W. Sweet, *A History of the North Indiana Conference* (Indianapolis: W. K. Stewart Company, 1917), 28. See the *Western Christian Advocate,* 11 July 1849.

107 Samuel C. Cooper was born in Baltimore in 1799 and spent most of his ministry in Indiana. He was remembered as a "shrewd businessman" and "one of the most popular preachers in the Conference." He served as presiding elder in Fort Wayne from 1849 through 1851 and died in 1856. Herrick and Sweet, *A History of the North Indiana Conference,* 58, 354.

108 A. S. Johns, *Sketch of Early Methodism in Fort Wayne,* 10.

109 Johnson was then serving as an agent for the Female College; in 1849 he was appointed to "labor for the benefit of the mariners at Fort Wayne"; he died December 8, 1850, at the age of forty-six, and was buried at Fort Wayne.

Brenton's home at 802 West Wayne Street underwent extensive restoration in 1989.

110 A. S. Johns, *Sketch of Early Methodism in Fort Wayne,* 12; *Trustee Minute Book of the M. E. Church, March 24, 1846-February 7, 1870,* December 21, 1849, 16. The lots were owned by Robert Brackenridge, a member of the congregation.

111 Sinex was born at New Albany, Indiana, in 1824; he was graduated from Asbury University (A. B. and A. M.) in 1845; after one year in Fort Wayne he established Asbury Female College in his hometown; in 1853, he became president of Bloomington Female College. He served as president of Albion College, Michigan, (1856-64) and president of the University of the Pacific (1867-72). Sinex died in 1898. *Alumni Register* (Greencastle, Indiana: Depauw University, 1900).

112 In April 1850, the exercises were held in the Berry St. Church; one student wrote: "We have it in the Methodist Church; the examinations occupy three days and the last evening they read their compositions." Maria Hubbell to Cousin Helen, February 14, 1850, Maria Hubbell Collection, Indiana State Library, Indianapolis, Indiana.

113 *Fort Wayne Times,* 24 April 1851.

114 Conference Minutes, 1849, quoted in Herrick and Sweet, *A History of the North Indiana Conference,* 1: 22.

115 *Ibid.,* 1: 24, quoting the *Western Christian Advocate,* 14 June 1848.

116 *Fort Wayne Times,* 21 June 1851, citing the *Marion [Grant Co.] Journal,* 28 June and 19 July 1851.

117 *Fort Wayne Sentinel,* 7 June 1851.

118 "In the year 1824-25, Gabriel Richard, a Roman Catholic priest, held his seat in Congress as the delegate from the then Democratic territory of Michigan. In the Spring of the year 1829, the Rev. Henry A. Muhlenberg . . . became a member of the House of Representatives." *Ibid.,* 12 June 1851.

119 *Fort Wayne Times,* 12 June 1851 and 26 June 1856 (quoting the *Huntington Observer*); *Fort Wayne Sentinel,* 11 June 1851.

120 *The Congressional Globe, Vol., 24,* 24 April 1852, 1181; 11 August 1852, 2189; 15 February 1853, 654.

121 Brenton was defeated by Judge E. M. Chamberlain, 6,875 to 5,966.

122 A. C. Huestis had served as president of the college from September 1847 to May 1848; the Reverend G. H. Rounds until July 30, 1849; the Reverend Cyrus Nutt until September 3, 1850; A. C. Huestis (acting president) until April 19, 1852; the Reverend S. T. Gillette to September 24, 1852. At this time, the faculty consisted of A. C. Huestis, A. M., mathematics and natural science; the Reverend R. D. Robinson, A. M., adjunct teacher of mathematics; Miss Lewis, French, painting and drawing; Miss Mary F. Wood, primary department and music. *Fort Wayne Sentinel,* 22 April 1852; William C. Ringenberg, *Taylor University: The First 125 Years* (Grand Rapids, Mich.: William B. Eerdmans Publishing Company, 1973), 30-32. Brenton was reelected president in June 1853 by a "meeting of the stockholders of the Fort Wayne Collegiate Institute." *Fort Wayne Times,* 8 June 1853.

123 Address of Samuel Brenton, 6 October 1853, *Fort Wayne Times,* 2 November 1853.

124 *Ibid.,* 28 September 1854.

125 *The Doctrines and Discipline of the Methodist Episcopal Church* (New York: T. Mason and G. Lane, 1836), 188. Herrick and Sweet, *A History of the North Indiana Conference,* 1: 46.

126 *Fort Wayne Sentinel,* 22 September 1854.

127 *Fort Wayne Standard,* 6 July 1854.

128 *The Congressional Globe,* 14 January 1856, 231. Griswold, *Pictorial History of Fort Wayne,* 1: 437.

129 *Appendix to the Congressional Globe, 34th Congress, 1st Sess.,* 20 March 1856, 196.

130 *Ibid.,* 24 July 1856, 939, 940.

131 William Orlando Lynch, "Population Movements in Relation to the Struggle for Kansas," in *Indiana University Studies,* vol. 12 (Bloomington, Ind.: Indiana University, 1914), 383-404.

132 *Fort Wayne Sentinel,* 15 and 26 November 1856.

133 *Fort Wayne Times,* 20 September 1855.

134 The number of ballots cast increased from 13,465 (1854) to 20,688 (1856).

135 The average age, at the time of death, of the eighteen clergy of the North Indiana Conference who died between 1844 and 1860, was forty years.

136 *The Congressional Globe,* remarks of Representatives Petit and Bennett, 23 December 1857; *Fort Wayne Times,* 2 April 1857.

137 The ministers who served the Wayne Street Church during that time were Reuben Davisson Robinson (1851), F.

A. Hardin (1852), James Armstrong Beswick (1853), Hawley Baxter Beers (1854), Asahel S. Kinnan (1855-56), Francis Asbury Sale (1857), Lewis Dale (1858), and Charles Martindale (1859-60).

[138] *Fort Wayne Times,* 19 January 1853.

[139] *Fort Wayne Sentinel,* 20 February 1858.

[140] *Fort Wayne Republican,* 21 July 1858.

[141] *Dawson's Daily Times,* 28 March 1859. For more on Quinn, see chapter "African Methodists."

[142] *Fort Wayne Republican,* 21 July 1858.

[143] Herrick and Sweet, *A History of the North Indiana Conference,* 1: 52.

[144] *Trustee Minute Book of the M. E. Church, March 24, 1846-February 7, 1870.* Pastors of the Berry Street Church during the 1850s were: Henry Clark Benson (1850), Milton Mahin (1851), Charles W. Miller (1852-53), J. D. G. Pettijohn (1854-55), Lawson W. Monson (1856), John H. Hull (1857), Almon Greenman (1858), and Valentine M. Beamer (1859-60).

[145] Herrick and Sweet, *A History of the North Indiana Conference,* 1: 56. The Reverend Reuben Davisson Robinson succeeded Brenton as president in 1855, serving until 1866. Debt eventually caused the school's demise; in 1890 it became Taylor University and later moved to Upland, Indiana.

[146] *Dawson's Daily Times,* 30 September 1859. The German Methodists continued to worship at this site until 1875 when the congregation disbanded. See *Panoramic View of the City Fort Wayne, Allen County, Indiana, 1880, Looking Southeast* (Old Fort Reproductions).

[147] The president of the synagogue, Frederick Nirdlinger, pledged ten dollars.

[148] *Dawson's Daily Times,* 4 June 1859.

Chapter 4

[1] The Reverend Julien Benoit, who served in Fort Wayne from 1840 to 1885, wrote: "The old Jesuit missionaries that may have visited Fort Wayne when it was a mere trading-post have left here no record of their labors." Julien Benoit, "Catholic Church," in T. B. Helm, *History of Allen County, Indiana* (Chicago: Kingman Brothers, 1880), 94. Benjamin F. Stickney, the Indian agent at Fort Wayne in 1817, said that the Miami never had schools or missionaries among them since they moved into the three-rivers area from western Indiana in the early 1700s. W. A. Brice, *History of*

Fort Wayne (Fort Wayne: D. W. Jones and Son, 1868), 291.

[2] *Journal of Jean de Bonnecamps,* 17 October 1750, Archives of the Marine, Paris, France; quoted in *The Jesuit Relations and Allied Documents,* Reuben Gold Thwaites, ed., 73 vols. (Cleveland: Burrow Bros. Co., 1901), 69: 189. De Bonnecamps returned to France in 1759.

[3] Payet was born in 1749, ordained in 1774, and later returned to Canada. *The Collections of the Wisconsin Historical Society,* Reuben G. Thwaites, ed., vol. 18, 493; Cyprien Tanguay, *Répertoire Général du Clergé Canadien* (Quebec: 1893), 140.

[4] *A Narrative of the Old Frontier, Henry Hay's Journal from Detroit to the Miami River,* Milo M. Quaife, ed. (Madison: State Historical Society of Wisconsin, 1915), 221, 224. Original in the Detroit Public Library. Payet may have been the unknown "missionary of the gospel of peace" who tradition says offered "the sacrifice of the mass somewhere near the site of the present St. Joseph hospital." See John F. Lang, "The Catholic Church in Allen County," in Robert S. Robertson, *The Valley of the Upper Maumee River,* 2 vols. (Madison Wis.: 1889) 2: 411.

[5] During the Revolutionary War, the political sentiment of most of the local French-speaking residents was pro-British; the Bishop of Quebec, in his zeal for the British cause, excommunicated all who joined with the Americans and, years later, refused the sacrament to all who had not remained faithful to the British crown. In contrast, the first American bishop, the Rt. Reverend John Carroll, assisted the patriot cause at the request of the Continental Congress in 1774. H. J. Alerding, *The Diocese of Fort Wayne* (Fort Wayne: Archer Printing Co., 1907), 14.

[6] *American Catholic Historical Researches,* vol. 27 (American Catholic Historical Society of Philadelphia), 131.

[7] Benedict Flaget to Edward Fenwick, 17 June 1832, UNDA.

[8] William McNamara, *The Catholic Church on the Northern Indiana Frontier, 1789-1844* (Washington, D. C.: The Catholic University of America, 1931), 13.

[9] Francis Badin, the younger brother of Stephen Badin, served in the Detroit Diocese; Anthony Ganihl, of the Diocese of Bardstown, was journeying to a mission on the Raisin River. Gabriel Richard to M. Duclaux, January 1824, St. Sulpice Seminary Archives, Paris; Thomas T. McAvoy, *The Catholic Church in Indiana* (New York: Columbia University Press, 1940), 151.

A local Catholic wrote (ca. 1870-1890): "The first Mass was celebrated [at Fort Wayne] in a log house, at or about the place where C. Orff or B. Trentman now reside. This house was not occupied at the time and was fitted up for the occasion. It afterwards was the home of Mr. Scott, the father-in-law of the lamented Dr. Thompson . . . . At this first Mass many children, as well as Indians and French, were regenerated in holy waters of baptism . . . . The priest who officiated on this occasion was Father Renaud. It was not long after this when Father Badin . . . secured by purchase [in 1831] the beautiful site where the magnificent Cathedral, Sisters' School, Bishop's house, boys' school and Pastoral residence are now established." Wm. B. Walter, *Five Books in One Volume* (Fort Wayne, Ind.: R. C. F. Rayhouser, 1894), Book 5: 9. The unidentifiable "Renaud" may be a corruption, through oral tradition, of "Richard."

[10] Isaac McCoy, *History of Baptist Indian Missions* (Washington: William M. Morrison, 1840), 133.

[11] Charles Furman to Absalom Peters, 19 February 1830, AHMS. In 1831, John B. Dubois, a faithful Catholic, pledged five dollars to the salary of the Presbyterian minister, the only clergyman living in Fort Wayne at that time. J. L. Williams, *Historical Sketch of the First Presbyterian Church, Fort Wayne, Indiana*, 2nd edit. (Fort Wayne: Daily News Printing House, 1881), 28.

[12] John F. Noll, *The Diocese of Fort Wayne: Fragments of History, vol. 2* (1941), 14. Before 1789, Catholics in the British colonies from New Hampshire to Georgia had been subject to the Vicars Apostolic of the district of London, England.

[13] Badin, in later years, sometimes signed himself "proto-sacerdos" (first priest).

[14] Badin hoped, in vain, that the facilities of the recently vacated Baptist Carey Mission, founded by Isaac McCoy in 1822, would be made available.

[15] Julien Benoit, "Catholic Church," in T. B. Helm, *History of Allen County, Indiana*, 94. Comparet came to Fort Wayne in 1820 as an agent of the American Fur Company to establish an Indian trading post; he was later active in a variety of business enterprises and served as Justice of the Peace and County Commissioner.

[16] *Cathedral Records: 1831-1857*, Cathedral of the Immaculate Conception Archives, Fort Wayne, Indiana. In 1831, Badin made entries in the register between January 23 and February 20, and on May 29.

[17] "Father" Béquette was an illiterate silversmith who came to Fort Wayne about 1823, and employed as many as forty persons making "ear bobs for Miami belles." B. J. Griswold, *The Pictorial History of Fort Wayne, Indiana*, 2 vols. (Chicago: Robert O. Law Co., 1917), 1: 258.

[18] *Catholic Telegraph*, 14 July 1832. Ghislain Bohême was then a deacon; he assisted at the mission through the summer and then returned to his studies at Cincinnati.

[19] In June 1833, Wayne Lodge was disbanded and the hall was sold; when the lodge was reorganized in 1840, Comparet was named treasurer. T. B. Helm, *History of Allen County, Indiana*, 100.

[20] Bishop Flaget had served as pastor at Vincennes from 1792 to 1795, and was then recalled by Bishop Carroll to Baltimore; in 1810 he was consecrated bishop of Bardstown, Kentucky. He never visited northern Indiana.

[21] Picot, a native of France, had been ordained at Bardstown and was sent to Vincennes. He incurred debts there and, unable to pay, was jailed; later, Bishop Flaget suspended him from his priestly functions for "disobedience." Thomas T. McAvoy, *The Catholic Church in Indiana*, 179-182.

[22] Stephen T. Badin to the Indian Commissioner, 10 October 1832, quoted in *American Catholic Historical Researches*, vol. 25 (American Catholic Historical Society of Philadelphia), 25.

[23] Thomas T. McAvoy, *The Catholic Church in Indiana*, 180; J. Herman Schauinger, *Stephen T. Badin: Priest in the Wilderness* (Milwaukee: Bruce Publishing Co., 1956), 241.

[24] James E. Deery, "The First Orphan's Home of Indiana," *Catholic Historical Society of Indiana* (December 1937), 1-4; John F. Noll, *The Diocese of Fort Wayne*, 36.

[25] The Reverend Louis DeSeille, a Flemish priest, carried on the work of the mission until his death in 1837.

[26] Ghislain Bohême to Frederick Résé, Pentecost 1833, UNDA; Ghislain Bohême to John E. Purcell, 26 May 1833, UNDA; Bohême Baptismal Record, UNDA; Thomas T. McAvoy, *The Catholic Church in Indiana*, 185-186. The local Presbyterian pastor, James Chute, wrote: "At present we have but one school in town, and this is taught by a Catholic. He calculates to continue his school until spring, when he intends to establish himself in business." James Chute to Absalom Peters, 17 December 1832, AHMS.

[27] *Cathedral Records: 1831-1857*, Cathedral of the Immaculate Conception Archives, Fort Wayne, Indiana.

[28] The trading house of Comparet & Colerick was located on Columbia St.; Colerick was later named county recorder and clerk of the circuit court; in 1853 he built Colerick's Hall, and in 1858, Colerick's Public Bathhouse.

[29] Charles Blanchard, ed., *History of the Catholic Church in Indiana*, 2 vols. (Logansport, Ind.: A. W. Bowen & Co., 1898), 1: 145.

[30] For a few months at least, the orphanage seems to have operated for both Indian and white children. In 1842, the land came into the possession of the Congregation of Holy Cross, which established Notre Dame University, to which place Badin's remains were removed in 1906.

[31] Stephen T. Badin to John B. Purcell, Cincinnati, 10 May 1834, UNDA.

[32] See *The United States Catholic Almanac: or Laity's Directory. . .for 1833, 1834, 1835, 1836, 1837* (Baltimore:

James Myres, 1836).

33 Cicero, *In Catilinam,* 1: 1.

34 Stephen Badin to John B. Purcell, 23 September 1834, UNDA. The "Dutch language" is *Deutsch,* German.

35 J. Herman Schauinger, *Stephen T. Badin,* 49-51; Mary Borromeo Brown, *The History of the Sisters of Providence of Saint Mary-of-the-Woods* (New York: Benzinger Brothers, 1949), 312.

36 Stephen T. Badin to John B. Purcell, 15 February and 23 September 1834, UNDA; J. Herman Schauinger, *Stephen T. Badin,* 252. Subscriptions to the *Catholic Telegraph* were secured for Comparet, Jesse Aughinbaugh, and John Dubois.

37 Stephen T. Badin to John B. Purcell, 22 September 1834, UNDA. Badin also procured on contract a "glebeland" about three miles outside of Fort Wayne.

38 James Chute to Absalom Peters, March 22 1834, AHMS.

39 Agreement between John T. Barr (Henry Rudisill, agent) and John B. Bruno, John B. Béquette, and Francis Comparet, Trustees of the Catholic Church, 18 July 1831, Diocese of Fort Wayne-South Bend Archives, Fort Wayne, Indiana.

40 Stephen T. Badin to Simon Bruté, 7 January 1835, UNDA.

41 J. Herman Schauinger, *Stephen T. Badin,* 2.

42 B. J. Griswold, *The Pictorial History of Fort Wayne, Indiana,* 1: 111, n3. See E[dward]. F. C[olerick]., *Indianapolis News,* 6 July 1891; reprinted as *Cannibals of Indiana,* Ivan Gerould Grimshaw, ed. (Fort Wayne: Allen County-Fort Wayne Historical Society, 1958), 2.

43 Hugh McCulloch, *Men and Measures of Half A Century* (New York: C. Scribner's Sons, 1888), 112.

44 Stephen T. Badin to Simon Bruté, 7 January 1835, UNDA.

45 The Reverend Anthony Foucher, born at Ouiatenon (near Lafayette) July 22, 1741, became a parish priest in Canada, dying in 1812. Charles Blanchard, ed., *History of the Catholic Church in Indiana,* 1: 141.

46 James Bayley, *Memoirs of Right Reverend Simon Gabriel Bruté* (New York: 1861), 70-75.

47 It was not the custom at this time to refer to a priest as "Father." Bruté addressed his clergy as Monsieur (abbreviated "M.") or Mister; occasionally the clergy addressed their bishops as "Doctor" (for their Doctor of Divinity degree); rarely does any priest refer to himself or another with the title "Father." Formal salutations to the superiors of religious orders, however, were "Reverend Father" and "Reverend Mother." Protestants, during the 1820s to 1850s, occasionally used "Father" as a title of respect for their elderly clergy. By the late 1850s, the use of "Father" for Catholic priests became more common.

48 Simon Bruté to John Timon, 28 May 1835, UNDA.

49 Simon Bruté to Frederick Rése, 4 March, 8 January 1835, UNDA.

50 B. J. Griswold, *The Pictorial History of Fort Wayne, Indiana,* 1: 323.

51 David Burr to Governor Noah Noble, 30 December 1835, cited in Dorothy Riker and Gayle Thornbrough, eds., *Messages and Papers of Noah Noble* (Indianapolis: Indiana Historical Collections, 1958), 38: 419-423.

52 Mary Borromeo Brown, *The History of the Sisters of Providence of Saint Mary-of-the-Woods,* 314. "Down" in Ireland meant north. The Irish conflicts were renewed in Indiana when the railroad was built: Mother Theodore Guérin wrote in 1854: "The Irishmen who work on the railroad have been fighting like lions day and night with guns and all sorts of weapons for the past three days. Our Father Corbe is the only one who can appease them." Mother Theodore's Diary, February 1854, SMWA, *Ibid.,* 315.

53 James Chute to Absalom Peters, 8 July 1835, AHMS.

54 Simon Bruté to the Leopoldine Society, quoted in H. J. Alerding, *The Diocese of Fort Wayne,* 26. Felix Matthieu Ruff made entries in the Fort Wayne parish register between August 9 and October 10, 1835, as a "missionaire apostolique."

55 Peg O'Connor, in the diocesan edition of *Our Sunday Visitor,* 30 October 1960, 10B, suggests (without documentation) that a log church named St. Mary's might have been built during the winter, between Badin's departure and Lalumière's arrival; that a second log church named St. Joseph's was built in the three months between Lalumière's departure and Ruff's arrival; and that both of these "temporary structures" were later supplanted by St. Augustine's, built by Müller. None of this hypothesis is supported by the letters of Bruté and Lalumière, or the histories of Benoit or Lang, or the reminiscences of early settlers; all speak of one frame church.

56 Gabriel Bruté to John Timon, 28 May 1835, UNDA.

57 *United States Catholic Almanac: or Laity's Directory . . . for 1836,* 36.

58 Two organizations which assisted the Diocese of Vincennes were the Leopoldine Society in Vienna, Austria—which had a special interest in German-speaking missions—and the Society for Propagating the Faith in Lyons, France—which raised 9,000,000 francs for missionary work in the United States, between 1822 and 1850. The Ludwig Missions Society of Bavaria also supported missionary work among Germans, and donated one thousand florins to the Sisters of Providence at St. Mary-of-the-Woods.

59 Hercule Brassac to Anthony Blanc, March 8, 1836, UNDA. The *United States Catholic Almanac. . .for 1837* (composed in the fall of 1836) lists Ruff as "occasionally" visiting "Peru, Miamiport, Wabashtown, Salomic, Gros *(sic)*."

60 Tervooren, a seminarian at Münster, Germany, came to New York in 1830; in 1834, he was censured by Bishop J. Dubois for "his unbecoming conduct, and his flight from America." In December 1833, he had asked to be sent to Cincinnati, and later offered his services to Bruté for Fort Wayne. Bruté demurred, "May the Lord preserve us from such priests as Tervooren." He was never listed as a priest of the Vincennes diocese. Finbar Kenneally, ed., *United States Documents in the Propaganda Fide Archives: A Calendar, 7 vols.* (Washington, D. C.: Academy of American Franciscan History, 1973), *Index,* 146; Simon Bruté to Frederick Résé, 4 March 1835, UNDA.

61 In *The Metropolitan Catholic Almanac and Laity's Directory. . .for 1837* (Baltimore: James Myres, 1836), 121, the Fort Wayne listing was: "St. Joseph's, Rev. Francis J. Claude *(sic)* ; St. Mary's, Rev. Lewis *(sic)* Muller."

62 Simon Bruté to Messrs. François and Müller, 13 September 1836, UNDA.

63 Ibid.

64 Ibid.

65 V. Eduard Milde to Simon Bruté, 29 December 1836, Leopoldine Society Letters, UNDA. The chief patron of the Society was Archduke Rudolph; members were to contribute five kreutzers each week, and certain indulgences were granted for their gifts and prayers. Between 1829 and 1846, the Society sent $330,000 to America. Raymond Payne, "Annals of the Leopoldine Association," *Catholic Historical Review,* 1905 (Catholic University of America Press), 1: 52-57.

66 Simon Bruté to Messrs. François and Müller, 13 September 1836, UNDA.

67 Simon Bruté to Claude François, 13 September 1836, UNDA.

68 This early "St. Mary's" should not be confused with St. Mary's German Catholic Church established in 1849. See the *The Metropolitan Catholic Almanac and Laity's Directory. . .for 1838* and *1839.* No name for the church was reported in the 1840 edition; in 1841, "St. Augustus" was listed.

69 Eight years later Müller's English was still so poor that Bishop J. J. Chanche of Natchez would not accept him as a missionary until he "acquired a good command of English." J. J. Chance to Propaganda Fide, 21 June 1844, Finbar Kenneally, ed., *United States Documents in the Propaganda Fide Archives,* 3: 336.

70 Simon Bruté to J. Claude François, 10 March 1837,

UNDA. The letter was not received by François until May 6.

71 In 1838, Petit accompanied the Potawatomis on their forced march from northern Indiana to their western reservation, and died in St. Louis from the rigors of the journey.

72 Simon Bruté to J. Claude François, 25 May 1837, UNDA; Simon Bruté to Bishop Rosati, 9 July 1837, UNDA. See Mary Salesia Godecker, *Simon Bruté de Rémur: First Bishop of Vincennes* (St. Meinrad, Indiana: Abbey Press, 1931), 311.

73 Simon Bruté to V. Eduard Milde, Vienna, 19 January 1839, Leopoldine Society Letters, UNDA.

74 Simon Bruté to J. Claude François, 27 May 1838, UNDA.

75 Ibid, 17 October 1838.

76 *Cathedral Records: 1831-1857,* Cathedral of the Immaculate Conception Archives, Fort Wayne, Indiana.

77 John W. Dawson," Charcoal Sketches of Old Times in Fort Wayne," nos. 3 and 7; *Fort Wayne Daily Sentinel,* 14 and 23 March 1872. The First Presbyterian Church was completed in 1837; the other organized "religious societies" were Methodist, Lutheran, and Baptist. Dawson also remarked, "Here I cannot forget to make honorable mention of two gentlemen, long since dead, whose munificence toward the [Catholic] Church was great . . . Captain John B. Bourie and Mr. Francis Comparet."

78 Simon Bruté to J. Claude François, 16 September 1838, UNDA.

79 Jesse Hoover to Charles Hall, 19 March 1838, AHMS.

80 Simon Bruté to J. Claude François, 1 October 1837, UNDA

81 Ibid., 13 June 1839.

82 Célestin de la Hailandière to John B. Purcell, 16 January and 29 February 1840, UNDA.

83 *Biographical Sketch oj Rt. Rev. Julian Benoit . . . by a Clergyman of the Episcopal Household* (Fort Wayne: J. J. Jocquel, 1885), 4.

84 *Ibid.*

85 Benoit first served at Leopold (near Evansville) and ministered to the canal laborers in the area; a year later he was at St. Mary's Church (near Rome) in Perry County, and visited Cassidy and Troy Stations. See *The Metropolitan Catholic Almanac and Laity's Directory. . .for 1839* and *1840.*

86 Simon Bruté to Anthony Blanc, 23 February 1839, UNDA.

87 Charles Blanchard, ed., *History of the Catholic Church in Indiana,* 1: 193.

88 Julien Benoit, "Catholic Church," in T. B. Helm, *History of Allen County, Indiana,* 95. New France (Nouveau Gaul or Nouvelle France) later became Academy (Académie).

Benoit's parish soon included Warsaw, Rome City, Lima (Lagrange Co.), and Girardot Settlement (Ege); he sometimes went on sick calls as far as Muncie; Bishop Purcell of Cincinnati also requested him to visit Defiance, Ohio, when the canal was being developed in that area.

89 Joseph Dwenger, in Charles Blanchard, ed., *History of the Catholic Church in Indiana,* 1: 206.

90 *Biographical Sketch of Rt. Rev. Julian Benoit . . . by a Clergyman of the Episcopal Household,* 17.

91 Blanc had been pastor at Vincennes in 1818-1819 and served parishes in Daviess County before he was named to the see of New Orleans in 1826.

92 Célestin de la Hailandière to Anthony Blanc, 14 January 1841, UNDA.

93 Edward Sorin, *Chronicles Of Notre Dame Du Lac From The Year 1841,* translated by J. M. Toohey (1895), 21, Indiana Province Archives, Congregation of Holy Cross, Notre Dame, Indiana.

94 John F. Noll, *The Diocese of Fort Wayne: Fragments of History,* 109.

95 Rudolf had been ordained by the Bishop of Strasbourg in 1839. On October 29, 1844, he was sent to Oldenburg, Indiana; he died there on May 29, 1866.

96 F. C. D. Wyneken, *The Distress of the German Lutherans in North America* (Erlangen, Germany: 1843); translated by D. Adolph Harless (Fort Wayne, Ind.: Concordia Theological Seminary Press, 1982), 44.

97 The local Episcopal minister challenged a visiting Universalist clergyman to a debate in 1844. See chapter, "Episcopalians."

98 Alexander T. Rankin to Michael E. Shawe, 19 August 1842, printed in the *Fort Wayne Sentinel,* 27 August 1842.

99 "Letters From Indiana - No. 4," *Fort Wayne Sentinel,* 14 May 1842. William W. Steevens published another challenge to Rankin in the *Fort Wayne Sentinel,* 14 January 1843.

100 *Fort Wayne Sentinel,* 20 August 1842.

101 *Ibid.,* 27 August 1842.

102 *Ibid.*

103 *Ibid.,* 24 September 1842.

104 *Ibid.,* 8 October 1842.

105 Charles Beecher to Milton Badger, 2 October 1845, AHMS.

106 *Fort Wayne Sentinel,* 30 September 1843. Shawe also lectured at Fort Wayne in 1845.

107 Appeals to Governor Whitcomb for Weinzoepflen's release were made by several Protestant women of Evansville, as well as by Mrs. James. K. Polk, who learned of the case when she and the president-elect were traveling on the Ohio River on their way to Washington. Mary Borromeo Brown, *The History of the Sisters of Providence of Saint Mary-of-the-Woods,* 217.

108 *Fort Wayne Sentinel,* 21 January 1843. Maria Monk published anti-convent literature, ghost-written by the Reverend J. J. Slocum, that "took the country by storm." The Reverends W. C. Brownlee and Robert J. Breckinridge lectured widely on anti-Catholic themes. See Ray Allen Billington, *The Protestant Crusade, 1800-1860* (New York: Macmillan Co., 1938), 45, 62-65, 99-108.

109 John Hughes, *The Decline of Protestantism and its Causes* (New York: 1850), 26.

110 *Catholic News-Letter,* June 1846, quoted in John F. Noll, *The Diocese of Fort Wayne: Fragments of History,* 51.

111 Julien Benoit to Augustin Martin, 1 July 1843, SMWA.

112 On September 17, 1844, the *Fort Wayne Times* announced that St. Augustine's Institute "resumed its annual session on Tuesday last."

113 Frederick Steber to Edward Sorin, 7 March 1844, Indiana Province Archives, Congregation of Holy Cross, Notre Dame, Indiana. Brother John's letters to Sorin imply that he was alone. The records are not clear: "The Council ordered Br. Joseph from Pokagan to Fort Wayne." *Register of the Particular Council of the Brothers (1841-1845),* December 4, 1843, Indiana Province Archives, Congregation of Holy Cross, Notre Dame, Indiana. Another record notes: "Fort Wayne school opened December 1, 1843. One Brother at first, then another in German." *Extracts From the Archives of the Brothers of Holy Cross,* Aiden O'Reilly, comp. (typescript, 1951), 199, UNDA.

114 B. J. Griswold, *The Pictorial History of Fort Wayne, Indiana,* 1: 385, 431. Walter resigned his position at the Catholic school in July 1847 and, for the next forty years, took an active role in affairs of the Catholic Church in Fort Wayne. He was elected to the city council in 1853 and was vocal in his opposition to the establishment of free public schools; Walter was also a lifelong advocate of the causes of total abstinence and prohibition.

115 Wm. B. Walter, *Five Books in One Volume,* Book 1: 2.

116 *Fort Wayne Sentinel,* 5 and 19 October 1844.

117 Julia Baker Stapleford, 5 January 1835, in *As I Remember* (Fort Wayne, Ind.: Public Library of Fort Wayne and Allen County, 1960), 36.

118 *Minor Chapter Record Book, 1847-1854,* 27 August 1847, Indiana Province Archives, Congregation of Holy Cross, Notre Dame, Indiana.

119 Julien Benoit to Edward Sorin, 12 February 1847, 17 March 1851, UNDA.

120 Edward Sorin, *Chronicles Of Notre Dame Du Lac From The Year 1841,* translated by J. M. Toohey (1895), 141, 142, Indiana Province Archives, Congregation of Holy Cross, Notre Dame, Indiana.

121 *Ibid.,* 346. Br. Bernadine (Francis Ryan) was director in 1859; Br. Stanislaus (Manasses Kane) arrived in 1860. *Extracts From the Archives of the Brothers of Holy Cross,* Aiden O'Reilly, comp. (1951), 200, UNDA. In 1862, Benoit built a brick schoolhouse at Jefferson and Clinton streets; between 1869 and 1908, it had an average enrollment of 250 boys. When the Brothers opened Central Catholic High School in 1909, they relinquished the grade school to the Sisters of Providence.

122 Müller and Bohême went to Mississippi. Bohême served as a confederate chaplain under Gen. Stonewall Jackson and died in Virginia. In 1842, François began a mission for slaves in the Diocese of Natchez; he later became a Lazarist and died of cholera in Louisiana. J. J. Chance to Propaganda Fide, 21 June 1844, Finbar Kenneally, ed., *United States Documents in the Propaganda Fide Archives,* 3: 336. Augustin Martin, Hailandière's vicar general, quit the diocese in 1846.

123 Mother Theodore to Sister Mary, quoted in Mary Borromeo Brown, *The History of the Sisters of Providence of Saint Mary-of-the-Woods,* 385.

124 Mary Borromeo Brown, *The History of the Sisters of Providence of Saint Mary-of-the-Woods,* 384.

125 Célestin de la Hailandière to John B. Purcell, 11 June and 1 August 1844, UNDA.

126 Joseph Dwenger, quoted in Charles Blanchard, ed., *History of the Catholic Church in Indiana,* 1: 206.

127 Julien Benoit to Augustin Martin, 19 July 1843, SMWA.

128 Benoit told Mother Theodore that he had confronted the bishop on her behalf: "While you were imprisoned . . . I was carrying on a vigorous correspondence with His Lordship, which nearly ended in my extermination." Mary Theodosia Mug, ed., *Journals and Letters of Mother Theodore Guérin* (Saint-Mary-of-the-Woods, Ind.: Providence Press, 1937), 216.

129 Julien Benoit to Mother Theodore, 14 November 1845, SMWA.

130 Mary Borromeo Brown, *The History of the Sisters of Providence of Saint Mary-of-the-Woods,* 538.

131 Mother Theodore wrote to the Bishop of Le Mans: "We shall take on a new mission, Fort Wayne, in the northern part of the state. They intend to give us a brick house with a small meadow. That is all they can do." Mother Theodore to J. Bouvier, 21 July 1846, SMWA.

132 Julien Benoit to Mother Theodore, 17 July 1846, SMWA. In the housebook at Fort Wayne, Mother Theodore

wrote: "To testify her gratitude to this generous benefactor, the superior general obliges herself and her Sisters residing now at Fort Wayne, and those who will come after them, to recite every day one Our Father and Hail Mary for the spiritual and temporal needs of their founder."

133 Booth Tarkington, in *The Two Rebels,* wrote that Sr. Basilide was a great favorite of her pupils, among whom were his mother and, later, three cousins.

134 Benoit wrote, "I brought back a seven-hundred-pound bell with a very pretty tone, a Spanish one, cast in 1787, and paid two hundred dollars of my own money for it." Julien Benoit to Augustin Martin, 19 July 1843, SMWA. After a fire destroyed the church sometime after 1861, the bell was recast into two bells: one was given to the Brothers' school; the other, which was placed in the convent court, was used at St. Augustine's Academy until 1949; it was later placed in the Cathedral Museum.

135 *Fort Wayne Sentinel,* 10 October 1846.

136 For details of the removal, see chapter, "Missions to the Miamis."

137 Neyron had first trained as a physician and had served as a surgeon in the Napoleonic Wars.

138 Charles Blanchard, ed., *History of the Catholic Church in Indiana,* 1: 195.

139 Julien Benoit to Edward Sorin, 12 February 1847, UNDA.

140 Julien Benoit to Augustin Martin, 3 February 1847, SMWA.

141 Sr. Marie Thérèse joined the faculty in August 1847; Sr. Gabriella and Sr. Philomene came in 1848.

142 Julien Benoit to Augustin Martin, 14 October 1847, SMWA.

143 Mother Theodore to J. Kundek, 6 December 1853, SMWA.

144 Mary Borromeo Brown, *The History of the Sisters of Providence of Saint Mary-of-the-Woods,* 539. The Academy closed on December 23, 1938, and its students were received into Catholic High School, which opened across the block on January 3, 1939.

145 In the 1850 census, 2,439 German-born residents were enumerated in Allen County, nearly twice the number of all other immigrants combined.

146 Rudolf left Fort Wayne in November 1844; the Reverend Alphonse Munschina (who, with Hamion, had been sent by the bishop of Strasbourg) served as an assistant from January 1845 to February 1846; the Reverend Anthony Carius (a young Alsatian who had been recruited by Hailandière in Paris in 1845) served from April to June 1846.

147 No American had yet enrolled in the seminary. In 1839, Bruté reported: "Of the Seminarians, four are Irish and one German-Swiss. To prepare a native clergy is a funda-

mental object, but it is difficult in view of the ardor of this country for temporal matters and the needs that families have for their children as soon as they can be useful to them." Simon Bruté to V. Eduard Milde, Vienna, 19 January 1839, Leopoldine Society Letters, UNDA.

148 Hailandière requested the dispensation "super defectu aetatis." Célestine de la Hailandière to Propaganda Fide, 1 January 1846, Finbar Kenneally, ed., *United States Documents in the Propaganda Fide Archives,* 2: 88.

149 The first members of the council were Joseph Sommers, B. Rekers, Martin Noll, G. Fox, H. Engel, and the pastor.

150 *Constitution des Deutscher Römisch Catholischer St. Josephs-Schulvereins an der Mutter-Gottes Kirche zu Fort Wayne, Ind., Verfasst im Jahre 1847* (Fort Wayne: Indiana Staatszeitung). A primary purpose of the Schulverein was to raise funds for the school. Unlike all other parishes served by the Sisters of Providence, the German congregation paid the order a flat fee; in 1853, it remitted $200 for the annual service of one teacher. Mother Theodore to J. Kundek, 6 December 1853, SMWA.

151 The families were Bernard Meyer, Nicholas Jostvert, Henry and Lucas Hoevel, and Bernard Voors.

152 The *Wahrheitsfreund* (St. Gall, Switzerland, 5 February 1852) reported that the German Catholics in Fort Wayne opened St. Paul Orphan Asylum on January 25, 1848: "Its beginnings were hard but, by 1855, it had gained a firm foothold." Mary Carol Schroeder, *The Catholic Church in the Diocese of Vincennes, 1847-1877* (Washington, D. C.: The Catholic University of America Press, 1946), 111.

153 Ernest Audran to Célestin de la Hailandière, August 1848, UNDA.

154 *Fort Wayne Times,* 28 August 1847.

155 John F. Lang, "The Catholic Church in Allen County," in Robert S. Robertson, *The Valley of the Upper Maumee River,* 2: 416. In 1900, the Diocesan Directory began listing the church as "St. Mary's."

156 Charles Beecher to Milton Badger, 31 October 1849, AHMS.

157 Julien Benoit to Mother Theodore, 23 July 1849, SMWA.

158 *Fort Wayne Times,* 20 September 1849.

159 Henry Fletter in *Fort Wayne Sentinel,* 26 March 1910.

160 Sr. Marie Joseph was named superior in 1849, assisted by Sr. Gabriella and Sr. Mary Celestia (the first Irish-born women to enter the order), Sr. Lawrence, Sr. Martina, and Sr. Clotilde. On March 17, 1851, Sr. Marie Joseph died of tuberculosis at Fort Wayne. Sr. St. Vincent Ferrer was named superior in May 1851. In 1854, two sisters were at St. Mary's German school and seven at St.

Augustine's. A Fort Wayne resident, Sr. Josephine (**Mary** Glutting), entered the order in 1851.

161 Julien Benoit to Mother Theodore, 21 September 1849, SMWA.

162 *Fort Wayne Sentinel,* 1 October 1849.

163 Charles Beecher to Milton Badger, 31 October 1849, AHMS.

164 Julien Benoit to Mother Theodore, 11 August 1852 and 23 August 1854, SMWA.

165 Mary Borromeo Brown, *The History of the Sisters of Providence of Saint Mary-of-the-Woods,* 566.

166 Charles Blanchard, ed., *History of the Catholic Church in Indiana,* 1: 148. This was Badin's last visit to Fort Wayne; he died in Cincinnati on April 19, 1853.

167 *Fort Wayne Times,* 20 December 1849.

168 John F. Lang, "The Catholic Church in Allen County," in Robert S. Robertson, ed., *The Valley of the Upper Maumee River,* 2: 417.

169 Julien Benoit to Anthony Blanc, 24 March 1852, UNDA.

170 Augustin Martin, Natchatoches, La., to Anthony Blanc, 22 June 1852, UNDA.

171 Maurice de St. Palais to John Purcell, 12 August 1853, UNDA.

172 Julien Benoit to Peter Paul Lefevere, Detroit, Mich., 20 September 1852, UNDA.

173 Julien Benoit to Mother Theodore, 11 August 1852, SMWA. "Mother Theodore . . . [offered] continual prayers for Father Benoit's return, and eventually, owing to intervention on her part, which smoothed away his difficulties, and to the open regret at his absence manifested by Bishop de Saint-Palais on his return from Europe, their former pastor was soon back." Mary Borromeo Brown, *The History of the Sisters of Providence of Saint Mary-of-the-Woods,* 555; Maurice de St. Palais to Mother Theodore, 8 November 1852, SMWA.

174 Julien Benoit to Stephen Rousselon, 5 May 1853; Julien Benoit to Anthony Blanc, 7 July 1853; Augustin Martin to Anthony Blanc, 29 July 1853; Maurice de St. Palais to John Purcell, 12 August 1853; Julien Benoit to Anthony Blanc, 19 October 1855, UNDA.

175 August Bessonies to John Purcell, 2 February 1854, UNDA. Bessonies continued in the Diocese of Vincennes, serving in Jeffersonville and Indianapolis; he became Vicar General in 1871 and a Roman Prelate in 1884.

176 Julien Benoit to Anthony Blanc, 19 October 1855, UNDA.

177 Julien Benoit to John Purcell, 2 September 1871, UNDA. In this letter Benoit was responding to accusations of fraud by those opposed to his nomination for bishop in 1871, as well to as an inquiry from the Vatican to Purcell on

the allegations. Cardinal Prefect Alexander Barnabo to John Purcell, 15 November 1871, UNDA.

[178] William Warren Sweet estimated that "perhaps a third of the Germans coming to the West were Catholic." *The Story of Religion in America* (New York: Harper and Brothers, 1939), 373.

[179] The census of 1850 enumerated 3908 foreign born residents of Allen County (33.7 percent of the population): Germany, 2439 (21 percent); France, 554 (4.8 percent, the largest number of French natives in any Indiana county); Ireland, 424 (3.7 percent); England, 197 (1.7%); Canada, 124; Switzerland, 96; Scotland, 56; Wales, 6.

[180] Charles H. Banet identifies French Town (also called Lasselleville) as "east of Calhoun St. and south of the Wabash Railroad"; others suggest a neighborhood bordered by "Buchanan, Savannah, Pontiac, and John streets" and "Hanna, Dewald, Lasselle and Lafayette streets." See *French Immigrants in Allen County, Indiana: 1850-1870,* Charles H. Banet, ed. (Fort Wayne, Ind.: Public Library of Fort Wayne and Allen Co., 1981), 24; *Fort Wayne Journal Gazette,* 14 January 1909, 8 and 5 July 1914.

[181] *Articles D'Incorporation & Constitution de la Société Bienfaisance Lafayette de Fort Wayne, Indiana,* art. 16, sec. 11, Miscellaneous Record 294, Allen County Courthouse, Fort Wayne, Indiana.

[182] Susan McCulloch to Maria Halsey, 13 January 1845, McCulloch Papers.

[183] *Dawson's Daily Times,* 14, 15, 17, and 19 March 1859. The St. Patrick's School Society also had French and German members. See George R. Mather, "Fort Wayne's First St. Patrick's Day Celebration In 1859," in *Today's Catholic,* vol. 65, no. 11 (March 1991), 20-21.

[184] *Fort Wayne Sentinel,* 24 June 1854; Carl F. Brand, "The History of the Know-Nothing Party in Indiana," in *Indiana Magazine of History,* vol. 18 (1922), 79, 201.

[185] *Fort Wayne Times,* 31 November 1853, 7 and 14 December 1853; *Fort Wayne Sentinel,* 10 December 1853. This was not the first or last time Dawson was "thrashed" by an irate reader. In 1861 he was appointed governor of Utah by President Lincoln, and died in 1877 as a result of injuries inflicted by angry Mormons.

[186] *Fort Wayne Times,* 11 January 1855.

[187] Mary Borromeo Brown, *The History of the Sisters of Providence of Saint Mary-of-the-Woods,* 704.

[188] "Letters From Indiana - No. 7," *Fort Wayne Sentinel,* 30 July 1842.

[189] In 1850, the Diocese of Cincinnati was made an archdiocese, with six suffragan sees in its Province, including Vincennes; Bishop Purcell was named archbishop.

[190] During the 1850s, Lüers used the umlaut in his name, even when writing in English, as did his Vicar General. See

John Lüers to John Purcell, 5 March 1858 and Julien Beniot to Edward Sorin, 29 May 1858, UNDA.

[191] John Purcell to Propaganda Fide, 30 April 1857; George Carrell to Propaganda Fide, 5 May 1857; M. J. Spaulding to Propaganda Fide, 11 May 1857; Finbar Kenneally, ed., *United States Documents in the Propaganda Fide Archives,* 6: 668, 669, 670. John Purcell to Anthony Blanc, 30 April 1859, UNDA. Charles Blanchard, ed., *History of the Catholic Church in Indiana,* 1: 79n.

[192] Charles Blanchard, ed., *History of the Catholic Church in Indiana,* 1: 153.

[193] John Lüers to John Purcell, 20 February 1858, UNDA.

[194] Ibid., 5 March 1858, UNDA.

[195] Ibid., 9 April 1858, UNDA.

[196] The *Lafayette City Directory for 1858* (Lafayette, Ind.: R. K. Polk & Co.), 125, noted: "The large square of ground on the corner of Alabama and Ohio in the southern part of the city has recently been purchased by the Bishop, at a cost of $10,000 on which is contemplated to build a cathedral and Episcopal residence." A Catholic in Lafayette later wrote: "The gift was to be from the city, and the project was voted down in the city council by one vote, and that the vote of the *member from the first ward.* History and tradition have consigned, or should consign, his name to oblivion." John A. Wilstach, *St. Mary's Church* (Lafayette, 1893), quoted in H. J. Alerding, *The Diocese of Fort Wayne,* 34.

[197] John Lüers to John Purcell, 5 October 1859, UNDA.

[198] Ibid., 5 January and 5 October 1859; John Lüers to P. P. Lefevre, 15 April 1860; UNDA.

[199] John Lüers to John Purcell, 17 April 1858, UNDA.

[200] Ibid., 12 March 1860, UNDA.

[201] Augustin Martin to Anthony Blanc, 12 March 1853, UNDA; Charles Blanchard, ed., *History of the Catholic Church in Indiana,* 1: 207.

[202] Julien Benoit to John Purcell, 26 December 1859, UNDA.

[203] John Purcell to Anthony Blanc, 9 July 1859; John Lüers to John Purcell, 21 March 1859, UNDA. Archbishop Hughes of New York, as well as Bishops Odin and Elder, also endorsed Benoit's candidacy for coadjutor of New Orleans; Benoit eventually became "second on the list." Anthony Blanc to John Purcell, 29 September 1859, UNDA.

[204] Julien Benoit to Edward Sorin, 29 May 1858, UNDA. Benoit had been invited to "join the diocese of Cleveland." *Biographical Sketch of Rt. Rev. Julian Benoit . . . by a Clergyman of the Episcopal Household,* 11.

[205] Julien Benoit to Anthony Blanc, 22 February 1860, UNDA.

[206] John Lüers to John Purcell, 5 October 1859, UNDA.

[207] *Fort Wayne Sentinel,* 25 June 1858; *Fort Wayne Republican,* 1 September 1858.

208 Sr. Catherine (who had taught German at St. Augustine's Academy in 1846) and Sr. Edward (Magdalena Marendt) began teaching at St. Mary's School in the fall of 1854; "after New Year 1855 . . . they were able to take possession of the dwelling which had been prepared for them in the German parish." Sr. Maria (Caroline Vicaire) was added to the faculty in 1856. "Fort Wayne German School," *The Book of Establishments,* SMWA.

209 "Bishop St. Palais moved Faller to the Diocese of Vincennes before the division (1857) to avoid losing Faller's family fortune which he frequently used on church projects." James Divita, 15 May 1991, letter to the author. Faller left Fort Wayne in March 1857 to be come pastor of the Church of the Annunciation in New Albany; he later served parishes in Terre Haute, Cannelton, Tell City, Madison, Jennings County, and returned to New Albany in 1886. "Faller. . . lived abstemiously . . . preferring to give his means to the aid of his parishioners rather than to the vulgar display of his wealth or the gratification of selfish ambition." Charles Blanchard, ed., *History of the Catholic Church in Indiana,* 2: 180.

210 *Fort Wayne Sentinel,* 10 September 1859; *Dawson's Daily Times,* 14 October 1859 and 7 April 1860; *Fort Wayne Republican,* 9 September 1858 and 2 November 1859.

211 Julien Benoit to Edward Sorin, 12 January 1859, UNDA.

212 *Fort Wayne Sentinel,* 8 January 1859.

213 *Fort Wayne Times,* 3 February 1859.

214 John Lüers to John Purcell, 20 January 1859, UNDA.

215 Blanc's permission presumed Lüers's reciprocity, allowing the southern prelate in the future to collect in the Diocese of Fort Wayne. John Lüers to Anthony Blanc, 8 May 1859, UNDA.

216 Julien Benoit to Anthony Blanc, 12 June 1859, UNDA.

217 *Dawson's Daily Times,* 16 May 1859.

218 John Purcell to Anthony Blanc, 9 July 1859, UNDA.

219 Committee members were Henry Baker, Michael Hedekin, Morris Cody, and Jacob Kintz, each of whom donated a window to the cathedral. John F. Noll, *The Diocese of Fort Wayne: Fragments of History,* 106.

220 John Lüers to John Purcell, 13 January 1859, UNDA.

221 Julien Benoit to Anthony Blanc, 21 July 1859, UNDA.

222 Julien Benoit to Edward Sorin, November 4 and 10 December 1859, UNDA.

223 *Fort Wayne Sentinel,* 15 August and 20 October 1860.

224 In 1846, the American Bishops had chosen the Immaculate Conception as patroness of the United States; Pius IX issued the bull *Ineffabilis Deus* on the feast day of the Immaculate Conception, 8 December 1854.

225 *Fort Wayne Sentinel,* 15 December 1860.

226 *Biographical Sketch of Rt. Rev. Julian Benoit . . . by a Clergyman of the Episcopal Household,* 7.

227 Edward Sorin, *Chronicles Of Notre Dame Du Lac From The Year 1841,* translated by J. M. Toohey, 21, UNDA.

228 *Extracts From the Archives of the Brothers of Holy Cross,* Aiden O'Reilly, comp. (1951), 46, UNDA.

229 August Oechtering, Mishawaka, to Daniel E. Hudson, Notre Dame, 21 September 1899, UNDA.

230 John Lüers to John Purcell, 7 August 1868 and 12 March 1869, UNDA.

231 Benoit was placed second to Dwenger "because he does not know German, which is very important for the diocese." Cardinal Prefect Alexander Barnabo to John Purcell, 15 November 1871, UNDA.

232 Ibid., 6 January 1872.

233 Julien Benoit to John Purcell, 5 December 1871, UNDA.

234 Julien Benoit to Sister Euphrasie, 21 February 1882, SMWA. When Benoit's obituary was mistakenly published in December 1880, he wrote to the editor: "Your eulogy. . . is so grandiloquent, inflated and exaggerated, that I cannot, by any possibility, recognize myself, being in reality *vermis et no homo.*"

235 Charles Blanchard, ed., *History of the Catholic Church in Indiana,* 1: 201.

236 *Ibid.,* 1: 211.

237 *Biographical Sketch of Rt. Rev. Julian Benoit . . . by a Clergyman of the Episcopal Household,* 22.

Chapter 5

1 Martin Bargus, a Catholic, was the second German known to settle in Fort Wayne. Charles R. Poinsatte, *Fort Wayne During the Canal Era: 1828-1855* (Indianapolis: Indiana Historical Bureau, 1969), 57.

2 J[esse] L. Williams, *Historical Sketch of the First Presbyterian Church, Fort Wayne, Indiana,* [2nd edition] (Fort Wayne: Daily News Printing House, 1881), 28.

3 Rudisill to Barr, 8 January 1830, Rudisill Letterbook (in the possession of his heirs), cited in Charles R. Poinsatte, *Fort Wayne During the Canal Era: 1828-1855,* 55-56. Rudisill took his own advice and built his fortune on German immigrant labor, most of whom were young women and children. One German, who came to the area in 1834, recollected: "There was a rich German here who . . . . had

arrived early and built a large frame house; his name was Rudisill. He had a large paper mill, a large sawmill, a wool factory, and a cotton factory. In these mills and factories they got jobs, mostly the girls and the children." Gottfried Weber, *Buch,* translated by Antonius Holtmann (Cincinnati: 1877), 12, original held by the Igel family, Engler, Ohio.

4 Rudisill to Barr, 16 January 1830, Rudisill Letterbook, cited in Charles R. Poinsatte, *Fort Wayne During the Canal Era: 1828-1855,* 56.

5 H. G. Sauer and J. W. Miller, *Geschichte der Deutschen Ev.-Luth. St. Pauls-Gemeinde zu Fort Wayne, Ind., vom Jahre 1837 bis zum Jahre 1912* (St. Louis: Concordia Publishing House, 1887 and 1912), 10. Sauer's history, written in 1887 (chapters 1 and 2), was extended by Miller in 1912 (chapter 3).

6 John G. Morris, Fifty Years in the Lutheran Ministry (Baltimore: 1878), quoted in Concordia Historical Institute Quarterly, vol. 4, no. 4 (January 1932), 117.

7 Susan Man to Mrs. Frederick Halsey, 16 July, 18 August, and 19 September 1836, McCulloch Papers, Lilly Library, Bloomington, Indiana.

8 Ibid.

9 Ibid., 9 January and 23 April 1837. At the fiftieth anniversary of the founding of the congregation, charter members remembered Hoover's preaching as "sincere, convincing, and enjoyable." H. G. Sauer and J. W. Miller, *Geschichte der Deutschen Ev.-Luth. St. Pauls-Gemeinde zu Fort Wayne, Ind.,* 13.

10 Susan M. McCulloch, *Recollections* (1896), Allen County-Fort Wayne Historical Society, published as "The Recollections of Susan Man McCulloch," Wilhelmina and Clifford Richards, eds., *Old Fort News,* vol. 44, no. 3 (1981), 10.

11 Minutes and Baptismal Records of the First Evangelical Lutheran Church of Fort Wayne, Indiana, St. Paul's Lutheran Church Archives, Fort Wayne, Indiana, 4, 5; H. G. Sauer and J. W. Miller, *Geschichte der Deutschen Ev.-Luth. St. Pauls-Gemeinde.,* 13.

12 Susan Man to Mrs. Frederick Halsey, 4 March 1837, McCulloch Papers.

13 *Fort Wayne Sentinel,* 15 April 1837. The curriculum was "Reading, Spelling and Writing: $2.50 per 12 week term; Arithmetic, Grammar, History, Mental Philosophy, Chemistry, Botany, Retorick, Logick, Geometry, etc.: $4.00 per term; Water Colors and Embroidery: $6.00."

14 Susan Man to Mrs. Frederick Halsey, 4 March 1837, McCulloch Papers.

15 Ibid., 24 April 1837.

16 Jesse Hoover to Susan Man, 10 November 1837, McCulloch Papers. The "Smoky Retreat" was the lower level of the First Presbyterian Church where Hoover and

Man had taught. When Hoover decided to teach independently in the schoolhouse, the Presbyterians engaged William W. Steevens and Alexander McJunkin to direct their academy.

17 Ibid.

18 Ibid.

19 H. G. Sauer and J. W. Miller, *Geschichte der Deutschen Ev.-Luth. St. Pauls-Gemeinde,* 10. Hoover's sons were Henry Luther, born April 15, 1835, and Lewis Thompson (named for the local physician, Dr. Lewis G. Thompson), born October 23, 1837. Minutes and Baptismal Records of the First Evangelical Lutheran Church of Fort Wayne, Indiana.

20 S. R. Ball, William Corbin, A. T. Rankin, and Smalwood Noel to Milton Badger, December 1837, AHMS. The congregation "up the St. Mary's River" was the Friedheim Church in Adams County.

21 Samuel G. Lowry to Milton Badger, 9 January 1839, AHMS.

22 L. C. Rudolph, W. W. Wimberly, T. W. Clayton, *Indiana Letters: Abstracts of Letters from Missionaries on the Indiana Frontier to the American Home Missionary Society, 1824-1893,* vol. 1 (University Microfilms International, 1979), v.

23 Some of the poor Germans who had taken menial work in the Netherlands in the early eighteenth century, emigrated to America when the Dutch economy declined in the early 1830s.

24 Jesse Hoover to Charles Hall, 19 March 1838, AHMS.

25 Ibid.

26 Letters of the Rev. E. Keller, Ev. Lutheran Missionary in the West, to the Secretary of the Missionary Society of the Theological Seminary, Gettysburg, Pennsylvania, 14 December 1836, published in *The Lutheran Observer,* 17 March 1837; quoted in Rudolph F. Rehmer, "Letters of Lutheran Traveling Missionaries Keller and Heyer, 1835-1837," *Concordia Historical Institute Quarterly,* vol. 47, no. 2 (Summer 1974), 70-89.

27 William Warren Sweet, *Religion on the American Frontier, 1783-1840, vol. 2, The Presbyterians* (Chicago: Chicago University Press, 1936), 3.

28 Jesse Hoover to Charles Hall, 19 March 1838, AHMS.

29 Ibid.

30 John G. Morris, *Fifty Years in the Lutheran Ministry* (Baltimore: 1878), quoted in Concordia Historical Institute Quarterly, vol. 4, no. 4 (January 1932), 118.

31 Jesse Hoover to Charles Hall, 19 March 1838, AHMS; Susan Man McCulloch to Mrs. Frederick Halsey, 4 June 1838, McCulloch Papers.

32 John G. Morris, *Fifty Years in the Lutheran Ministry,* 118. Hoover was buried in the Broadway (McCulloch)

Cemetery; in 1849, the German congregation purchased a headstone whose inscription concluded, "Mir nach spricht Christus unser Held [Follow me, says Christ, our Hero]"; his remains were later removed to the Concordia Cemetery on Anthony Blvd.; the original headstone was placed in a garden adjacent to St. Paul's Lutheran Church on Barr St.

33 "Ich glaube, darum rede Ich." H. G. Sauer and J. W. Miller, *Geschichte der Deutschen Ev.-Luth. St. Pauls-Gemeinde,* 13.

34 Adam Wefel, Heinrich Trier, Konrad Nill, Henry Rudisill, to Charles Hall, July 1838, AHMS. The appeal was most likely written by Hoover's brother, David, who taught school at the county seminary. Rudisill, as postmaster, utilized his franking privilege to mail the letter without postage.

35 G. E. Hageman, *Friedrich Konrad Dietrich Wyneken: Pioneer Lutheran Missionary of the Nineteenth Century,* in the series *Men and Missions, III,* L. Fuerbringer, ed. (St. Louis: Concordia Publishing House, 1926), 13.

36 *Ibid,* 10.

37 *Ibid.,* 15. The man, whose name was Loeffler, later befriended Wyneken.

38 Buuck and his wife Margaretha emigrated from Windheim, Germany, in 1836, and journeyed to the Fort Wayne area in response to Henry Rudisill's advertisements in Baltimore; he was elected an elder of the Friedheim Church at its organization, February 28, 1838. Gale C. Buuck and Marvin L. Buuck, comps., *The Buuck Family in America: Sesquicentennial 1836-1986* (Fort Wayne, Indiana: 1987), 17.

39 Friedrich K. D. Wyneken to C. W. Wolff, 1 October 1838, cited in G. E. Hageman, *Friedrich Konrad DietrichWyneken: Pioneer Lutheran Missionary of the Nineteenth Century,* 16.

40 Friedrich K. D. Wyneken, *Die Noth der Deutschen Lutheraner in Nordamerika,* first published in *Zeitschrift fuer Protestantismus und Kirche* (Erlangen: 1843); reprinted in Pittsburgh, Pa. (1844). S. Edgar Schmidt, trans.,*The Distress of the German Lutherans in North America,* edited by R. F. Rehmer (Fort Wayne: Concordia Theological Seminary Press, 1982), 26, 27.

41 See chapter "Old School Presbyterians" for A. T. Rankin's comments on the financial crisis.

42 Alexander Rankin to Milton Badger, 4 September 1838, and Alexander Rankin to Charles Hall, 22 January 1839, AHMS.

43 Alexander Rankin to Charles Hall, 5 October 1839, AHMS.

44 In German, "jeanshose." H. G. Sauer and J. W. Miller, *Geschichte der Deutschen Ev.-Luth. St. Pauls-Gemeinde,* 21.

45 G. E. Hageman, *Friedrich Konrad Dietrich Wyneken: Pioneer Lutheran Missionary of the Nineteenth Century,* 24-27.

46 Johann Joseph Nuelsen to Johann Haesbaert, August 1839, *Ibid.,* 30.

47 H. G. Sauer and J. W. Miller, *Geschichte der Deutschen Ev.-Luth. St. Pauls-Gemeinde,* 22, 23; translated by Annelie Moxter-Collie.

48 Friedrich K. D. Wyneken to Milton Badger, 10 January 1840, AHMS (written in German, translated by the Society).

49 *Ibid.* Wyneken was referring to the theological rationalism in Germany which tried to "explain away" the supernatural.

50 Friedrich K. D. Wyneken to Milton Badger, 28 March 1840, AHMS.

51 H. G. Sauer and J. W. Miller, *Geschichte der Deutschen Ev.-Luth. St. Pauls-Gemeinde,* 20.

52 Friedrich K. D. Wyneken to Friedrich Schmidt, Pittsburgh, Pennsylvania, 25 January 1840, quoted in G. E. Hageman, *Friedrich Konrad Dietrich Wyneken: Pioneer Lutheran Missionary of the Nineteenth Century,* 20.

53 Letter of Friedrich K. D. Wyneken (February 1839), Minutes of the German Evangelical Lutheran Synod of Pennsylvania (Trinity Week, Allentown, 1839), Appendix 5: 8, 10-11, 13-14, quoted in Rudolph F. Rehmer, *New Light on F. K. D. Wyneken* (Lafayette, Ind.: Lafayette Sunday Visitor, 1981), 3. See Henry Waltmann, "The Struggle to Establish Lutheranism in Tippecanoe County, 1812-1850," *Indiana Magazine of History,* vol. 75, no. 1 (March 1979), 36.

54 Friedrich K. D. Wyneken to Milton Badger, 28 March 1840, AHMS. This is Wyneken's last report to the Society, as his A. H. M. S. commission was not renewed. The Society may have reasoned that, if the Synod could send him to Germany, they could send him to Fort Wayne. It is also possible that the A. H. M. S. knew nothing of Wyneken's plans and simply believed that their responsibility had ceased at the end of the original three year commitment from July 18, 1837 to July 18, 1840.

55 Husmann was thirty-two years old, a native of Hannover, and recently married; he was later accepted as a candidate for ordination by the Pennsylvania Ministerium. E. S. H. Husmann, "F. W. Husmann," in *Concordia Historical Institute Quarterly,* vol. 1, no. 1 (April 1928).

56 Jensen had come under the sponsorship of a "mission committee" in Stader. H. G. Sauer and J. W. Miller, *Geschichte der Deutschen Ev.-Luth. St. Pauls-Gemeinde,* 26.

57 *Ibid.,* 25.

58 At revival meetings, the "mourners' bench" was a

seat near the front reserved for those who had been brought to repentance and mourned their sins; it was also called the anxious seat.

59 G. E. Hageman, *Friedrich Konrad Dietrich Wyneken: Pioneer Lutheran Missionary of the Nineteenth Century,* 36-38, quoting Friedrich Lochner, who responded to Wyneken's call to minister in America, and became a leader in the Missouri Synod.

60 "Memoiren," in *Deutscher Kalender für das Jahr 1902…der Central Deutschen Konferenz der Bischöflichen Methodistenkirche* (Cincinnati: Jennings and Pyne, 1902), 95. See chapter "Methodists."

61 Friedrich K. D. Wyneken, *Die Noth der Deutschen Lutheraner in Nordamerika,* translated by S. Edgar Schmidt, 51.

62 *Ibid.,* 49.

63 *Der Deutsche Evangelische-Reformierte St. Johannis-Gemeinde.* See chapter "German Reformed."

64 Wyneken said that, because of the expense and distance, he had not been able to attend the meetings of the Synod.

65 G. E. Hageman, *Friedrich Konrad Dietrich Wyneken: Pioneer Lutheran Missionary of the Nineteenth Century,* 41. The Synod of the West dissolved in 1844.

66 See chapter "Methodists."

67 G. E. Hageman, *Friedrich Konrad Dietrich Wyneken: Pioneer Lutheran Missionary of the Nineteenth Century,* 48. Wyneken next served in Missouri as a teacher, pastor, and then president of the Missouri Synod. When his health failed in 1851, he returned to Indiana to live near the Friedheim Church; after three years he moved to Fort Wayne, where he remained until 1862, when he accepted a pastorate in Cleveland, Ohio. The Wynekens had thirteen children, eight boys (two of whom died in early childhood) and five girls. He died in California, while visiting his son, on May 4, 1876; his body lay in state in St. Louis, Fort Wayne, and Cleveland, where he was buried.

68 Wilhelm Sihler, *Lebenslauf von W. Sihler bis zu seiner Ankunft in New York* (St. Louis: Druckerei Des Lutherischen Concordia Verlags, 1879), 143.

69 Sihler's son, Ernest, born at Fort Wayne in 1853, recalled: "Although the bulk of the German settlers came from Westphalia and Hannover, *every* part of Germany was represented, from East Prussia to the Rhine, from Bremen to the Black Forest; so that, as a young boy, I became familiar with the dialects of Mecklenburg and Pomerania, of Bremen and Minden—the latter a veritable hive of ever more newcomers—of Bavaria and with the guttural articulation of the Swiss." Ernest G. Sihler, *From Maumee to Thames and Tiber* (New York City: New York University Press, 1930), 16.

70 Friedrich Wilhelm Husmann, *Diary on My Ministry. . .From the Middle of October 1845,* translated by Otto F. Stahlke (Fort Wayne: Concordia Theological Seminary Press, 1987), 1.

71 J. H. Jaebker and C. H. F. Fricke (later Frincke).

72 In 1829, Sihler had published a collection of essays, *Symbolik des Antlitzes* (Symbolism of Countenance) for which the University of Jena awarded him an honorary doctorate of philosophy.

73 See James Lewis Scharf, *Wilhelm Löhe's Relation to the American Church: A Study in the History of Lutheran Mission* (Inaugural Dissertation, Ruprech-Karl University of Heidelberg, 1961).

74 The students arrived in August 1846, accompanied by Candidate C. A. W. Roebbelen, who soon accepted a call to a congregation in Liverpool, Ohio. Sihler opened the seminary in October; in November Candidate Karl A. Wolter arrived to assist in teaching. Wolter was remembered as an "eloquent preacher;" he died in the cholera epidemic of 1849. H. G. Sauer and J. W. Miller, *Geschichte der Deutschen Ev.-Luth. St. Pauls-Gemeinde,* 36.

75 Carl Mauelshagen, *American Lutheranism Surrenders to the Forces of Conservatism* (Athens, Georgia: University of Georgia, 1936), 162. See Herbert G. Bredemeier, *Concordia College, Fort Wayne, Indiana: 1839-1957* (Fort Wayne, Ind.: Fort Wayne Public Library, 1978).

76 Wilhelm Sihler, St. Louis, to Susanna Sihler, Fort Wayne, 12 November 1851, quoted in Lewis W. Spitz, *Life in Two Worlds: Biography of William Sihler* (St. Louis: Concordia Publishing House, 1968), 69, 70. The Sihlers raised five sons and four daughters: Christian became a physician in Cleveland; Ernest was a noted classicist and professor at New York University; Frederick entered his father-in-law's drug business; William taught at Luther College, Iowa; Carl became a Fort Wayne banker; Elizabeth was a college teacher; and Marie, Lily, and Johanna married.

77 *Minutes of the Voters' Assembly of St. Paul's Ev. Lutheran Church, 1837-May 16, 1856,* 19 June 1846, St. Paul's Lutheran Church Archives, Fort Wayne, Indiana.

78 Wilhelm Sihler, *Lebenslauf von W. Sihler, als Lutherischer Pastor u. s.w.* vol. 2 (New York: Lutherischer Verlags-Verein, 1880), 58, 62.

79 In October 1845, Husmann became pastor of three congregations: St. Paul (now Emmanuel) Lutheran Church in Marion Township (Soest), eight miles southeast of Fort Wayne; St. John at Bingen, near Decatur; and St. Peter at Fuelling, Adams County.

80 Friedrich Wilhelm Husmann, *Diary on My Ministry . . .From the Middle of October 1845,* 54. This diary was kept to fulfill a pre-ordination requirement of the Pennsylvania Ministerium.

[81] *Synodal Bericht der Deutschen Evangelisch-Lutherischen Synode von Missouri, Ohio und andern Staaten vom Jahre 1848* (Chicago), 25, quoted in Herbert G. Bredemeier, *Concordia College,* 54.

In 1861, the seminary was moved to St. Louis, and a Gymnasium and secondary school in that city were moved to Fort Wayne. "The outbreak of the Civil War in April 1861 lent unexpected urgency to the move. Missouri, unlike Indiana, granted theological students exemption from military service." Erich H. Heintzen, *Prairie School of the Prophets: The Anatomy of a Seminary, 1846-1976* (St. Louis: Concordia, 1989), 55-56.

In 1857, the Lutheran Teachers Seminary was moved from Milwaukee to Fort Wayne. H. G. Sauer and J. W. Miller, *Geschichte der Deutschen Ev.-Luth. St. Pauls-Gemeinde,* 38.

[82] In 1850, English grammar was added to the school curriculum. In 1856, the corner stone for an English "Male Academy" was laid on the Seminary campus and classes commenced on November 16, 1857, under the direction of S. Sutermeister; the school was closed after one year for lack of patronage and funds. In 1858, Pastor Stephan was "requested to deliver addresses in English"; he was "peacefully dismissed" soon afterwards. *Minutes of the Voters' Assembly of St. Paul's Ev. Lutheran Church, 1837-May 16, 1856,* 17 August 1850, 1 September 1858; *Fort Wayne Sentinel,* 21 November 1857.

[83] The congregation also called itself "The First English Lutheran Church of the Holy Trinity."

[84] Friedrich Wilhelm Husmann, *Diary on My Ministry . . . From the Middle of October 1845,* 30. Albaugh next preached there on May 17, 1846, *Ibid.,* 37.

[85] Wilhelm Sihler, *Lebenslauf von W. Sihler,* 2: 36.

[86] *Minutes of the Voters' Assembly of St. Paul's Ev. Lutheran Church, 1837-May 16, 1856,* July 1846.

[87] Rudisill did "more than any other man, through his personal influence with the Germans, to make the Democratic party a ruling power in the county." Wallace A. Brice, *History of Fort Wayne from the Earliest Known Accounts of This Point to the Present Period* (Fort Wayne: Jones & Son, 1868), appendix, 16-17. Rudisill had been appointed postmaster in 1831, under President Jackson's spoils policy, and served for ten years. He had established flouring, wool carding, flax seed oil, and saw mills.

[88] H. G. Sauer and J. W. Miller, *Geschichte der Deutschen Ev.-Luth. St. Pauls-Gemeinde,* 9.

[89] Rudisill also voted against Wyneken's request to be allowed to accept the Baltimore pastorate. *Minutes of the Voters' Assembly of St. Paul's Ev. Lutheran Church,* 18 November 1844.

[90] J. W. Dawson, "Early Masonic History," in T. B. Helm, *History of Allen County, Indiana* (Chicago: Kingman Brothers, 1880), 101-103. Later, Sihler required all who applied for membership "to appear in person and be <u>asked</u> if he is a member of a secret society." *Minutes of the Voters' Assembly of St. Paul's Ev. Lutheran Church, 1837-May 16, 1856,* 1 March 1851.

[91] Rudisill's daughter, Eliza—who was confirmed by Albaugh in 1851 and remained a member of Trinity English Lutheran Church until her death in 1929—was often quoted by Pastor Paul H. Krauss: "Henry Rudisill desired a Lutheran Church in which the faith of the fathers would be shared in English, the language of the children, and one which would be open to all Christians." Richard G. Frazier, letter to the author, April 3, 1987.

[92] *Record Book,* 3, Trinity English Lutheran Church Archives, Fort Wayne, Indiana. Organizing members were Henry Rudisill, Emanuel Rudisill, Samuel Cutshall, John A. Maier, Jacob Kline, Charles Ruch, Ann Edwards, Elizabeth Rudisill, Henry J. Rudisill, Elizabeth J. Maier, Peter Brewer, Judith Brewer, Adam Rudisill, and Sarah Rudisill.

[93] In 1925, the bell was installed in the belfry of the new church at Wayne, Fairfield, and Ewing Streets.

[94] "Memorandum of Agreement," 1 August 1846, First Presbyterian Church of Fort Wayne Archives. On March 10, 1863—when the English Lutherans were building a new church—the Presbyterian Trustees reported that the "deed to the Lutheran Church [had been] approved and executed."

[95] *First Presbyt. Church Trustees Record No. 1, Apr. 12, 1843 to Dec. 22, 1868,* 18 January 1847, First Presbyterian Church of Fort Wayne Archives. Although this resolution is dated five months after the sales agreement was negotiated, it may be assumed that the English Lutherans were worshipping in the Presbyterian meetinghouse after August 1, 1846.

[96] F. W. Husmann wrote that Albaugh visited his Marion Township congregation five times between November 1845 and April 1846.

[97] *Fort Wayne Times,* 6 September 1949 and 17 December 1849. The Rudisills may have wished to have the ceremonies conducted in the larger, although unfinished, Presbyterian Church.

[98] *Record Book,* 6. It appears that this entry was made at a later time, in an attempt to reconstruct an original roll of pastors, officers and members.

In 1852, Albaugh was suspended by the Ministerium of the Eastern District, and expelled the following year for failure to furnish "satisfactory evidence of repentance and reparation . . . treating the Ministerium with contempt by persisting in defiance of its resolution to perform all ministerial acts . . . and addressing to it a very insulting letter." *Minutes of the Eastern District of the Ohio Synod, 1853,* 23,

Ohio Synod Archives, Wittenberg University Library, Springfield, Ohio. Albaugh later engaged in business in St. Louis and, for a number of years, taught in the Immanuel Lutheran parochial school there.

99 Another son, Henry Joseph George Bartholomew, was born on April 9, 1852.

100 The English District protested the "intolerant, oppressive, and inconsistent" behavior of the Ohio Synod in a matter concerning the Capitol University in Columbus, Ohio.

101 In 1858, Bartholomew was serving churches at Constantine and Three Rivers, Michigan; from 1865 to 1881, he served Zion Evangelical Church in Lima, Ohio and St. John's Church in Elida; he died of typhoid fever in Lima on September 23, 1882, at the age of fifty-seven, and was buried in Fort Wayne. *Minutes of the Twenty-Seventh Annual Convention of the English District of the Joint Synod of Ohio... May 16 to May 22, 1883* (Columbus, Ohio: J. L. Trauger, 1883), 7.

102 *Minutes of the Second Convention of the Evangelical Lutheran Synod of Northern Indiana, September 18-20, 1856* (Indianapolis: Elder & Harness, Printers, 1856), 10.

103 *Minutes of the Eleventh Annual Convention of the Evangelical Lutheran Synod of Northern Indiana, Sept. 21 to Oct. 1, 1865* (Fort Wayne: Jenkinson & Hartman, Printers, 1865), 6.

104 *Fort Wayne Republican,* 26 May 1858.

105 Charles Ebersold, *Dawson's Daily Times,* 1 November 1856.

106 *District Synod of Ohio Minutes of the Twentieth Convention... 1876* (Canton, Ohio: A. M. Gregor & Son, Printers, 1876), 37. Ruthrauff was a tutor at Jefferson college while studying for the ministry; the Allegheny Evangelical Lutheran Synod then licensed him to serve a congregation at Schellburg in Bedford County, Pennsylvania; in 1852, he was ordained by the Pittsburgh Synod (General Synod).

107 *Dawson's Daily Times,* 13 April 1859. In September, Ruthrauff was formally installed as pastor at a morning worship service, at which Professor F. W. Conrad of Dayton, Ohio, preached the sermon.

108 *Minutes of the Voters' Assembly of St. Paul's Ev. Lutheran Church, January 11, 1857-July 5, 1867,* 15 April 1860, St. Paul's Lutheran Church Archives, Fort Wayne, Indiana.

109 *Dawson's Daily Times,* 23 November 1859.

110 When a committee of the Evangelical Lutheran Synod of Northern Indiana endorsed another Synod's "abhorrence of the evils of American slavery" and recommended that they "labor and pray for [its] abolition," the Synod president, D. Smith, insisted that his name be recorded in the negative.

Minutes of the Fifth Annual Convention of the Evangelical Lutheran Synod of Northern Indiana, September 22-25, 1859 (Indianapolis: Elder & Harness, Printers, 1859), 19. The most vocal antislavery clergy in Fort Wayne were Methodist, Baptist, and Presbyterian.

111 *Dawson's Daily Times,* 25 November 1859.

112 *Ibid; Fort Wayne Sentinel,* 17 December 1859.

113 *Dawson's Daily Times,* 28 February 1860.

114 *Ibid.,* 2 July 1860.

115 In 1864, the congregation reported 112 communicants, and 60 Sunday School scholars with 18 teachers. *Minutes of the Tenth Annual Convention of the Evangelical Lutheran Synod of Northern Indiana, Sept. 21 to Oct. 1, 1864* (Fort Wayne: Jenkinson & Hartman, Printers, 1864), Appendix A.

116 In 1865, Ruthrauff was elected president of the Evangelical Lutheran Synod of Northern Indiana, and consequently served as its delegate to General Synod's National convention. The following year, Trinity English Lutheran's new church facility was the site of the historic meeting of the General Synod at which the rupture occurred leading to the formation of the General Council of the Evangelical Lutheran Church in North America. Ruthrauff's and his congregation's sympathy was with the General Council.

On June 5, 1867, Ruthrauff resigned his Fort Wayne pastorate to accept the call of Christ Church, Easton, Pennsylvania. After two and a half years, he was induced by the Executive Committee on Home Missions to undertake a mission at Akron, Ohio, where in two years, he led the congregation in building a new church. When his health failed, he went to St. John's Church at Zanesville, Ohio, where he served for eight years until his death in May 1876, in his fiftieth year. Di*strict Synod of Ohio Minutes of the Twentieth Convention... 1876,* 38, 39.

117 "We the undersigned trustees," 25 March 1846, St. Paul's Lutheran Church Archives.

11 See C. W. Schaeffer, *Early History of the Lutheran Church in America* (Philadelphia: Lutheran Book Store, 1868), 142.

119 Between 1830 and 1870, the Lutheran increase in America was three times that of the general population. From 1830 to 1845 the average annual emigration of Germans was 40,000; in the decade of the fifties, nearly a million Germans came to America, of which the majority were Lutherans. See William Warren Sweet, *The Story of Religion in America* (New York: Harper & Brothers, 1939), 373-375, and Carl E. Schneider, *The German Church on the American Frontier* (St. Louis: Eden Publishing House, 1939), 1-5.

120 *Fort Wayne Times,* 20 June 1846.

121 *Ibid.,* 28 August 1847.

122 *Ibid.*, 5 October 1854 and *Fort Wayne Sentinel,* 7 October 1854. The statement was signed: "Rev. Dr. W. Sihler, Rev. Dr. W. Föhlinger, Ch. Piepenbrink, L. Friebel, Ch. Woerking, G. Thieme."

123 *Ibid.*

124 *Fort Wayne Times,* 25 January 1855.

125 *Fort Wayne Sentinel,* 27 July 1846.

126 *Fort Wayne Times,* 19 July 1855.

127 August F. Crämer had come from Frankenmuth, Michigan, in 1850; he succeeded Karl A. Wolter, the school's first regular professor.

128 These children were from the parochial school; Sunday schools were not established in the German Lutheran churches of the Missouri Synod at this time.

129 Friedrich Föhlinger was named St. Paul's second "Vikar" on June 22, 1853, and served for over four years. Other assistant pastors were Ernst Ludwig Hermann Kühn (1852-1853), Martin Stephan (1858-1860), and Julius C. Renz (1860-1861).

130 *Fort Wayne Times,* 11 July 1855, signed "A Visitor."

131 *Dawson's Daily Times,* 26 September 1855.

132 Letter of E. Fair, Lena, Illinois, January 15, 1857, to the *Lutheran Observer,* reprinted in *Fort Wayne Times,* 23 April 1857. The "apartment" or "closet" was the sacristy, to which the clergyman retired during the hymns and offering.

133 H. G. Sauer and J. W. Miller, *Geschichte der Deutschen Ev.-Luth. St. Pauls-Gemeinde,* 40, translated by Annelie Moxter-Collie.

134 Strauss conducted his first wedding on September 23, 1852, and signed the register "A. Strauss, Lutheran Minister." Marriage Records, Allen County Courthouse.

135 *Geschichte der Evangelisch-Lutherischen St. Johannis-Gemeinde zu Ft. Wayne, Indiana* (Columbus, Ohio: Lutherische Verlagshandlund, 1903), translated by Carl H. Amelung and Herbert A. Just, 7, 15-17.

Later histories of St. John's (the congregation adopted "St. John" in the twentieth century) repress the early conflict and allege that the congregation was organized because these emigrants spoke "a different dialect of German . . . [and] did not feel at home among the people of St. Paul's." See *100th Anniversary: 1853-1953, St. John Evangelical Lutheran Church* (Fort Wayne, Ind.: 1853).

136 *Certificate of Election of the Trustees of the German Evangelical Lutheran St. John's Congregation of Fort Wayne, August 23, 1856,* St. John Evangelical Lutheran Church Archives, Fort Wayne, Indiana.

137 A professor at the German Lutheran Seminary wrote that "the congregation contained an element that would not tolerate church discipline and order." Henry W. Diederich, "History of the German Evangelical Lutheran Church in Allen County," in Robert S. Robertson, *The Valley of the Upper Maumee River,* 2 vols. (Madison, Wis.: Brant and Fuller, 1889), 1: 471.

138 *Minutes of the Voters' Assembly of St. Paul's Ev. Lutheran Church, 1837-May 16, 1856,* October 1854.

139 *Geschichte der Evangelisch-Lutherischen St. Johannis-Gemeinde zu Ft. Wayne, Indiana,* 8.

140 *Ibid.,* 19.

141 Wilhelm Sihler, *Lebenslauf von W. Sihler,* 2: 112-116; Carl S. Mundinger, *Government in the Missouri Synod* (St. Louis: Concordia Publishing House, 1947), 188, 189n. Mundinger concludes: "Everybody in his congregation and many people in the Missouri Synod knew that he was a former Prussian army officer, and that fact probably contributed somewhat to the apocryphal accounts of his sternness."

142 H. G. Sauer and J. W. Miller, *Geschichte der Deutschen Ev.-Luth. St. Pauls-Gemeinde,* 30. Husmann noted that Sihler, on December 27, 1846, preached a "simple, clear, emphatic and edifying" sermon. Friedrich Wilhelm Husmann, *Diary on My Ministry. . . From the Middle of October 1845,* 74.

143 Wilhelm Sihler, *Lehre und Wehre,* vol. 31 (May 1879), 137-45, quoted in Lewis W. Spitz, *Life in Two Worlds: Biography of William Sihler,* 95.

144 Lewis W. Spitz, *Life in Two Worlds: Biography of William Sihler,* 74. The pastor of St. John's German Reformed Church, the Reverend John A. Bayer, complained that Sihler preached against him: "A shocking oppostion I have to contend with. Dr. Sihler. . . speaks against prayer meetings, Bible classes, tracts, Sunday Schools—and nobody but a Lutheran of the old stamp can be saved!!" John A. Bayer to Milton Badger, 18 September 1845, AHMS.

145 Lewis W. Spitz, *Life in Two Worlds: Biography of William Sihler,* 48.

146 Sihler's views on women's education may have moderated when his youngest daughter, Elizabeth, insisted on a college education, studied in Berlin, and subsequently taught at Mount Holyoke College in Massachusetts. In her diary she consoled herself that, as a single woman, she would at least escape the worse fate of being a minister's wife. *Ibid.,* 49.

147 *Ibid.,* 119. Sihler enjoyed swimming, riding, cigars, and beer.

148 *Ibid.,* 108. *Der Lutheraner,* February and March 1863; later reprinted in Baltimore in a pamphlet, *Slavery Viewed in the Light of the Holy Scriptures.*

149 The editor of the Whig/Republican *Fort Wayne Times,* John Dawson, called the German-Lutheran Democrats, "Sihlerites."

150 In 1850, the German Singing Society, at their Washington's Birthday concert at Second Presbyterian Church, announced: "The avails are to be devoted to the

relief of the German and Hungarian refugees." *Fort Wayne Times,* 21 February 1850. At the German Fourth of July celebration, a resolution lamented "the deplorable defeat of the cause of freedom in Europe." *Fort Wayne Times,* 27 July 1850.

[151] *Fort Wayne Times,* 5 October 1854.

[152] Lewis W. Spitz, *Life in Two Worlds: Biography of William Sihler,* 118.

[153] "A prolific writer of half a dozen books, numerous pamphlets, and over a hundred articles in church periodicals, [Sihler] was more a religious publicist than a scholar or original thinker. . . . He made no creative response to the intellectual trends of the day." *Ibid.,* 173.

[154] H. G. Sauer and J. W. Miller, *Geschichte der Deutschen Ev.-Luth. St. Pauls-Gemeinde,* 49, translated by Annelie Moxter-Collie. Sihler died a few months later, on October 27, 1885.

[155] Jesse Hoover to Charles Hall, 19 March 1838, AHMS.

Chapter 6

[1] Indiana's first Protestant church was organized in 1798 on Owens (Silver) Creek near Charlestown, at the Falls of the Ohio River. For more on Isaac McCoy, see chapter "Missions to the Miamis."

[2] Jones was born in Newcastle County, Delaware, in 1736; he long served the upper Freehold Baptist church in New Jersey. When he suspected the British would arrest him for his patriot preaching he moved to Pennsylvania and was appointed chaplain in the continental army. During the War of 1812, at the age of seventy-six, he again served as an army chaplain.

[3] John Cooke, *Diary of Captain John Cooke, 1794,* 21 September and 19 October 1794 (Fort Wayne: Public Library of Fort Wayne and Allen County, 1953), n.p.; cited in *Fort Wayne Gazette,* 17 June 1873; original in Harrisburg, Pennsylvania.

[4] Charles E. Furman to Absalom Peters, 19 February 1830, AHMS.

[5] J. L. Williams, *Historical Sketch of the First Presbyterian Church, Fort Wayne, Indiana* (Fort Wayne: John W. Dawson, 1860), 21-22. Williams also wrote: "There are those yet living who can bear grateful testimony to seasons of marked religious enjoyment in the union meetings of that period, held amid these rude surroundings, with so little of the elegance, or even the convenience, with which Christian congregations in Fort Wayne are now blessed."

[6] J. L. Williams, *Historical Sketch of the First Presbyterian Church,* 17.

[7] John W. Dawson, *Fort Wayne Daily Sentinel,* 3 April 1872.

[8] Ann Turner, Fort Wayne, Indiana, to Jesse L. Holman, Aurora, Indiana, 18 May 1833, Jesse L. Holman Correspondence, 1820-1840, Franklin College Library, Franklin, Indiana.

[9] "The First Baptist Church," anon., in Robert S. Robertson, *Valley of the Upper Maumee River,* 2 vols. (Madison, Wis.: Brant & Fuller, 1889), 2: 302.

[10] Presenting their letters of transfer were Richard Worth, Elizabeth Worth, John Fairfield, Jane Fairfield, William Worth, Merriam Sawtell, Sarah Swop, Ann Archer, Hannah Worth, Elizabeth Morgan. Baptized were Ann Girard, Mahaly Worth, Charles Swop, David Worth, Richard Worth, Jr., and Elizabeth Morgan. John Fairfield was named Clerk, and Richard Worth, Deacon. *Church Record Book "B" 1842 to 1869,* First Baptist Church Archives, Fort Wayne, Indiana.

[11] The honorific title "elder" was loosely applied by Baptists at this time to both ordained ministers and lay preachers, and was without technical significance.

[12] David Benedict, *A General History of the Baptist Denomination in America and Other Parts of the World* (New York: Lewis Colby and Company, 1848), 874. The author states that "elder R. Tisdale appears to have been distinguished for assiduity and success."

[13] The short-lived mission of the Christian Church (Disciples of Christ) in Fort Wayne (1846-1848) insisted on believer baptism by immersion. See chapter, "Swedenborgian, Universalist, and Christian."

[14] Joseph Morgan, Fort Wayne, to Jesse L. Holman, Aurora, 27 February 1837, Jesse L. Holman Correspondence. Morgan's wife, Elizabeth, was a charter member of the congregation, but he never joined.

[15] S. R. Ball, William Corbin, A. T. Rankin, and Smalwood Noel to Milton Badger, December 1837, AHMS.

[16] Other churches in the association were Dayton, Delphi, Grand Prairie, Logansport, Bethel, Frankfort, Hopewell, and Rossville. William T. Stott, *Indiana Baptist History* (Franklin, Ind.: 1908), 170.

[17] Corbin died in late 1841 or early 1842.

[18] John F. Cady, *The Origin and Development of the Missionary Baptist Church in Indiana* (Berne, Ind., Berne Witness Co., 1942), 140.

[19] *The Regular Baptist,* April 1839.

[20] "History of the First Baptist Church, Fort Wayne," *Huntington Baptist Association Minutes, 1867,* 6-7.

[21] The only new member received during 1839 came by a letter of transfer. *Church Record Book "B" 1842 to 1869,* 12.

22 See John F. Cady, *The Origin and Development of the Missionary Baptist Church in Indiana* , 31-63.

23 *Baptist Home Missions in North America,* H. L. Morehouse, ed. (New York: Baptist Home Mission Rooms, 1883), 331.

24 F. K. D. Wyneken, *Die Noth der Deutschen Lutheraner in Nordamerika,* first printed in *Zeitschrift fuer Protestantismus und Kirche* (Erlangen: 1843); reprinted in Pittsburgh, Pa. (1844). S. Edgar Schmidt, trans.,*The Distress of the German Lutherans in North America,* edited by R. F. Rehmer (Fort Wayne: Concordia Theological Seminary Press, 1982), 31-32.

25 Baptist Home Missionary Society Records, American Baptist Historical Society, Rochester, New York.

26 The Huntington, Fort Wayne, and Crooked Creek churches left the Tippecanoe Association, probably for geographical convenience, to join with four other previously unaffiliated congregations in this new association. David Benedict, *A General History of the Baptist Denomination in America and Other Parts of the World,* 874.

27 Gildersleeve also may have assumed some preaching responsibilities for the Huntington Baptist Church in 1841-42.

28 *Church Record Book "B" 1842 to 1869,* 11.

29 *Ibid.,* 25-37.

30 The lot was later designated 514 East Washington Street.

31 *Church Record Book "B" 1842 to 1869,* 25-26.

32 Combs's denominational obituary states: "He preached for more than fifty years, during which time hundreds were led by him to Christ . . . . He spent the last eighteen years of his life in Butler county, where he did much lasting good." Combs died there in 1884.

33 *Church Record Book "B" 1842 to 1869,* 29.

34 *Ibid.,* 31.

35 *Ibid.,* 32.

36 *First Presbyterian Church Session Record No. 2: July 1, 1831 to Dec. 22, 1868,* 23 August 1843, First Presbyterian Church Archives, Fort Wayne, Indiana.

37 *Church Record Book "B" 1842 to 1869,* 30.

38 "Letters From Indiana—No. VII," *Fort Wayne Sentinel,* 30 July 1842.

39 Charles Beecher to Milton Badger, 16 September 1844, AHMS.

40 "The First Baptist Church," anon., Robert S. Robertson,*Valley of the Upper Maumee River,* 2: 303.

41 Sleeper had most recently served the Huntington Church, 1843-46. In August 1847, he was in New Jersey laboring as a missionary (1847-49); he later served New Jersey congregations at Canton Church (five years) and at Dividing Creek (three years). Sleeper died in Vincent, Pennsylvania, March 19, 1865.

42 *Minutes of the Huntington Baptist Association, 1845,* 6.

43 Mason was born in Cheshire, Berkshire County, Massachusetts in 1805 and grew up in Orleans County, New York. He studied medicine, then theology, was ordained in 1833, and initially served churches in Ohio; Mason died at Bloomington, Illinois, February 2, 1854.

44 *Church Record Book "B" 1842 to 1869,* 43.

45 "The First Baptist Church," anon., Robert S. Robertson,*Valley of the Upper Maumee River,* 2: 303.

46 *Fort Wayne Times,* 1 January 1848.

47 *Minutes of the Huntington Baptist Association, 1847,* 15-17.

48 Charles Beecher to Milton Badger, 19 July 1847, AHMS.

49 *Church Record Book "B" 1842 to 1869,* 47.

50 *Minutes of the Huntington Baptist Association, 1846,* 6-7.

51 The Church Record Book states: "S. B. Searl has become insane and gone to New York." A later church history says he was "stricken down with malaria."

52 *Church Record Book "B" 1842 to 1869,* 48.

53 *Fort Wayne Times,* 29 October 1855. Amalgamation meant miscegenation.

54 B. J. Griswold, *The Pictorial History of Fort Wayne, Indiana,* 2 vols. (Chicago: Robert O. Law Company, 1917), 1: 415.

55 *Minutes of the Huntington Baptist Association, 1849,* 5-6. After 1857, Burroughs's name no longer appears on the association's list of ministers.

56 *The Standard,* 4 January 1855.

57 *Fort Wayne Sentinel,* 20 January 1849.

58 *Fort Wayne Times,* 29 March 1849.

59 Home Mission Society grants to the Fort Wayne mission were: 1841, $150; 1842, $100; 1843, $25; 1844, $75; 1845, $95.19; 1847, $150; 1848, $50; 1849, $84.56; 1850, $162.50; 1851, $239.50; 1852, $150; 1853, $150; 1854, $150. Baptist Home Missionary Society Records.

60 *Fort Wayne Sentinel,* 22 November and 27 December 1851.

61 "The First Baptist Church," anon., in Robert S. Robertson,*Valley of the Upper Maumee River,* 2: 303.

62 Ibid.

63 *Fort Wayne Times,* 3 May 1855.

64 *Ibid.*

65 *Church Record Book "B" 1842 to 1869,* 73.

66 *Dawson's Daily Times,* 21 July 1855.

67 *Fort Wayne Times,* 1 January 1857.

68 *Church Record Book "B" 1842 to 1869,* 82.

69 "The First Baptist Church," anon., in Robert S.

Robertson, *Valley of the Upper Maumee River,* 2: 303. Wilkens concluded his ministry on July 8, 1860, and went to Michigan.

70 J. F. Cady states: "The Baptist constituency in particular was drawn from the humbler strata of the indigenous elements of the population." *The Origin and Development of the Missionary Baptist Church in Indiana,* 8.

Chapter 7

1 See Edward Rochie Hardy, Jr., "Kemper's Missionary Episcopate: 1835-1859," *Historical Magazine of the Protestant Episcopal Church,* vol. 4, no. 3 (September 1935). In 1837, the Diocese of Indiana was carved out of the "Northwest Diocese"; Kemper then continued as the "acting" or "missionary bishop" of Indiana, while retaining the title of Bishop of Missouri.

2 Jackson Kemper to Elizabeth Kemper, 31 August 1837, Jackson Kemper Papers, State Historical Society of Wisconsin, Madison, Wisconsin.

Kemper and Johnson also visited Michigan City, LaPorte, South Bend, Mishawaka, Lima, Delphi, Americus, and Lafayette. *The Church Worker,* Diocese of Indiana, March 1884, 7.

3 "Spirit of Missions," vol. 2, 165, quoted in Edward Rochie Hardy, Jr., "Kemper's Missionary Episcopate: 1835-1859," *Historical Magazine of the Protestant Episcopal Church,* vol. 4, no. 3 (September, 1935), 198.

4 Benjamin Hutchins, "Protestant Episcopal Church" in *Combined History of Edwards, Lawrence and Wabash Counties, Illinois* (Philadelphia: J. L. McDonough & Co., 1883), 165, 166.

5 Jackson Kemper to Henry J. Hutchins, 30 August 1839, Letterbook/Diary, vol. 83, Jackson Kemper Papers.

6 Hutchins wrote: "We took the stage at Maumee City and in two days reached Fort Wayne. The stage goes from either place every other day and meets at Defiance, which is about half way, every evening." "The road . . . has been much improved and a good strong tray coach runs upon it." Benjamin Hutchins to Jackson Kemper, 17 May 1839 and 11 March 1840, Jackson Kemper Papers.

7 Henry Hutchins seems to have made the management of his son's career his full time job, and sustained an active correspondence with Kemper on the subject.

8 The "academy building" was Alexander McJunkin's schoolhouse, located on the east side of Lafayete St. between Berry and Wayne streets.

9 Benjamin Hutchins to Jackson Kemper, 17 May 1839, Jackson Kemper Papers.

10 Ibid.

11 Hutchins lodged with the Huxfords for his first "two or three weeks" in Fort Wayne. Letter of Sarah Huxford, 1894, Trinity Episcopal Church Archives, Fort Wayne, Indiana.

12 Benjamin Hutchins to Jackson Kemper, 17 May 1839, Jackson Kemper Papers.

13 Ibid., 27 May 1839.

14 Ibid., 21 June 1839.

15 Vestry Minutes of Christ Church, 6 August 1839, Trinity Episcopal Church Archives.

16 Benjamin Hutchins to the Vestry, 16 November 1839, Trinity Episcopal Church Archives.

17 Huxford, Broom, Moon, and Stophlet to Hutchins, 18 November 1839, Trinity Episcopal Church Archives.

18 Benjamin Hutchins to Jackson Kemper, 2 December 1839, Jackson Kemper Papers.

19 Jackson Kemper to Benjamin Hutchins, 5 December 1839, Letterbook/Diary, vol. 85, Jackson Kemper Papers.

20 In 1842, Hutchins became rector of St. John's Episcopal Church in Albion, Illinois; he died there in his 87th year. In 1857 it was reported in Fort Wayne: "The Rev. Benjamin Hutchings *(sic),* a clergyman in the Episcopal Church, Albion, Illinois (formerly of this city) we find it announced in one of the church journals, has lost, in a little over a month, namely from April 24 to May 31, eight of his children—two sons and six daughters, whose ages varied from one to eighteen years. What was the disease which so fearfully decimated a single family, we do not find stated." *Fort Wayne Sentinel,* 4 July 1857. One son, Harry, survived this epidemic of scarlet fever.

21 Benjamin Hutchins, Philadelphia, to Jackson Kemper, 11 March 1840, Letterbook/Diary vol. 22: 79, Jackson Kemper Papers.

22 Jackson Kemper to Elizabeth Kemper, 20 July 1840 and 6 August 1843, Jackson Kemper Papers.

23 Jackson Kemper Diaries, 16 and 17 July 1840, Jackson Kemper Papers.

24 Kemper's sermon topics and texts are some of the earliest recorded in Fort Wayne: "a. m. . . . on love of Christ; p. m. . . . on temporal benefits of Christianity; night . . . on Felix." Ibid., 19 July 1840.

25 Ibid.

26 Ibid., 20 July 1840. Isaac DeGroff Nelson later served on the vestry, and was elected Senior Warden in 1866.

27 Ibid.

28 Ibid., 21 and 22 July 1840.

29 In June 1841, Kemper lamented: "The list of vacancies is much too long . . . . Fort Wayne . . . ought, if possible, to be supplied immediately." *Journal of Proceedings of the*

Fourth Annual Convention of the Protestant Episcopal Church in the Diocese of Indiana, June 1841, 29.

30 *Fort Wayne Sentinel,* 1 October 1842.

31 "A. B." (pseud.), "Letters From Indiana - No. III," *Fort Wayne Sentinel,* 30 April 1842.

32 Bessie Kerran Roberts, *Fort Wayne's Family Album* (Fort Wayne: Cummins Printing Co., 1960), 78, quoting Ferry's daughter, Eudora Ferry Boyles.

33 Peter Bailey, "Historical Address," read at the semi-centennial anniversary of Trinity Parish, Fort Wayne, 20 May 1894; cited in the *Fort Wayne Sentinel,* 20 May 1915.

34 Bailey mentions two Irish-born teachers, Miss Cornelia Hotchkiss (who married Michigan Supreme Court Judge James Campbell) and his wife's sister, Miss Livia Penton (who married Hibben Porter); although Sunday school classes had been held in Fort Wayne since 1825, these are among the earliest recorded names of teachers. Ibid.

35 Ibid.

36 Jackson Kemper Diaries, February, 1844, Jackson Kemper Papers. Halsted was offered the choice of Fort Wayne, Delphi, and Logansport; after visiting Delphi, he choose Fort Wayne.

37 Jacob Hull, senior warden; Peter P. Bailey, junior warden; Lucien P. Ferry and R. M. Lyon, vestrymen. Vestry Minutes, 25 May 1844, Trinity Episcopal Church Archives.

38 Halsted usually signed himself "Minister of the Parish and Missionary"; once he termed himself "Presbyter." The vestry referred to him as the "Rev. Mr. Halsted," "pastor," "minister," "missionary minister," and "rector." At no time, during these formative years, was the Episcopal clergyman called priest or father.

39 Jackson Kemper to Elizabeth Kemper, 23 August 1844, Jackson Kemper Papers.

40 Vestry Minutes, 5 May 1845, Trinity Episcopal Church Archives.

41 *Fort Wayne Times,* 1 November 1845. Halsted reported that the parish library consisted "of about fifty volumes." *Journal of Proceedings of the Eighth Annual Convention of the Protestant Episcopal Church in the Diocese of Indiana,* June 1845, 24.

42 A Universalist minister later preached in the courthouse "once a month." Charles Beecher to Amelia Ogden, 20 May 1845, Beecher-Stowe Family Papers, 1798-1856, Schlesinger Library, Radcliffe College, Cambridge, Massachusetts. Charles Beecher to Milton Badger, 16 December 1844, AHMS.

43 *Articles of Religion, As Established by the Bishops, the Clergy, and Laity of the Protestant Episcopal Church in the United Sates of America* (Philadelphia: 1801), Art. 17: "Of Predestination and Election."

44 Erasmus Manford, *Twenty-five Years in the West* (Chicago: H. B. Manford, 1885), 167. T. B. Helm, in *History of Allen County Indiana* (Chicago: Kingman Brothers, 1880), 99, says the debate was held on two evenings during the week of September 11-18, 1843; there is, however, no record of an Episcopal clergyman in Fort Wayne during 1843.

45 *S. W. Sentinel-Extra. The Town of New Harmony and the Rev. Benjamin Halsted* (Evansville, Indiana: Alexander Burns Jr., April 1842), 2.

46 A portion of Halsted's pique with the Owenites stemmed from his difficulty in securing a suitable facility for Sunday worship: "The only place which we can use for public worship is a public lecture room, in which an infidel society has a claim." Benjamin Halsted, New Harmony, to Jackson Kemper, St. Louis, 15 December 1841, Jackson Kemper Papers.

47 Peter P. Bailey, "Historical Address." Bailey was active in Whig politics and later served as a judge; in 1858 he became editor of the *Fort Wayne Republican;* in 1865 he organized the Merchant's National Bank and became president of the Fort Wayne and Cincinnati Railroad. He died in Fort Wayne in 1899.

48 *Fort Wayne Sentinel,* 2 November 1844.

49 Charles Beecher to Milton Badger, 16 September 1844, AHMS.

50 Ibid., 16 December 1844.

51 M. P. Eggleston, "Calvary Parish and Its Rector," *St. Mary's Church News* (Lexington, Mississippi: 1889).

52 Jackson Kemper to Elizabeth Kemper, 4 September 1845, Jackson Kemper Papers.

53 Jackson Kemper, Letterbook/Diary, vol. 107, 16 October 1845, Jackson Kemper Papers.

54 B. Halsted to the Vestry of Trinity Church, 1 December 1845, Trinity Episcopal Church Archives.

55 On Whitsunday 1847, Halsted visited Trinity Church to preach and administer communion. In 1852, he became missionary at Athens, Tennessee; in 1854, he founded St. Mary's Church in Lexington, Mississippi, which he served until his death in 1888. Peter Bailey, who had retired to Jackson, Mississippi, wrote in 1894: "Rev. Mr. Halsted died ...in Lexington, Miss., where he had resided for thirty years, honored and respected by all who know him. I frequently met him at our diocesan councils in Mississippi. He had not forgotten the incident of the political meeting on a Sunday in Fort Wayne, nor Dr. Anderson, nor Major Edsell and the barrel of flour." Peter Bailey, Historical Address.

56 Jackson Kemper to Benjamin Halsted, Letterbook, 21 January 1846, Jackson Kemper Papers.

57 *Indiana Convention Journal,* cited in Edward Rochie Hardy, Jr., "Kemper's Missionary Episcopate: 1835-1859," *Historical Magazine of the Protestant Episcopal Church,*

vol. 4, no. 3 (September, 1935), 207.

58 Ibid.

59 Peter P. Bailey to John W. Mitchell, 11 October 1844, Bailey Letters, Allen County-Fort Wayne Historical Society, Fort Wayne, Indiana. The Oxford Movement, then led by John Henry Newman, held that apostolic succession and the sacraments were the true source of divine grace; when Newman joined the Roman Catholic Church in 1845, the Anglo-Catholics (also called Tractarians, Puseyites, and the Oxford Movement) gained influence under the leadership of Edward Pusey.

60 Ibid., 18 May 1846.

61 Jackson Kemper, Letterbook/Diary, vol. 107, 23 May 1846, Jackson Kemper Papers.

62 Ibid., 21 August 1847. The "cheap plan" may have been by Richard Upjohn, who later published *Upjohn's Rural Architecture: Designs, Working Drawings, and Specifications For a Wooden Church and Other Rural Structures* (New York: George P. Putman, 1852).

63 Charles Beecher to Milton Badger, 19 July 1847, AHMS. When Bishop Kemper conducted worship on July 17, 1847, an afternoon service was scheduled at the Methodist Church, in addition to morning prayer at the courthouse. *Fort Wayne Times,* 10 July 1847.

64 Vestry Minutes, 17 February 1848, Trinity Episcopal Church Archives.

65 Peter P. Bailey to John W. Mitchell, 10 April 1848, Bailey Letters.

66 *Fort Wayne Sentinel,* 15 April 1848.

67 There was no other meeting of the vestry recorded during Power's stay; apparently Powers declined the rectorship when it was offered. Peter Bailey noted: "Our clergyman is liked very much, but whether we shall be able to support him is not yet certainly known." Peter Bailey to John W. Mitchell, 2 May 1848, Bailey Letters.

68 *Fort Wayne Sentinel,* 12 August 1848.

69 Jackson Kemper, Letterbook, 11 August 1848, Jackson Kemper Papers. Powers may have left Fort Wayne before receiving this letter.

70 *Journal of Proceedings of the Eleventh Annual Convention of the Protestant Episcopal Church in the Diocese of Indiana,* June 1848, 19.

71 Newspaper advertisements indicate Bishop Kemper conducted services in the courthouse in May 1846 and July 1847. Parish records show that he visited in July 1840, July 1843, August 1844, August 1845, May 1846, July 1847, and October 1848.

72 Vestry to Joseph Large, 12 October 1848, Trinity Episcopal Church Archives.

73 In his annual report to the Diocese, Large described "the addition to their Church" which doubled "the former number of sittings. This addition makes the Church in the form of a cross; the main body or nave being 58 by 22, with one central aisle; the transept 16 by 6, and the chancel 14 by 9. The organ is placed in one of the transepts. A beautiful chancel window of stained glass, made in Buffalo, was presented to the Church by two gentlemen of the parish, P. P. Bailey and Wilfred Smith, Esqs." *Journal of Proceedings of the Thirteenth Annual Convention of the Protestant Episcopal Church in the Diocese of Indiana,* June 1850, 49. Large modestly did not mention that he had pledged to pay the cost of one of the three windows.

74 *Fort Wayne Sentinel,* 6 June 1849.

75 The bishop traveled to Fort Wayne from his home in Lafayette by canal boat: "At Delphi I was joined by the Rev. Mr. Phelps, and at Peru by the Rev. Mr. Harriman . . . . On Thursday morning, May 23, I consecrated the neat and commodious parish Church, recently enlarged and improved by the introduction of stained glass windows at the east end and the transept, and a new arrangement of the chancel and its appendages, by the name of Trinity Church. The request to consecrate was read by the Rev. Mr. Halsted of Mishawaka." *Journal of Proceedings of the Thirteenth Annual Convention of the Protestant Episcopal Church in the Diocese of Indiana,* June 1850, 23.

76 David Miller, "George Upfold," in *A History of the Episcopal Diocese of Indianapolis: 1838-1988,* Joyce Marks Booth, ed. (Dallas, Texas: Taylor Publishing Co., 1988), 39.

77 When Missouri, Indiana, and Iowa in turn became independent dioceses, Kemper, in 1854, became bishop of Wisconsin, his favorite part of the original see. He was instrumental in the founding of Nashotah House and Racine College. In 1868, at the age of seventy-nine, he attended the Council of Bishops in England and was honored with an LL.D. degree by Cambridge University. At the time of his death, two years later at his home in Delafield, Wisconsin, he had established seven dioceses, founded three colleges, and planted the Episcopal Church in the Northwest.

78 George Upfold, Diaries, 15 May 1863 (written at Bristol, Elkhart County), Indiana Historical Society, Indianapolis, Indiana. After the initial visit, Upfold visited Fort Wayne at least once a year: 3rd Sunday after Easter in 1851 and 1852; 4th Sunday after Easter in 1853; 28 April 1854; 14 February 1855; 5-8 October 1855; 20-24 November 1856 (Thanksgiving); 30 May-6 June 1857 (Diocesan Convention); 24-26 April 1858; 10-11 April 1859; 25-26 June 1959; 26-29 May 1860; 13-17 March 1861; 15-19 August 1861; 11-16 December 1861; 1 May 1862; 18-24 April 1863; 25 September 1863; 30 March-1 April 1864; 15-18 April 1864.

79 Joseph K. Edgerton, *Private Journal No. 4,* 20 July 1851, Allen County Public Library, Fort Wayne, Indiana.

The minutes of the Methodist Church Trustees record Edgerton's resignation from that board at the end of 1849; he appears at his first vestry meeting May 29, 1851.

[80] *Fort Wayne Times,* 21 November 1850. Other local clergy speaking in the series were the Reverends J. H. Sinex, J. G. Riheldaffer, S. Brenton, and J. M. Meeson.

[81] *Fort Wayne Sentinel,* 14 December 1850.

[82] In June 1852, Large reported: "During last summer we commenced the erection of a parsonage, which by contract, was to have been completed by the 1st of December last. It is not yet done, however—though I hope to remove my family into it in the course of a few weeks." *Journal of Proceedings of the Fifteenth Annual Convention of the Protestant Episcopal Church in the Diocese of Indiana,* June 1852, 52.

[83] David Miller, "George Upfold," in *A History of the Episcopal Diocese of Indianapolis: 1838-1988,* Joyce Marks Booth, ed., 35.

[84] Vestry Minutes, 12 September 1851, Trinity Episcopal Church Archives.

[85] A number of episcopal clergy had been attracted from other communions. The Reverend J. W. Ray, who served as pastor of the Second Presbyterian Church in Fort Wayne (and who had previously served in Kalamazoo near Bruce) later joined the Episcopal Church and served as a lay delegate to the 1859 Diocesan Convention.

[86] *Fort Wayne Times* (dated January 25, 1855), published 1 February 1855.

[87] The writer refers to Jonathan Edwards, pastor of First Presbyterian Church; Charles Beecher, who had concluded his ministry at Second Presbyterian Church five years before; and William J. Chaplin, a Universalist minister from Kosciusko County who occasionally preached in the court-house.

[88] *Fort Wayne Times,* 15 February 1855. The use of the Dutch word "patroon" suggests that Bailey, from New York City, wrote this rejoinder.

[89] Bruce assumed the rectorship of St. Paul's Church in Alton, Illinois, in 1859. In 1870, at the age of 52, he became a missionary in Arkansas, serving St. John's Church in Helena, where he remained until his death in 1895.

[90] Letter of James Lloyd Breck, 30 May 1840, cited in Edward Rochie Hardy, Jr., "Kemper's Missionary Episcopate: 1835-1859," *Historical Magazine of the Protestant Episcopal Church,* vol. 4, no. 3 (September, 1935), 204.

[91] *Fort Wayne Sentinel,* 6 June 1857.

[92] Tigar's wife, Catherine Shimeall, was a member of the parish, and their five children were baptized in the church; a native of England, Catherine's brother was an Episcopal clergyman serving Trinity Church in Brooklyn; she died in 1848.

[93] *Dawson's Daily Times,* 7 April 1859.

[94] *Fort Wayne Republican,* 20 October 1858.

[95] *Fort Wayne Sentinel,* 3 May 1856. Pattison went on to serve parishes in Portage City, Wisconsin (1858-60); Dutchess County, New York (1860-68); Bethel, Connecticut (1868-81); he died in Bethel on April 10, 1881 at age 50.

[96] George Upfold, Diary, 1857-1862, "Introduction," written 2 January 1863.

[97] Vestry Minutes, 10 June 1858, Trinity Episcopal Church Archives. On July 11, 1858, the Reverend John Long of Scranton, Pennsylvania officiated at Sunday worship. *Fort Wayne Republican,* 7 July 1858.

[98] *Fort Wayne Republican,* 6 October 1858.

[99] *Ibid.,* 20 October 1858.

[100] Battin was called to the Cooperstown parish in 1848; he resigned in 1858 in a altercation with his vestry over the administration of some minor fund. According to that church's historian, Battin was a "vigorous personality... and brought to the parish the kind of leadership it had not before experienced .... It seems clear to me that Mr. Battin was a Tractarian; . . . it had been customary to administer the Sacrament of the Lord's Supper once a quarter. Under Battin, it was celebrated once a month and on all major feasts." George E. DeMille, *Christ Church Parish History, 1810-1960* (1960), 16-18.

[101] *Fort Wayne Republican,* 7 September 1859, announcing "the third term of this now popular school." Martha Bandriff Hanna remembered "Rev. S. H. Battin's school—the morning session lasting until one o'clock." *Reminiscences of Old Fort Wayne* (Fort Wayne: Public Library of Fort Wayne and Allen County, 1906), n. p.

[102] *Fort Wayne Republican,* 18 January 1860.

[103] George A. Irvin, who had had been appointed the city's first Superintendent of Schools in 1857, resigned in 1863, upon his ordination to the Presbyterian ministry and enlistment as a chaplain in the Union Army. He was succeeded by S. S. Green.

[104] Stephen H. Battin to the Church Wardens and Vestry, 6 July 1863, Trinity Episcopal Church Archives.

[105] On August 18, 1863, Bishop Upfold dismissed Battin to the Diocese of Ohio; a necrology report states that he was "thrice rector of Christ Church, Jersey City." He died February 23, 1893.

[106] Vestry Minutes, 13 July 1863, Trinity Episcopal Church Archives.

[107] Ibid., 28 December 1863. Charles Crosby Miller was a church architect from Toledo, Ohio.

[108] Ibid., 24 October 1865.

[109] At the age of sixty-two, Large was asked to resign because of "a growing apathy and indifference to his ministration, and a want of that congeniality of feeling that should

exist between a rector and the members of his parish." Ibid., March 22, 1872. Some "want of congeniality" had been aggravated by his strident public opposition to the Woman's Rights Movement. (See chapter "Women's Societies.) Large later served churches in Michigan; he died at age eighty in Galveston, Texas, April 18, 1890. He was buried in Fort Wayne next to his wife; his daughter had continued to reside in Fort Wayne, where she co-directed a musical school.

110 *Fort Wayne Times,* 5 January 1853.

Chapter 8

1 *The Liberator,* vol. 11 (July 23, 1841), 118, cited in Dorothy C. Bass, "Their Prodigious Influence: Women, Religion and Reform in Antebellum America," in *Women of Spirit: Female Leadership in the Jewish and Christian Traditions,* Rosemary Ruether and Eleanor McLaughlin, eds. (New York: Simon and Schuster, 1979), 280.

2 Dorothy C. Bass, "Their Prodigious Influence: Women, Religion and Reform in Antebellum America," in *Women of Spirit: Female Leadership in the Jewish and Christian Traditions,* Rosemary Ruether and Eleanor McLaughlin, eds., 281.

3 James Chute to Absalom Peters, 27 January 1834, AHMS.

4 Ibid.

5 Susan Man to Mary A. Hawkins, 27 October 1836; Susan Man to Marie Halsey, 9 January 1837, McCulloch Papers, Lilly Library, Bloomington, Indiana.

6 Jesse Hoover to Susan Man, 10 November 1837, McCulloch Papers.

7 Sarah Huxford to the 50th Anniversary Committee, 1894, Trinity Episcopal Church Archives, Fort Wayne, Indiana.

8 *Dawson's Daily Times,* 29 and 31 May 1860, 4 June 1860; *Fort Wayne Sentinel,* 2 June 1860.

9 *Fort Wayne Sentinel,* 19 March 1859.

10 *Ibid.,* 1 October 1859. In 1861, the Thiriza Association became the Ladies Hebrew Benevolent Society.

11 *Minutes of the Voters' Assembly of St. Paul's Ev. Lutheran Church, 1837-1856,* 8 August 1846, St. Paul's Lutheran Church Archives, Fort Wayne, Indiana.

12 Susan Man McCulloch to Maria Halsey, 26 February 1846, McCulloch Papers.

13 *Fort Wayne Times,* 27 February 1847. See Chapter "Old School Presbyterians" for the account of Wood's attack on the Presbyterian Women's Fair in 1843.

14 *Dawson's Daily Times,* 9 June 1856.

15 *Fort Wayne Times,* 14 February 1850.

16 Ellen C. Parsons, "History of Woman's Organized Missionary Work as Promoted by American Women," in *Woman in Missions: Papers and Addresses Presented at the Woman's Congress of Missions, October 2-4, 1893,* E. M. Wherry, comp. (New York: American Tract Society, 1894), 85.

17 See Helen Barrett Montgomery, *Western Women in Eastern Lands* (New York: The MacMillen Co., 1911).

18 Ellen C. Parsons, "History of Woman's Organized Missionary Work as Promoted By American Women," in *Woman in Missions: Papers and Addresses Presented at the Woman's Congress of Missions, October 2-4, 1893,* E. M. Wherry, comp., 86.

19 J[esse] L. Williams, *Historical Sketch of the First Presbyterian Church, Fort Wayne, Indiana, With Early Reminiscences of the Place* (Fort Wayne, Ind.: John W. Dawson, 1860), 22.

20 *Fort Wayne Times,* 28 June 1845.

21 *Ibid.,* 14 August 1847.

22 John M. Lowrie, *Adam and His Times* (Philadelphia: Presbyterian Board of Publication, 1861), 49.

23 "An Address: Delivered at the anniversary celebration of the Methodist Sabbath School in the City of Fort Wayne, Jan, 27, 1845. By Joseph K. Edgerton." *Fort Wayne Times,* 8 March 1845.

24 The date of the founding of the Fort Wayne Female Benevolent Society is unknown; financial reports to the public were made in the early 1840s; in 1845 the president signed her report "M. E. H." *Ibid.,* 22 February 1845.

25 *Dawson's Daily Times,* 22 November 1855.

26 *Fort Wayne Times,* 24 April 1847.

27 *Ibid.,* 10 January 1856.

28 *Fort Wayne Sentinel,* 10 January 1856. Alida Hubbell had come to Fort Wayne in 1836 to teach school with Susan Man; she married a local merchant, Royal W. Taylor, and was active in the Second Presbyterian Church. In 1893, she was one of the leaders of the Woman's Club League that successfully petitioned the city council to impose a tax for library purposes.

29 *Fort Wayne Times,* 18 January 1856.

30 *Ibid.,* 21 January 1856.

31 *Ibid.,* 22 January 1856.

32 *Fort Wayne Daily Times,* 9 May 1856. Louisa E. Sturgis was a daughter of Alexander Ewing, who settled in Fort Wayne in 1822; she married Dr. Charles E. Sturgis, a prominent physician and politician, and was a member of First Presbyterian Church; she died March 10, 1887, at the age of sixty-eight. Mary J. Read Randall was born in Washington, Indiana, and married a young lawyer, Franklin P. Randall; they moved to Fort Wayne in 1838, and later

joined the Episcopal Church; she died in Fort Wayne on December 30, 1912.

33 W. J. Rorabaugh, *The Alcoholic Republic: An American Tradition* (New York: Oxford University Press, 1979), 8.

34 *Fort Wayne Times,* 31 May 1854.

35 *Fort Wayne Sentinel,* 1 April 1874. Other leaders in the Allen County Temperance Society were B. W. Oakley, J. W. Dawson, C. B. Oakley, C. W. Allen, James Humphrey, John Cochrane, Isaac Jenkinson, Charles Case, L. M. Ninde, M. F. Barber, and I. N. McAbee.

36 *Ibid.,* 16 June 1855.

37 *Fort Wayne Times,* 22 February 1855.

38 M[ary] F. Thomas, Fort Wayne, February 20, 1855, *The Lily,* 1 April 1855. Lucretia P. Wright had come to Fort Wayne from Ohio; after Fort Wayne she lectured in Lima, Ohio.

39 *Fort Wayne Standard,* 22 February 1855.

40 *Fort Wayne Times,* 19 March 1856. Carrie Nation, who achieved notoriety in the 1890s for her "hatchetation" of "joints" (her words), was only nine years old at this time. Temperance advocates also called such places "tippling houses" and "liquor hells."

41 Some of the same persons who supported the antislavery and temperance movements also embraced the cause of peace; in June 1851, a state-wide convention met in Indianapolis to endorse the objects of the World Peace Convention which was to meet in Frankfurt-Am-Main later that year. *Indiana State Sentinel* (Indianapolis), 15 June 1851.

42 Alice Hamilton, *Exploring the Dangerous Trades* (Boston: Little, Brown and Company 1843), 23, 24.

43 *Fort Wayne Sentinel,* 28 March 1846.

44 In 1847, the Indiana legislature had granted married women the right to devise property and to control real estate; at the Constitutional Convention, Owen sought to include personal property in these rights, and to then safeguard these gains by putting them in the constitution. Richard W. Leopold, *Robert Dale Owen, A Biography* (Cambridge, Mass.: Harvard University Press, 1940), 273.

45 See Rex M. Potterf, *The Constitution of Indiana Made in 1851* (Fort Wayne-Allen County Public Library, n. d.), 12-16, 23-29.

46 *Fort Wayne Times,* 2 January 1851.

47 Eliza (pseud.), "The Rights of Women," *Ibid.,* 25 December 1851.

48 Eliza (pseud.), "Rights of Females," *Ibid.,* 11 December 1851.

49 B. J. Griswold, *The Pictorial History of Fort Wayne, Indiana,* 2 vols. (Chicago: Robert O. Law Company, 1917), 2: 428. Lindley. M. Ninde was described as a "forceful and skillful advocate . . . . Though lacking in many of the qualities of a polished orator, he is nevertheless one of the most convincing speakers before a jury." Robert S. Robertson, *Valley of the Upper Maumee River,* 2 vols. (Madison, Wis.: Brant & Fuller, 1889), 2: 509. For his successful defense of an African-American visitor, see chapter, "The African Methodists."

50 John Witherspoon Scott to Beulah C. Ninde, 14 November, 1851, Ninde-Puckett Letters, Lewis G. Thompson Collection, Allen County-Fort Wayne Historical Society, Fort Wayne, Indiana. Scott was principal of the Oxford Female Institute from 1849 to 1854; Ninde had attended this school during its first year of operation, 1849-1850. *First Catalogue of the Oxford Female Institute at Oxford, O.: 1849-50* (Cincinnati: John D. Thorpe, 1850). Scott's daughter, Caroline Lavina Scott, was Ninde's schoolmate; a mutual friend told Ninde: "I hear Carrie Scott has been carrying on quite a flirtation with Mr. Ben Harrison this winter. I think she need not say any thing more about young beaus." Anna Howell to Beulah C. Ninde, 18 March 1851, Ninde-Puckett Letters.

51 Elizabeth Cady Stanton, Susan B. Anthony, and Matilda Joslyn Gage, eds., *History of Woman Suffrage,* 3 vols. (Rochester, N. Y.: Susan B. Anthony, 1889), 1: 292.

52 *Ibid.,* 1: 306.

53 *Preamble and Constitution of the Woman's Rights Association of Indiana, Art. 6,* Indiana State Library, Indianapolis, Indiana.

54 "Reminiscences by Dr. Mary F. Thomas and Amanda M. Way," in Elizabeth Cady Stanton, Susan B. Anthony, and Matilda Joslyn Gage, eds., *History of Woman Suffrage,* 1: 306. Mary Thomas's letter to the Dublin convention was postmarked "North Manchester," where her relative, Mrs. L. A. Frame, resided; Thomas, her husband, and three children, Laura, Bolena, and Julia, lived at first on a rented farm in Aboite Township. Fayne E. Harter, comp., *Federal Census of Allen Co., Indiana, Indexed* (Graybill, Ind.: 1968), 415.

55 "In the early 1840s, the Thomases were involved in the formation of a utopian socialist community at Marlborough in Stark County, Ohio. Later, their affiliations were with the Congregational or Progressive Friends, a radical abolitionist and reform splinter sect from the Hicksite Friends." Thomas D. Hamm, letter to the author, "1st Month 15, 1991."

56 Florence M. Adkinson, "The Mother of Women," in *Woman's Journal* (29 September 1888), 308.

57 "Proceedings of the Woman's Rights Convention, Held in Richmond, Indiana, October 15th and 16th, 1852," Indiana State Library, Indianapolis, Indiana.

58 *Fort Wayne Weekly Times,* 11 April 1854. The Thomas's office was located on the "North West corner of Main and Calhoun Sts., in the Phoenix Block"; their adver-

tisement ran weekly until their departure from Fort Wayne in August 1856.

[59] *The Lily,* 15 February 1856.

[60] *Ibid.,* 1 July 1856.

[61] *Ibid.,* 15 July 1855. The daughter's interest in typesetting was most likely sparked by a plea by Amelia Bloomer, editor of *The Lily,* (then published in Vernon, Ohio) who lamented: "We wish we could say that our compositor is a *woman,* as we greatly desire to have the work done by female hand. But that we cannot do . . . . and so we must entrust it to men till we can learn a woman to do it—or find one who has already learned the trade." *Ibid.,* 2 January 1854.

[62] *Ibid.,* 15 April 1856. The Fort Wayne Mercantile Institute (located in the same building as the Thomases' office) made an effort to attract women students: "Being impressed with the necessity of Ladies acquainting themselves more thoroughly with business transactions, the Principal has set up apartments with neatness, elegance and convenience, expressly for them. The Ladies' Department is entirely separate from the male, having separate entrances from the street, and will remain permanently connected with the Institution." *Fort Wayne Jeffersonian,* 16 July 1856.

[63] *Ibid.,* 1 July 1856.

[64] The Thomases may have converted to Methodism during their eight years in Fort Wayne.

[65] "Reminiscences by Dr. Mary F. Thomas and Amanda M. Way," in Elizabeth Cady Stanton, Susan B. Anthony, and Matilda Joslyn Gage, eds., *History of Woman Suffrage,* 1: 308.

[66] *The Lily,* 1 October 1857, Indiana State Library, Indianapolis, Indiana. This was one of the last issues Thomas published.

[67] Hugh McCulloch, who practiced law in Fort Wayne, said: "In Indiana and in many other States before this [woman's rights] movement was commenced, the dower of widows whose husbands had died without providing for them by will was one-third part of the rents and profits for life of the lands of which their husbands were the owners, and these lands in a new country were often unimproved. I knew of many instances in which the widows of men who were extensive land-owners were left without any means of support." Hugh McCulloch, *Men and Measures of Half a Century* (New York: C. Scribner's Sons, 1888), 52.

[68] "Reminiscences by Dr. Mary F. Thomas and Amanda M. Way," in Elizabeth Cady Stanton, Susan B. Anthony, and Matilda Joslyn Gage, eds., *History of Woman Suffrage,* 1: 309. During the Civil War, Dr. Mary F. Thomas served on the Sanitary Commission and later assisted her husband, a contract surgeon, in a hospital for refugees in Nashville, Tennessee. Although her husband later switched his prac-

tice to dentistry, she continued to be active in medicine and, in 1887, was elected president of the Wayne County Medical Society. In 1880, she was elected president of the American Woman Suffrage Association; five years later, she resigned as president of the state suffrage association because of her declining health; she died in Richmond, in 1888, at the age of seventy-two. See Frederick C. Waite, "The Three Myers Sisters—Pioneer Women Physicians," in *Medical Review of Reviews* (March 1933).

[69] *Cincinnati Daily Gazette,* 29 January, 1859, cited in Pat Creech Scholten, "A Public 'Jollification:' The 1859 Women's Rights Petition before the Indiana Legislature," *Indiana Magazine of History,* vol. 72, no. 4 (December 1976), 347.

[70] "O" (pseud.), *Fort Wayne Standard,* 22 February 1855.

[71] The Young Men's Literary Society was founded in 1846; during 1855 and 1856, it published the *Summit City Journal.* In 1856, the Society merged its organization and library with the recently established Workingman's Institute and Library.

[72] Emerson, who came from Cincinnati, presented her evening lecture at the "Baptist Meeting House . . . Admittance 15 cts." *Fort Wayne Standard,* 17 August 1854. Emerson was a speaker at the National Woman's Rights Convention held in Cincinnati in 1855. *The Lily,* 15 October 1855.

[73] *Fort Wayne Times,* 12 January 1853.

[74] *Fort Wayne Daily Times,* 24 January, 1856. By the mid-1850s, the Bloomer costume was being abandoned; Stone said that her friends "left it off with the feeling that the large freedom they gained for their feet bore no comparison to the bondage that beset their spirits." Alice Stone Blackwell, *Lucy Stone: Pioneer of Woman's Rights* (Boston: Little, Brown, and Company, 1930), 106.

[75] *Fort Wayne Times,* cited in B. J. Griswold, *The Pictorial History of Fort Wayne, Indiana,* 1: 415.

[76] *The Lily,* 15 November 1854.

[77] The incident was not the first time that women felt unsafe on Fort Wayne's streets after dark. In 1849, when "a respectable lady was accosted on the street and grossly insulted by a set of ruffians," a local editor called for the City Council to "speedily take some steps to prevent the outrages which are almost nightly committed." Even a walk home from church after an evening service was not without risk; two sisters, returning from Second Presbyterian Church, were "assailed by a ruffian from whom they escaped by taking refuge in Mr. William's House." The reporter lamented that "ladies have no security for night walking without a protector." Daytime walks could also provide unpleasant moments for women: "A beggar regards it as his

prerogative to authoritatively demand alms. . . and to anathematize the man or woman who would refuse"; and some local men vowed to give a "coat of tar and feathers" to the "little Scoundrel who has for the past year been exposing his person to little girls and unprotected ladies." *Fort Wayne Times,* 14 June 1849; *Dawson's Daily Times,* 23 March 1860; *Fort Wayne Times,* 19 February 1859; *Dawson's Daily Times,* 26 July 1859.

[78] *Fort Wayne Times,* 24 May 1854. Women in the nineteenth century wore over fifteen pounds of skirts and petticoats, plus their stays. Bloomers, which were cut moderately full and gathered in above the footwear, allowed the skirts to be cut halfway between the knee and the ankle. Indiana women attended the National Dress Reform Association meeting in June 1856. See Charles Nelson Gatty, *The Bloomer Girls* (New York: Coward-McCann, 1968)

[79] *Fort Wayne Daily Times,* 26 January 1856.

[80] A. T. Rankin, pastor of the First Presbyterian Church, joined to protest some church leaders' snide remarks about women speakers: "Illiberal attacks upon *women* [have been] manifest in some of the splendid college chapels of Indiana, where, under the influence of popular feeling, the orator will step out of his way to give women a slap, and a learned D. D. will nod a cordial assent. One will insinuate and another will come out in open attack upon *women,* and that too where a free discussion of slavery is not permitted . . . . Let those collegiate gentlemen debate the subject of slavery and abolition with the *women* whose discretion and intelligence they depreciate and doubtless they will be as glad to escape as they were to encounter." *Proceedings of the Indiana Convention, Assembled to Organize a State Anti-Slavery Society, held in Milton, Wayne Co., September 12th, 1838* (Cincinnati, Samuel A. Alley, 1838), 20.

[81] Hugh McCulloch remembered Stone's eloquence: "I had heard many men with lusty lungs and clear voices speak in the same hall [in Fort Wayne], and I knew how much effort was required by them to make themselves heard. And yet here was a small young woman whose sweet, silvery tones reached every ear in a crowded hall as if they had been trumpet-tongued. She spoke without notes and with great earnestness and feeling, but there was no straining for effect, nothing like mere declamation, in her manner of speaking." Hugh McCulloch, *Men and Measures of Half a Century,* 51.

[82] Alice Stone Blackwell, *Lucy Stone: Pioneer of Woman's Rights,* 80, 92, 94, 99. Blackwell's sisters, Elizabeth and Emily, were pioneer women physicians; his brother Samuel later married Antoinette L. Brown, Stone's friend and Oberlin classmate, and the country's first theologically trained woman to be ordained to the ministry.

[83] *Fort Wayne Sentinel,* 26 January 1856.

[84] *Fort Wayne Daily Times,* 26 January 1856.

[85] *Fort Wayne Sentinel,* 26 January 1856.

[86] *Ibid.*

[87] *Ibid.,* 24 June 1854.

[88] "T" (pseud.), *Fort Wayne Weekly Times,* 28 February 1856. Most likely, "T" was Mary F. Thomas. "Lizzie B." described "T" as "a woman of that city [Fort Wayne], competent in intellect, clear in argument, and just in conclusion, [who] did lift up her voice in reply. . . [in] the manner of a woman who is honest, earnest, and true." *Ibid.,* 21 February 1856.

[89] "Lizzie B." (pseud.), *Ibid.,* 21 February 1856. Letters debating the subject of women's rights continued to be published until May 3, 1856, when the editor of the *Sentinel* declared that he was discontinuing the "personal controversies."

[90] *Fort Wayne Times,* 24 April, 7 August, and 11 September 1851.

[91] J. Edwards, *Aspects of Society* (Fort Wayne, Ind.: T. N. Hood, 1855), 25.

[92] John W. Lowrie, *Adam and His Times,* 49.

[93] *Dawson's Daily Times,* 2 and 9 June 1860.

[94] Lewis W. Spitz, *Life in Two Worlds: Biography of William Sihler* (St. Louis: Concordia Publishing House, 1968), 49.

[95] *Fort Wayne Daily Gazette,* 30 March 1871.

[96] Vestry Minutes, 22 March 1872, Trinity Episcopal Church Archives, Fort Wayne Indiana.

[97] *Dawson's Daily Times,* 4 February 1860; *Fort Wayne Sentinel,* 11 February 1860. See Grace Greenwood, *Recollections of My Childhood and Other Stories* (Boston: Ticknor, Reed, and Fields, 1854) and *Records of Five Years* (Boston: Ticknor and Fields, 1867).

[98] *Dawson's Daily Times,* 2 March 1860. Soon after her visit to Fort Wayne, Montez suffered a paralytic stroke; she died in a boarding house in New York City in January 1861. See [Charles Burr] *Lectures of Lola Montez, Including Her Autobiography* (Philadelphia: T. B. Peterson & Bros., 1858).

[99] *Fort Wayne Republican,* 22 September 1858.

[100] *Fort Wayne Times,* 9 November 1859.

[101] *Dawson's Daily Times,* 3 May 1860.

[102] The Lodge of Good Templars was founded in Fort Wayne on March 1, 1859. *Ibid.,* 7 February 1860; B. J. Griswold, *The Pictorial History of Fort Wayne, Indiana,* 1: 450.

[103] Elizabeth Cady Stanton, Susan B. Anthony, and Matilda Joslyn Gage, eds., *History of Woman Suffrage,* 3: 533.

[104] Beulah C. Ninde continued to be a leader of the woman's movement in Fort Wayne: in July 1873, she helped establish the Home for the Friendless (to care for indigent

women) and was elected president of its board of managers, and later treasurer; in 1887, she was elected president of the Twelfth District Woman's Suffrage Association. She died June 6, 1892 and was survived by her husband and five children. B. J. Griswold, *The Pictorial History of Fort Wayne, Indiana,* 1: 491, 495; *Fort Wayne Gazette,* June 9, 1892.

[105] Alice Hamilton, *Exploring the Dangerous Trades,* 24. Susan B. Anthony also spoke in Fort Wayne in 1878 and 1887. Emerine Hamilton (who was elected a vice-president of the Twelfth District Woman's Suffrage Association in 1887) counted Anthony and Willard as "personal friends"; upon her death, Hamilton received a "tribute of respect" at the 1890 (22nd) convention of the National-American Woman Suffrage Association. Susan B. Anthony and Ida Husted Harper, eds., *History of Woman Suffrage, vol. 4* (Rochester, N. Y.: Susan B. Anthony, 1902), 4: 174.

Chapter 9

[1] "Dismissed" meant transferred, not discharged.

[2] Samuel Merrill, Fort Wayne, to David Merrill, Peachham, Vermont, 26 October 1843. Merrill Papers, Indiana State Historical Society, Indianapolis, Indiana.

[3] A decade later, the *Fort Wayne Daily Times* reported: "Dr. Wm. C. Anderson, late president of Miami University . . . accepted the call of the 1st Presbyterian Church in San Fransisco . . . . He has labored for some years under a disease of the throat, which has materially interfered with his ministerial duties . . . . We rejoice to learn he has so far recovered as to be able to engage in the work of the ministry with renewed zeal." Copied from the *Cincinnati Gazette,* 21 September 1855.

[4] Anderson remained in Fort Wayne until the fall, when the Reverend Hugh S. Dickson was called to the church. He then ministered briefly in Washington, Pennsylvania, and Dayton, Ohio, before going to Europe for his health. He was president of Miami University, Ohio (1849-1854); pastor in Chillicothe, Ohio (1854-1855); pastor, First Presbyterian Church, San Francisco (1855-1863); pastor in Cincinnati, Ohio, and Junction City, Kansas, where he died, August 28 1870.

[5] Jesse L. Williams, quoted by "Historian," *Fort Wayne Daily Gazette,* 15 May 1878 (first published by the Presbyterian Historical Society in the *Philadelphia Presbyterian*).

[6] William C. Anderson, quoted in George W. Allison, *Forest, Fort and Faith: Historical Sketches of the Presbytery of Fort Wayne* (Fort Wayne: 1945), 40.

[7] After his visit to Fort Wayne in 1877, Henry Ward Beecher reminisced in the *Christian Union* about "the little courthouse where we preached two thundering weeks and gathered the Second Presbyterian Church." B. J. Griswold, *The Pictorial History of Fort Wayne, Indiana,* 2 vols. (Chicago: Robert O. Law Company, 1917), 1: 381.

[8] *Fort Wayne Daily Gazette,* 15 May 1878.

[9] L. C. Rudolph, *Hoosier Zion: The Presbyterians in Early Indiana* (New Haven: Yale University Press, 1963), 148.

[10] Oral tradition from the Reverend R. Dean Cope, pastor emeritus of Westminster Presbyterian Church, Fort Wayne (formerly Second Presbyterian Church), and the last stated clerk of the old Fort Wayne Presbytery.

[11] Charles Beecher to Amelia Ogden, 20 May 1845, Beecher-Stowe Family Papers, Schlesinger Library, Radcliffe College, Cambridge, Massachusetts.

[12] Technically, a Stated Supply was not formally called by the congregation but was appointed annually by the presbytery, upon petition by the session. It was the usual designation for pastors of mission churches receiving financial aid. Both James Chute and Alexander T. Rankin at First Presbyterian Church had been Stated Supplies.

[13] Presbyterians were fond of titling their churches with numbers: by 1855, there was a Sixth Presbyterian Church in Pittsburgh and a Seventh Presbyterian Church in Cincinnati.

[14] "The Recollections of Susan McCulloch," Wilhemina and Clifford Richards, eds., *Old Fort News,* vol. 44, no. 3 (Allen County-Fort Wayne Historical Society, 1981), 6.

[15] Hugh McCulloch, *Men and Measures of Half a Century* (New York: C. Scribner's Sons, 1888), 140-144.

[16] Harriet Beecher Stowe bought Charles a fine Amati violin on their European tour in 1853.

[17] Lyman Beecher Stowe, *Saints, Sinners, and Beechers* (Indianapolis: Bobbs Merrill Co., 1934), 336.

[18] In her "Concluding Remarks" of the later editions of *Uncle Tom's Cabin,* Harriet wrote: "The story of 'old Prue,' in the second volume, was an incident that fell under the personal observation of a brother of the writer, then collecting-clerk to a large mercantile house, in New Orleans. From the same source was derived the character of the planter Legree. Of him her brother thus wrote, speaking of visiting his plantation, on a collecting tour: 'He actually made me feel of his fist, which was like a blacksmith's hammer, or a nodule of iron, telling me that it was "calloused with knocking down niggers." When I left the plantation, I drew a long breath, and felt as if I has escaped from an ogre's den.'"

[19] Reminiscences of Jane Merrill Ketchem, Merrill Papers, 76.

[20] Henry Ward Beecher to Lyman Beecher, Indianapolis, 13 September 1844, Beecher-Stowe Family Papers; quoted in Jane Shaffer Elsmere, *Henry Ward Beecher: The*

Indiana Years, 1837-1847 (Indianapolis: Indiana Historical Society, 1973), 210.

21 Henry Ward Beecher to Charles Beecher, September 1844, quoted in Charles Beecher, ed., *Autobiography, Correspondence, Etc., of Lyman Beecher D. D.*, 2 vols. (New York: Harper and Brothers, 1864), 2: 476.

22 Charles Beecher to Milton Badger, 16 September 1844, AHMS.

23 Joseph K. Edgerton, *Private Journal No. 3,* 21 July 1844, 170, Allen County Public Library, Fort Wayne, Indiana.

24 Charles Beecher to Milton Badger, 16 September 1844, AHMS.

25 Susan M. McCulloch to Mary I. Man, 20 November 1844, McCulloch Papers, Lilly Library, Bloomington, Indiana.

26 *Fort Wayne Times,* 19 April 1844; it was first published in a report of the Essex County (Massachusetts) Education Society and reprinted in the B*oston Recorder.*

27 Hugh McCulloch, *Men and Measures of Half a Century,* 149.

28 Lyman Beecher, *A Plea for the West,* 2nd ed. (Cincinnati: 1835), 12.

29 Hugh McCulloch, *Men and Measures of Half a Century,* 148.

30 *Ibid.,* 141.

31 George W. Allison, *Forest, Fort and Faith: Historical Sketches of the Presbytery of Fort Wayne,* 12.

32 Susan M. McCulloch to Mary I. Man, 20 November 1844, McCulloch Papers.

33 Charles Beecher to Amelia Ogden, 20 May 1845, Beecher-Stowe Family Papers.

34 Joseph K. Edgerton, *Private Journal No. 3,* 10 and 17 November 1844, 227, 230, 231, 233.

35 Susan M. McCulloch to Mary I. Man, 20 November 1844, McCulloch Papers.

36 Julia Merrill, Fort Wayne, to Jane Merrill, Indianapolis, 20 September 1845, Merrill Papers.

37 Susan M. McCulloch to Mary I. Man, 20 November 1844, McCulloch Papers.

38 Taylor and McCulloch, as non-members, were allowed to serve as Trustees; Asa Fairfield joined the congregation in 1864. Their wives, however, were charter members. The funeral of Elizabeth Rockhill, wife of William, was conducted in Second Presbyterian Church in May 1859.

39 Charles Beecher to Milton Badger, 27 October 1845, AHMS.

40 Charles Beecher to Amelia Ogden, 20 May 1845, Beecher-Stowe Family Papers. The new church was located on the south side of Berry Street between Webster and Ewing streets, facing Cass Street.

41 Susan M. McCulloch to Maria Halsey, 26 February 1846, McCulloch Papers.

42 *Fort Wayne Times,* 22 February 1846.

43 Charles Beecher, *Tracts for the Times, no. 19, The Bible a Sufficient Creed: Being Two Discourses Delivered at the Dedication of the Second Presbyterian Church, Fort Wayne, Iowa* (sic), *February 22, 1846* (Boston: Office of the Christian World, 1846), 41, 42, 44.

44 Susan M. McCulloch to Maria Halsey, 26 February 1846, McCulloch Papers.

45 Benjamin W. Oakley, John Hamilton, and Frederick H. Tyler (elders); Royal W. Taylor and Hugh McCulloch (trustees).

46 Charles Beecher, *The Bible a Sufficient Creed,* 2.

47 Peter P. Bailey, senior warden in the Episcopal Church, worried about Beecher's unorthodoxy; when a friend sent him a tract, he replied, "I received your tract entitled, 'How shall I understand the scriptures'.... I think it ... so good that I enclosed it with a polite note to our New School minister who, only the evening before, had, as I was told, announced to his congregation that, though he was a Presbyterian minister and had assented to the 'Confession of Faith' of that church, yet it contained things which he did not believe, and that he intended to tell his Synod and Presbytery the same, and that, hencefore, the Bible should be his only creed. I could not help but think that, in the reading of that creed with the help of this tract, he might yet find the church." Peter P. Bailey to John W. Mitchell, 19 January 1846, Bailey Letters, Allen County-Fort Wayne Historical Society, Fort Wayne, Indiana.

48 Charles Beecher, *The Bible a Sufficient Creed,* 40.)

49 George William Allison, *Forest, Fort, and Faith: Historical Sketches of the Presbytery of Fort Wayne,* 13.

50 Hugh McCulloch, 29 June 1846, to "Dear Sir," McCulloch Papers.

51 George William Allison, *Forest, Fort, and Faith: Historical Sketches of the Presbytery of Fort Wayne,* 13.

52 Charles Beecher to Milton Badger, 3 August 1846, AHMS.

53 Charles Beecher to Amelia Ogden, 20 May 1845, Beecher-Stowe Family Papers.

54 Henry Ward Beecher's resignation in 1847 from Second Presbyterian Church in Indianapolis evoked only mild regret among his parishioners. Samuel Merrill said, "We have liked him as a preacher but many in the Ch[urch], as I now learn, complain much of him as a Pastor." Samuel Merrill to David Merrill, 5 September 1847, Merrill Papers.

55 Julia Merrill, Fort Wayne, to Kate Merrill, Indianapolis, 4 September 1845, Merrill Papers.

56 Charles Beecher to Milton Badger, 16 September

1844, AHMS.

57 Ibid., 10 February 1847.

58 Ibid., 5 April 1847.

59 Ibid.

60 Ibid., 16 September 1844.

61 See the Smithsonian Institution collection of early American viols in the Museum of American History, Washington, D. C.

62 At the church dedication they "had a bass viol and a violin to aid the choir." Susan McCulloch to Maria Halsey, 26 February 1846, McCulloch Papers.

63 Catherine Beecher to Mary Dutton, 31 May 1845, penned on her copy of Charles Beecher's letter to Amelia Ogden, 20 May 1845, Beecher-Stowe Family Papers.

64 *Fort Wayne Times,* 15 November 1845.

65 Charles Beecher to Milton Badger, 4 February 1850, AHMS.

66 The first donation party was organized in March 1845, and then in each succeeding winter.

67 *Fort Wayne Sentinel,* 13 January 1849.

68 Charles Beecher to Milton Badger, 10 February 1847, AHMS.

69 Julia D. Merrill, Fort Wayne, to "one and all, both great and small," Indianapolis, 20 September 1845, Merrill Papers.

70 Charles Beecher to Milton Badger, 19 July 1847, AHMS.

71 *Fort Wayne Sentinel,* 6 November 1847.

72 *Fort Wayne Times,* 4 October 1849.

73 *Ibid.,* 8 November 1849.

74 *Ibid.*

75 *Ibid.,* 28 August 1847

76 By 1850, the Sons of Temperance in Indiana had raised $12,000 to lobby the State Legislature for temperance legislation. In 1854, they allied themselves with a coalition of Know Nothings, Whigs, and antislavery Democrats. In Fort Wayne, the Methodists supported the Sons of Temperance, which in 1847 numbered about forty members.

77 Charles Beecher to Milton Badger, 19 July 1847, AHMS.

78 Proceedings of the Presbytery of Fort Wayne (New School), May 1847, published in the *Fort Wayne Sentinel,* 22 May 1847.

79 *Fort Wayne Sentinel,* 22 May 1847.

80 Charles Beecher to Lyman Beecher, 1 October 1845, Beecher-Stowe Family Papers.

81 *Fort Wayne Times,* 13 April 1845. Also serving on the committee were Jesse L. Williams, F. S. Avaline, and Thomas Hatfield.

82 *Ibid.,* 3 March 1845.

83 *Ibid.,* 14 August 1847.

84 *Ibid.,* 21 August 1847.

85 Most historians agree that the Ewings were "aggressive, unscrupulous, but capable operators." R. Carlyle Buley, *The Old Northwest: Pioneer Period, 1815-1840,* 2 vols. (Bloomington, Indiana: Indiana University Press, 1951), 2: 321.

86 *Fort Wayne Times,* 27 July 1848. For more on William G. Ewing and the election campaign, see Mark E. Neely, Jr., "'Perfidious Whig Rascals': A Businessman Runs for Congress in Fort Wayne, 1847," *Old Fort News,* vol. 44, no. 1 (1981).

87 Susan McCulloch wrote, "Mr. Beecher preaches good *practical* sermons." Susan McCulloch to Maria Halsey, 8 February 1847, McCulloch Papers.

88 Charles Beecher to Milton Badger, 5 February 1846, AHMS.

89 *Fort Wayne Times,* 29 November 1849.

90 Julia D. Merrill, Fort Wayne, to Elizabeth Bates, Indianapolis, 21 September 1845, Merrill Papers.

91 Charles Beecher, *The Incarnation; or Pictures of the Virgin and Her Son, With an Introductory Essay, by Mrs. Harriet Beecher Stowe* (New York: Harper & Brothers, 1849), 27. Beecher may have been the first resident of Fort Wayne to have a book published and distributed nationally.

92 "The Second Presbyterian Church," in T. B. Helm, *History of Allen County, Indiana* (Chicago: Kingman Brothers, 1880), 97.

93 *Manual of the Second Presbyterian Church, Fort Wayne, Indiana* (Fort Wayne: T. S. Taylor & Co., 1869), 10. Taylor was designated a Temporary Supply (invited by the session, but not confirmed by the Fort Wayne Presbytery); Blood was formally called as a Stated Supply (the terms of employment were approved by the Presbytery). Ray (Temporary Supply) had previously served a parish in Kalamazoo, Michigan; his poem, "A Ride Around Fort Wayne," was published in the *Fort Wayne Times,* 16 October 1851; he later demitted the Presbyterian ministry, joined the Episcopal Church, and was named a lay delegate to the 1859 Diocesan Convention.

94 Hugh McCulloch, Indianapolis, to Charles Beecher, Newark, New Jersey, 9 February 1852, McCulloch Papers.

95 In 1851, Beecher was granted a dismissal by the Fort Wayne Presbytery (New School) to the Congregational Association of New York and Brooklyn. *Minutes of the Fort Wayne Presbytery (New School),* Presbyterian Historical Society, Philadelphia, Pennsylvania.

96 Susan McCulloch, New York City, to Hugh McCulloch, Fort Wayne, 29 March 1852 and 13 April 1852, McCulloch Papers.

97 The speech was given on July 22, 1852. *Fort Wayne Times,* 5 August 1852. McCulloch never tired of moral and

religious themes; in January 1851, he lectured on "Mohomet and His Religion."

98 *Fort Wayne Times,* 8 December 1852. The community service was held at the First Presbyterian Church. For Freeman's remarks on slavery, see chapter "African Methodists."

99 "The Second Presbyterian Church," in T. B. Helm, *History of Allen County, Indiana,* 97. Freeman next served congregations at Aurora (1854-1883) and Petersburg (1885-1893); in retirement, he served a church at St. Joseph, Missouri, (1893-1900) until his death at age seventy-nine.

100 *Fort Wayne Times,* 3 May 1855. See chapter "Baptists."

101 *Fort Wayne Times,* 20 February 1860.

102 *Ibid.,* 27 November 1856. This is a rebuttal of the *Sentinel's* critique.

103 *Fort Wayne Republican,* 8 and 15 September 1858.

104 Isaac Lesser, *The Occident and American Jewish Advocate,* vol. 17, October 1859, 166-168.

105 *Encyclopaedia of the Presbyterian Church in the U. S. A.,* Alfred Nevin, ed. (Philadelphia: Presbyterian Encyclopaedia Publishing Co., 1884), 170.

106 "The Second Presbyterian Church," in T. B. Helm, *History of Allen County, Indiana,* 97. In 1867, Curtis was called to the First Presbyterian Church of Newburg, Ohio (later designated the South Presbyterian Church of Cleveland); he received the degree of Doctor of Divinity from Marietta College.

107 In September 1870, when the Old School and New School wings of the Presbyterian Church were about to reunite, twenty-five members of Second Presbyterian Church—who were of Congregational heritage and sympathy—withdrew to organize the Plymouth Congregational Church.

108 Charles Beecher, *The Duty of Disobedience to Wicked Laws: A Sermon on the Fugitive Slave Law* (New York: J. A. Gray, 1851), 21. The sermon was delivered on a Sunday evening in mid-November, 1850.

109 *Fort Wayne Times,* 13 March 1851.

110 Sarah and Charles Beecher, Newark, New Jersey, to Susan McCulloch, Fort Wayne, 21 January 1852, McCulloch Papers.

111 Quoted in Milton Rugoff's *The Beechers: An American Family in the Nineteenth Century* (New York, Harper & Row, 1981), 413.

Chapter 10

1 Dickson was born in Rathfriland, County Down, Ireland, November 13, 1812. He was graduated from Union College (1839) and Princeton Theological Seminary (1842); the church at Bardstown was his first charge.

2 See chapter "German and French Reformed."

3 Minutes of the Fort Wayne (Old School) Presbytery, quoted in George William Allison, *Forest, Fort, and Faith: Historical Sketches of The Presbytery of Fort Wayne* (Fort Wayne: 1945), 16.

4 Joseph K. Edgerton, "Private Journal No. 3," 22 December 1844, 248, Allen County Public Library, Fort Wayne, Indiana.

5 Elizabeth Wines, Springfield, Indiana, to Susan C. Williams, Fort Wayne, Indiana, 15 January 1845, Allen County-Fort Wayne Historical Society, Fort Wayne, Indiana.

6 Susan Man McCulloch to Mary A. Hawkins, 3 November 1845, McCulloch Papers, Lilly Library, Bloomington, Indiana.

7 William Wesley Woollen, *Biographical and Historical Sketches of Early Indiana* (Indianapolis: Hammond & Co., 1883), 80.

8 Alexander Davidson, Indianapolis, to Davidson, Lexington, Virginia, 28 July 1843, quoted in L. C. Rudolph, *Hoosier Zion* (New Haven: Yale University Press, 1963), 181.

9 Charles Beecher stated that all but one of the men of his congregation voted Whig. Charles Beecher to Milton Badger, 16 December 1844, AHMS.

10 Usually written seraphine or seraphina, the instrument was an early form of the harmonium, a bellows operated reed organ.

11 *Fort Wayne Times,* 22 November 1845. The organ was built by Henry Hitzfield. Miss Sykes was the daughter of the new headmistress of the Presbyterian school.

12 *Ibid.,* 7 June 1845.

13 *Fort Wayne Times,* 4 October 1845; *Fort Wayne Sentinel,* 28 September 1844. This school may have been designed to succeed the Fort Wayne Female Seminary which opened on October 2, 1843, under the direction of Miss M. L. Wallace in the house "formerly occupied by the Rev. A. T. Rankin;" its sponsors were Samuel Hanna, Allen Hamilton, Henry Rudisill, and Hugh McCulloch.

14 *Ibid.,* 5 October 1846.

15 Steevens had begun his teaching career in Fort Wayne in the fall of 1837, at the First Presbyterian Church.

16 *Fort Wayne Sentinel,* 3 August 1844.

17 *Ibid.,* 5 October 1846.

18 James Greer (or Grier) was born at Pleasant Valley, New York, in 1815; he was graduated from the College of New Jersey (Princeton) in 1836. After teaching school for four years, he enrolled in Princeton Theological Seminary

and was ordained in 1842. He served as a stated supply at Constantine, Michigan (1844-1845) and LaPorte, Indiana (1846-1847). While teaching in Fort Wayne, he supplied the pulpits at Cedar Creek (1850) and Eel River (Coesse) (1851). Greer left Fort Wayne in 1851, and taught in Virginia, Georgia, Kentucky, Tennessee, eventually becoming president of Richmond College at Richmond, Missouri. He died in 1890. *Necrology Report Presented to the Alumni Association of Princeton Theological Seminary* (Princeton, N. J.: C. S. Robinson, 1890), 42.

[19] *Fort Wayne Sentinel,* 5 June 1847. Greer stated that his academy was "limited to 25 pupils in the upper room of a two story house opposite the First Presbyterian Church. Each student is expected to provide desk and chair."

[20] *Ibid.,* 25 October 1845.

[21] H. S. Dickson to the Trustees of First Presbyterian Church, 12 January 1846, First Presbyterian Church Archives, Fort Wayne Indiana.

[22] A year later, the elders heard this report: "Sometime since, the trunk of Charles Engleman, formerly a respectable young man, was opened by the citizens of Fort Wayne under a suspicion of roguery, in which was found a letter of introduction, written by Samuel C. Evans, a member of this church, to a female of ill fame, which letter was publicly read in the streets of Fort Wayne. This mournful case has been a subject of conversation in the Session." *First Presbyt. Church Session Records No. 3, 1845-1869,* 15 February 1847, First Presbyterian Church Archives.

[23] *First Presbyt. Church Session Records No. 3, 1845-1869,* 29 January 1847, First Presbyterian Church Archives. Concern about the evils of dancing was not peculiar to Methodists, Baptists, and Presbyterians: both the Reverends Stephen Badin and Jesse Hoover, the first Catholic priest and Lutheran minister in Fort Wayne, condemned dancing and denied the sacraments to those who persisted in the practice. See chapters "Catholics" and "Lutherans."

[24] *Fort Wayne Times,* 10 July 1847.

[25] Martha Brandriff Hanna, "Early Days," in *Reminiscences of Old Fort Wayne* (Fort Wayne and Allen County Library, 1906), n.p. In 1848, Mary Ann Wall and Margaret Forsyth had been cited to appear before the session for their "attendance of dancing parties and . . . willfully absenting themselves from the Lord's Table."

[26] *Fort Wayne Times,* 20 June 1846.

[27] *Ibid.,* 29 August 1846.

[28] *Ibid.,* 29 November 1845. The "destitute" were those persons lacking Bibles. For more on Stephen Ball, see chapter "Methodists."

[29] The blight on the potato crop in 1845 and 1846, which provided 80 percent of the Irish diet, caused the death of a million Irish and precipitated the migration of another million to North America.

[30] John F. Noll to Allen Hamilton, 14 January 1847, Hamilton Papers, Allen County-Fort Wayne Historical Society, Fort Wayne, Indiana.

[31] McCulloch's wife wrote: "We were trying to get up an 'Irish supper.' The ladies appointed me one of the committee and, as my husband was very much interested in the cause, I took an active part." Susan Man McCulloch to Maria Halsey, 11 April 1847, McCulloch Papers.

[32] Most local Catholics contributed to the cause through St. Augustine's Church, which sent $232 to Archbishop Hughes in New York City; most Protestants contributed though the community appeals. The Presbyterian, Methodist, English Lutheran, and Baptist congregations each received special offerings. *Fort Wayne Sentinel,* 26 June 1847.

[33] David Hoge Colerick's father, John Colerick, was an Irish patriot and publisher, who was imprisoned for his political activity, and later escaped to America.

[34] *Fort Wayne Times,* 13 March 1847.

[35] *Fort Wayne Times,* 5 April 1845. The paper later reported that in "the late epidemic . . . in April twenty-six were buried in the Protestant burying ground . . . only one by May 24." *Ibid.,* 21 June 1845.

[36] *Ibid.,* 13 March 1847.

[37] *Ibid.,* 4 April 1846.

[38] *Ibid.,* 31 May 1845.

[39] *Ibid.,* 2 January 1847.

[40] *Ibid.,* 27 February 1847.

[41] *Fort Wayne Sentinel,* 6 March 1847; *Fort Wayne Times,* 13 March 1847.

[42] *Fort Wayne Times,* 3 April 1847.

[43] Susan Man McCulloch to Maria Halsey, 11 April 1847, McCulloch Papers.

[44] *Fort Wayne Times,* 17 April 1847.

[45] S. Noel, S. Hanna, W. Paul, J. H. Robinson, J. S. Williams, and J. Cochrane to H. S. Dickson, 14 April 1847, First Presbyterian Church Archives.

[46] H. S. Dickson to the Session, 15 April 1847, First Presbyterian Church Archives.

[47] J. Robinson, clerk, to H. S. Dickson, 20 April 1847, First Presbyterian Church Archives.

[48] H. S. Dickson to the Session, 22 April 1847, First Presbyterian Church Archives. Charles Beecher reported: "Mr. Dickson left . . . partly thro' the influence of his wife's relatives in Phila. and partly owing to a newspaper controversy between himself and the Editor of the Whig *Times and Press.* This controversy was not wholly to his advantage, and altho' his congregation met and resolved that they reposed confidence in him, and desired his further stay, yet as they made no allusion whatever to the circumstances which had occurred, Mr. D. was not satisfied." Charles

Beecher to Milton Badger, 19 July 1847, AHMS.

49 *First Presbyt. Church Trustee Record No. 1, 1843-1868,* 2 November 1847, First Presbyterian Church Archives.

50 Alice Hamilton, *Exploring the Dangerous Trades* (Boston: Little, Brown and Company, 1943), 23, 24. Emerine Hamilton received a "tribute of respect" at the 1890 convention of the National-American Woman Suffrage Association. See Susan B. Anthony and Ida Husted Harper, eds, *History of Woman Suffrage, Vol. 4* (Rochester, N. Y.: Susan B. Anthony, 1902), 174.

51 *First Presbyt. Church Trustee Record No. 1, 1843-1868,* 2 November 1847, First Presbyterian Church Archives.

52 *Ibid.,* 13 March 1848.

53 Hawes next served the Concord Church, near Pittsburgh, Pennsylvania (1848-1850); then parishes in Huntington, Pennsylvania; Waukesha, Wisconsin (where he was professor of languages at Carroll College); and Beloit, Wisconsin. He was called to Madison, Indiana, in 1857 and died there four years later at the age of thirty-six. *Encyclopedia of the Presbyterian Church in the United States of America,* Alfred Nevin, ed. (Philadelphia: Presbyterian Publishing Co., 1884), 310.

54 When only men voted, there were 31 votes; when both men and women voted the total was 105—suggesting that the women members were determined to demonstrate their interest in the issue by attending the meeting in full force.

55 *Fort Wayne Sentinel,* 30 March 1848. Robinson and his wife soon joined the Second Presbyterian Church; in August 1854, they reunited with First Presbyterian Church.

56 Charles Beecher to Milton Badger, 19 July 1847, AHMS. Beecher called Riheldaffer "a brother indeed." Ibid., 27 May 1850.

57 *Fort Wayne Times,* 10 February 1848.

58 The Trustees had resolved: "When the building is completed, the pews (leaving out the one fifth of free pews) shall be equitably valued, so that their aggregate valuation shall be equal to the whole cost of the church, including the cost of the ground, and that they then be sold to the highest bidder, taking the valuation as the minimum price." Samuel Hanna paid $300 for a choice location; William G. and George W. Ewing (attenders, but not members) deeded eighty acres of land, valued at $2.50 an acre, in payment for a pew. Each pew would also be subject to an "assessment to be based upon the original valuation—and such taxes and assessments shall be a lien and charge upon said pews." Trustees Report No. 2, First Presbyterian Church Archives.

59 *Fort Wayne Times,* 3 February 1848.

60 Hugh McCulloch, "An Address to the Indiana State Teachers Association," *Indiana State Journal,* vol. 4 (November 1859), 321-335, and (December 1859), 353-360.

61 *Fort Wayne Times,* 17 February 1848; *Fort Wayne Sentinel,* 18 November 1848.

62 *Fort Wayne Sentinel,* 11 January 1851. Rufus Morgan French, who was born in Norwich, Connecticut, in 1822, returned to Fort Wayne where he was a contractor, woolen mill owner, and hardware merchant.

63 *First Presbyt. Church Session Records No. 3, 1845-1869,* 5 May 1851, First Presbyterian Church Archives. Riheldaffer served as pastor, Central Church, St. Paul, Minnesota (1852-1865); principal, St. Paul Female Seminary (1858-1870); principal, Minnesota State Reform School, St. Paul (1868-1886); pastor, Redwood Falls, Minnesota (1886 to his death in 1891). *Biographical Catalogue of the Princeton Theological Seminary, 1815-1931,* Edward Howell Roberts, comp. (Princeton, N. J.: Princeton Theological Seminary, 1933), 144.

64 J. G. Riheldaffer to the Session of the 1st Pres. Ch. of Fort Wayne, 2 November 1852, First Presbyterian Church Archives.

65 Glenn was a twenty-three-year-old native of Pittsburgh, Pennsylvania; after graduation from Duquesne College he studied theology at Allegheny and Oxford Seminaries; in June 1850, he was ordained by the Michigan Presbytery and was sent to serve the congregations in Murray, Wells Co., and Warren, Huntington Co. (The Michigan Presbytery of the General Synod of the Associate Reformed Church of the West had jurisdiction in Indiana north of the 40th parallel.) Most likely, Glenn continued to care for these neighboring charges after establishing the Fort Wayne "vacancy;" in 1852 he "demitted" his three-county appointment and later served a parish in Salem, Indiana (1854-1858); from 1859 to 1881 he assumed pastorates in Pennsylvania; he died in 1883. James Brown Scouller, *A Manual of the United Presbyterian Church of North America, 1751-1887,* 2nd edit. (Pittsburgh: United Presbyterian Board of Publication, 1887), 346.

66 *Fort Wayne Times,* 20 March 1851.

67 In 1782, the Covenanters (the Reformed Presbytery) and Seceders (the Associate Synod) united to form the Associate Reformed Synod.

68 Associate Reformed Presbyterian congregations in the Presbytery of Indiana were: New Zion (Spring Hill), Caledonia, Shiloh (Mays), Bethesda (Milroy), Richland (Rush County), Glenwood (Vienna in Rush County), First Indianapolis, Princeton, Bloomington, Eden (Gibson County); in the Presbytery of Michigan: Camden, Burnett's Creek, Oswego, New Paris, Rossville, Providence, Murray, Warren, Lafayette, Hebron, Albany, Frankfort, Salem, Somerset, Bethel, and Tipton. Minutes of the Eleventh General Synod of the Associate Reformed Church of the West, *United Presbyterian and Evangelical Guardian,* vol.

5, no. 2 (June 1851), 93-98; John W. Meloy, "A History of the Indiana Presbytery of the United Presbyterian Church," *Indiana Magazine of History,* vol. 31, no. 1 (March 1935), 22, 27.

69 John W. Dawson remembered "with pleasure" Joseph H. McMaken, who kept the "Mansion House . . . . He was an honest man, and long an Associate Judge of the Circuit Court." *Fort Wayne Daily Sentinel,* 15 March 1872.

70 *First Presbyt. Church Session Records No. 3, 1845-1869,* November 1851, First Presbyterian Church Archives. The 1850 Census enumerated 56 Scottish-born residents of Allen County, 0.5 percent of the population.

71 *Fort Wayne Times,* 12 October 1851 and 15 January 1852.

72 Minutes of the Twelfth General Synod of the Associate Reformed Church of the West, in *United Presbyterian and Evangelical Guardian,* vol. 6, no. 2 (June 1852), 110; Minutes of the Second Synod of the Associate Reformed Church of the West, 1852, *The United Presbyterian and Evangelical Guardian,* vol. 6, no. 6 (October 1852), 312.

73 James Brown Scouller, *A Manual of the United Presbyterian Church of North America, 1751-1887,* 2nd edit., 498. Miller continued as a missionary in his denomination; he died in Iowa in 1867.

74 James Albert Woodburn, "United Presbyterian Beginnings," *Indiana Magazine of History,* vol. 30, no. 1 (March 1934), 20.

75 The last pastor of the congregation was a licentiate, John R. McCalister, who arrived in Fort Wayne in February 1854. *Fort Wayne Times,* 15 February 1854. In October 1855 McCalister was ordained by the Presbytery of Illinois, and the Fort Wayne congregation, according to A. R. P. records, was "disorganized." William Melancthon Glasgow, *Cyclopedic Manual of the United Presbyterian Church of North America* (Pittsburgh: United Presbyterian Board of Publication, 1903), 440.

In 1893, the United Presbyterian Church (the successor to the A. R. P.) established a short-lived congregation in Fort Wayne on South Lafayette St. near Pontiac St. under the leadership of the Reverend A. McDowell.

76 This seminary grew out of Hanover College and located at New Albany in 1839; in 1859 it moved to Chicago where it was successively named the "Seminary of the Northwest," "McCormick," the "Presbyterian Seminary of Chicago," and again "McCormick."

77 Alice Hamilton, *Exploring the Dangerous Trades,* 27. She lamented that this building was later "replaced by a rough-stone, pseudo-Richardson monstrosity."

78 *Minutes of the Fort Wayne Presbytery (O. S.),* 16 June 1852, cited in George William Allison, *Forest, Fort, and Faith: Historical Sketches of The Presbytery of Fort Wayne,* 17.

79 *Ibid.,* 18.

80 *Ibid.,* 19.

81 *Fort Wayne Times,* 28 December 1853.

82 Martha Brandriff Hanna remembered receiving a Bible for "committing the Shorter Catechism to memory" in the Sunday School. Martha Brandriff Hanna, "Early Days," in *Reminiscences of Old Fort Wayne* (Fort Wayne and Allen County Library, 1906), n.p.

Montgomery Hamilton, son of Allen and Emerine, attempted to pass on to his children his love for the Bible and the catechism. His daughter, Alice, wrote: "He insisted that my sister Edith and I learn the Westminster Catechism, and many a struggle we had over that heathenish production . . . . The Bible was more familiar to us than any other book, and as is true of everything we learned in childhood, it is so deeply imprinted in my memory that more often than not when I hear it read in church I can keep just a little ahead of the minister." Alice Hamilton, *Exploring the Dangerous Trades,* 27.

83 *Minutes of the Fort Wayne Presbytery (O. S.),* 10 February 1853, Presbyterian Historical Society, Philadelphia, Pa., cited in George William Allison, *Forest, Fort, and Faith: Historical Sketches of The Presbytery of Fort Wayne,* 19.

84 Martha Brandriff Hanna, "Early Days," in *Reminiscences of Old Fort Wayne,* n.p.

85 A Presbyterian supported school was also operating at St. John's Reformed Church (a member of the Fort Wayne Presbytery until 1856), as well as New Lancaster, Kendallville, and Swan. The Presbyterian Board of Education appropriated a total of $875 to the presbytery in subsidies for these schools. All had closed by 1858 (except St. John's which had transferred into the German Reformed Synod); the enterprise proved to be costly and, after 1870, was abandoned by the denomination. See L. J. Sherrill, *Presbyterian Parochial Schools* (New Haven: 1932) and Thomas J. Hardin, The Academies of Indiana," *Indiana Magazine of History,* vol. 10 (1914), 350-358.

86 Jacob W. Lanius was a twenty-six-year-old graduate of Jefferson College, who had attended Allegheny Theological Seminary. At Fort Wayne, he continued his studies for the ministry under the direction of Jonathan Edwards; in the fall of 1854, was licensed to preach by the Fort Wayne Presbytery. Lanius taught at the Presbyterian Academy one academic year (1854-55) and then moved with his wife, Jane A. H. Gordon, to Amite, Mississippi, where he served the Unity Church. In 1856, he accepted the call of the congregation in Waveland, Indiana, and was ordained. In the fall of 1858, he went to Nashville City, Tennessee, to serve the Edgefield Church, where he died of dysentery on August 9,

1859. Joseph M. Wilson, *The Presbyterian Historical Almanac and Annual Remembrancer of the Church for 1861* (Philadelphia: Joseph M. Wilson, 1861), 95.

[87] B. J. Griswold, *The Pictorial History of Fort Wayne, Indiana,* 2 vols. (Chicago: Robert O. Law Company, 1917), 1: 384, 421. Irvin (who later changed the spelling to Irwin) was born in Madison, Indiana, March 25, 1820. He graduated from Hanover College (1843), taught school in Newcastle, Kentucky (1843-44), earned a Master of Arts from Hanover College (1846), and then taught at Paris, Kentucky. *The Journal of Hanover College,* vol. 3, no. 4 (January 1897), 166. Other teachers at the Presbyterian school were John H. Jacobs and a Mrs. Mills.

[88] J. Randolph Kirby, "Fort Wayne Common School Crusaders: The First Year for Free Schooling, April 1853-March 1854," *Old Fort News,* vol. 42, no. 1 (1979), 23.

[89] George William Allison, *Forest, Fort, and Faith: Historical Sketches of The Presbytery of Fort Wayne,* 19.

[90] Irvin had been licensed to preach by the Fort Wayne Presbytery (O. S.) in April 1856; he served for a brief period in 1858 as Stated Supply at the Unity Church; after the Civil War he served a church at Fort Scott and later at Council Grove, Kansas. He died at Anaheim, California, October 8, 1896.

[91] *Fort Wayne Times,* 7 July 1855.

[92] J. Edwards, *Aspects of Society* (Fort Wayne, Ind.: T. N. Hood, 1855), 24, 25.

[93] *Fort Wayne Standard,* 1 February 1855. Case was briefly an editor for this newspaper. As a lawyer, he defended local black clients; in Congress, he introduced a bill to abolish slavery in the District of Columbia.

[94] *Fort Wayne Times,* 25 January 1855.

[95] *First Presbyt. Church Trustee Record No. 1, 1843-1868,* 25 June 1855, First Presbyterian Church Archives.

[96] Jonathan Edwards to John Findley Crowe, 9 June 1855, Hanover College Archives. After two years at Hanover, Edwards resigned because its Board was unable to pay his full salary. (In October 1855, the Fort Wayne Presbytery had agreed to assume the new president's salary for the academic year; by February, however, only three churches had contributed at total of twenty-eight dollars.) Edwards successively became pastor of the West Arch St. Church, Philadelphia, Pennsylvania (1857-66); president, Washington and Jefferson College (1866-69); pastor, Second Presbyterian Church, Baltimore, Maryland (1869-71); pastor, First Presbyterian Church, Peoria, Illinois (1871-77); professor of theology, Danville Theological Seminary, Danville, Kentucky (1877-81); pastor, Seventh Presbyterian Church, Cincinnati, Ohio (1881-85); pastor, Long Branch, New Jersey (1885-87); pastor, Meadville, Pennsylvania (1887-91). He received the degrees of Doctor of Divinity from Princeton in 1856 and Doctor of Letters from Lafayette College in 1866. He died in Peoria, Illinois in 1891.

[97] William D. Howard, "A Memoir of the Author," forward to *The Prophet Elisha,* by John M. Lowrie (Philadelphia: Presbyterian Board of Publication, 1869), 7, 15.

[98] Lowrie had been elected pastor on September 3, 1855, but did not assume the position for thirteen months; perhaps ill health, which in 1847 had forced him to resign his position in New Jersey, delayed his acceptance of the call. During part of the interim, the Reverend J. H. Burns supplied the pulpit.

[99] *Fort Wayne Times,* 1 January 1857; *Dawson's Daily Times,* 2 April 1860.

[100] *Ibid.,* 22 January 1857. In 1860 Lowrie spoke to the Institute on "Mohammedanism."

[101] See chapter "Women's Societies."

[102] John M. Lowrie, *Adam and His Times* (Philadelphia: Presbyterian Board of Publication, 1861), 49, 60.

[103] John M. Lowrie, *The Lessons of Our National Sorrow: A Discourse . . . Succeeding the Death of Abraham Lincoln* (Fort Wayne: Jenkinson & Harman, 1865), 14.

[104] George William Allison, *Forest, Fort, and Faith: Historical Sketches of The Presbytery of Fort Wayne,* 15.

[105] *Ibid.,* 41.

[106] William D. Howard, *A Memoir of the Author,* prefixed to John M. Lowrie, *The Prophet Elisha,* 18.

[107] *Fort Wayne Sentinel,* 27 March 1858. These prayer meetings in Fort Wayne were part of what came to be called the Revival of 1857-8. The financial panic of 1857 "had much to do with starting one of the most unusual revivals in the history of religious awakenings. It was . . . a lay movement and its impact was principally urban. It began suddenly [at a prayer meeting] in the financial center of New York City . . . . By the spring of 1858 twenty daily union prayer meetings were being held in different parts of the city. The movement quickly spread to other cities . . . . It has been estimated that at least 100,000 professed conversion within 4 months . . . and that the total ingathering of new members into the churches throughout the country as the direct result of the revival was more the 1,000,000." William Warren Sweet, *The Story of Religion in America* (New York: Harper & Brothers, 1950), 310-311.

[108] *Fort Wayne Weekly Republican,* 12 May 1858. Dickson went on to serve churches in New York City and Lewisburg, Pennsylvania; he later retired to Philadelphia where he died in 1887. *Biographical Catalogue of the Princeton Theological Seminary, 1815-1931,* Edward Howell Roberts, comp., 108. On December 18, 1871, Mrs. Dickson met with women of First, Second, and Third Presbyterian Churches to organize the Fort Wayne auxiliary of the Ladies

Foreign Missionary Society.

109 J. L. Williams, *Historical Sketch of First Presbyterian Church, Fort Wayne, Indiana* (Fort Wayne: John W. Dawson, 1860), 15.

Chapter 11

1 Reformed Churches are those European bodies who, during the Protestant Reformation, undertook to reform their faith "according to the Word of God" under the leadership of Huldreich Zwingli and John Calvin. As Lutheranism spread north—creating state churches in northern Germany, Denmark, Sweden, Finland, and Norway—the Reformed movement spread in central Europe to create the Reformed churches of Switzerland, the Netherlands, France, Bohemia, Hungary, and the British Isles.

2 Early in the eighteenth century, those Germans who were Reformed in their confessional allegiance began to emigrate to America, mostly from the Palatine region, the largest number settling in southern Pennsylvania. Because of political turmoil in the Palatinate, the Reformed churches of Germany were unable to assist their expatriate brethren in America in any significant way; what little help was available came from the Dutch Reformed Church.

3 In the Dutch and German Reformed churches of Europe and America, the Classis is the regional governing body, consisting of all ministers and representative elders from congregations in the district.

4 Marie Johnson, "St. John's First Hundred Years" in *Centennial Souvenir and History, St. John's Evangelical and Reformed Church* (Fort Wayne: 1944), unnumbered second page.

5 See chapter "Lutherans."

6 *Minutes of the Voter's Assembly of the St. Paul's Ev. Luth. Church,* June 1844, St. Paul's Lutheran Church Archives, Fort Wayne, Indiana.

7 Susan McCulloch to Maria Halsey, January 13, 1845, McCulloch Papers.

8 Carroll was born in 1781 or 1782. In 1842 he was stationed at Humbersville, Holmes Co., Ohio; the following year he served two congregations in Richland and Knox Townships, Ohio, within the bounds of the Sandusky Classis. Henry Harbaugh, *Fathers of the Reformed Church,* 12 vols. (Lancaster, Pennsylvania: Sprenger & Westhaeffer, 1857), 4: 492.

9 *Minutes of the Voter's Assembly of the St. Paul's Ev. Luth. Church,* 12 July 1844.

10 The trustees were George Nill, Conrad Dreiblebiss, Christian Siebold, and Rudolph Jasper.

11 Lot 443 in "Hanna's Addition" was purchased at a cost of $200; in 1852 and 1854 the adjoining lots 442 and 444 were purchased.

12 *Fort Wayne Times,* 28 August 1847.

13 Carroll went on to serve churches in Millersburg, Ohio, and Bloomfield, Indiana. He died in 1857 at the age of seventy-five years.

14 Bayer first appears in the records of the West Pennsylvania Classis in 1831, as an ordained minister from Rheinbaiern, Germany. Henry Harbaugh, *Fathers of the Reformed Church,* 5: 421.

15 John A. Bayer to Milton Badger, 3 July 1846, AHMS.

16 See chapter "Early Presbyterians" for details on the Society; by 1845, it had already provided partial financial support for the first three ministers of First Presbyterian Church, the first two pastors of the Lutheran congregation, and the minister of the newly organized Second Presbyterian Church.

17 Jacob Laisner et. al. to the Board of the Amer. Home Miss. Society, 18 June 1845, AHMS.

18 Charles Beecher to Milton Badger, 1 August 1845, AHMS.

19 Ibid.

20 John A. Bayer to Milton Badger, 18 September 1845, AHMS.

21 Ibid.

22 Ibid.

23 Ibid. The German Methodists, who were erecting a church in Fort Wayne, were more successful in attracting the "temperance minded" emigrant. See chapter "Methodists."

24 Ibid., 16 March 1846.

25 Ibid.

26 See chapter "New School Presbyterians."

27 John A. Bayer to Milton Badger, 15 May 1846, AHMS.

28 Charles Beecher to Milton Badger, 23 April 1846, AHMS.

29 Bayer discontinued his relationship with the Erie Classis at this time and may have withdrawn from the ministry; he returned to Dansville, New York, which may have been his wife's hometown.

30 Charles Beecher to Milton Badger (attached to Bayer's letter to Badger), 13 September 1846, AHMS.

31 *Record of the Session of the German Presbyterian Church at Fort Wayne, Indiana, 1850-1854,* Presbyterian Historical Society, Philadelphia, Pennsylvania.

32 See chapter "Old School Presbyterians."

33 George W. Allison, *Forest, Fort, and Faith: Historical Sketches of the Presbytery of Fort Wayne* (Fort Wayne: 1945), 55.

34 Henry Harbaugh, *Fathers of the Reformed Church,*

6: 287-293.

[35] I Timothy 4: 14, *King James* version.

[36] No churches were organized, and this ministry was at length discontinued. George W. Allison, *Forest, Fort, and Faith: Historical Sketches of the Presbytery of Fort Wayne,* 21.

[37] See Carl Wittke, *Refugees of Revolution: The German Forty-Eighters in America* (Philadelphia: University of Pennsylvania Press, 1952).

[38] See James Pula, *The French in America, 1488-1974* (Dobbs Ferry, New York: Oceana Publications, 1975).

[39] Most of the French in Fort Wayne before 1825 were Catholics of Canadian (Quebec) heritage; most of the French immigrants of the 1840-1860 era were from Department Doubs (especially from Besancon, Montbeliard, and Belfort), Department Haute Saone, Department Haute Rhin, and Alsace. Charles Banet, St. Joseph's College, Rensselaer, Indiana: unpublished research.

[40] In 1854, the baptisms of David Louis Richard, Albin Alfred Yoquelet, and Jean Auguste Chevelier are recorded in French, and state that the parents came from the Canton of Berne. Marie Johnson, "St. John's First Hundred Years," 4.

[41] Family names were Rosseloz, Racine, Richard, Schafter, Carel, Évard, and Yoquelet. *Records of the Session of the German Presbyterian Church at Fort Wayne, Indiana, 1850-1854.*

[42] Niel was born in France in 1796. "In 1832 he united with the Reformed Church of France and was inducted into the ministry of that church. In 1838 he married and was sent as a missionary to Canada; after laboring there for about 10 years, he removed to N. Y. City and soon connected with the O. S. branch of the Presbyterian Church. He afterwards labored for sometime as a missionary in San Domingo; then for a time in New Orleans; and then in the bounds of the Presbytery of Fort Wayne, Ind. In 1861 he removed to Mt. Eaton [Wayne County, Ohio], and took charge of the Reformed French Church." He died there December 17, 1870. Joseph P. Moore, *History of the Churches in Fort Wayne Presbytery: To which is added Biographical Sketches of deceased Ministers* (Swan, Indiana: manuscript, 20 July 1876), Presbyterian Historical Society, Philadelphia, Pa., 79.

[43] George W. Allison, *Forest, Fort, and Faith: Historical Sketches of the Presbytery of Fort Wayne,* 21. Allison states that this French congregation was located at "Vera Cruz (or Newville)."

[44] Apparently the congregation divided on the issue of Benz's adequacy; there is no record of his subsequent service in the German Reformed Church.

[45] Klein was born January 13, 1829, at Weingarten, Baden, Germany, and emigrated to Sandusky, Ohio, in 1849.

Two years later he entered the Theological Seminary at Tiffin, Ohio—at the same time taking courses at Heidelberg College—and was ordained by the Tiffin Classis in 1854. He resigned his Fort Wayne pastorate in 1868 to serve as professor of systematic theology at Mission House, Wisconsin. He next served Zion Reformed Church in Louisville, Kentucky (1870-1878), and the church at Gallion, Ohio (1878-1888). He was elected president of the General Synod in 1872; Ursinis College awarded him the degree of Doctor of Divinity. In his later years, he served as president of the Reformed Orphans Home of Fort Wayne. He died at Louisville, Kentucky, April 5, 1902. *The Reformed Messenger,* 17 April 1902; *Reformed Church Almanac,* 1903.

[46] *The Reformed Messenger,* 16 April 1856.

[47] In 1870, the school was taken over by the Fort Wayne Public Schools as a "German Department."

[48] *Fort Wayne Weekly Republican,* 5 May 1858 and 2 June 1858. It was officially named the "Synod of the German Reformed Church in Ohio and Adjacent States."

[49] On June 26, 1934, the (German) Reformed Church in the United States merged with the Evangelical (Lutheran) Synod of North America to form the Evangelical and Reformed Church. In July 1961, this body was united with the Congregational Christian Churches to create the United Church of Christ.

On November 27, 1983, St. John's merged with a stepdaughter congregation to form Grace St. John's United Church of Christ, and sold its facilities at the original site. In 1989, these buildings were demolished.

Chapter 12

[1] Isaac McCoy, *History of Baptist Missions* (Washington, D. C.: William M. Morrison, 1840 [Johnson Reprint Corporation, 1970]), 156.

[2] *bid.,* 75.

[3] In 1812, an English merchant visiting Indiana Territory wrote: "Slavery was originally prohibited, but the law has been relaxed in favour of the new settlers who have slaves, and there are now 237 slaves in this territory." John Melish, *Travels in the United States of America, in the years 1806 and 1807, and 1809, 1810, and 1811,* 2 vols. (Philadelphia: T. & G. Palmers, 1812), 2: 157. According to *The American Almanac* (Bureau of the Census), Indiana Territory had 137 slaves in 1800, 247 in 1810, 190 in 1820, and 3 in 1840.

[4] Major Joseph Jenkinson, commandant of Fort Wayne in 1813-1814, complained that some of the local French

residents had so "corrupted [his slave] Ephraim by their ideas" that he was forced "to cool the fellow off, by two very hard whippings." Joseph Jenkinson to Sarah Jenkinson, 14 March 1814, cited in B. J. Griswold, *The Pictoral History of Fort Wayne, Indiana,* 2 vols. (Chicago: Robert O. Law Company, 1917), 1:216.

5 J. Randolph Kirby, "The Appearance of Blacks in Fort Wayne Before 1820," *Old Fort News,* vol., 48, no. 2 (Fort Wayne, Indiana: Allen County-Fort Wayne Historical Society, l985).

6 McCoy mentions a stableman, a bootblack, a gravedigger named John, and Priscilla Burdoin, who had made a handkerchief. Isaac McCoy Papers, 1808-1874, Kansas State Historical Society, Topeka, Kansas, 13 reels microfilm (National Historical Publications Commission, n. d.) 1: 760, 786, 779.

7 On September 28, 1824, Ben Harris paid a $10 down payment on lot 108 on the south side of Berry Street, but did not complete the purchase. On September 19, 1825, Benjamin James, bought lot 130 on the northeast corner of Wayne and Calhoun Streets. J. Randolph Kirby, "Notes on the Emergence of a Black Community in Fort Wayne between 1820 and 1850," taped lecture (Allen County-Fort Wayne Historical Society, 24 February 1985).

8 *Fort Wayne Daily Sentinel,* 23 March 1872. See also *Dawson's Daily Times,* 21 April 1860.

9 Emma Lou Thornbrough, *The Negro in Indiana* (Indianapolis, Indiana: Indiana Historical Bureau, l957), 62.

10 Joseph P. Edsell and John Winton were elected overseers on April 3, 1842.

11 The name was also spelled Canady and Kennedy.

12 J. Randolph Kirby, "Notes of the Emergence of a Black Community in Fort Wayne between 1820 and 1850."

13 *Minutes of the Annual Conferences of the Methodist Episcopal Church For the Years 1839-1845* (New York: T. Mason and G. Lane, 1840-1846), 309, 537, 657.

14 The A. M. E. Discipline stated, "Indiana Conference shall include the States of Indiana, Illinois, Minnesota, Michigan, Wisconsin, and Iowa." Benjamin T. Tanner, *An Apology for African Methodism* (Baltimore: 1867), 305.

15 *Minutes of the Indiana Annual Conference of the Methodist Episcopal Church, 1851* (New York: T. Mason and Lane, 1852), 34.

16 Quinn spent his retirement in Richmond, died there in 1873, and was buried in the Earlham College cemetery.

17 Daniel A. Payne, *History of the African Methodist Episcopal Church* (Nashville, Tenn.: Publishing House of the A. M. E. Sunday-School Union, 1891 [reprint: Arno Press and The New York Times, New York, 1969]), 170-171.

18 Benjamin T. Tanner, *An Apology for African Methodism,* 313.

19 Daniel W. Payne, *History of the African Methodist Episcopal Church,* 184.

20 *Fort Wayne Standard,* 10 August 1854.

21 Benjamin T. Tanner, *An Apology for African Methodism,* 318.

22 The 1850 Allen County Census enumerated 100 "Free Colored" (0.59 percent of the population) who reported their birthplaces as Indiana (47), Ohio (26), Virginia (19), Kentucky (5), North Carolina (4), Tennessee (1), South Carolina (1), and Maryland (1).

23 Lot 296 in Hanna's First Addition was purchased on May 16, 1849, from the estate of Absalom Holcomb, John Rogers, administrator. Allen County Probate Order Book D, 111, 241, 244-246; Probate Final Record G, 180; Deed Record K, 408.

24 Daniel A. Payne, *History of the African Methodist Episcopal Church,* 161.

25 George N. Black was an ordained Deacon in the Indiana District of the A. M. E. Church. *Journal of Proceedings of the Annual Conference of the African Methodist Episcopal Church, for the District of Indiana* (Indianapolis: Rawson Vaille, 1854), 7. Black was a native of Kentucky and owned property in Fort Wayne valued at $800; his wife Elizabeth, was originally from Virginia; in 1850 they had five children under the age of ten years. *1850 Federal Census of Allen Co., Indiana,* F. E. Harter, comp. (Graybill, Indiana: 1968), 54.

26 On November 16, 1850, the indenture was drawn between the titleholders and George Nelson Black for $10. According to Indiana law at that time, each man's wife was required to sign for the sale. These women are some of the first identified black women in Fort Wayne: Susan Fisher, Nancy Elliot, Caroline Canada (who signed with an X), and Elizabeth Black. Henry signed his name Canady. Allen County Deed Record O, 553; Deed Record M, 720.

27 "Robert E. Fleming vs. Canada, Elliot et al., Trustees of the African Methodist Episcopal Church," Book 5, 144, file box 216 (15 July 1863), and Book 6, 130, file box 216 (11 November 1863), Allen County Circuit Court, State of Indiana.

28 See Emma Lou Thornbrough, *The Negro in Indiana.*

29 Isaac McCoy, *History of Baptist Missions,* 156.

30 *Fort Wayne Times,* 25 January and 15 February 1855, signed "X."

31 *Indiana House Journal, 1850-1851,* 39. See John D. Barnhardt and Donald F. Carmony, *Indiana: From Frontier to Industrial Commonwealth,* 2 vols. (New York: Lewis Historical Publishing Co., 1954), 1: 90-104.

32 Rankin wrote: "Slavery and colonization have always had my decided opposition." *The Philanthropist*

(Cincinnati, Ohio), 25 February 1837; reprinted in *The Friend of Man* (Utica, New York), 20 March 1837.

33 William W. Findlay, "Appeal of Wm. W. Findlay, To the Colored People of Indiana," [Covington, Indiana, 6 April 1849] *The African Repository and Colonial Journal* (Washington, D. C.: American Colonization Society, 1850-1892), vol. 25, no. 6, June 1849, 177, 178. Findlay's "Appeal" was submitted to the A. C. S. by their Indiana agent, the Reverend James Mitchell, a black Methodist minister, who describes the writer as "a man of good character and a member of the African Methodist Church . . . very much esteemed by the citizens of Covington . . . . He might live there in peace all his days, and be much respected too; but he is not happy in his social position, as is evident in the language of the circular, nor do we wonder at this when we consider the circumstance that surrounds the colored man in this land. But it is a matter of astonishment that colored men of intelligence and independence would submit to social oppression, when they can escape from it."

Findlay later wrote that he had become "true Liberian in feeling" and stated that more emigrants were needed in Liberia to help protect the African-Americans from hostile native tribes. *Indiana Daily State Sentinel,* Indianapolis, 9 August 1852.

34 "Voice from the Colored Citizens of Fort Wayne, Indiana." *Anti-Slavery Bugle,* Salem, Ohio, 11 August 1849.

35 Although the Colonization Society complained that the Fort Wayne statement was "pretty strong language," it admitted that, on the issue of the "emancipation of slaves or the amelioration of their condition," it would maintain "the strictest impartiality." *The African Repository and Colonial Journal,* vol. 25 (Washington, D. C.: American Colonization Society, October 1849), 310-313. Other African-American communities also made anti-colonization statements that summer, but it was the Fort Wayne resolution that provoked a response. See the *Anti-Slavery Bugle,* Salem, Ohio, 14 July and 4 August 1849, for the statements of the communities in Cleveland and Columbus, Ohio.

36 *Fort Wayne Times,* 9 October 1851.

37 Frederick Hoover, quoted in B. J. Griswold, *The Pictorial History of Fort Wayne, Indiana,* 1: 290-292.

38 Marion Clinton Miller, *The Antislavery Movement In Indiana* (Ann Arbor: dissertation at University of Michigan, 1938), 170.

39 William M. Cockrum, *History of the Underground Railroad as It was Conducted by the Anti-Slavery League, Including Many Thrilling Encounters between Those Aiding the Slaves to Escape and Those Trying to Recapture Them* (Oakland City, Indiana: J. W. Cockrum Printing Co., 1915), 226. Wilbur Henry Seibert, "Light on the Underground Railroad," in the *American Historical Review* (Washington,

D. C.: American Historical Association, 1895), 1: 458-459.

40 Local tradition says that the Vermilyea House, fourteen miles southwest of Fort Wayne on the canal towpath, was a "station" on the Underground Railroad.

41 Addison Coffin, *Life and Travels of Addison Coffin* (Cleveland, Ohio: William G. Hubbard, 1897), 88-89.

42 Gwendolyn J. Crenshaw, *Catalogue: "Bury Me in a Free Land": The Abolitionist Movement in Indiana, 1816-1865* (Indianapolis: Indiana Historical Bureau, 1986), 30. *A Map of Indiana: Showing its History, Points of Interest* (Indiana Dept. of Natural Resources: revised 1984), describes this as the "Most Famous of the 'Underground Railroad' Routes." For a critical view of the Underground Railroad, see Larry Gara, *The Liberty Line: The Legend of the Underground Railroad* (Lexington: University Press, 1961).

43 *Fort Wayne Sentinel,* 12 December 1857.

44 B. J. Griswold, *The Pictorial History of Fort Wayne, Indiana,* 1: 415.

45 *Fort Wayne Sentinel,* 26 February, 1889. Burroughs was born in Vermont in 1808. He established a stationary store in Fort Wayne; in 1844 he became Sealer of Weights and Measures; in 1849-1850 he supplied the pulpit of the Baptist Church; *The Standard* was published from 1854 to 1856. Robert S. Robertson, *Valley of the Upper Maumee River* (Madison, Wisconsin: Brant and Fuller, 1889), 303.

46 *Compilation of the Statutes of Tennessee, 1836* (Nashville: J. Smith, 1836), 279.

47 *Fort Wayne Sentinel,* 7 December 1850.

48 *Fort Wayne Times,* 12 December 1850.

49 Editorial by Thomas Tigar, *Fort Wayne Sentinel,* 7 December 1850.

50 Dorothy Riker and Gayle Thornbrough, comps., *Indiana Election Returns* (Indianapolis: Indiana Historical Bureau, 1860), 388.

51 *Fort Wayne Times,* 4 June 1853.

52 *Ibid.,* 9 August 1855.

53 *Ibid.*

54 Ninde was a "birth-right" Quaker who came to Fort Wayne in 1850, opened a law office, and was later named a judge; with his wife, Beulah, he became an ardent supporter of the woman's rights movement. See chapter "Woman's Societies."

55 Case also served as prosecuting attorney of the court of common pleas; in 1857, he was elected to two terms in congress, where he introduced a bill to abolish slavery in the District of Columbia. During the Civil War he served as colonel in an Indiana regiment; after 1865 he moved to New Orleans for his health. *Fort Wayne Gazette,* 27 February 1873.

56 *Fort Wayne Times,* 9 August 1855.

57 *The Standard,* 1 February 1855.

58 Sermon delivered at the First Presbyterian Church, 25 November 1852. *Fort Wayne Times,* 8 December 1852.

59 Lewis W. Spitz, *Life in Two Worlds: Biography of William Sihler* (St. Louis: Concordia Publishing House, 1968), 108. Sihler's views supporting slavery were published in *Der Lutheraner,* February and March 1863.

60 *The Standard,* 4 January 1855.

61 *The Doctrines and Discipline of the Methodist Episcopal Church, The Twenty-First Edition* (New York: N. Bangs and T. Mason, 1821), 186.

62 See chapter "Methodists" for Brenton's congressional speeches against slavery.

63 *Fort Wayne Sentinel,* 20 September 1854.

64 See Fort Wayne newspapers, especially the *Sentinel,* during the congressional elections of the 1850s and the controversy surrounding the Dred Scott Decision, Nebraska Bill, and "Bleeding Kansas."

65 *The Standard,* 6 July 1854.

66 *Fort Wayne Sentinel,* 12 September 1857.

67 *Ibid.,* 3 October 1857.

68 Case carried the Tenth Congressional District with a plurality of 749, in spite of losing in Allen County by 768 votes.

69 *Fort Wayne Sentinel,* 11 November 1856.

70 *Ibid.,* 21 March 1857.

71 *Fort Wayne Times,* 31 May 1854, signed "R. S."

72 Stowe was the sister of the Reverend Henry Ward Beecher, then an active abolitionist serving the Plymouth Congregational Church in Brooklyn, New York, and the Reverend Charles Beecher, who had served the Second Presbyterian Church in Fort Wayne from 1844 to 1850. Charles Beecher had contributed some material for his sister's book from his experiences in Louisiana. See chapter "New School Presbyterians."

73 The play was continually on the American stage from 1852 to 1931. It has been alleged that Stowe obtained some of her material from Indiana; see Jacob Piatt Dunn, "Indiana's Part in the Making of the Story 'Uncle Tom's Cabin,'" *Indiana Magazine of History,* 7 (1902), 112-118.

74 *Fort Wayne Daily Times,* 18 December 1855.

75 *Dawson's Daily Times,* 23 February 1859.

76 Isaac H. Julian, "Legislation of Indiana Respecting Colored People," *Fort Wayne Standard,* 14 September 1854. Julian was the younger brother of the abolitionist reformer and politician, George W. Julian. See Patrick W. Riddleberger, *George Washington Julian, Radical Republican* (Indianapolis: Indiana Historical Bureau, 1966).

77 Isaac H. Julian, "Legislation of Indiana Respecting Colored People," *Fort Wayne Standard,* 14 September 1854.

78 *Ibid.*

79 *Ibid.,* 28 March 1859.

80 Earlier that year, a black preacher addressed a white audience on the subject of slavery; a biased editor reported: "The Rev. Tabbs Scroggs, a big darkie from somewhere, proposed on last night to enlighten the whites on the subject of slavery. What a humbug to catch gulls. It is pretty near time that such lubber-lifters have found their proper place. What is strange, the Daily [Republican] of his friend Peter [Bailey], of this morning, omits mention of his African brother." *Fort Wayne Times,* 20 January 1859. "Scroggs" may be a mocking pseudonym substituted by the editor to insult the black preacher. Quinn was six feet three inches tall and weighed more than 250 pounds.

81 The U. S. Census registered a decline in Fort Wayne's black population from 102 in 1850, to 63 in 1860, and only 27 in 1870. During the same period the white population grew from 4,800 in 1850, to 10,000 in 1860; in 1870 the city's total population was enumerated to be 17,718.

82 "Turner Chapel A. M. E. History," in *Anniversary Program* (Fort Wayne, Ind.: 15 August 1985), 2.

83 Of the original A. M. E. church trustees of 1849, only George Fisher was in Fort Wayne in 1869; he was elected treasurer of the reorganized congregation on December 12, 1872, with trustees W. L. Steward, William Hurdle, and John Hall, with the Reverend Jason Bundy. T. B. Helm, *History of Allen County* (Chicago: Kingman Brothers, 1880), 96.

84 The donor put a condition in the deed that, if the land should cease to be used by the A. M. E. Church for religious purposes, then the title to the land should be vested in a society which would use it for the purpose of establishing an orphan's home for black and white children. Assisting developing congregations in Fort Wayne was a special interest of Mrs. Hamilton: in 1867, she had furnished the funds to secure land for a Presbyterian Sunday School mission (later to become Third Presbyterian Church) on the northeast corner of Calhoun and Holman Streets.

85 *Fort Wayne Daily Democrat,* 10 February 1870.

Chapter 13

1 Thomas Morris, "Journal of Captain Morris" (1764) in *Miscellanies in Prose and Verse* (London: 1791), 23 (Ann Arbor, Mich: University Microfilms, Inc., 1966), reprinted in the *Old Fort News*, vol. 6, no. 1 (Fort Wayne: Allen County-Fort Wayne Historical Society, 1941), 7. In 1780, "a man called George, a partner of Israel," was living in Miamitown, who may have been Levi. "LaBalme Papers," *Michigan Pioneer and Historical Collections* 19 (Lansing, Michigan:

Wyncoop Hallenbeck Crawford Co., 1877), 578.

2 See Nellie A. Robertson, "John Hayes and the Fort Wayne Agency," *Indiana Magazine of History,* vol 39, no. 3 (September 1943), 223, 226.

3 Mrs. Eliza Brouillet wrote in 1904 that she had in her possession "a family Bible [prayer book?] and other evidences of her grandfather's Jewish faith." See Harry Simonoff, *Jewish Notables in America: 1776-1865* (Greenberg Publishing Co., 1956).

4 John Reynolds, *Pioneer History of Illinois* (Belleville, Ill.: N. A. Randall, 1852), 186-188, quoted in Joseph Levine, *John Jacob Hays: The First Known Jewish Resident of Fort Wayne* (Fort Wayne, Indiana: Jewish Historical Society, 1973), 5.

5 In 1825, all the Jews in the Ohio valley, except three, were of English ancestry; by 1830, these were outnumbered by German Jews. David Philipson, "The Jewish Pioneers of the Ohio Valley," *American Historical Society,* vol. 8 (New York: 1900), 47-48.

6 *Fort Wayne Sentinel,* 20 and 27 January, 3 February 1849.

7 *Schreiben eines Deutschen Juden, an den Presidenten des Congresses de Vereinigten Staaten,* 1783 (original in the Deutches Museum, Leipsig), published by Mendelssohn in 1787, quoted in I. Harold Sharfman, *Jews of the Frontier* (Chicago: Henry Regnery Company, 1977), 89.

8 *Allgemeine Zeitung des Judentums* 24 (1839), quoted in I. Harold Sharfman, *Jews on the Frontier,* 299.

9 *Fort Wayne Times,* 14 August 1847.

10 Abram Vossen Goodman, "A Jewish Peddler's Diary: 1842-1843," *American Jewish Archives,* no. 3 (Cincinnati, Ohio: June 1951), 99, 108, 109.

11 *Ibid.*

12 Harold Sharfman, *Jews on the Frontier,* 103.

13 Sigmund and Lena Redelsheimer left their three-year-old son, David, in Germany, where he "received a fair German education"; at the age of fourteen he came to Fort Wayne. Robert S. Robertson, *The Valley of the Upper Maumee,* 2 vols. (Madison, Wis.: Brant & Fuller, 1889), 1: 408; B. J. Griswold, *Pictorial History of Fort Wayne, Indiana,* 2 vols. (Chicago: Robert O. Law Company, 1917), 1: 347.

14 *Ibid.,* 1: 384. "All of the earliest [Jewish] settlers [of Muncie, Indiana] were of French extraction, having been born and raised in the town of Forbach, in Lorraine." Alexander L Schonfield, *Sketch of the Jewish Congregation in the City of Muncie, Indiana* [written May 13, 1922], (Fort Wayne, Ind.: Indiana Jewish Historical Society, 1977), 2.

15 Charles Beecher to Milton Badger, 5 February 1846, AHMS.

16 Nirdlinger's obituaries said Hechingen; other sources say Nördlingen.

17 Nirdlinger died in Fort Wayne in 1873 at the age of sixty-three after residing in Fort Wayne for "nearly thirty years;" he was, therefore, born in 1810, arrived in Pennsylvania in 1826, and seems to have come to Fort Wayne in 1846. (His son Albert was born in Alabama in 1845.) What Nirdlinger did in the preceding twenty years is not recorded; he appears suddenly in Fort Wayne history in 1846 as a prosperous merchant. (The first advertisement for his "New York Emporium" appears in the *Fort Wayne Times,* 19 December 1846.) Isaac Goldberg, in the biography of Nirdlinger's grandson, *George Jean Nathan* (New York: Simon and Schuster, 1926), 44, incorrectly asserts "Nirdlinger was a cattleman and frontier trader who later did his share in building up Fort Wayne as a mid-Western trading post." Most likely he was one of the many young south-German peddlers who eventually settled in town; this would explain Nirdlinger's sensitivity to the newspaper attack on local Jewish peddlers.

18 B. J. Griswold, *Pictorial History of Fort Wayne, Indiana,* 1: 451.

19 Located at the southeast corner of Main and Harrison streets, the home of Frederick Nirdlinger and his wife, Hannah Mysorson, was later described as a "big brick house, with a thick cornice all around, and nearly covered with a green vine . . . a fountain in the middle of the yard spraying into an aquarium." It no longer exists. Mrs. A. J. Detzer, quoted in Bessie K. Roberts, "Unity and Peace," *Old Fort News,* vol. 8, no. 1 (Fort Wayne, Ind.: Allen County-Fort Wayne Historical Society, 1943), 3.

20 Purchased for $200 on October 13, 1848, the plot was adjacent to what is now McCulloch Park on Broadway.

21 *The Occident and American Jewish Advocate,* vol. 15 (April 1857), 45.

22 The bylaws stipulated that "discussion, as well as the books of society, will be conducted in the German language."

23 Signed by Frederick Nirdlinger, president; Sigmund Redelsheimer, vice president; Isaac Wolf, treasurer; Isaac Lauferty, secretary; Daniel Guggenheimer, Abraham Oppenheimer, Isidor Lichtenheim, Salomon Stahl, trustees.

24 Constitution and Bylaws, *Verein Fur Krankensbesuche Und Todesbestattung, October 26, 1848,* translated by Frances Lowens, Achduth Vesholom Temple Archives, Fort Wayne Indiana. (American Jewish Archives microfilm numbers 436, 436A.)

25 *Fort Wayne Times,* 18 October 1845.

26 *Ibid.,* 16 December 1847.

27 *Fort Wayne Sentinel,* 20 January 1849.

28 The *Lagrange Democrat* had reported the week before, "We understand the smallpox is raging to a consid-

erable extent in Fort Wayne."

[29] Nirdlinger was in partnership with a relative who operated another "F. & J. Nirdlinger" at 81 North 3rd St., Philadelphia, Pennsylvania, and did the buying for the Fort Wayne store; in 1852, Abraham Oppenheimer became a partner in the local firm. *Fort Wayne Times,* 19 December 1846 and 1 December 1852.

[30] F. & J. Nirdlinger dealt in the wholesale, as well as retail, trade; most likely some of these local Jewish peddlers were customers.

[31] *Fort Wayne Sentinel,* 27 January 1849.

[32] "Jew peddler" was a label sometimes applied to any peddler, but the word "Jew," at that time, had a derogatory connotation and Jews themselves preferred to be termed "Israelites" or "Hebrews."

[33] *Fort Wayne Sentinel,* 27 January 1849.

[34] *Ibid.,* 3 February 1849.

[35] *Fort Wayne Times,* June 12 1851.

[36] Founded by Isaac Leeser, a hazzan in Philadelphia, this journal published news of orthodox congregations.

[37] The earliest record of Salomon's presence in Fort Wayne shows him officiating at a wedding on September 27 and October 16, 1850. Marriage Records, Allen County Courthouse, Fort Wayne, Indiana.

[38] In the congregational documents he signed his name "Salomon"; it was always printed "Solomon" in the English language Jewish papers. The congregation always referred to him as cantor or prayer leader, but the Gentile community referred to him as Rabbi or minister. See the *Fort Wayne Sentinel,* 17 November 1855.

[39] Minutes of the Congregation, 10 October 1853, Achduth Vesholom Temple Archives.

[40] *The Occident and American Jewish Advocate,* vol. 16 (Summer 1858), 362. This spelling is from the congregational minutes of October 6, 1861, when the name was officially changed to "Achdath Veshalom," later written Achduth Vesholom.

[41] "A Member," Fort Wayne, February 1857, *Occident and American Jewish Advocate,* vol. 15 (April 1857), 45; *Williams' Fort Wayne Directory, City Guide, and Business Mirror: Volume 1: 1858-59,* C. S. Williams, comp. (Fort Wayne: C. L. Hill, 1858), [17]. The room above the hall was rented to a member for $25 a year and this sum was then paid to another member to serve as the janitor *(shammes).*

[42] Revised Constitution and Bylaws, 4 May 1856, Achduth Vesholom Temple Archives.

[43] The school was later held in Pratt's Hall at the northwest corner of Calhoun and Main streets. *The American Hebrew,* vol, 64, no. 6 (9 December 1898), 173.

[44] The Eppsteins had four daughters and two sons, all of whom had emigrated to the United States; one daughter married Marx Frank of Fort Wayne.

[45] *Fort Wayne Sentinel,* 5 April 1879 (obituary).

[46] *Fort Wayne Times,* 21 October 1858.

[47] The English teacher was a Mr. Walter; later they hired a Mr. Hamilton.

[48] *The Occident, and American Jewish Advocate,* vol. 15 (April 1857), 45, 46.

[49] Bessie K. Roberts, "Unity and Peace," *Old Fort News,* 7.

[50] "Her husband, Block *(sic),* was a reformed Jew, who had been converted to Christianity through the winning ways of Kezia rather than by biblical arguments, at least so 'twas told." Kezia died August 25, 1856; her tombstone in the Broadway (McCulloch) Cemetery was inscribed, "Kezia, wife of Rev. Aaron Block *(sic)* . . . aged 24." *Fort Wayne Daily News,* 31 May 1884.

[51] *Fort Wayne Times,* 25 June 1857.

[52] *Fort Wayne Republican,* 12 December 1858.

[53] This phrase suggests that Bloch had come to Fort Wayne under the auspices of the Society for Meliorating the Condition of the Jews, a Christian missionary organization which offered economic assistance to converted Jews. Rabbi Isaac Mayer Wise of Cincinnati warned Jews of this society which, he said, "does not refuse to stoop to most disgraceful means to parade the name of a convert or two to the public." *The Israelite,* vol. 3, no. 6 (19 August 1854), 44; quoted in W. William Wimberley, II, *The Jewish Experience in Indiana Before the Civil War: An Introduction* (Fort Wayne: Indiana Jewish Historical Society, July 1976), 2, 13.

[54] *Dawson's Daily Times,* 21 March 1859.

[55] Minutes of the Congregation, 11 August 1861, Achduth Vesholom Temple Archives.

[56] Isaac Leeser, *The Occident and American Jewish Advocate,* vol. 15 (July 1857), 309.

[57] Anonymous, *Ibid.,* vol. 15 (1858), 588; dated "Rosh Hodesh Adar, 5618."

[58] *Ibid.,* 579, 588.

[59] Albert, who had been born in Alabama in 1845, was the oldest of eight Nirdlinger children and remained in Fort Wayne; Sam and Frank, theatrical entrepreneurs in Philadelphia, changed their name to "Nixon"; Charles Frederic graduated from Harvard University and became a playwright; Ella attended Notre Dame convent, married Charles Narét-Nathan of France, and was the mother of drama critic George Jean Nathan; Max was in the clothing business in Fort Wayne, manufactured baseball bats for the A. G. Spaulding Company, and became president of the Northwestern Baseball League in 1884; also Eli, who died in 1873 at the age of 23, and Dolly Leopold. See Bessie K. Roberts, "Unity and Peace," Old Fort News, vol. 8 (February 1943); also K. White, "A Study of Jewish Businessmen in Fort

60 Wayne, Indiana as Reflected in the City Directories of 1861 through 1872," unpublished typescript (1979), American Jewish Archives, Hebrew Union College, Cincinnati, Ohio.

60 The opening words of Leviticus, the Torah reading for that Sabbath.

61 The bracketed explanation was inserted by the editor of the Occident, Isaac Leeser.

62 *The Occident and American Jewish Advocate,* vol. 16 (1858), 93-94; the letter is dated March 24, 1858.

63 *Ibid.,* 94-95.

64 Minutes of the Congregation, August 1861 and June 1865, Achduth Vesholom Temple Archives. The women's Thiriza Association, which in 1861 became the Ladies' Hebrew Benevolent Society, tried to help the needy with its limited funds. In April 1870, the congregation voted to send $5.00 to the poor in Russia.

65 *Fort Wayne Times,* 14 June 1845.

66 *Ibid.,* 31 May 1849. Not all of the appeals from Palestine were for the poor. The *Fort Wayne Times* reported on January 11, 1849, that "Great efforts are now being made by the Jews throughout the world for the rebuilding of the Temple at Jerusalem . . . permission to that effect having recently been given them by the Turkish governmen t. . . . At the [New York City] Coliseum, was a Greek rabbi, who comes here specially commissioned to receive money for the enterprise."

67 Isaac Leeser, *The Occident and American Jewish Advocate,* vol. 10 (Summer 1852), 263.

68 Minutes of the Congregation, 4 April 1858, Achduth Vesholom Temple Archives.

69 Anonymous, *Occident and American Jewish Advocate,* vol. 15 (Fall 1858), 587.

70 The German Methodists had built this church in 1846; by the fall of 1859, "under the ministerial charge of Rev. Barth, [they] . . . erected a neat frame house as a place of worship in the western part of the city." *Dawson's Daily Times,* 30 September 1859. *The American Hebrew,* vol. 64, no. 6 (9 December 1898), 173, incorrectly reports that it was the "Heidelberg Reformed Church."

71 When, in October, Nirdlinger was again named president, a local newspaper reported, "Frederick Nirdlinger was on yesterday elected generalissimo of the Hebrew Society of this city." *Dawson's Daily Times,* 10 October 1859.

72 *The Occident and American Jewish Advocate,* vol. 20 (May 1862).

73 *Dawson's Daily Times,* 11 July 1859.

74 Isaac Leeser, *The Occident and American Jewish Advocate,* vol. 17 (August 1859), 132.

75 Signed "Benoni," *Ibid.,* vol. 17 (August 1859), 114.

76 Isaac Leeser *The Occident and American Jewish Advocate,* vol., 17 (October 1859), 166-168.

77 Solomon's temple was so oriented, but synagogues are situated to face Jerusalem.

78 *Dawson's Daily Times,* 24 September 1859.

79 *Fort Wayne Sentinel,* 24 September 1859.

80 Isaac Leeser *The Occident and American Jewish Advocate,* vol. 17 (October 1859), 166-168.

81 Peter Bailey, *Fort Wayne Republican,* 28 September 1859.

82 Isaac Leeser, *The Occident and American Jewish Advocate,* vol. 17 (October 1859), 166-168.

83 Peter Bailey, *Fort Wayne Republican,* 28 September 1859.

84 Jewish visitors were from Wabash, Warsaw, Auburn, LaPorte, and Huntington, Indiana; Van Wert, Bryan, and Cleveland, Ohio; St. Louis, Missouri and Philadelphia, Pennsylvania. *The Occident and American Jewish Advocate,* vol. 17 (October 1859), 166-168.

85 *Ibid.*

86 *Ibid.*

87 *Ibid.*

88 *Ibid.,* 174.

89 *Dawson's Daily Times,* 7 October 1859.

90 Jacob Radar Marcus, *Memoirs of American Jews: 1775-1865,* vol. 3 (Philadelphia: Jewish Publication Society of America, 1955), 1.

91 Isaac Mayer Wise, *The Israelite,* vol. 6, no. 27 (6 January 1860), 214.

92 The "Parnas" (Hebrew: "manager") is the chief officer of the congregation, usually a person of means who contributes substantially to the support of the synagogue.

93 The mystical books of the medieval cabala, which teach that every letter, word, number and accent of Scripture contains a hidden meaning.

94 *Dawson's Daily Times* had announced: "Rev. Dr. Wise, editor of the Israelite at Cincinnati, will lecture at the Hebrew Church, Fort Wayne, at 7 1/2 this night." 21 December 1859.

95 *The Israelite,* vol. 6, no. 27 (6 January 1860), 214. Wise organized the Union of American Hebrew Congregations in 1873 and, in 1875, was the founder and first president of Hebrew Union College in Cincinnati; he returned to Fort Wayne on January 7, 1876, to deliver the dedication address of the second synagogue.

96 Minutes of the Congregation, April 1857 and October 1857, Achduth Vesholom Temple Archives.

97 Ibid., 16 and 26 July 1860.

98 Quoted in Frances Lowen's 1948 translation of the minutes; her 1988 search of the minutes, however, finds no mention of Rosenthal's discharge. Because there is no current record of any meeting between October 13, 1861 and April 20, 1862, the translator suggests that the minutes

concerning Rosenthal's "moral life" have been lost.

99 *The Occident and American Jewish Advocate,* vol. 20 (August 1862), 2A.

100 In the nineteenth century, a rabbi was trained to teach and decide matters of Jewish law, and ordination by another rabbi indicated this competence. He did not ordinarily lead in worship, a responsibility of the cantor or prayer leader; nor did he render pastoral care, the duty of the whole congregation. A rabbi, however, might be invited to preach at special occasions, such as before holidays. Rabbi Richard Safran of congregation Achduth Vesholom stated: "To a large extent, the modern American rabbi has been Protestantized."

101 Minutes of the Congregation, 10 August 1862, Achduth Vesholom Temple Archives.

102 Ibid., July 1863.

103 Ibid., 8 October 1865.

104 Marx Frank, in his Jubilee address in 1898, incorrectly stated that "Mayer Eppstein gave to that little band the first glimpse of Reformed Judaism." Reprinted in *Centennial Souvenir, 1848-1948, Achduth Vesholom* (Fort Wayne, Indiana: 1848).

105 The traditionalists suggested the ritual of the Julian Strass Synagogue of Philadelphia.

106 Minutes of the Congregation, 22 October 1865, Achduth Vesholom Temple Archives.

107 Fannie Bronstein said, "I have been told by two of Rev. Rubin's grandchildren that some of the members of the congregation threw stones at the windows of his home on West Main Street, next to the old Interurban Station. These dissenters finally resigned and organized another congregation." (Address to the Annual Meeting of the Congregation, 20 May 1961, typescript), Achduth Vesholom Temple Archives.

108 In December 1869, the officers voted that the delinquent dues of six members "should be collected by a lawyer." Minutes of the Congregation, Achduth Vesholom Temple Archives.

109 They elected V. Jacobson, president; Leopold Falk, secretary; Simon Freiberger, Marx Graff, and Jacob Becker, trustees.

110 *The Occident and American Jewish Advocate,* vol. 23 (July, August and September 1865).

111 Isaac Leeser, *The Occident and American Jewish Advocate,* vol. 23 (November 1865), 382-383.

112 Minutes of the Congregation, 14 August 1866, Achduth Vesholom Temple Archives.

113 Nirdlinger never again held office; Lauferty was elected president in 1868, 1869, and 1870.

114 Minutes of the Congregation, 14 August 1866, Achduth Vesholom Temple Archives.

Chapter 14

1 The Associate Reformed Presbyterian effort to establish a congregation is described in chapter "Old School and Associate Reformed Presbyterians."

2 Knox County, Ohio, 5 November 1828, Record of Deeds, vol. G, 504; deed facsimile in H. Kenneth Dirlan, *John Chapman: By Occupation a Gatherer and Planter of Appleseeds* (Mansfield, Ohio, [published by the author] 1853), 26.

3 *Report of the Society for Printing, Publishing and Circulating the Writings of Emanuel Swedenborg,* Manchester, England, 14 January 1817, quoted in Robert C. Harris, *Johnny Appleseed Sourcebook* (Fort Wayne, Ind.: Public Library of Fort Wayne and Allen County, n.d.), 12. First published in *Old Fort News,* vol. 9, nos. 1-2 (Fort Wayne, Ind.: March-June 1945).

4 Chapman was born in Leominster, Massachusetts, on September 26, 1774.

5 Marguerite Beck Block, *The New Church in the New World* (New York: Holt, Rinehart and Winston, 1932), 171. By 1833, the society at Madison had disappeared from the New Church records.

6 New Church tradition suggests that Chapman was converted by Judge John Young of Greensburg, Pennsylvania. Young's obituary in 1840 said: "It was he who supplied 'Johnny Appleseed' with the New Church literature which the latter spread among the early settlers in Ohio." Carl T. Odhner, *Annals of The New Church,* vol. 1 (Bryn Athyn, Pa.: Academy of the New Church, 1904), 451.

7 Marguerite Beck Block, *The New Church in the New World,* 113.

8 *Ibid.,* 115.

9 J. H. Newton, *History of Venango County, Pennsylvania* (Columbus, Ohio: J. A. Caldwell, 1879), 120, 451.

10 R. I. Curtis, "John Chapman, alias 'Johnny Appleseed,'" *Ohio Pomological Society Transactions* (Columbus, Ohio: 1859), 68.

11 Carl T. Odhner, *Annals of The New Church,* 1: 534.

12 Reminisces of E. Vandorn, *Ohio Liberal,* Mansfield, Ohio, 13 and 20 August 1873. "A descendant of Jonathan's [half] sister [Persis Chapman Broom] is authority for the statement that her Uncle Jonathan never bartered [bargained or haggled for] anything, it being contrary to his religious scruples to do so, and that the money he sometimes received or the entertainment and shelter he was accorded was voluntarily bestowed, and not necessarily in direct return for value given. He himself gave to all alike, asking nothing." Mrs. Samuel R. Taylor, "The Story of the Townships of Allen County," in B. J. Griswold, *The Pictorial History of Fort Wayne, Indiana,* 2 vols. (Chicago: Robert O. Law Company,

1917), 1: 603.

13 *Some Letters of William Schlatter: 1814 to 1825* (typescript from letter books), New Church Theological School Library, Cambridge, Massachusetts, 52.

14 *Ibid.,* 108.

15 *Ibid.,* 16 April 1821.

16 *Ibid.,* 20 March 1820.

17 *Journal of the Proceedings of the Fifth General Convention of the Receivers of the Doctrines of the New Jerusalem* (Boston, Mass.: The General Convention of the New Jerusalem, 1822); reprinted as *The Early Journals of the General Convention of the New Jerusalem, Part I, Journals 1-8, 1817-1826* (Boston: Massachusetts New Church Union, 1888), 8.

18 Robert Price, *Johnny Appleseed: Man and Myth* (Bloomington, Ind.: Indiana University Press, 1954), 184.

19 George W. Brackenridge, in *Reminiscences of Old Fort Wayne,* Laura Case Woodworth et al., comps. (Fort Wayne, Ind.: Public Library of Fort Wayne and Allen County, 1906 [reprint]), n. p.

20 Tract Book, Allen County Records. See Robert C. Harris, *Johnny Appleseed Sourcebook,* 15.

21 John W. Dawson wrote: "In the autumn of 1830 . . . he planted a nursery on what was then called the Taylor farm, near the canal lock, just east of this city—another at that time . . . just below the city on the north side of the River Maumee, and then taking a quantity of apple-seed he journeyed to Elkhart prairie, near Goshen . . . . [Later] he planted the one on the south bank of the Maumee River, about ten miles from here, in Milan township . . . . the very nursery which was inventoried as of his personal estate, and which contained there 15,000 trees . . . . Another orchard he planted somewhat later on the St. Mary's, about nine miles up from this city, south side. Another was on the land of David Archer. . . at the northwest corner of said land, on the St. Joseph [Leo] Road." John W. Dawson, "Johnny Appleseed," *Fort Wayne Sentinel,* 21 and 23 October 1871.

22 *Ibid.*

23 *Hamilton-Taber Acct. Book,* 136, Allen Hamilton Papers, Allen County-Fort Wayne Historical Society, Fort Wayne, Indiana.

24 John W. Dawson, "Johnny Appleseed," *Fort Wayne Sentinel,* 21 and 23 October 1871.

25 Marguerite Beck Block, *The New Church in the New World,* 9.

26 J. H. Newton, *History of Venango County, Pennsylvania,* 595.

27 "Report of the Society for Printing, Publishing and Circulating the Writings of Emanuel Swedenborg," Manchester, England, 14 January 1817, quoted in Robert C. Harris, *Johnny Appleseed Sourcebook,* 12.

28 *Fort Wayne Sentinel,* 22 March 1845.

29 Carl T. Odhner, *Annals of The New Church,* 1: 533.

30 John W. Dawson, "Johnny Appleseed," *Fort Wayne Sentinel,* 21 and 23 October 1871.

31 Robert Price, *Johnny Appleseed: Man and Myth,* 31.

32 George W. Brackenridge, in *Reminiscences of Old Fort Wayne,* Laura Case Woodworth et al., comps., n. p.

33 Lorenzo Dow was an itinerant preacher who often spoke about the work of the devil in his hearers.

34 John W. Dawson, "Johnny Appleseed," *Fort Wayne Sentinel,* 21 and 23 October 1871. William D. Haley, "Johnny Appleseed—A Pioneer Hero," *Harper's New Monthly Magazine* 43 (November, 1871). Dawson states that Payne was "killed by the Indians, and his head severed from his body, and carried on a pole as a trophy. . . in the northern part of this State, soon after his visit here."

35 *Fort Wayne Sentinel,* 22 March 1845; Robert S. Robertson, *Valley of the Upper Maumee River,* 2 vols. (Madison, Wis.: Brant & Fuller, 1889), 1: 152.

36 John W. Dawson, "Johnny Appleseed," *Fort Wayne Sentinel,* 21 and 23 October 1871.

37 George Field, *Memoirs, Incidents & Reminiscences of the Early History of the New Church in Michigan, Indiana, Illinois and Adjacent States; and Canada* (Toronto, Canada: R. Carswell & Co., 1879), 17, 29, 37, 65, 192.

38 See Robert W. Gladish, *Swedenborg, Fourier and the America of the 1840s* (Bryn Athyn, Pa.: Swedenborg Scientific Association, 1983).

39 None of the recollections of Chapman by Fort Wayne residents mentions a local convert. His New Church obituary stated that "several earnest members of the Church are known to have received their first knowledge of the Doctrines from Johnny Appleseed." Carl T. Odhner, *Annals of The New Church,* 1: 534.

40 Marguerite Beck Block, *The New Church in the New World,* 219.

41 Chapman died at the age of 71 of the "winter plague" in Fort Wayne on March 18, 1845, at the home of Richard Worth, Sr., and was buried in the family plot of David Archer. See Steven Fortriede, *Johnny Appleseed: The Man Behind the Myth* (Fort Wayne, Ind.: Fort Wayne Public Library, 1978), 37-51.

42 One settler said that Chapman "seemed to be as much at home with the red men of the forest as with his own race." J. H. Newton, *History of Venango County, Pennsylvania,* 595.

43 Chapman's warning cry was said to have been: "The spirit of the Lord is upon me, and he hath anointed me to blow the trumpet in the wilderness, and sound an alarm in the forest; for, behold, the tribes of the heathen are round about your doors, and a devouring flame followeth after them." A.

Banning Norton, *A History of Knox County, Ohio* (Columbus, Ohio: R. Nevins, Printer, 1862), 140.

44 Carl T. Odhner, *Annals of The New Church,* 1: 533.

45 *Ibid.*

46 Robert S. Robertson, *Valley of the Upper Maumee River,* 1: 151.

47 John W. Dawson, "Johnny Appleseed," *Fort Wayne Sentinel,* 21 and 23 October 1871.

48 Matthew 6:25, *Authorized* (King James) *Version.*

49 Emanuel Swedenborg, *Arcana Coelestia,* No. 6872 (New York: American Swedenborg Printing and Publishing Society, 1908), 9: 135.

50 Charles Beecher to Milton Badger, 28 March 1845, AHMS.

51 *Dawson's Daily Times,* 28 May 1859.

52 Charles Furman to Absolom Peters, 19 February 1830, AHMS.

53 Hugh McCulloch, *Men and Measures of Half a Century* (New York: C. Scribner's Sons, 1880), 107. In 1834, Thompson was employed "to attend the poor house . . . at two shillings per mile for visits, and one shilling for each dose of medicine prescribed." B. J. Griswold, *The Pictorial History of Fort Wayne, Indiana,* 1: 319.

54 *Ibid.,* 1: 302, 319.

55 J. L. Williams, *Historical Sketch of the First Presbyterian Church, Fort Wayne, Indiana, With Early Reminiscences of the Place* [2nd edit.] (Fort Wayne, Ind.: Daily News Printing House, 1881), 27.

56 Lewis G. Thompson to Wilson L. Thompson, 17 August 1840, Lewis G. and Wilson L. Thompson Letters, Indiana State Library, Indianapolis, Indiana.

57 Hugh McCulloch to Eunice Hardy, 12 March 1834, Connie Hurni Collection, Hicksville, Ohio. Hugh McCulloch, who defended Thompson, reported that the case "produces much excitement"; the identity of the Methodist minister and the outcome of the legal action are unknown.

58 Lewis G. Thompson to Wilson L. Thompson, 6 March 1842, Lewis G. and Wilson L. Thompson Letters. The Reverend Burroughs Westlake, born in 1792, had served congregations in Maryland and Ohio before coming to Indiana in 1836; he died in Logansport in 1845.

59 Erasmus Manford, *Twenty-five Years in the West* (Chicago: H. B. Manford, Publisher, 1885), 167. The "Restitution" is the final restoration of all things and persons to harmony with God's will.

60 The anonymous author of "First Universalist," in *History of Allen County, Indiana,* T. B. Helm, ed. (Chicago: Kingman Brothers, 1880), 99, gives the date of September 7-18, 1843, for Manford's first visit to Fort Wayne. This date is problematical because there was no Episcopal clergyman in Fort Wayne until May 1844. Manford wrote: "In 1843 I

moved from Lafayette to Terre Haute"; some time after this he visited Fort Wayne. Charles Beecher's letters suggest that Manford lectured during the fall of 1844.

61 Charles Beecher to Milton Badger, 16 December 1844, AHMS.

62 Ernest Cassara, ed., *Universalism in America: A Documentary History* (Boston: Beacon Press, 1871), 6. The issue of future punishment was contentious in Universalism, dividing its members between the "Restorationists" who held that there would be a "just retribution for sin" after death, and the "Ultra Universalists" who believed that all would enter heaven at death. In 1899, the Universalist Church adopted as a principle of faith: "We believe in the certainty of just retribution for sin."

63 "Of Predestination and Election" (Art. 17), *Articles of Religion, As Established by the Bishops, the Clergy, and Laity of the Protestant Episcopal Church in the United States of America* (Philadelphia: 1801).

64 Thomas Starr King, cited in Ernest Cassara, ed., *Universalism in America: A Documentary History,* 6.

65 In 1851, Erasmus Manford moved to St. Louis where he published the *Golden Era* and later *Manford's Magazine.* He was a lifelong teetotaler and devoted considerable effort to the cause of temperance. Although most Universalists were strong abolitionists, Manford, perhaps influenced by his Missouri environment, would not advocate full abolition, but favored a form of gradual emancipation. He supported equal rights for women, and was one of the first Protestant clergymen to advocate the ordination of women to the ministry. See Russell E. Miller, *The Larger Hope: The First Century of the Universalist Church in America, 1770-1870* (Boston: Unitarian Universalist Association, 1979), 337, 501, 523, 537, 558, 626.

66 Charles Beecher to Milton Badger, 16 December 1844, AHMS.

67 *Trumpet and Universalist Magazine* 25, 15 June 1844, 205. Foster had been ordained in 1842 to serve a congregation at Perryville; he later organized churches at Indianapolis (1853), Logansport (1857), and Muncie (1859); he died in 1897.

68 *Christian Record,* February 1858.

69 "First Universalist," in *History of Allen County, Indiana,* T. B. Helm, ed., 99.

70 Charles Beecher to Amelia Ogden, 20 May 1845, Beecher-Stowe Family Papers, Schlesinger Library, Radcliffe College, Cambridge, Massachusetts.

71 Charles Beecher to Milton Badger, 16 September 1844, AHMS.

72 Charles Beecher to Amelia Ogden, 20 May 1845, Beecher-Stowe Family Papers.

73 Universalist preachers whose presence in Fort Wayne

was reported in local newspapers were: J. George, June 1846; Erasmus Manford, November 1846 and November 1848; W. J. Chaplin, June 1847, January 1849, January 1851, February 1855, June and September 1857; Charles Craven, June 1848; P. Hathaway, January 1849; T. C. Eaton, February and March 1859. *Fort Wayne Times:* 20 June and 14 November 1846; 1 and 15 June 1848; 10 January 1849; 16 January 1851; 15 February 1855; 4 June and 26 September 1857; 11 September 1858. *Fort Wayne Sentinel:* 12 June 1847; 27 January and 28 April 1849; 25 January 1851; 14 October 1854; 4 June 1857; 2 March 1859. *Fort Wayne Republican,* 9 February 1859.

Jonathan Kidwell, the "contentious preacher and author . . . died in Fort Wayne in mid-1849." David Johnson, *To Preach or Fight: Universalism in the Queen City of the West, 1800-1849* (Tucson, Ariz.: Philomath Press, 1973), 100.

[74] L. H. Newton, "Perry Township Churches," *History of Allen County, Indiana,* T. B. Helm, ed., 168. The congregation, which affiliated with the St. Joseph's Valley Association of Universalists, later built a church at the cost of $1500; the congregation was dissolved in 1891.

[75] *Fort Wayne Sentinel,* 26 September 1857.

[76] This congregation leased the old Jewish synagogue (formerly Bethel German M. E. Church) on the west side of Harrison between Wayne and Washington streets; the congregation dissolved in 1888.

[77] "First Universalist," *History of Allen County, Indiana*, T. B. Helm, ed., 99. Another Fort Wayne resident who became a minister of the Christian Church was N. A. Rayhouser, who served a congregation at South Bend in 1856.

[78] *Fort Wayne Sentinel,* 19 June 1847. Chaplin later published the *Christian Pulpit* at Michigan City; he died in Wolcottville in 1885 and was buried at Pierceton.

[79] In 1961, the denomination's name returned to Fort Wayne: following the merger of the Universalist Church of America and the American Unitarian Association to form the Unitarian Universalist Association, the local Unitarians added "Universalist" to their congregation's title.

[80] Elmo Arnold Robinson, "Universalism in Indiana," *Indiana Magazine of History,* vol. 13, no. 2 (June 1917), 186.

[81] *Fort Wayne Times,* 6 December 1845.

[82] For a discussion of the principles that united early Christian churches in Indiana, see Henry K. Shaw, *Hoosier Disciples* (St. Louis: Bethany Press, 1966).

[83] In the nineteenth century this movement was variously known as the Christian Church, the Church of Christ, and the Disciples of Christ. During the 1840s and 1850s, however, the title "Disciples" was seldom, if ever, used by leaders of the Christian Church in Indiana.

[84] *Christian Record,* August 1846, 51.

[85] *Ibid.,* 53.

[86] *Ibid.,* September 1846, 72-73.

[87] Mathes's image of the "old Lady" referred to the Catholic Church, a derogatory allusion drawn from Revelation 17, 1-6: "I saw a woman sitting on the scarlet-colored beast . . . on her forehead was written . . . 'Babylon the great, mother of harlots, and of earth's abominations.'"

[88] *Christian Record,* September 1846, 73.

[89] *Ibid.,* 74. At the State Meeting in October, Mathes reported that he had "spent thirty-six days on the tour. . . for which he received $36, being one dollar per day and his expenses. Br. Hopkins reports that he has spent sixty days on the mission, and has received $40." *Ibid.,* November 1846. Hopkins died in Kokomo, Indiana in 1874, at the age of fifty-four.

[90] *Minutes of the State Meeting, Christian Meeting House, Greensburg, Ia., October 2-4, 1846,* cited in the *Christian Record,* November 1846, 151, 152.

[91] Madison Evans, *Biographical Sketches of the Pioneer Preachers of Indiana* (Philadelphia: J. Challen & Sons, 1862), 80.

[92] *Ibid.,* 99, 100.

[93] J. B. New to J. M. Mathes, 27 November 1846, *Christian Record,* January 1847, 221.

[94] *Ibid.,* 12 February 1847; *Ibid.,* April 1847, 316.

[95] Madison Evans, *Biographical Sketches of the Pioneer Preachers of Indiana,* 95.

[96] *Christian Record,* 11 March 1847; *Ibid., April 1847,* 317.

[97] New's report was dated May 26, 1847. Commodore Wesley Cauble, *Disciples of Christ in Indiana: Achievements of a Century* (Indianapolis, Ind.: Meigs Publishing Co., 1930), 88. Fifteen years later Hodgkins was described as "an able advocate of primitive Christianity"; Madison Evans, *Biographical Sketches of the Pioneer Preachers of Indiana,* 95.

[98] *First Presbyt. Church Session Record No. 3, April 22, 1845 to Oct. 2, 1869,* 31 March 1847, First Presbyterian Church Archives, Fort Wayne, Indiana.

[99] Dickson's reference to a "change of heart" and "regeneration" refers to the Christian Church's adoption of Alexander Campbell's view of experimental religion. See D. Newell Williams, "The Gospel as the Power of God to Salvation: Alexander Campbell and Experimental Religion," in *Lectures in Honor of the Alexander Campbell Bicentennial, 1788-1988* (Nashville, Tennessee: Disciples of Christ Historical Society, 1988), 127-148.

[100] J. B. New to J. M. Mathes, 13 April 1847; *Christian Record,* May 1847, 351. Mrs. Ball may have been ill at the time of her immersion, for five months later it was reported

that she had "departed this life . . . in the midst of great bodily weakness and pain." H. St. John Van Dake, "To the saints," 2 December 1847; *Ibid.,* January 1848.

[101] *Fort Wayne Sentinel,* 14 August 1847.

[102] In 1849, the local Episcopal Church increased the frequency of its celebration of Holy Communion to twelve times a year.

[103] "The Church of Christ in Fort Wayne to the saints and faithful ministers of Christ Jesus, assembled at Greensburg," 24 September 1847; signed, "Elders: David Browand, H. U. Armstrong, and D. B. Rich; Deacons: J. B. Griffith, Robert Campbell, and John Miller." *Christian Record,* November 1847, 155-157.

[104] *Ibid.,* 157.

[105] *Ibid.,* December 1847, 186.

[106] *Ibid.,* 187.

[107] *Fort Wayne Times,* 1 June 1848.

[108] Charles Beecher to Milton Badger, 28 March 1845, AHMS.

[109] *Fort Wayne Times,* 22 June 1848.

[110] *Christian Record,* November 1848.

[111] *Minutes of the State Meeting of Preachers, Elders, and members of the Christian Congregations in the State of Indiana, held at the Church at Little Flat Rock, in Rush County, Indiana, commencing Friday, the 29th of September, 1848.* Cited in the *Christian Record,* November 1848.

[112] *Dawson's Daily Times,* 28 August 1855.

[113] Van Dake continued to be active in the leadership of the Christian Church, and fifty years later was described as "one of the best known preachers in Indiana." *The Christian Evangelist,* 19 March 1903. He died in May 1869, at his home in Lebanon, Indiana.

[114] *Christian Record,* April 1856, 123.

Reflections

[1] *Journal of Jean de Bonnecamps,* 17 October 1750, Archives of the Marine, Paris, France; quoted in *The Jesuit Relations and Allied Documents,* Reuben Gold Thwaites, ed., 69: 189; Gerald T. Hopkins, *A Mission to the Indians,* 48; J. L. Williams, *Historical Sketch of First Presbyterian Church, Fort Wayne, Indiana,* 14; Riley to Tiffin, 14 November 1820, quoted in T. B. Helm, *History of Wabash County, Indiana,* 78.

[2] A. B., "Letters From Indiana—No. III," *Fort Wayne Sentinel,* April 30, 1842.

Sources Cited

Unpublished Sources

Allen County Courthouse, Fort Wayne, Indiana.
Allen County Probate Order Book, Circuit Court Records, Deed Records, Marriage Records, Miscellaneous Record, Probate Final Records, Tract Book.

American Home Missionary Society Papers. Letters of S. R. Ball, John A. Bayer, Charles Beecher, James Chute, Charles E. Furman, Allen Hamilton, Jesse Hoover, Daniel Jones, Samuel G. Lowry, Smalwood Noel, Alexander T. Rankin, Adam Wefel, Friedrich K. D. Wyneken. The Amistad Research Center, Tulane University, New Orleans, Louisiana. Microfilming Corporation of America, 1975.

Antislavery Papers. Clements Library, Ann Arbor, Michigan.

Articles D'Incorporation & Constitution de la Societé Bienfaisance Lafayette de Fort Wayne, Indiana. Miscellaneous Record 294, Allen County Courthouse, Fort Wayne, Indiana.

Bailey, Peter P. Letters. Allen County-Fort Wayne Historical Society, Fort Wayne, Indiana.

Baptist Home Missionary Society Records. American Baptist Historical Society, Rochester, New York.

Beecher, Charles. Beecher-Stowe Family Papers: 1798-1856. Schlesinger Library, Radcliffe College, Cambridge, Massachusetts.

Bronstein, Fannie. "Address to the Annual Meeting of the Congregation." May 20, 1961. Achduth Vesholom Temple Archives, Fort Wayne Indiana.

Congregation of Holy Cross, Indiana Province Archives, Notre Dame, Indiana.
Register of the Particular Council of the Brothers: 1841 1845.
Minor Chapter Record Book: 1847-1854.
Letters of Julien Benoit, Edward Faller, Joseph F. Rudolf, Frederick Steber.

Crowe, John Findley. Letters. Hanover College Archives.

de Bonnecamps, Jean. Journal. Archives of the Marine [Archives des Colonies], Paris, France.

Divita, James. Letter to the author, 15 May 1991.

Documents and Records. Diocese of Fort Wayne-South Bend Archives, Fort Wayne, Indiana.

Dunlap, E. Dale. "The System of Itineracy in American Methodism." DePauw University Archives, Greencastle, Indiana. Typescript, n.d.

Edgerton, Joseph K. "Private Journal No. 3, Commenced October 27, 1843." "Private Journal No. 4, Commenced December, 16, 1845." Allen County Public Library, Fort Wayne, Indiana.

Ewing Letters. Allen County-Fort Wayne Historical Society, Fort Wayne, Indiana.

First Baptist Church Archives, Fort Wayne Indiana Church Record Book B: 1842 to 1869.

First Presbyterian Church Archives, Fort Wayne, Indiana.
First Presbyt. Church Session Record No. 2: July 1, 1831 to April 20, 1845.
First Presbyt. Church Session Record No. 3: April 22,

317

1845 to Oct. 2, 1869.

First Presbyt. Church Trustees Record No.1: Apr. 12, 1843 to Dec. 22, 1868.

Session Correspondence with H. S. Dickson and J. G. Riheldaffer.

Trustees Report No. 2.

Frazier, Richard G. Letter to the author, April 3, 1987.

Hamilton Papers. Allen County-Fort Wayne Historical Society, Fort Wayne, Indiana.

Hamm, Thomas D. Letter to the author, "1st Month 15, 1991."

Hawfield, Michael C. "Religion and the Origins of Fort Wayne." Paper presented at the Spring History Conference of the Indiana Historical Society, May 5-6, 1989, at Clifty Falls State Park, Indiana.

Holman, Jesse L. Correspondence: 1820-1840. Franklin College Library, Franklin, Indiana.

Hubbell, Maria. Letters. Indiana State Library, Indianapolis, Indiana.

Huxford, Sarah. Letter. 1894. Trinity Episcopal Church Archives, Fort Wayne, Indiana.

Jefferds, Oliver. Reminiscences: 1812-1900. Allen County-Fort Wayne Historical Society, Fort Wayne, Indiana.

Johns, A[lfred] S. "Sketch of Early Methodism in Fort Wayne." Fort Wayne, August 30, 1901. Allen County-Fort Wayne Historical Society, Fort Wayne, Indiana.

Kemper, Jackson. Papers. The State Historical Society of Wisconsin, Madison, Wisconsin.

Ketchem, Jane Merrill. Reminiscences. Indiana Historical Society, Indianapolis, Indiana.

Kingsbury Papers. Chicago Historical Society Library, Chicago, Illinois.

Kirby, J. Randolph. "Notes on the Emergence of a Black Community in Fort Wayne Between 1820 and 1850." Allen County-Fort Wayne Historical Society, Fort Wayne, Indiana. Audio-tape, February 24, 1985.

McCoy, Isaac. Papers, 1808-1874. Kansas State Historical Society, Topeka, Kansas. National Historical Publications Commission, microfilm, n. d.

McCulloch, Hugh and Eunice Hardy. Letters. Connie Hurni Collection, Hicksville, Ohio. Typescript.

McCulloch, Hugh and Susan Man. Papers. Lilly Library, Bloomington, Indiana.

Merrill Papers. Indiana Historical Society, Indianapolis, Indiana.

Miller, Marion Clinton. "The Antislavery Movement In Indiana." Ph.D. diss., University of Michigan, 1938.

Minutes of the Congregation, 1848-1887. 3 vols. Achduth Vesholom Temple Archives, Fort Wayne, Indiana. Microfilm nos. 436, 436A, American Jewish Archives, Hebrew Union College, Cincinnati, Ohio.

Minutes of the Eastern District of the Ohio Synod. Ohio Synod Archives, Wittenberg University Library, Springfield, Ohio.

Minutes of the Fort Wayne Presbytery (New School). Presbyterian Historical Society, Philadelphia, Pennsylvania.

Moore, Joseph P. "History of the Churches in Fort Wayne Presbytery: To which is added Biographical Sketches of deceased Ministers." Swan Indiana: July 20, 1876. Presbyterian Historical Society, Philadelphia, Pennsylvania.

Ninde-Puckett Letters. Lewis G. Thompson Collection. Allen County-Fort Wayne Historical Society, Fort Wayne, Indiana.

Parish Records, 1831-1857. Cathedral of the Immaculate Conception Archives, Fort Wayne, Indiana.

Proceedings of the Woman's Rights Conventions: 1851-1859, 1869-1881. Indiana State Library, Indianapolis, Indiana.

Rankin, Alexander T. Diary. State Historical Society of Colorado, Denver.

Rankin, John. "Life of Rev. John Rankin: Written by Himself in his Eightieth Year." 1873. Western Reserve Historical Society, Cleveland, Ohio. Typescript.

Rankin, Mary Burt. "A. T. Rankin." 1957. Chapman House, Ripley, Ohio. Typescript.

Record Book. Trinity English Lutheran Church Archives, Fort Wayne, Indiana.

Record of the Session of the German Presbyterian Church at Fort Wayne, Indiana: 1850-1854. Presbyterian Historical Society, Philadelphia, Pennsylvania.

Records of the Wardens and Vestrymen. Trinity Episcopal Church Archives, Fort Wayne Indiana.

Rudisill, Henry. Letterbook. In the possession of his heirs.

St. Mary-of-the-Woods Archives, Terre Haute, Indiana.
Book of Establishments.
Letters of Julien Benoit and Augustin Martin.
Mother Theodore's Diary.

St. Paul's Lutheran Church Archives, Fort Wayne, Indiana.
Minutes and Baptismal Records of the First Evangelical Lutheran Church of Fort Wayne, Indiana: 1837-1844.
Minutes of the Voters' Assembly of St. Paul's Ev. Lutheran Church: 1837-1884.

Scharf, James Lewis. "Wilhelm Löhe's Relation to the American Church: A Study in the History of Lutheran Mission." Inaugural Dissertation, Ruprech-Karl University of Heidelberg, Germany, 1961.

Schlatter, William. Letterbooks: 1814 to 1825. New Church Theological School Library, Cambridge, Massachusetts. Typescript.

Sorin, Edward. "Chronicles Of Notre Dame Du Lac From The Year 1841." Translated by John M. Toohey. 1895. Congregation of Holy Cross, Indiana Province Archives, Notre Dame, Indiana. Typescript.

Steevens, William W. Letters. Allen County-Fort Wayne Historical Society, Fort Wayne, Indiana.

Titus, Charles H. "Travel Journal: 1843." Henry E. Huntington Library, San Marino, California (Manuscript HM 29181).

Thompson, Lewis G. and Wilson L. Letters. Indiana State Library, Indianapolis, Indiana.

Trustee Minute Book of the M. E. Church, March 24, 1846 to February 7, 1870. Allen County-Fort Wayne Historical Society, Fort Wayne, Indiana.

University of Notre Dame Archives, Notre Dame, Indiana.
Archdiocese of Cincinnati Records. Letters of Stephen T. Badin, Ghislain Bôheme, Simon Bruté, Benedict J. Flaget, John Henry Lüers, Gabriel Richard.
Archdiocese of New Orleans Records. Letters of Anthony Blanc, Julien Benoit, Simon Bruté.
Audran, Ernest. Papers.
Diocese of Detroit Records. Letters of Simon Bruté; Baptismal Register of Ghislain Bôheme.
Diocese of Vincennes Records. Letters of Simon Bruté, Célestin de la Hailandière, Jean S. Bazin, Maurice de St. Palais.
"Extracts From the Archives of the Brothers of Holy Cross." Aiden O'Reilly, comp. Typescript, 1951.
Propaganda Fide Records.

Upfold, George. Diaries. Indiana Historical Society, Indianapolis, Indiana.

Vaudreuil Papers. Provincal Archives, Quebec, Canada.

Vaughn, Alfred J. and Thomas H. Harvey. Letters to the Office of Indian Affairs. National Archives, Washington, D. C.

Weber, Gottfried. "Buch." Cincinnati: 1877. Original held by the Igel family, Engler, Ohio. Photocopy.

Wells Papers. Allen County-Fort Wayne Historical Society, Fort Wayne, Indiana.

Wetmore, Allyn C. "Allen Hamilton: Evolution of a Frontier Capitalist." Ph.D. diss., Ball State University, 1974.

White, K. "A Study of Jewish Businessmen in Fort Wayne, Indiana as Reflected in the City Directories of 1861 through 1872." 1979. American Jewish Archives, Hebrew Union College, Cincinnati, Ohio. Typescript.

Wines, Elizabeth. Letters. Allen County-Fort Wayne Historical Society, Fort Wayne, Indiana.

Published Sources

Adkinson, Florence M. "The Mother of Women." *Woman's Journal* (29 September 1888).

Alerding, H[erman] J[oseph]. *The Diocese of Fort Wayne: 1857-1907. A Book of Historical Reference: 1669-1907.* Fort Wayne: Archer Printing Co., 1907.

Allison, George W. *Forest, Fort, and Faith: Historical Sketches of the Presbytery of Fort Wayne.* Fort Wayne: 1945.

The American Almanac. Bureau of the Census, 1831.

American Catholic Historical Researches, vols. 25, 27. American Catholic Historical Society of Philadelphia.

The American Sunday School Union, Sixth Annual Report. Philadelphia: 1830.

Anson, Bert. *The Miami Indians.* Norman, Okla.: University of Oklahoma Press, 1970.

Anthony, Susan B., and Ida Husted Harper, eds. *History of Woman Suffrage, Vol. 4: 1883-1900.* Rochester, N. Y.: Susan B. Anthony, 1902.

Articles of Religion, As Established by the Bishops, the Clergy, and Laity of the Protestant Episcopal Church in the United States of America. Philadelphia: 1801.

Auburn Theological Seminary: General Biographical Catalogue, 1818-1918. Auburn, N. Y.: Auburn Seminary Press, 1918.

Bailey, Peter. "Historical Address," [read at the semicentennial of Trinity Episcopal Church] Fort Wayne, May 20, 1894. *Fort Wayne Sentinel,* May 20, 1915.

Banet, Charles H., ed. *French Immigrants in Allen County, Indiana: 1850-1870.* Fort Wayne: Allen County Public Library, 1981.

Barnhardt, John D., and Donald F. Carmony. *Indiana: From Frontier to Industrial Commonwealth,* 2 vols. New York: Lewis Historical Publishing Co., 1954.

Bass, Dorothy C. "Their Prodigious Influence: Women, Religion and Reform in Antebellum America." In *Women of Spirit: Female Leadership in the Jewish and Christian Traditions,* edited by Rosemary Ruether and Eleanor McLaughlin. New York: Simon and Schuster, 1979.

Bayley, James. *Memoirs of Right Reverend Simon Gabriel Bruté.* New York: 1861.

Beecher, Charles, ed. *Autobiography, Correspondence, Etc., of Lyman Beecher D.D.,* 2 vols. New York: Harper and Brothers, 1864.

_____. *The Duty of Disobedience to Wicked Laws: A Sermon on the Fugitive Slave Law.* New York: J. A. Gray, 1851.

_____. *The Incarnation; or Pictures of the Virgin and Her Son, With an Introductory Essay, by Mrs. Harriet Beecher Stowe.* New York: Harper & Brothers, 1849.

_____. *Tracts for the Times, no. 19, The Bible a Sufficient Creed: Being Two Discourses Delivered at the Dedication of the Second Presbyterian Church, Fort Wayne, Iowa,* [sic] *February 22, 1846.* Boston: Office of the Christian World, 1846.

Beecher, Lyman. *A Plea for the West,* 2nd ed. Cincinnati: 1835.

Beggs, Stephen R. *Pages from the Early History of the West and Northwest.* Cincinnati: Methodist Book Concern, 1868.

Benedict, David. *A General History of the Baptist Denomination in America and Other Parts of the World.* New York: Lewis Colby and Company, 1848.

Benoit, Julien. "Catholic Church." In *History of Allen County, Indiana,* edited by T. B. Helm. Chicago: Kingman Brothers, 1880.

Billington, Ray Allen. *The Protestant Crusade, A Study of the Origins of American Nativism: 1800-1860.* New York: Macmillan Co., 1938.

_____. *Westward Expansion: A History of the American Frontier.* New York: Macmillan Co., 1914.

Biographical Sketch of Rt. Rev. Julian Benoit . . . by a Clergyman of the Episcopal Household. Fort Wayne: J. J. Jocquel, 1885.

Blackwell, Alice Stone. *Lucy Stone: Pioneer of Woman's Rights.* Boston: Little, Brown, and Company, 1930.

Blanchard, Charles, ed. *History of the Catholic Church in Indiana,* 2 vols. Logansport, Ind.: A. W. Bowen & Co., 1898.

Block, Marguerite Beck. *The New Church in the New World.* New York: Holt, Rinehart and Winston, 1932.

Brackenridge, George W. "I am surprised . . ." In *Reminiscences of Old Fort Wayne,* edited by Laura Case Woodworth, Carolyn Randall Fairbank, and Martha Brandriff Hanna. Fort Wayne: Allen County Public Library, 1906.

Brand, Carl F. "The History of the Know-Nothing Party in Indiana." *Indiana Magazine of History* 18 (March, June, and September 1922).

Bredemeier, Herbert G. *Concordia College, Fort Wayne, Indiana: 1839-1957.* Fort Wayne: Allen County Public Library, 1978.

Brice, Wallace A. *History of Fort Wayne from the Earliest*

Known Accounts of This Point to the Present Period. Fort Wayne: D. W. Jones & Son, 1868.

Brown, Mary Borromeo. *The History of the Sisters of Providence of Saint Mary-of-the-Woods, vol. 1, 1806-1856.* New York: Benziger Brothers, Inc., 1949.

Booth, Joyce Marks, ed. *A History of the Episcopal Diocese of Indianapolis: 1838-1988.* Dallas: Taylor Publishing Co., 1988.

Buley, R. Carlyle. *The Old Northwest: Pioneer Period, 1815-1840,* 2 vols. Bloomington, Indiana: Indiana University Press, 1951.

[Burr, Charles.] *Lectures of Lola Montez, Including Her Autobiography.* Philadelphia: T. B. Peterson & Bros., 1858.

Buuck, Gale C., and Marvin L. Buuck, comps. *The Buuck Family in America* (1986).

Cady, John F. *The Origin and Development of the Missionary Baptist Church in Indiana.* Berne, Ind.: The Berne Witness Co., 1942.

Carvin, Earl L. "The Methodist Church in Fort Wayne, Indiana." In *History of the First Wayne Street United Methodist Church, Fort Wayne, Indiana*. Fort Wayne: Allen County Public Library, 1975.

Cassara, Ernest, ed. *Universalism in America: A Documentary History.* Boston: Beacon Press, 1871.

Catechism of the Methodist Episcopal Church, No. 1. New York: Hunt & Eaton, 1884.

Cauble, Commodore Wesley. *Disciples of Christ in Indiana: Achievements of a Century.* Indianapolis: Meigs Publishing Co., 1930.

Centennial Souvenir, 1848-1948, Achduth Vesholom. Fort Wayne, Indiana: 1948.

Clark, Elmer T., J. Manning Potts, and Jacob L. Payton, eds. *The Journal and Letters of Francis Asbury.* Nashville: Abingdon Press, 1958.

Cockrum, William M. *History of the Underground Railroad as It was Conducted by the Anti-Slavery League, Including Many Thrilling Encounters between Those Aiding the Slaves to Escape and Those Trying to Recapture Them.* Oakland City, Ind.: J. W. Cockrum Printing Co., 1915.

Coffin, Addison. *Life and Travels of Addison Coffin.* Cleveland: William G. Hubbard, 1897.

Colerick, Edward F. *Cannibals of Indiana.* Occasional Publication No. 6, edited by Ivan Gerould Grimshaw. Fort Wayne: Allen County-Fort Wayne Historical Society, 1958.

Compilation of the Statutes of Tennessee, 1836. Nashville: J. Smith, 1836.

Constitution and Discipline of the Methodist Protestant Church. Baltimore: Book Committee of the Methodist Protestant Church, 1853.

Constitution des Deutscher Römisch Catholischer St. Josephs-Schulvereins an der Mutter-Gottes Kirche zu Fort Wayne, Ind., Verfasst im Jahre 1847. Fort Wayne: Indiana Staatszeitung, n.d.

The Constitution of the Presbyterian Church in the United State of America. Utica, N. Y.: William Williams, 1822.

Cooke, John. *Diary of Captain John Cooke, 1794 .* Fort Wayne: Allen County Public Library, 1953.

Cramton, Thomas J. "The First Church Church Building in Fort Wayne." In *Old Fort Bulletin.* Fort Wayne: Allen County-Fort Wayne Historical Society, January-February 1976.

Crenshaw, Gwendolyn J. *Catalogue: "Bury Me in a Free Land:" The Abolitionist Movement in Indiana, 1816-1865.* Indianapolis: Indiana Historical Bureau, 1986.

Curtis, R. I. "John Chapman, alias 'Johnny Appleseed.'" In *Ohio Pomological Society Transactions.* Columbus, O.: 1859.

Dawson, John W. "Charcoal Sketches of Old Times in Fort Wayne." Nos. 3, 6, and 7. In *Fort Wayne Daily Sentinel,* 14, 20, and 23 March 1872. Reprinted in *Old Fort News* (January-March 1959), edited by Alene Godfrey.

_____. "Early Masonic History." In *History of Allen County, Indiana,* edited by T. B. Helm. Chicago: Kingman Brothers, 1880.

_____. "Johnny Appleseed." In *Fort Wayne Daily Sentinel,* October 21 and 23, 1871.

Deery, James E. "The First Orphan's Home Of Indiana." *Catholic Historical Society of Indiana* (December 1937).

DeMille, George E. *Christ Church Parish History, 1810-1960*. Cooperstown, N. Y.: 1960.

Deutscher Kalender für das Jahr 1902 . . . der Central Deutschen Konferenz der Bischöflichen Methodistenkirche. Cincinnati: Jennings and Pyne, 1902.

Diederich, Henry W. "History of the German Evangelical Lutheran Church in Allen County." In *The Valley of the Upper Maumee River*, vol. 1, edited by Robert S. Robertson. Madison, Wis.: Brant and Fuller, 1889.

Dirlan, H. Kenneth. *John Chapman: By Occupation a Gatherer and Planter of Appleseeds*. Mansfield, Ohio: [published by the author], 1853.

District Synod of Ohio Minutes of the Twentieth Convention . . . 1876. Canton, O.: A. M. Gregor & Son, 1876.

The Doctrines and Discipline of the Methodist Episcopal Church, The Twenty-First Edition. New York: N. Bangs and T. Mason, 1821.

The Doctrines and Discipline of the Methodist Episcopal Church. New York: T. Mason and G. Lane, 1836.

Douglass, Paul F. *The Story of German Methodism: Biography of an Immigrant Soul*. Cincinnati: Methodist Book Concern, 1939.

Dunn, Jacob Piatt. *Indiana and Indianans*. Chicago: American Historical Society, 1919.

_____. "Indiana's Part in the Making of the Story 'Uncle Tom's Cabin.' " *The Indiana Magazine of History* 7 (1902).

Edson, Hanford A. *Contributions to the Early History of the Presbyterian Church in Indiana, Together with Biographical Notices of the Pioneer Ministers*. Cincinnati: Winona Publishing Co.: 1898.

Edwards, J. *Aspects of Society: A Lecture Delivered Before the Young Men's Literary Association of Fort Wayne, Ind., January 22d 1855*. Fort Wayne: T. N. Hood, 1855.

Eggleston, M. P. "Calvary Parish and Its Rector." In *St. Mary's Church News*. Lexington, Mississippi: 1889.

Elsmere, Jane Shaffer. *Henry Ward Beecher: The Indiana Years, 1837-1847*. Indianapolis: Indiana Historical Society, 1973.

Esarey, Logan. *A History of Indiana*. Boston: Harcourt Brace & Co., 1905.

Evans, Madison. *Biographical Sketches of the Pioneer Preachers of Indiana*. Philadelphia: J. Challen & Sons, 1862.

Field, George. *Memoirs, Incidents & Reminiscences of the Early History of the New Church in Michigan, Indiana, Illinois and Adjacent States; and Canada*. Toronto: R. Carswell & Co., 1879.

Findlay, William W. "Appeal of Wm. W. Findlay, To the Colored People of Indiana." *African Repository and Colonial Journal* 25 (June 1849).

Finley, James B. *Life Among the Indians; or, Personal Reminiscences and Historical Incidents Illustrative of Indian Life and Character*. Cincinnati: Cranston & Curts, 1857.

First Catalogue of the Oxford Female Institute at Oxford, O.: 1849-50. Cincinnati: John D. Thorpe, 1850.

"First Universalist." In *History of Allen County, Indiana*, edited by T. B. Helm. Chicago: Kingman Brothers, 1880.

Fortriede, Steven. *Johnny Appleseed: The Man Behind the Myth*. Fort Wayne: Allen County Public Library, 1978.

Gara, Larry. *The Liberty Line: The Legend of the Underground Railroad*. Lexington: University Press, 1961.

Gatty, Charles Nelson. *The Bloomer Girls*. New York: Coward-McCann, 1968.

Geschichte der Evangelisch-Lutherischen St. Johannis-Gemeinde zu Ft. Wayne, Indiana. Columbus, O.: Lutherische Verlagshandlund, 1903.

Gladish, Robert W. *Swedenborg, Fourier and the America of the 1840's*. Bryn Athyn, Pa.: Swedenborg Scientific Association, 1983.

Glasgow, William Melancthon. *Cyclopedic Manual of the United Presbyterian Church of North America*. Pittsburgh: United Presbyterian Board of Publication, 1903.

Godecker, Mary Salesia. *Simon Bruté de Rémur: First Bishop of Vincennes*. St. Meinrad, Ind.: Abbey Press, 1931.

Goldberg, Isaac. *George Jean Nathan*. New York: Simon

and Schuster, 1926.

Golder, C., John H. Horst, J. G. Schaal. *Geschichte der Zentral Deutschen Konferenz, Einschiesslich der Unsangsgeschichte des deutschen Methodismus.* Cincinnati: Jenning & Graham, 1907.

Goodman, Abram Vossen. "A Jewish Peddler's Diary: 1842-1843." *American Jewish Archives* 3 (June 1951).

Greenwood, Grace. *Recollections of My Childhood and Other Stories.* Boston: Ticknor, Reed & Fields, 1854.

_____. *Records of Five Years.* Boston: Ticknor & Fields, 1867.

Griswold, B. J. *The Pictorial History of Fort Wayne, Indiana,* 2 vols. Chicago: Robert O. Law Company, 1917.

Hageman, G. E. *Friedrich K. D. Wyneken: Pioneer Lutheran Missionary of the Nineteenth Century.* Men and Missions, vol. 3, edited by L. Fuerbringer. St. Louis: Concordia Publishing House, 1926.

Haley, William D. "Johnny Appleseed—A Pioneer Hero." In *Harper's New Monthly Magazine* (November 1871).

Hamilton, Alice. *Exploring the Dangerous Trades.* Boston: Little, Brown and Company, 1943.

Hanna, Martha Bandriff. "Early Days." In *Reminiscences of Old Fort Wayne,* edited by Laura Case Woodworth, Carolyn Randall Fairbank, and Martha Brandriff Hanna. Fort Wayne: Allen County Public Library, 1906.

Harbaugh, Henry. *Fathers of the Reformed Church,* 12 vols. Lancaster, Pa.: Sprenger & Westhaeffer, 1857.

Hardin, Thomas J. "The Academies of Indiana." *Indiana Magazine of History* 10 (1914).

Hardy, Jr., Edward Rochie. "Kemper's Missionary Episcopate: 1835-1859." *The Historical Magazine of the Protestant Episcopal Church* 4, no. 3 (September 1935).

Harris, Robert C. "Johnny Appleseed Sourcebook." *Old Fort News* 9, nos. 1 and 2 (March and June 1945). [Reprinted as a pamphlet by the Public Library of Fort Wayne and Allen County, n.d.]

Harter, Fayne E., comp. *Federal Census of Allen Co., Indiana, Indexed.* Graybill, Ind.: 1968.

Hartman, Grover L. *A School for God's People: A History of the Sunday School Movement in Indiana.* Indianapolis: Central Publishing Company, 1980.

Heintzen, Erich H. *Prairie School of the Prophets: The Anatomy of a Seminary, 1846-1976.* St. Louis: Concordia, 1989.

Helm, T. B., ed. *History of Allen County, Indiana.* Chicago: Kingman Brothers, 1880.

Herrick, H. N., and William W. Sweet. *A History of the North Indiana Conference of the Methodist Episcopal Church, From its Organization, in 1844, to the Present.* Indianapolis: W. K. Stewart Company, 1917.

Holliday, F. C. *Indiana Methodism.* Cincinnati: Hitchcock and Walden, 1873.

_____. *Life and Times of Allen Wiley, A.M.* Cincinnati: S. Swormstedt & A. Poe, 1853.

Hopkins, Gerald T. *A Mission to the Indians from the Indian Committee of the Baltimore Yearly Meeting to Fort Wayne in 1804, Written at the Time, with an Appendix, compiled in 1862, by Martha E. Tyson.* Philadelphia: T. Ellwood Zell, 1862.

Howard, Timothy. *A History of St. Joseph County, Indiana.* Chicago: Lewis Publishing Co., 1907.

Howard, William D. "A Memoir of the Author." Forward to *The Prophet Elisha,* by John M. Lowrie. Philadelphia: Presbyterian Board of Publication, 1869.

Hughes, John. *The Decline of Protestantism and its Causes.* New York: 1850.

Husmann, E. S. H. "F. W. Husmann." In *Concordia Historical Institute Quarterly* 1, no. 1 (April 1928).

Husmann, Friedrich Wilhelm. *Diary on My Ministry. . . From the Middle of October 1845.* Translated by Otto F. Stahlke. Fort Wayne: Concordia Theological Seminary Press, 1987.

Huntington Baptist Association Minutes, 1841-1853, 1867. 1842; Lafayette: M. Bemiss, 1843; Fort Wayne, People's Press, 1844; Logansport, Pharos Press, 1845; Logansport: S. A. Hall, 1846; Peru: John H. Scott, 1847; 1848; Huntington: Indiana Herald, 1849; Logansport: S. A. Hall, 1850; Wabash: Knight & Scott, 1851; Wabash: Gazette, 1852; Logansport: Pharos Press, 1853.

Hutchins, Benjamin. "Protestant Episcopal Church." In *Combined History of Edwards, Lawrence and Wabash Counties, Illinois.* Philadelphia: J. L. McDonough & Co., 1883.

Indiana House Journal, 1850-1851.

In Memoriam: Rev. James Chute. Fort Wayne: 1874.

Johnson, David. *To Preach or Fight: Universalism in the Queen City of the West, 1800-1849.* Tucson, Ariz.: Philomath Press, 1973.

Johnson, Marie. "St. John's First Hundred Years." In *Centennial Souvenir and History, St. John's Evangelical and Reformed Church.* Fort Wayne: 1944.

Journal of Proceedings of the Annual Conference of the African Methodist Episcopal Church, for the District of Indiana. Indianapolis: Rawson Vaille, 1854.

Journal of Proceedings of the [2nd through 28th] *Annual Convention of the Protestant Episcopal Church in the Diocese of Indiana.* June 1840 through June 1862.

Journal of the Proceedings of the Fifth General Convention of the Receivers of the Doctrines of the New Jerusalem. Boston: The General Convention of the New Jerusalem, 1822. Reprinted as *The Early Journals of the General Convention of the New Jerusalem, Part I, Journals 1-8, 1817-1826.* Boston, Mass.: Massachusetts New Church Union, 1888.

Keith, Ben. F. *History of Maria Creek Church.* Vincennes, Ind.: A. V. Crotts & Co., 1889.

Kenneally, Finbar, ed. *United States Documents in the Propaganda Fide Archives: A Calendar,* 7 vols. Washington, D. C.: Academy of American Franciscan History, 1973.

Kinietz, W. Vernon. *The Indians of the Western Great Lakes, 1615-1760.* Ann Arbor: University of Michigan Press, 1940.

Kirby, J. Randolph. "The Appearance of Blacks in Fort Wayne Before 1820." *Old Fort News* 48, no. 2 (1985).

_____. "Fort Wayne Common School Crusaders: The First Year for Free Schooling, April 1853-March 1854." *Old Fort News* 42, no. 1 (1979).

Lafayette City Directory for 1858. Lafayette, Ind.: R. L. Polk, & Co., 1858.

Lang, John F. "The Catholic Church in Allen County." In *The Valley of the Upper Maumee River,* vol. 2, edited by Robert S. Robertson. Madison, Wis.: 1889.

Leopold, Richard W. *Robert Dale Owen, A Biography.* Cambridge, Mass.: Harvard University Press, 1940.

Letters of the Rev. E. Keller, Ev. Lutheran Missionary in the West, to the Secretary of the Missionary Society of the Theological Seminary, Gettysburg, Pa. [Peoria, December 14, 1836:] *The Lutheran Observer,* March 17, 1837. "Letters of Lutheran Traveling Missionaries Keller and Heyer, 1835-1837," edited by Rudolph F. Rehmer. *Concordia Historical Institute Quarterly,* vol. 47, no. 2 (Summer 1974).

Levine, Joseph. *John Jacob Hays: The First Known Jewish Resident of Fort Wayne.* Fort Wayne: Indiana Jewish Historical Society, 1973.

Lowrie, John M. *Adam and His Times.* Philadelphia: Presbyterian Board of Publication, 1861.

_____. *The Lessons of Our National Sorrow: A Discourse. . . Succeeding the Death of Abraham Lincoln.* Fort Wayne: Jenkinson & Hartman, 1865.

Lynch, William Orlando. "Population Movements in Relation to the Struggle for Kansas." *Indiana University Studies* 12 (1914).

Manford, Erasmus. *Twenty-five Years in the West.* Chicago: H. B. Manford, 1885.

Manual of the Second Presbyterian Church, Fort Wayne, Indiana. Fort Wayne: T. S. Taylor & Co., 1869.

Marcus, Jacob Radar. *Memoirs of American Jews: 1775-1865.* Philadelphia: Jewish Publication Society of America, 1955.

Marine, A. "Methodist Episcopal Church." In *History of Allen County,* edited by T. B. Helm. Chicago: Kingman Brothers, 1880.

Mather, George R. "Fort Wayne's First St. Patrick's Day Celebration in 1859." In *Today's Catholic* 65, no. 11 (March 1991).

Mauelshagen, Carl. *American Lutheranism Surrenders to the Forces of Conservatism.* Athens, Ga.: University of Georgia, 1936.

McAvoy, Thomas T. *The Catholic Church in Indiana.* New

York: Columbia University Press, 1940.

McClune, James. *History of the Presbyterian Church in the Forks of Brandywine, Chester County, Pa., From A. D. 1735 to A. D. 1885, With Biographical Sketches of the Deceased Pastor of the Church.* Philadelphia: J. B. Lippincott Co., 1885.

McCormick, Calvin. *The Memoir of Miss Eliza McCoy.* Dallas: [published by the author] 1892.

McCoy, Isaac. *History of Baptist Indian Missions: Embracing Remarks on the Former and Present Condition of the Aboriginal Tribes; Their Settlement Within the Indian Territory and Their Future Prospects.* Washington, D. C.: William M. Morrison, 1840.

_____. *Periodical Account of Baptist Missions Within the Indian Territory for the Year Ending December 31, 1836, Published by Isaac M'Coy, Shawanoe Baptist Mission House, Indian Territory.*

McCulloch, Hugh. "An Address to the Indiana State Teachers Association." *Indiana State Journal* 4 (November 1859 and December 1859).

_____. *Men and Measures of Half a Century.* New York: C. Scribner's Sons, 1888.

McCulloch, Susan Man. "The Recollections of Susan McCulloch." Edited by Wilhemina and Clifford Richards. *Old Fort News* 44, no. 3 (1981).

McKee, Irving. *The Trail of Death.* Indianapolis: Indiana Historical Society, 1941.

McNamara, William. *The Catholic Church on the Northern Indiana Frontier, 1789-1844.* Washington, D.C.: Catholic University of America, 1931.

Mead, Seth, comp. *Hymns and Spiritual Songs.* Richmond, Va.: 1807.

Melish, John. *Travels in the United States of America, in the years 1806 and 1807, and 1809, 1810, and 1811.* Philadelphia: T. & G. Palmers, 1812.

Meloy, John W. "A History of the Indiana Presbytery of the United Presbyterian Church." *Indiana Magazine of History* 31, no. 1 (March 1935).

The Metropolitan Catholic Almanac and Laity's Directory . . . for 1837 . . . 1838 . . . 1839 . . . and 1840. Baltimore: James Myres, 1837-1840.

Miller, Adam. *Experience of German Methodist Preachers.* Cincinnati: Methodist Book Concern, 1859.

Miller, Russell E. *The Larger Hope: The First Century of the Universalist Church in America, 1770-1870.* Boston: Unitarian Universalist Association, 1979.

Minutes of the Annual Conferences of the Methodist Episcopal Church For the Years 1839-1845, 1852. New York: T. Mason and G. Lane, 1840-1846, 1853.

Minutes of the Annual Conventions of the Evangelical Lutheran Synod of Northern Indiana, 1855 to 1865. Indianapolis: Elder & Harness, Printers; Fort Wayne: Jenkinson & Hartman.

Minutes of the General Assembly of the Presbyterian Church, 1837.

Minutes of the Synod of Ohio, 1876 . Canton, O.: A. M. Gregor & Son, 1876.

Minutes of the Twenty-Seventh Annual Convention of the English District of the Joint Synod of Ohio . . . May 16 to May 22, 1883. Columbus, O.: J. L. Trauger, 1883.

Montgomery, Helen Barrett. *Western Women in Eastern Lands.* New York: Macmillan Co., 1911.

Morehouse, H. L., ed. *Baptist Home Missions in North America.* New York: Baptist Home Mission Rooms, 1883.

Morris, John G. *Fifty Years in the Lutheran Ministry.* Baltimore: 1878.

Morris, Thomas. "Journal of Captain Morris [1764]." *Miscellanies in Prose and Verse* . London: 1791. Ann Arbor: University Microfilms, 1966. *Old Fort News* 6, no. 1 (1941).

Mug, Mary Theodosia, ed. *Journals and Letters of Mother Theodore Guérin.* Saint Mary-of-the-Woods, Ind.: Providence Press, 1937.

Mundinger, Carl S. *Government in the Missouri Synod.* St. Louis: Concordia Publishing House, 1947.

Murray, Andrew E. *The Skyline Synod; Presbyterianism in Colorado and Utah.* Denver: Golden Bell Press, 1971.

Nast, Albert J. *Souvenir of the Ninetieth Anniversary of the Organization of German Methodism.* Cincinnati: Nast Memorial Church, September 4-9, 1928.

Necrology Report Presented to the Alumni Association of Princeton Theological Seminary. Princeton, N. J.: C. S. Robinson, 1890.

Neely, Mark E., Jr. " 'Perfidious Whig Rascals': A Businessman Runs for Congress in Fort Wayne, 1847." *Old Fort News,* vol. 44, no. 1, 1981.

Nevin, Alfred, ed. *Encyclopaedia of the Presbyterian Church in the U.S.A.* Philadelphia: Presbyterian Encyclopaedia Publishing Co., 1884.

Newton, J. H. *History of Venango County, Pennsylvania.* Columbus, O.: J. A. Caldwell, 1879.

Newton, L. H. "Perry Township Churches." In *History of Allen County, Indiana,* edited by T. B. Helm. Chicago: Kingman Brothers, 1880.

Noll, John F. *The Diocese of Fort Wayne: Fragments of History, vol. 2.* 1941.

Norton, A. Banning. *A History of Knox County, Ohio.* Columbus, O.: R. Nevins, 1862.

Norwood, Frederick A. *History of the North Indiana Conference 1917-1956, Vol. 2.* Winona Lake, Ind.: Light and Life Press, 1957.

Nottingham, Elizabeth K. *Methodism and the Frontier: Indiana Proving Ground.* New York: Columbia University Press, 1941.

Odhner, Carl T. *Annals of The New Church,* vol. 1. Bryn Athyn, Pa.: Academy of the New Church, 1904.

Overton, Julie M. *The Ministers and Churches of the Central German Conference (Methodist).* Thomson, Ill.: Heritage House, 1975.

Panoramic View of the City Fort Wayne, Allen County, Indiana, 1880, Looking Southeast. Old Fort Reproductions, n.d.

Parkman, Francis. *LaSalle and the Discovery of the Great West.* Boston: Little, Brown & Co., 1904.

Parsons, Ellen C. "History of Woman's Organized Missionary Work as Promoted By American Women." In *Woman in Missions: Papers and Addresses Presented at the Woman's Congress of Missions, October 2-4, 1893,* edited by E. M. Wherry. New York: American Tract Society, 1894.

Payne, Daniel A. *History of the African Methodist Episcopal Church.* Nashville, Tenn.: Publishing House of the A. M. E. Sunday-School Union, 1891.

Philipson, David. "The Jewish Pioneers of the Ohio Valley." *American Historical Society,* 8 (1900).

Poinsatte, Charles R. *Fort Wayne During the Canal Era: 1828-1855.* Indianapolis: Indiana Historical Bureau, 1969.

_____. *Outpost in the Wilderness: Fort Wayne, 1708-1828.* Fort Wayne: Allen County-Fort Wayne Historical Society, 1976.

Potterf, Rex M. *The Constitution of Indiana Made in 1851.* Fort Wayne: Allen County Public Library, n. d.

Price, Robert. *Johnny Appleseed: Man and Myth.* Bloomington, Ind.: Indiana University Press, 1954.

Proceedings of the Indiana Convention, Assembled to Organize a State Anti-Slavery Society, held in Milton, Wayne Co., September 12th, 1838. Cincinnati: Samuel A. Alley, 1838.

Prucha, Francis Paul. *American Indian Policy in the Formative Years: The Indian Trade and Intercourse Acts, 1770-1834.* Cambridge, Mass.: Harvard University Press, 1962.

Pula, James. *The French in America, 1488-1974.* Dobbs Ferry, New York: Oceana Publications, 1975.

Quaife, Milo M., ed. *A Narrative of the Old Frontier: Henry Hay's Journal from Detroit to the Miami River.* Madison, Wis.: State Historical Society of Wisconsin, 1915.

Reed, Isaac. *The Christian Traveler in Five Parts including Nine Years and Eighteen Thousand Miles.* New York: J. and J. Harper, 1828.

Rehmer, Rudolph F. *New Light on F. K. D. Wyneken.* Lafayette, Ind.: Lafayette Sunday Visitor, 1981.

Report of the Society for Printing, Publishing and Circulating the Writings of Emanuel Swedenborg. Manchester, England: January 14, 1817.

Reynolds, John. *Pioneer History of Illinois.* Belleville, Ill.: N. A. Randall, 1852.

Riddleberger, Patrick W. *George Washington Julian, Radical Republican.* Indianapolis: Indiana Historical Bureau, 1966.

Riker, Dorothy, and Gayle Thornbrough, comps. *Indiana Election Returns.* Indianapolis: Indiana Historical Bureau, 1960.

_____, eds. *Messages and Papers Relating to the Administration of Noah Noble, Governor of Indiana, 1831-1837.* Indianapolis: Indiana Historical Bureau, 1958.

Ringenberg, William. "Fort Wayne Methodist College." In *Old Fort News* 35, no. 3 (1972).

_____. *Taylor University: The First 125 Years.* Grand Rapids, Mich.: William B. Eerdmans Publishing Company, 1973.

Roberts, Bessie Kerran. *Fort Wayne's Family Album.* Fort Wayne: Cummins Printing Co., 1960.

_____. "Unity and Peace." *Old Fort News* 8, no. 1 (1943).

Roberts, Edward Howell, comp. *Biographical Catalogue of the Princeton Theological Seminary, 1815-1931.* Princeton, N. J.: Princeton Theological Seminary, 1933.

Robertson, Nellie A. "John Hayes and the Fort Wayne Agency." *Indiana Magazine of History* 39, no. 3 (September 1943).

Robertson, Nellie A., and Dorothy Riker, eds. *John Tipton Papers,* 3 vols. Indianapolis: Indiana Historical Commission, 1942.

Robertson, Robert S. *History of the Maumee River Basin, Allen County, Indiana.* 2 vols. [Vol. 2 and 3 of *History of the Maumee River Basin from the Earliest Account to Its Organization into Counties,* edited by Charles Elihu Slocum.] Indianapolis: Bowen & Slocum, 1905.

_____. *Valley of the Upper Maumee River, With Historical Account of Allen County and the City of Fort Wayne, Indiana. The Story of its Progress from Savagery to Civilization.* 2 vols. Madison, Wis.: Brant & Fuller, 1889.

Robinson, Elmo Arnold. "Universalism in Indiana." *Indiana Magazine of History* 13, nos. 1 and 2 (March and June 1917).

Rorabaugh, W. J. *The Alcoholic Republic: An American Tradition.* New York: Oxford University Press, 1979.

Rudolph, L. C. *Hoosier Zion: The Presbyterians in Early Indiana.* New Haven: Yale University Press, 1963.

Rudolph, L. C., W. W. Wimberly, and Thomas W. Clayton. *Indiana Letters: Abstracts of Letters from Missionaries on the Indiana Frontier to the American Home Missionary Society, 1824-1893,* 3 vols. Ann Arbor: University Microfilms International, 1979.

Rugoff, Milton. *The Beechers: An American Family in the Nineteenth Century.* New York: Harper & Row, 1981.

Sadtler, William A. *Under Two Captains.* Philadelphia: General Council Press, 1902.

Sauer H. G., and J. W. Miller. *Geschichte der Deutschen Ev.-Luth. St. Pauls-Gemeinde zu Fort Wayne, Ind., vom Jahre 1837 bis zum Jahre 1912.* St. Louis: Concordia Publishing House, 1887 and 1912.

Schaeffer, C. W. *Early History of the Lutheran Church in America.* Philadelphia: Lutheran Book Store, 1868.

Schauinger, J. Herman. *Stephen T. Badin: Priest in the Wilderness.* Milwaukee: Bruce Publishing Co., 1956.

Schneider, Carl E. *The German Church on the American Frontier.* St. Louis: Eden Publishing House, 1939.

Scholten, Pat Creech. "A Public 'Jollification:' The 1859 Women's Rights Petition before the Indiana Legislature." *Indiana Magazine of History* 72, no. 4 (December 1976).

Schonfield, Alexander L. *Sketch of the Jewish Congregation in the City of Muncie, Indiana.* May 13, 1922. Fort Wayne: Indiana Jewish Historical Society, 1977.

Schroeder, Mary Carol. *The Catholic Church in the Diocese of Vincennes, 1847-1877.* Washington, D. C.: Catholic University of America Press, 1946.

Scouller, James Brown. *A Manual of the United Presbyterian Church of North America, 1751-1887,* 2nd edit. Pittsburgh: United Presbyterian Board of Publication, 1887.

Seibert, Wilbur Henry. "Light on the Underground Railroad." *American Historical Review* 1 (1895).

Sharfman, I. Harold. *Jews of the Frontier.* Chicago: Henry Regnery Company, l977.

Shaw, Henry K. *Hoosier Disciples.* St. Louis: Bethany

Press, 1966.

Sherrill, L. J. *Presbyterian Parochial Schools.* New Haven: Yale University Press, 1932.

Sihler, Ernest G. *From Maumee to Thames and Tiber.* New York City: New York University Press, 1930.

Sihler, Wilhelm. *Gespräche zwischen zwie Lutheranern über den Methodismus,* 4th ed. St. Louis: M. C. Barthel, 1878; English edition: *A Conversation between Two Lutherans on Methodism.* St. Louis: Publishing House of the Evangelical Lutheran Church of Mo., Ohio and other States, 1877.

_____. *Lebenslauf von W. Sihler bis zu seiner Ankunft in New York.* St. Louis: Druckerei Des Lutherischen Concordia Verlags, 1879.

_____. *Lebenslauf von W. Sihler, als lutherischer Pastor u. s. w.* New York: Lutherischer Verlags-Verein, 1880.

_____. "Slavery Viewed in the Light of the Scriptures." Baltimore: 1864. First published (in German) in *Der Lutheraner,* February and March 1863.

Simonoff, Harry. *Jewish Notables in America: 1776-1865.* New York: Greenberg Publishing Co., 1956.

Smith, John C. *Early Methodism in Indiana.* Indianapolis: J. M. Olcott, 1879.

Smith, J. L. *Indiana Methodism.* Valparaiso: 1892.

Smith, Timothy S. *Missionary Abominations Unmasked or a View of the Carey Mission.* South Bend, Ind.: Beacon, 1833.

Spitz, Lewis W. *Life in Two Worlds: Biography of William Sihler.* St. Louis: Concordia Publishing House, 1968.

Stanton, Elizabeth Cady, Susan B. Anthony, and Matilda Joslyn Gage, eds. *History of Woman Suffrage, vol. 1: 1848-1861* (2nd edit.) and *vol. 3: 1876-1885.* Rochester, N. Y.: Susan B. Anthony, 1889.

Stott, William T. *Indiana Baptist History.* Franklin, Ind.: 1908.

Stowe, Harriet Beecher. *Uncle Tom's cabin, or, Life among the lowly.* Boston: J. P. Jewett, 1852.

Stowe, Lyman Beecher. *Saints, Sinners, and Beechers.*

Indianapolis: Bobbs Merrill Co., 1934.

Swedenborg, Emanuel. *Arcana Coelestia.* New York: American Swedenborg Printing and Publishing Society, 1908.

Sweet, William Warren. *Circuit-Rider Days in Indiana.* Indianapolis: W. K. Stewart Co., 1916.

_____. *Methodism in American History.* New York: Abingdon Press, 1933, revised 1953.

_____. *Religion on the American Frontier, 1783-1840.* Vol. 2. *The Presbyterians.* Chicago: Chicago University Press, 1936.

_____. *The Story of Religion in America.* New York: Harper & Brothers, 1950.

Synodal Bericht der Deutschen Evangelisch-Lutherischen Synode von Missouri, Ohio und andern Staaten vom Jahre 1848. Chicago: n.d.

Tanner, Benjamin T. *An Apology for African Methodism.* Baltimore: 1867.

Tarkington, Joseph. *Autobiography, Written in 1887, with Introduction by Rev. Thomas A. Goodwin, D. D.* Cincinnati: Curts & Jennings, 1899.

Teas, Thomas Scattergood. "Journal of Thomas Scattergood Teas." In *Indiana as Seen by Early Travelers,* edited by Harlow Lindley. Indianapolis: 1916.

Telford, John, ed. *The Letters of the Rev. John Wesley, A. M.* London: Epworth Press, 1931.

Thornbrough, Emma Lou. *The Negro in Indiana.* Indianapolis: Indiana Historical Bureau, 1957.

Thwaites, Reuben G., ed. *Jesuit Relations and Allied Documents,* 73 vols. Cleveland: Burrow Bros. Co., 1901.

"The Town of New Harmony and the Rev. Benjamin Halsted." *S. W. Sentinel-Extra.* Evansville, Indiana: Alexander Burns Jr., Printer, April 1842.

"Turner Chapel A. M. E. History." *Anniversary Program.* Fort Wayne: August 15, 1985.

The United States Catholic Almanac: or Laity's Directory ...for 1833, 1834, 1835, 1836. Baltimore: James Myres.

Upjohn, Richard. *Upjohn's Rural Architecture: Designs,*

Working Drawings, and Specifications For a Wooden Church and Other Rural Structures. New York: George P. Putman, 1852.

Vandorn, E. "Reminiscences." In *Ohio Liberal.* Mansfield, Ohio: 13 and 20 August 1873.

"Voice from the Colored Citizens of Fort Wayne Indiana." *Anti-Slavery Bugle* [Salem, Ohio] 4, no. 50 (11 August 1849). [Reprinted as "Sentiments in Indiana . . . No Colonization." *African Repository and Colonial Journal* 25 (October 1849).]

Waite, Frederick C. "The Three Myers Sisters—Pioneer Women Physicians." *Medical Review of Reviews* (March 1933).

Walter, W[illia]m B. *Five Books in One Volume.* Fort Wayne: R. C. F. Rayhouser, 1894.

Wehr, Paul W. *James Hanna.* Fort Wayne: Allen County Public Library, 1971.

Williams, C. S., comp. *Williams' Fort Wayne Directory, City Guide, and Business Mirror: Volume 1 - 1858-59.* Fort Wayne: C. L. Hill, 1858.

Williams, D. Newell. "The Gospel as the Power of God to Salvation: Alexander Campbell and Experimental Religion." In *Lectures in Honor of the Alexander Campbell Bicentennial, 1788-1988.* Nashville, Tennessee: Disciples of Christ Historical Society, 1988.

Williams, J[esse] L. *Historical Sketch of the First Presbyterian Church, Fort Wayne, Indiana, With Early Reminiscences of the Place.* Fort Wayne: John W. Dawson, 1860. 2nd edit.: Fort Wayne: Daily News Printing House, 1881.

Wilson, Joseph M.. *The Presbyterian Historical Almanac and Annual Remembrancer of the Church for 1861, vol. 3. . .1867, vol. 9.* Philadelphia: Joseph M. Wilson, 1861 . . . 1867.

Wilstach, John A. *St. Mary's Church.* Lafayette, Ind.: 1893.

Wimberley II, W. William. *The Jewish Experience in Indiana Before the Civil War: An Introduction.* Fort Wayne: Indiana Jewish Historical Society, 1976.

Winger, Otho. *The Last of the Miamis.* North Manchester, Ind.: 1935.

Winter, George. *The Journals and Indian Paintings of George Winter, 1837-39.* Indianapolis: Indiana Historical Society, 1948.

Wittke, Carl. *Refugees of Revolution: The German Forty-Eighters in America.* Philadelphia: University of Pennsylvania Press, 1952.

Woehrmann, Paul. *At the Headwaters of the Maumee: A History of the Forts of Fort Wayne.* Indianapolis: Indiana Historical Society, 1971.

Woodburn, James Albert. "United Presbyterian Beginnings." *Indiana Magazine of History* 30, no. 1 (March 1934).

Woodworth, Laura Case, Carolyn Randall Fairbank, and Martha Brandriff Hanna, comps. *Reminiscences of Old Fort Wayne.* Fort Wayne: Allen County Public Library, 1906.

Woollen, William Wesley. *Biographical and Historical Sketches of Early Indiana.* Indianapolis: Hammond & Co., 1883.

Wyeth, Walter M. *Isaac McCoy: A Memorial.* Philadelphia: W. N. Wyeth, 1895.

Wyneken, Friedrich K. D. "Die Noth der Deutschen Lutheraner in Nordamerika." *Zeitschrift fuer Protestantismus und Kirche.* Erlangen, Germany: 1843. Reprinted in Pittsburgh: 1844.

_____. *The Distress of the German Lutherans in North America.* Translated by S. Edgar Schmidt; edited by R. F. Rehmer. Fort Wayne: Concordia Theological Seminary Press, 1982.

Young, Calvin. *Little Turtle.* Indianapolis: Sentinel Printing Co., 1917.

Newspapers and Periodicals

American Hebrew. (December 1898).

Anti-Slavery Bugle. (14 July, 4 and 11 August 1849).

Catholic News-Letter. (June 1846).

Catholic Telegraph. (14 July 1832).

Christian Evangelist. (19 March 1903).

Christian Record. (August, September, November, 1846;

January, February, March, April, May, August, November, December 1847; January, November 1848; April 1856).

Cincinnati Daily Gazette. (29 January 1859).

Dawson's Daily Times. (July 1855 to September 1864).

Fort Wayne Daily News. (31 May 1884).

Fort Wayne Gazette. (30 March 1871; 17 June 1873; 9 June 1892).

Fort Wayne Jeffersonian. (16 July 1856).

Fort Wayne Weekly Republican. (May 1858 to March 1860).

Fort Wayne Standard. (July 1854 to June 1855).

Fort Wayne [Weekly] Sentinel. (March 1841 to April 1860).

Fort Wayne [Weekly] Times [and People's Press]. (January 1845 to August 1860).

Friend of Man. (29 March 1837).

Indianapolis News. (6 July 1891).

Israelite. (January 1860).

Journal of Hanover College. (January 1897).

Lagrange Democrat. (January 1849).

Liberator. (23 July 1841).

Lily. (2 January and 15 November 1854; 15 April, 1 July, and 15 October 1855; 15 February, 15 April, and 1 July 1856; 1 October 1857).

Lutheran Observer. (March 1837).

Occident and American Jewish Advocate. (1852-1865).

Our Sunday Visitor. (30 October 1960), 10B.

Philanthropist. (25 February 1837).

Reformed Messenger. (16 April 1856; 17 April 1902).

Regular Baptist. (April 1839).

Trumpet and Universalist Magazine. (June 1844).

United Presbyterian and Evangelical Guardian. (June 1851, June 1852 and October 1852).

List of Illustrations

Index

336

Wall, Mary Ann, 300

Wallace, Matthew, 21, 24

Walter, William B., 83-84, 92

Walther, C. F. W., 111, 122, 213

Watters, Mrs. John P., 267

Way, Amanda M., 156

Wayne Street Methodist Church, 59, 64-65; clergy, 253, 254; *see also* Methodists

Wayne, Anthony, 4, 5, 125

Wefel, Adam, 101

Weinzoepflen, Roman, 82-83

Wells, William, 4, 6, 12, 203

Weninger, Francis X., 97

Westlake, Burroughs, 242, 254, 314

Weutz, Joseph, 94

Whitcomb, James, 244

White Skin, 73

Wiley, Allen, 42, 45, 46

Wilkins, Stephen, 134

Willard, Frances, 187

Williams, Jesse L., 8, 30, 38, 97, 154, 164, 177, 182, 183

Williams, Susan Creighton, 41, 179

Wilson, William, 59

Wines, Elizabeth, 31, 41, 138, 179

Wines, Marshall W., 31, 38, 138

Winter, George, 4

Wise, Isaac M., 213, 229-231, 232

Wiskehelaehqua, 14

Woerking, Christian, 285

Wolf, Abraham, 231

Wolf, Isaac, 224, 227

Wolter, Karl A., 282

Woman's rights, 155-162; clerical opposition, 122, 160, 292, 295; clerical support, 193, 295; Presbyterians vote woman's suffrage, 187, 194

Woman's Rights Association of Allen County, 162

Woman's Rights Association of Indiana, 156, 157, 293

Women's societies, 149-162; Female Benevolent Society, 153; Female Temperance Meetings, 154-155; Presbyterian (O. S.), 36, 149-150, 151, 152, 185, 188; Methodist, 65, 150, 151, 185; Catholic, 90, 91, 150; Baptist, 132, 150; Episcopal, 143, 148, 150, 151; English Lutheran, 150; Jewish, 150, 227, 311

Wood, George W., 151, 178, 185-187, 221

Wood, Mary F., 270

Work, Henry, 267

World Peace Convention, 293

Worth, David, 286

Worth, Hannah, 286

Worth, Mahaly, 286

Worth, Richard, Elizabeth, and Richard, Jr., 286

Worth, William, 286

Worthington, Ellis, 139

Wright, Joseph A., 207

Wright, Lucretia, 155

Wyneken, Friedrich K. D., 36, 50, 81, 104-110, 123, 195; on Baptists, 128

Wyneken, Marie Buuck, 108, 109

Young Men's Literary Society, 57, 157, 191